WAISTCOATS

From the Hopkins Collection

*c.*1720-1950

Photography by Alan Hopkins
Text by Vanessa Hopkins

Series Editor Jenny Tiramani

THE SCHOOL OF HISTORICAL DRESS

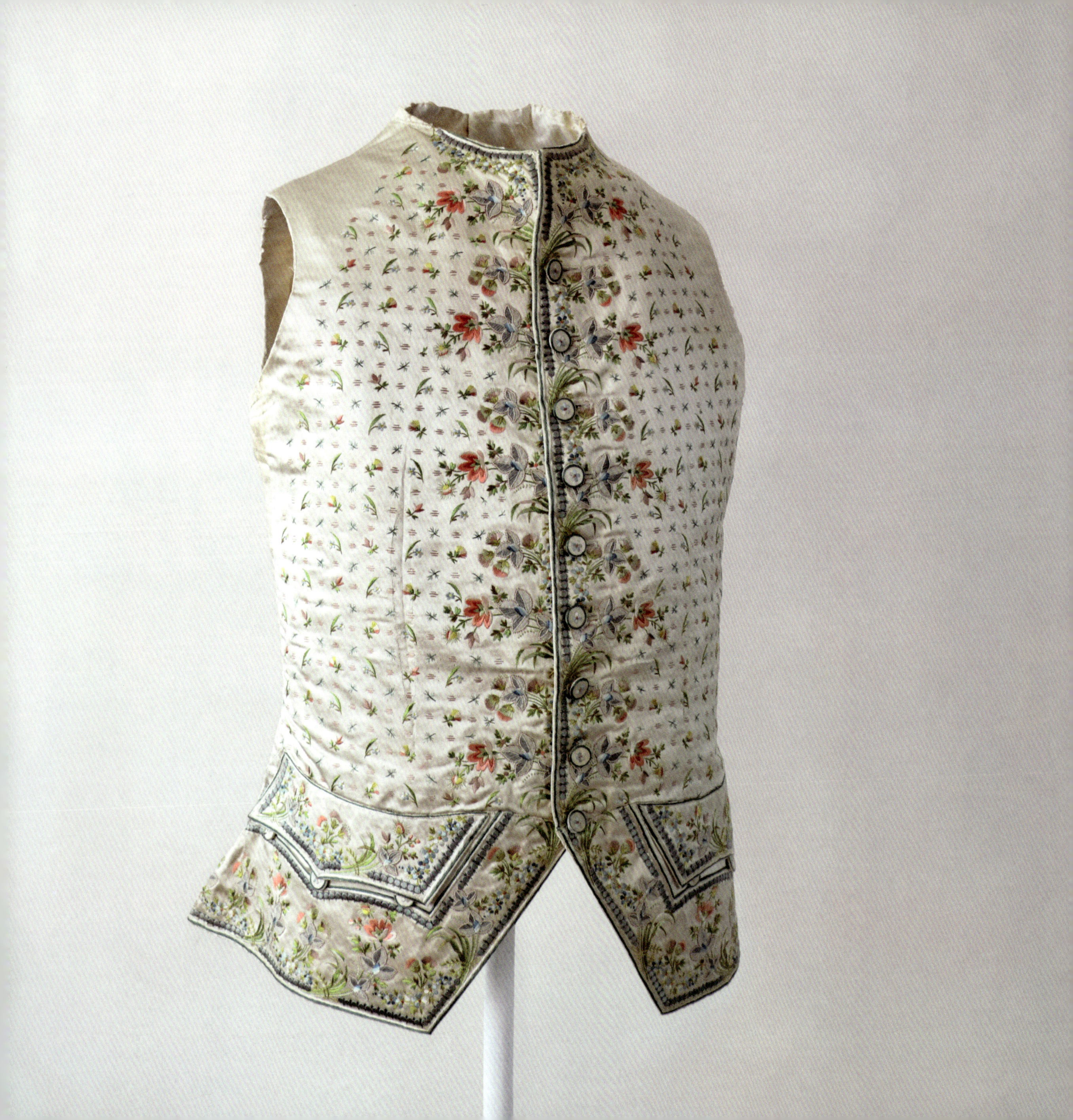

Foreword

Now in my ninth decade, I have seen waistcoats come and go a number of times over the years. I have always thought them magical ingredients in any man's wardrobe adding style, decoration and panache to the dullest suit or even, dare I say it, the ubiquitous jeans. I recall them returning briefly into fashion as part of the post World War II neo-Edwardian revival. Indeed I spent part of my grant to go up to the university on one in claret silk flecked with gold. They were not to figure again until the 1980s when they became a means whereby I could liven up my obligatory directorial suit at the V&A. These all came from Tommy Nutter in Savile Row and one in particular I cherished which was of a brilliant yellow watered silk. Once again they vanished to resurface in the second decade of this century when Favourbrook in Jermyn Street revived them to wear with formal morning dress. I wore a floral one at Prince William's wedding and another beneath an evening suit which was also made for me in the form of a purple velvet frock coat. They are all in the collection of the Fashion Museum in Bath.

The brilliant photographer John Swannell photographed me in the latter.

What follows is a wonderful book, not only visually exciting and discriminating but also exact in terms of factual historical information. It is a publication which will hold its own as the standard work on the subject.

Roy Strong
Patron
The School of Historical Dress

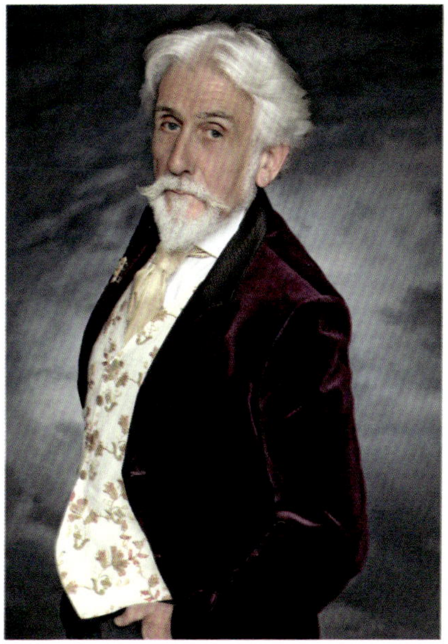

Roy Strong photographed by John Swannell.

First published by The School of Historical Dress, 2017
52 Lambeth Road, London SE1 7PP
www.theschoolofhistoricaldress.org.uk

A catalogue record for this book is available from the British Library.

Hardback edition
ISBN 978 0 9931744 1 4

10 9 8 7 6 5 4 3 2 1
2021 2020 2019 2018 2017

Copy editor and proof reader Chris Allen
Cover design Lizzie Ballantyne
Design Vanessa Hopkins

Printed by Empress, London

***Front cover:* A waistcoat in silk velvet, 1840-1855.**
HC.W-6.88-2
The velvet has polychrome warp stripes, with narrow weft stripes of cream silk, and uncut velvet which contrasts with the cut pile and creates a check pattern. The waistcoat has a roll collar and five blue patterned silk thread-covered buttons (page 216). There are two welted pockets, and a curved breast pocket in the left forepart. The lining is fawn cotton twill and the back is in dark brown silesia, with a backstrap and a pale metal buckle to adjust the waist.

Back cover: The back of the silk velvet waistcoat on page 111. It is in dark brown silesia with a pair of tabs with three pairs of brass eyelets and a dark brown narrow linen tape for lacing.

***Page 2:* A waistcoat in cream silk satin, 1770-1785.**
HC.W-4.81
It has polychrome floral embroidery of scattered sprigs over the foreparts and sprays on the borders and pocket flaps. The back has been much altered; the original was cream silk twill, but this has been cut short, and pieces of linen and wool have been inserted into the centre back. At some point, darts, now unpicked, have been taken in the middle of each forepart. The front edges and forepart skirts are faced with cream silk satin, and the lining is plain white silk, which may not be original. The nine satin-covered buttons have an embroidered flower motif (page 216).

Thank you

Special thanks to:
Richard Davin
Sam Hopkins
Johannes Pietsch, Bayerisches Nationalmuseum
Claire Thornton, The School of Historical Dress

Also:
Dale and Margaret Barter
George Clarke
Jacqueline Durran
Giana Ferguson
Andrew Gray
Joanna Hashagen, The Bowes Museum
Peter Headlam-Morley
Susan North, V&A
Stephen Nye, Guildhall Museum, Rochester
Linda Park
Sébastien Passot
John Swannell
David Walters
Julius Walters

THE SCHOOL OF HISTORICAL DRESS

The School of Historical Dress was established in 2009 to promote all aspects of historical dress, most particularly through surviving objects and documents. The Janet Arnold Archive is the foundation of this, and the Hopkins Collection has much to contribute in making objects available for study.

Previous publications: *Footwear: Shoes and Boots from the Hopkins Collection*, Alan and Vanessa Hopkins, 2015

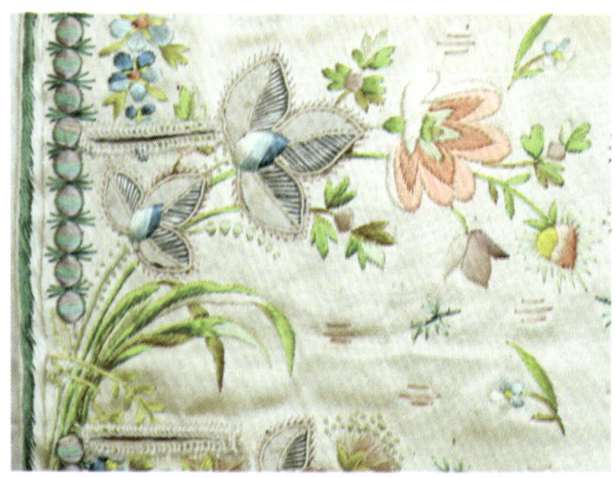

Detail of the embroidery on the waistcoat on page 2. The discs in the vertical row on the left-hand side have been worked over card, and gimp outlining pieces of appliquéd linen can be seen.

Contents

Measurements are given in inches:
1 inch (1″) = 2.54 centimetres.

Introduction

Alan and Vanessa Hopkins have been collecting historical clothing, textiles and accessories in the United Kingdom for more than forty years. *Waistcoats from the Hopkins Collection* is the second in a series of books focusing on different groups of items from this large and significant collection that spans a period from the seventeenth to the twentieth century.

Garments called 'waistcoats', both knitted and of woven fabrics, were documented for more than two hundred years before the first example featured here, and were worn for warmth underneath outer layers of clothing, for informal wear and for sports such as tennis.

Waistcoats are defined as 'close-fitting garments' in *The Academy of Armory*, published in 1688.[1] Written in the transitional period during which the staple garments of men's dress changed from doublet and hose to coat and breeches, the book notes the evolving nature of waistcoats in two entries that appear on a list of garments comprising a man's suit of clothes. First there is an entry for '**Waistcoat**, is [*sic*] close Garment worn under a Doublet, and within the Waist-band of the Breeches', while the second entry details the newer fashion in the following context: '**A Street bodied Coat**, this is close to the Body and Arms, and is usually worn without a Doublet, having under it a Waistcote with side or deep skirts almost to the Knees. These kind of Waistcoats are called Chates [Cheats]; because they are to be seen rich and gaudy before, when all the back part is no such thing'.

The terms 'waistcoat' and 'vest' have both been used in the past, but in the course of the twentieth century 'vest' became the usage in the U.S.A., and 'waistcoat' the term in the U.K. We have used the name 'waistcoat' throughout. There are 337 waistcoats in the Hopkins Collection, 150 of which are included here, together with nine un-made-up (or unpicked) panels. The prominence of waistcoats in men's dress from 1720 to 1950 varied from time to time. For example, from about 1870 coats were commonly worn with the buttons fastened, so waistcoats went largely unseen until it became fashionable to wear coats open again in the 1890s. After 1870 the fabrics and decoration of waistcoats became more subdued, and often matched the jacket or trousers, or formed part of a suit.

The dates given for each waistcoat have taken into account the fact that some were not necessarily of the latest fashion. The tailor would have made a waistcoat to suit the taste of the individual customer, so dating can hardly ever be precise. In addition, some have been altered as the wearer changed size, or were passed on to another person, or were used for fancy dress at a date later than their creation.

All the waistcoats featured here are probably English, unless otherwise stated. Most examples are for men, and the majority are sleeveless, although eight women's waistcoats and three with sleeves have been included.

The larger tailors' establishments throughout the period covered would often send out simpler items such as waistcoats to be stitched by female outworkers once the fabric had been cut by the tailor. They were then brought back to the tailor for fitting, and afterwards finished by the outworkers. The 1861 census has a waistcoat maker, Jane Wade, living and working in one room of an artisans' lodging house at 47 Charles Square in Hoxton, the former home of The School of Historical Dress.

Jenny Tiramani
The School of Historical Dress

1 Randle Holme, The Academy of Armory, 1688, Book III, chapter III, pp. 95 & 96.

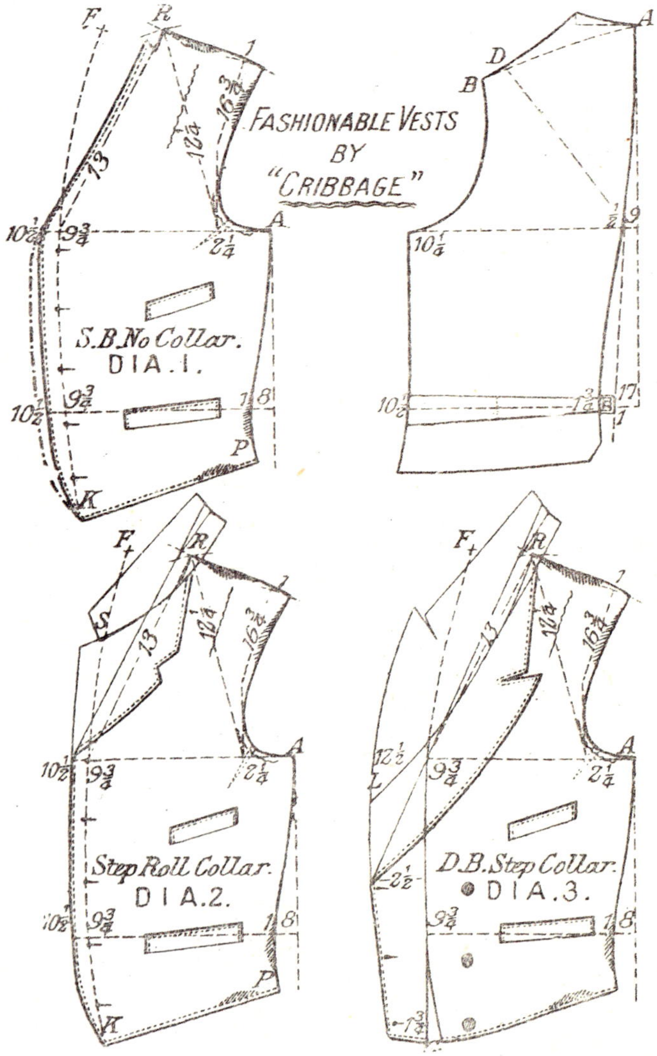

A Neglected Subject.

Vest making is too often designated "a woman's job," or, at best, something with which a man may "piece out time." This discreditable state of affairs is quite incomprehensible when we remember that the normal, and every departure from that standard, requires the same speciality of treatment as a coat.

Aim, first of all, at making the pockets as thin, neat and firm as possible. Stretch and shrink the shoulder section as indicated, so that it may correctly define the hollow of shoulder. Slightly strain out the hollow of waist and bottom as shown—this will be found a more effective provision for prominent hips than either gusset or opening. Draw in bottom of front scye and press the fulness towards breast.

Well shrink canvas and carry it throughout foreparts. Snip and insert vees at shoulder (on the same principle as for a coat), reversing the operation at bottom of front scye by cutting out as indicated by dotted vee, and draw edges together. This special treatment of the canvas gives a desirable firmness, and materially preserves the form already given to the foreparts.

For no-collar vests keep the staytape a shade tight at back neck, easy for two or three inches below point R, about three quarters of an inch tight opposite breast, snug around bottom corners, and terminate about four inches from sideseams. When pressing out see that all is done in harmony with the previous manipulation.

The practice of filling out the shoulders with wadding is reprehensible, inasmuch as it prevents the coat from taking its proper position on the shoulders, "lifting it" where it should define the hollow.

The crease row of collar vests should be controlled with a bridle sufficiently firm to produce a snug fit without pulling it off at bottom of front.

The back may be of soft silesia or Italian cloth to match foreparts, if the latter it should be cut *across* the piece. Place the backstraps in the natural waist as shown on diagram. The interlinings should be of fast colours, and as light and delicately patterned as possible. Keep a pleat in forepart lining of about half an inch at shoulder seam to nothing at prominence of breast.

Extract from an article in *The Tailor and Cutter*, 1898.

WAISTCOATS

*c.*1720–1950

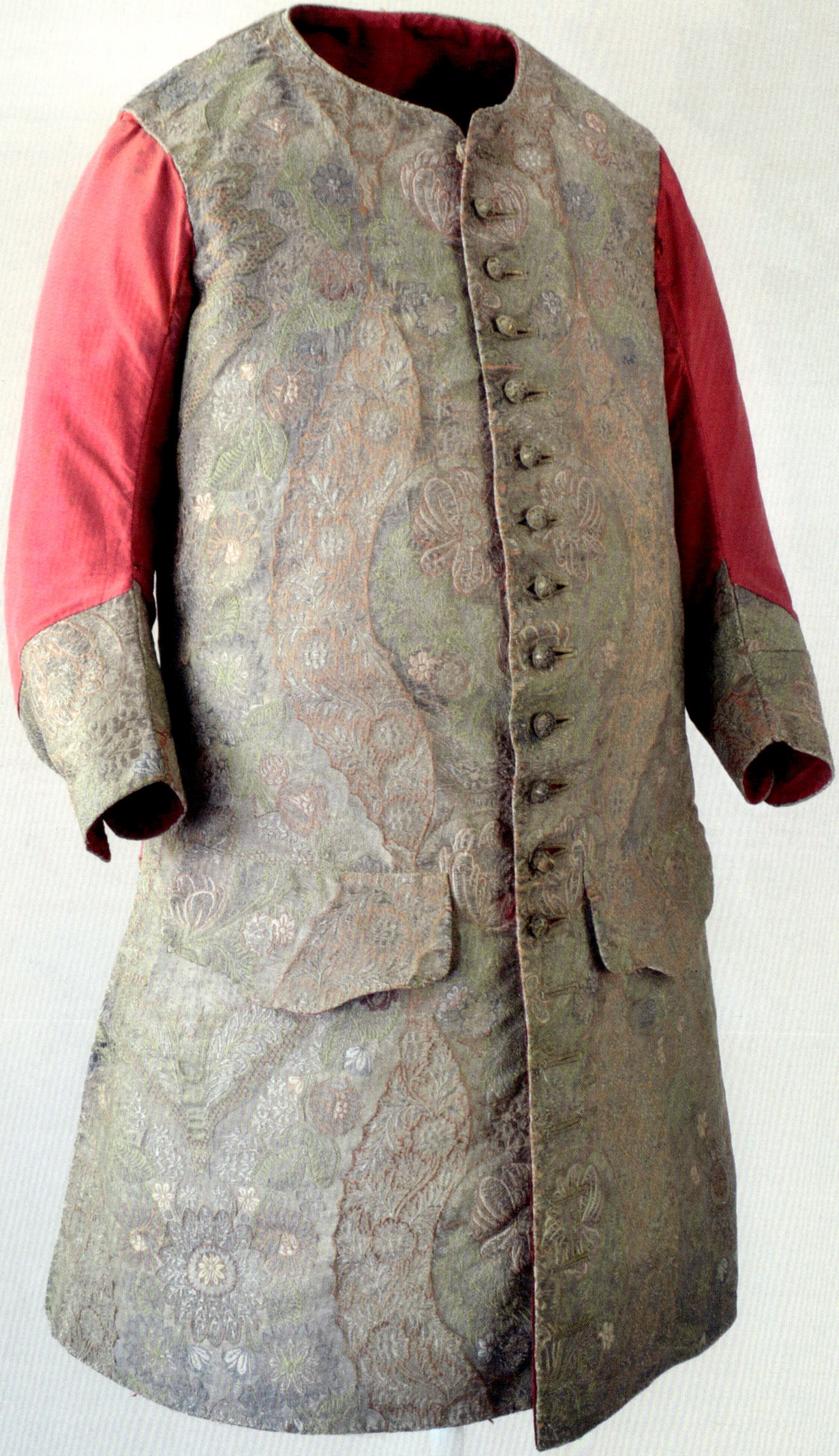

A waistcoat in silver-gilt, silver and polychrome silk brocade, 1720-1740.
HC.W-10.15-1

The brocade is quite faded except for the cuffs, and under the pocket flaps, where it has retained its original brightness. The waistcoat has sleeves in deep pink silk taffeta, with cuffs in the brocade. The back is in the deep pink taffeta, with a piece of the brocade round the back neck; the back skirts are also in the brocade, with pieced sections at the sides. It has been altered with pieces of the taffeta inserted in the side seams. The lining is the deep pink silk taffeta, except for the back skirts, which are lined in red calimanco, and this also lines the inserted side pieces. There are nineteen buttonholes and the lowest six are not open. The nineteen domed buttons are covered with tightly packed silver-gilt threads over a wooden mould, and have a pattern of silver-gilt purl interlaced over the top; the two on the level of the pockets show a lot of wear, which indicates that only these two were regularly used.

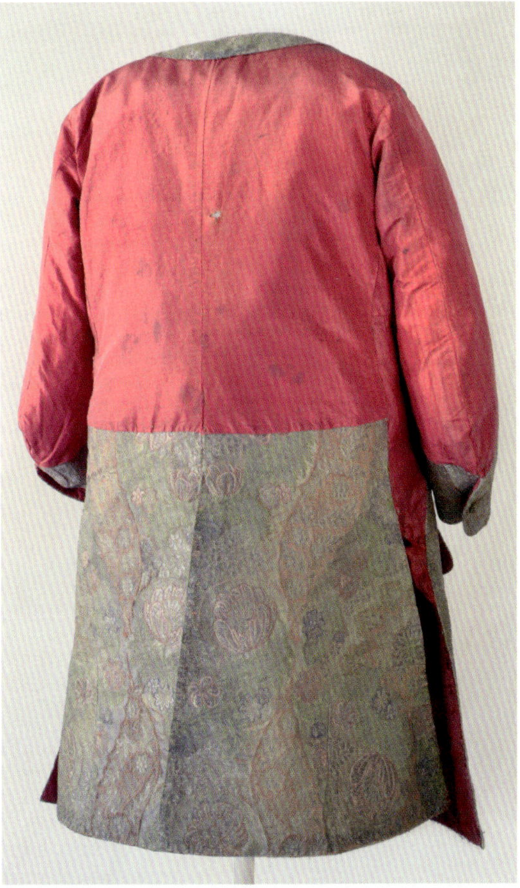

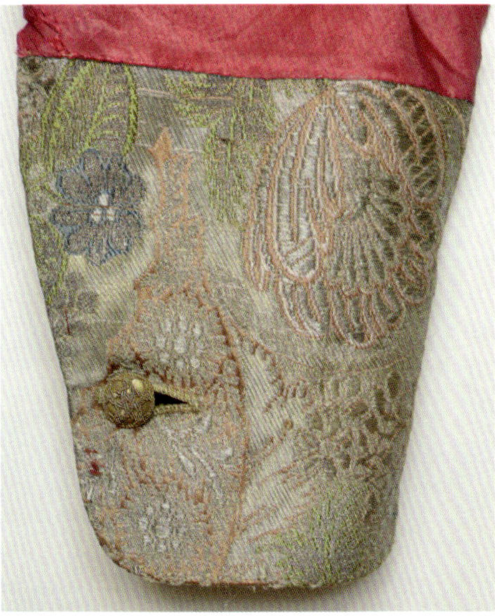

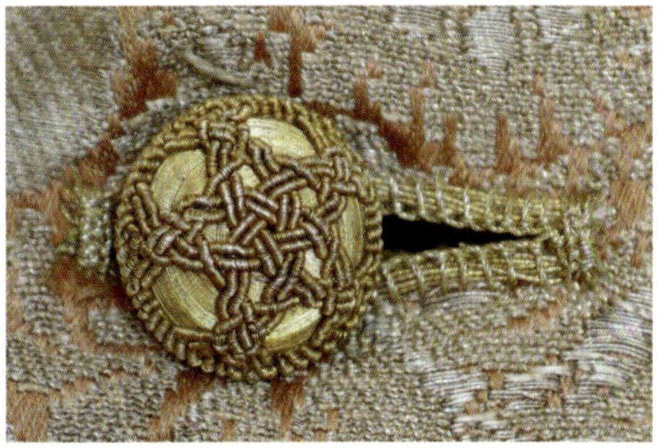

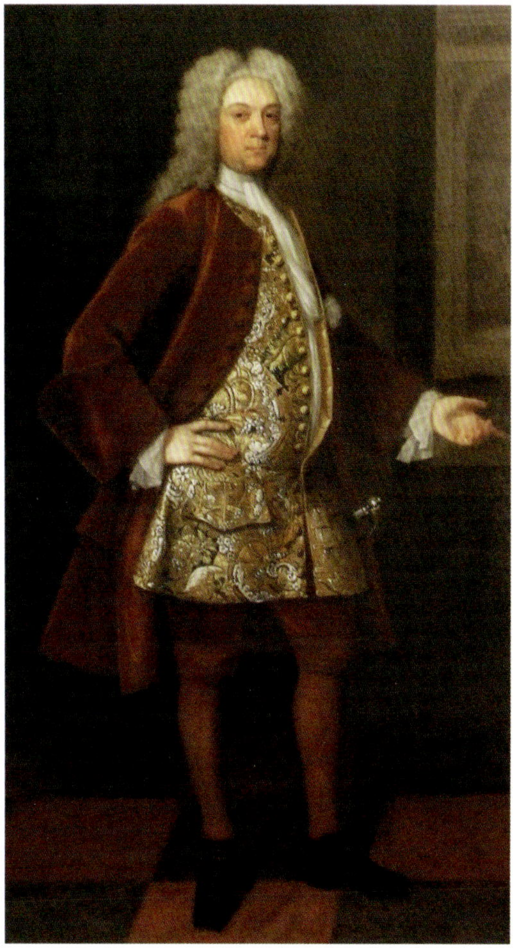

Sir Thomas Palmer, Bt, M.P. by Richard Phillips, 1722. Image courtesy of Guildhall Museum, Rochester.

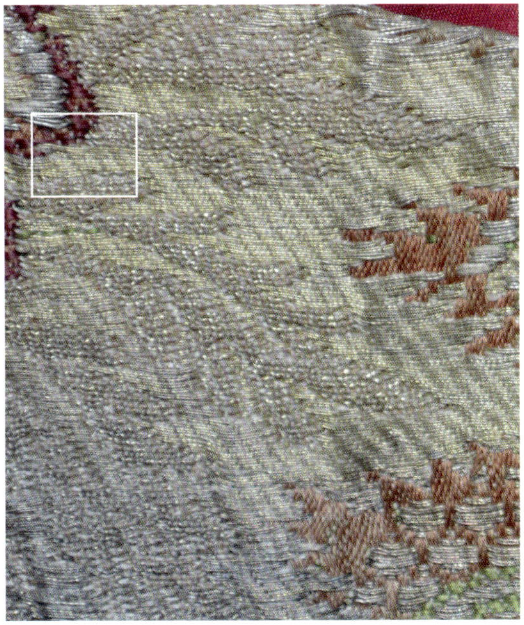

Detail from under the pocket flap, showing the unfaded brocade becoming faded lower down.

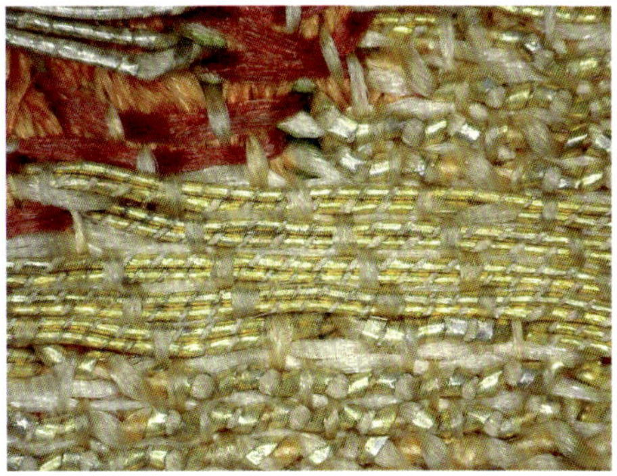

Detail outlined left, showing the silver-gilt filé and frisé threads.

The brocade has a stylised floral design mirrored across the centre of the fabric. The pattern is formed by polychrome silk and silver-gilt filé and frisé weft threads (page 211); it has a main warp of ivory silk and a supplementary warp of apricot silk which appears in the pattern.

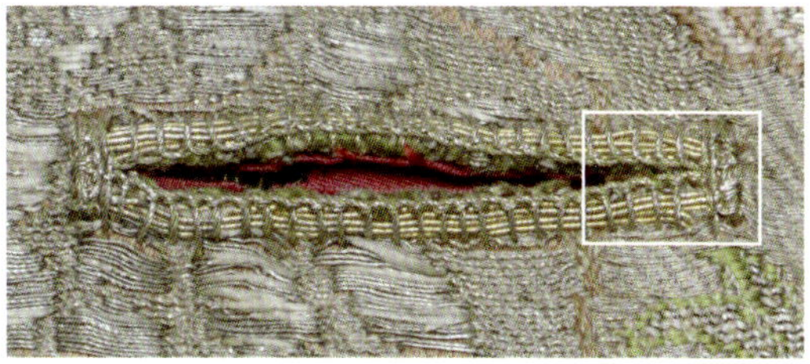

One of the buttonholes, formed from five silver-gilt filé threads buttonhole stitched with silver-gilt filé twist.

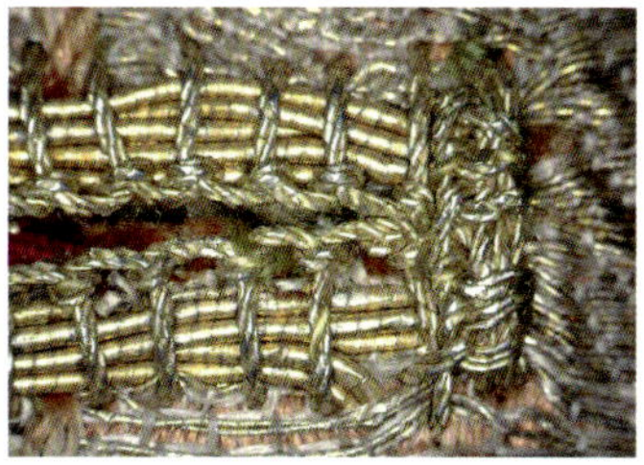

Right: Detail of the buttonhole outlined above.

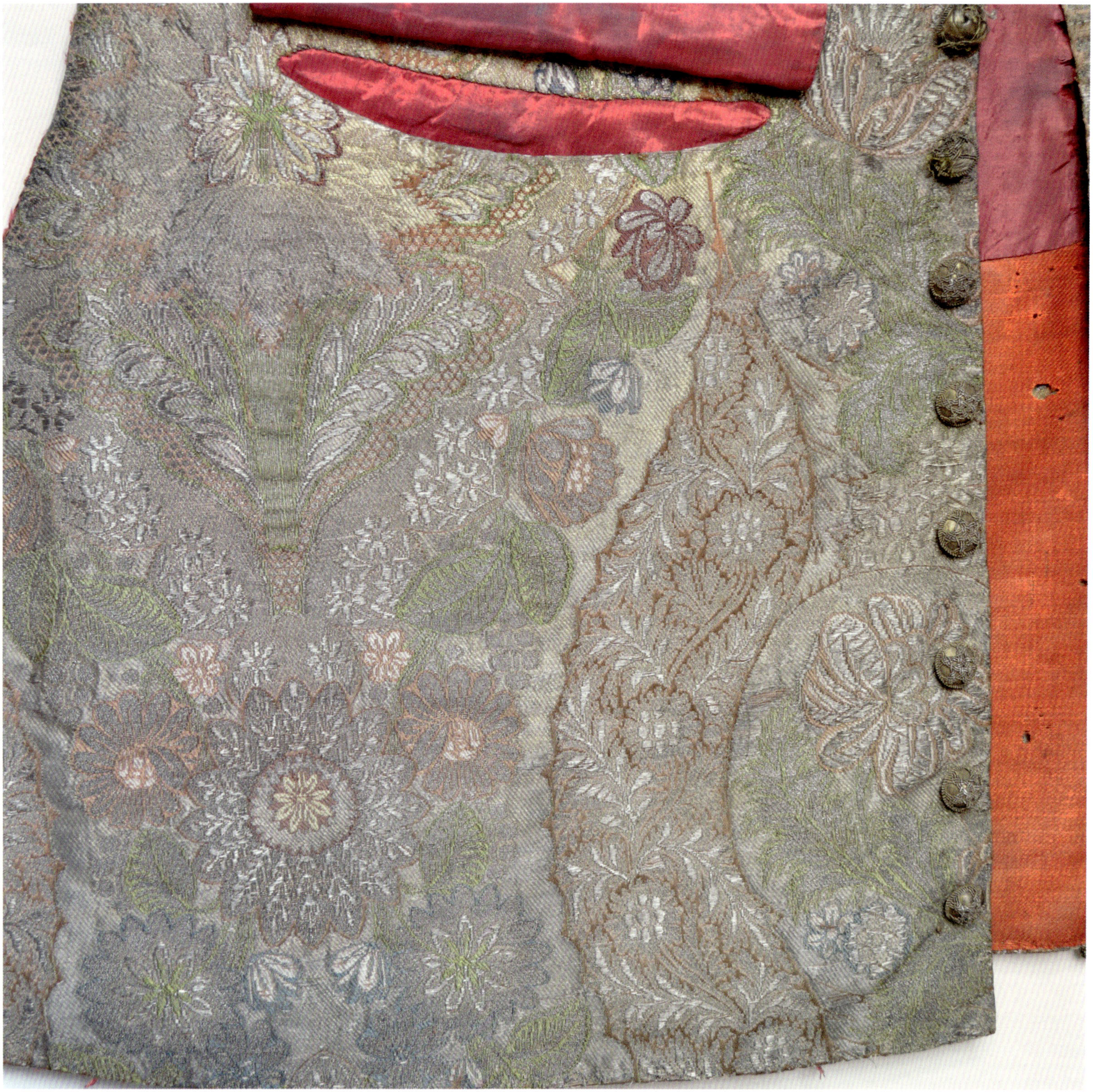

The right forepart skirt of the waistcoat on page 8, showing the original brightness of the brocade which has survived under the pocket flap. The deep pink taffeta lining and the red calimanco skirt lining can be seen at the right-hand edge of the picture.

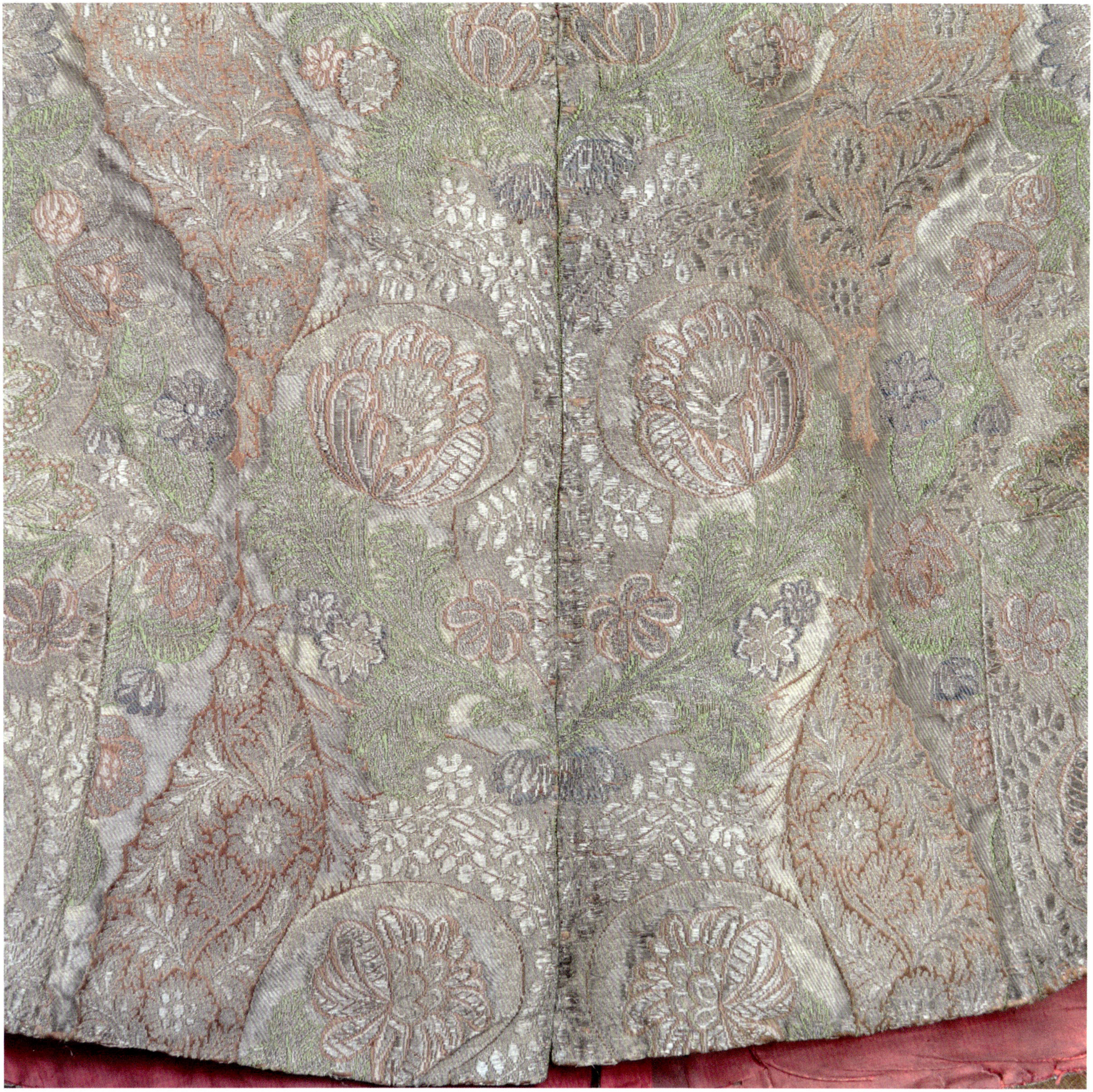

The back skirts of the waistcoat on page 8; the selvedge of the fabric runs along each edge of the centre back opening, where the pattern is mirrored. The pieced sections can be seen at the sides, with the taffeta lining of the foreparts visible at the bottom.

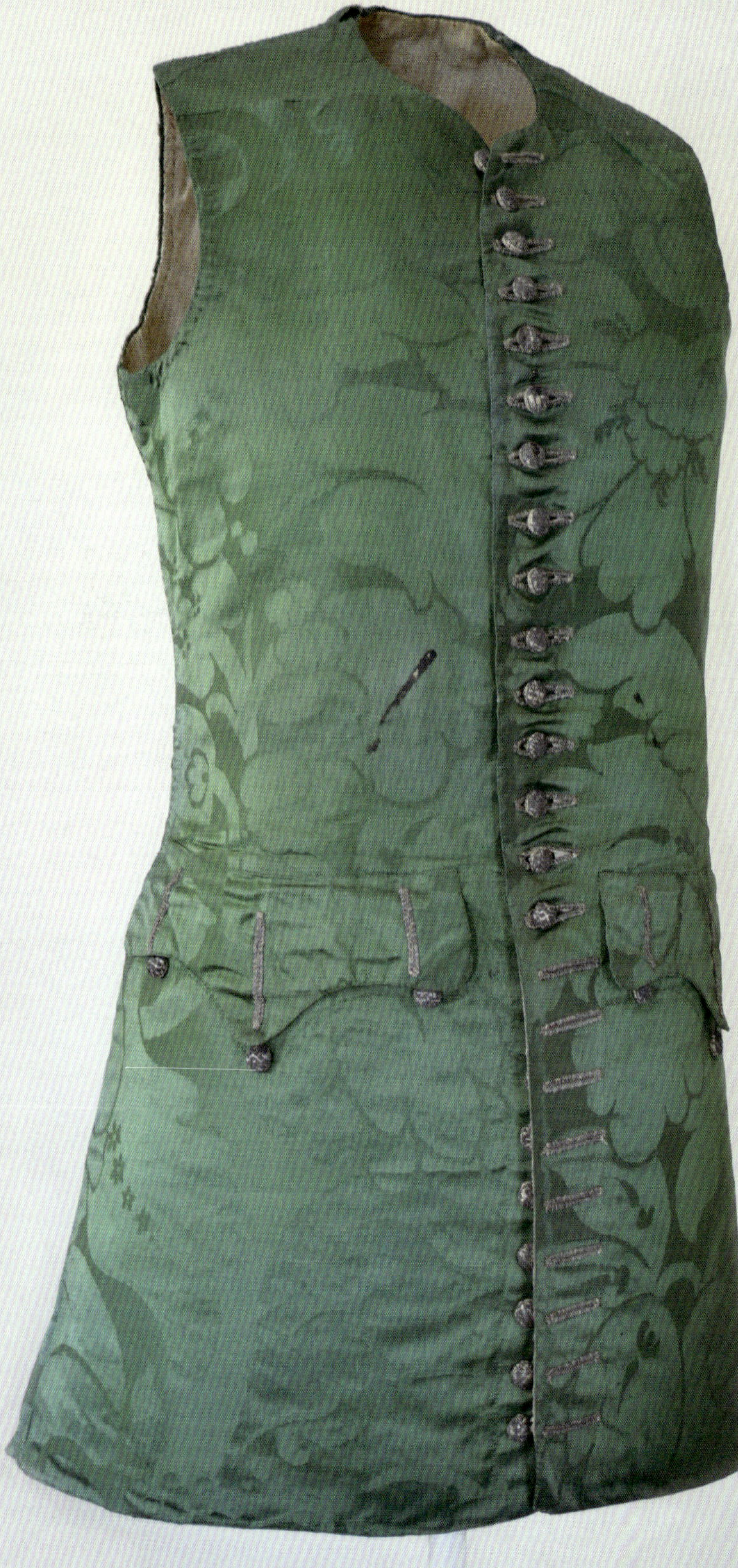

A waistcoat in green silk damask, 1725-1740.
HC.W-12.12

The damask design is very large, with no repeat in the entire length of the foreparts; the back is in a wool damask, with a different pattern that is mirrored across the centre back seam, and similarly large in scale. The foreparts and the back may have both been cut from earlier garments, and there are inset pieces at the shoulders, front and back, and at the sides of the back panels; a small piece of the damask was found in one of the pockets. The body of the waistcoat is lined with white fustian, and the skirts are lined with cream shagreen, a spotted silk with a pebbled surface; the front skirts are interlined with buckram. The twenty-four buttons are wooden moulds covered in linen threads with flat strips of silver over that and purl, or silver coils, forming a pattern of little squares (page 216). The buttonholes are formed by pasteboard strips covered in a fine silver filé thread which have been buttonhole stitched on to the waistcoat with a coarser filé thread. Only the top fifteen are open, the lower ones on the skirt are merely decorative. The facing behind the open buttonholes is made of strips of the cream silk shagreen with their edges turned in along the edges of the buttonholes; the lining of the skirts extends uncut behind the decorative buttonholes. The dark stain on the right forepart might be a splash of candle wax. This waistcoat may have been worn with a coat with cuffs in the same green silk damask.

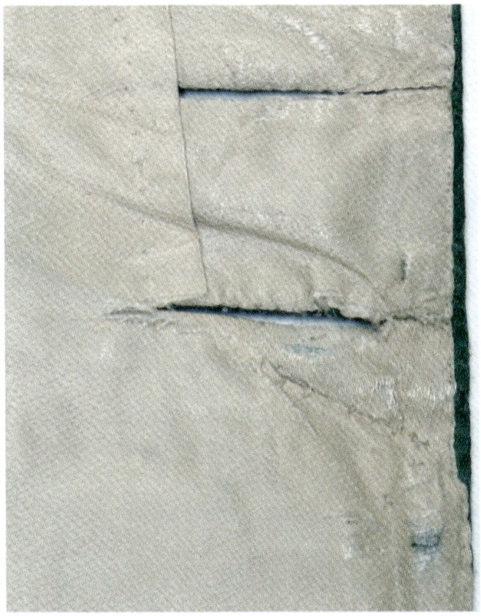

Inside the left front edge, showing the silk shagreen in strips behind the buttonholes and lining the front skirt.

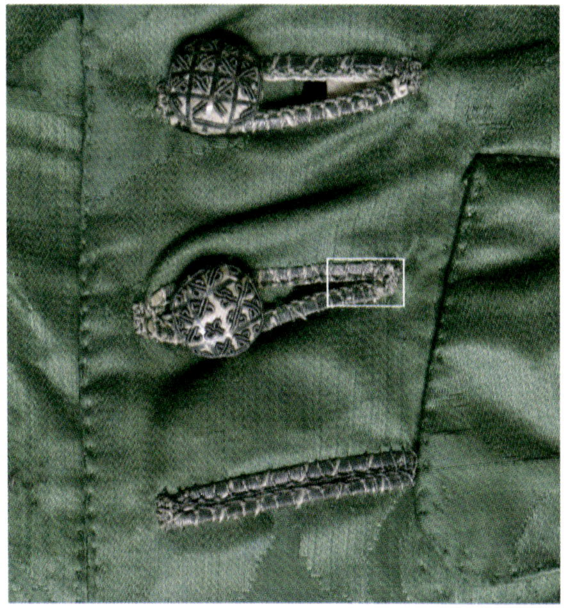

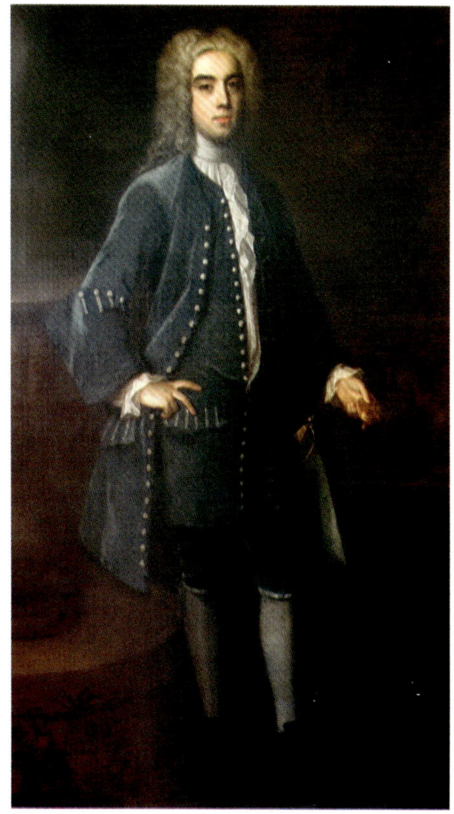

Portrait of a Young Man (detail), British School, 1730. © Amgueddfa Cymru / National Museum of Wales.

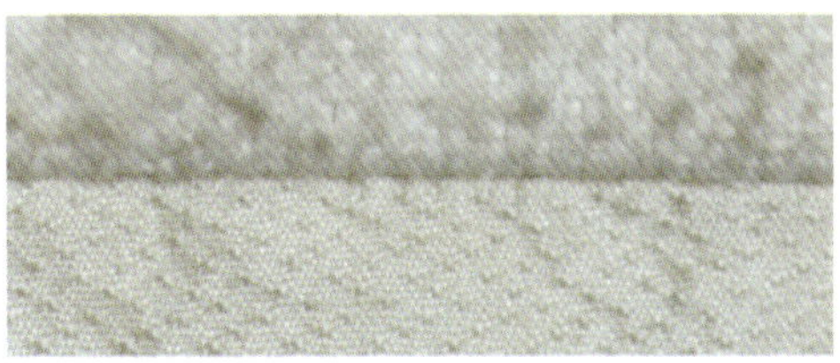

Detail of the lining showing fustian at the top and silk shagreen below.

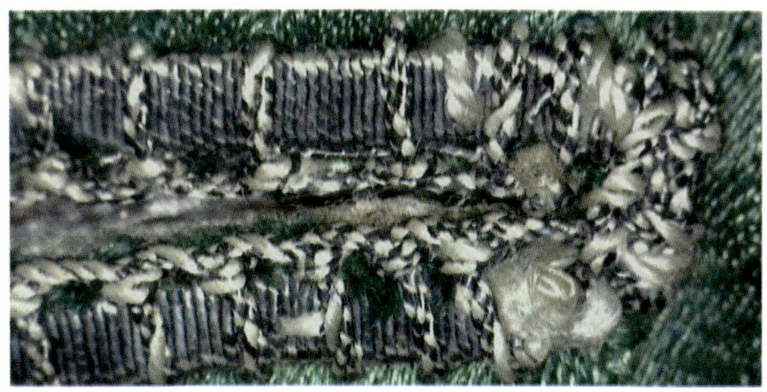

A buttonhole detail, outlined above.

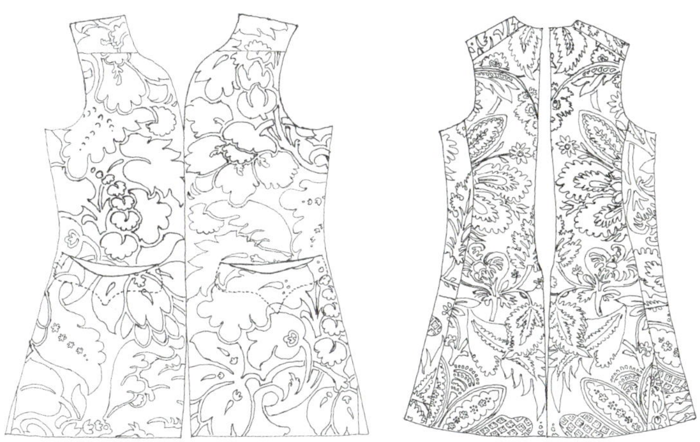

Sketch of the outlines of the silk damask pattern on the foreparts (left) and the wool damask pattern on the back (right). The centre back seam is shaped in to the waist. (Scale approximately 1:16)

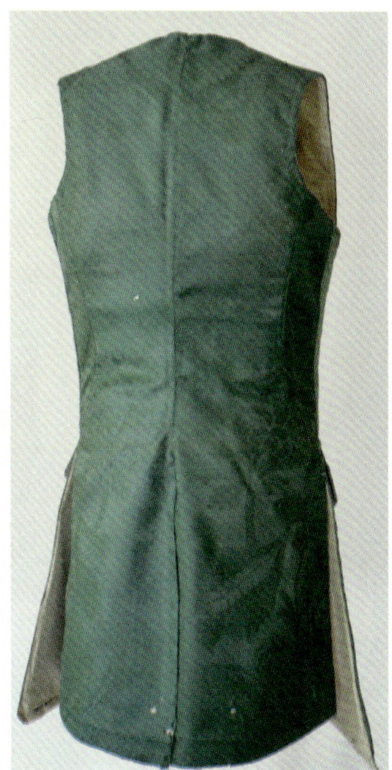

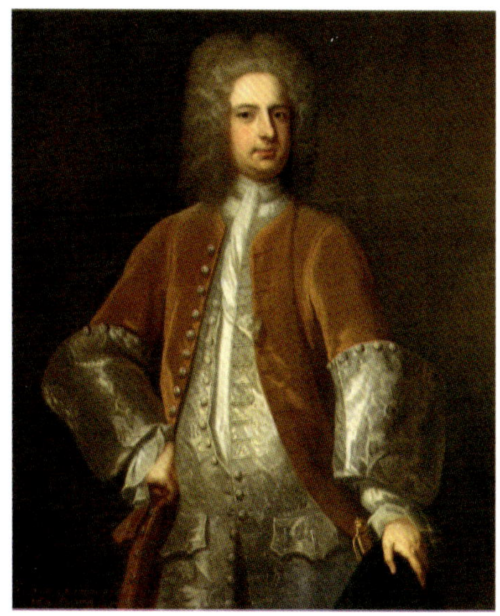

John Blathwayt (detail), attributed to Enoch Seeman the younger, 1720-1729, Dyrham Park, Gloucestershire. © National Trust.

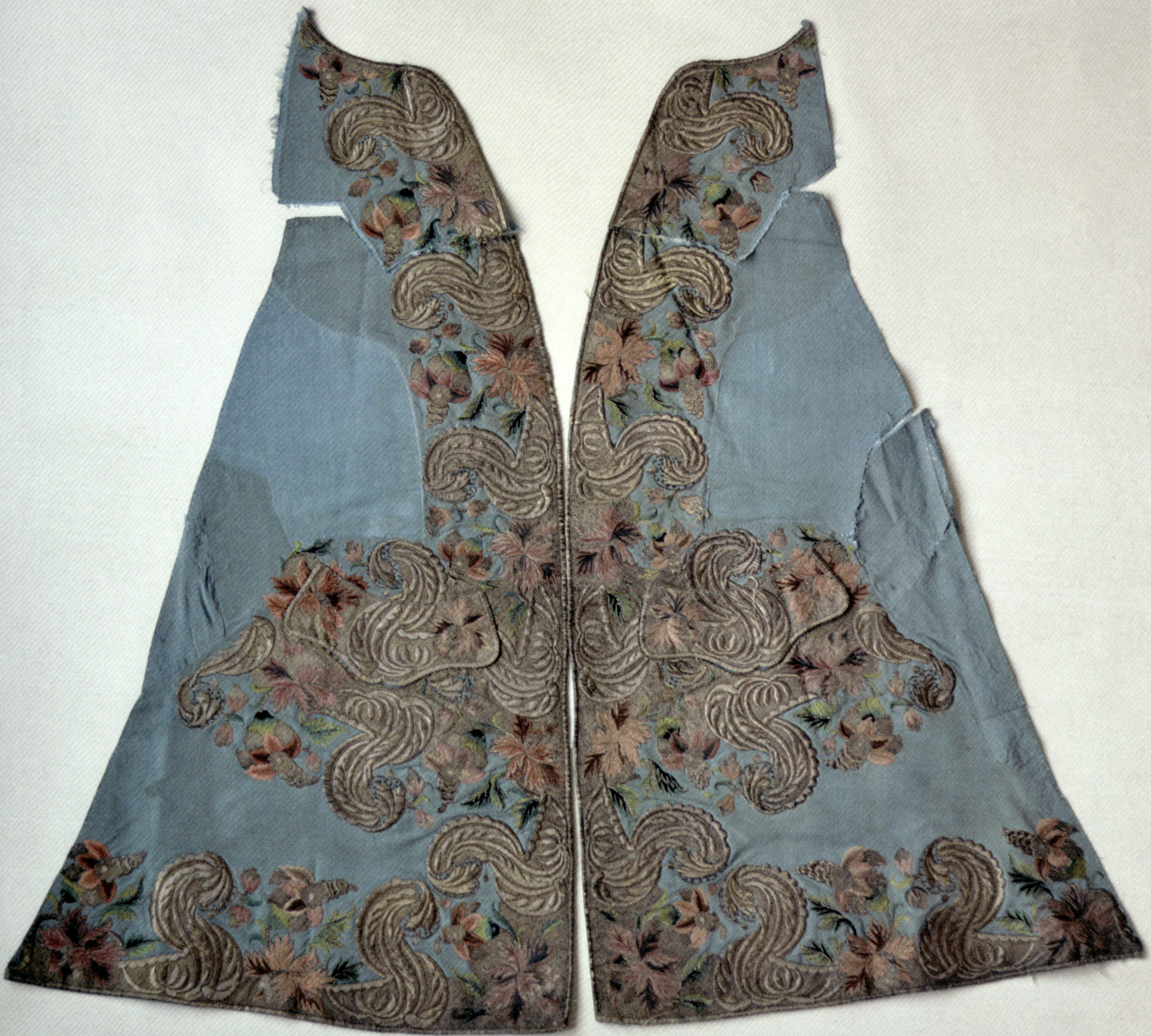

A pair of waistcoat foreparts in pale blue silk grosgrain with embroidery, 1735-1745. HC.W-11.92-1

They have been unpicked, and pieces at the top have been cut off and applied further down, where a cleaner patch is visible.

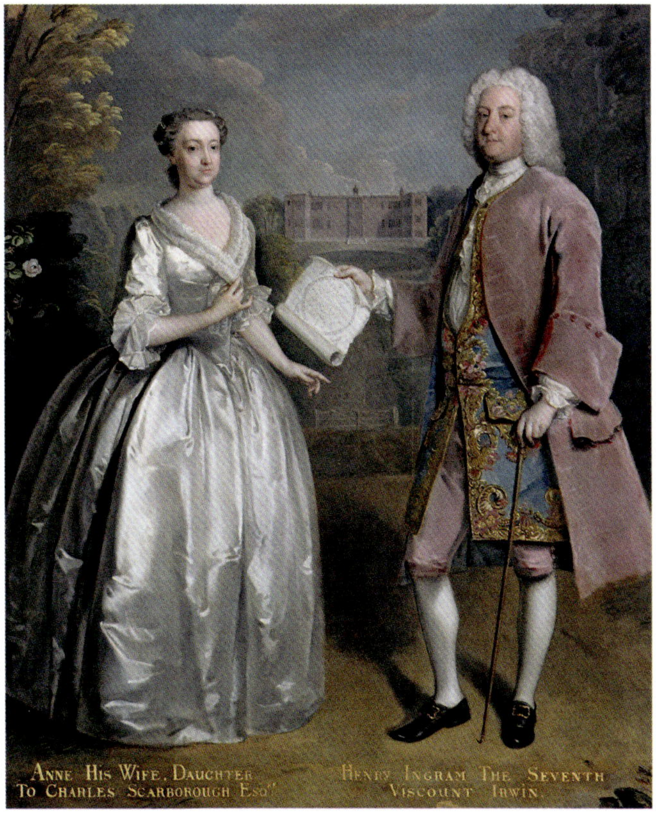

Portrait of Henry 7th Viscount Irwin and His Wife Anne (detail) by Philippe Mercier, 1742. © Leeds Museums and Art Galleries (Temple Newsam House), U.K.

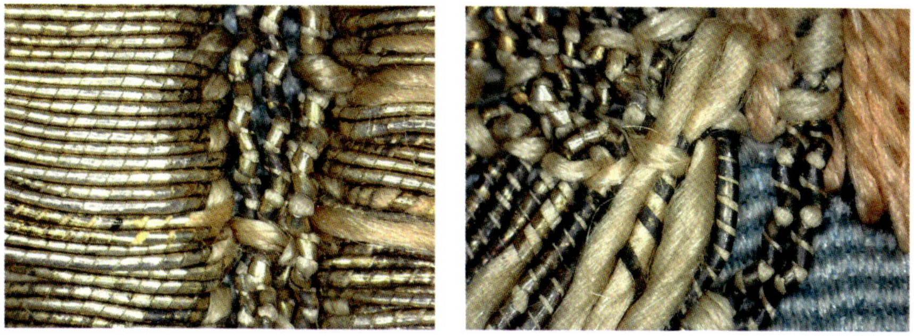

Two details of the embroidery, outlined below.

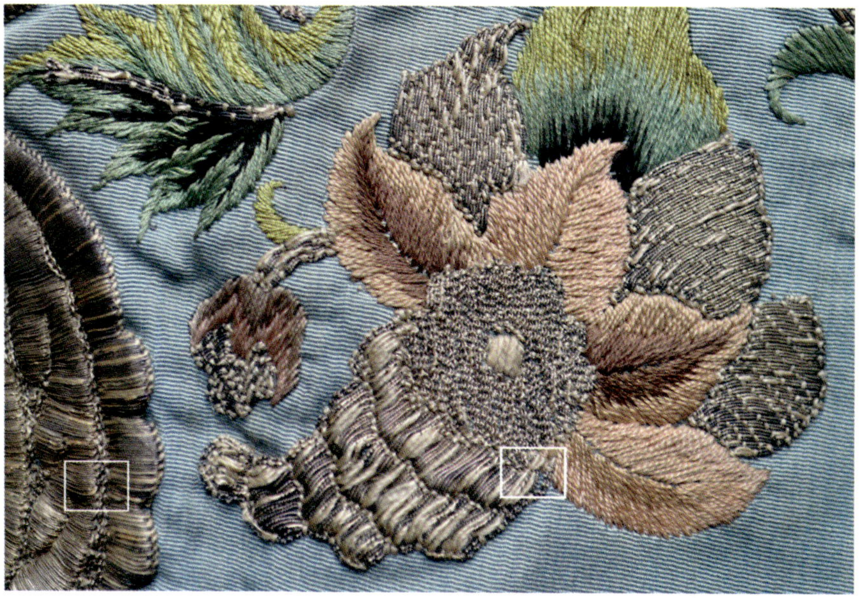

Above: Detail of the embroidery below the pocket on the left forepart.

Below: The back of the detail above.

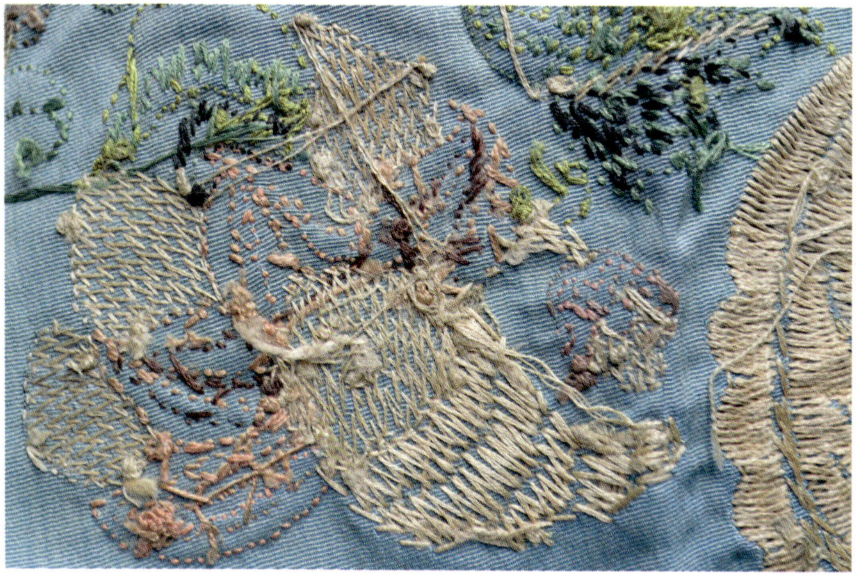

Silver and silver-gilt filé threads, purl and plate were worked in several techniques along with coloured silk twist of different thickness to give definition. The silk threads were worked first, in satin and overlapping satin stitches. Along the centre of the leaves and petals, the stitches chevron away from each other, so the angled silk threads catch the light differently.

Paired gilt threads were couched down with silk, working back and forth over a cut parchment shape, to give the raised effect. The warm beige and tan-coloured silk threads used to couch are now barely visible against the gilt, but would have appeared brighter when the waistcoat was worn, and can be seen clearly in the image of the reverse of the embroidery. Lengths of paired silver and silver-gilt filé threads were applied flat to the blue silk ground to form petal shapes, with alternate pairs being caught down to form a basket weave effect. The wavy silver-gilt filé thread, formed by wrapping a highly-twisted silk core in thin, fine metal strip, was also applied in pairs, all of these techniques being used to best reflect the light and give greater depth to the design.

Claire Thornton, *The School of Historical Dress.*

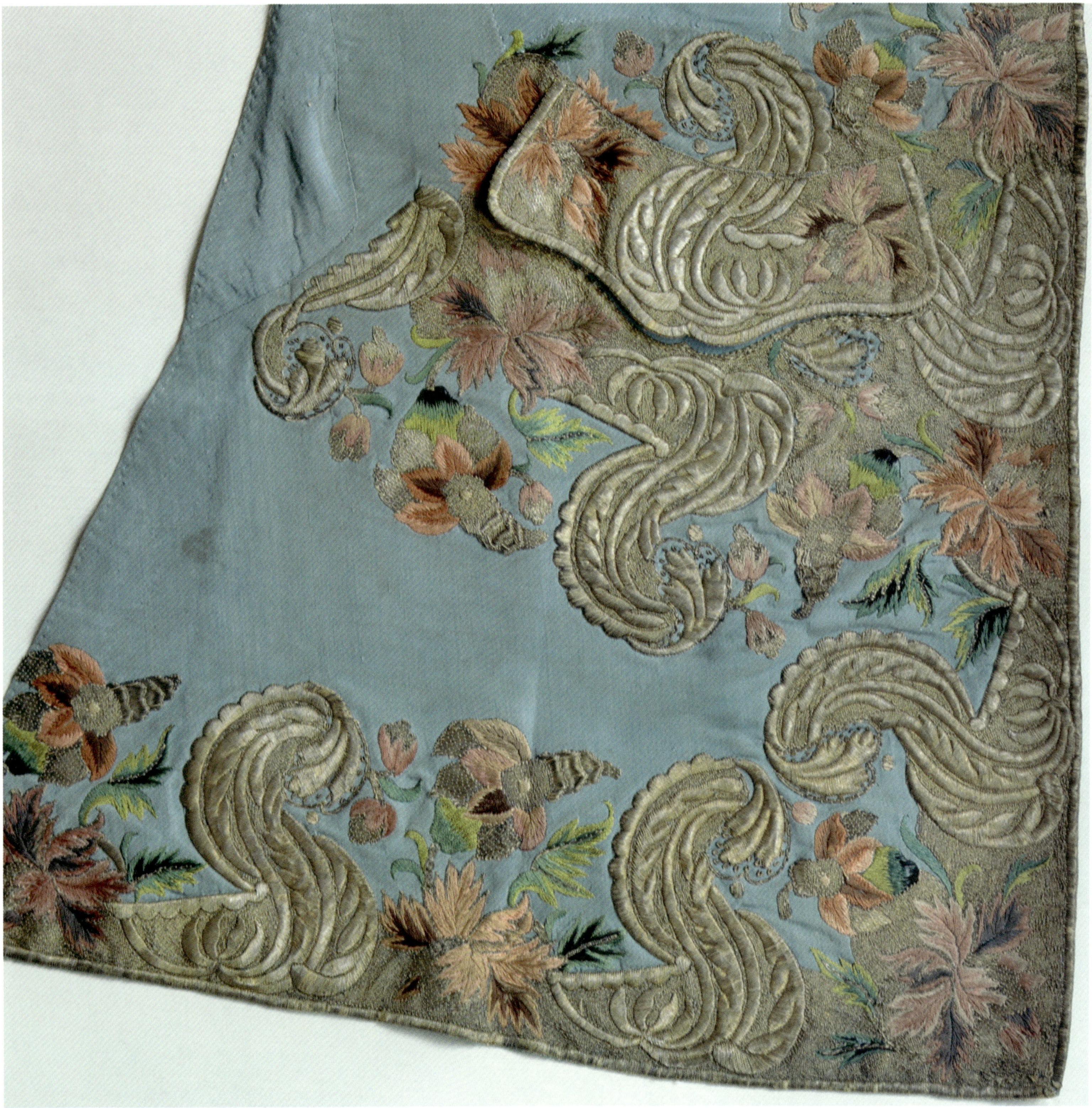

The skirt of the right forepart on page 14.

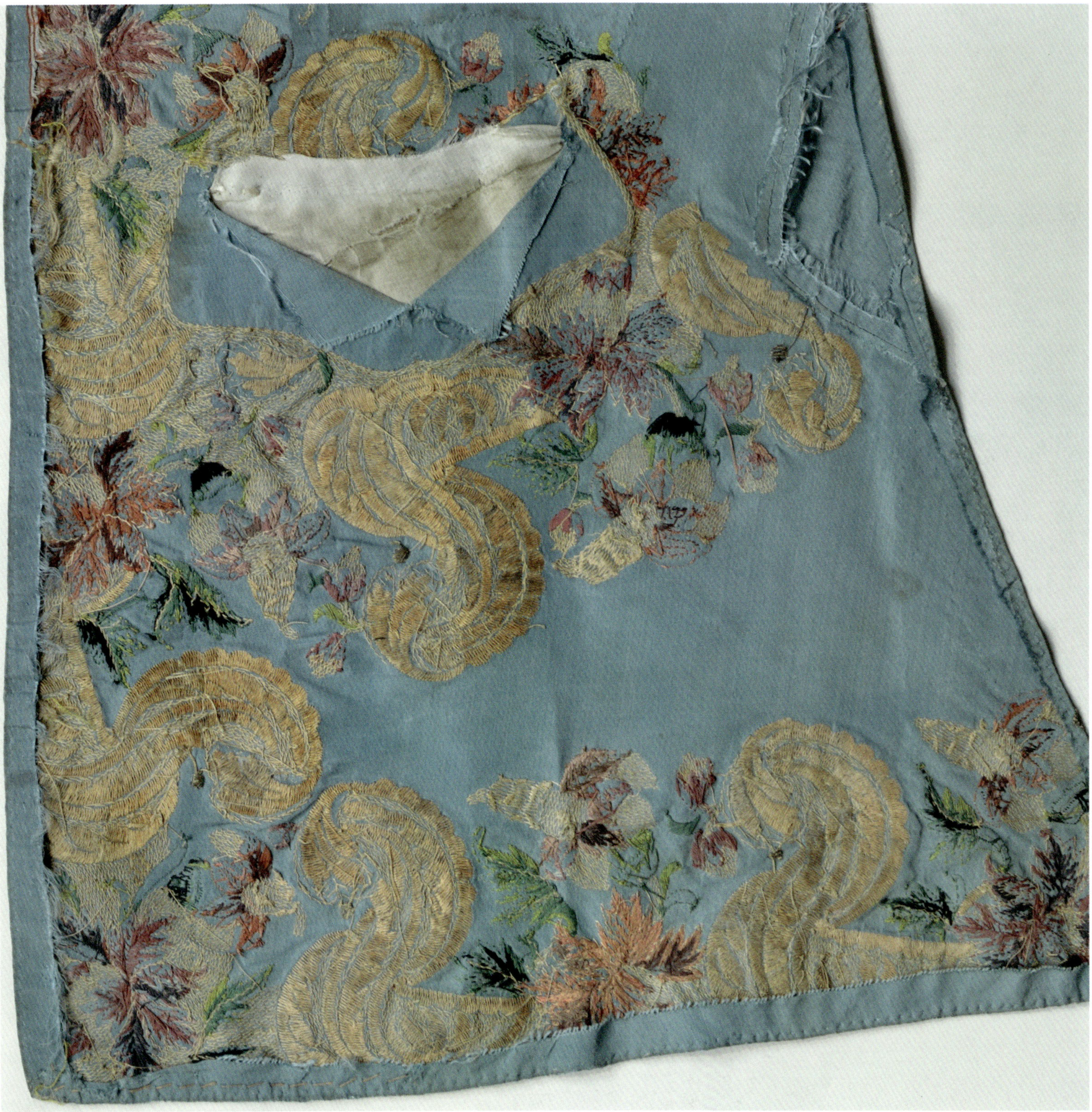

The back of the skirt of the right forepart on page 14.

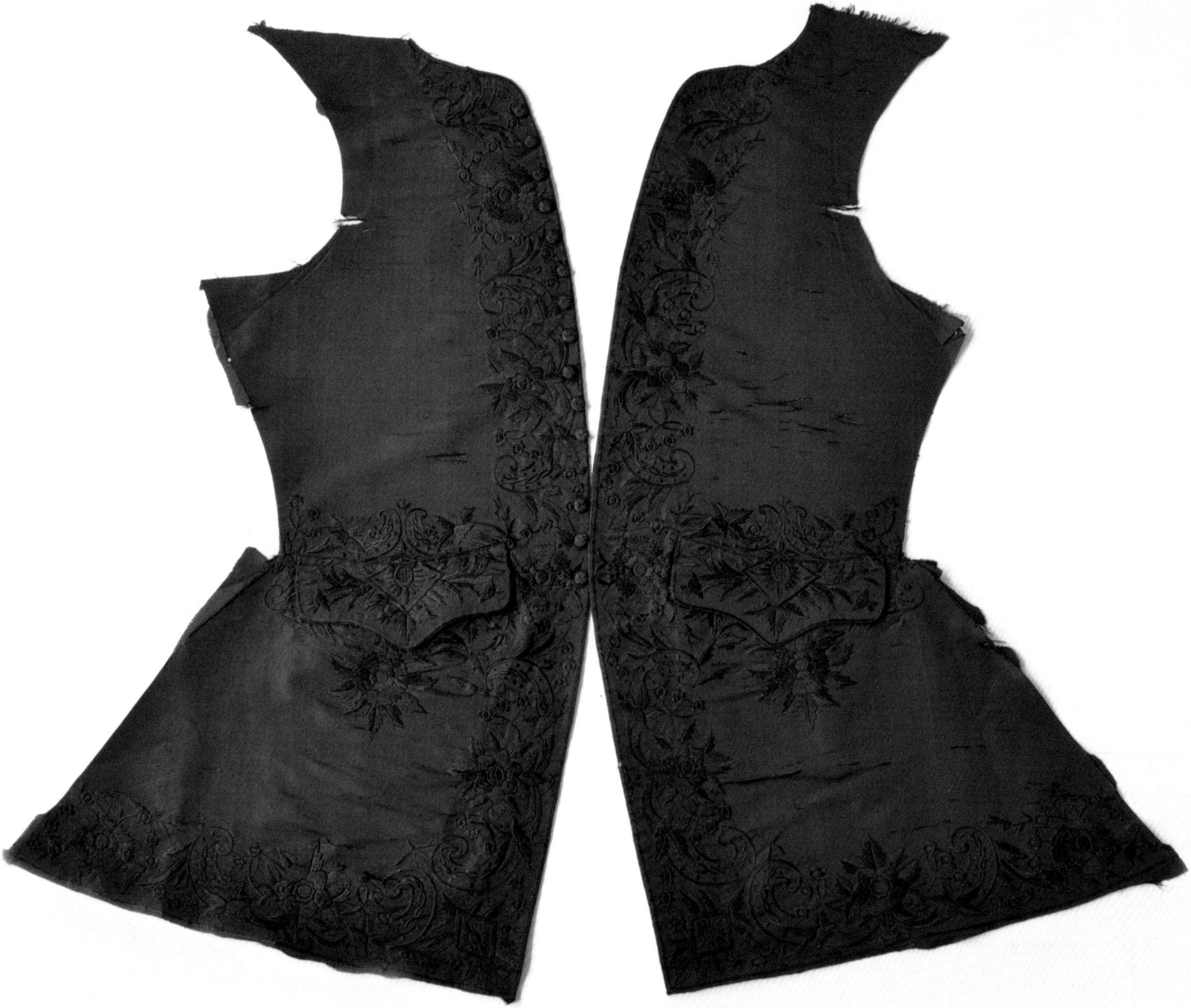

A pair of waistcoat foreparts in black silk grosgrain, 1735-1745.
HC.W-4.97-1

They have embroidered borders, and embroidery on the pocket flaps and around the pockets; this may have been done in China for the European market. The embroidery is done in overlapping satin stitch using black heavily twisted silk thread, and the use of stitches worked in different directions makes them catch the light differently, giving a slightly three-dimensional look to the design.

The foreparts have been made up and unpicked, and the fabric is quite fragile and splitting in places; they are made with a fly front, and one of the fifteen silk thread-covered buttons is missing. The front edges have an interlining of blue linen, and there is a strip of natural cotton on the inside front edge of the right forepart, behind the buttons. The pocket bags are still in place, made of a coarse natural cotton.

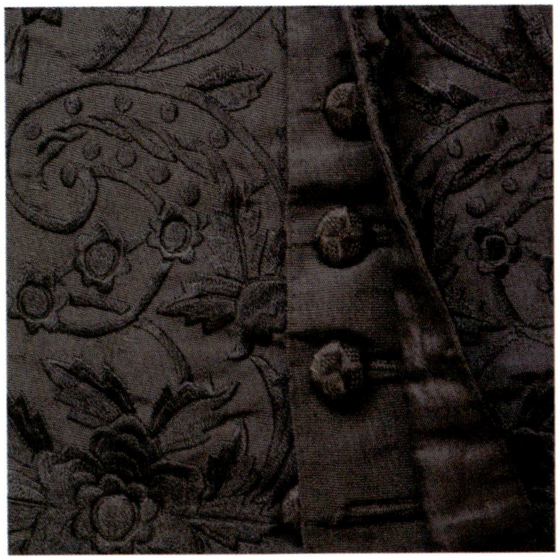

Detail of the fly front.

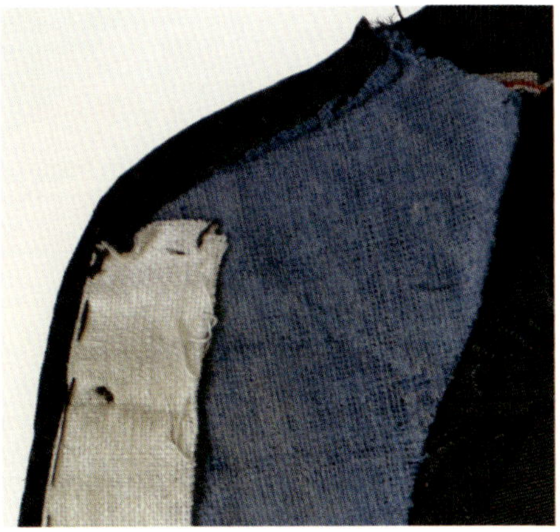

Detail of inside the top of the right forepart, where the blue linen interlining and natural cotton strip behind the buttons can be seen.

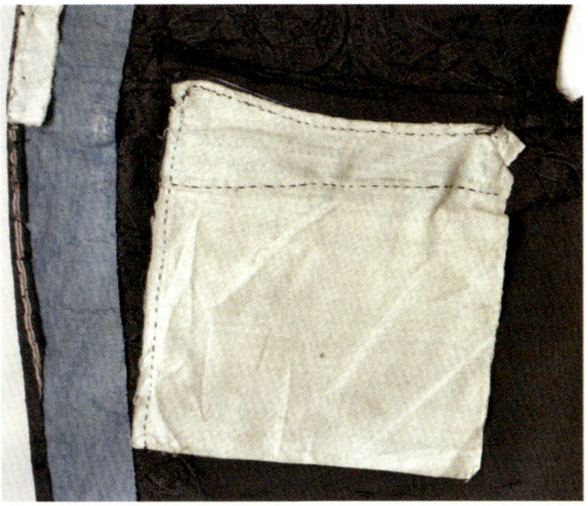

Inside the right forepart, showing one of the cotton pocket bags.

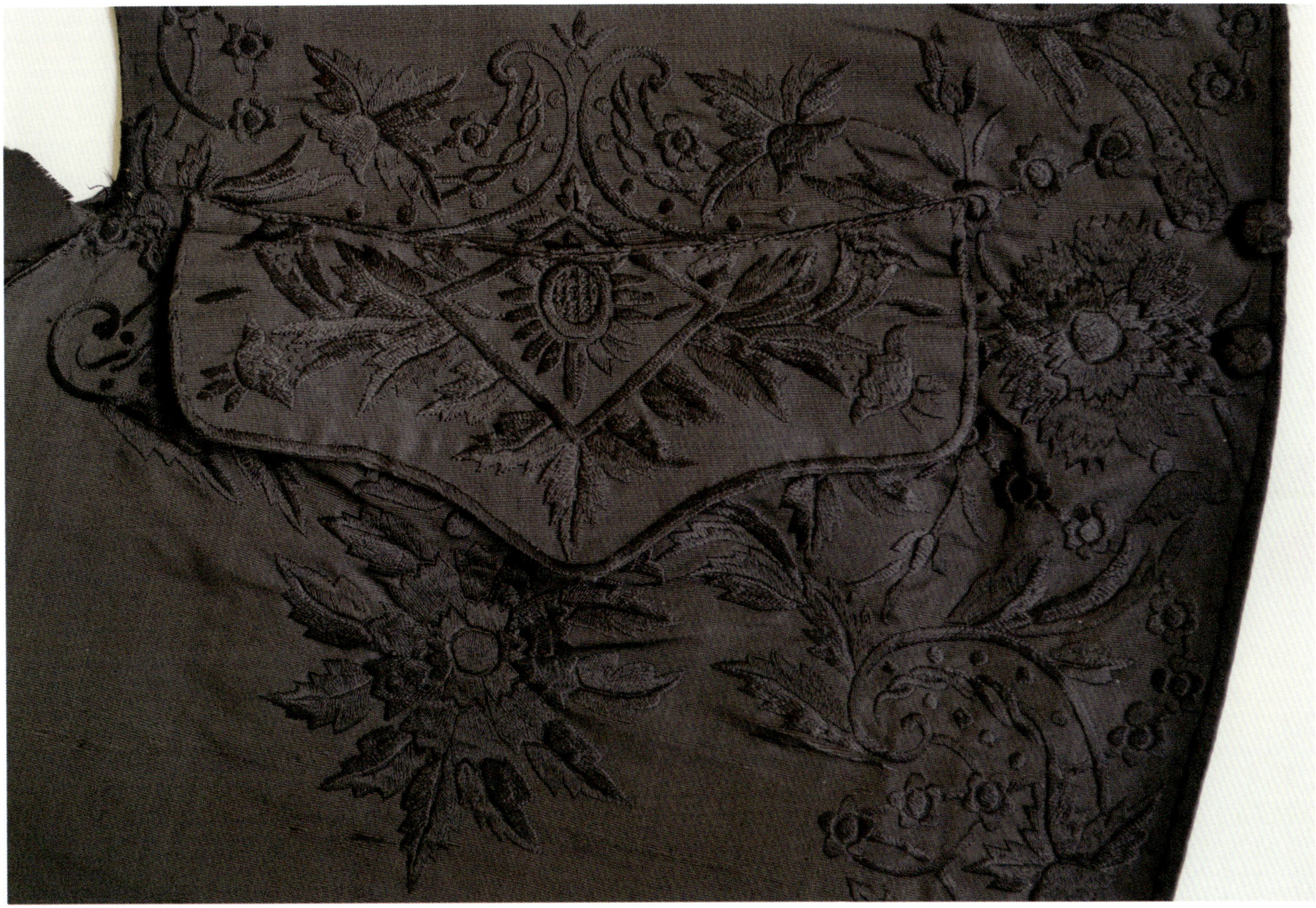

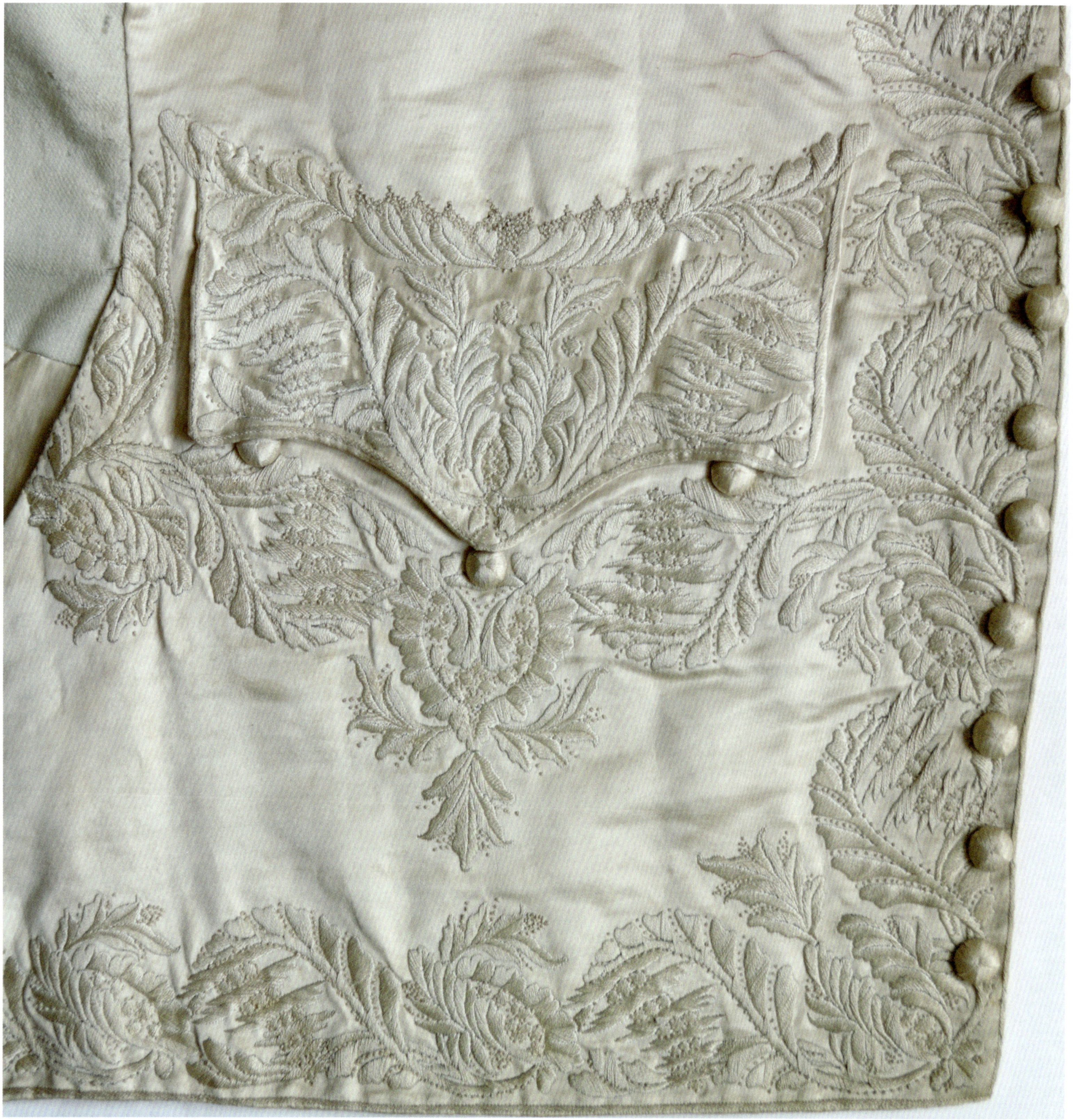

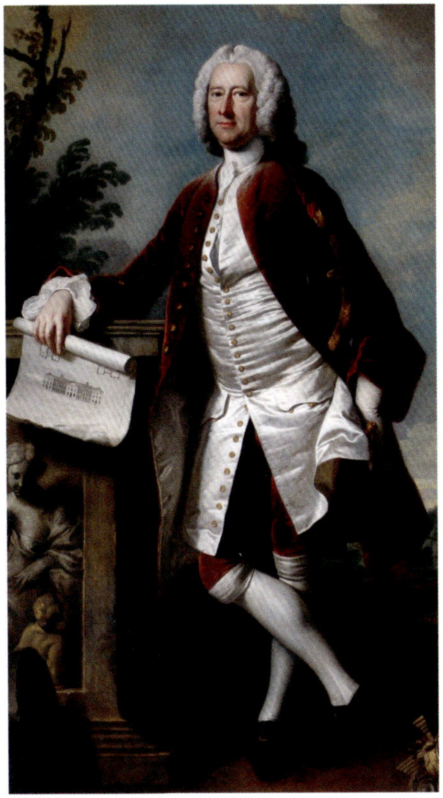

Portrait of Theodore Jacobsen (detail) by Thomas Hudson, 1746. © Coram in the care of the Foundling Museum, London. Jacobsen was a merchant of German descent, and architect of the Foundling Hospital.

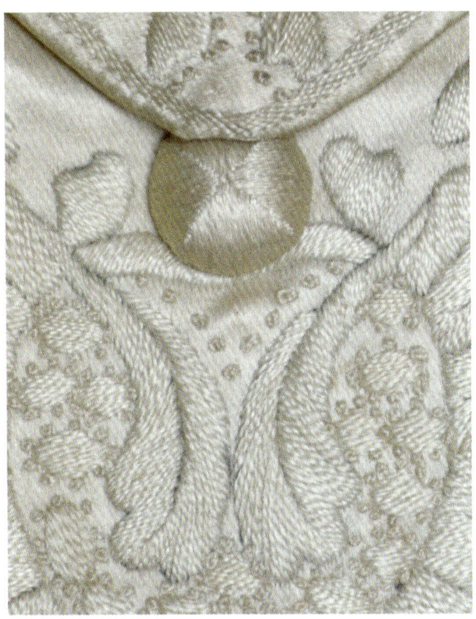

The button below the middle of the pocket flap.

A waistcoat in ivory silk satin, 1740-1760. HC.W-7.77

It has embroidery in matching twisted silk thread, of a stylised leafy pattern, bordering the foreparts, below the pockets and on the pocket flaps. The body is lined with ivory fustian and the skirt linings and forepart facings are ivory silk twill. The back skirts are in the ivory satin and are much pieced. There are fifteen buttonholes concealed by a fly front which extends from the neck to the level of the pockets, and twenty-one domed buttons, covered in silk threads, the lowest six being merely decorative. The back and the pocket bags are in ivory calimanco.

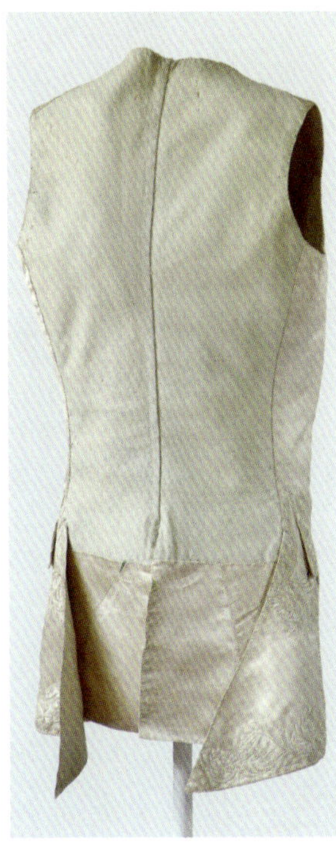

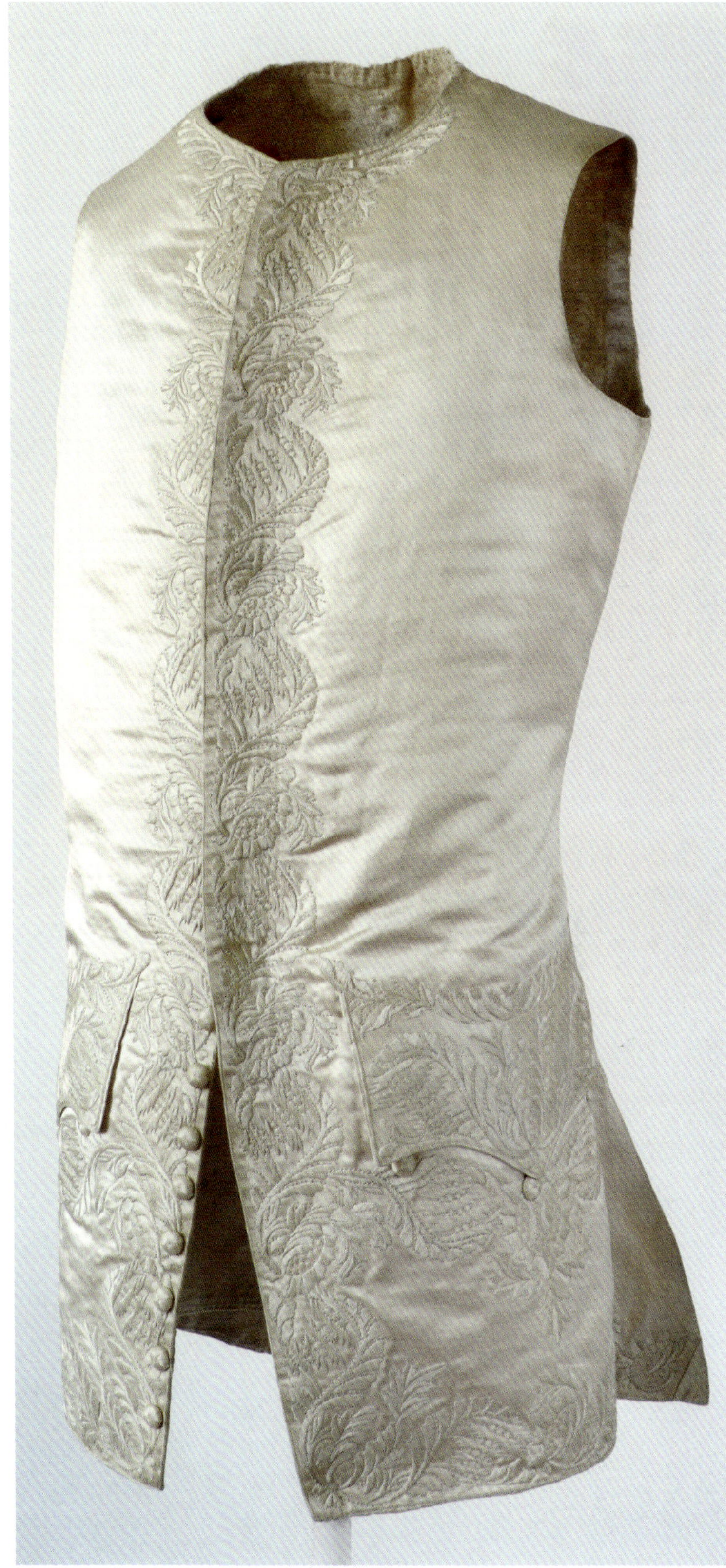

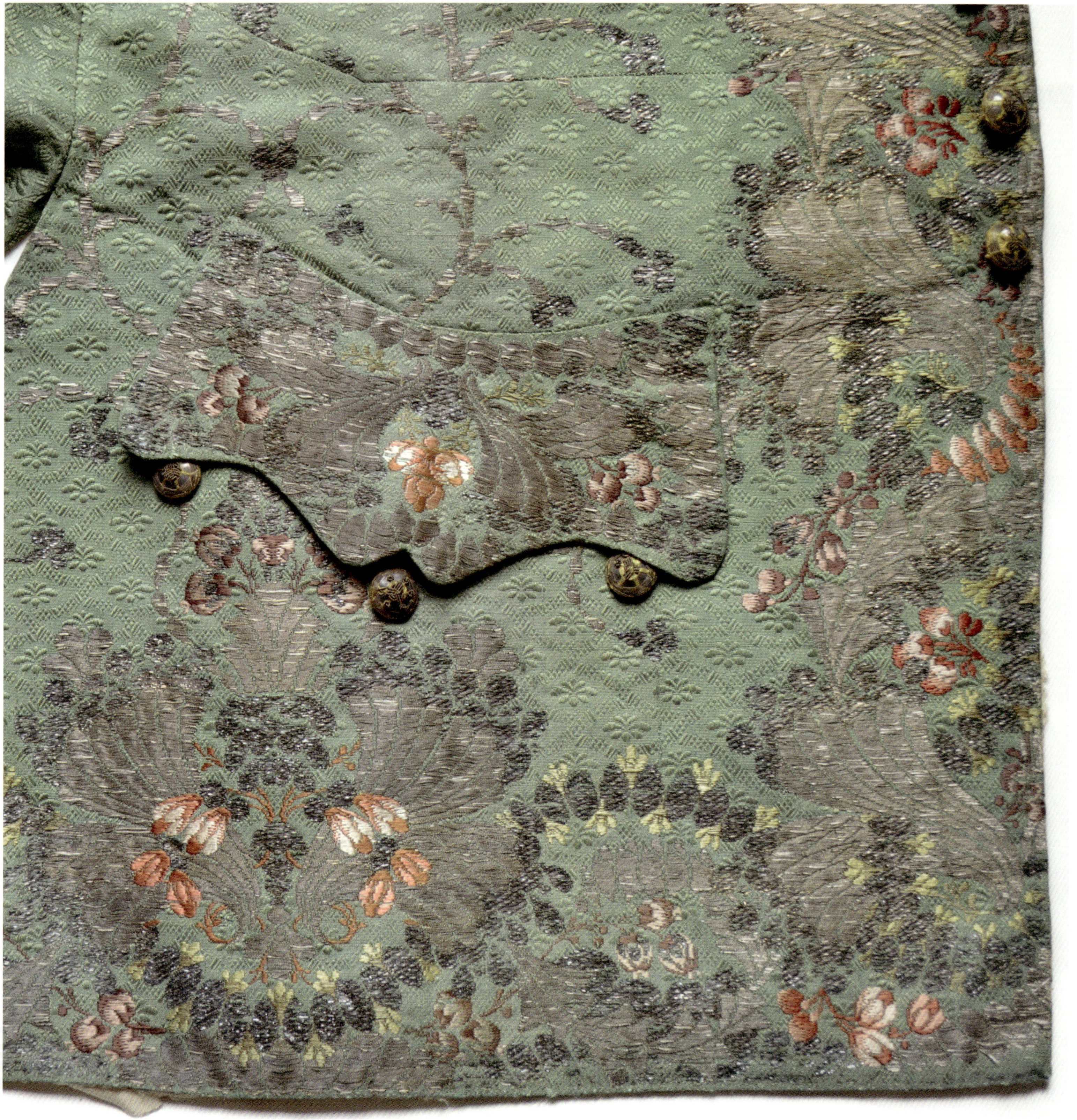

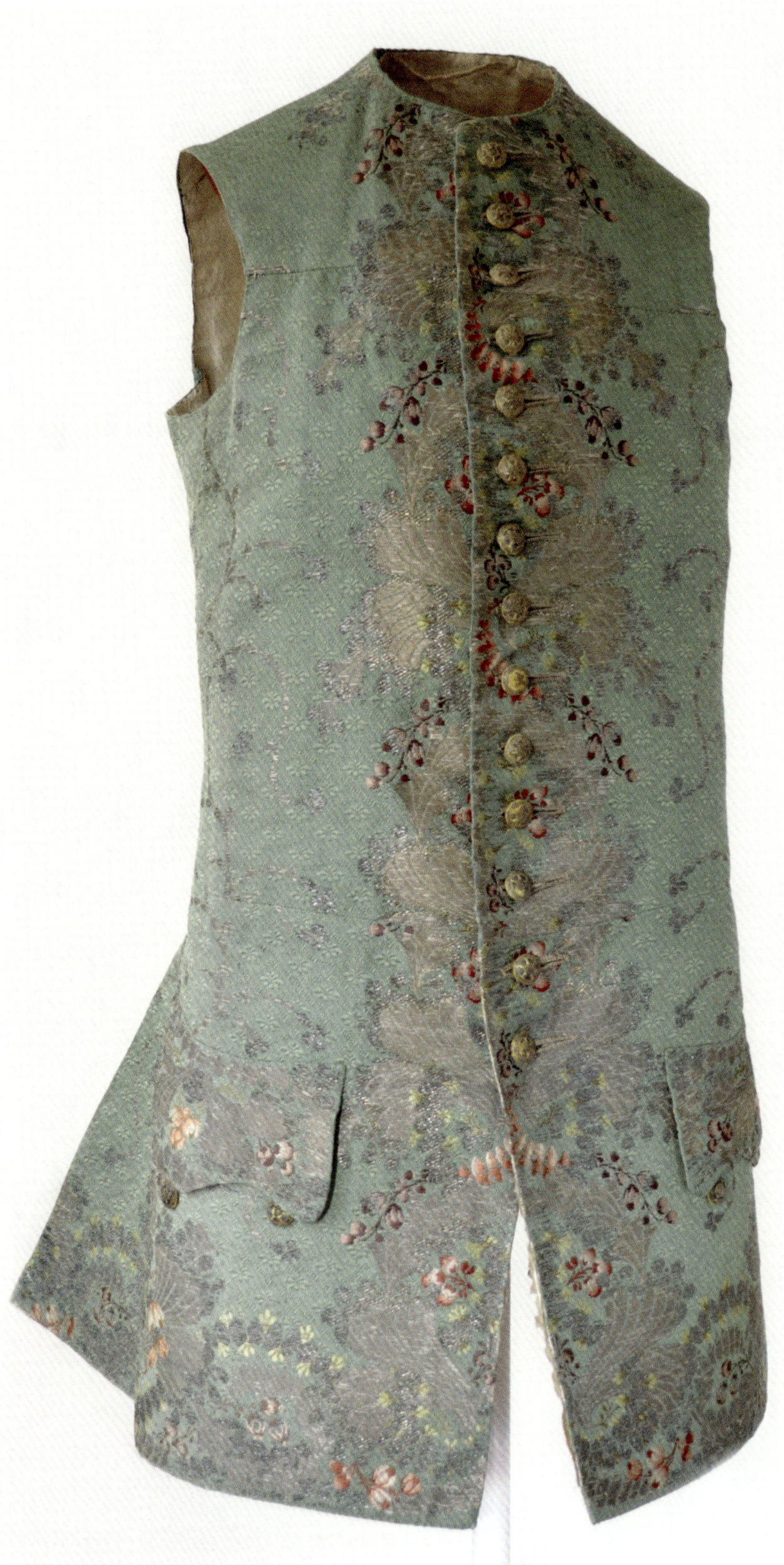

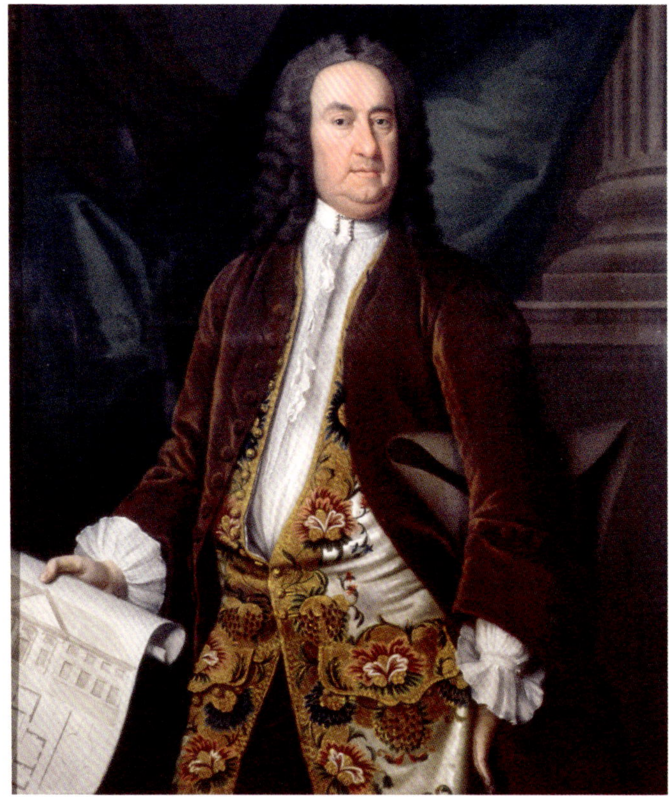

Richard Beau Nash (detail) by William Hoare, 1745. Image courtesy of Tunbridge Wells Museum and Art Gallery. Nash was the self-appointed Master of Ceremonies at the fashionable resort of Bath and later Tunbridge Wells.

A waistcoat in green silk, 1740-1760. HC.W-12.11

The foreparts have been woven to shape with a self pattern and a brocaded border in polychrome silks, silver filé and silver flat strip (page 211); there is a trailing pattern in the silver threads over the rest of the foreparts. The pocket flaps are also brocaded, with three buttons positioned below them. There are fourteen domed buttons down the front, decorated with silver-gilt (page 216). The back body is in plain green silk and the back skirts are in the green self-patterned silk with no brocading. The side seams have a narrow strip of this let in, to increase the size. The front halves of the foreparts and their skirts are lined with cream silk twill, which is disintegrating; this silk also lines the back skirts. The rest of the body is lined in natural linen, and there is a narrow strip of linen in the back neck as a loop for hanging up the waistcoat. Narrow darts have been taken from the front armholes to within ½" of the front edge, and there is a seam across the foreparts, at the waist, making them shorter than their original woven size. The foreparts have a thin layer of wool wadding, and the hems and front edges of the skirts are stiffened with buckram. This could have been part of a suit made from the unbrocaded self-patterned silk of the back skirts.

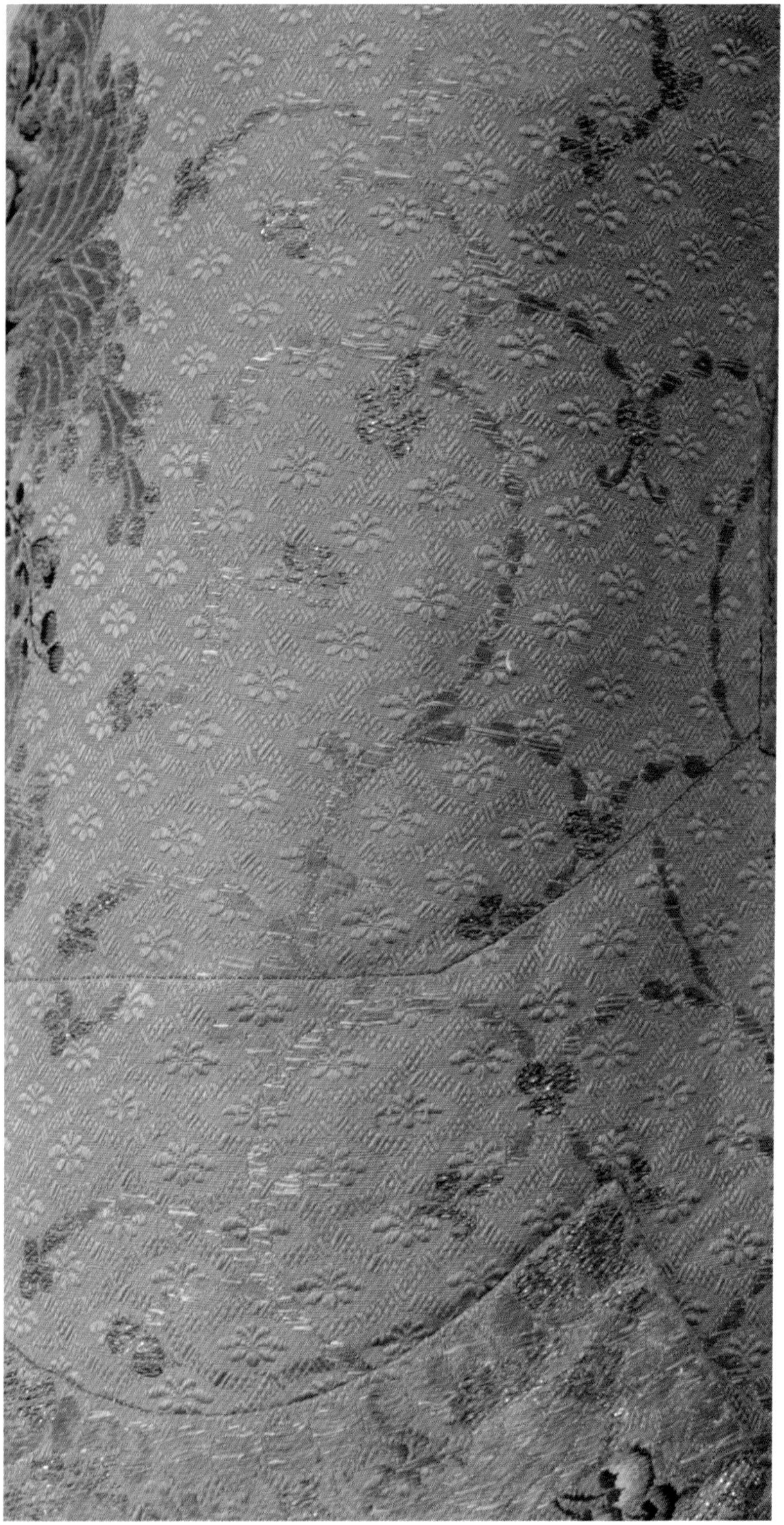

The side of the left forepart of the waistcoat on page 23; the seam can be seen across the forepart at the waist.

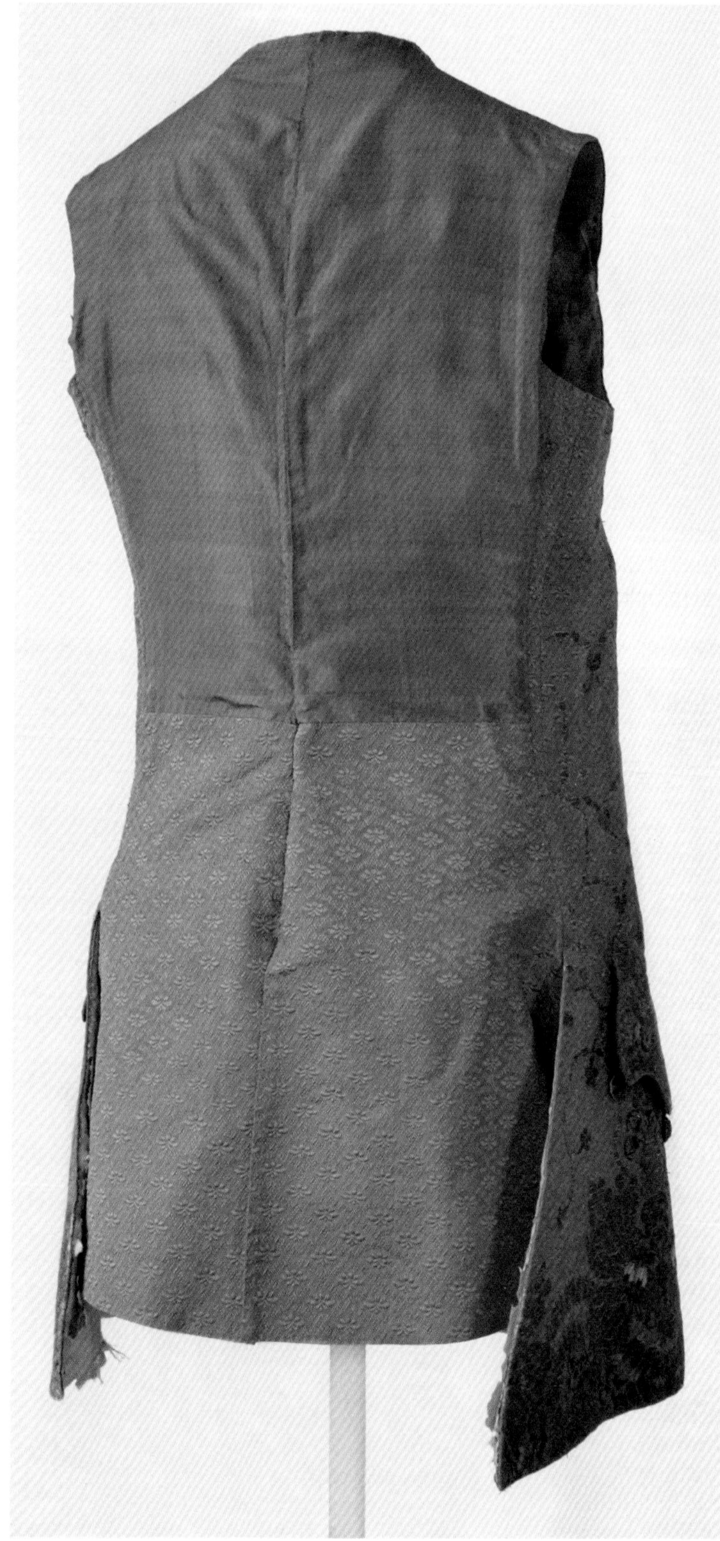

The back of the waistcoat on page 23, showing the skirt in self-patterned silk, with no brocading, and the plain silk back body.

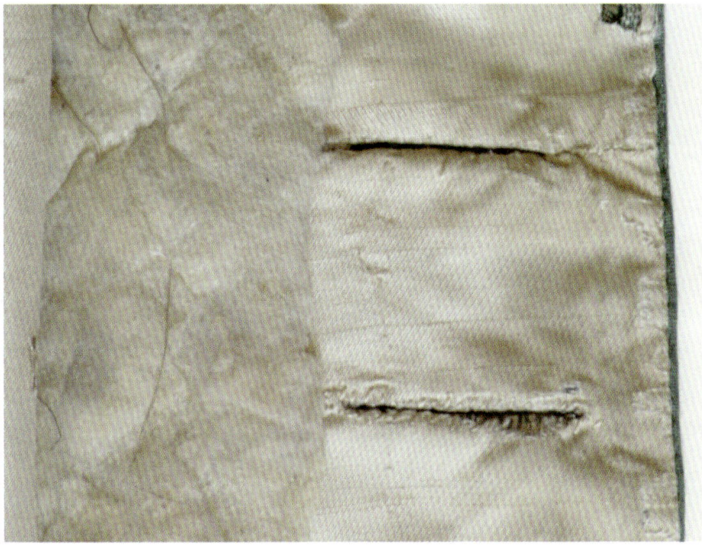

Detail of the cream silk twill facing of the left forepart, with buttonholes, and the edge of the wool wadding over the chest.

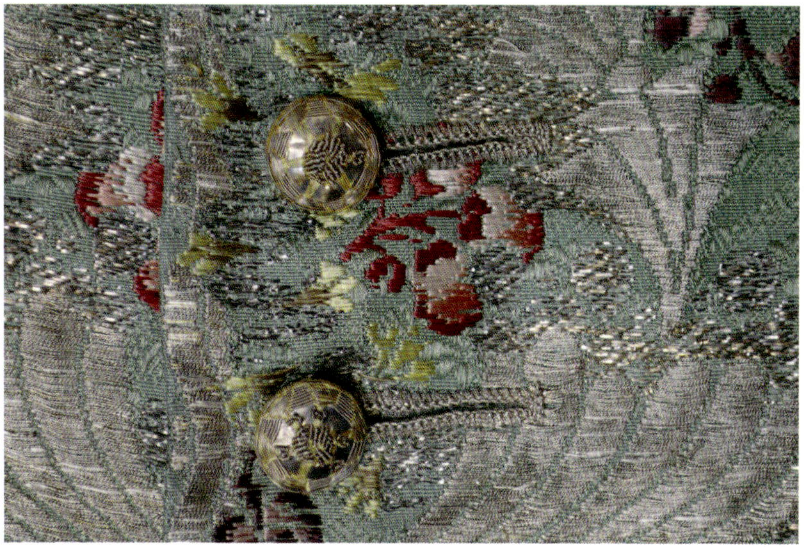

Detail of the buttons (page 216) and buttonholes.

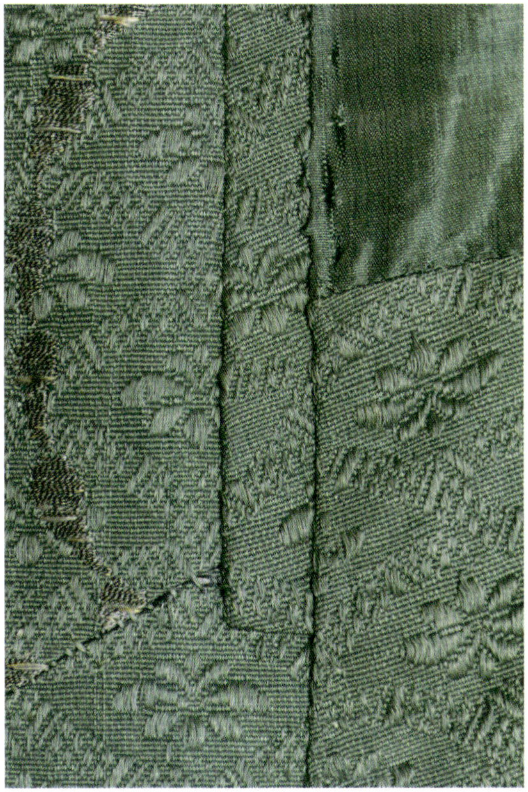

The left side seam at the waist; the plain silk of the back body is at the top on the right, joining the back skirt fabric, which has no silver pattern. Part of the narrow inserted piece in the side seam can be seen, and this would have increased the girth of the waistcoat.

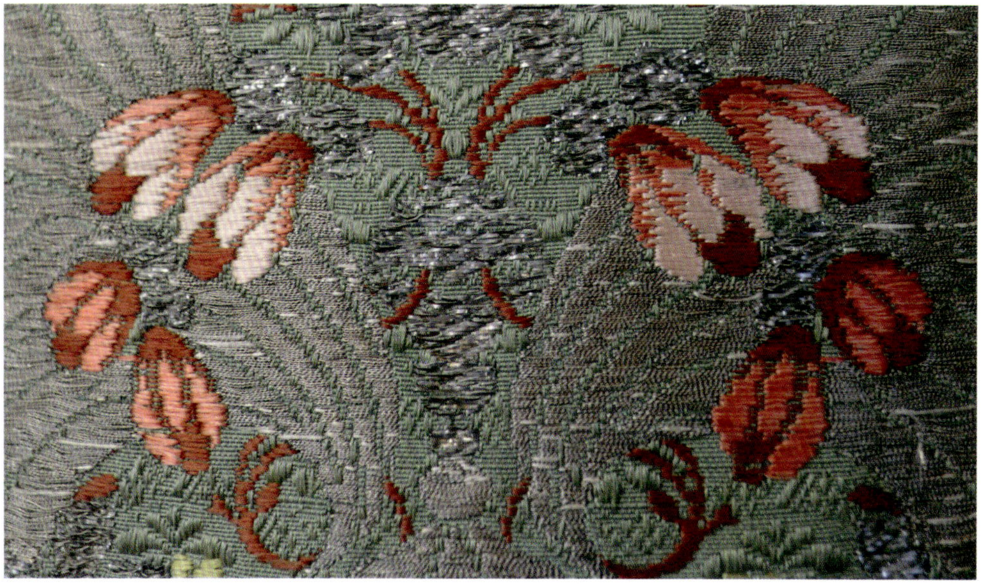

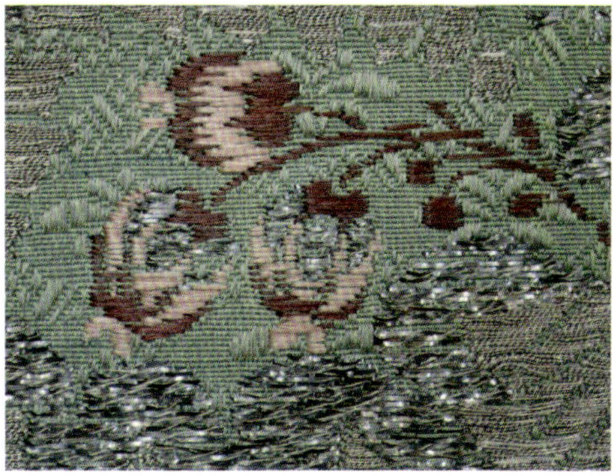

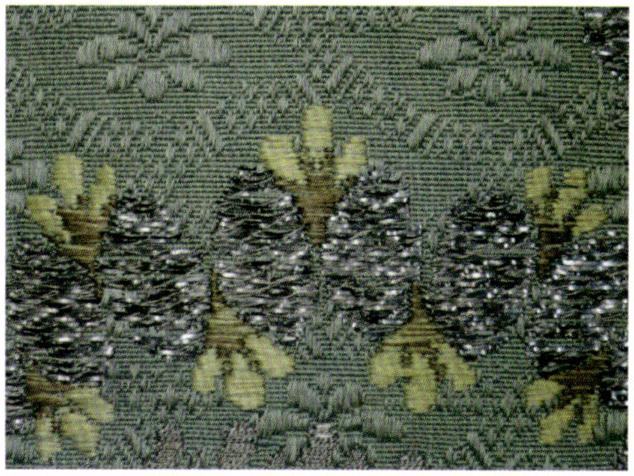

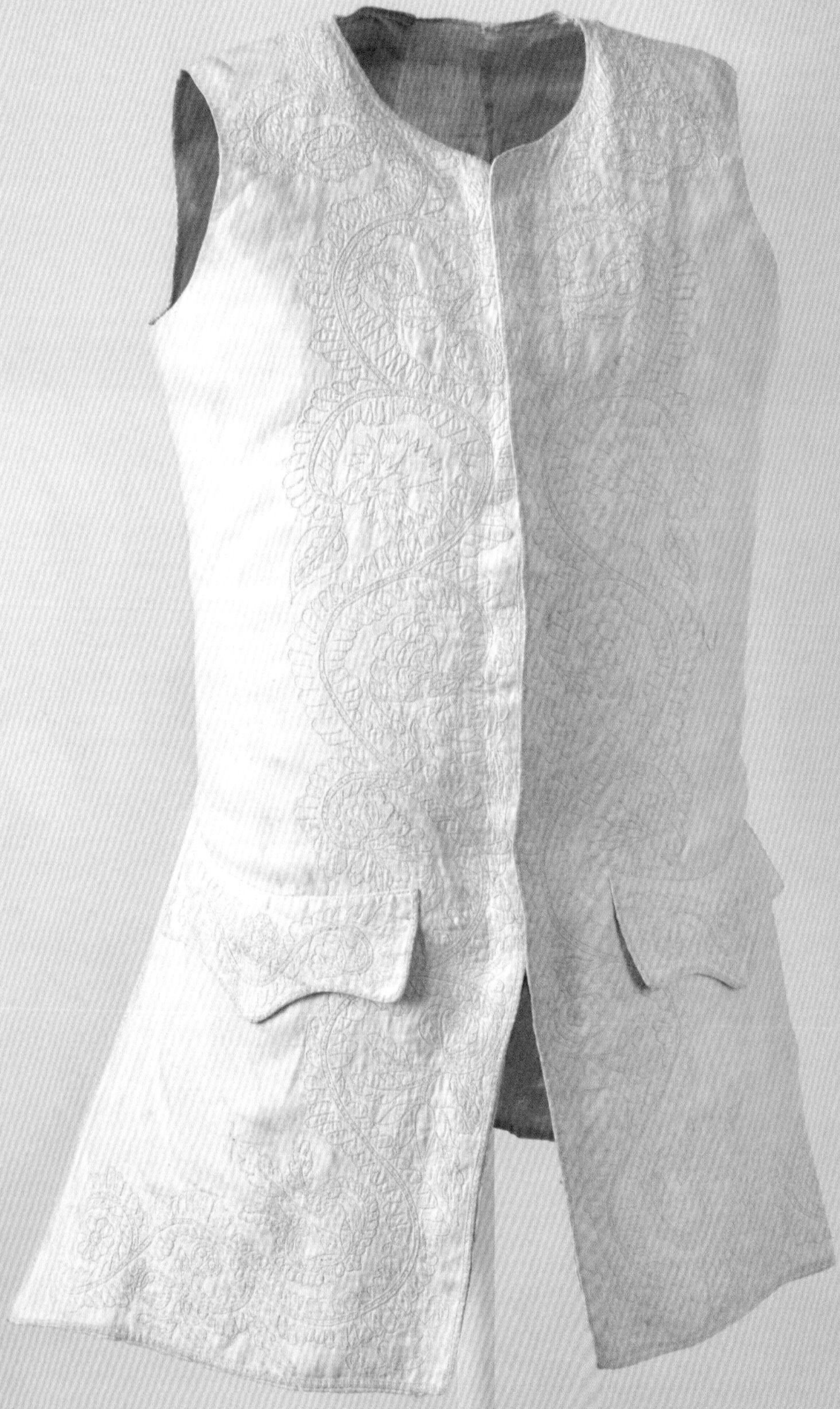

A waistcoat in white linen, 1740-1750.
HC.W-0.5

The foreparts have a wide border of embroidery, and this also appears on the pocket flaps which are only decorative as there are no pockets. It has a fly front, which goes down as far as the pocket flaps, with worked eyelet holes for removable buttons, which are now missing. The lining and the back are in white linen; an inserted panel of natural linen in the centre back is 2″ wide at the back neck widening to 4½″ where it stops at the level of the top of the pocket flaps. The waistcoat has been washed but now it is quite grubby.

The embroidery on this waistcoat is worked with a knotting technique. In the eighteenth century, knotting was considered a suitable pastime for ladies, and was simple to work, by making knots at even intervals on a thread drawn from a shuttle. When finished it could be couched on to a fabric ground, or applied as a fringe. Here though the knot itself is worked through the ground fabric, using a loosely spun linen thread, giving a subtle raised effect.

Claire Thornton, *The School of Historical Dress*

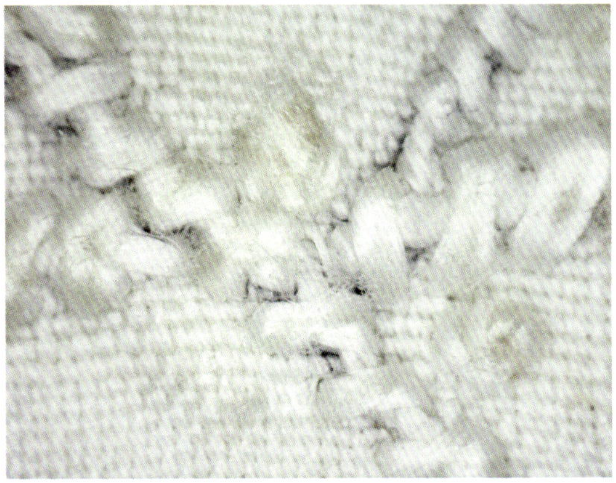

Detail of the embroidery, outlined in the image on the right; the inked lines of the pattern can be seen under the stitches.

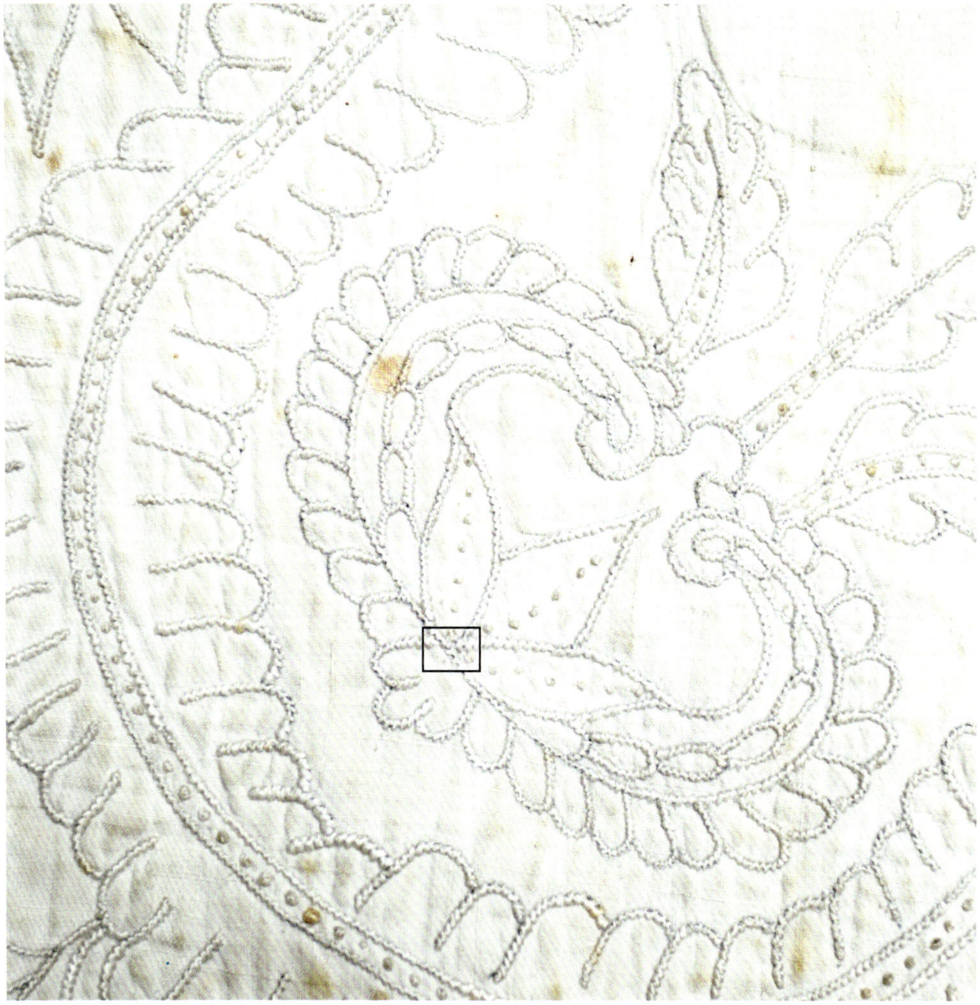

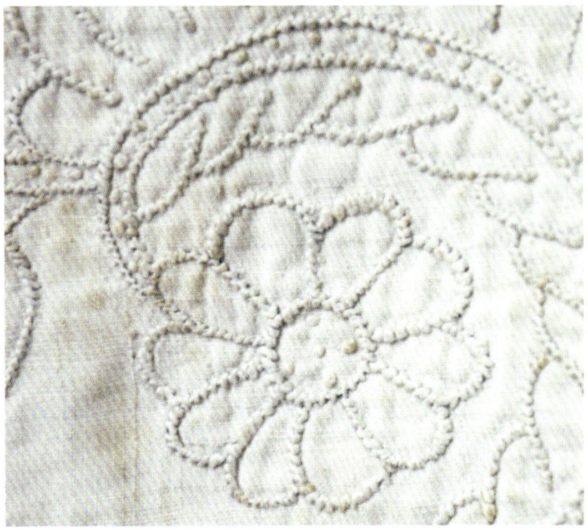

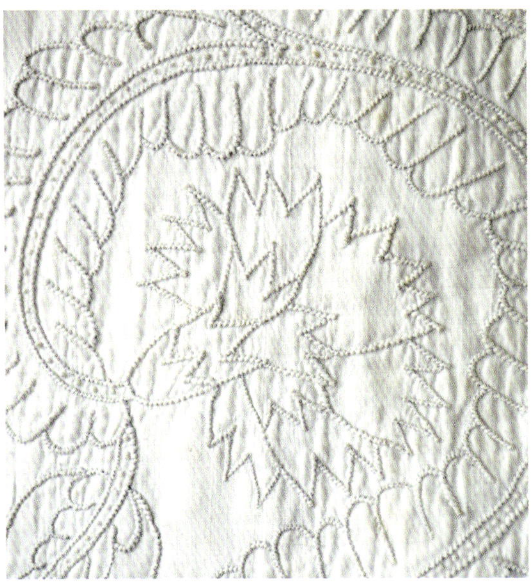

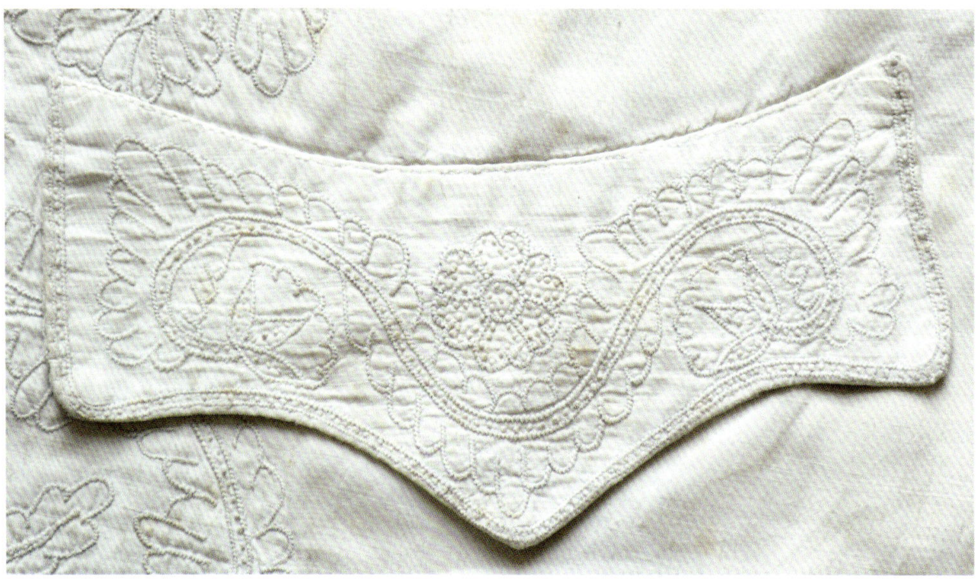

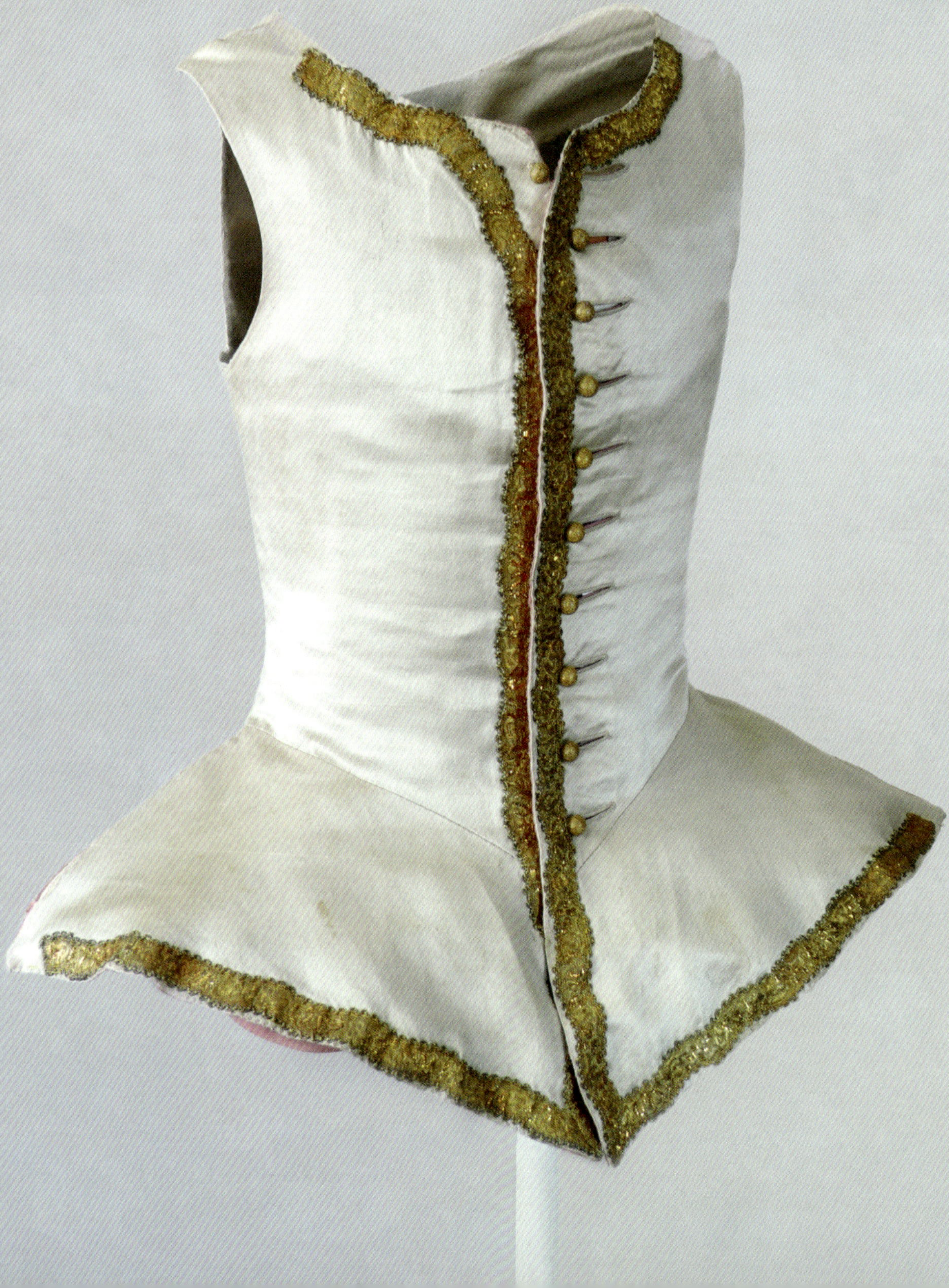

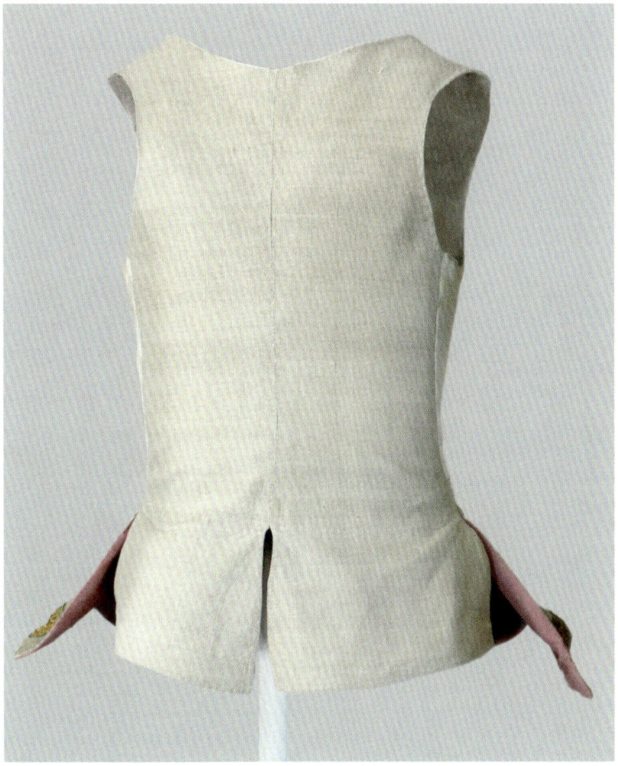

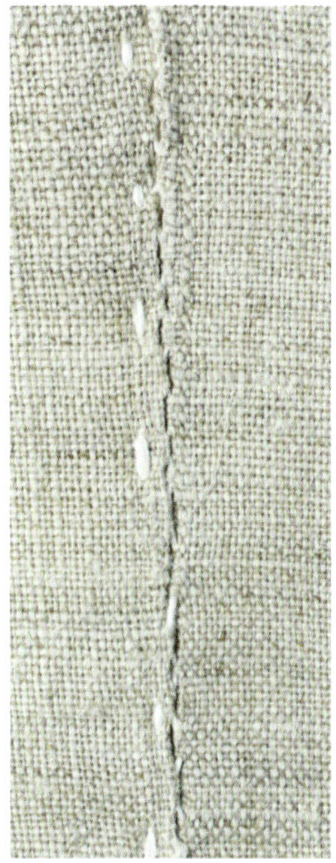

The centre back seam in the linen back of the waistcoat.

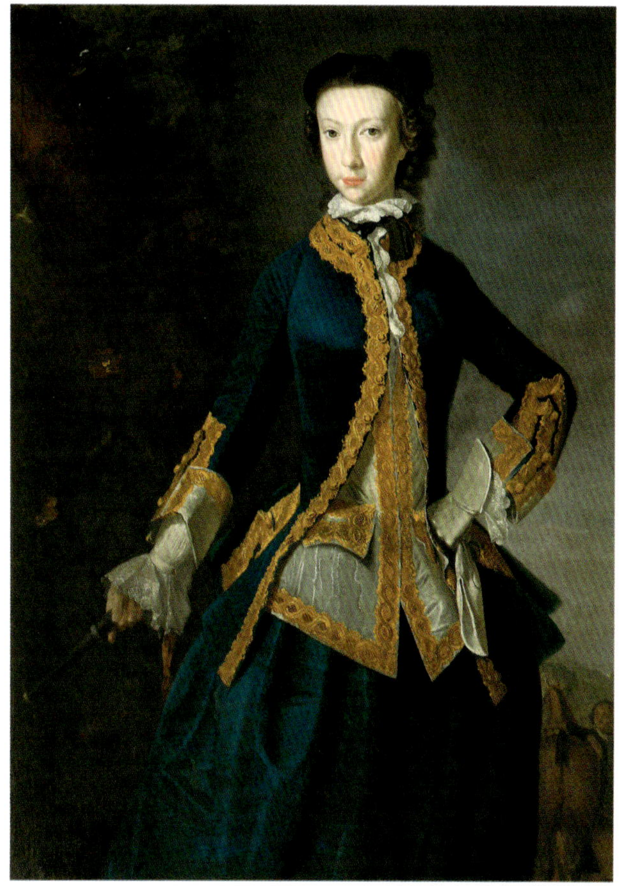

Detail of *Portrait of a Lady*, attributed to Robert Harvie (Scottish, active 1751-1763). © Christie's, London, 26 January 2011, Lot 249.

A waistcoat for a woman, in ivory silk satin, 1745-1760. HC.W-5.15

The waistcoat is French. The foreparts are edged with gold braid, and the ten gilt ball buttons are not original. The back is in natural linen with the body lined with ivory fustian and the back skirts unlined. The forepart bodies are lined with a greyer natural linen and the front skirts are lined with a pink silk and wool fabric. The front edge facings are also in the pink silk and wool, which is sewn on in separate strips on the left forepart with the edges turned in along the edges of the buttonholes.

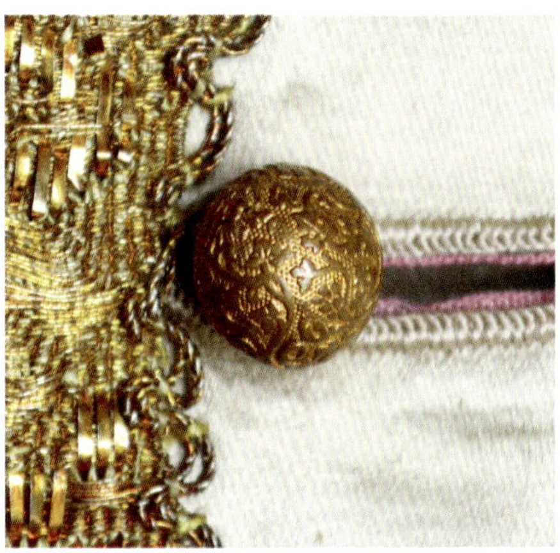

One of the buttons. They have the name A. P. & Cie, Paris, stamped on the back. This was a well-known firm of button makers in the late nineteenth and early twentieth centuries.

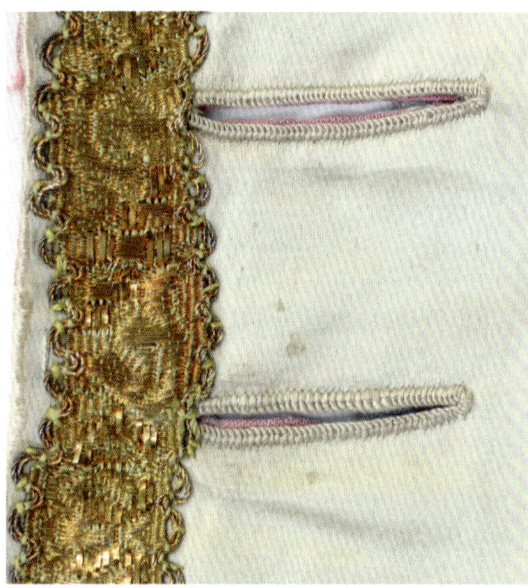

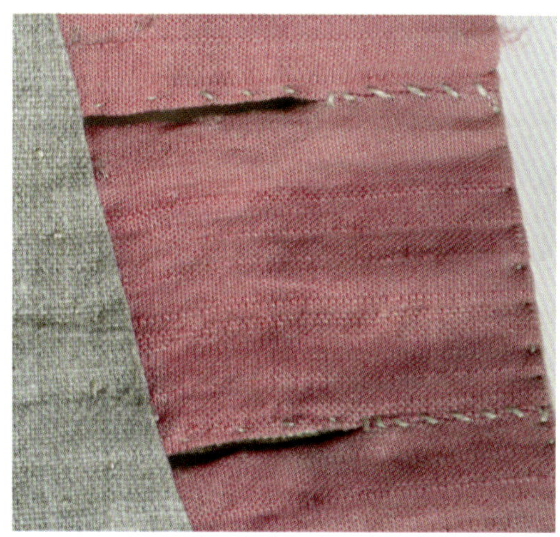

Inside the left front edge, showing the strips of pink silk and wool fabric behind the buttonholes, and the edge of the linen lining.

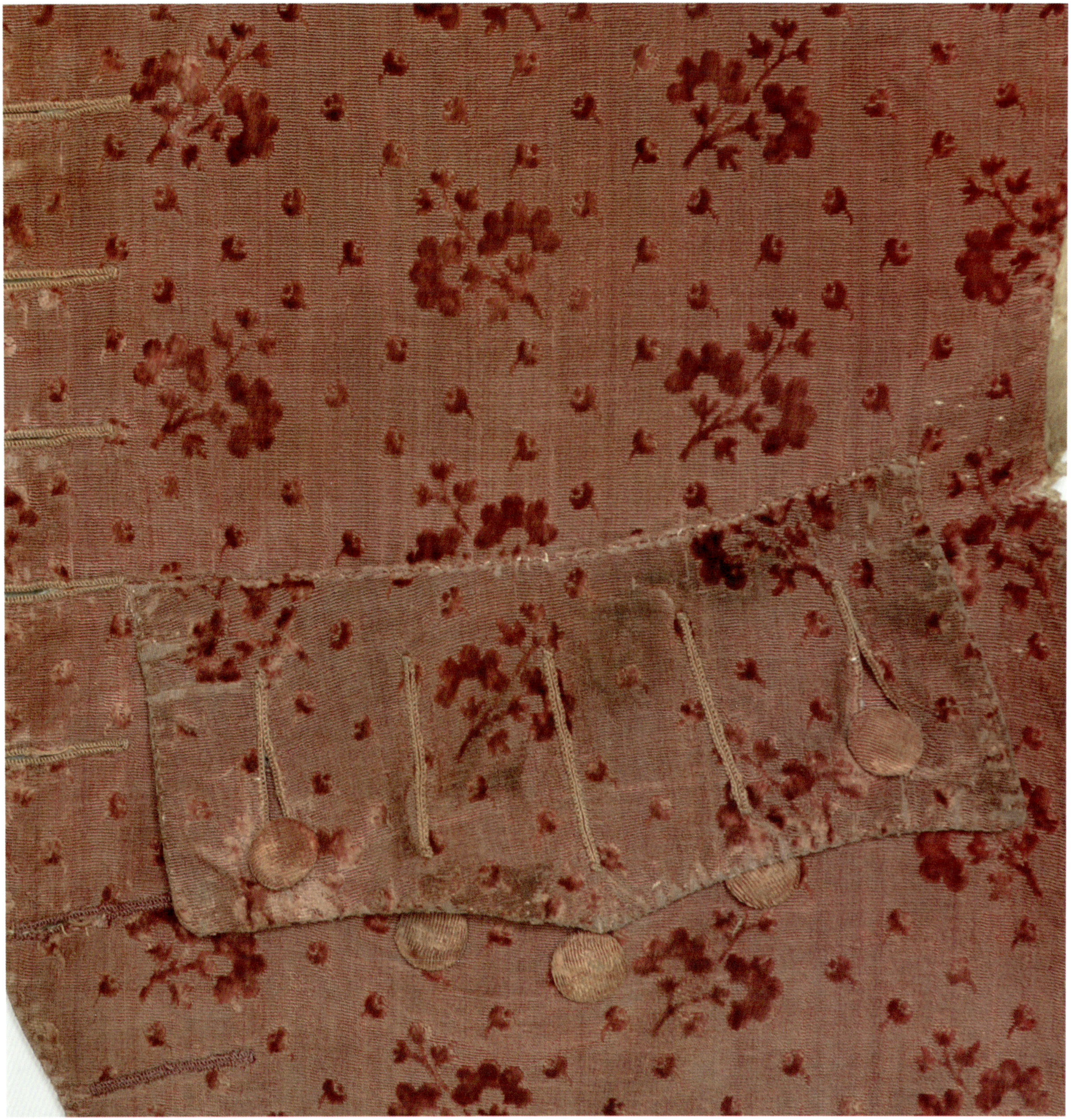

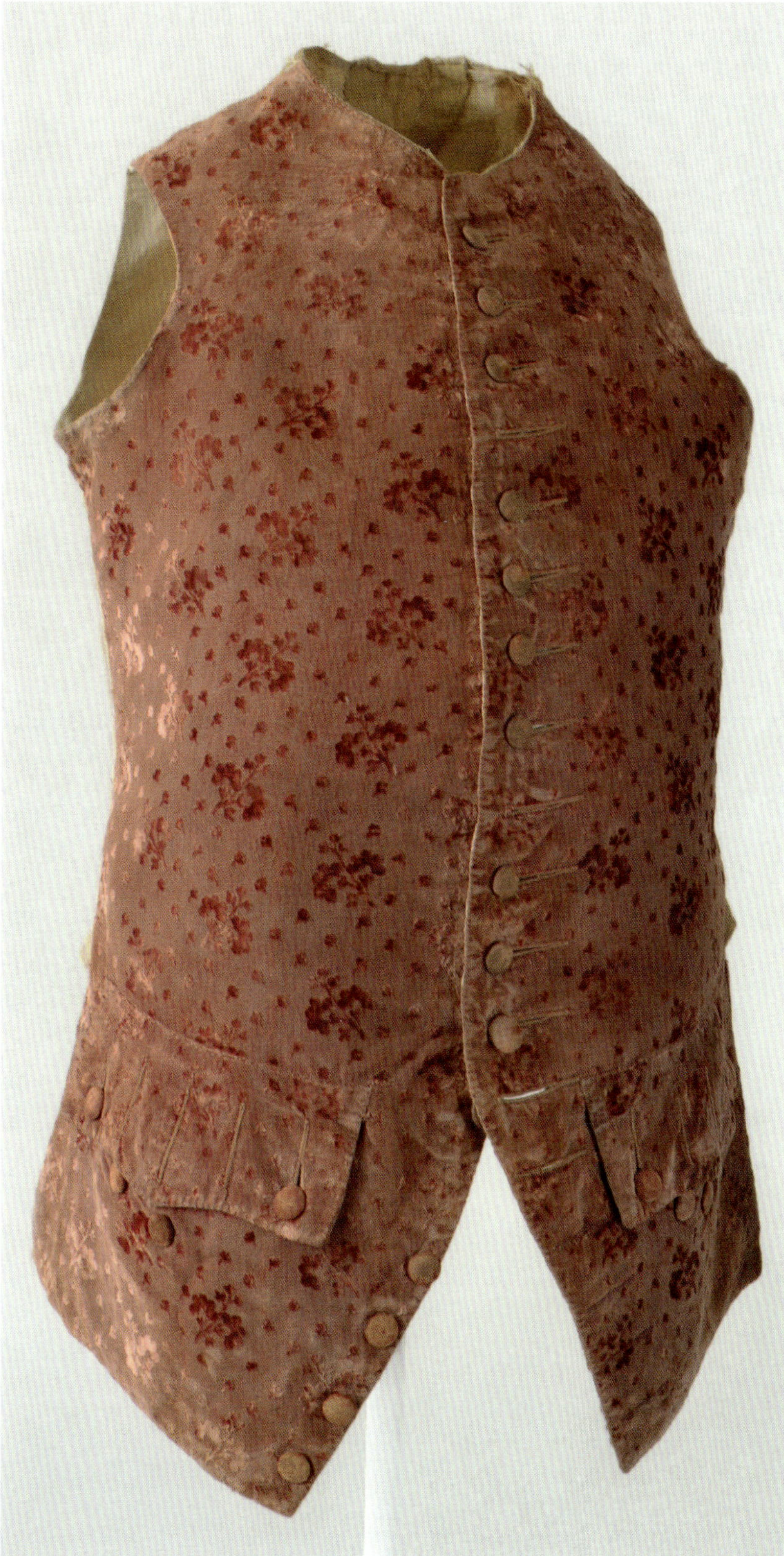

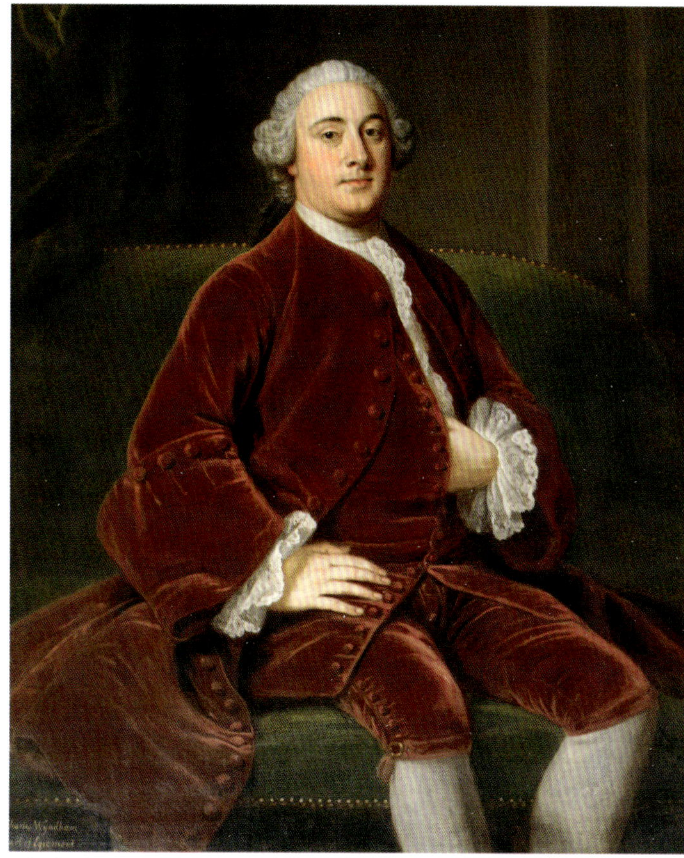

Charles Wyndham, 2nd Earl of Egremont (detail) by William Hoare of Bath, R.A., 1763, Petworth. © National Trust Images.

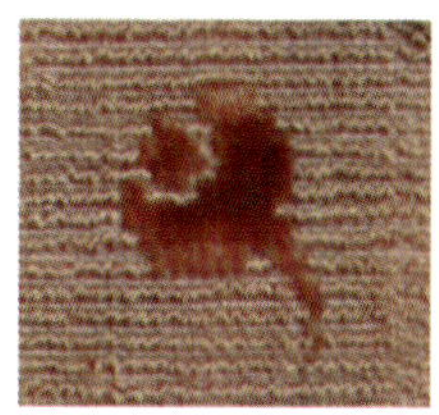

Left: Detail of the velvet showing the cut pile on a sprig and loops of the uncut pile on the ground.

A waistcoat in pink silk velvet, 1755-1765. HC.W-10.83

The pattern on the velvet is formed of flower sprays in cut pile on a ground of uncut pile, and the waistcoat was probably part of a suit. The back is in pale fawn silk faille lined with cream cotton twill, and has been altered, stopping short at the level of the top of the pockets. It has no back seam and has been split open for 2″ at the back neck to insert a crudely stitched gusset of fawn cotton. The foreparts have been relined with a cream silk taffeta, now disintegrating, which covers the original cream fustian lining. The front edges were originally faced with cream silk satin, and this lines the pocket flaps. Three of the eighteen covered buttons are missing on the front, and one button is missing from below the right pocket flap; the lowest four buttonholes are worked in a deeper shade of pink silk thread, and are not functional. The wooden mould from one of the missing buttons was found in a pocket (page 211).

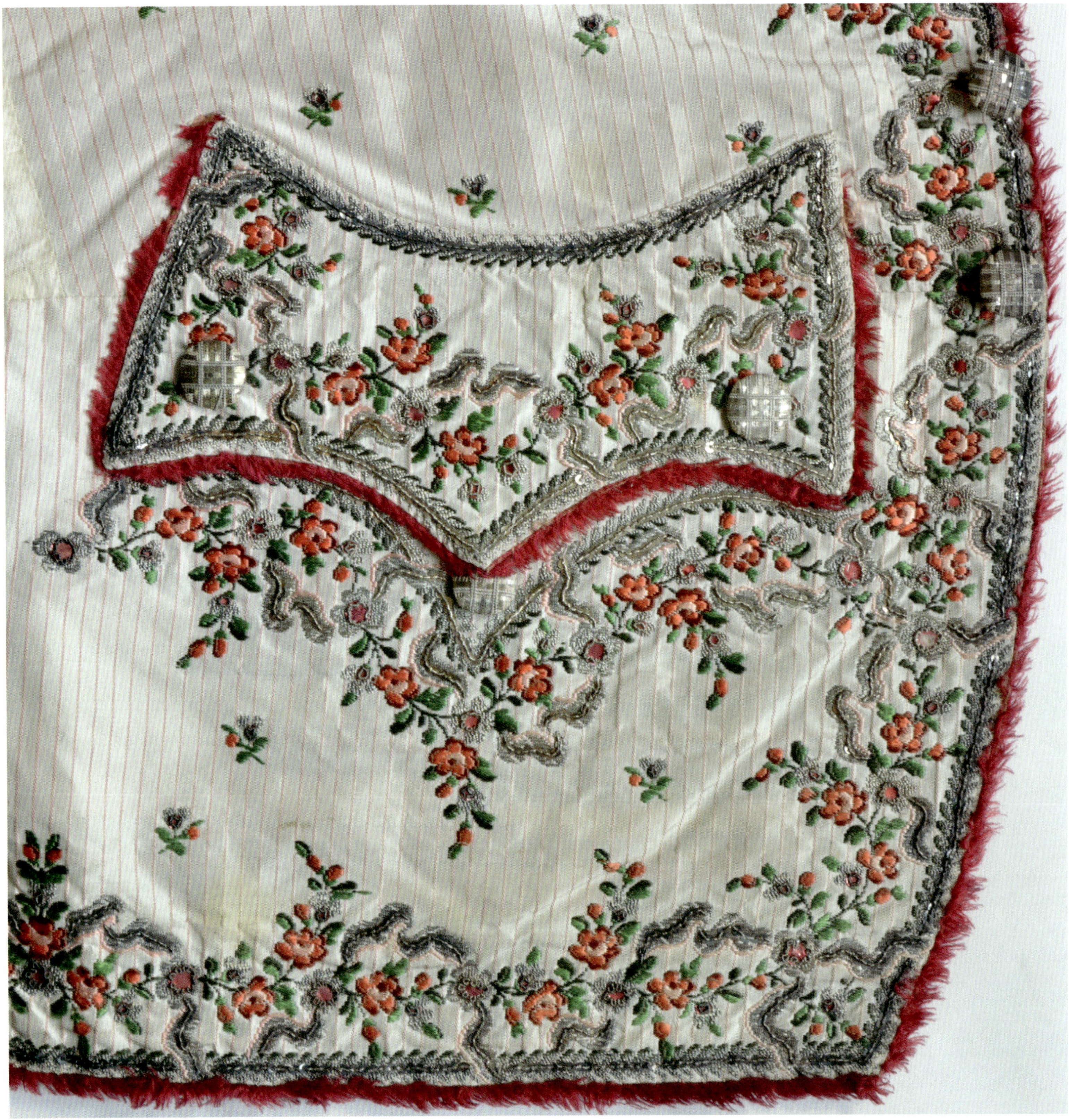

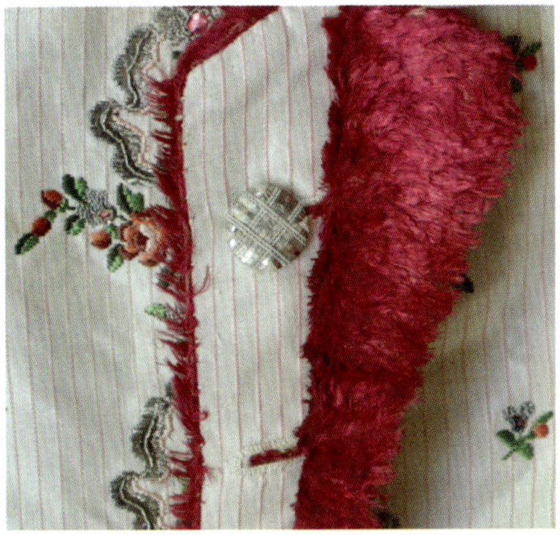

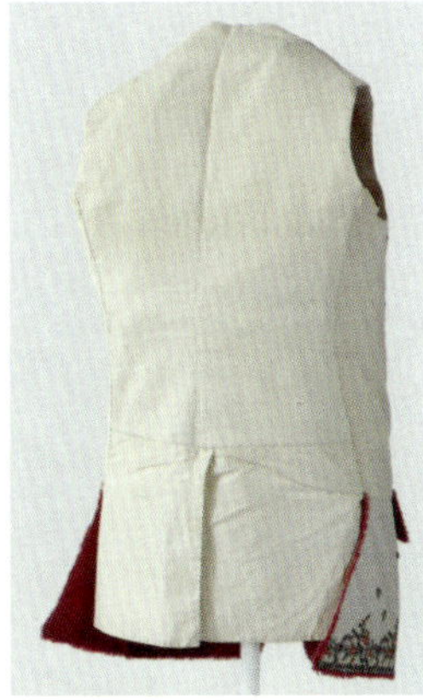

The top end of the fly front.

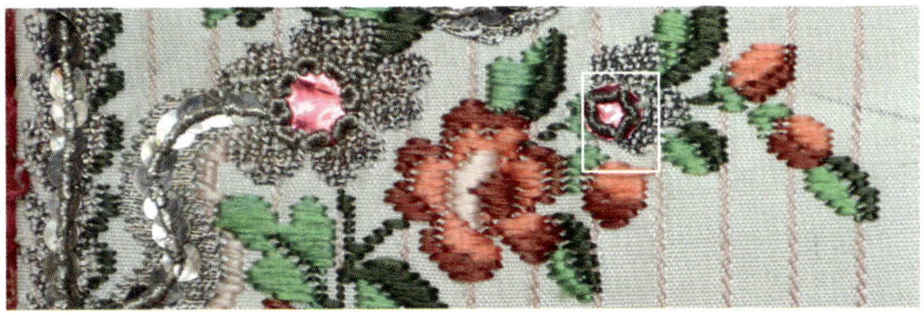

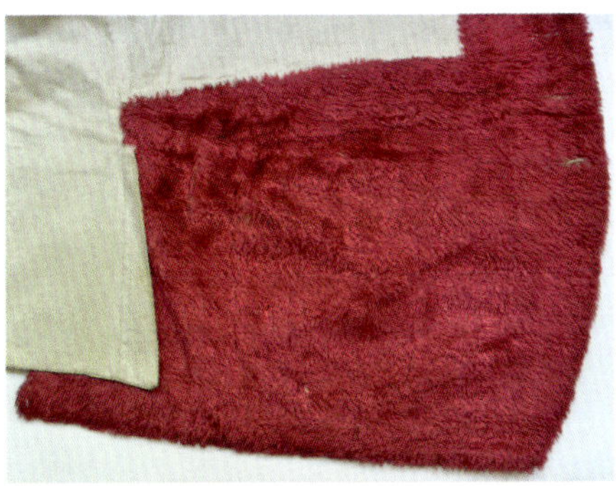

The silk shag lining of the left forepart skirt and the edge of the back linen lining.

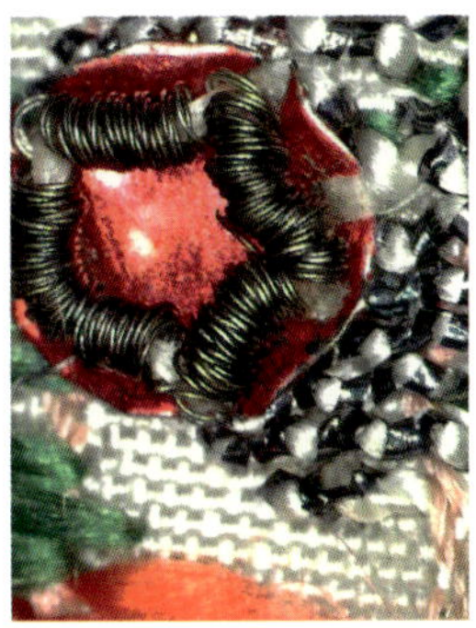

Detail outlined above.

A waistcoat in ivory silk taffeta, 1760-1775. HC.W-5.89-1

The silk has a narrow pink silk twill stripe; the forepart borders and pockets are woven to shape with a floral design in polychrome silks and threads of silver filé and frisé, and embroidered with silver purl, spangles, and pieces of red enamelled foil. There is a scattering of sprigs over the rest of the foreparts. The eleven buttons down the front are covered in silk threads, silver flat strip and silver filé, making a pattern of squares (page 216), but the waistcoat has a fly front which would conceal the buttons when done up. There are buttons at each end of the pocket flaps and one below the centre points. The front facings are in deep pink silk shag, and this also lines the forepart skirts and the pocket flaps. The foreparts and back bodies are lined in ivory linen; the back body is in cream wool twill and the back skirts are in cream silk taffeta. The side seams have sections of cream silk taffeta let in to them to increase the size of the waistcoat.

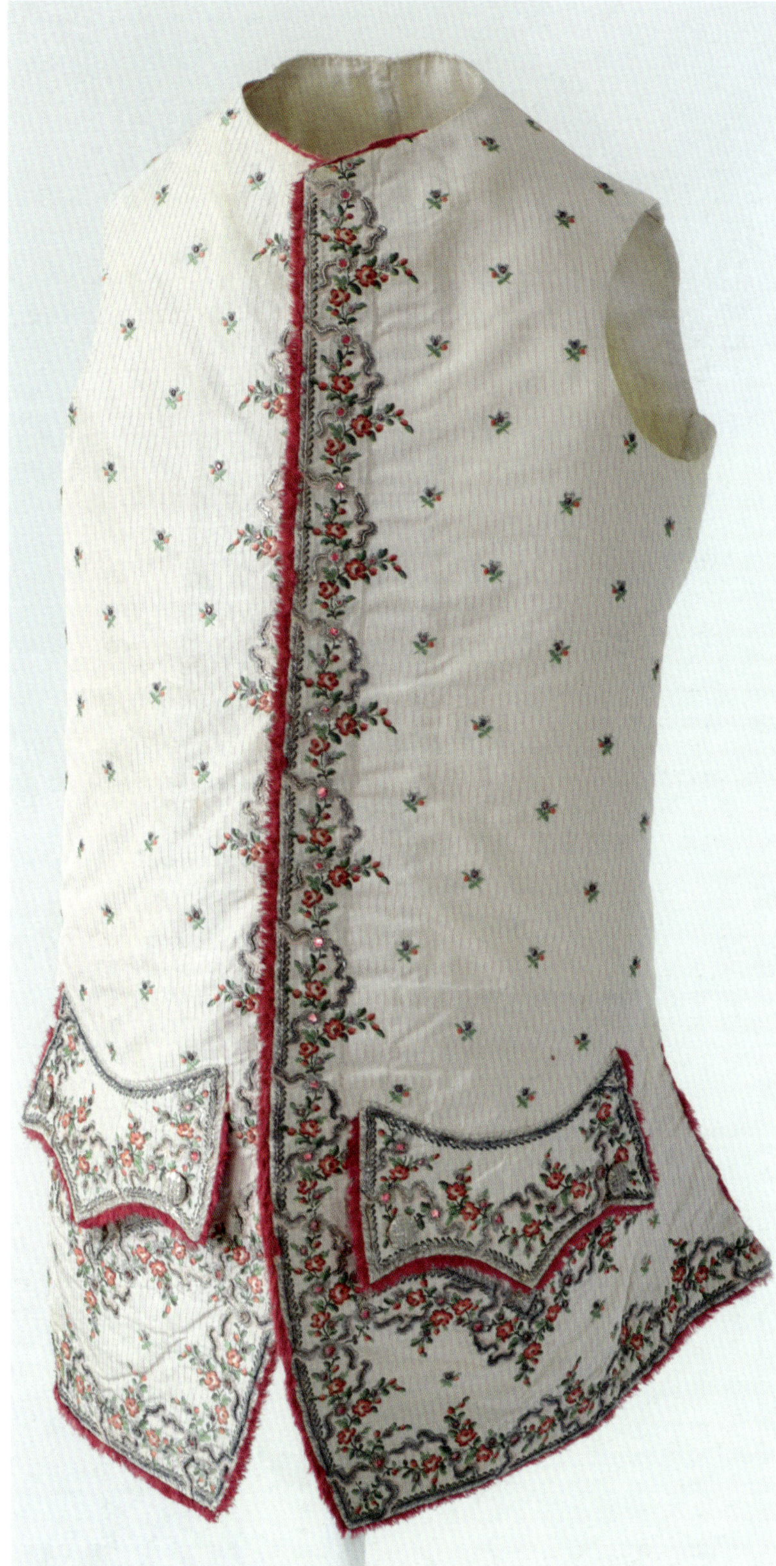

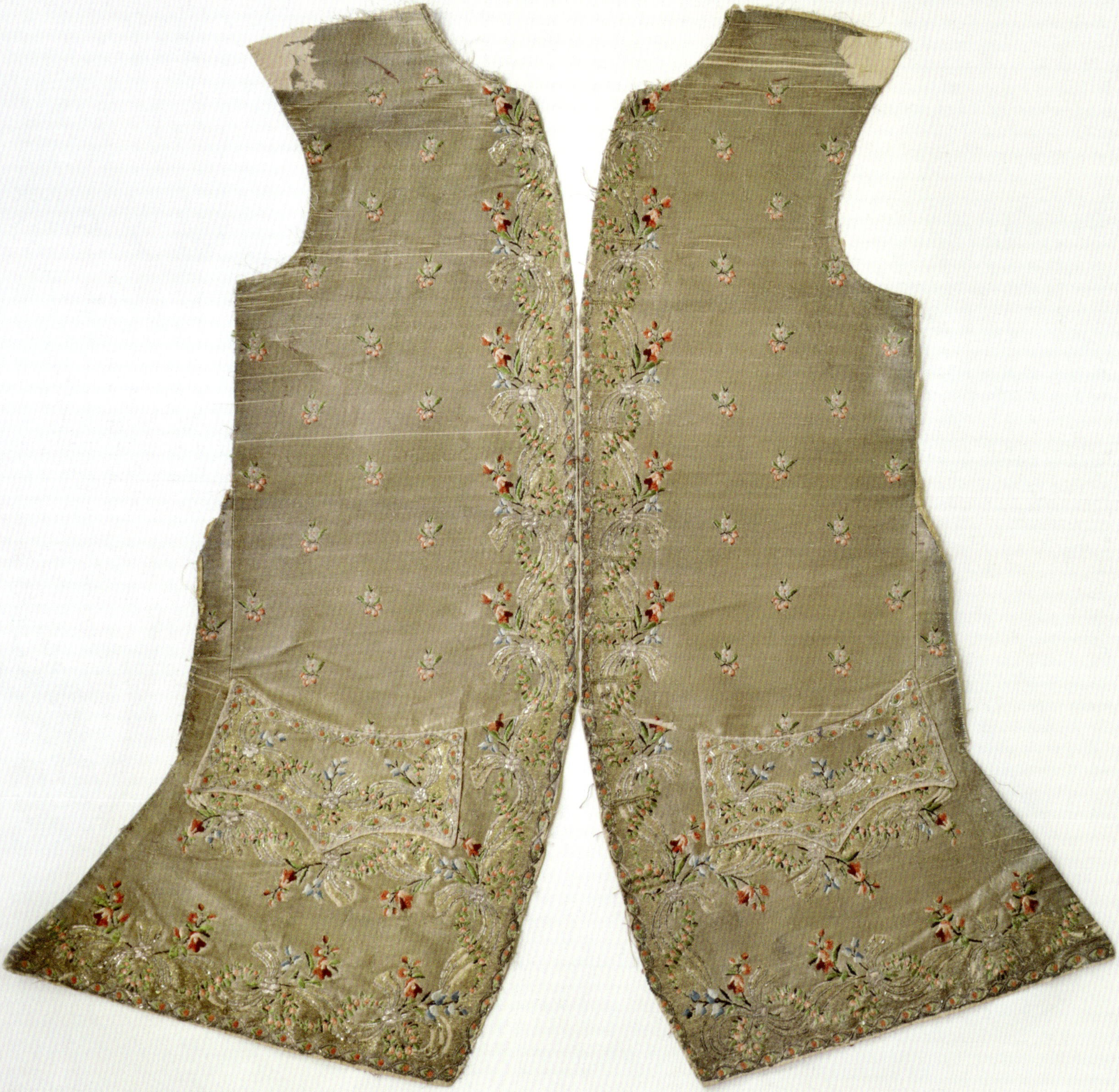

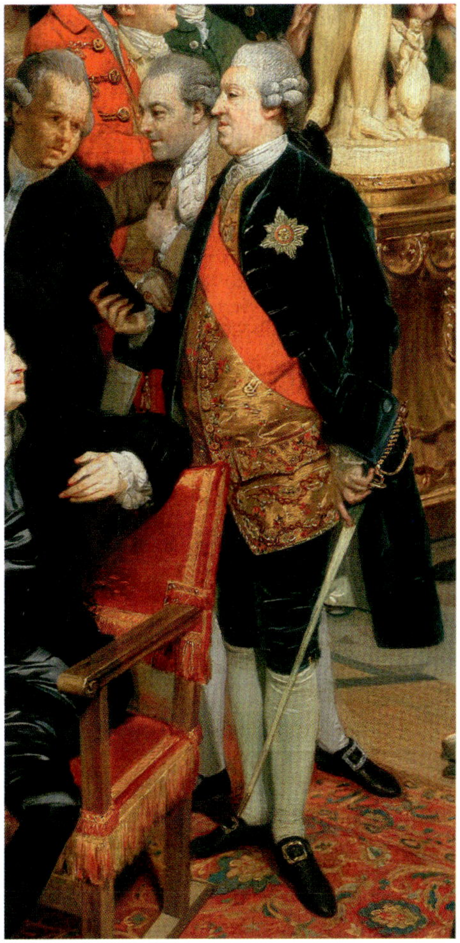

Sir Horace Mann in a detail from *The Tribuna of the Uffizi* by Johan Zoffany, 1774-1777. Royal Collection Trust / © Her Majesty Queen Elizabeth ll 2016. Sir Horace Mann (1706-1786) was the son of a London merchant; he served as the British diplomatic representative in Florence for most of his life, and was noted for his generous hospitality.

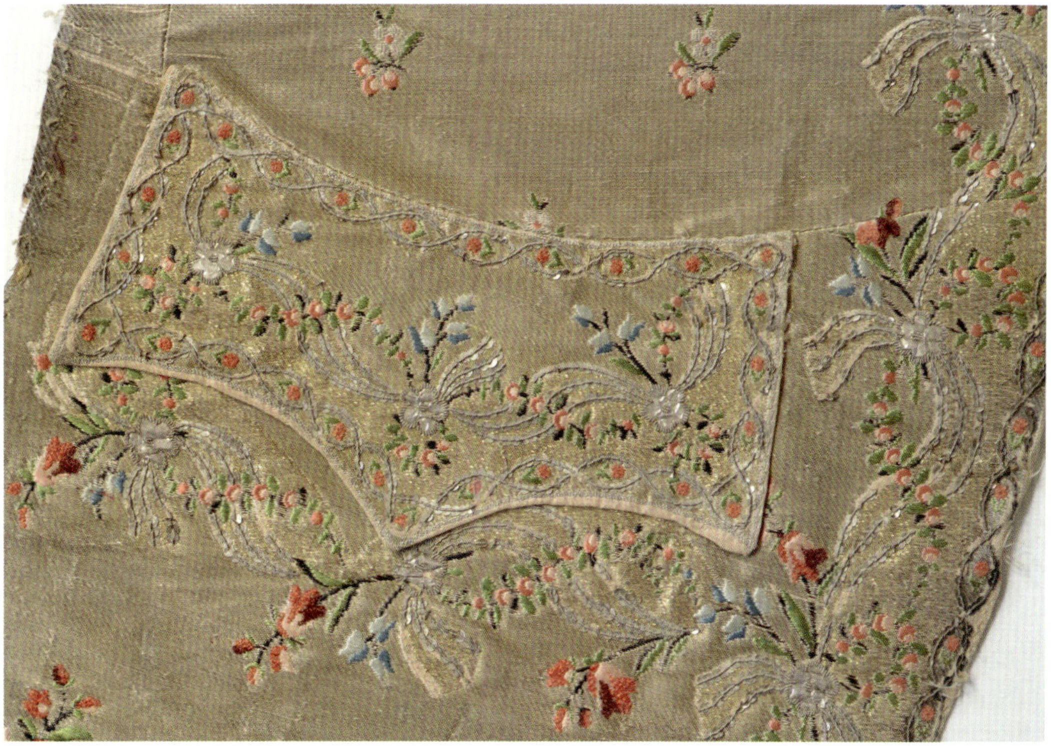

A pair of waistcoat foreparts in silver-gilt thread, 1760-1775. HC.W-2.12-2

They have a polychrome silk and chenille brocaded floral pattern woven to shape, on the front edges, hems, and on and below the pocket flaps, with sprigs scattered over the rest of the foreparts, and this has been embellished with silver-gilt spangles, purl and foil. The waistcoat has been unpicked and there are signs of wear at the shoulders; the buttons are missing.

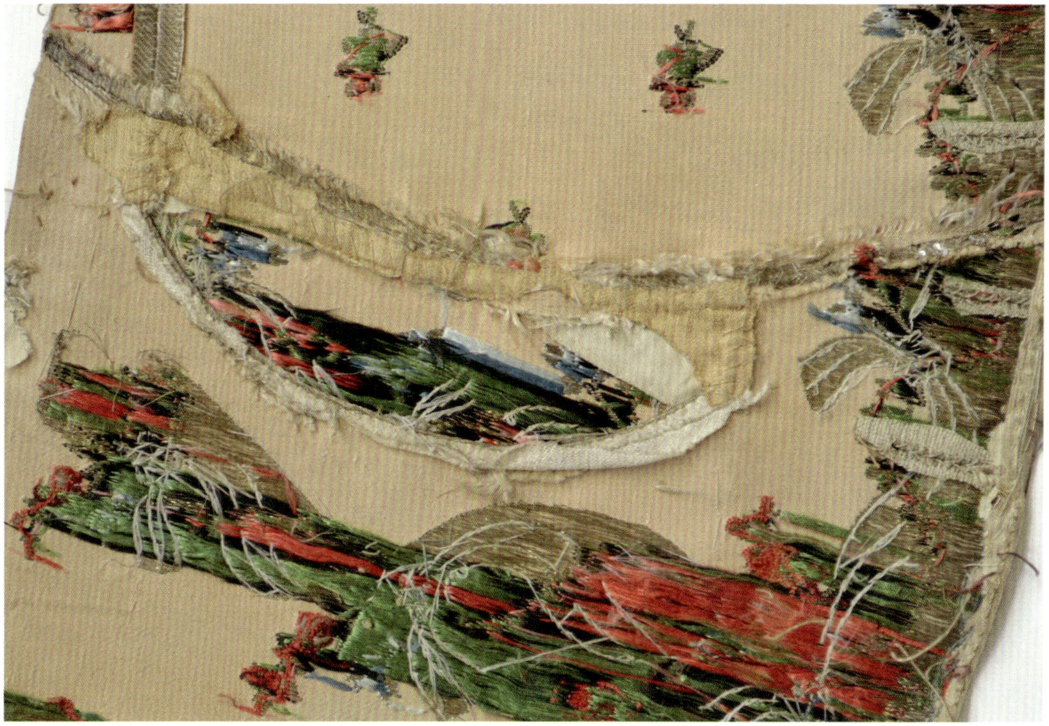

The back of part of the left forepart, showing the opening for the pocket and the seam that follows the top edge of the pocket flap. The coloured silks of the brocading are confined to the areas of the individual parts of the pattern.

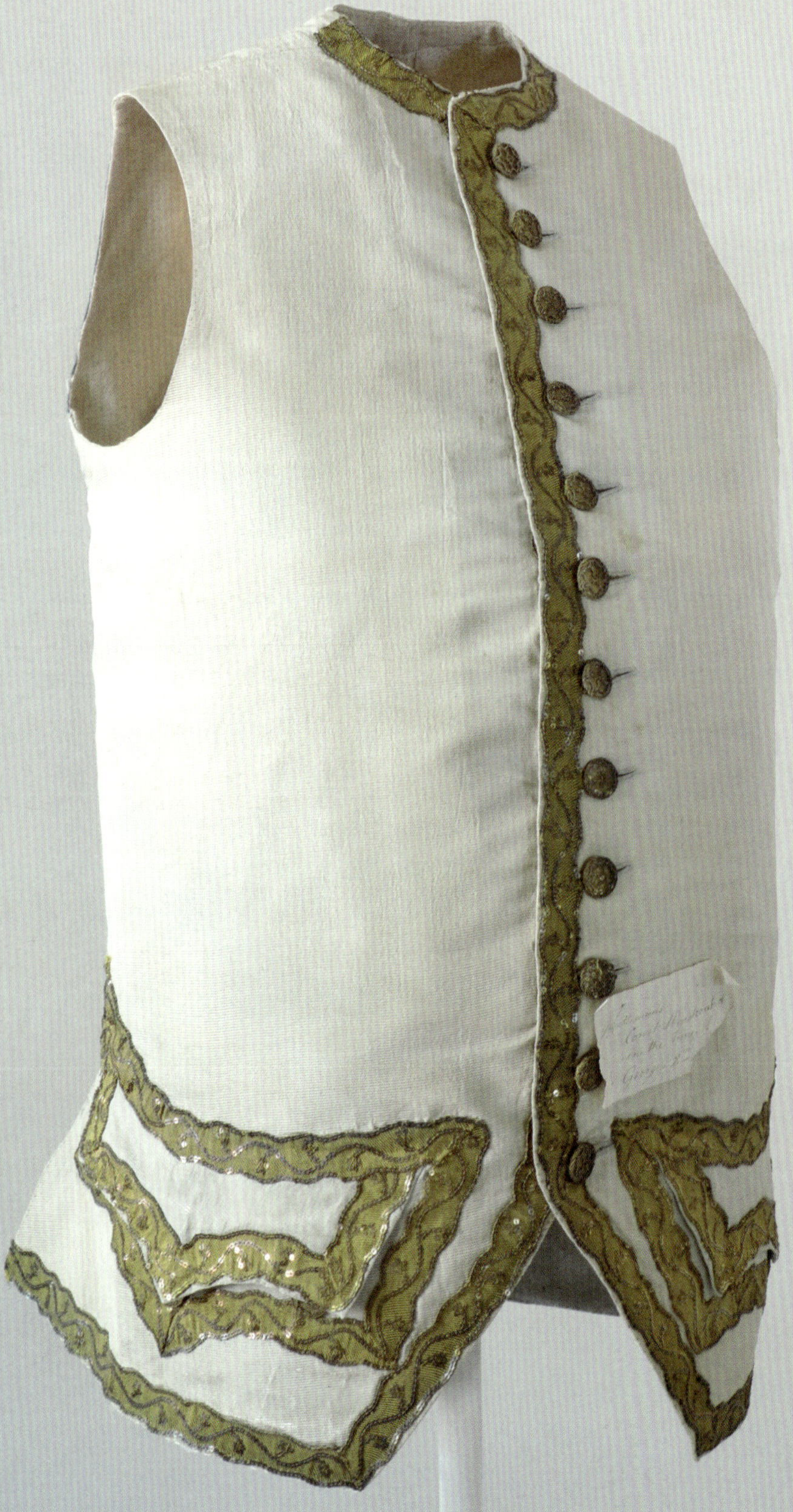

A waistcoat in silk ottoman, 1760-1775.
HC.W-10.03-3

The colour of the silk has faded from the original pale blue, which has only survived under the pocket flaps, as can be seen from the one pictured opposite. The waistcoat is trimmed with gold braid embellished with silver-gilt spangles (page 211); the buttons are similar, with added pieces of silver-gilt purl, and the buttonholes slant upwards. The back of the body is pale blue calimanco with a small yoke of the silk ottoman at the top, and the back skirts are also in the faded silk. The body is lined with ivory fustian, and the back skirts are lined with the pale blue calimanco; the front edges are faced with a pale blue twilled silk, and this also lines the front skirts and the pocket flaps.

A piece of paper is sewn on to the left forepart stating "Gentleman's Court Waistcoat in the time of George 2nd". This may be fanciful.

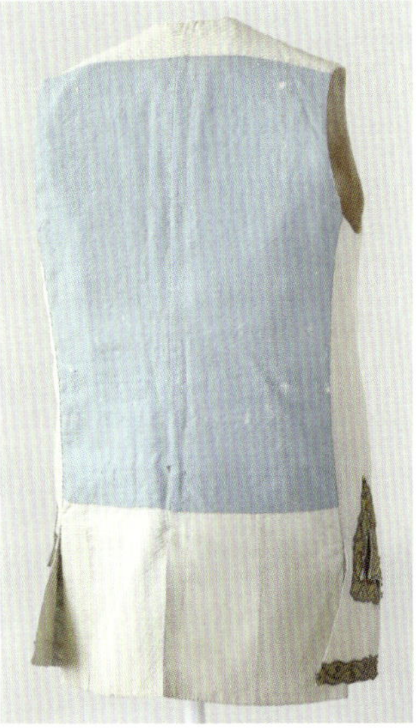

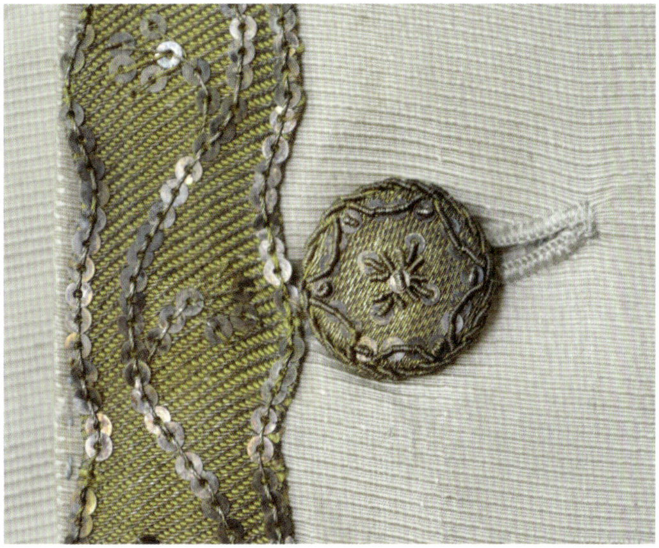

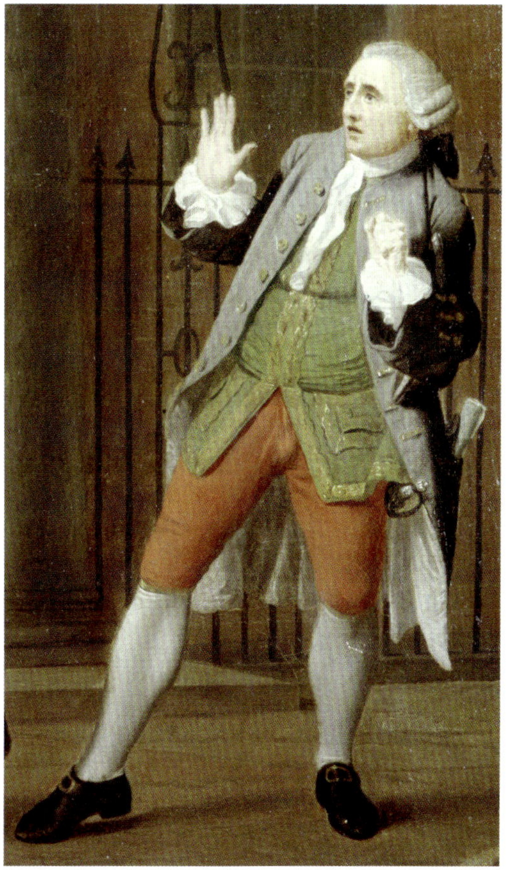

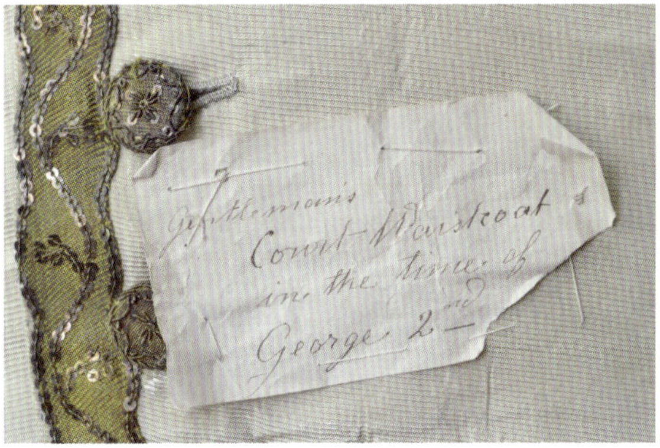

The piece of paper stitched to the left forepart.

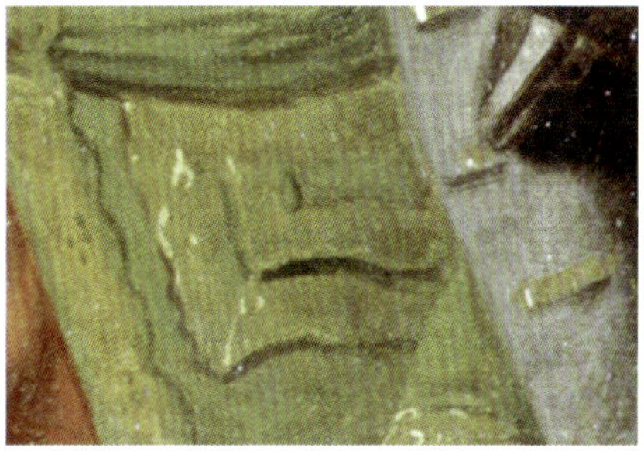

Two details from *A City Shower* by Edward Penny, 1764, Museum of London.

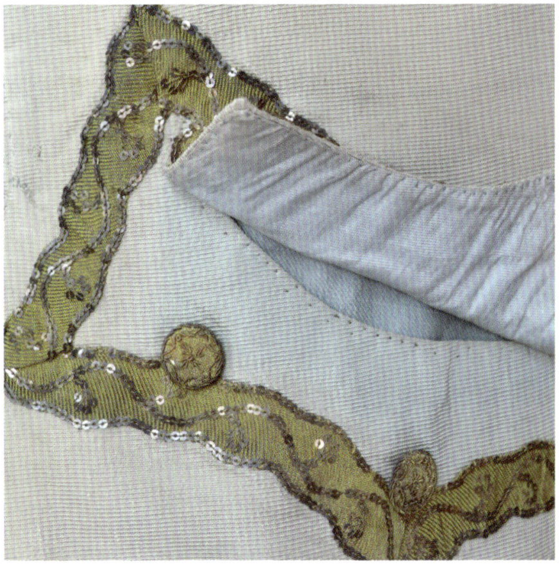

The unfaded blue colour under the pocket flap.

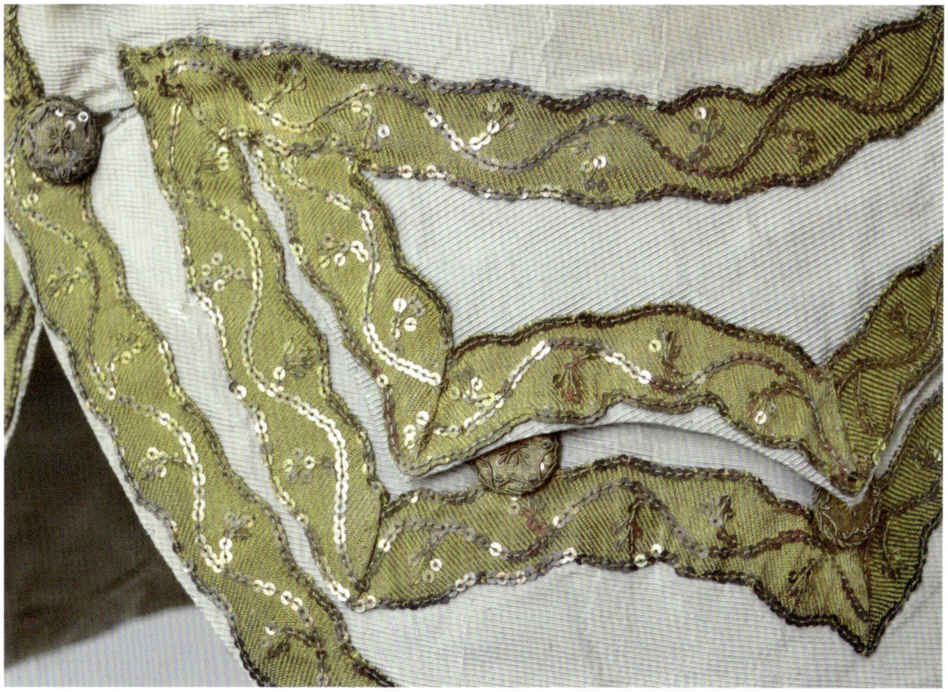

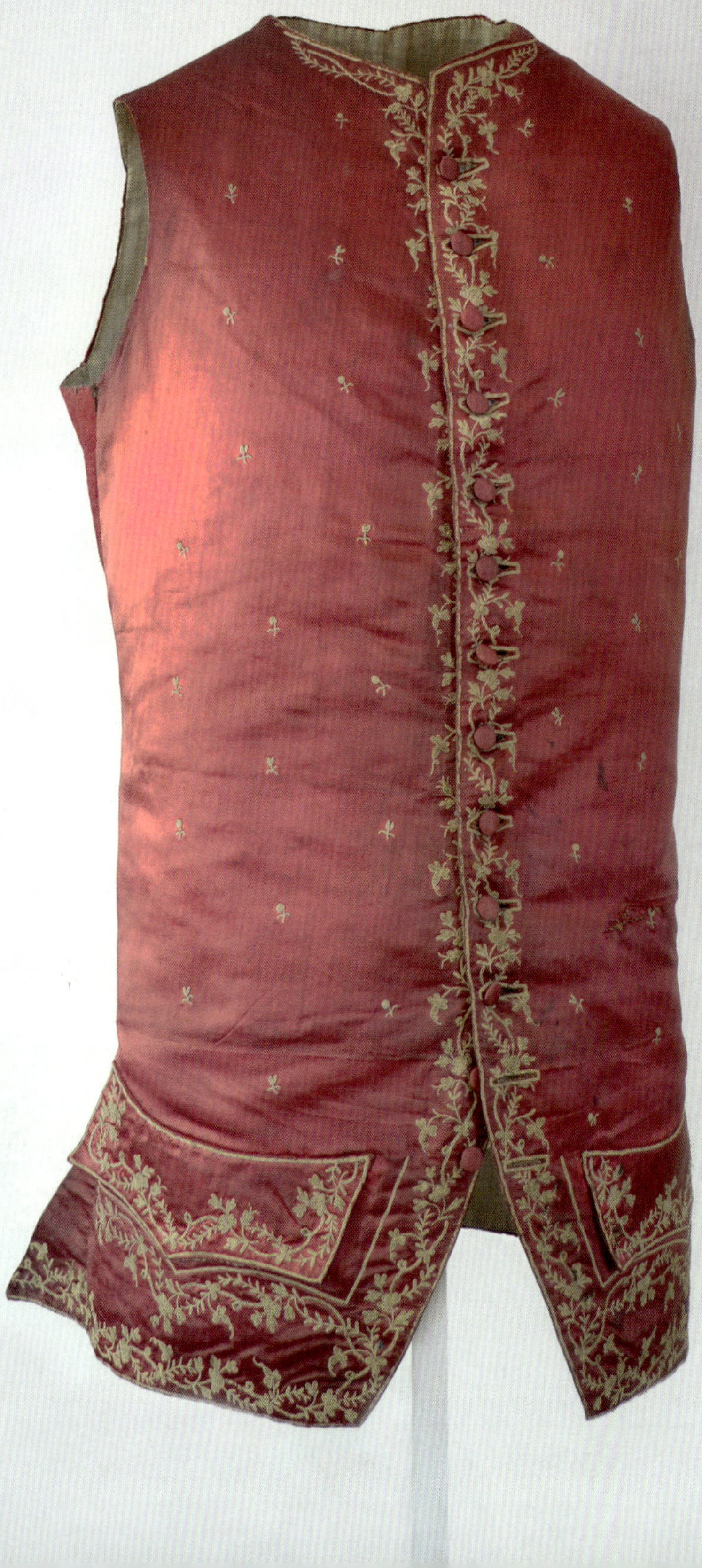

A waistcoat in crimson silk satin, 1770-1780.
HC.W-6.08-1

It has sprigs and a border of tambour embroidery in cream silk and a wispy form of chenille thread; this also appears on the pocket flaps which are purely decorative as there are no pockets. The thirteen buttons are covered in a matching coloured silk taffeta. The buttonholes are outlined in cream silk tambour work and the edges have been roughly oversewn in silk thread matching the satin; the oversewing with deeper green thread was done at a much later date. The back is in matching calimanco and has been crudely altered, at some point; the foreparts are lined in buff-coloured silk faille. The back is lined in natural linen, and the name C. Green is written in ink at the top of the right side of the lining. There were two pairs of black linen tapes on the back, to adjust the waist, but one tape is now missing. A tear below the waist at the side of the left front has been sewn up.

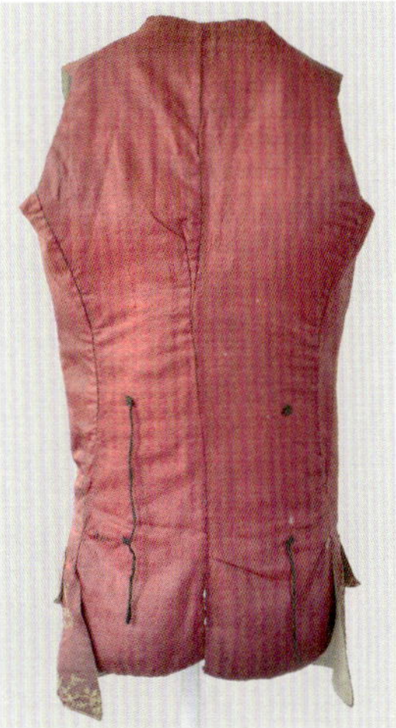

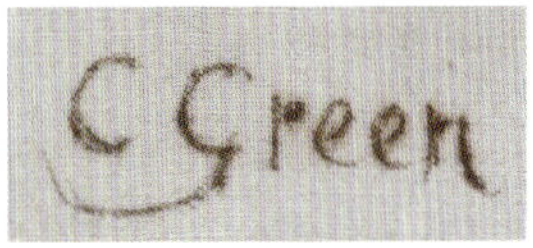

The name written on the lining.

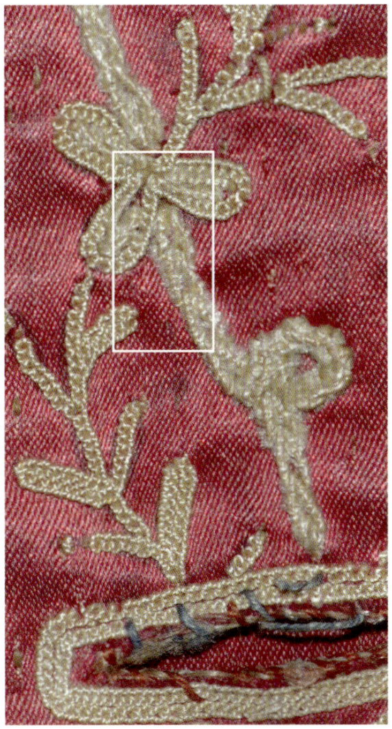

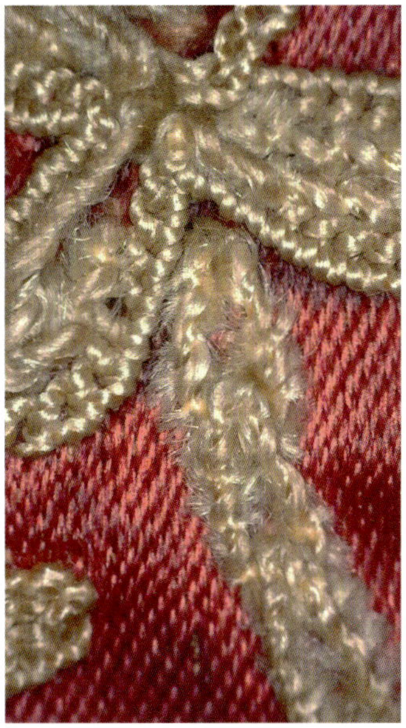

Detail of the embroidery, outlined left, showing the wispy chenille threads.

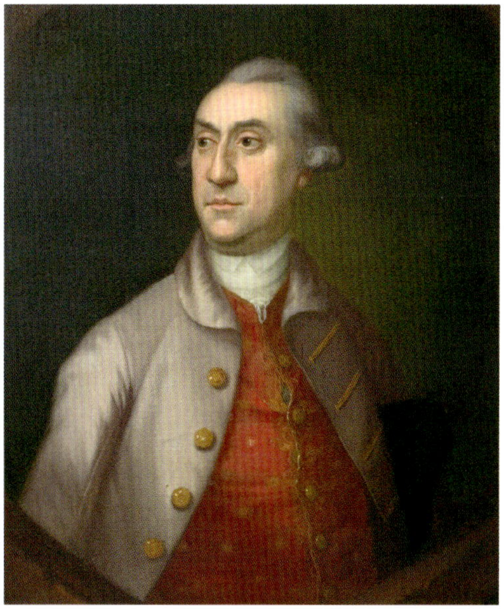

Portrait of a Gentleman by a follower of Joseph Wright of Derby, 1770s. Derbyshire County Council, Buxton Museum and Art Gallery.

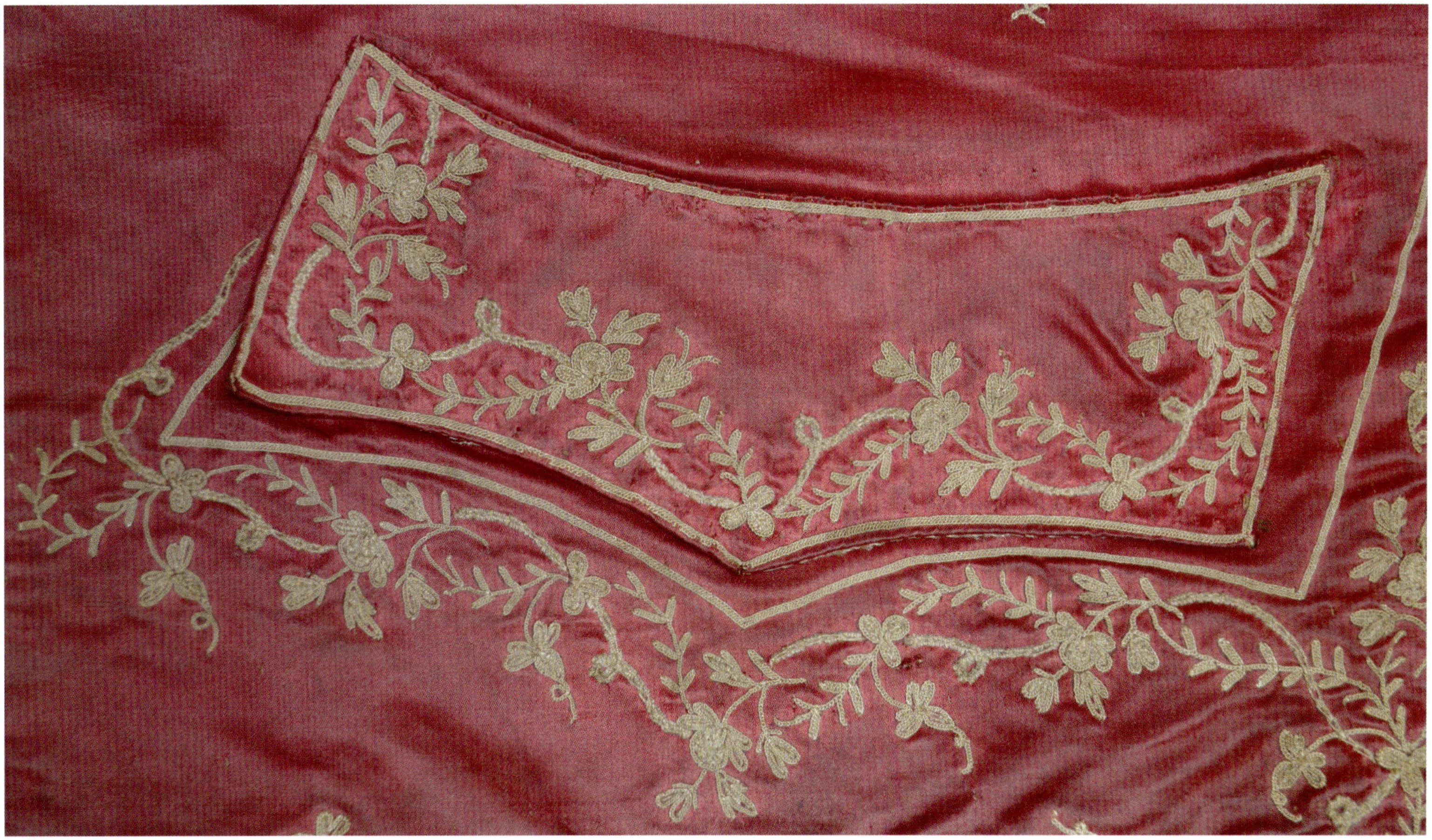

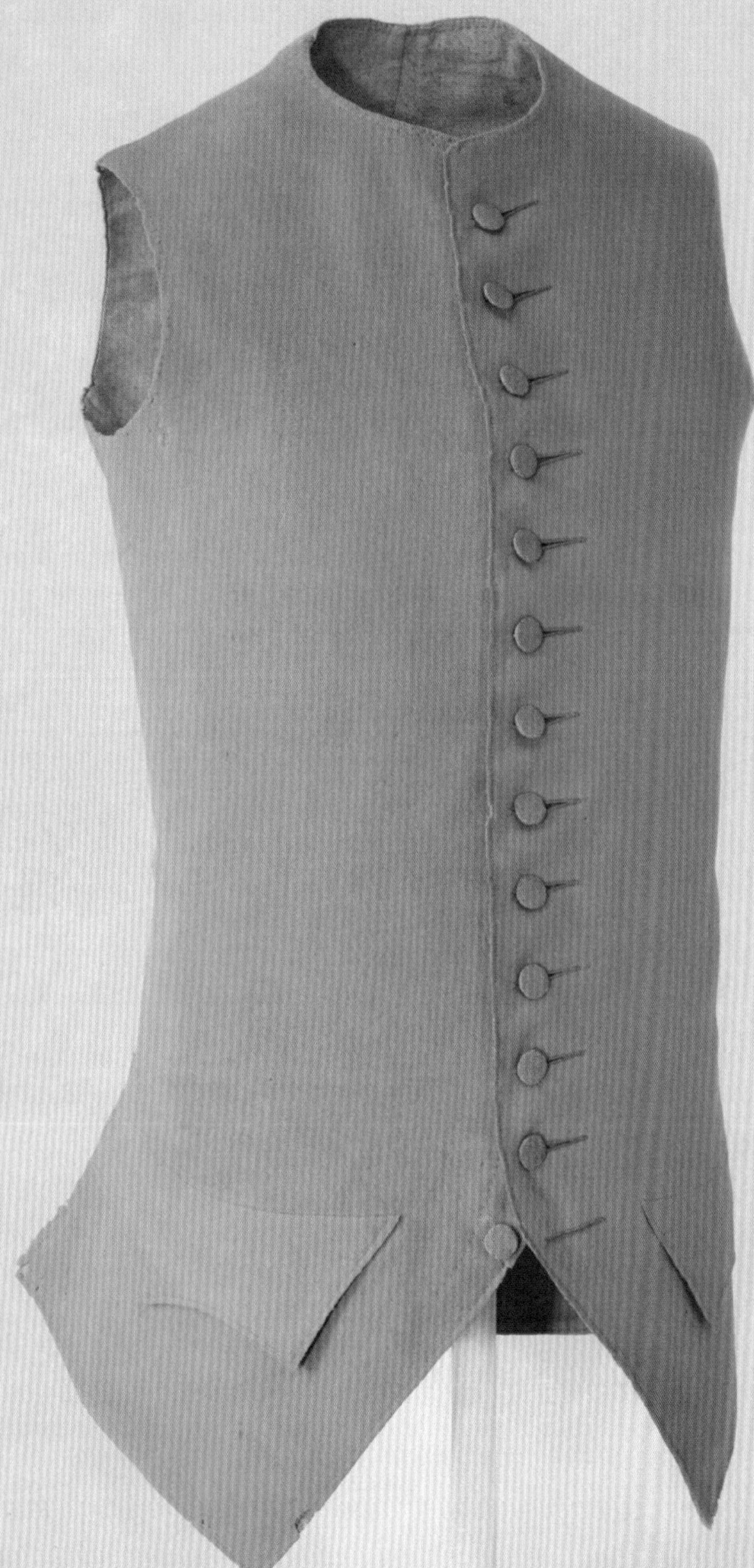

A waistcoat in green wool, 1770-1780.
HC.W-10.89-6

The wool is in a plain weave with a raised surface finished so closely that the cut edges are left raw and not hemmed or finished in any way. The waistcoat was probably part of a suit. The body is lined in fustian and the skirts are lined with a yellowy green calimanco, which also forms the back and front edge facings. The buttonholes are backed with separate strips of fabric and their folded edges form the inside edges of the buttonholes; their ends are covered by a folded strip of the calimanco facing. The buttons are covered with thick silk threads woven to look like fabric, with the ends drawn together underneath to form a shank.

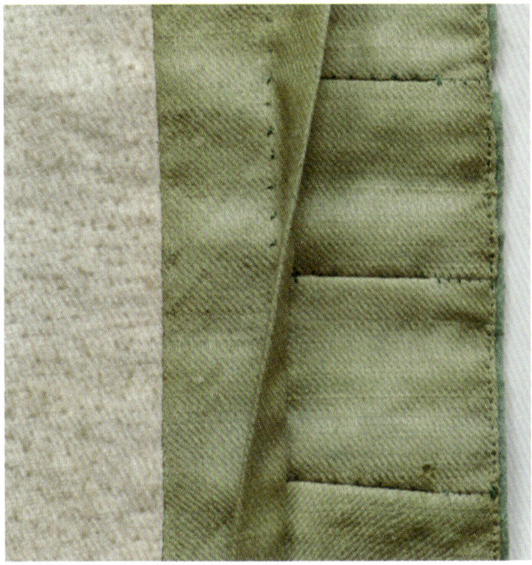

Detail inside one of the front edges, showing strips of the facing forming the edges of the buttonholes. The fustian lining can be seen on the left.

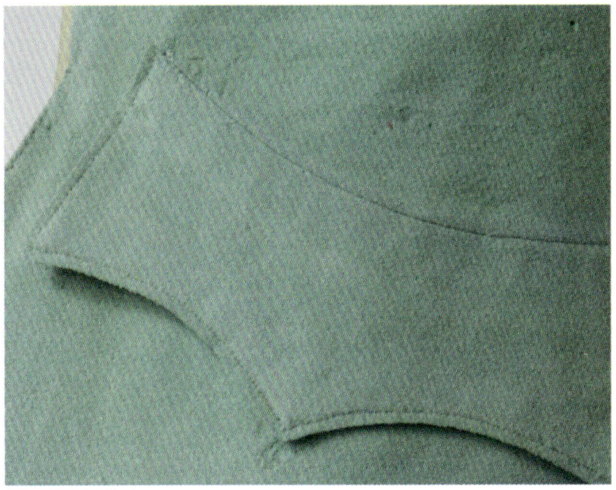

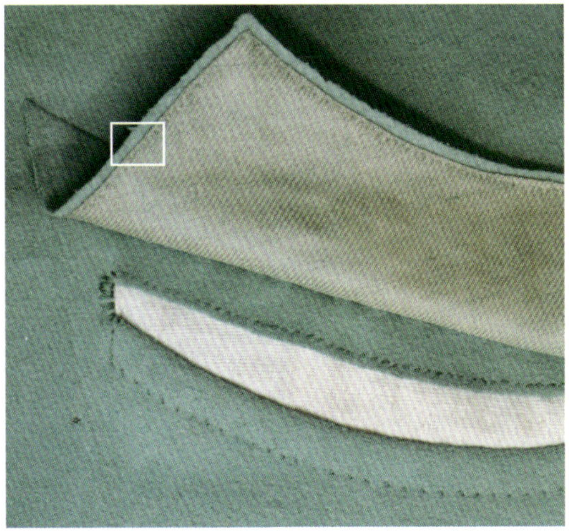

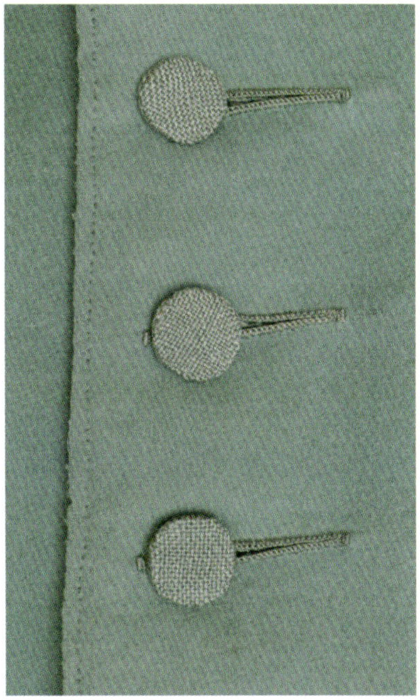

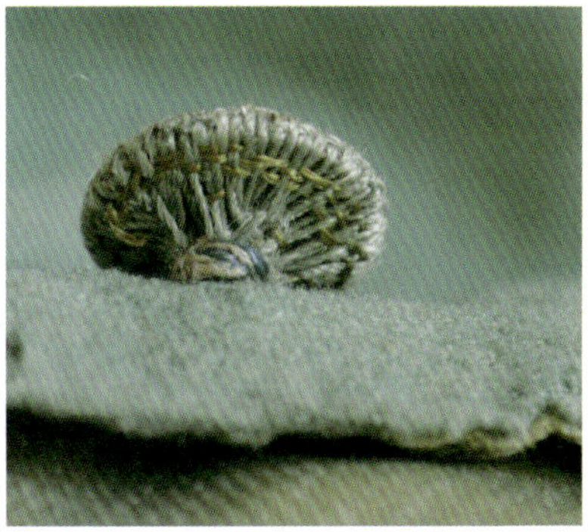

Underneath one of the buttons, showing the threads pulled in to form the shank.

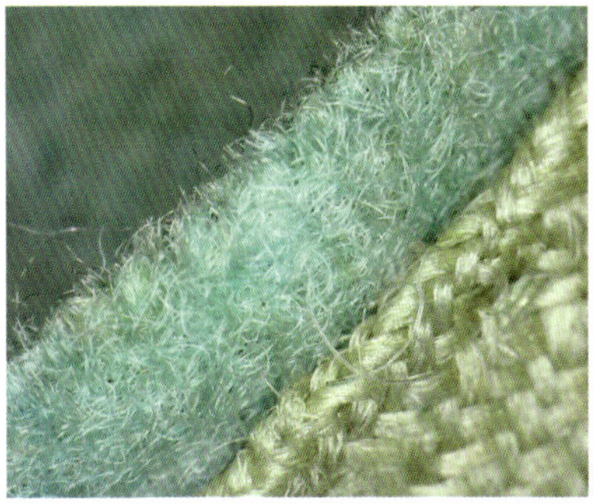

Detail of the edge of one of the pocket flaps, outlined left, showing the raw edge of the wool and the calimanco lining of the flap.

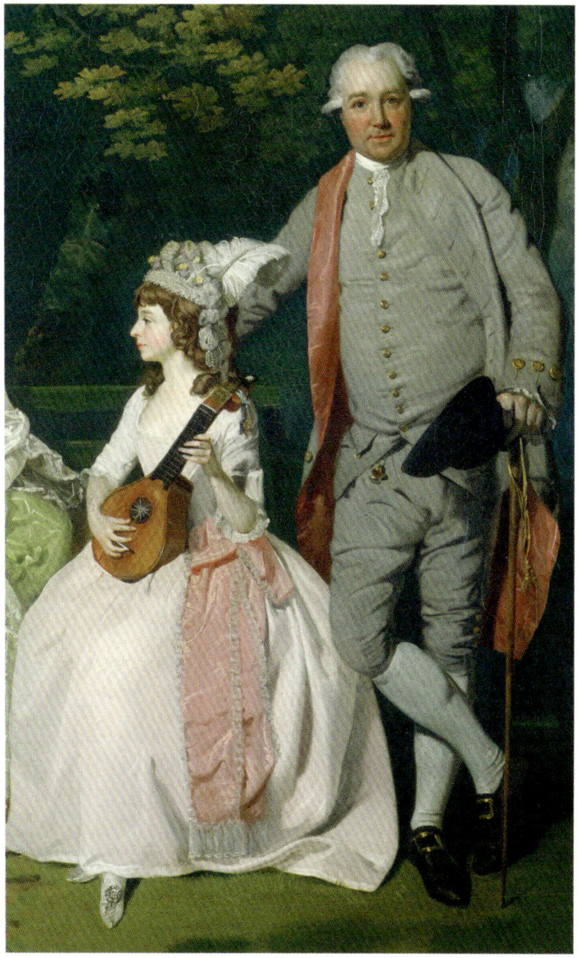

Detail from *Family Group* by Francis Wheatley, 1775-1780. Courtesy National Gallery of Art, Washington.

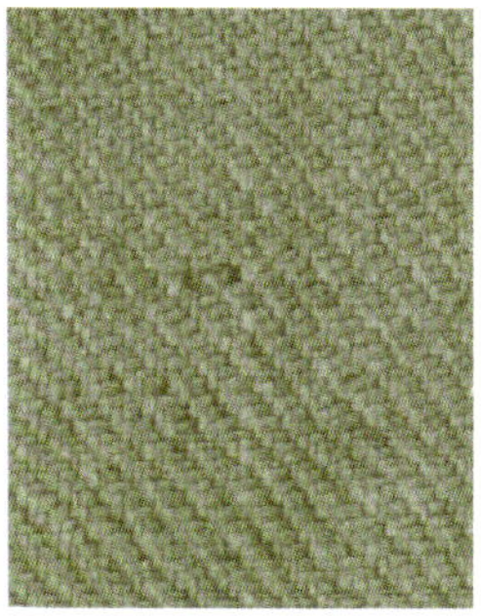

Detail of the calimanco, a glazed wool twill, which forms the back and the facings, and lines the pocket flaps. Glazed plain weave wool was also called calimanco.

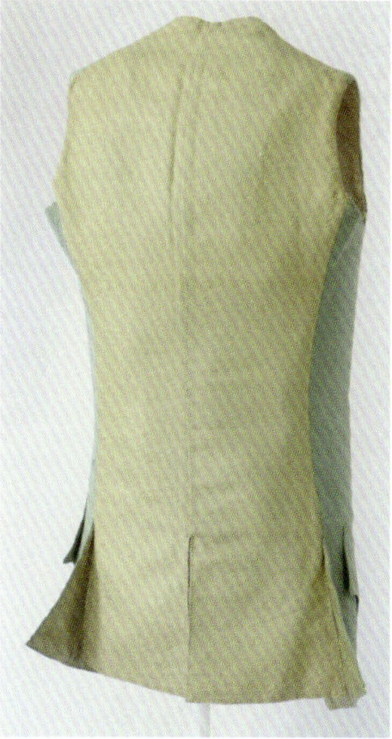

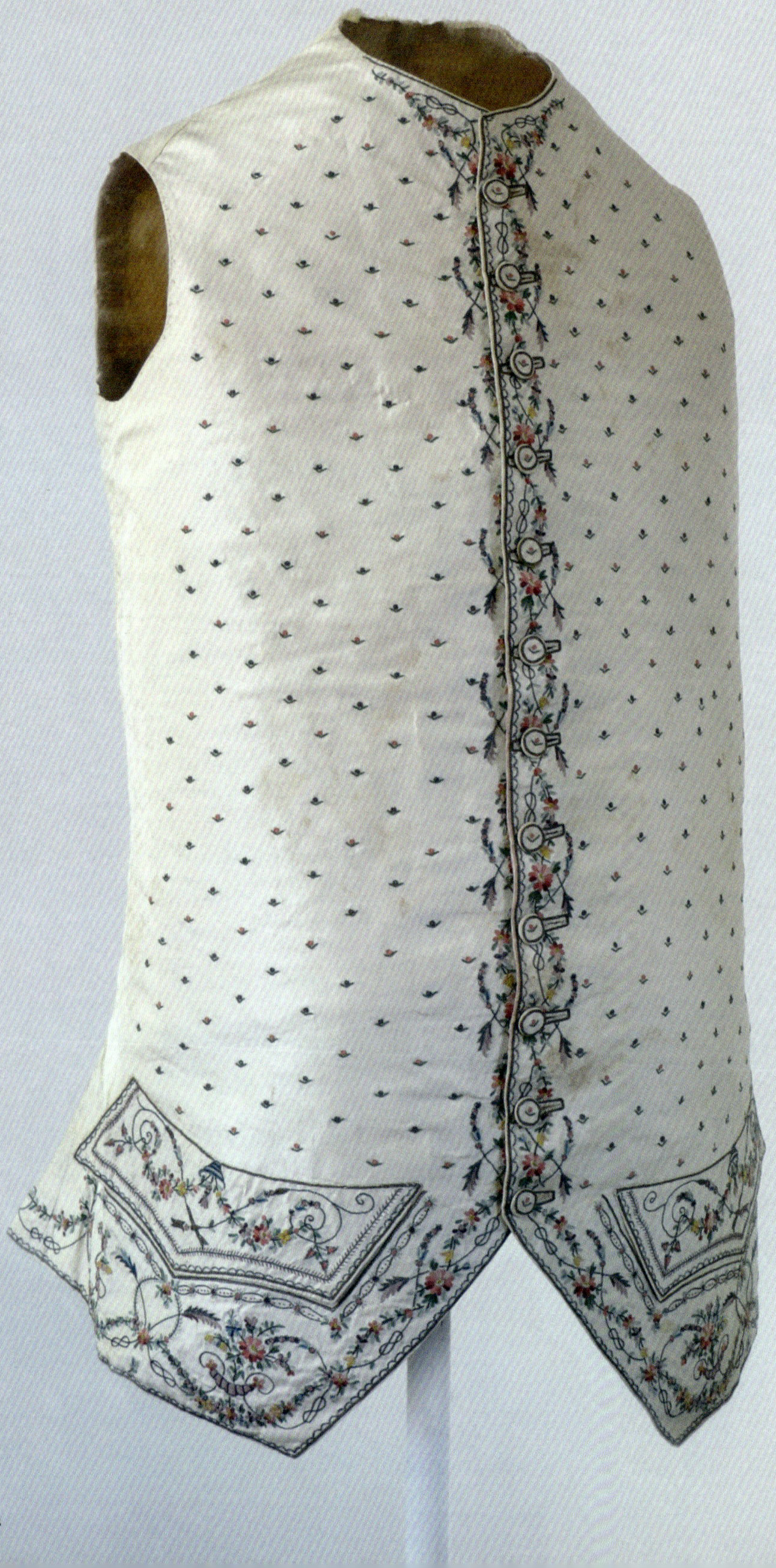

A waistcoat in cream silk faille, 1770-1780.
HC.W-10.89-7

It has tambour embroidery in polychrome silks and silver filé on the front edges, hems and the pocket flaps; there are scattered tiny sprigs over the foreparts. The back is in cream wool twill, and the lining is natural linen. The forepart front edges and hems are faced with cream silk twill, which also lines the back skirts. There are gussets of the silk twill under the armholes in the side seams, and triangles of the silk faille on the shoulders. The twelve covered buttons are embroidered.

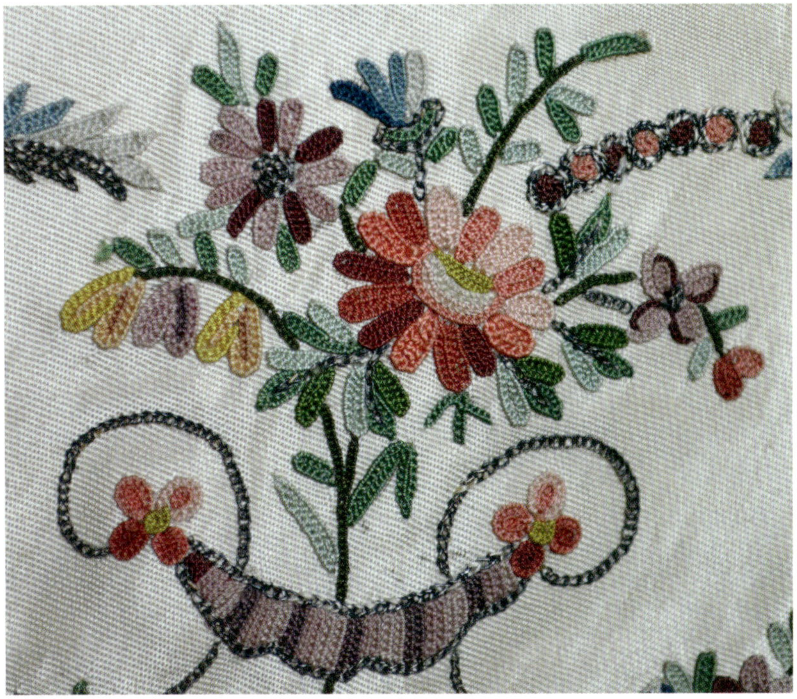

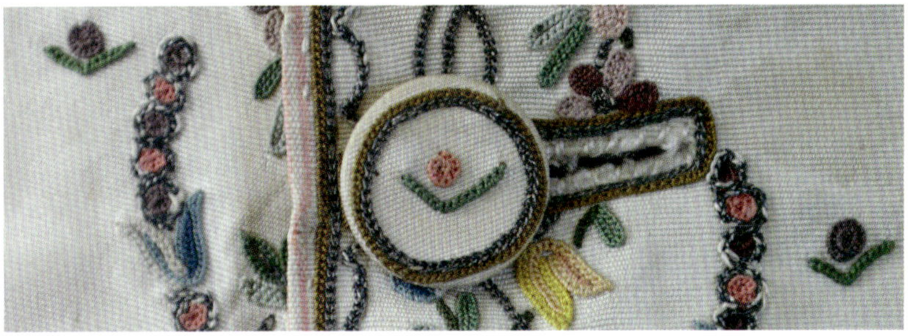

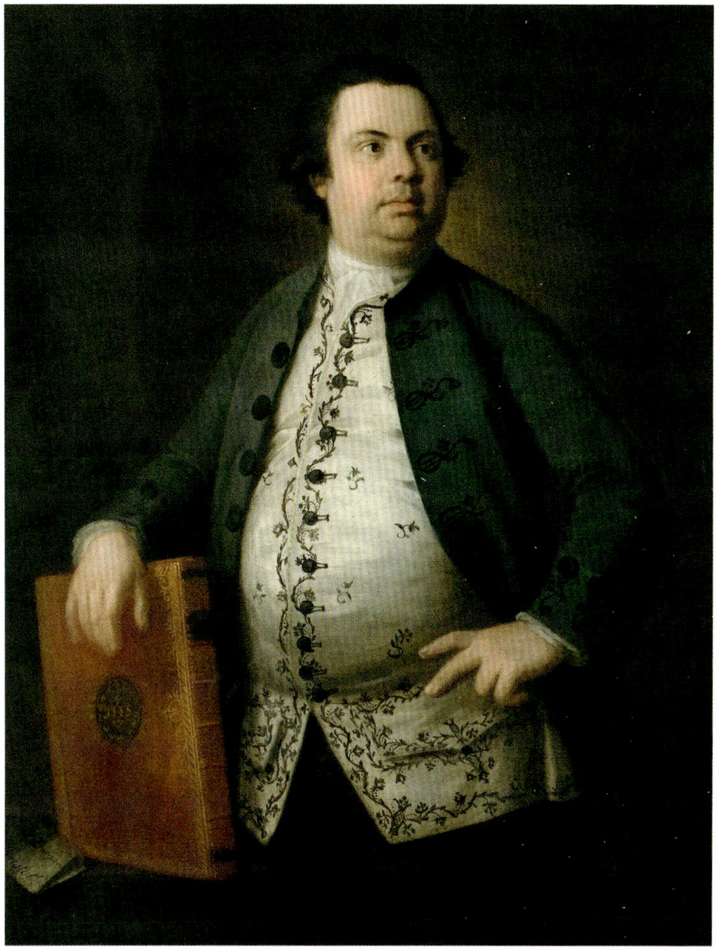

Henry Burgum of Bristol by John Simmons, 1775, The Georgian House Museum, Bristol. © Bristol Museums, Galleries & Archives.

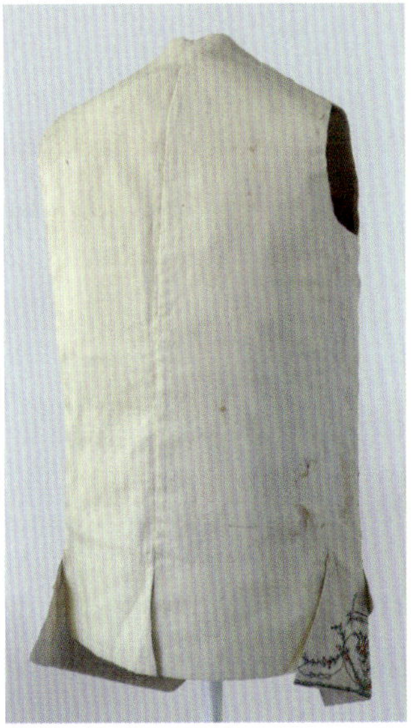

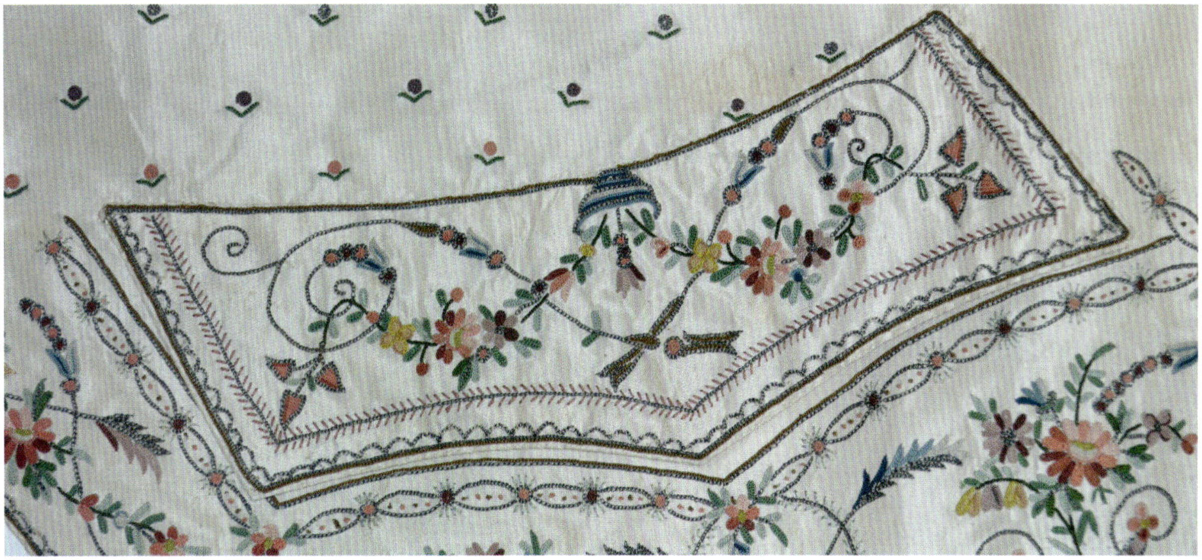

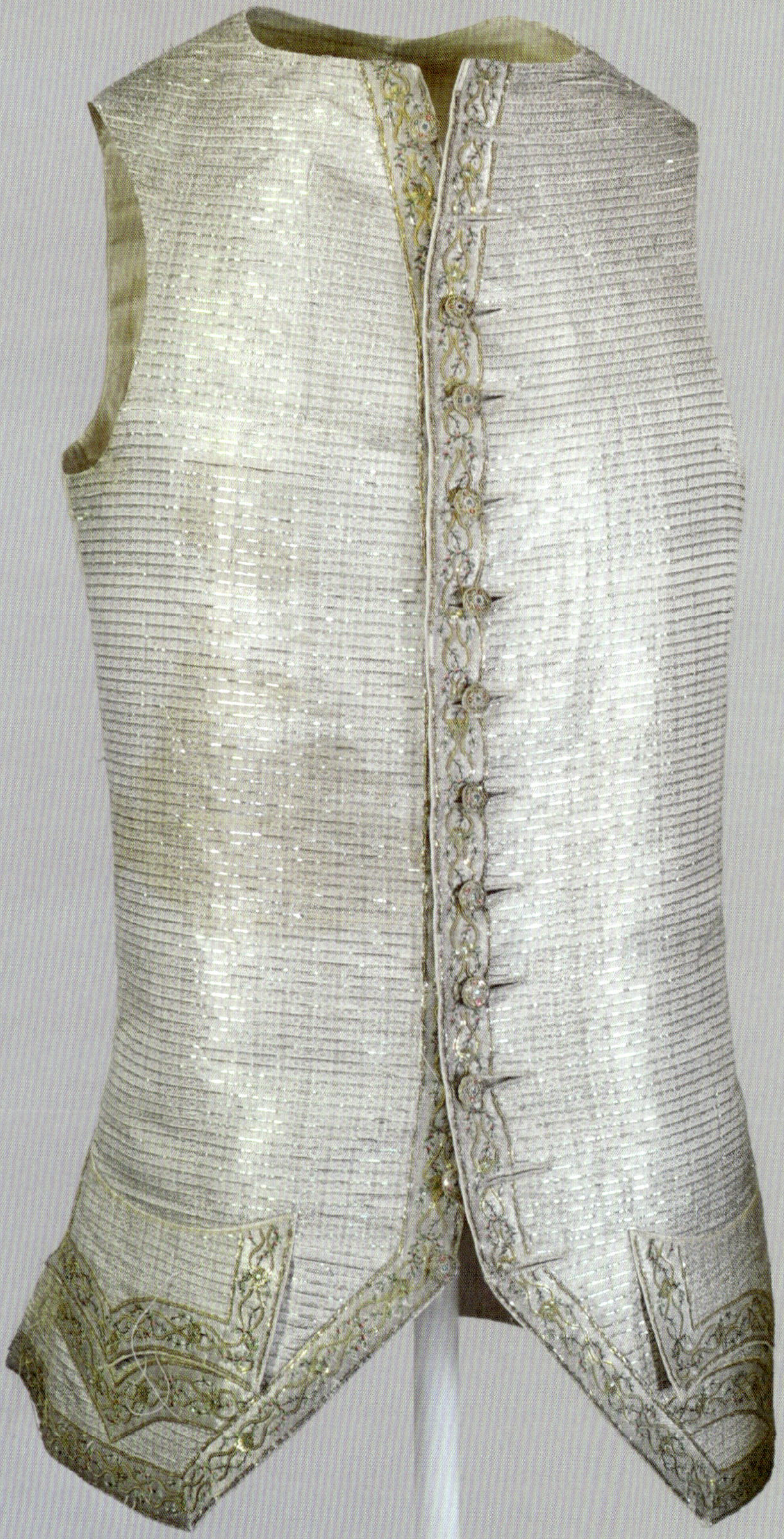

A waistcoat in silver figured silk, 1770-1780.
HC.W-2.12-1

The fabric has a small geometric pattern and spaced weft stripes of green enamelled silver flat strip. The foreparts and pocket flaps are bordered with embroidery of green, black and red silk threads, and silver-gilt spangles, silver-gilt purl and pieces of enamelled foil. The thirteen buttons have the same embroidery on them (page 216), and the buttonholes are worked in silver filé. The lining and back are in plain cream cotton, and the forepart facings and hems are in cream silk twill. There is a stain on the right forepart. Candlelight would have enhanced the glitter of the silver threads.

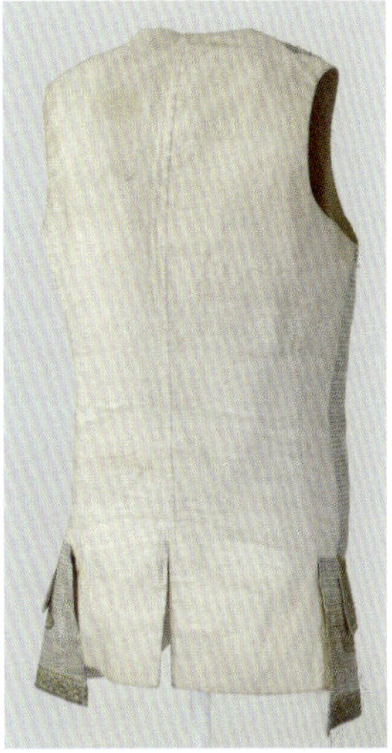

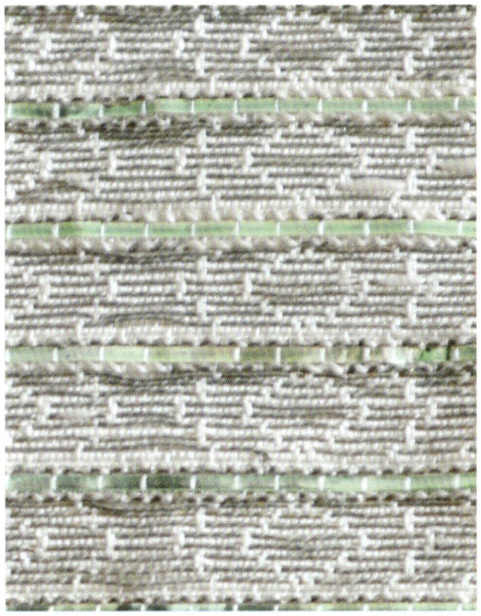

Left: The geometric pattern of the silver threads in the ground. This was known as a foot-figured pattern, as it was produced by pedals controlling the shafts of the loom.

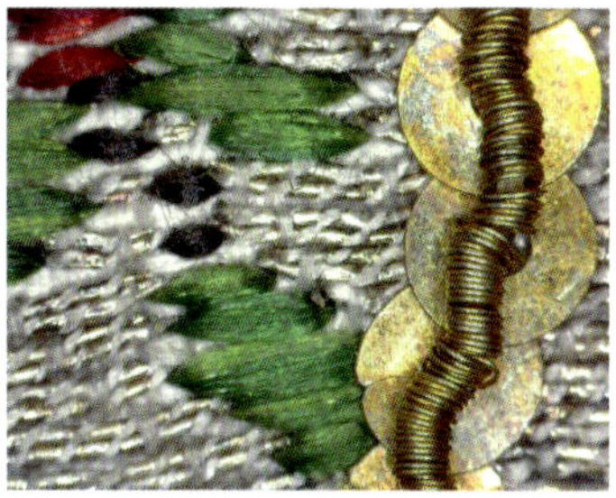

Detail outlined on the right.

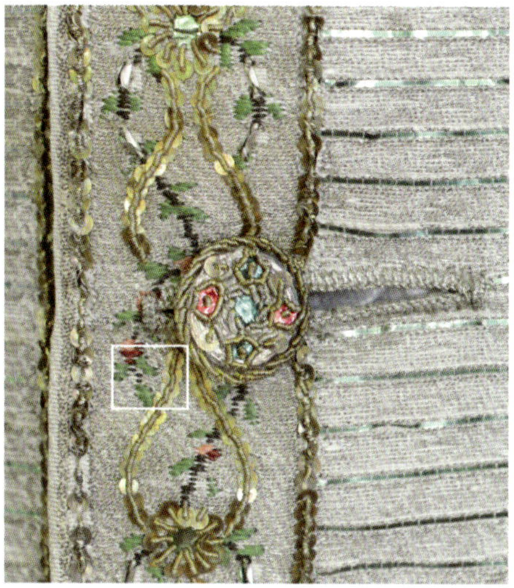

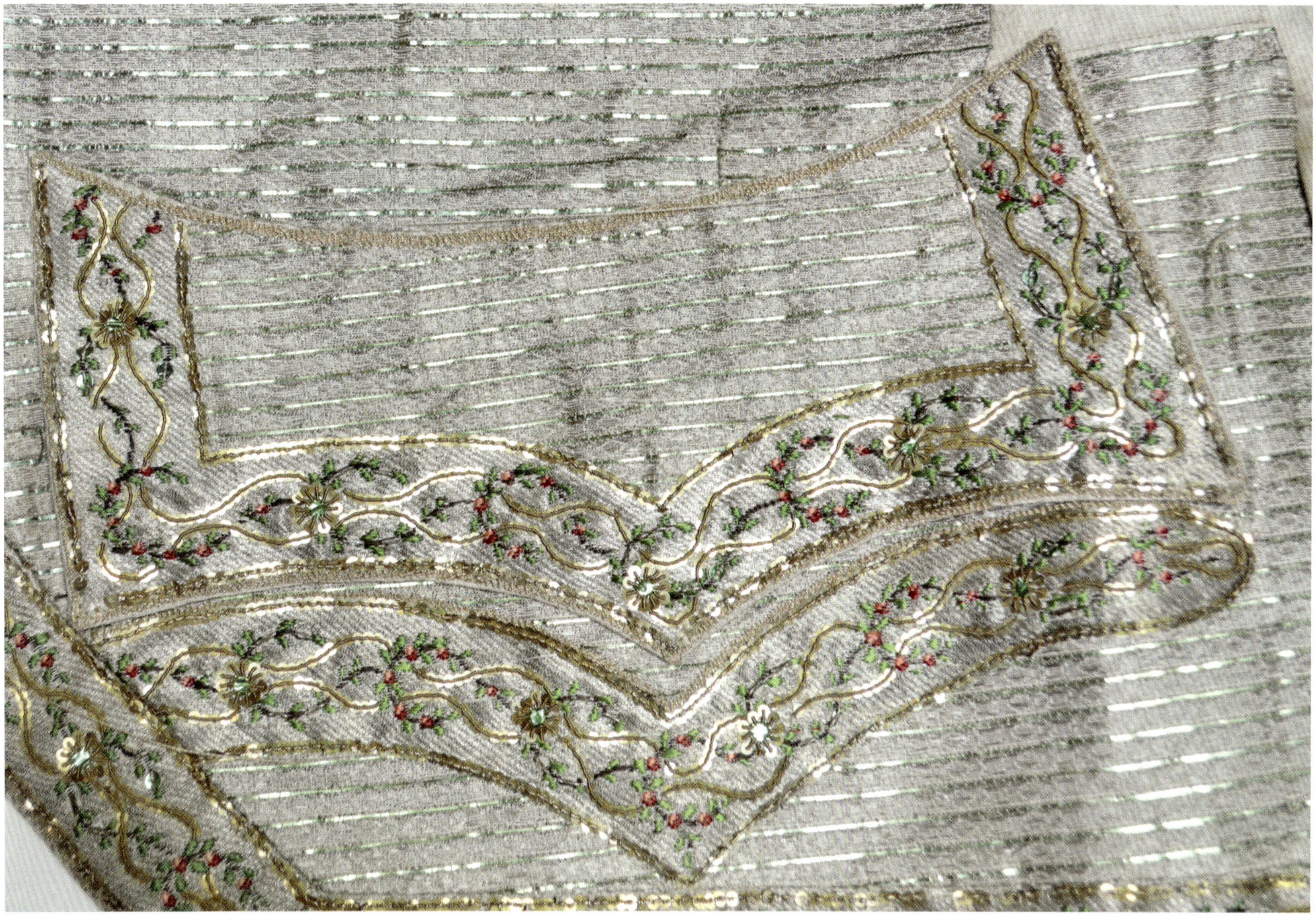

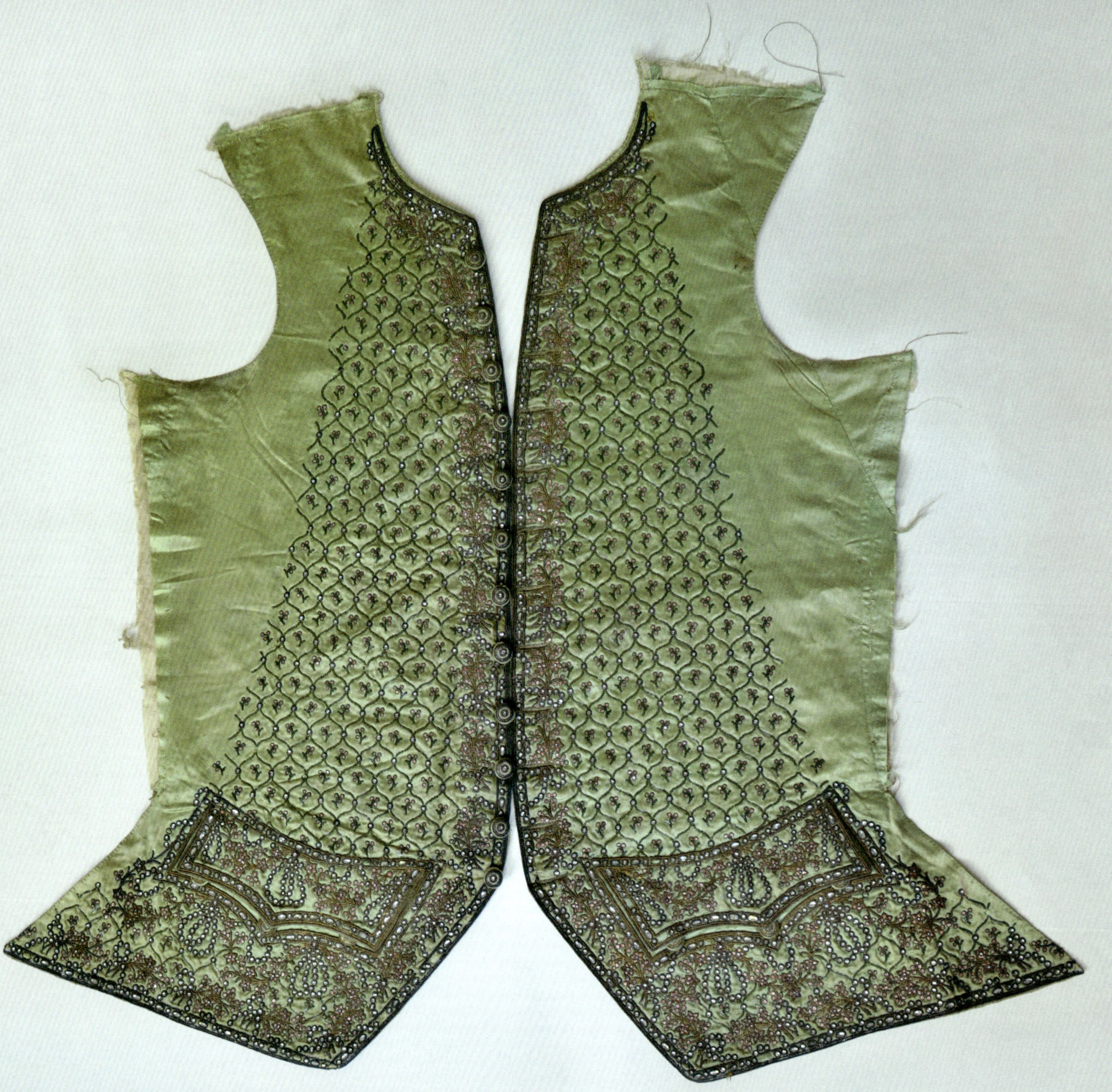

A pair of waistcoat foreparts in pale green silk satin, 1770-1785. HC.W-0.3

They have been used and unpicked. The embroidered ground pattern consists of silver spangles sewn on with green silk thread in a lattice pattern resembling that often used in quilting. This only covers the parts of the waistcoat which would be seen when a coat was worn; the rest of the foreparts are undecorated.

The front edges, hems and pocket flaps have additional embroidery of silver-gilt purl, spangles (page 211), pink enamelled foil and paste. The lining is cream silk twill, with a thin layer of wool between the foreparts and the lining.

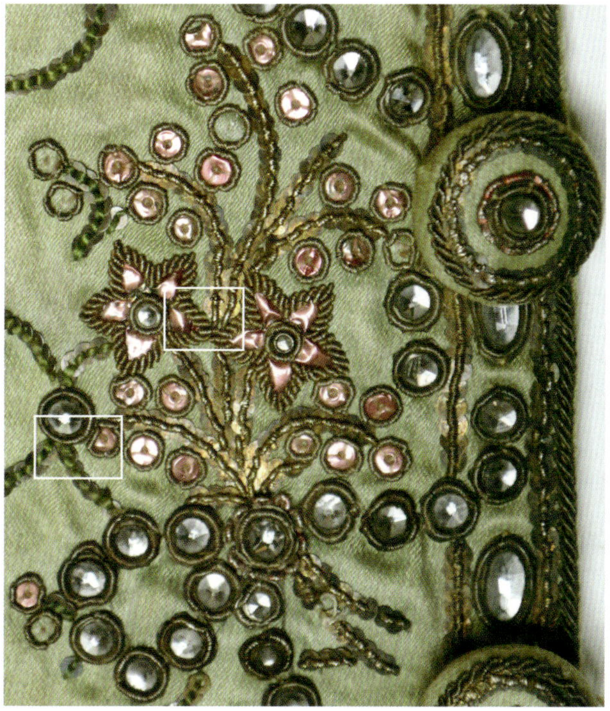

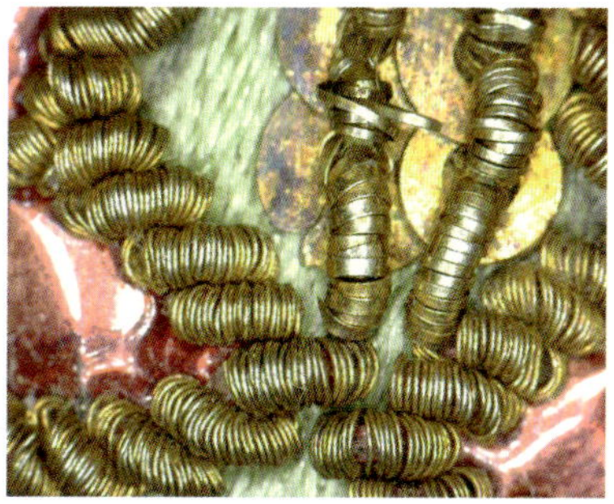

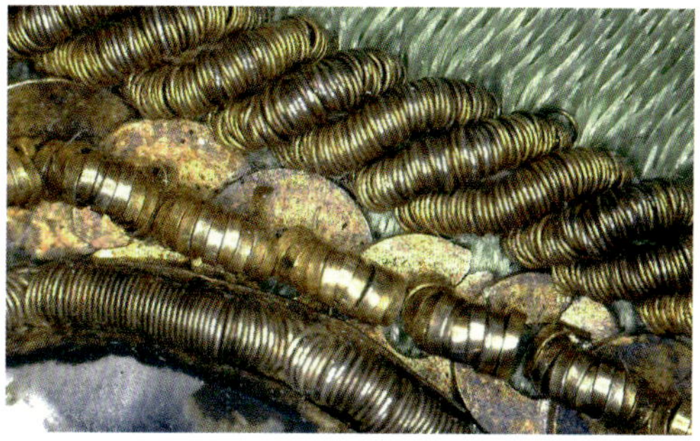

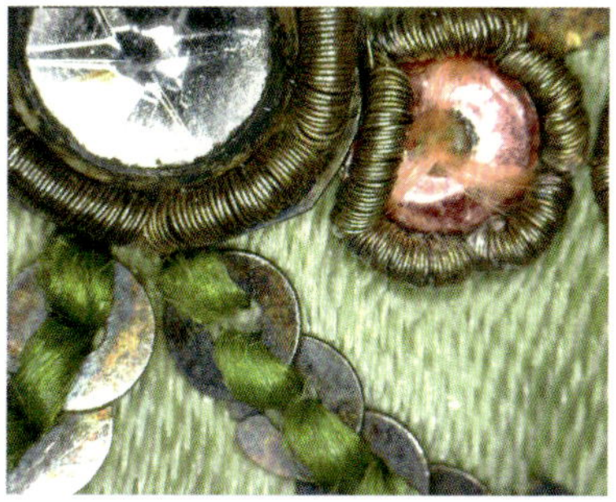

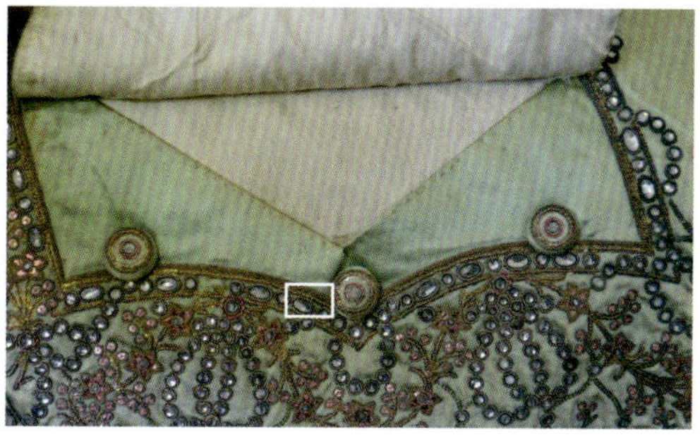

Above and top: Two details outlined on the left.

Under the pocket flap on the left forepart. The outlined detail is shown at the top.

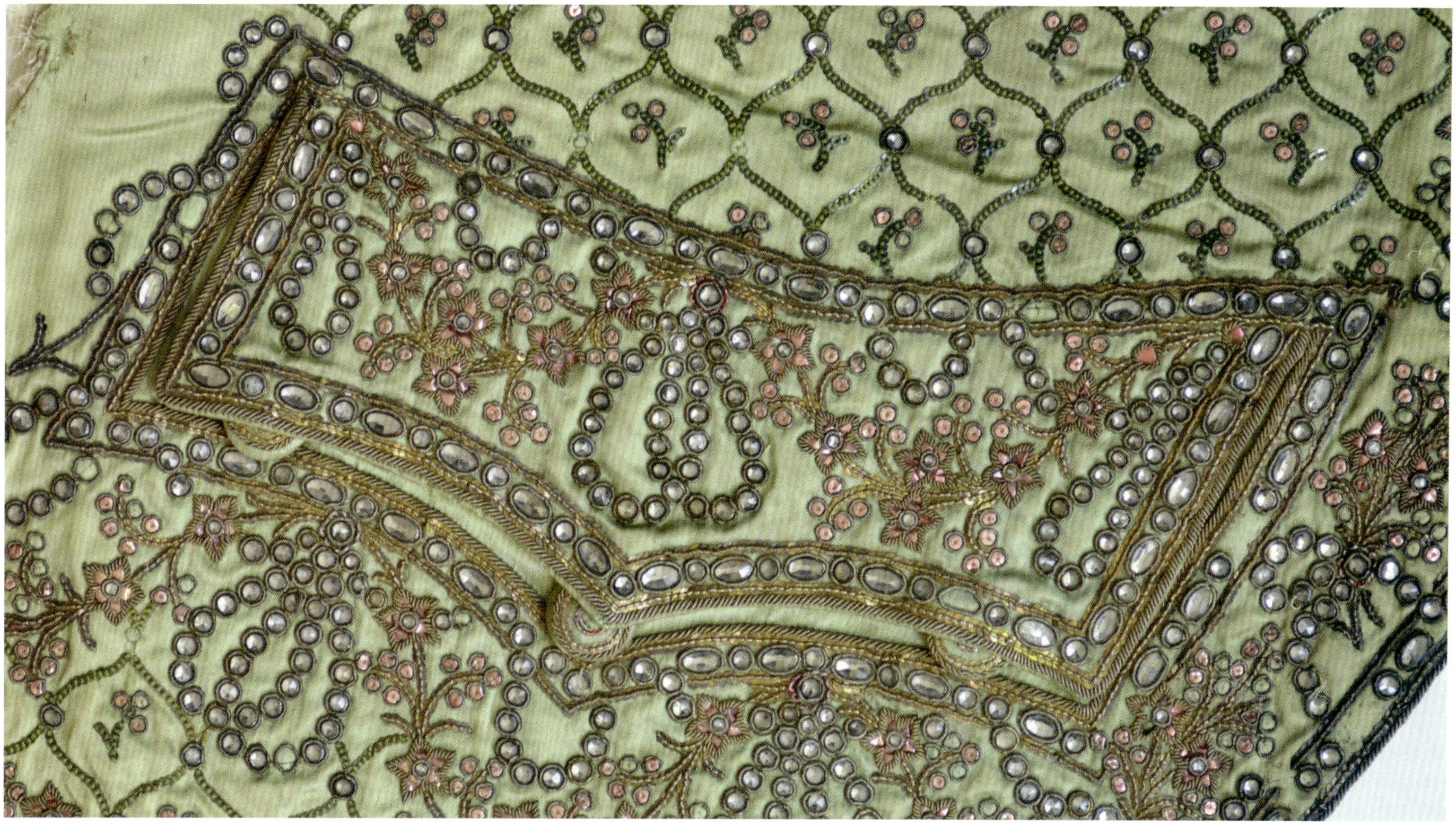

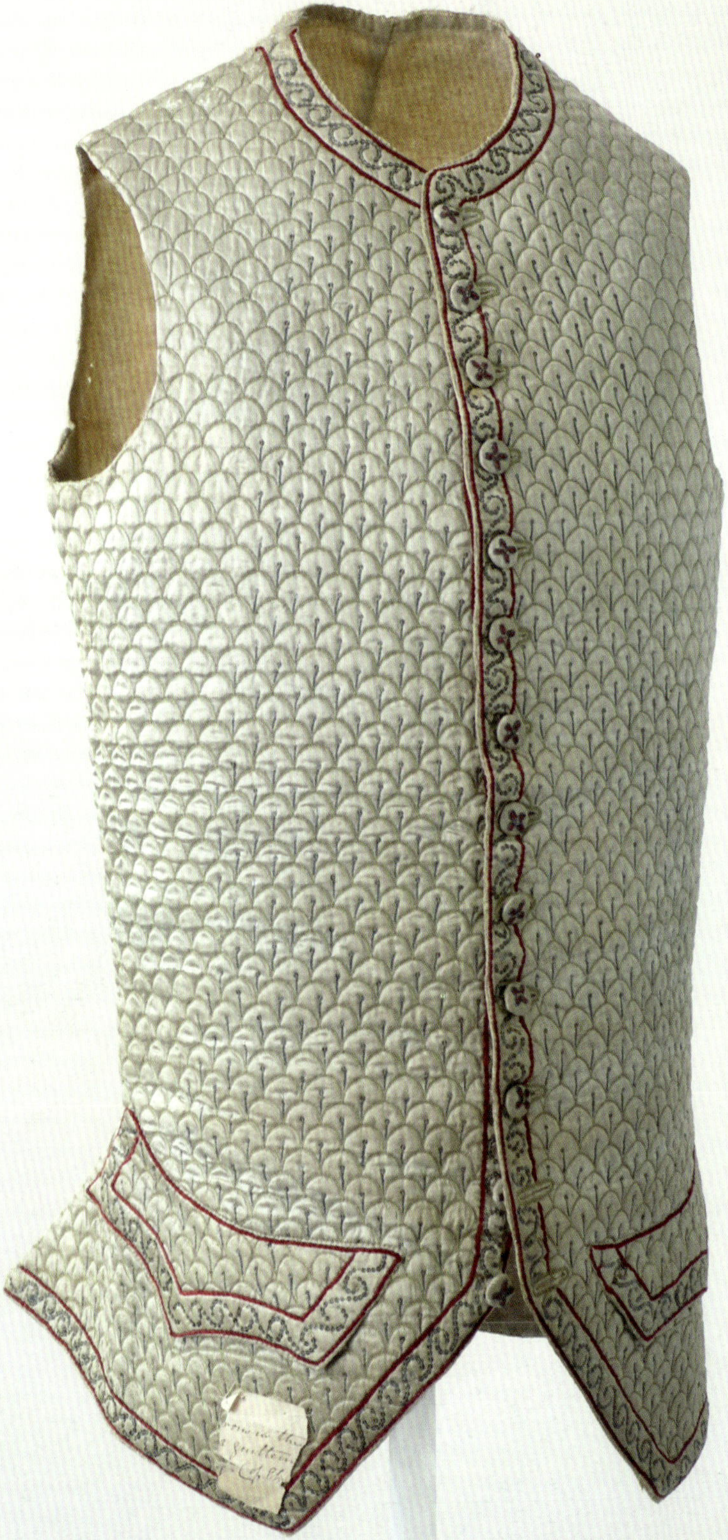

A waistcoat in pale green silk satin, 1775-1790. HC.W-3.92

The satin is quilted in a scales pattern with pale green silk chain stitch, and decorated with red chenille and silver filé embroidery, and silver spangles. The spangles on the quilting only cover the parts of the waistcoat which would remain visible when a coat was worn. The thirteen buttons are covered in the satin and embroidered with silver filé and red chenille petal shapes. The front edges are faced with cream silk twill, and this is sewn on in separate horizontal strips on the left forepart, with the edges turned in along the inside edges of the buttonholes. The buttonholes have been worked before the other decoration was done; they are outlined in the pale green silk chain stitch and the edges just oversewn in cream silk thread. The back was wool twill in a matching colour, but has been almost completely cut away, revealing the natural linen lining. Narrow gussets have been inserted in the side seams to let out the waist.

The piece of paper sewn on at the hem of the right forepart is now torn; the part on the left was found in the pocket, but the part on the right is missing. It says: "Waistcoat worn in the ... century, by a gentleman ... his wedding (of Chi..." and in the bottom left-hand corner it says "Titchener".

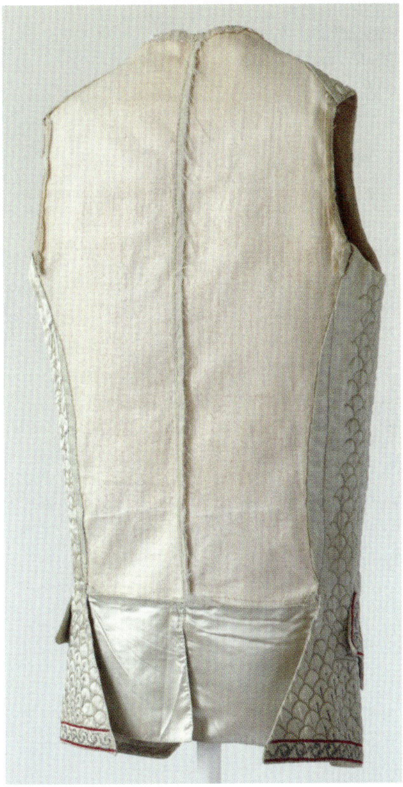

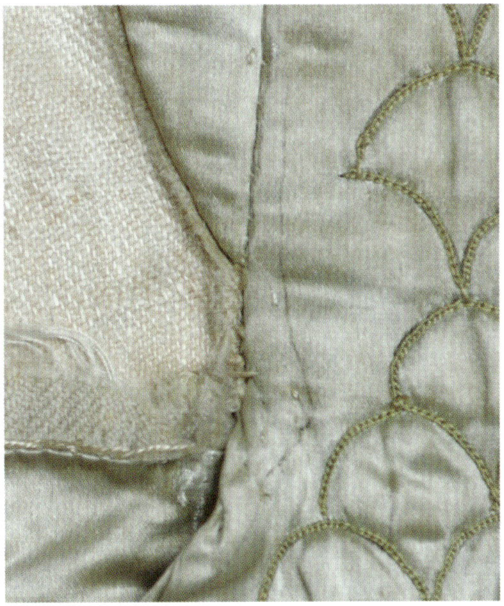

Detail of a side seam where the back skirts join the back. The remains of the wool twill back fabric can be seen in the seams, and also the end of a narrow gusset put in to let out the waist. There is a line drawn near the quilting which is where the seam was intended to be.

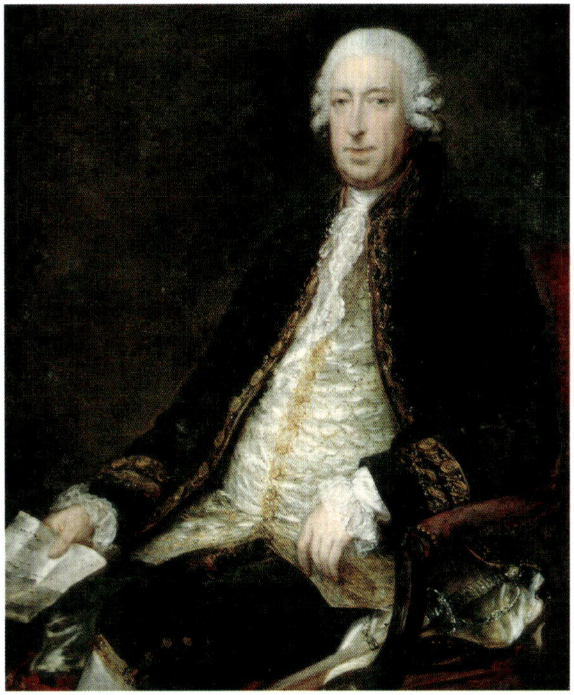

Lord George Sackville, Viscount Sackville by Thomas Gainsborough R.A., Knole. © National Trust Images / John Hammond.

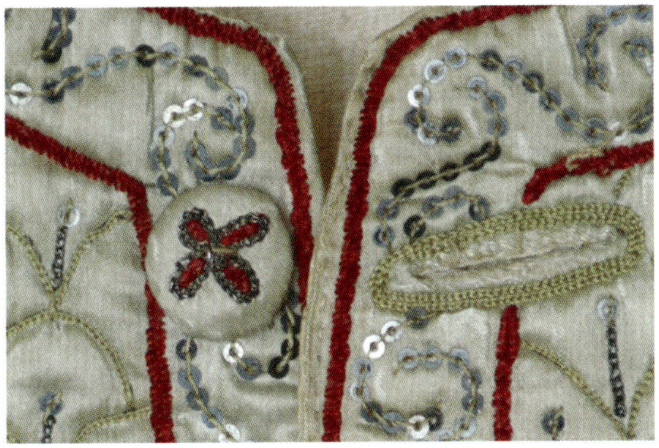

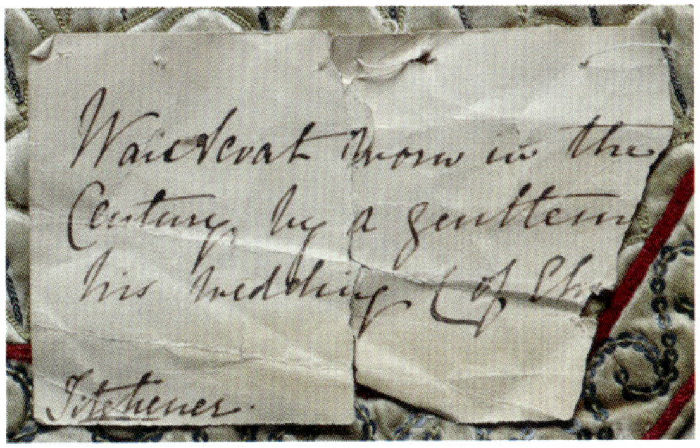

The piece of paper sewn on to the right forepart.

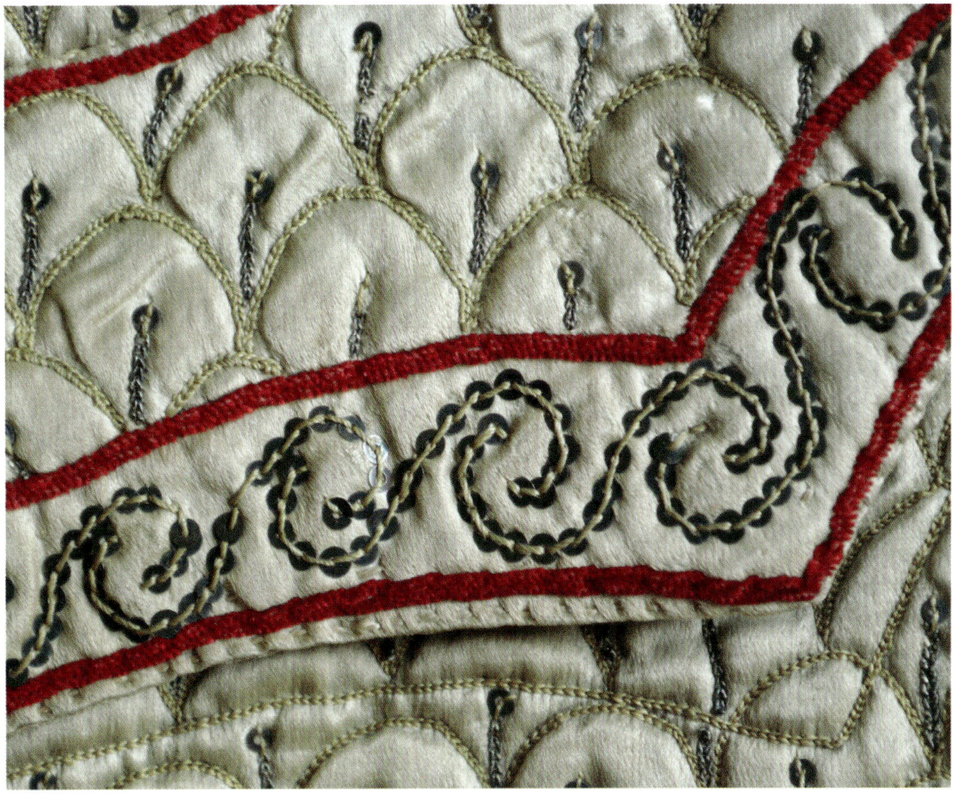

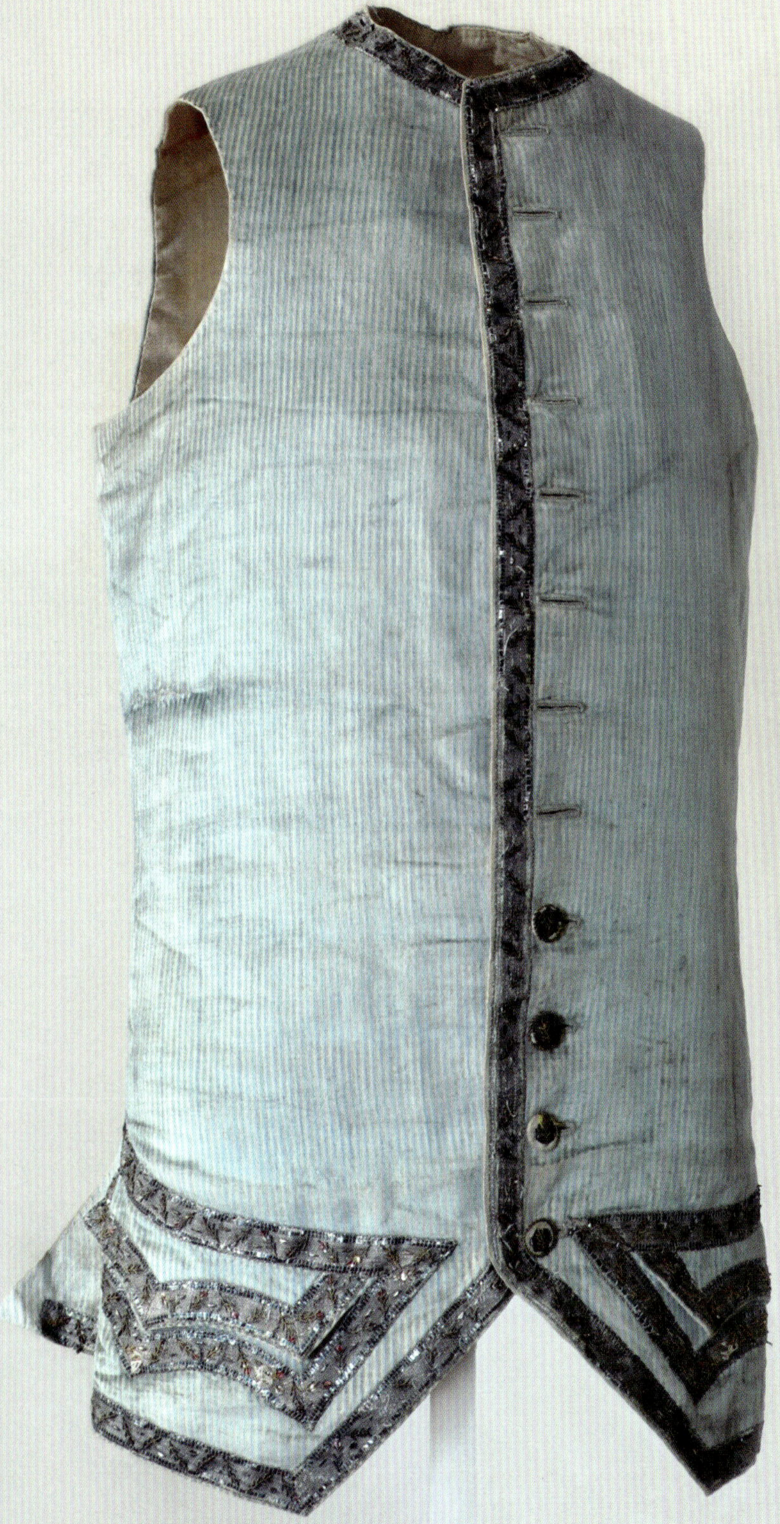

A waistcoat in silk velvet, 1775-1785.
HC.W-3.01-1

The velvet has a flattened pile, with narrow blue and ivory vertical stripes. The edges of the foreparts and pockets have applied silver braid decoration which has a double row of blue enamelled silver flat strips along the edges; there is added decoration of purl or silver-gilt coiled wire, and silver spangles, some of which are coloured pink. The waistcoat is lined with natural cotton, and the facings are in a cream silk twill, which also lines the front and back skirts. The back of the body is in blue wool and the skirts are in the velvet. The back of the waistcoat is open from just below the back neck, and held together with lacing through hand-worked eyelet holes; the lace is a plaited ivory wool cord with a single red thread in it, and it is knotted at the top and tied off at the bottom. There were twelve buttons but only four have survived; they were covered in linen with silver foil on top and decorated with silver-gilt purl. A tear at the side of the right forepart has been sewn up.

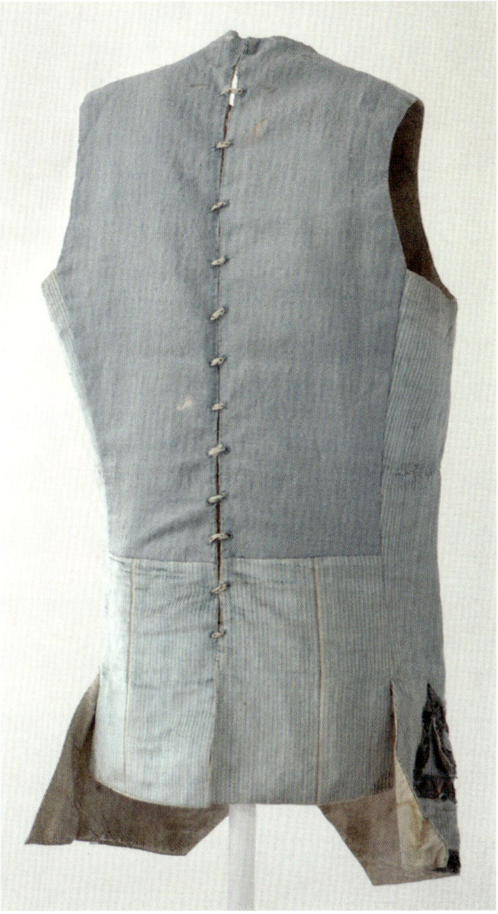

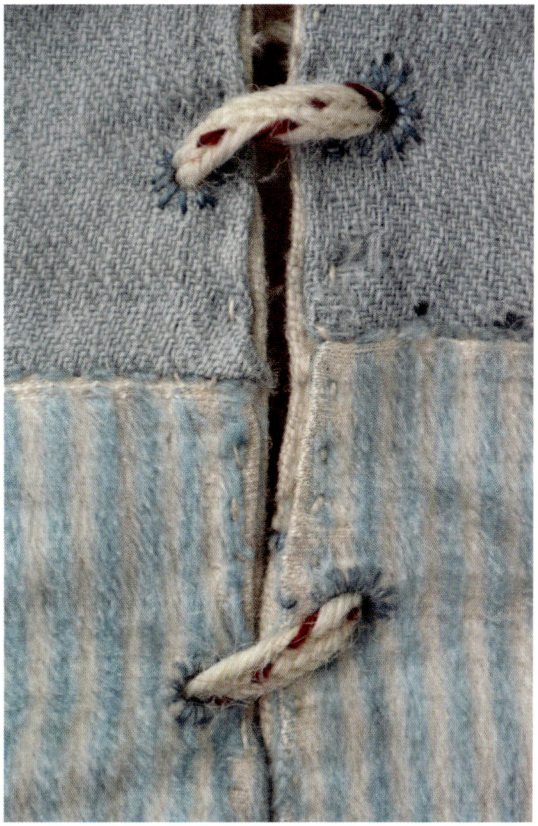

The centre back opening at the point where the skirts meet the body, showing the wool lacing cord and the hand-sewn eyelets.

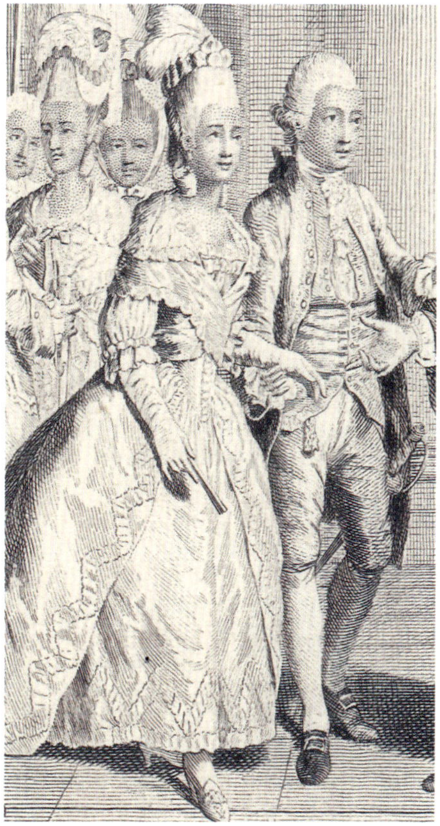

Detail of an illustration from *Sir Charles Grandison* by Samuel Richardson, 1778.

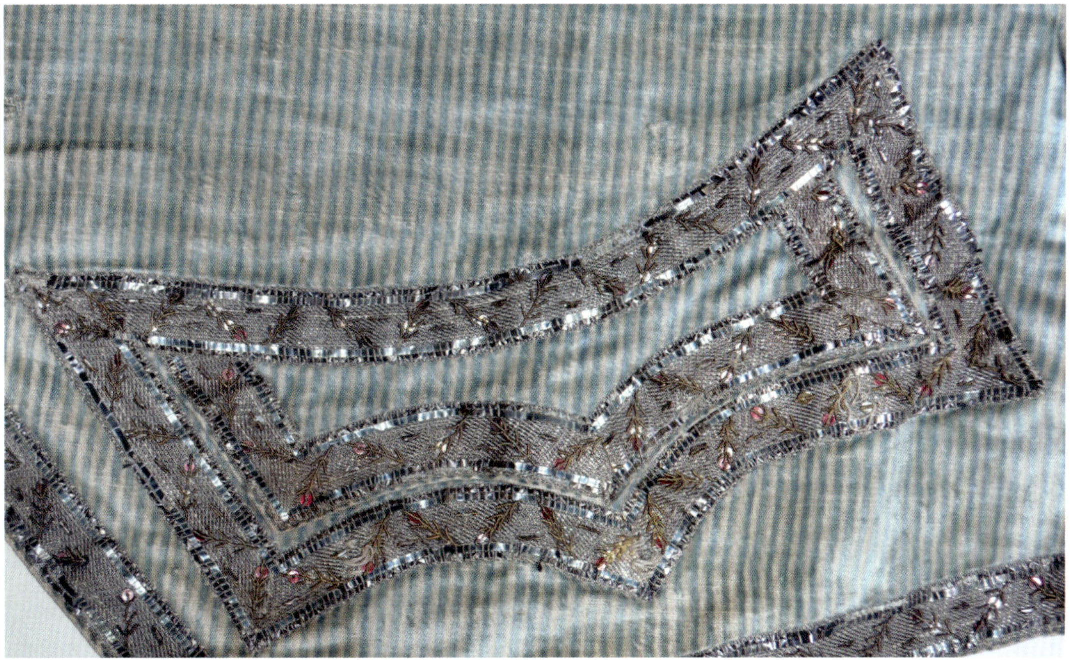

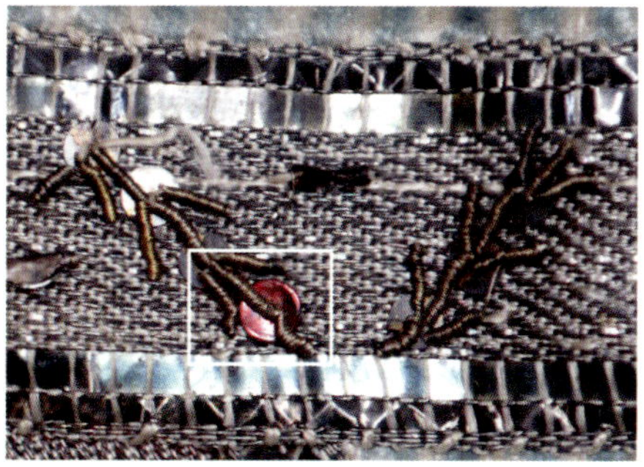

Detail of the silver braid, and below, the outlined section enlarged.

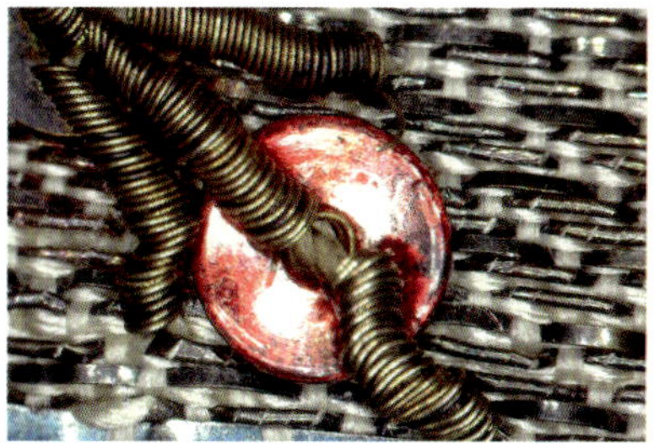

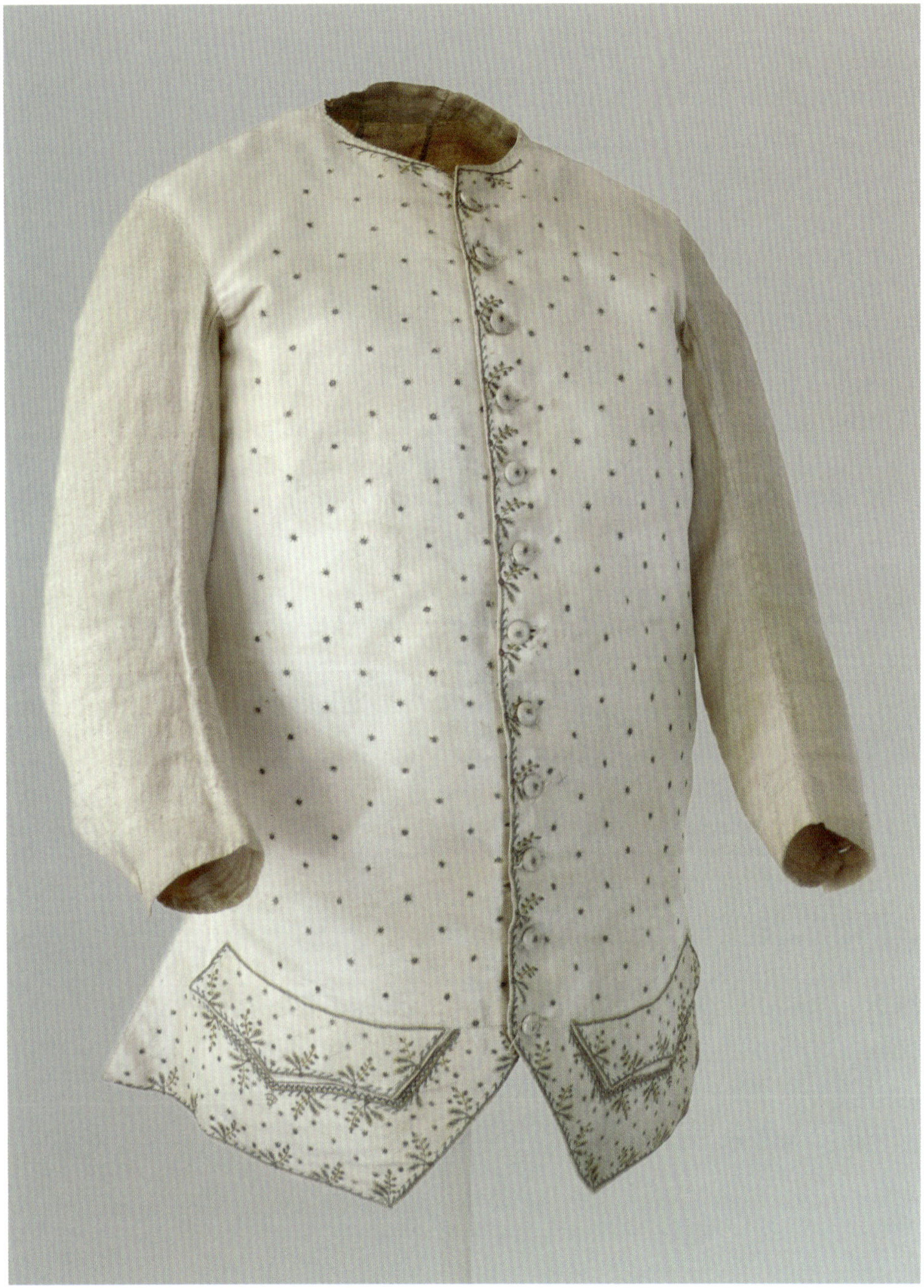

A waistcoat in ivory silk faille, 1770-1790. HC.W-4.14-1

There are embroidered spots in khaki-coloured silk and silver filé thread on the foreparts, and a leafy design on their borders, and on and below the pocket flaps. The waistcoat has sleeves in heavy natural cotton, which were not meant to be seen; they would have added warmth as well as controlling the fullness of the shirt, which would make putting on the coat easier. The cuffs have a covered button and buttonhole to close them. The foreparts are lined in the heavy cotton, and this forms the back which is unlined; there is a 2″-wide strip of natural linen let in to the centre back, which itself has an inserted gusset of heavy cotton at the bottom. The twelve covered buttons have an embroidered spot on them.

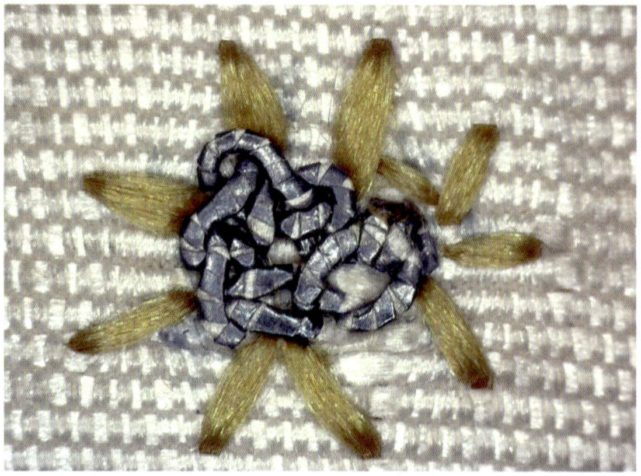

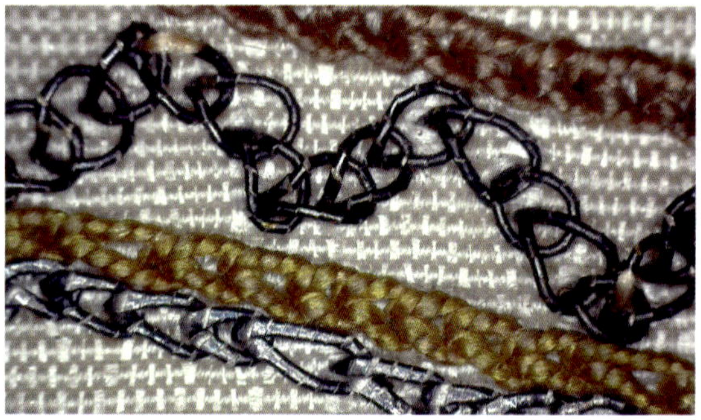

Two details of the embroidery on the pocket flap, outlined below.

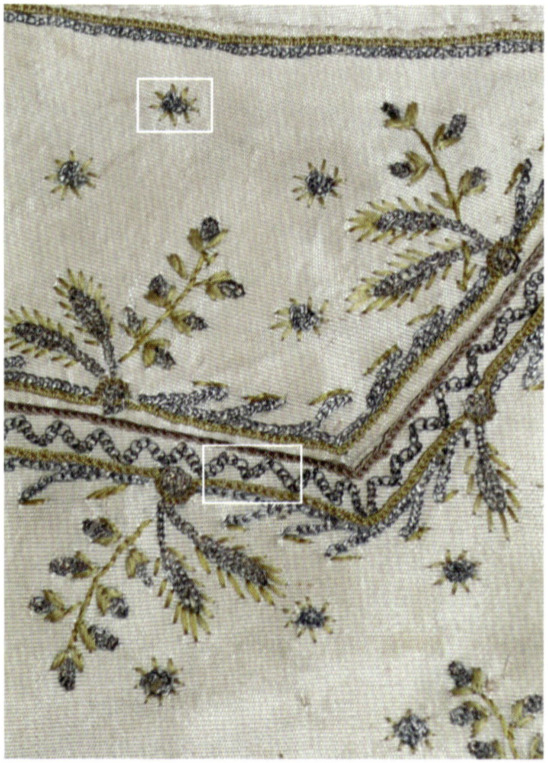

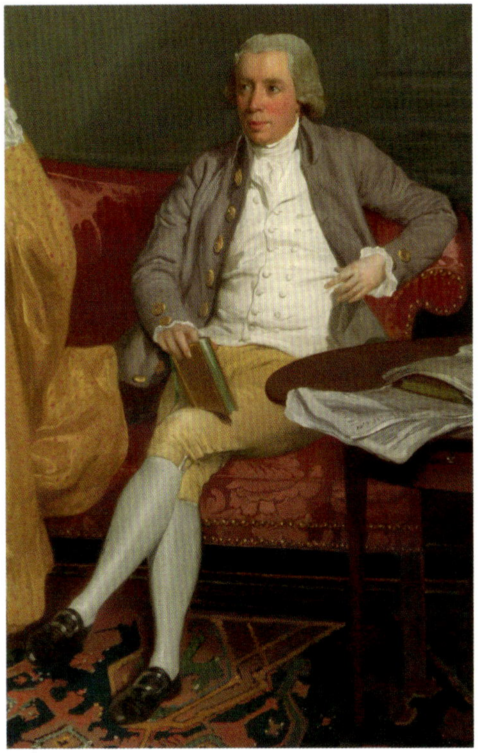

Detail from *The Saithwaite Family* by Francis Wheatley, *c.*1785. The Metropolitan Museum of Art. Gift of Mrs Charles Wrightsman, 2009. www.metmuseum.org

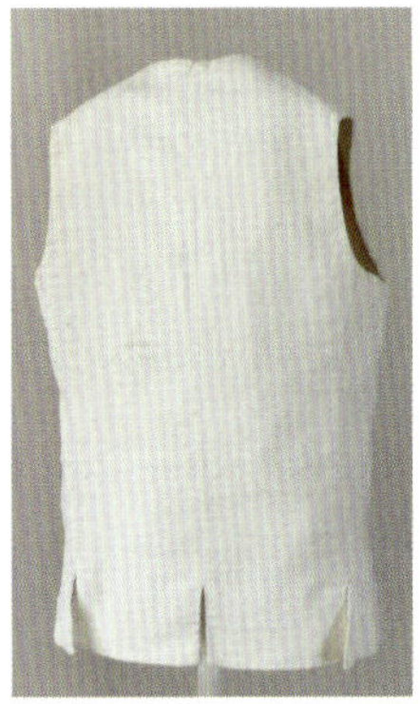

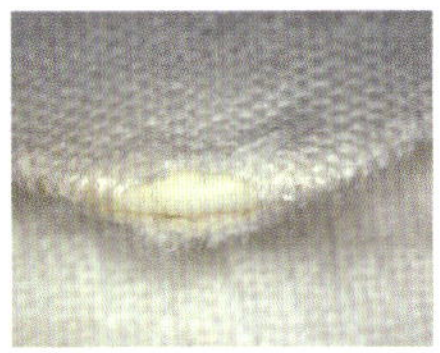

The edge of the bone mould of a button showing through the worn linen covering. Bone was used for buttons on washable waistcoats, since wood, as typically used, might stain the fabric when wet.

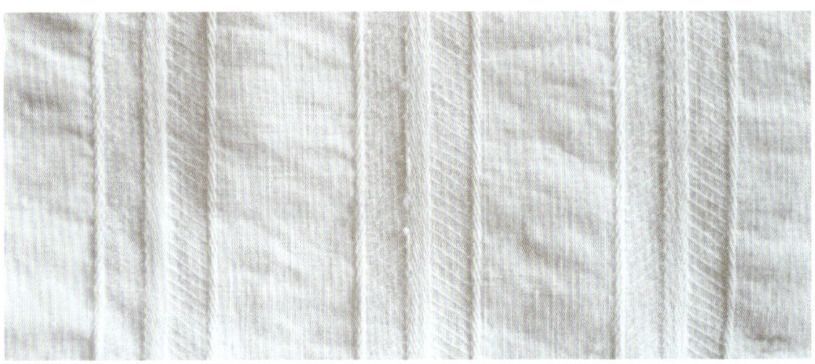

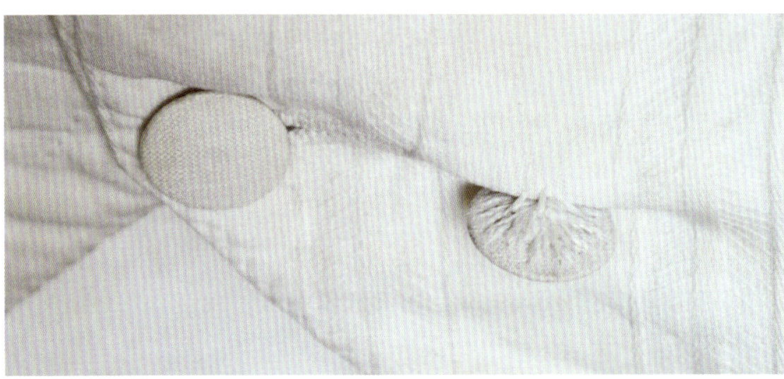

The lowest pair of buttons, showing the back of one, where it is stitched on.

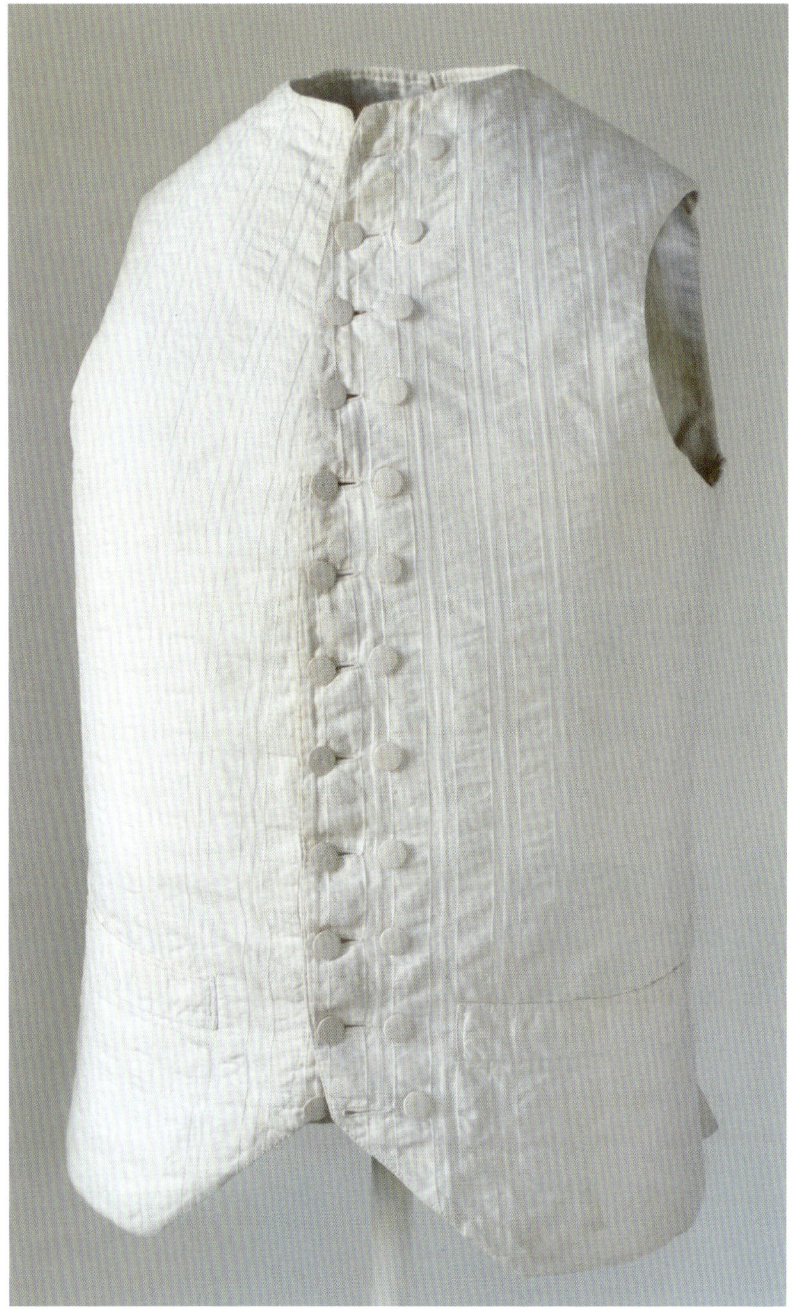

A waistcoat in white cotton seersucker, 1780-1795. HC.W-10.76-4

Seersucker was originally a striped silk and cotton fabric from India, the warp threads of the puckered stripes being at a slacker tension than the others. The waistcoat is narrowly double-breasted with twelve pairs of linen-covered buttons. The practical buttons are on the edge of the right forepart, and when done up they run down the centre of the waistcoat, as on a single-breasted garment; the decorative row has been added to one side, on the left forepart. The lining and back are in heavy white cotton. The pockets have welted tops, a style which appeared in the 1780s and gradually replaced pockets with flaps.

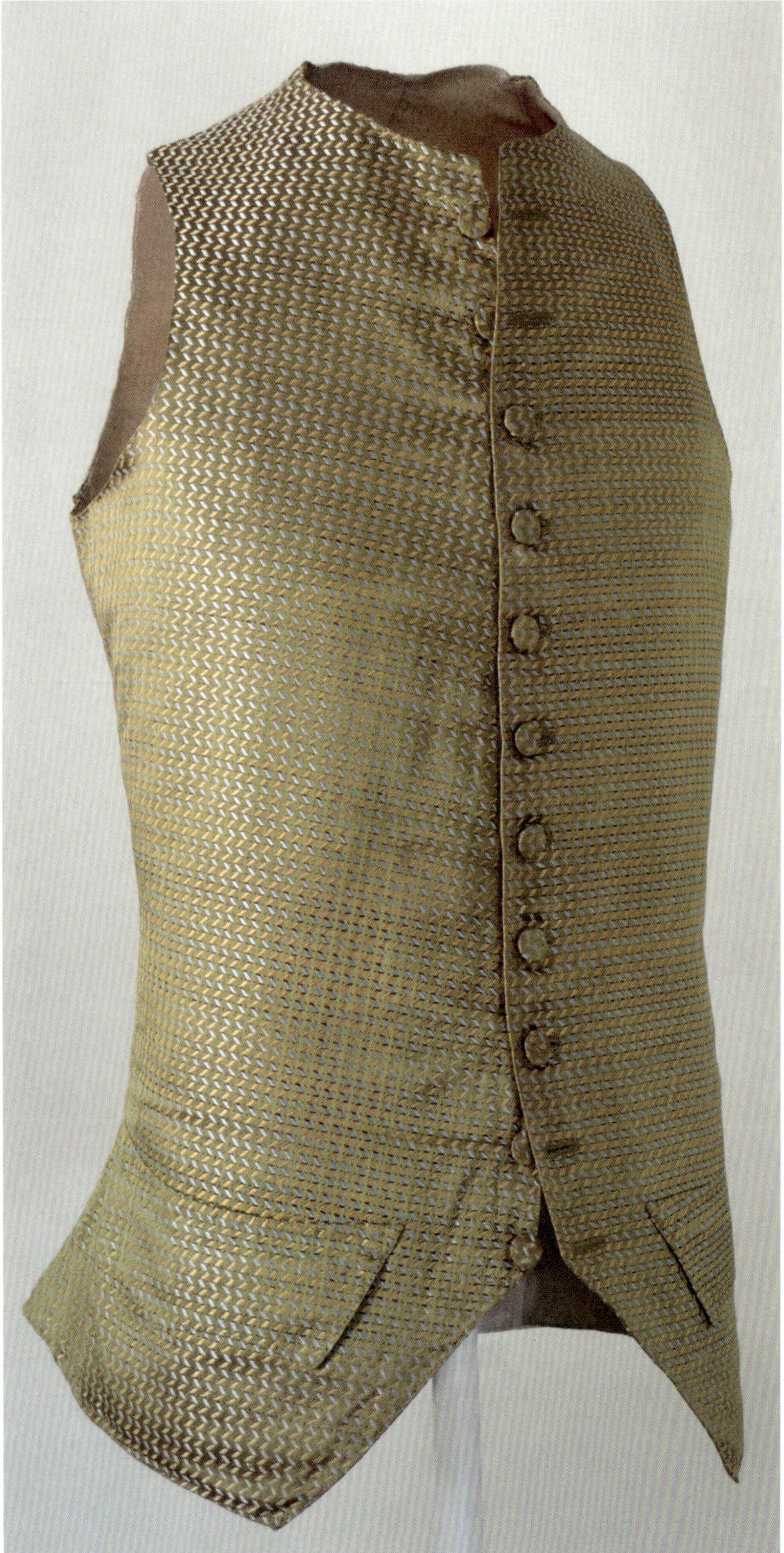

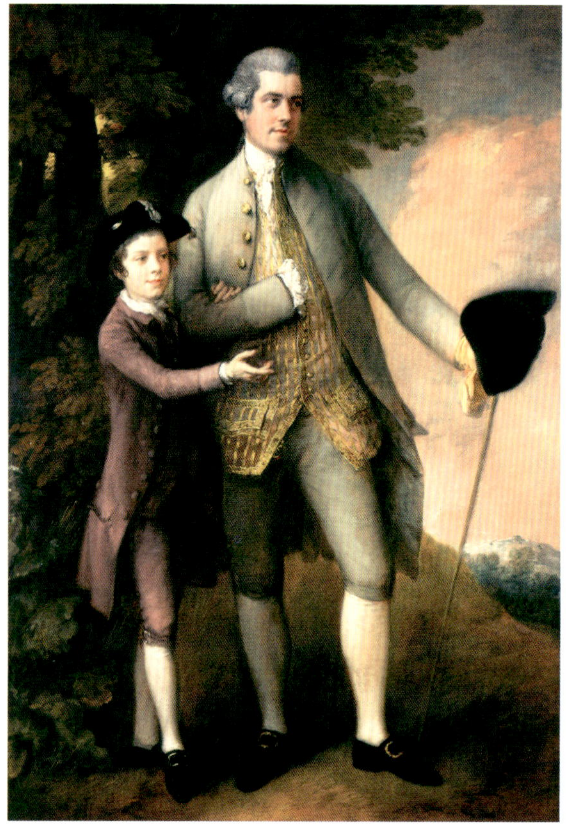

Thomas Rumbold and Son by Thomas Gainsborough, 1774.

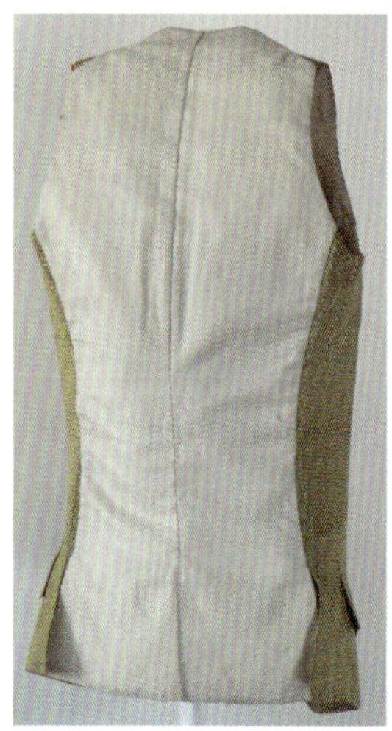

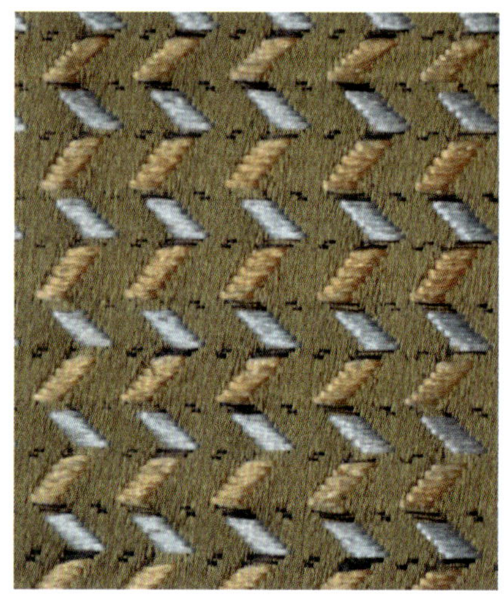

A waistcoat in khaki silk satin, 1770-1785. HC.W-7.89-1

The satin has a small geometric pattern in pale blue, gold and black. There are eleven self-covered buttons and the front facings are in a pale olive green silk twill, which also lines the front skirts. The rest of the lining is ivory fustian and the back is in cream calimanco. This may have been part of a suit.

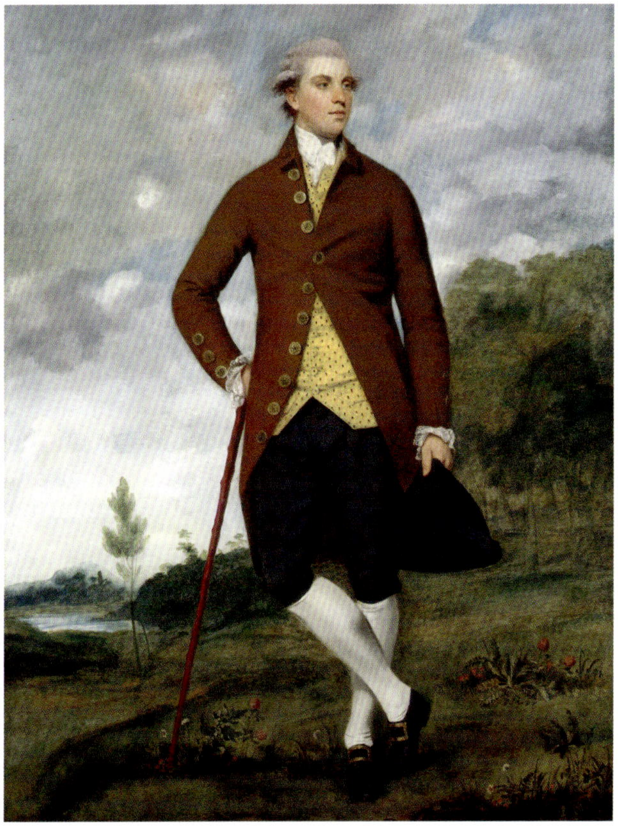

John Musters by Joshua Reynolds, 1777-1780. Courtesy National Gallery of Art, Washington.

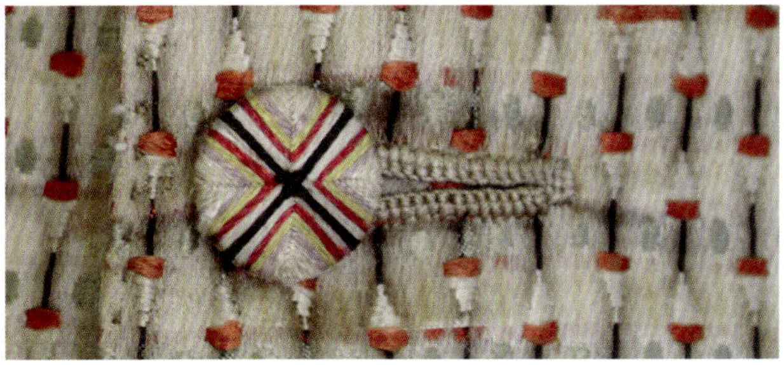

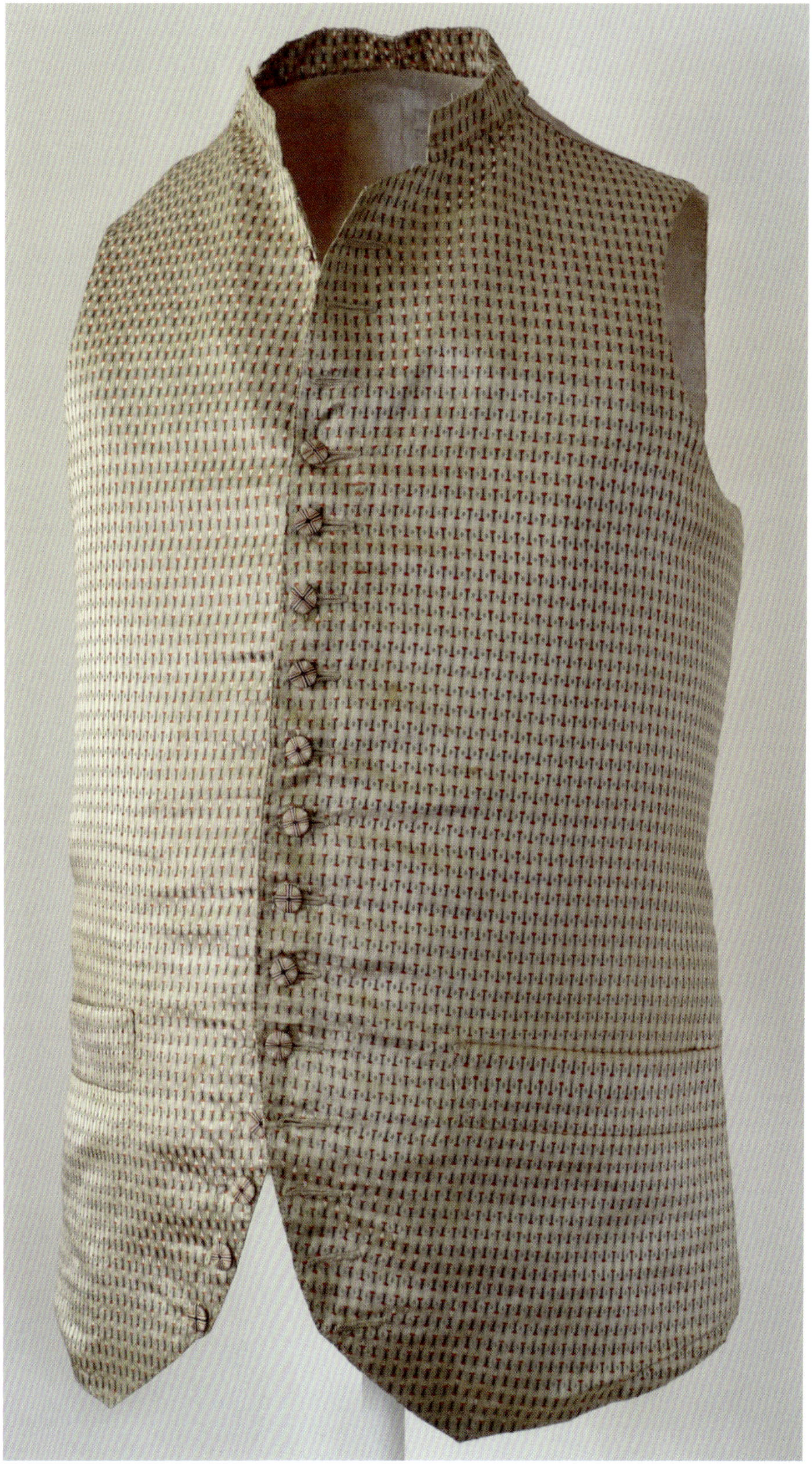

A waistcoat in deep cream silk satin, 1775-1785. HC.W-10.96-3

The satin has a small geometric pattern in red, green, ivory and black. The sixteen buttons are covered in matching threads geometrically arranged, and there are two welted pockets. The waistcoat is lined with ivory cotton and the back is in fawn wool twill with two pairs of cotton tapes to adjust the waist. The front facings behind the top five buttons are in the patterned silk, and below that the facings are in a plain cream silk twill, which also lines the hems of the foreparts. At some point the top edges had been folded back to form a V-shape opening, and the small stand collar has been cut, to align with this; the centre back seam has been taken in. This may have been part of a suit.

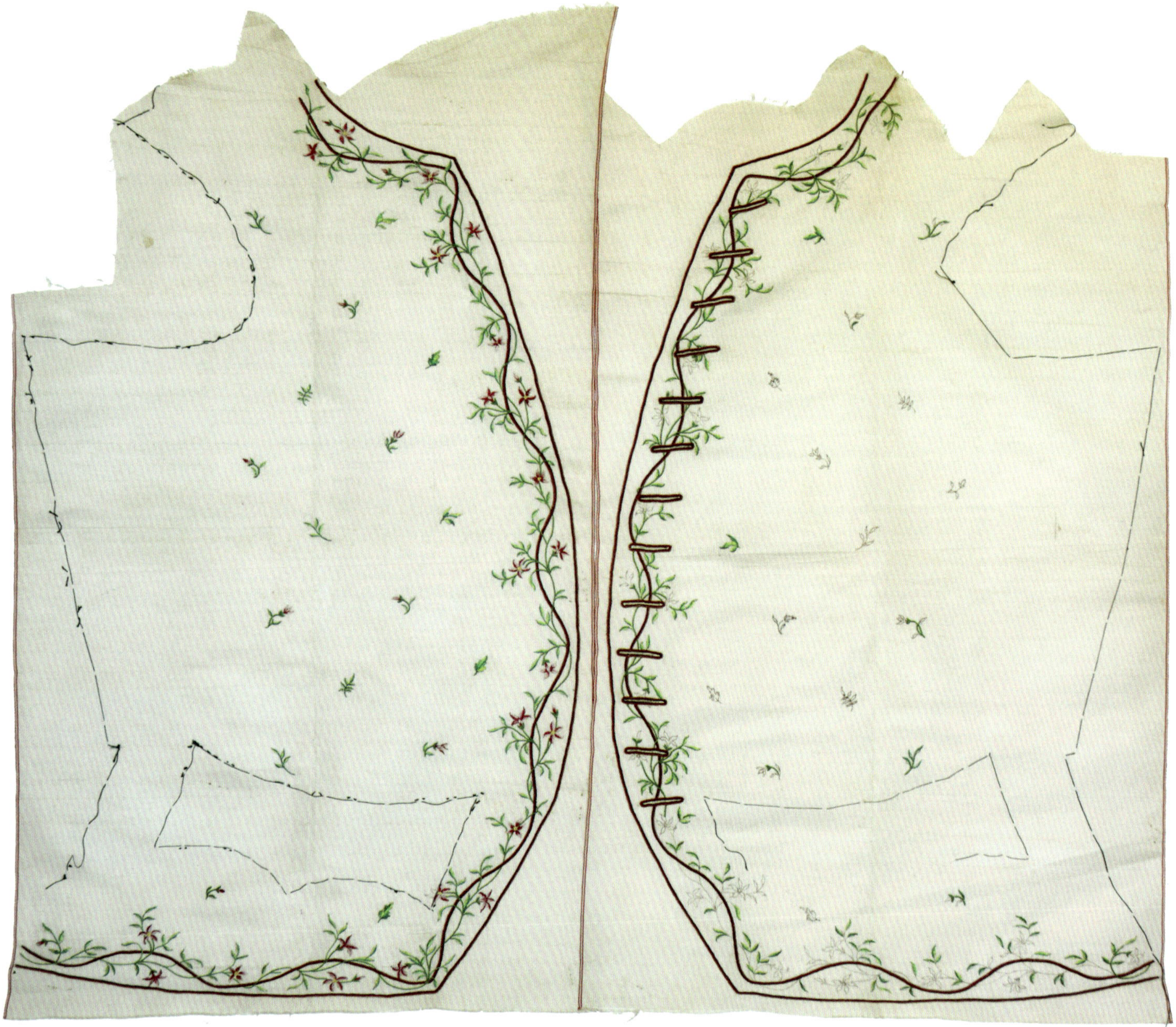

A pair of embroidered cream silk panels, 1770-1790.
HC.W-11.92-2

The silk is a type of cannelé; the shape of the waistcoat foreparts and the position of the pocket flaps have been outlined in dark green silk tacking stitches. The front edges have silk embroidery of brown lines and polychrome flower trails, and there is a scattering of sprigs over the rest of the foreparts. The work is unfinished and on the left forepart the outlines for the sprigs can be seen, drawn in ink.

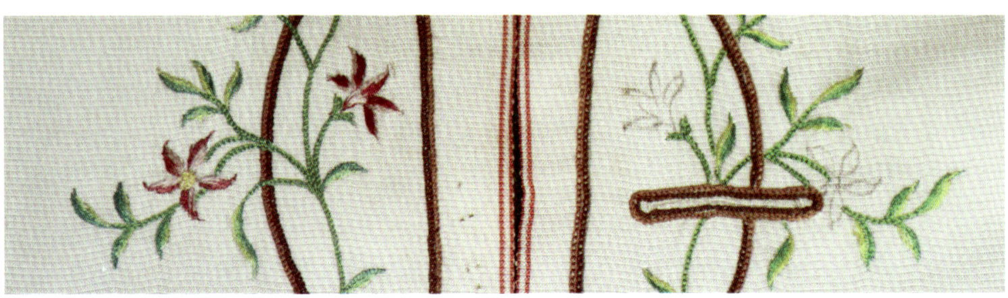

Detail of the front edges, with the finished flowers on the left and the inked outlines on the right.

A panel of white cotton twill, 1780-1800.
HC.W-0.33

It has silk tambour embroidery worked to shape for waistcoat foreparts and was probably made in India. There is an all-over pattern of leaves in green, and a border of black, yellow and ivory. Spaces have been left for the pocket welts, which have been worked separately at the bottom centre of the panel. The top sections of the facings are upside-down at the top centre, and there are tiny embroidered motifs in the centre and at the bottom, for buttons. The panel was probably made for the Countess of Melville, whose name is written in faint pencil on the bottom right-hand corner.

Below: Detail showing the faint pencilled name.

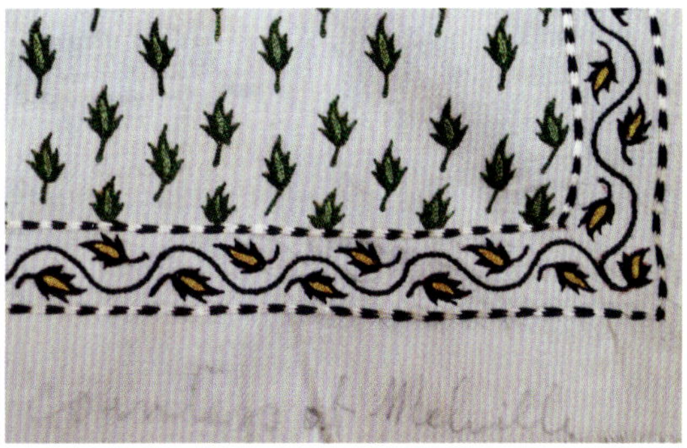

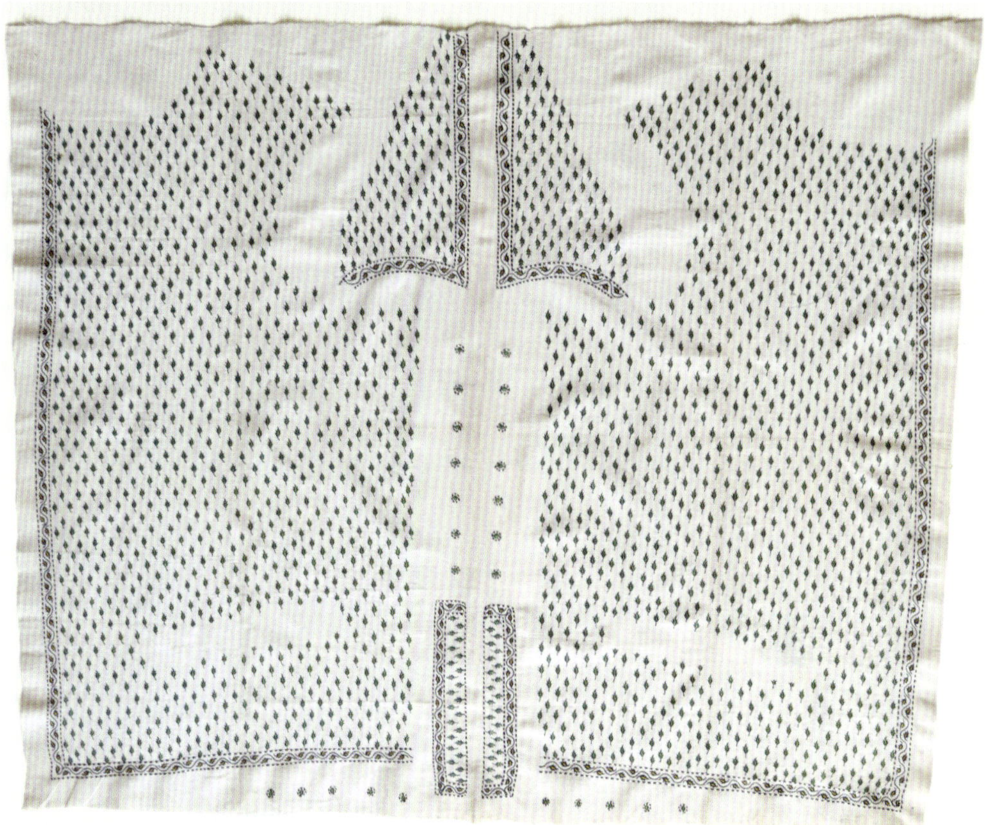

A pair of cream silk satin panels, 1785-1800.
HC.W-3.03-2

The embroidery of silver filé thread in chain stitch is worked to shape for waistcoat foreparts; between the stripes there are spots in cream silk. Shapes for the front sections of the collar, and the pocket welts are at the outside top corners of the panels, and below are shapes for the top of the facings, which would show when the waistcoat was worn open at the neck. Below that, down each edge are embroidered motifs for the buttons. The panels have a thin layer of wadding, creating a quilted effect.

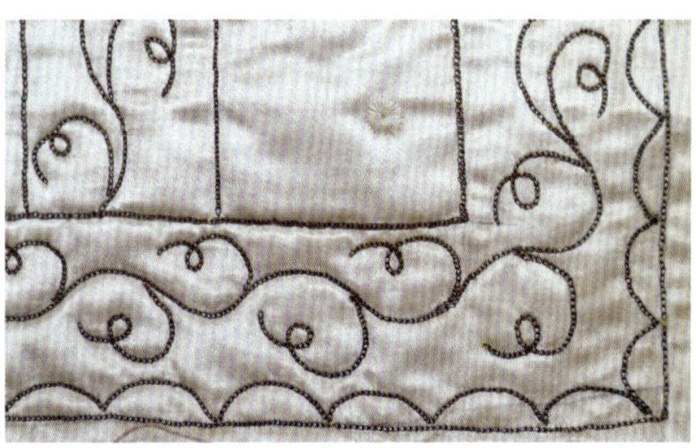

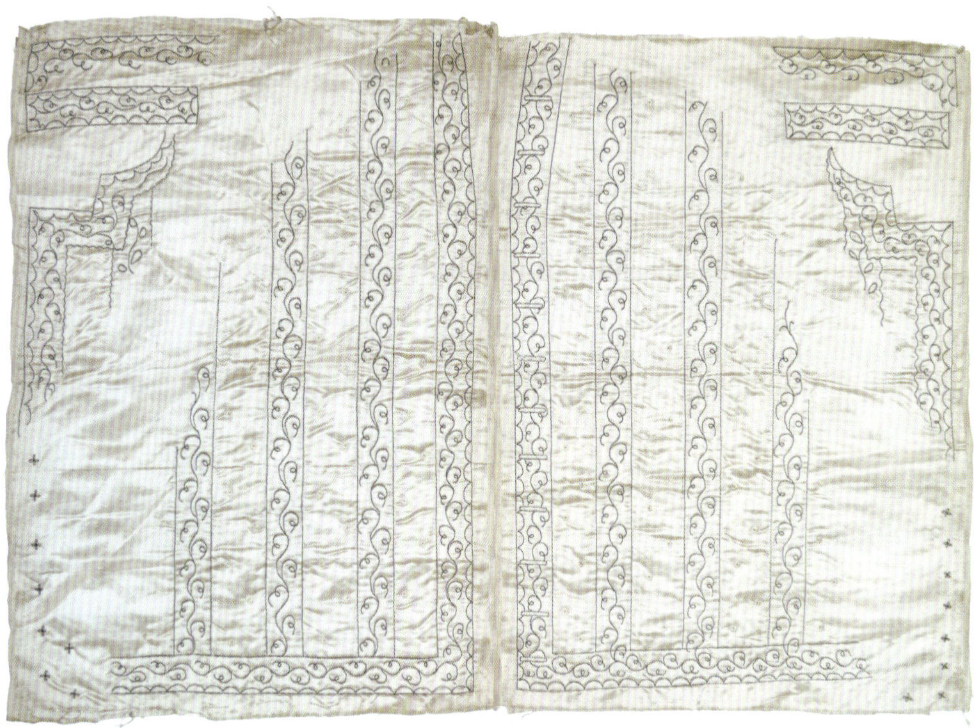

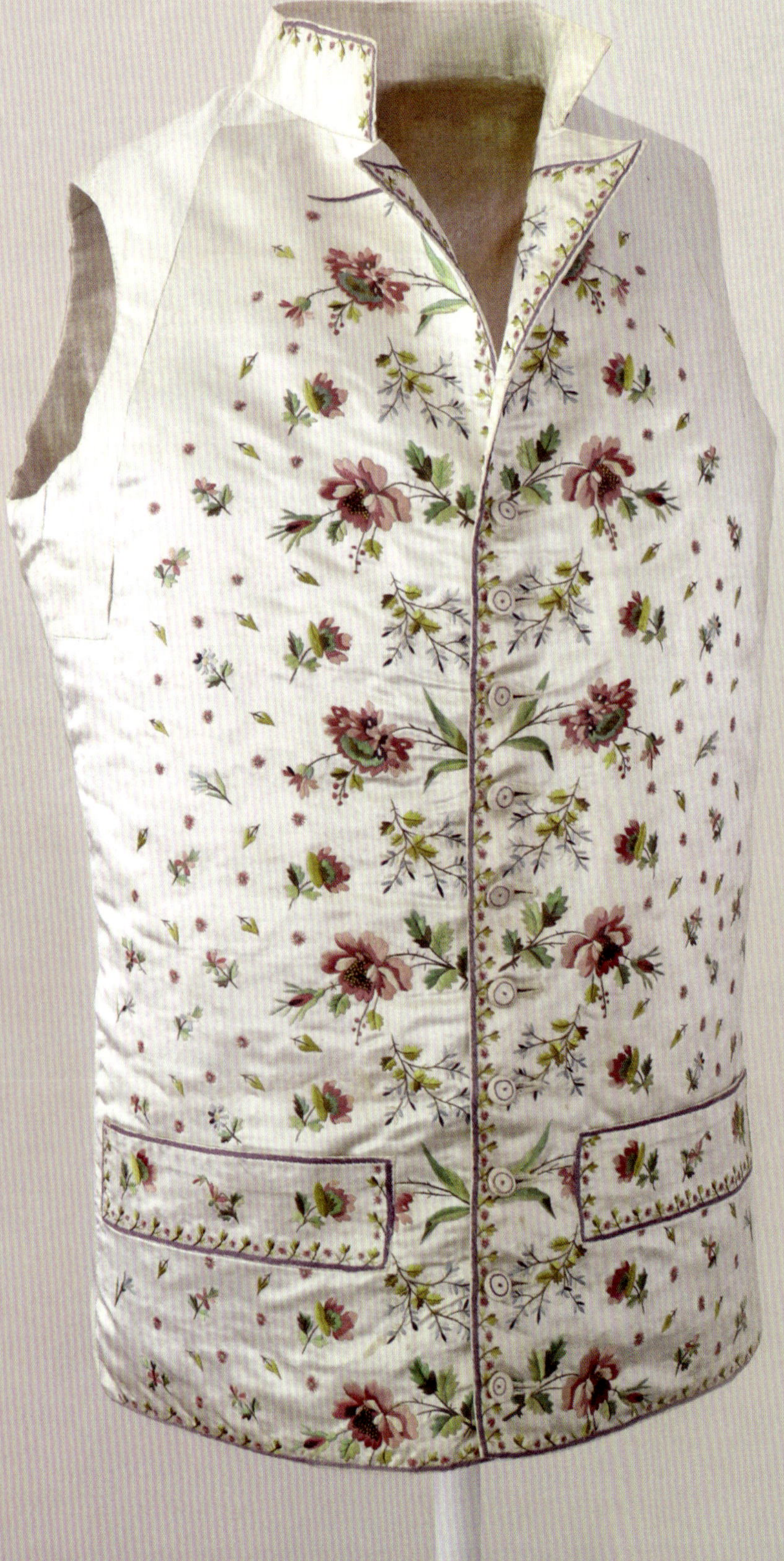

A waistcoat in white silk satin, 1784.
HC.W-11.14

This was worn by Cornelius Cayley for his wedding in 1784. The waistcoat has embroidery of flowers and leaves in polychrome silks on the foreparts and pocket welts. The top front edges of the foreparts are faced with the embroidered satin, which is also on the front sections of the stand collar. The embroidered lines at the neck suggest that the design of the waistcoat was intended to have more pointed revers but the foreparts have been cut higher, adding length, to accommodate a taller figure. The ten covered buttons have embroidered rings and dots on them. The front edges and hems of the foreparts are faced with cream silk twill, and this is also on the inside of the front sections of the collar band; the back of the collar is in natural linen. The lining is in ivory fustian and there is an interlining throughout, giving some padding. The back is in natural linen, with two pairs of cotton tape ties to adjust the waist.

The embroidered panels were evidently too narrow for the finished waistcoat, and there is piecing in ivory silk twill at the shoulders, beside the armholes, and in the side seams.

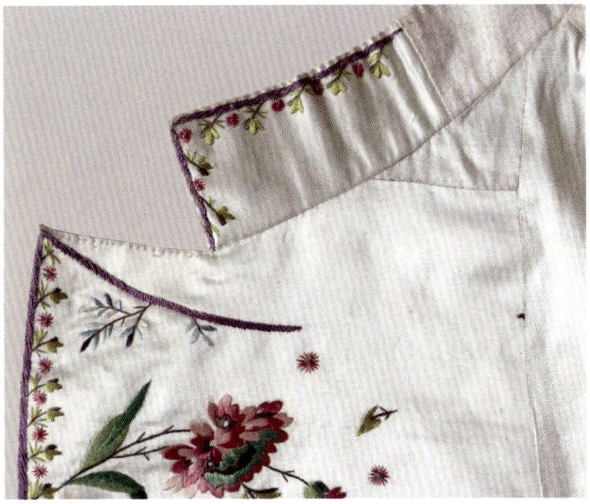

The top of the left forepart showing the intended top of the lapel; the piecing at the neck and the linen back of the collar can also be seen.

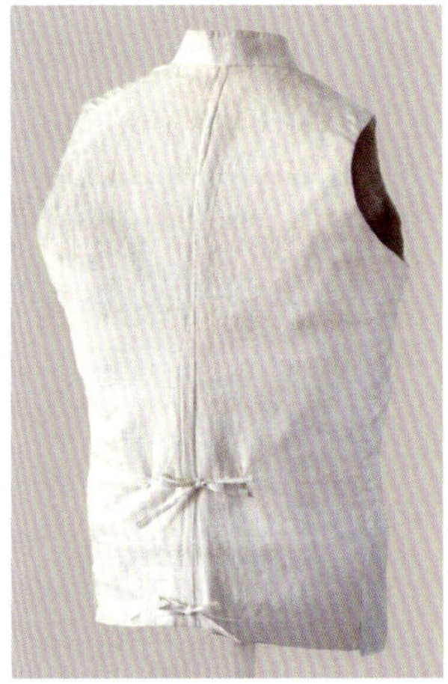

The tape ties on the back; these began to appear around this time.

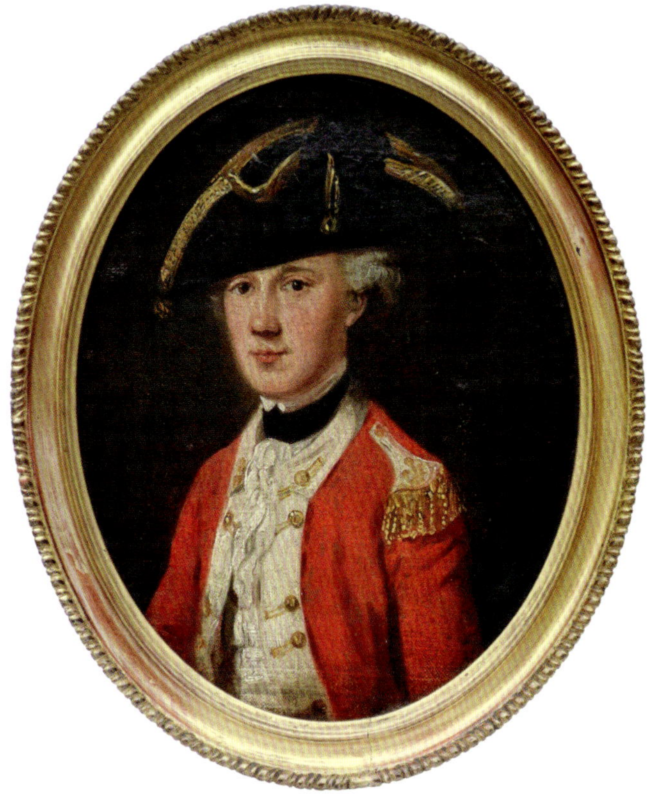

Cornelius Cayley in his uniform as a lieutenant in the Twentieth Regiment of Foot, probably around the time of his marriage in 1784. Privately owned.

Cornelius Cayley was born in 1762 in St. Petersburg, Russia, the son of John Cayley, the British consul, who was also a businessman running a Russian merchant partnership there. In 1784 Cornelius married Sarah Ward, in York, and spent most of his life running the English end of the family business. He died in 1836, in Sowerby, Yorkshire.

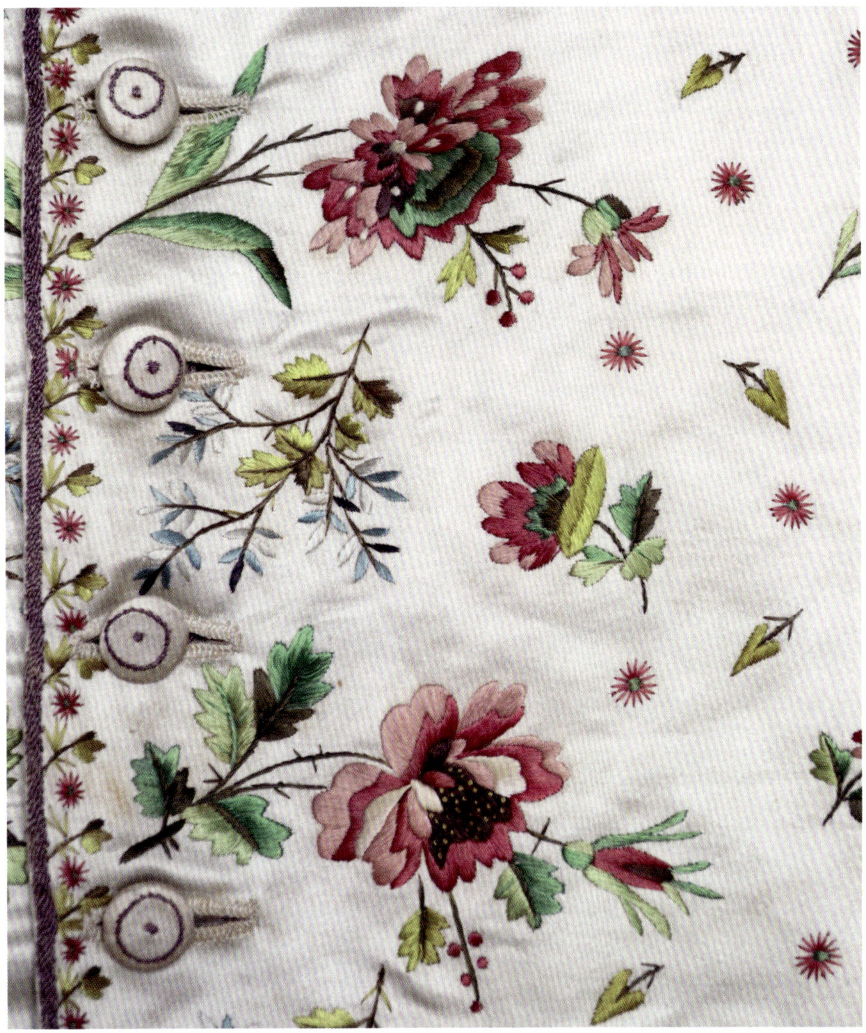

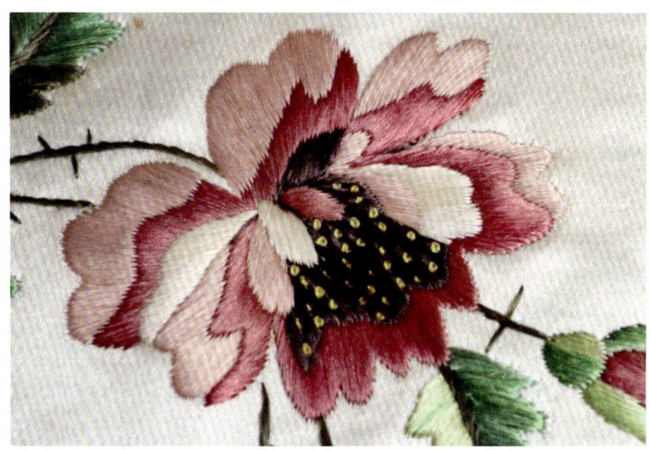

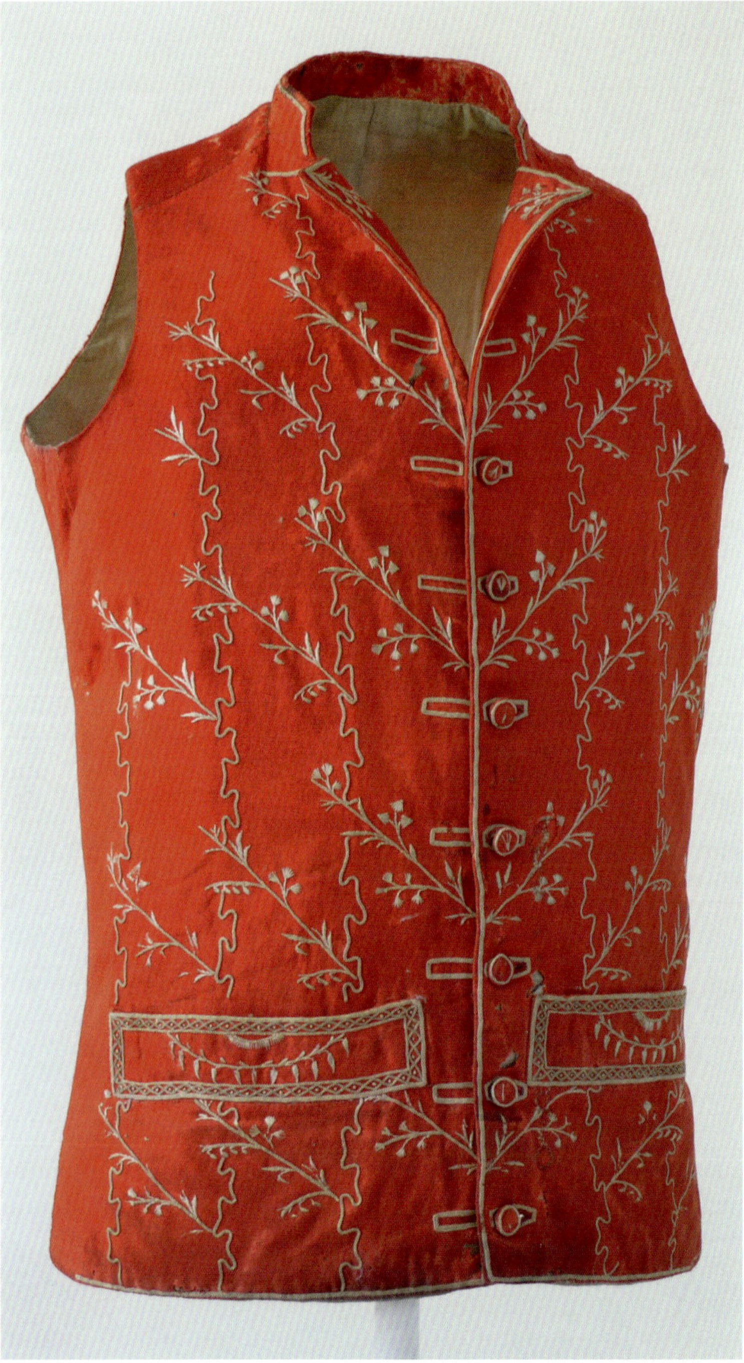

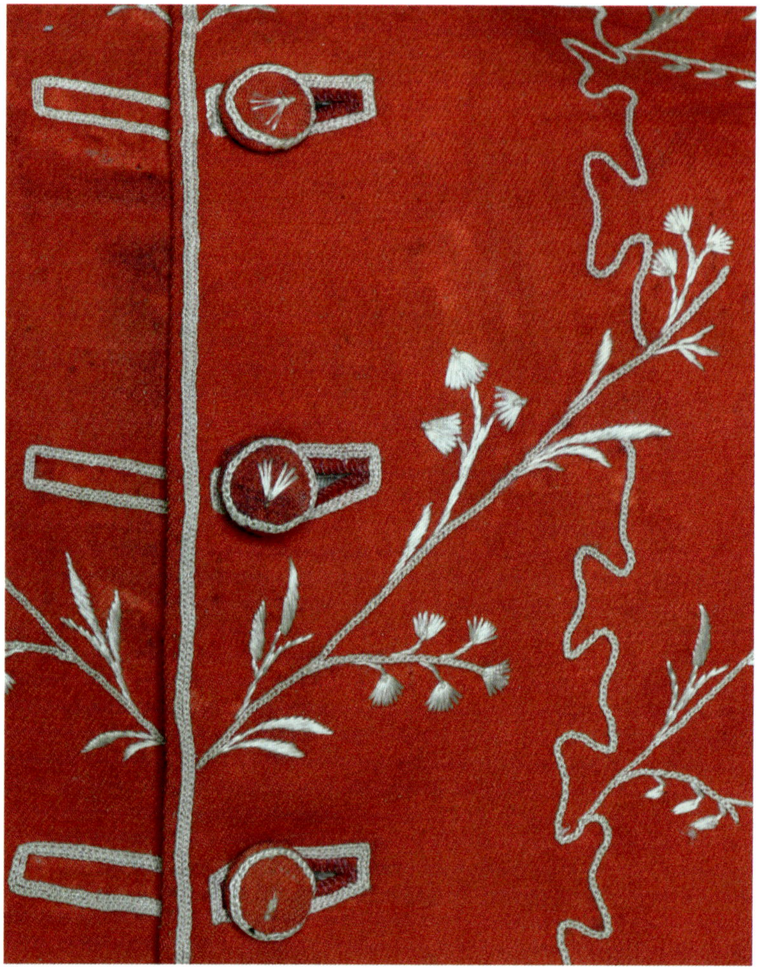

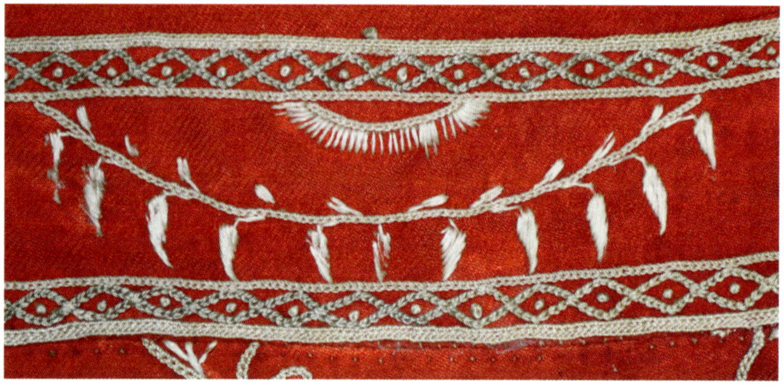

A waistcoat in scarlet fine wool twill, 1780-1790. HC.W-10.89-2

It has embroidery in cream twisted silk chain stitch with details in cream floss silk, in a design of stylised plant sprays and wiggly lines; this may have been done in India. The waistcoat has been well worn and has been darned and patched. It has a stand collar and two welted pockets, and the top of the forepart facings have a section of the embroidered red wool, which shows when they are folded open.

The lining is a coarse natural cotton, and the back is in red wool twill with the remains of a pair of tape ties to adjust the waist. There are nine buttonholes, of which the top two are not open, and the embroidery on the seven self-covered buttons has mostly worn away. There is another set of buttonhole shapes next to the buttons, which mirror the buttonholes, when the waistcoat is done up.

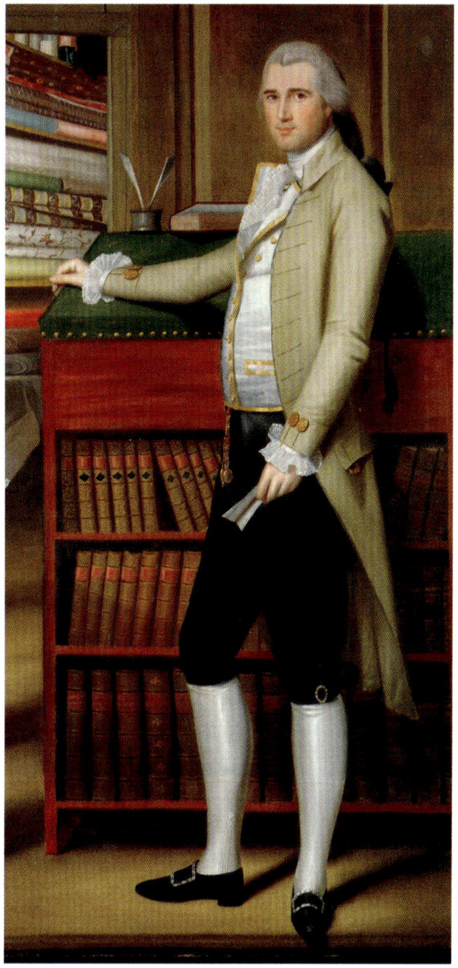

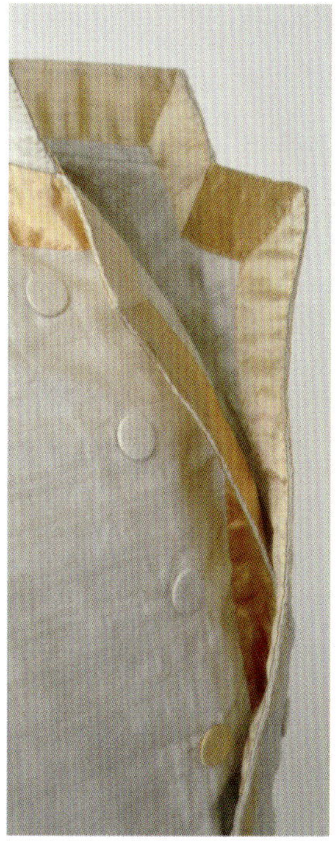

Left: Detail of *Elijah Boardman* by Ralph Earl, 1789. The Metropolitan Museum of Art. Bequest of Susan W. Tyler, 1979. www.metmuseum.org

Elijah Boardman was a dry goods merchant in New Milford, Connecticut.

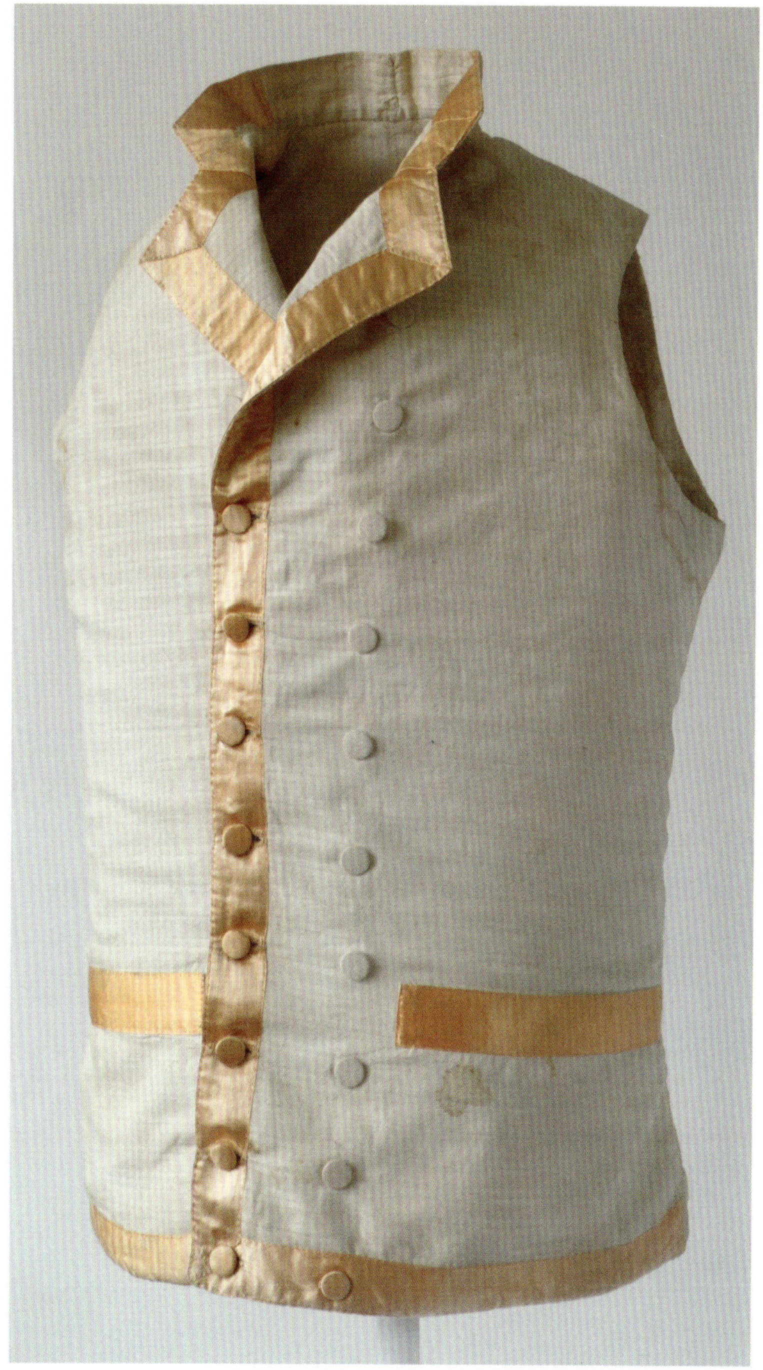

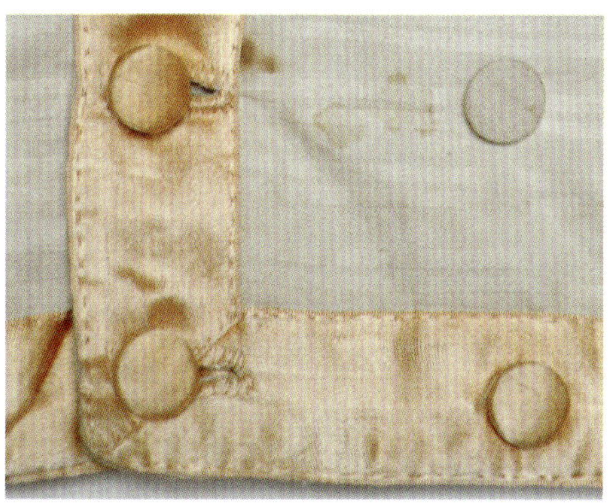

A waistcoat in natural cotton, 1780-1790. HC.W-10.89-4

The cotton has a horizontal double stripe of sateen. The foreparts are edged with an apricot silk satin ribbon, and this covers the pocket welts. The top sections of the facings are also edged with the ribbon, which extends inside the front parts of the stand collar, to show when the top of the waistcoat is open. The waistcoat is double-breasted with eight buttonholes and eleven pairs of buttons, the top three pairs being decorative.

The buttons are covered with the apricot satin of the ribbon edging where they appear on the ribbon, and a plain natural cotton to match the waistcoat fabric where they appear on that. The back is in a heavy natural cotton, and there are gussets of the same fabric on the shoulders and under the armholes. The lining is in the same heavy cotton except for the panel on the right side of the back, which is in fustian.

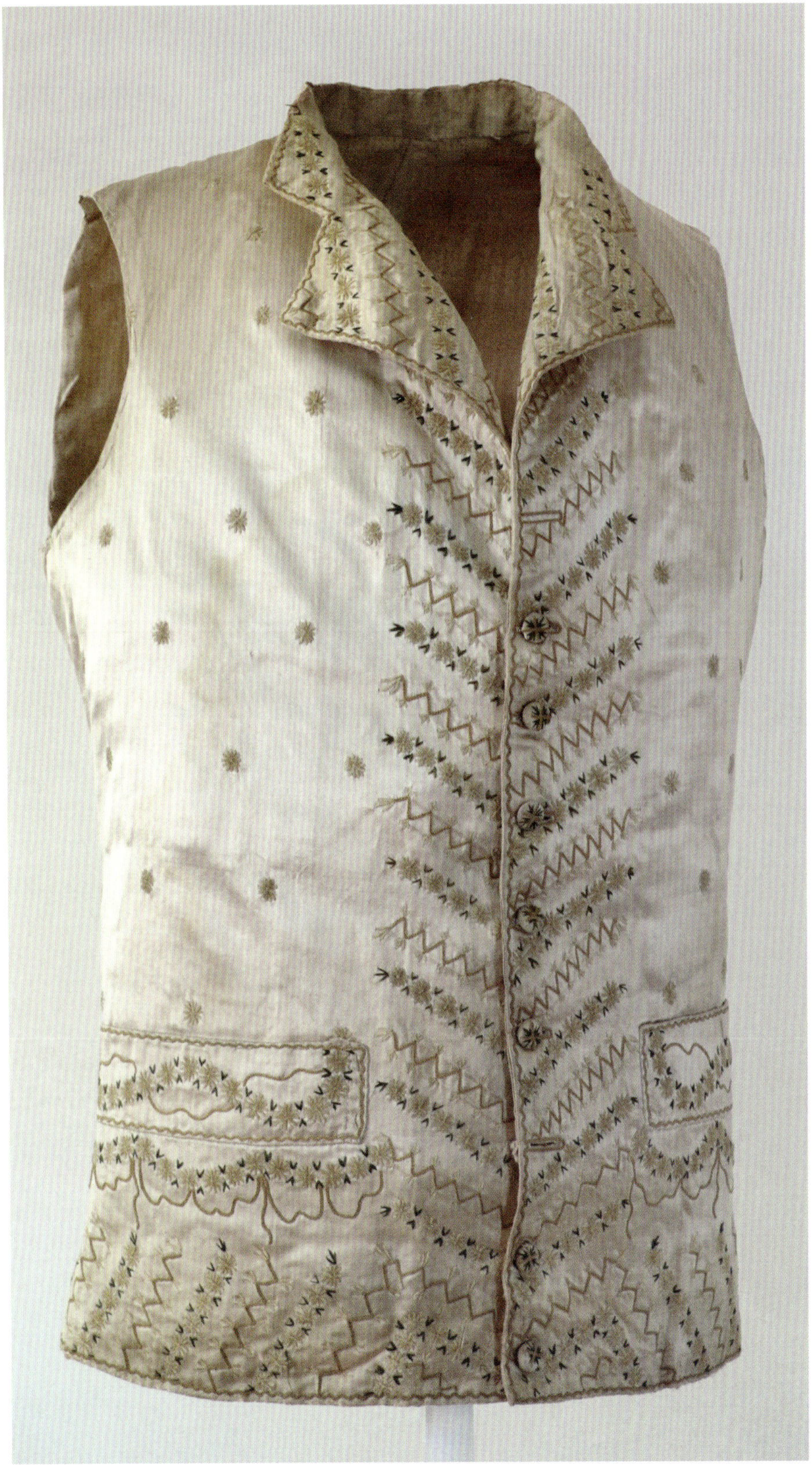

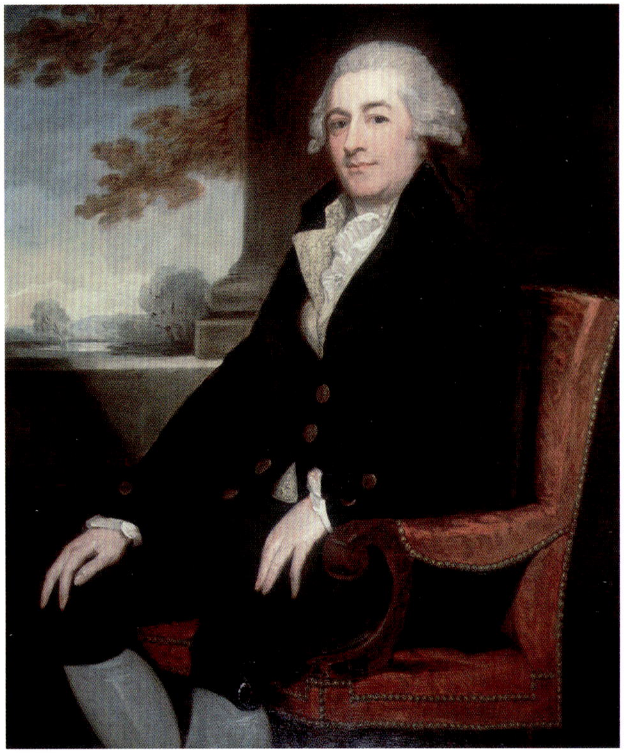

Edward Loveden by George Romney, 1787-1789. By permission of Llyfrgell Genedlaethol Cymru / The National Library of Wales, Aberystwyth.

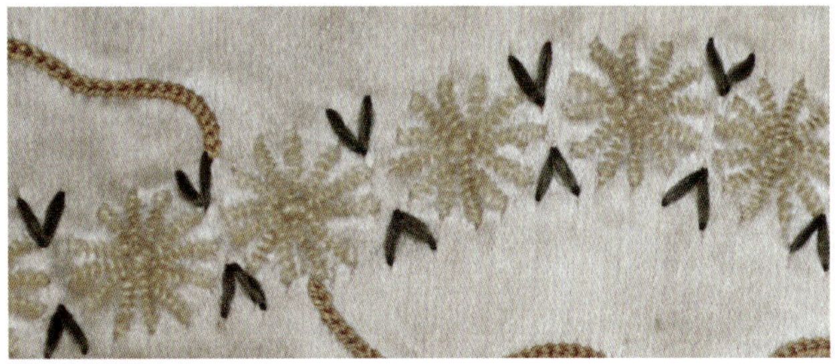

A waistcoat in cream silk satin, 1780-1790. HC.W-0.27

The foreparts have embroidery in fawn and olive green silk and cream chenille in a diagonal pattern on the front edges and hem, and also on, and below, the pocket welts. There are scattered star motifs in the cream chenille over the rest of the foreparts. The facings are cut with a step so that they extend up to the front edges of the inside of the stand collar, visible when the top of the waistcoat is folded open; these are also embroidered down to the level of the top button. There are eight covered buttons (page 216) with embroidered motifs, one of which has lost its wooden mould, and the top four of the twelve buttonholes are not open. The forepart hems are faced with cream silk twill. The lining is ivory fustian and the back is in a natural heavy cotton with two pairs of linen tape ties to adjust the waist.

A waistcoat in ivory silk satin, 1780-1790.
HC.W-12.80

The foreparts have borders embroidered with leaves in shades of brown silk, on stems of yellow ochre silk and green chenille. This embroidery is also on the welted pockets, and decorates the top of the satin forepart facings and each side of the front points of the collar, which would show when they were folded open. There are scattered embroidered motifs in brown silk and green chenille, and the nine satin-covered buttons have a star motif embroidered in shades of brown silk. The lining and back are in white cotton, and the forepart hems are faced in ivory silk twill. The centre back seam has been split open up to 5½″ from the top, and there are two pairs of linen tape ties to adjust the waist.

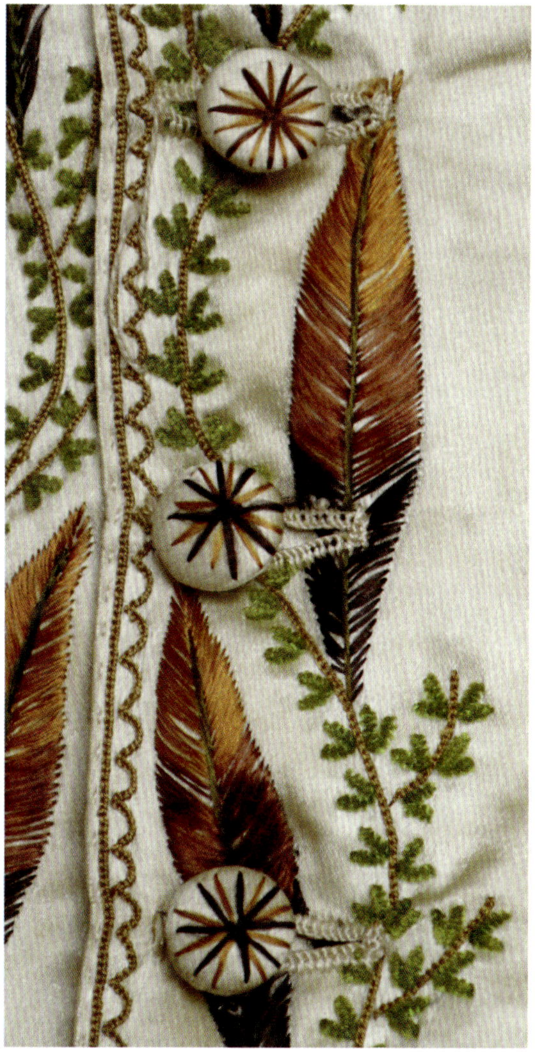

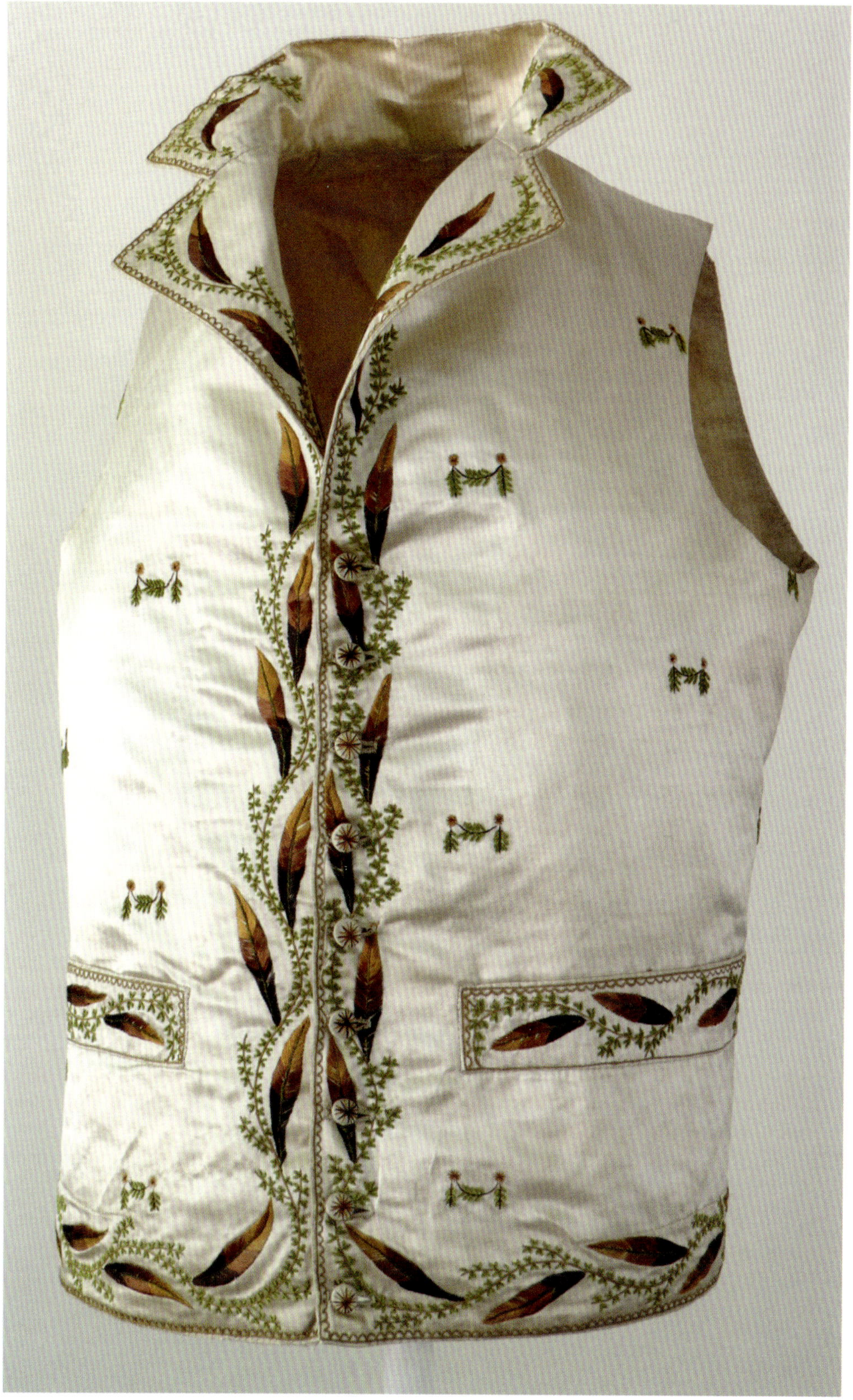

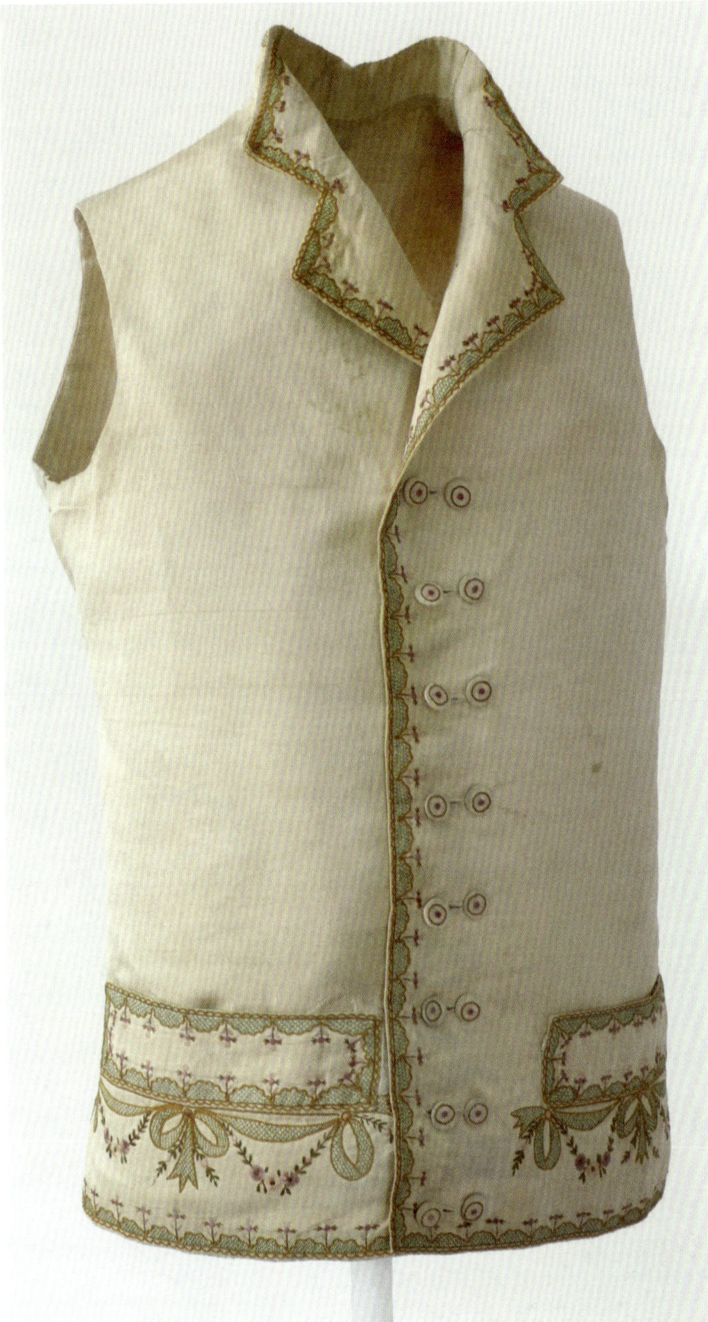

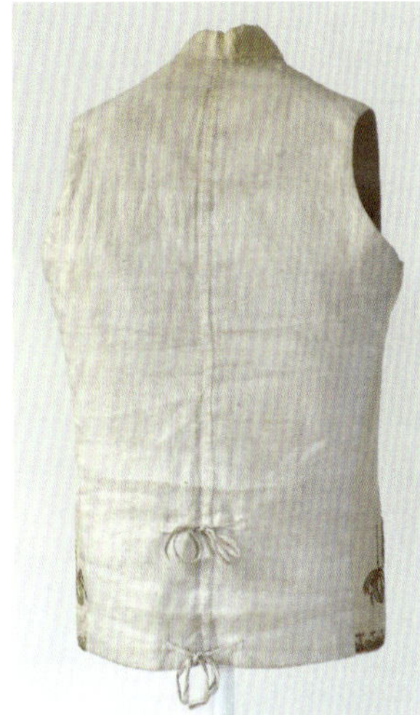

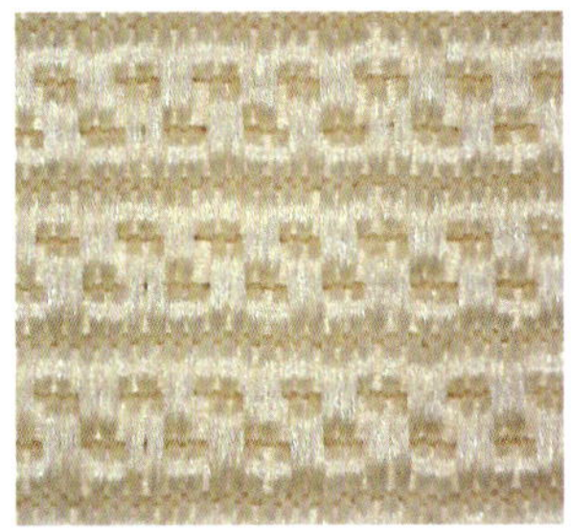

Detail of the cannelé, a warp patterned silk.

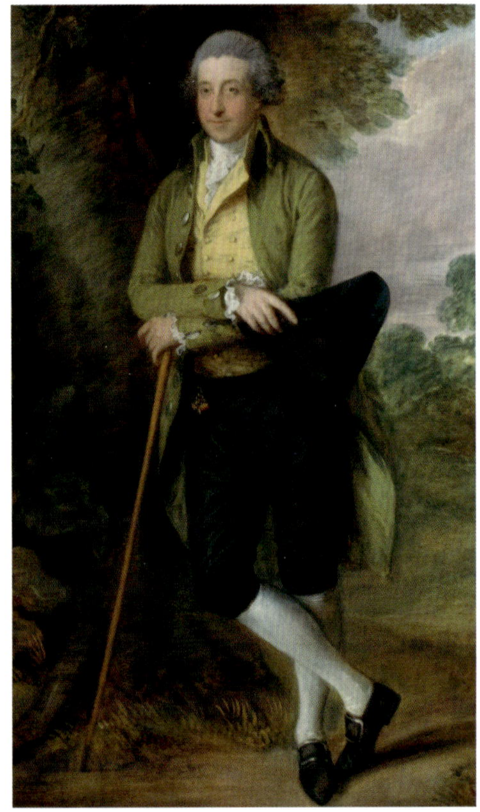

Arthur, 1st Marquess of Donegall, 1739-99 (detail), by Thomas Gainsborough, *c.*1780.
© National Museums of Northern Ireland. Collection Ulster Museum. BELUM.U35.

A waistcoat in cream silk, 1780-1790. HC.W-10.89-3

The silk is a type of cannelé. The waistcoat has embroidery in polychrome silks round the edges of the foreparts, on the pocket welts and below them. The front edge facings are embroidered at the top, and are cut with a step so that they extend up and face the front sections of the stand collar. The waistcoat is narrowly double-breasted with eight pairs of covered buttons, also embroidered. The lining and back are in heavy natural cotton, with two pairs of linen tapes on the back to adjust the waist.

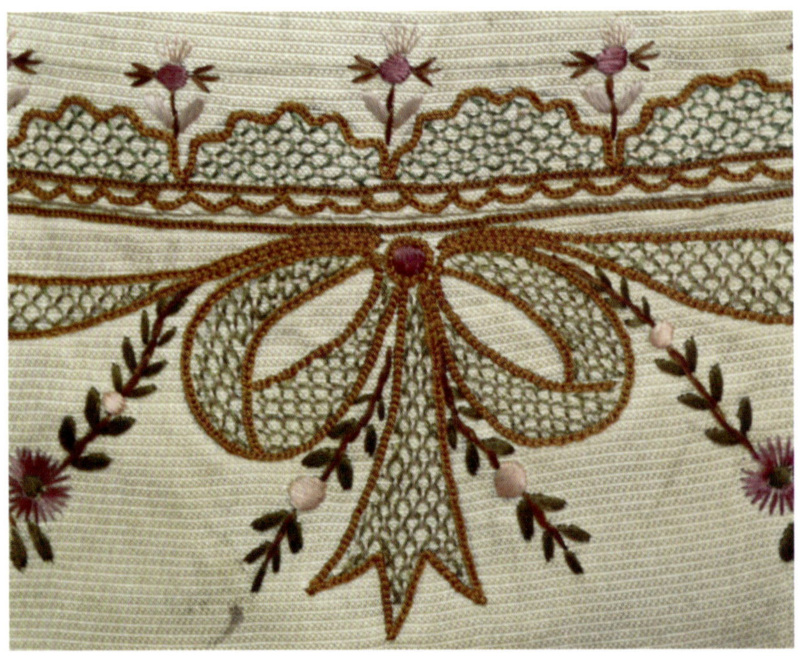

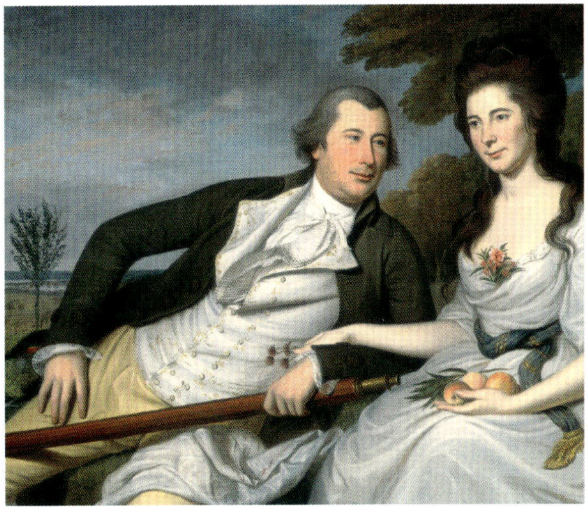

Detail from *Benjamin and Eleanor Ridgely Laming* by Charles Willson Peale, 1788. Courtesy National Gallery of Art, Washington.

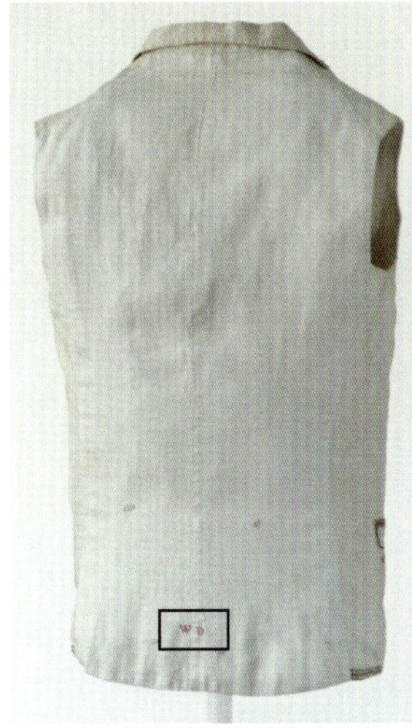

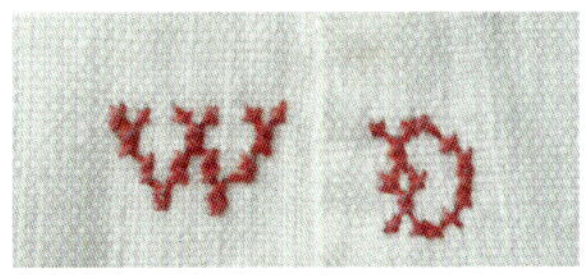

The initials embroidered on the back of the waistcoat.

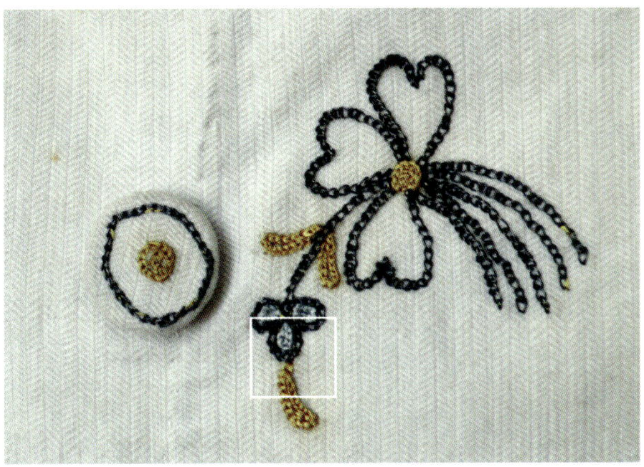

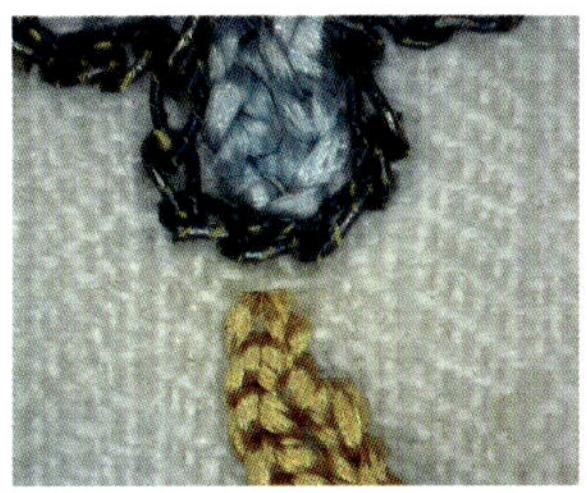

Detail of the embroidery outlined on the left.

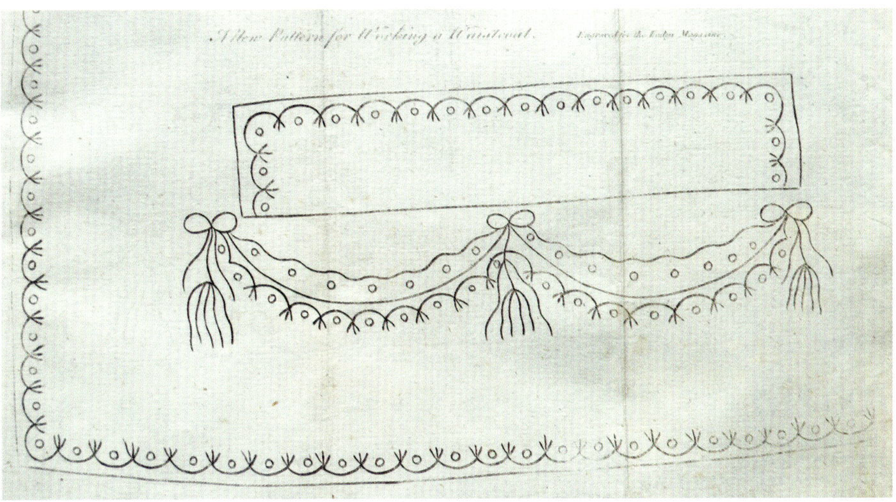

Pattern for embroidering a waistcoat from *The Lady's Magazine*, 1785.

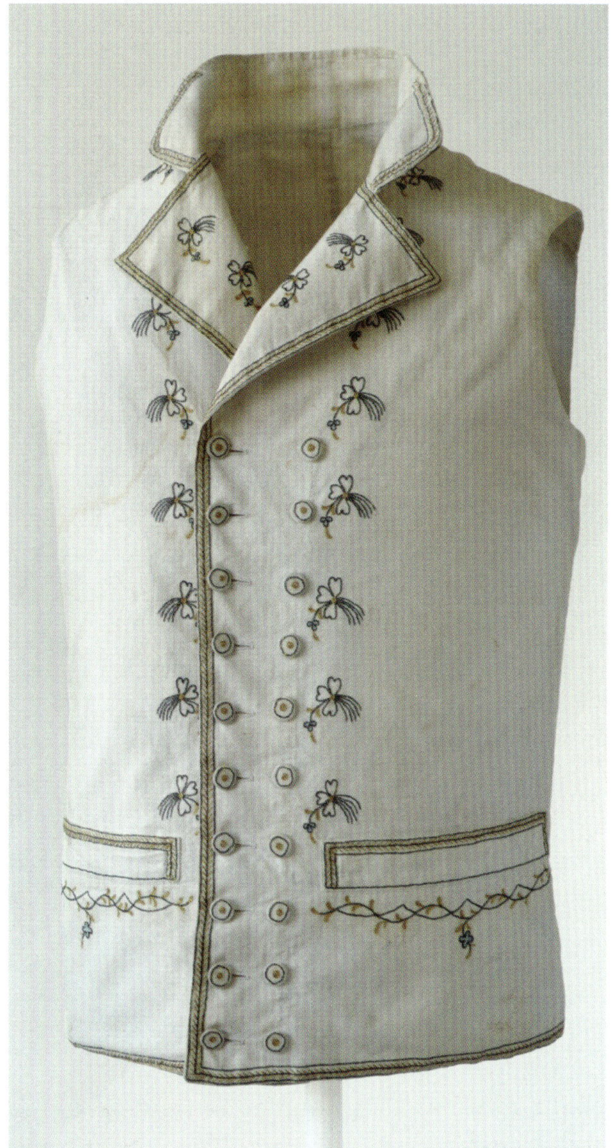

A waistcoat in ivory cotton, 1780-1790. HC.W-11.01

The cotton is in a chevron weave and has embroidery in silver filé with pale blue and gold-coloured silk threads, which forms a narrow border to the foreparts, welted pockets, the top half of the facings and the front edges of the collar. There are motifs below the pockets, beside the buttons and at the top of the facings. The waistcoat is double-breasted with embroidery on the ten pairs of covered buttons. The lining and the back are in white linen, and there were originally two pairs of tapes at the back to adjust the waist, which have been cut off. The initials W D are embroidered with red cotton in cross stitch, low down on the centre back. Marks on the inside of the collar suggest that at some point it was worn turned down, as shown in the back view, above centre.

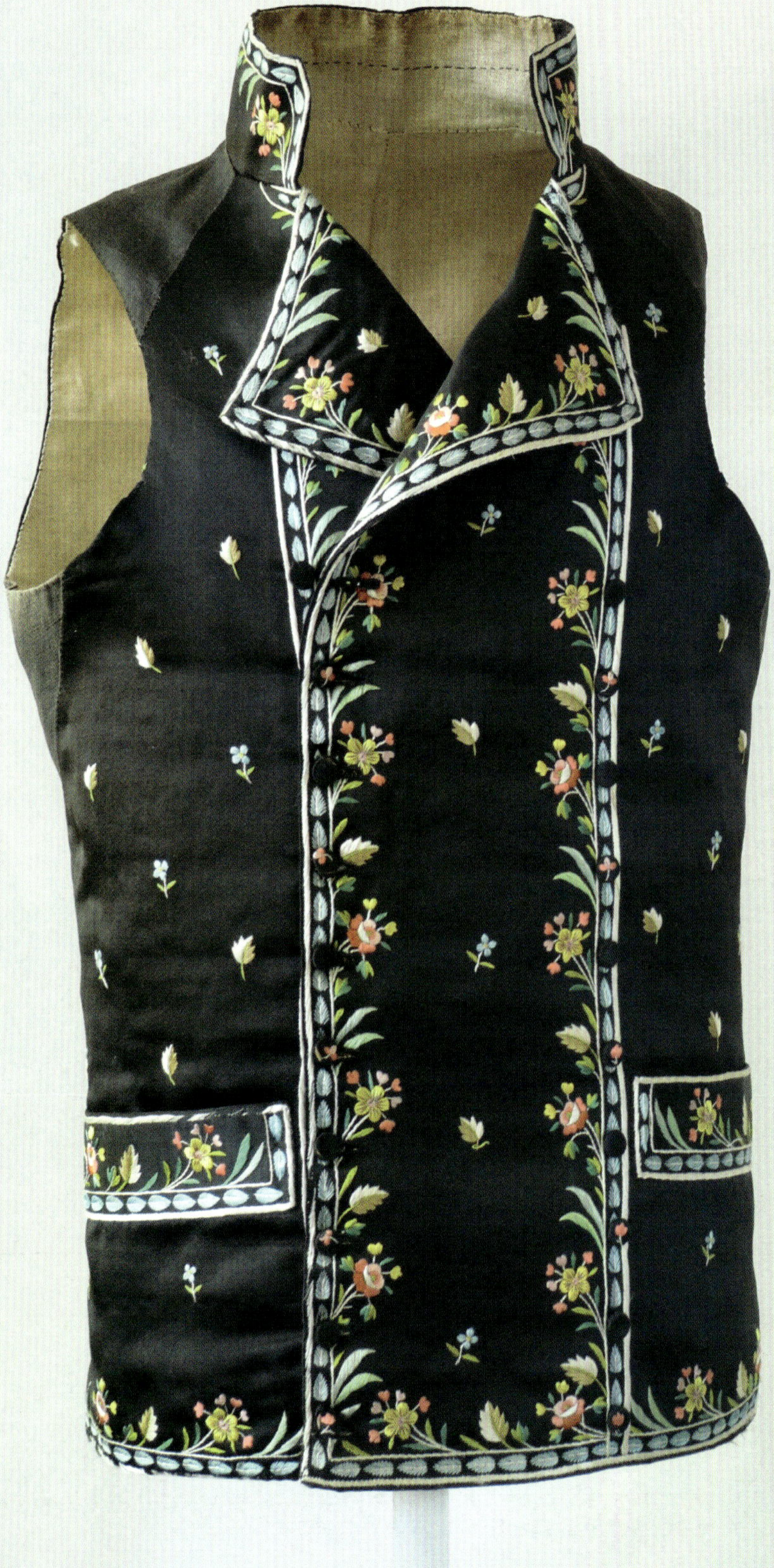

A waistcoat in black silk satin, 1785-1795.
HC.W-9.98-1

It is double-breasted with polychrome silk thread floral embroidery on the front edges and beside the opposite rows of buttons, giving the effect of a panel down the front of the foreparts. The top sections of the front facings are in the embroidered satin, forming wide revers. The embroidery is also on the forepart hems, the pocket welts and the front parts of the collar, and there are embroidered sprigs scattered over the foreparts. The ten pairs of buttons are covered in the black satin, and alternate pairs have an embroidered sprig. The back is black linen, now faded to dark brown, and this also forms the back of the stand collar. The back seam is open up to 4 1/2″ from the top, and held together by lacing, with a white cotton tape, knotted at the top, threaded through hand-stitched eyelets, and knotted at the bottom. There are inset pieces of a coarser linen on the shoulders and triangles of the same in the side seams, under the armholes. The waistcoat is lined with natural linen, and there is a pair of linen tapes sewn on the inside, near the bottom of each side seam, whose purpose is uncertain.

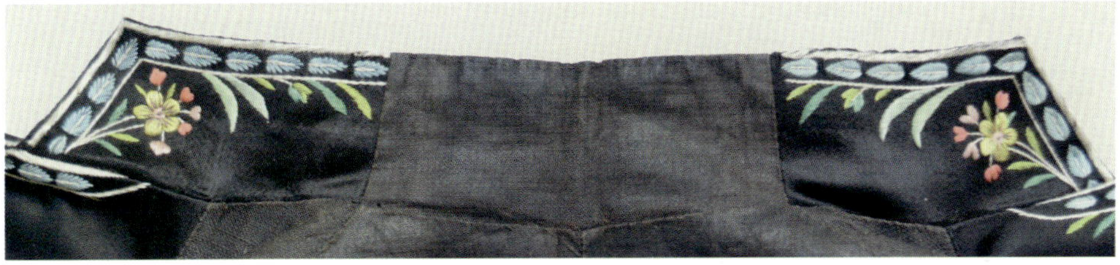

The collar, showing the embroidered front edges and the black linen section in the back.

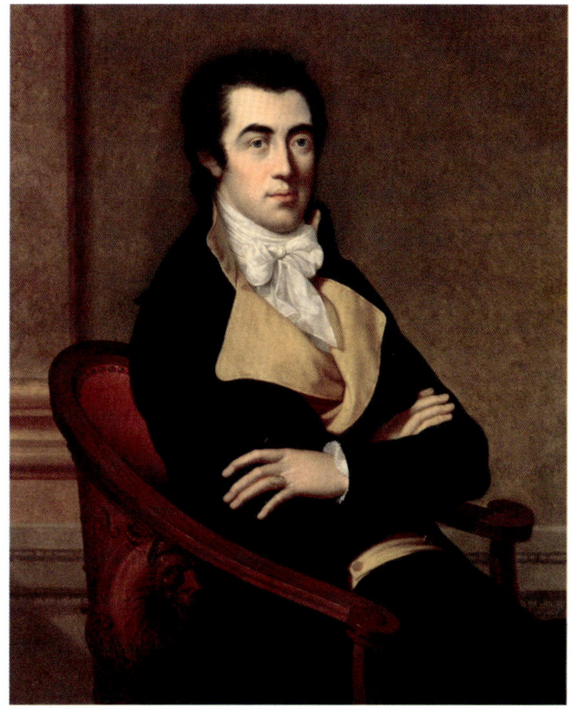

Henry Richard Fox (later Vassall), 3rd Baron Holland (detail) by Francis Xavier Fabre, 1795. © National Portrait Gallery, London.

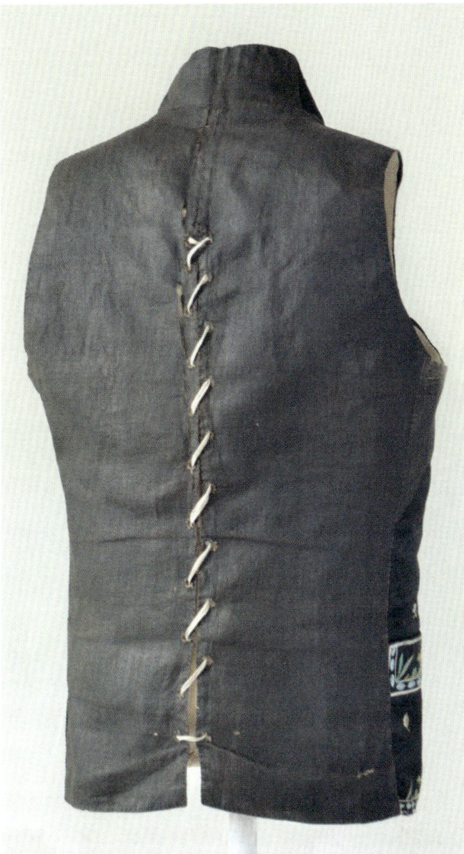

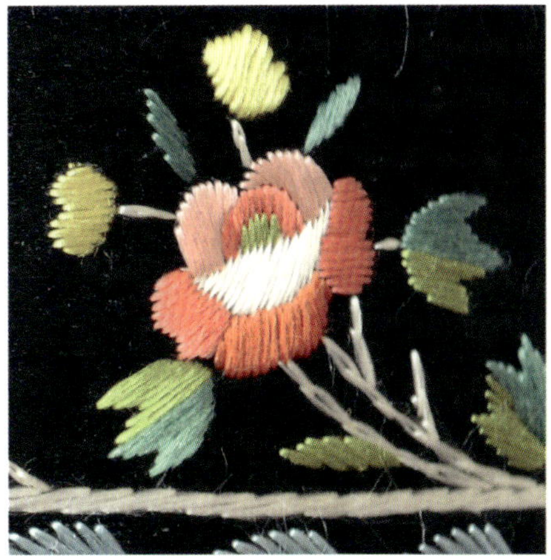

Detail of the embroidery on one of the pocket welts.

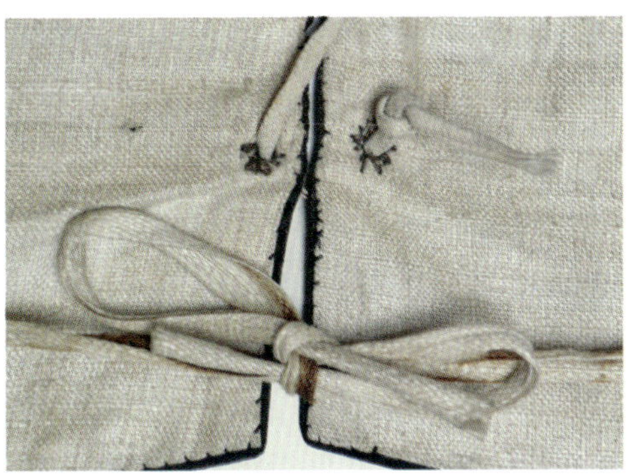

The bottom of the lacing inside the centre back hem and the inside tapes.

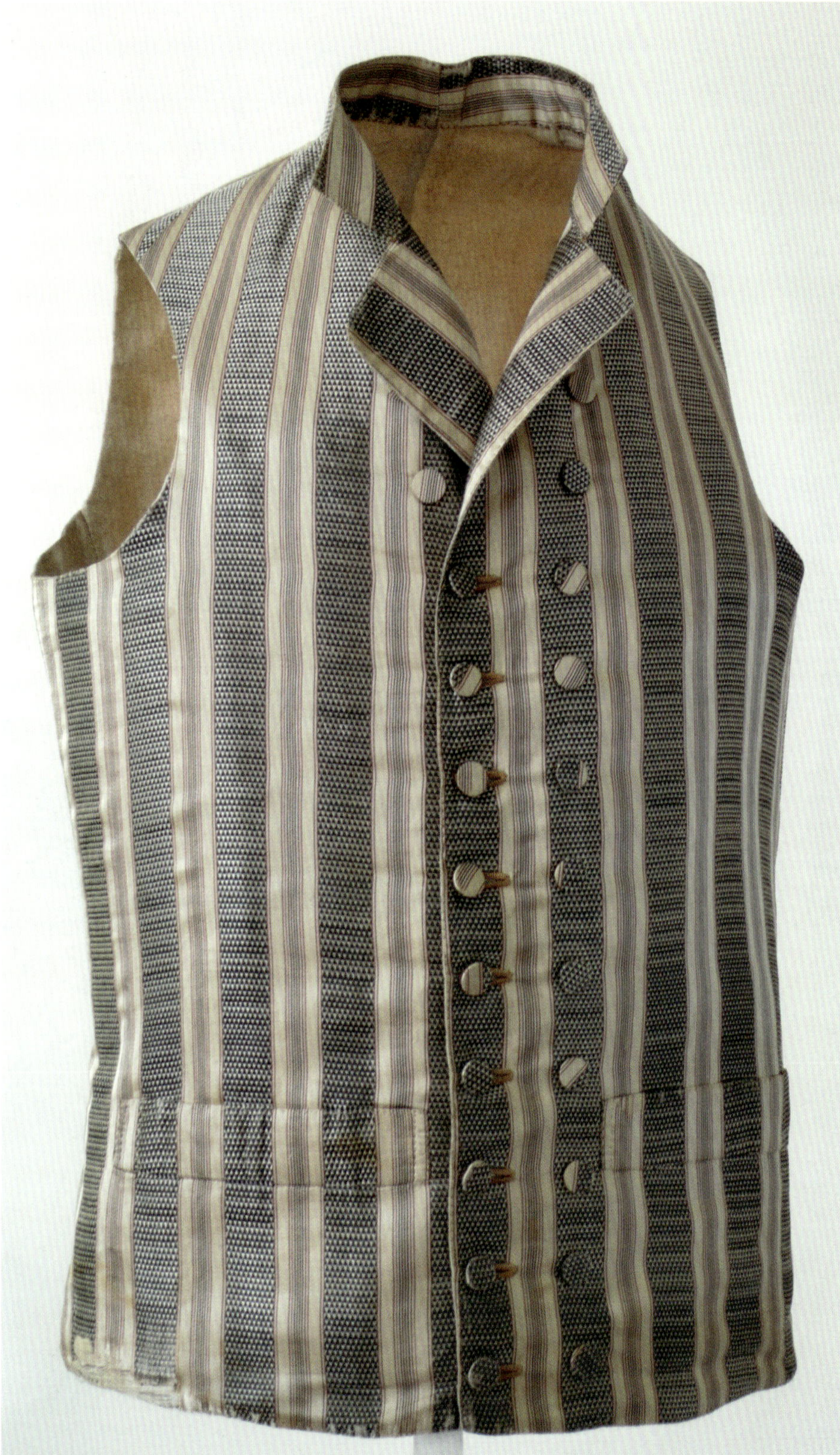

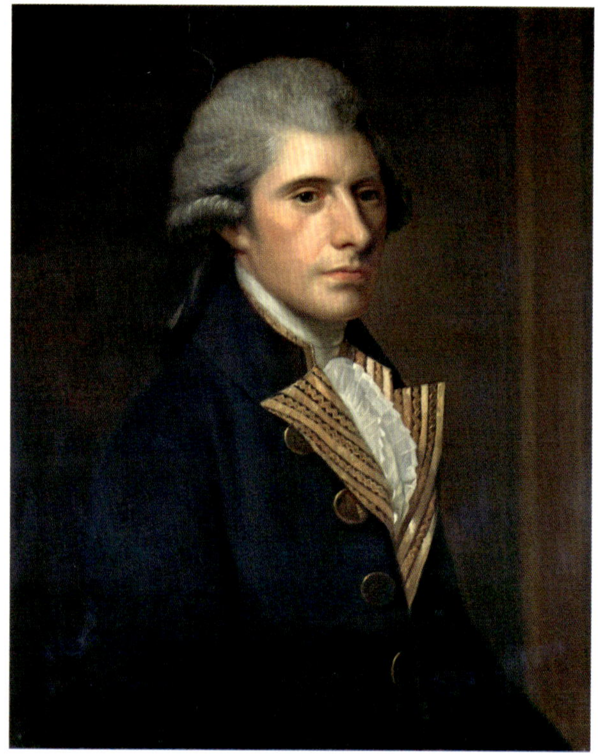

Mr. Dawson, son of William Dawson, M.C., at Bath. English School (late 18th century). © Victoria Art Gallery, Bath and North East Somerset Council.

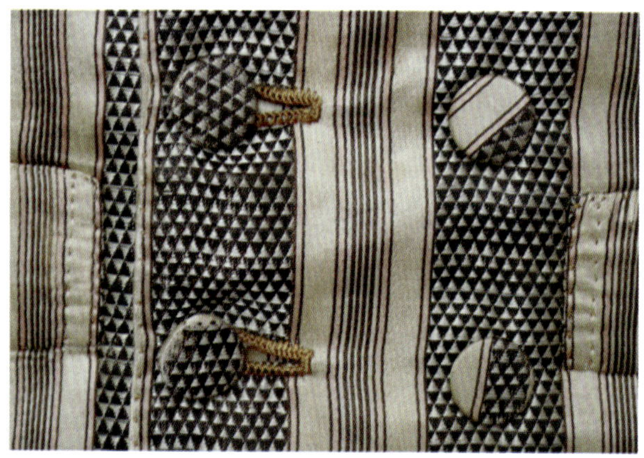

A waistcoat in striped silk, 1780-1795. HC.W-10.89-5

The pattern consists of a wide satin stripe in cream with narrow stripes of dark brown and pink, and a stripe of black warp and ivory weft forming little triangles. There is a stand collar and two welted pockets. The waistcoat is double-breasted with the striped silk as the top section of the facing, showing as revers when folded open. There are twelve pairs of self-covered buttons, of which the top three pairs are merely decorative. It is lined in ivory fustian and the back, which is in cream calimanco, has a 2″ opening at the bottom.

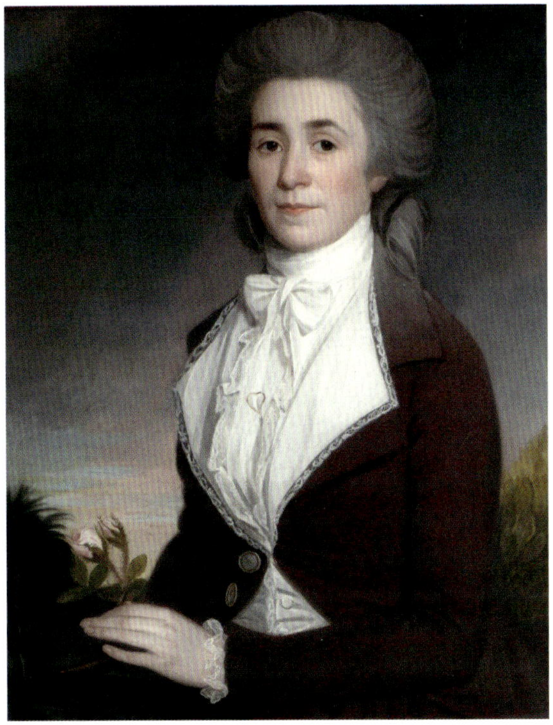

Sarah Webb by William Payne, *c*.1786. © Victoria Art Gallery, Bath and North East Somerset Council.

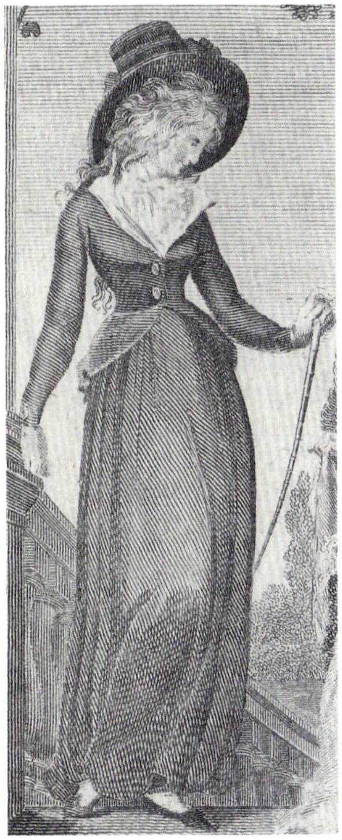

Fashion plate from *Lane's Ladies Museum*, 1786.

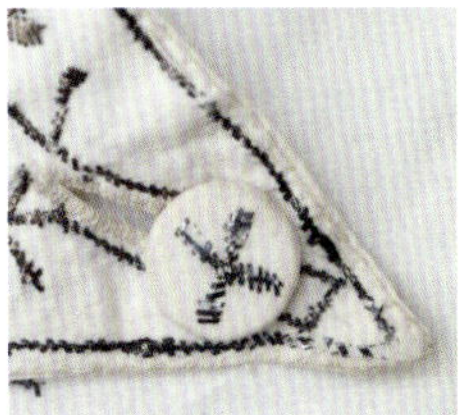

The button on the end of a lapel.

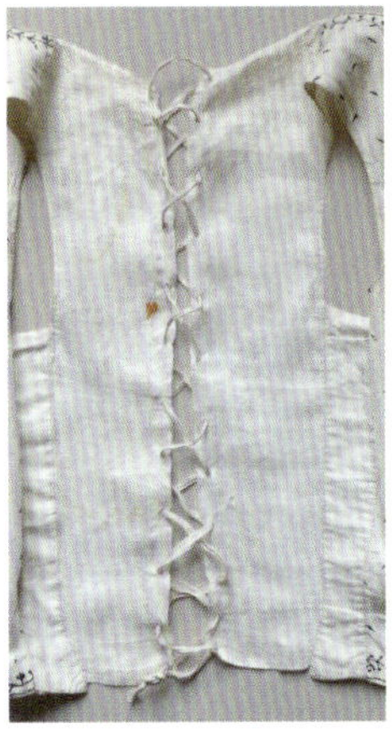

The back of the waistcoat.

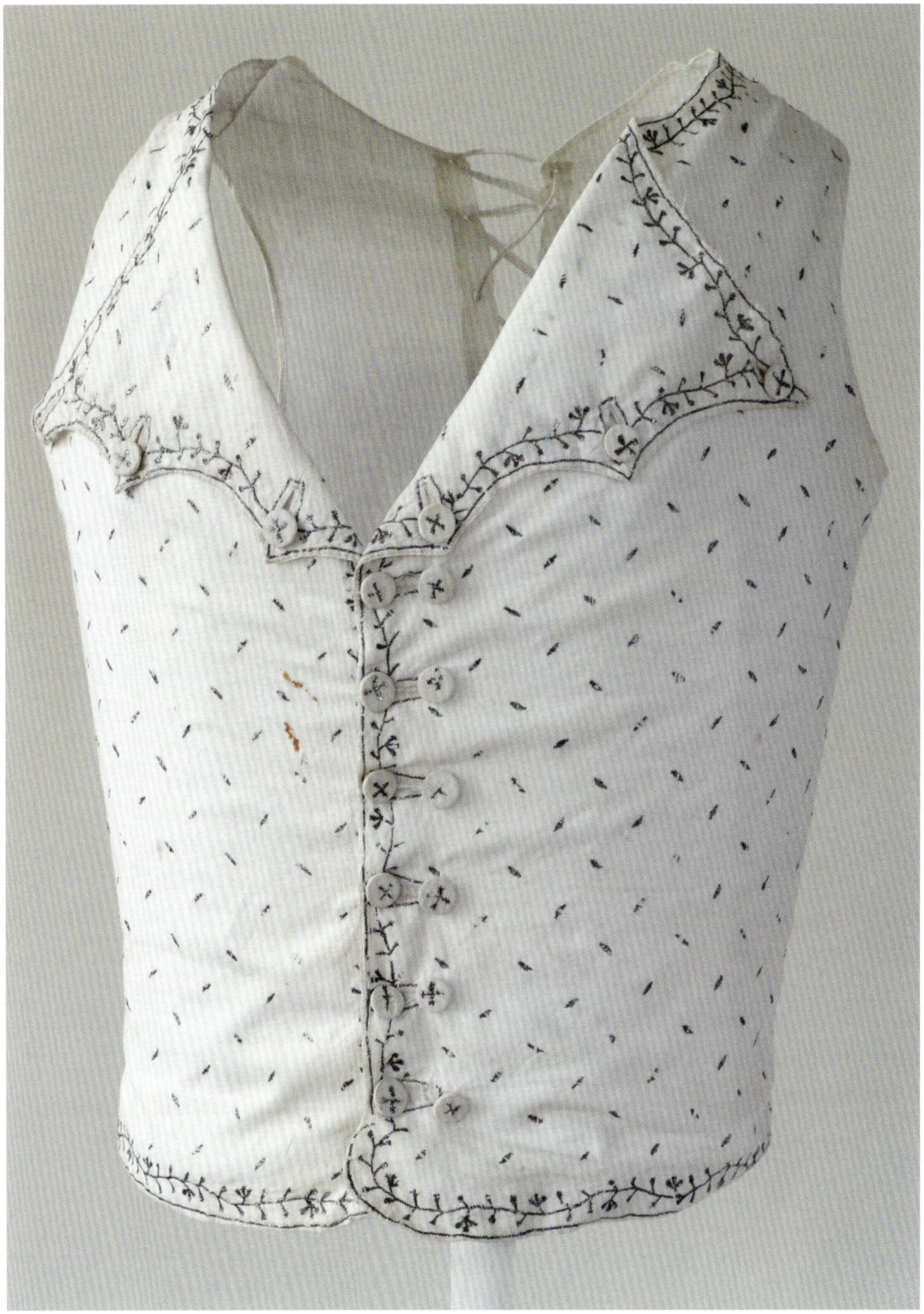

A woman's waistcoat in white cotton muslin, 1785-1795. HC.W-10.15-3

It has a border of silver flat strip embroidery, now tarnished, which also makes the tiny lozenge-shaped spots, and decorates the self-covered buttons. This was probably done in India, from where there was a growing trade in textiles at this time. The waistcoat is double-breasted and the lapels are buttoned down along their edges. The back is open with a white cotton tape lacing through hand-worked eyelets; it is in plain white cotton and unlined. The foreparts are lined with the same plain white cotton, and there are narrow strips of a heavier cotton inserted in the side seams.

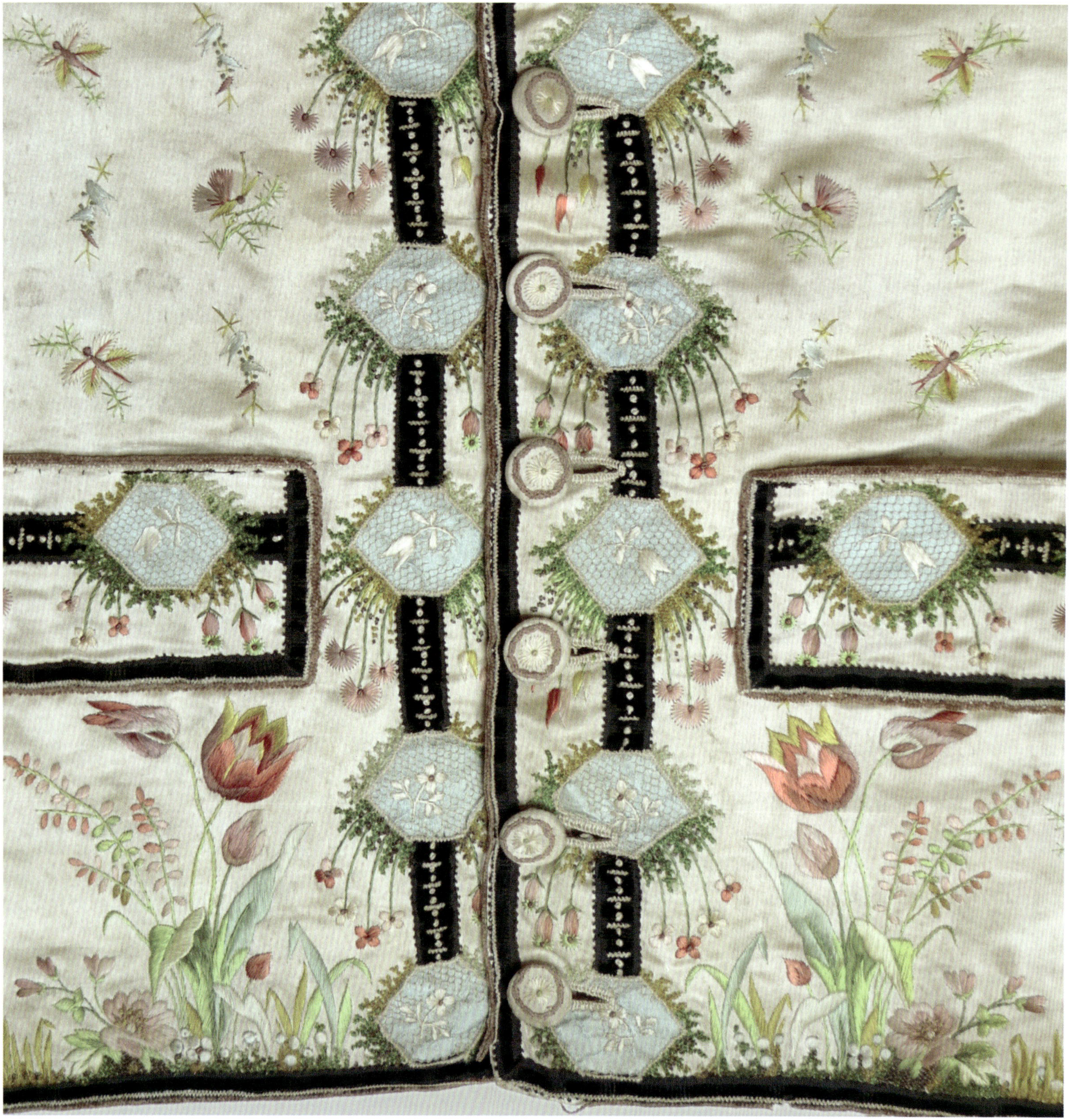

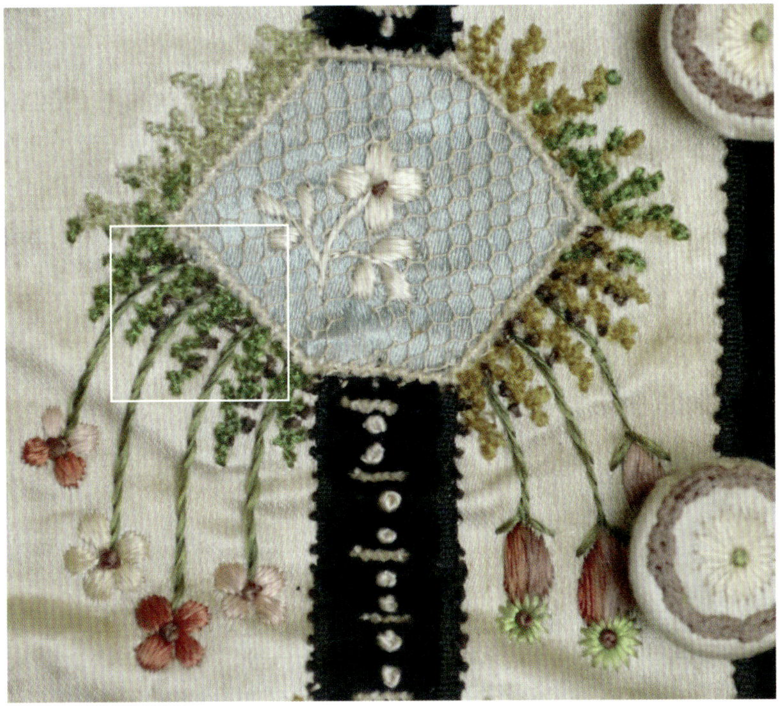

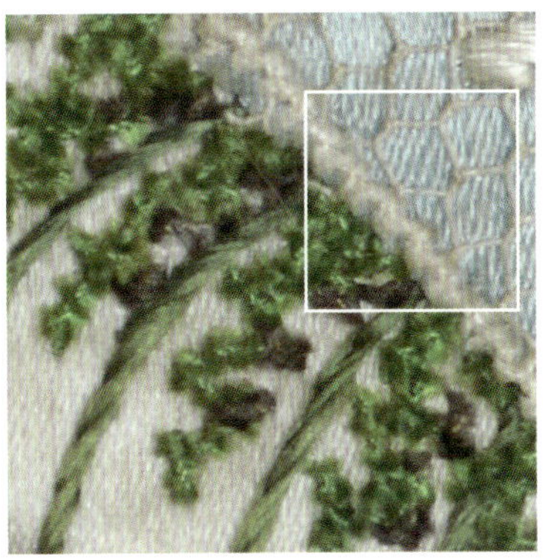

Detail, outlined above.

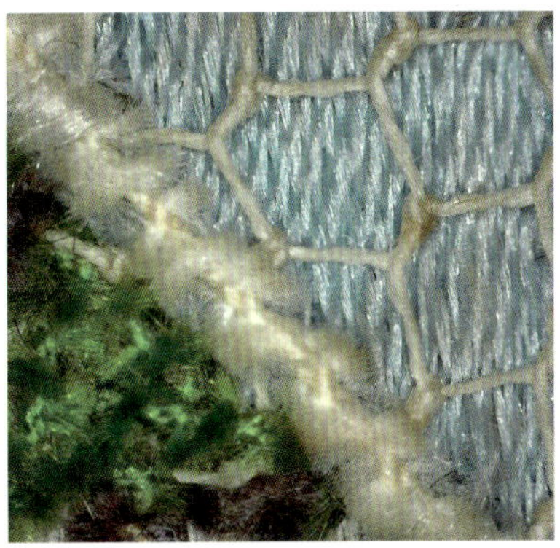

Detail, outlined left, showing the net and the chenille threads.

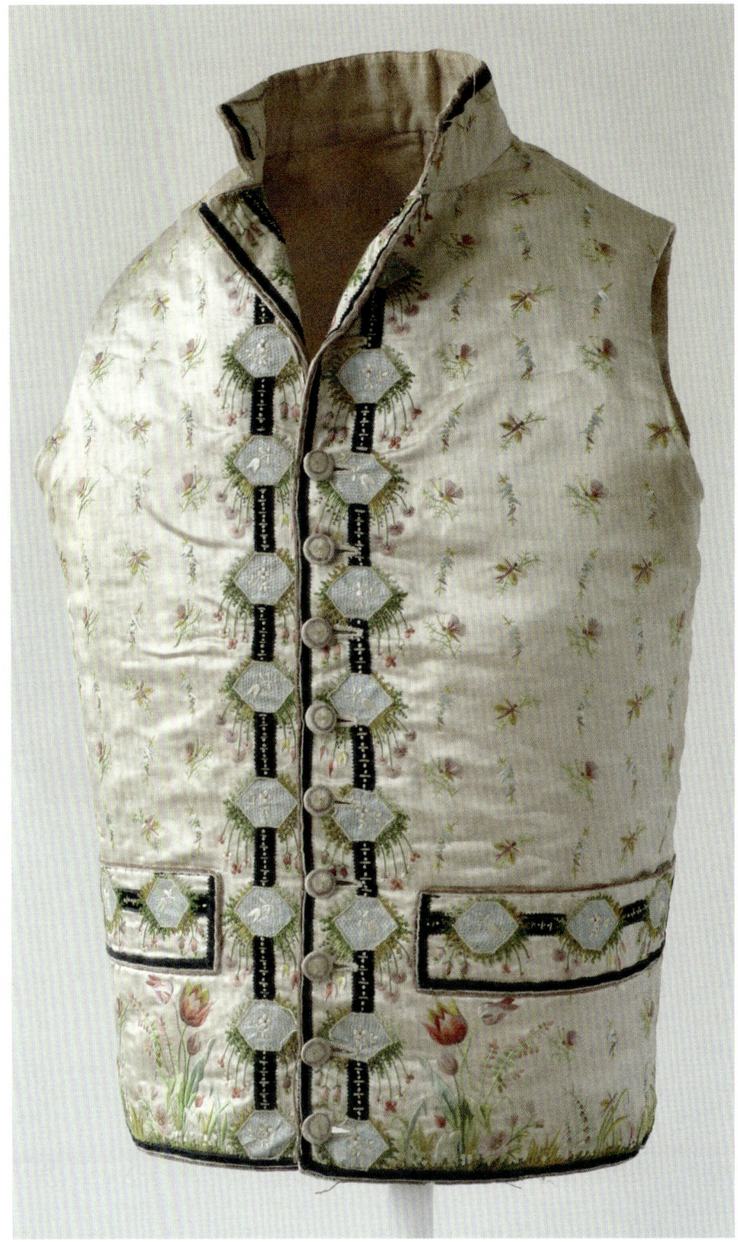

A waistcoat in cream silk satin, 1790-1800. HC.W-3.16

It has polychrome floral embroidery, in silk and chenille, bordering the foreparts, on the pocket welts, at the top of the facings and on both sides of the front ends of the stand collar. There are strips of black silk velvet ribbon with ivory stitching, and inset pieces of net with an embroidered motif in the centre. The embroidery on the hems is a naturalistic rendering of growing plants, and there are sprigs and insects scattered over the foreparts. The waistcoat lining and back are in heavy natural cotton, as is the back of the collar. The centre of the back has been cut open and there are three pairs of cotton tape ties on the back, to adjust the waist. The front edges and forepart hems are faced with cream silk twill and there are gussets of this at the top of the side seams. There are ten self-covered buttons, with embroidery on all but the top one, which is plain.

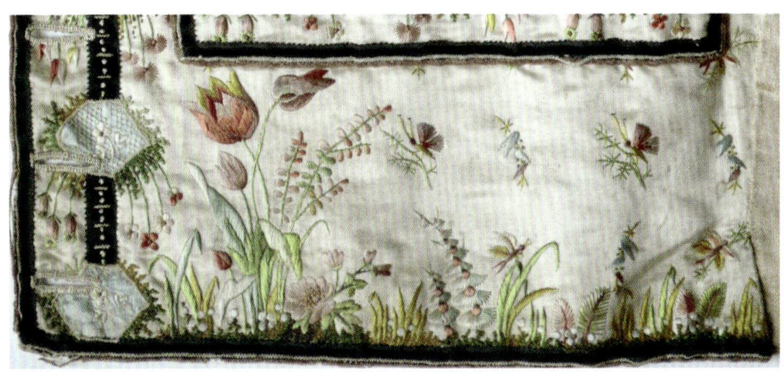

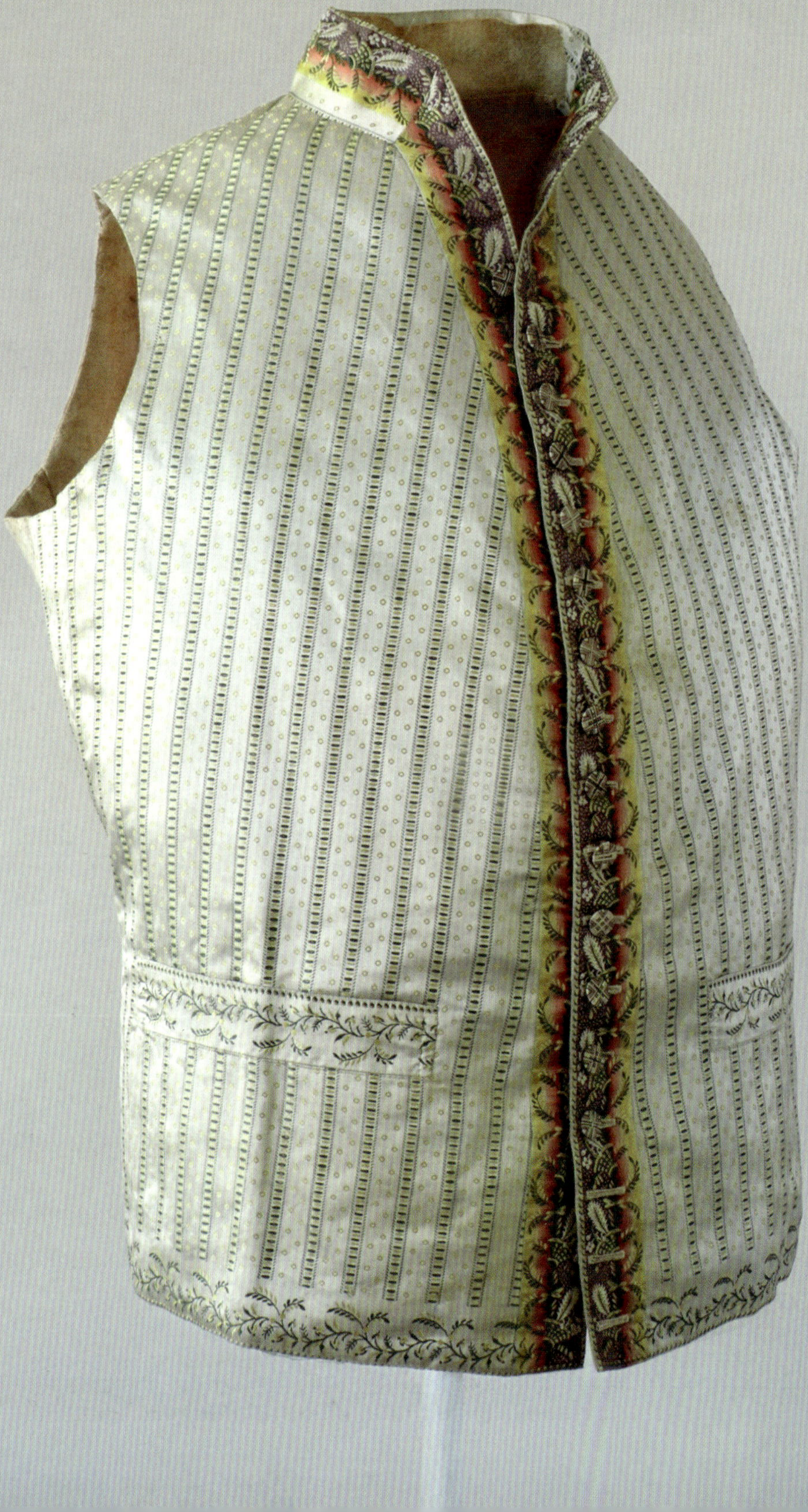

A waistcoat in silk satin, *c.*1790.
HC.W-9.98-2

The silk has woven ladder-patterned stripes in dark green and pale yellow, with rings between them. It has been woven to shape with a polychrome edge pattern of baskets with flowers, leaves and plumes, and a hem pattern of a leafy trail in dark green and pale yellow. This is the same design, in a different colourway, as a pattern found in a sample book for 1786-1789, from the Spitalfields silk weavers Maze and Steer, which is in the Victoria and Albert Museum. Although woven in one piece, the front edges of the foreparts have been cut and seamed on, to allow for shaping to fit the wearer. The pocket welts are made from the hem section of the fabric, and the stand collar is made from the front edge patterned silk. The top sections of the forepart facings are in the waistcoat silk, to show at the open neck. There are sixteen buttonholes and seventeen buttons covered in silk threads in a geometric pattern (page 216); the top button is decorative, and the lowest three are missing. The lining, the inside back of the collar and the back are in ivory fustian, with sections let in at the sides, and two pairs of cotton tape ties to adjust the size at the waist. The centre back seam has a 5″ opening at the bottom.

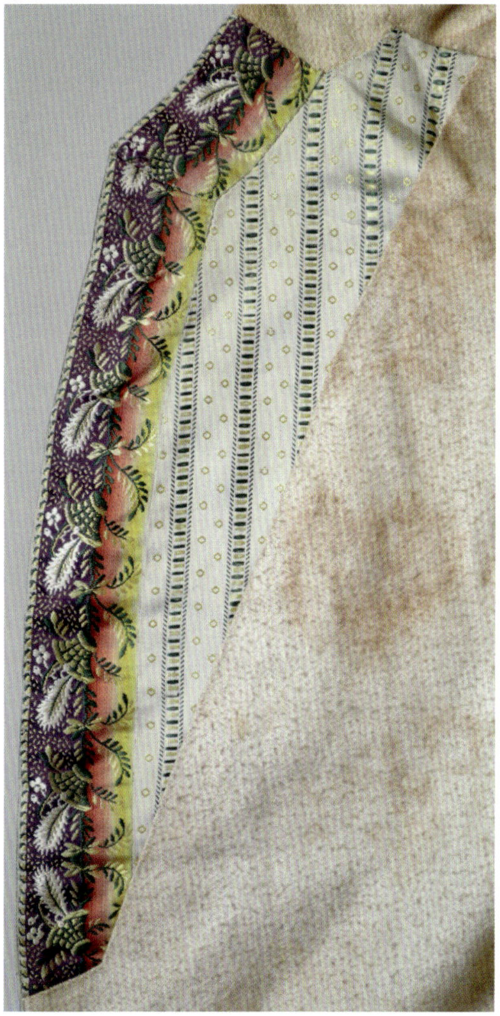

The top section of the right forepart facing joining the front of the inside edge of the collar.

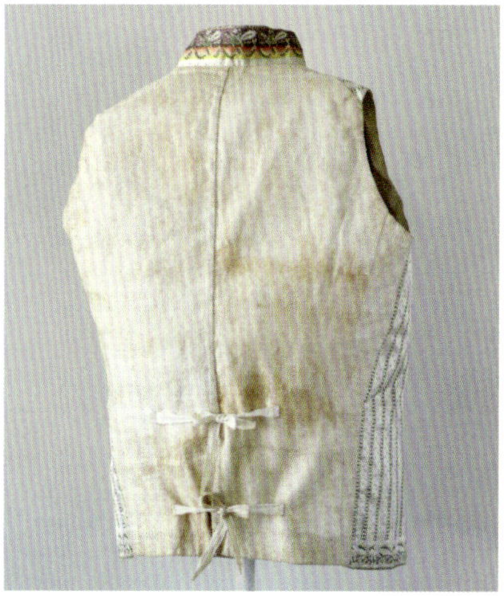

Charles Steer, nephew of a mercer, was apprenticed in 1765 to John Lambert, a silk weaver in Spitalfields, whose brother-in-law was James Maze, from a family of silk weavers. Maze and Steer are listed in several directories as Weavers at 2, Church Street (now Fournier Street), Spitalfields, between 1776 and 1790. They seem to have had a considerable output, as at least ten surviving waistcoats exist, made with silk that can be identified in the sample book mentioned opposite. *The London Gazette* has a notice that their co-partnership was dissolved by mutual consent on the 24th June 1788. Charles Steer continued to be listed at this address until 1800.

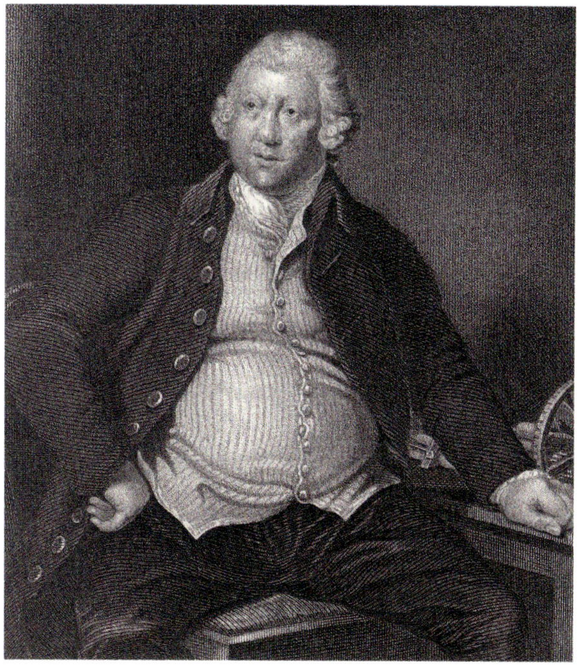

Engraving of the portrait of Sir Richard Arkwright by Joseph Wright of Derby, 1789-1790, in Derby Museum and Art Gallery.

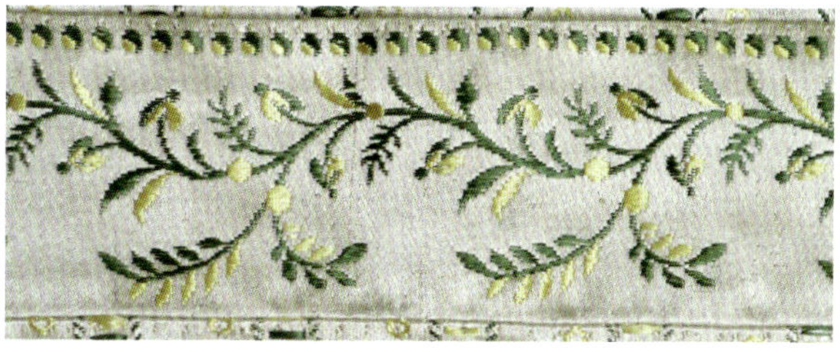

One of the pocket welts made out of the hem part of the fabric, used upside-down.

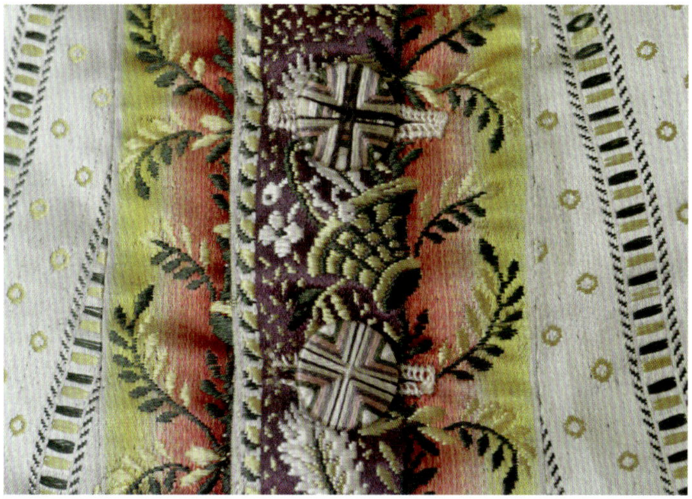

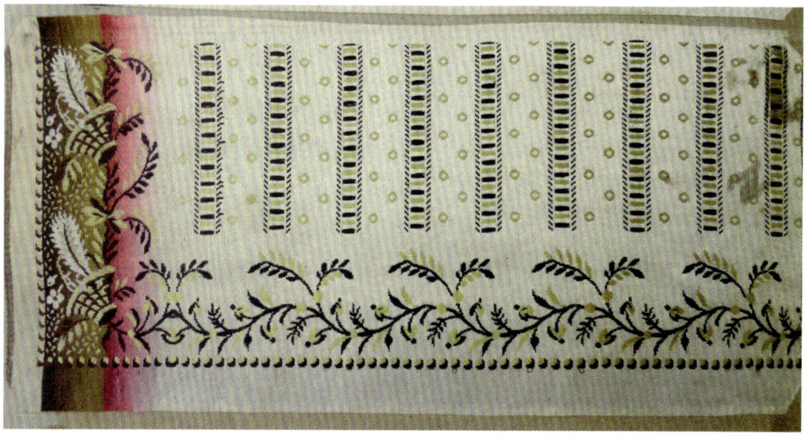

Pattern in a sample book from Maze and Steer, Spitalfields, "Fancy Vestings and Handkerchief Goods ... Winter 1789". © Victoria and Albert Museum, London.

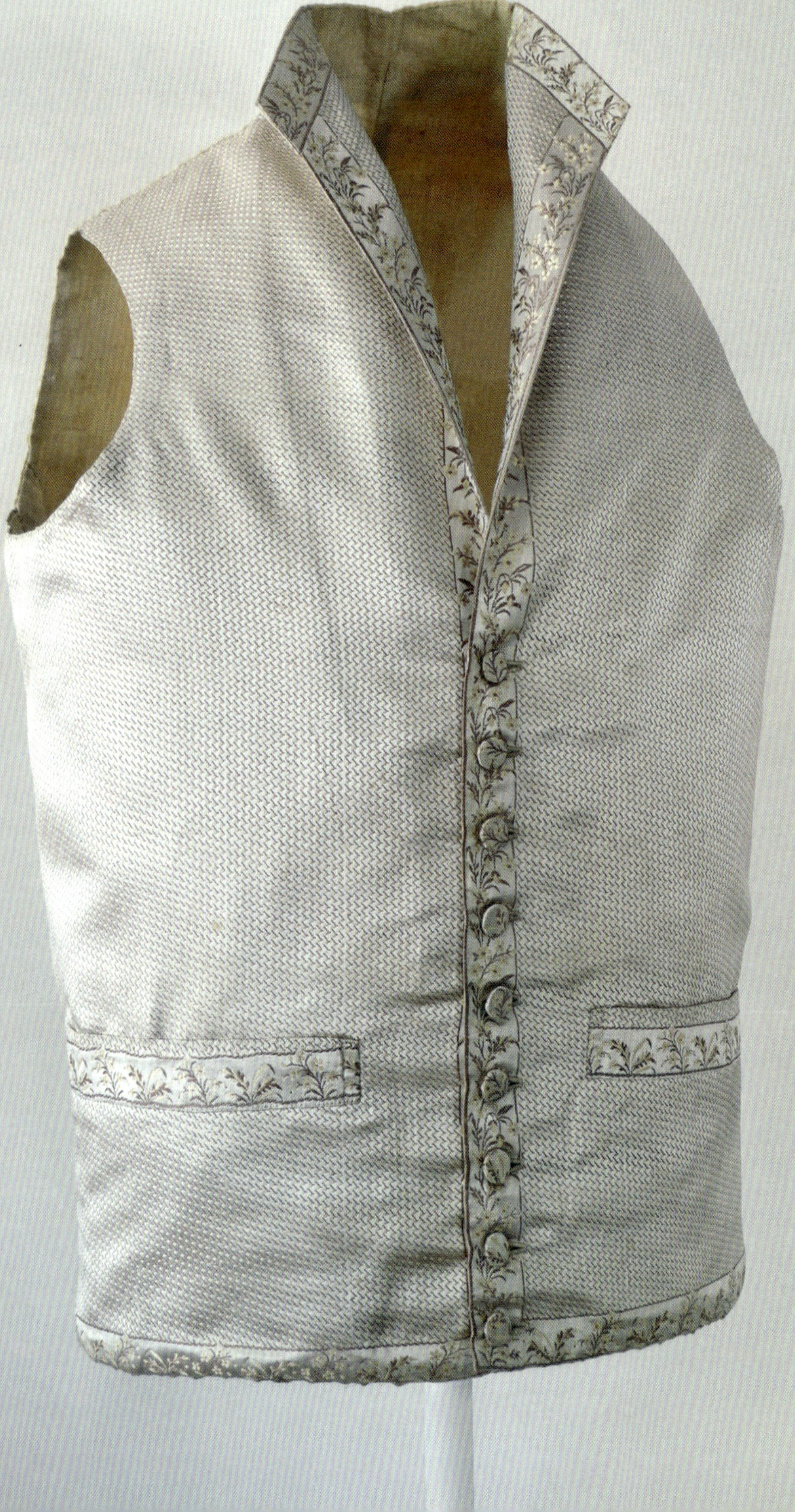

A waistcoat in beige silk satin, 1790-1800.
HC.W-5.82

The silk has a woven pattern in cream and nutmeg of an all-over tiny zig-zag and a border of flowers and leaves woven to shape. The border pattern is also on the pocket welts, and the foreparts are cut with the shoulder seam curving up at the neck, to form the front part of the collar, with a piece of the border pattern seamed on top. There are nine self-covered buttons. The upper part of the foreparts are faced with the silk, which shows when the tops are folded open. The waistcoat back is in cream cotton, which is cut high at the neck to form the back of the collar; there is a narrow gusset inserted in the centre back. The lining is in cream cotton and has no centre back seam or gusset, and there is a 1½″ opening in the centre of the back hem.

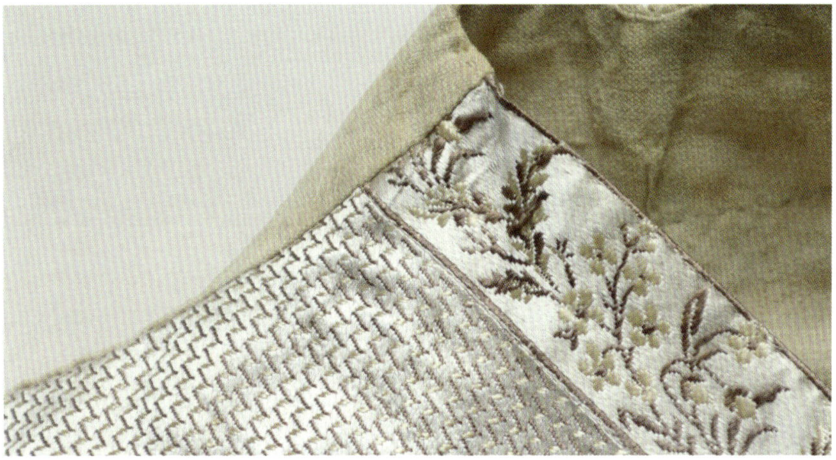

The shoulder seam curving up at the neck to join the collar.

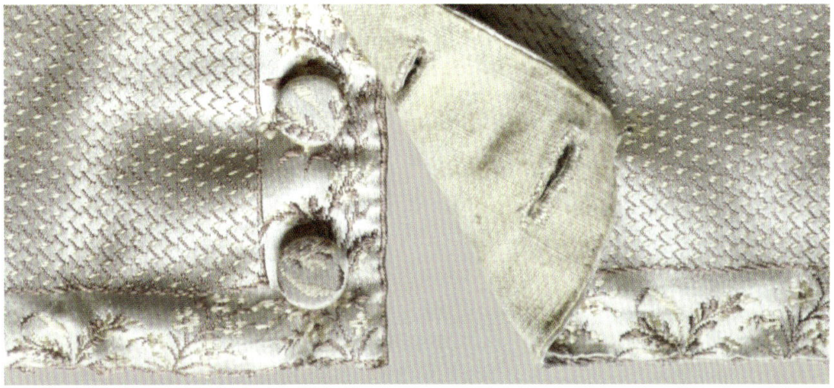

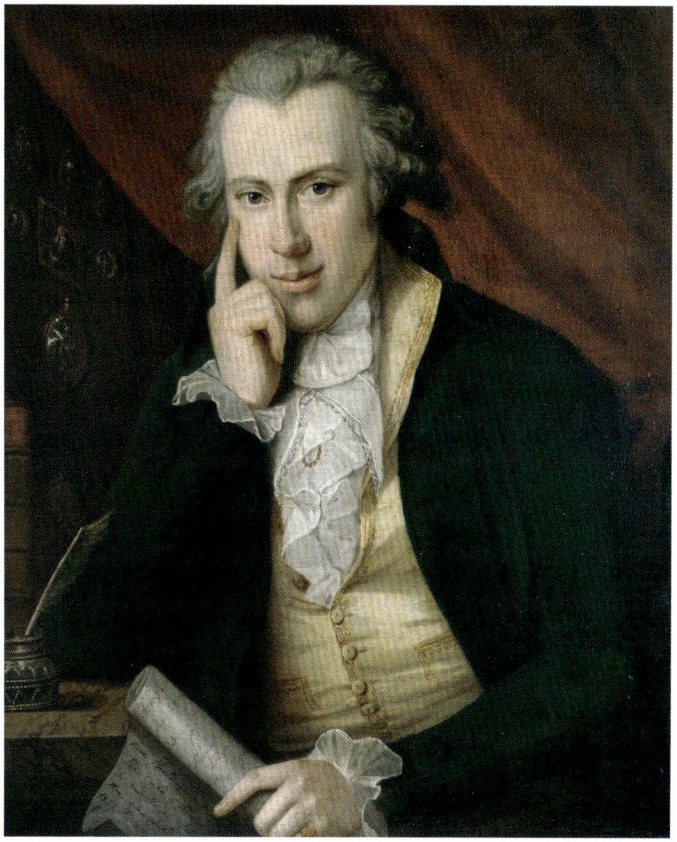

James Bisset by an unknown artist, 1793. © Leamington Spa Art Gallery and Museum (Warwick District Council).

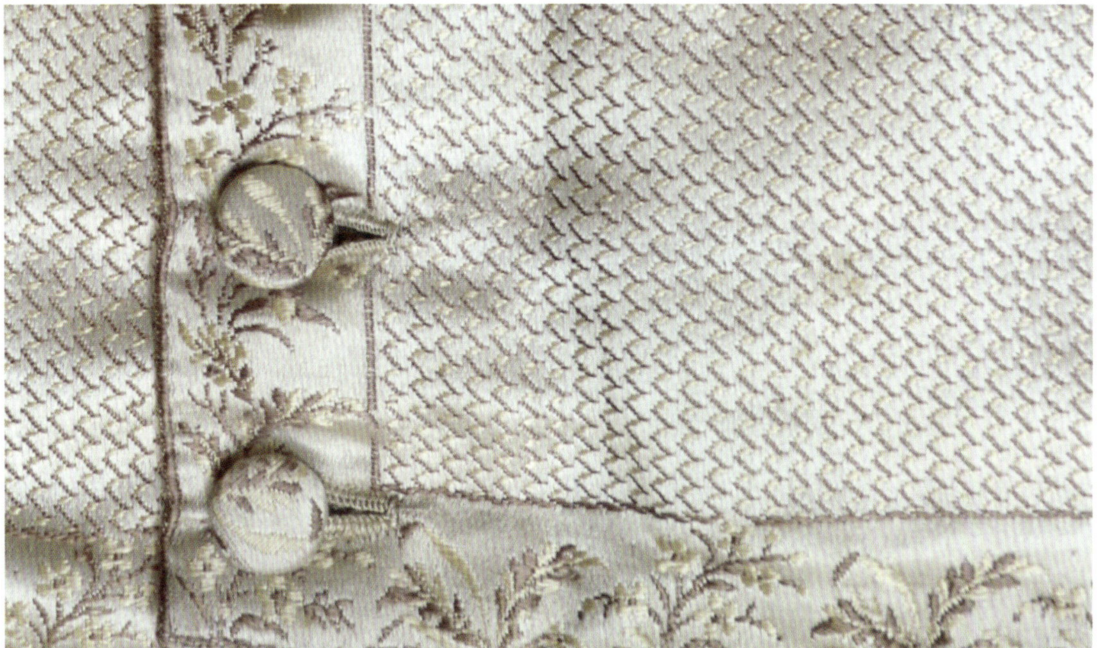

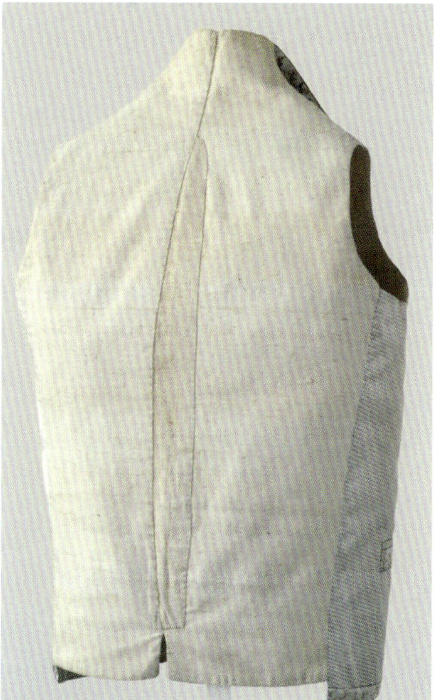

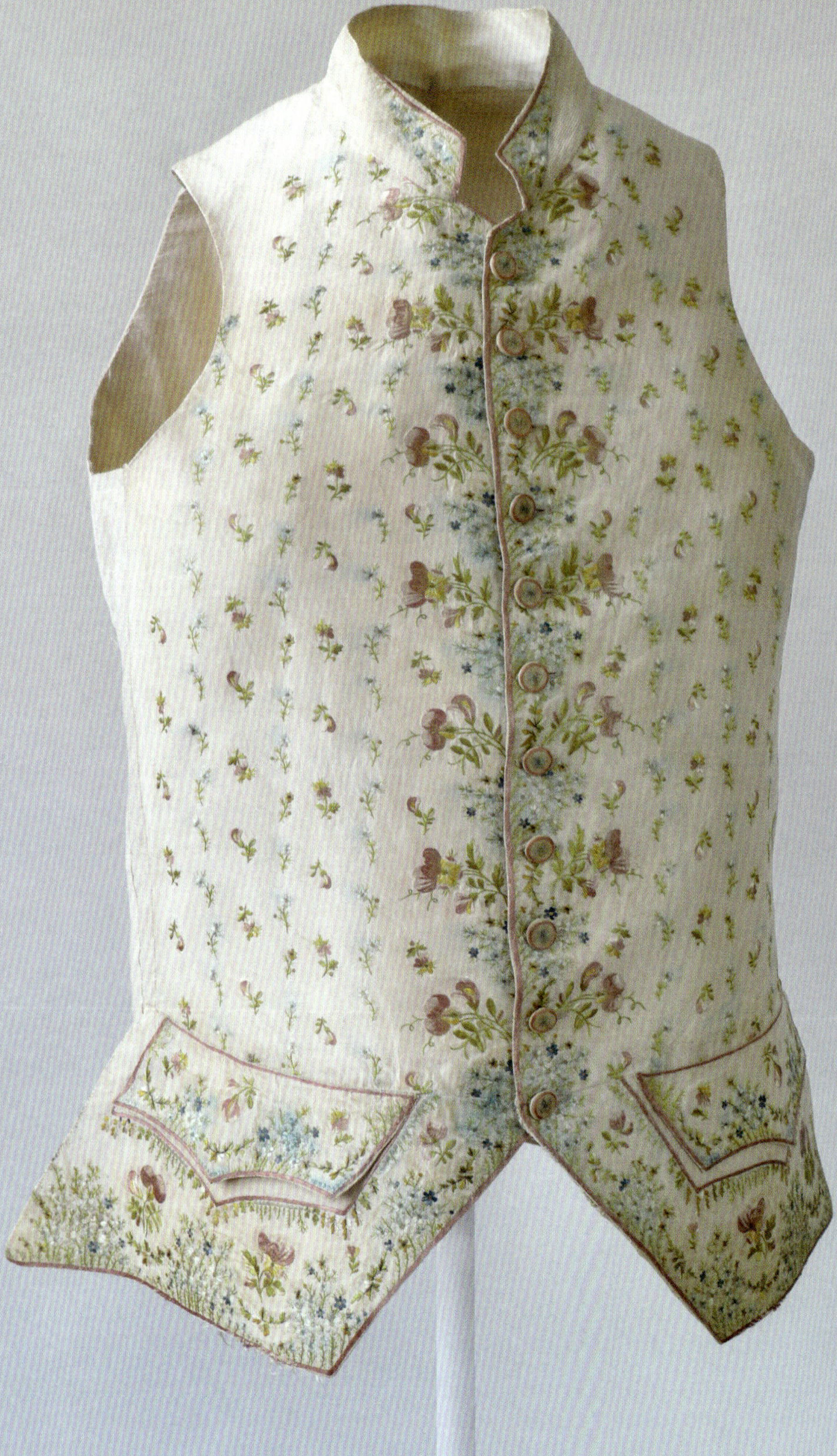

A waistcoat in cream silk faille, 1790-1810.
HC.W-3.75

By the end of the 18th century the style for court dress was beginning to fossilise, and this waistcoat may have been made for just such occasions; the shape is more typical of twenty years earlier but the collar is more up to date. There is polychrome floral silk embroidery bordering the foreparts and on the pocket flaps, and a scattering of sprigs. The waistcoat has been washed at some point and some colour, from the blue silk threads in the embroidery, has seeped into the surrounding silk. The back is in ivory plain cotton with two pairs of linen tape ties to adjust the waist; it is lined with the same cotton and the foreparts are lined with cream silk twill. The small stand collar is in cream silk ottoman with pieces of the embroidery appliquéd on to the front tips, and the eleven self-covered buttons are also embroidered.

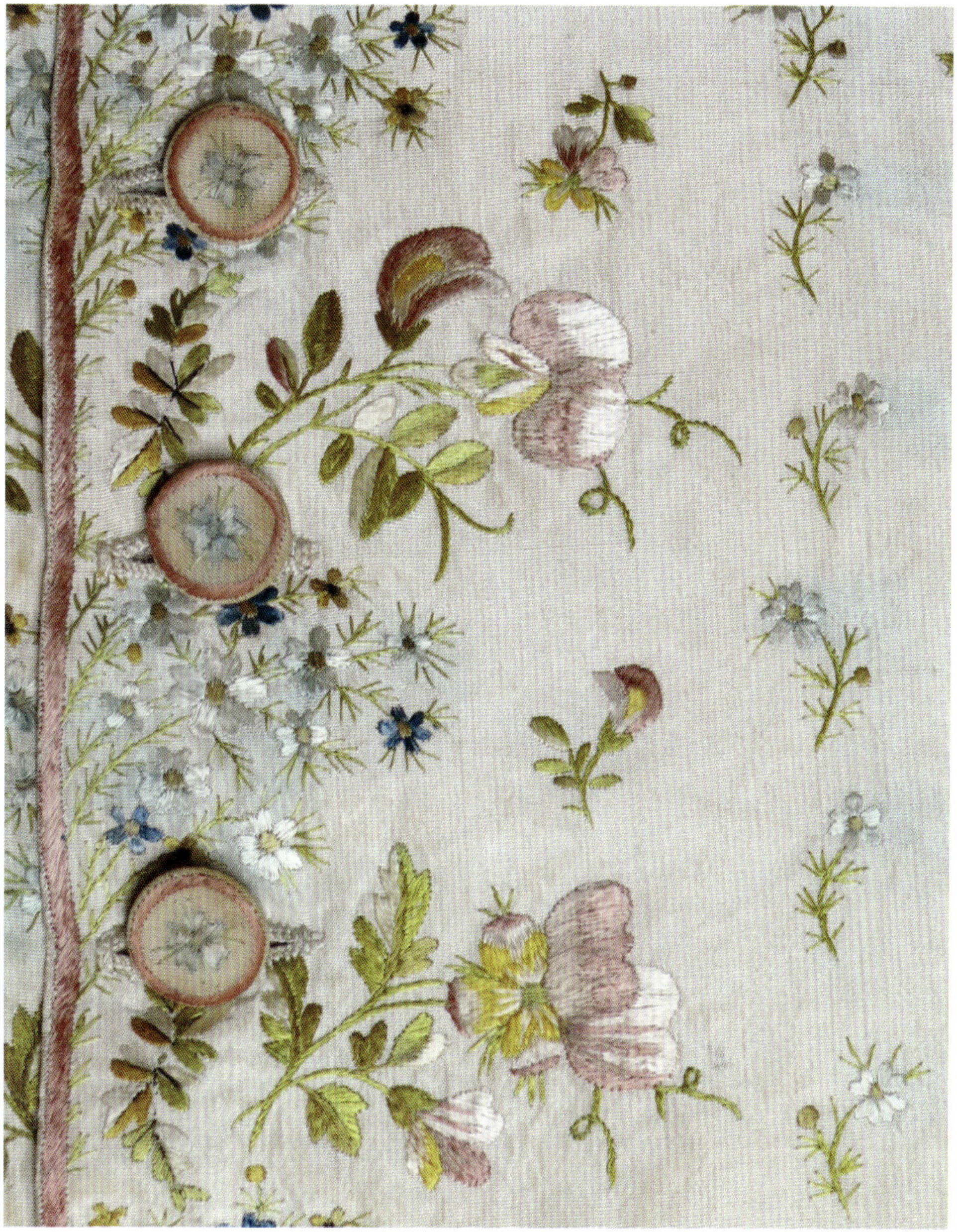

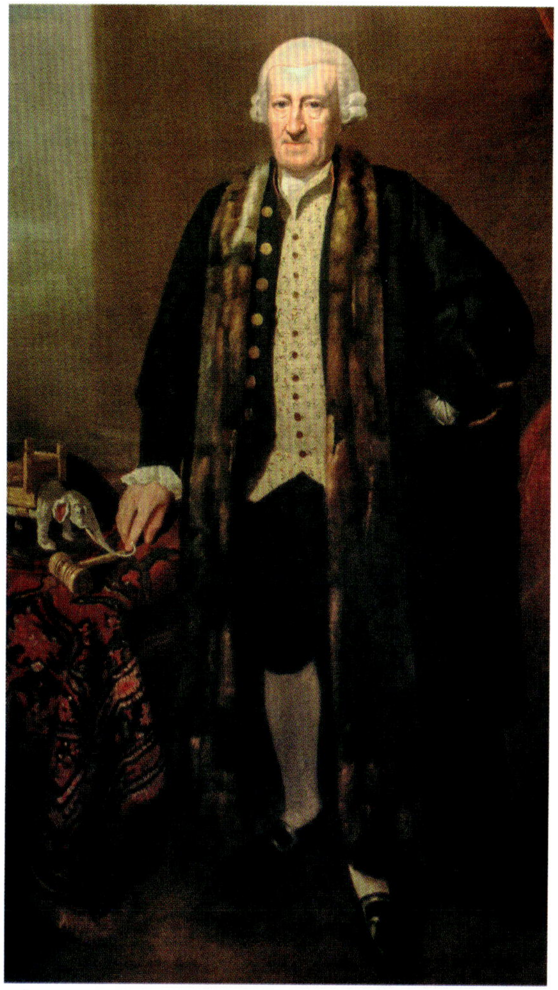

John Torr Foulds by an unknown artist, 1801, Cutlers Hall, London.

John Torr Foulds (1742-1815) was Chief Millwright, Surveyor and Engineer at the London Bridge Water Works from 1779, and was elected Master of the Worshipful Company of Cutlers in 1801.

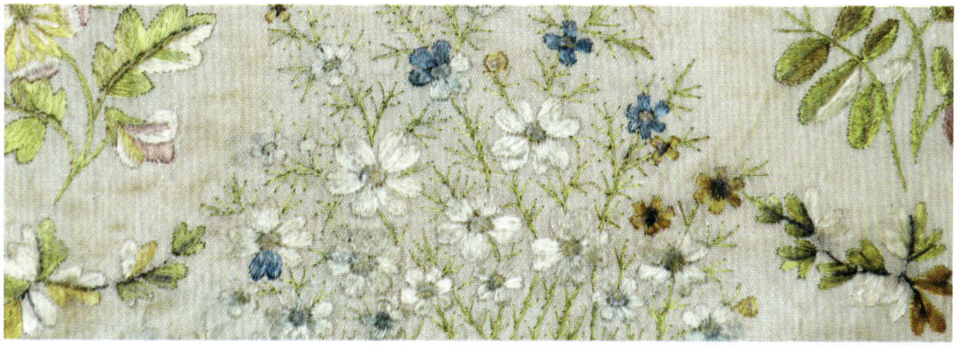

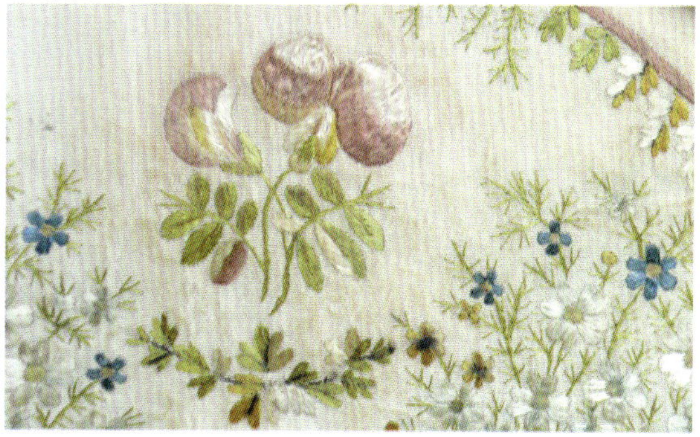

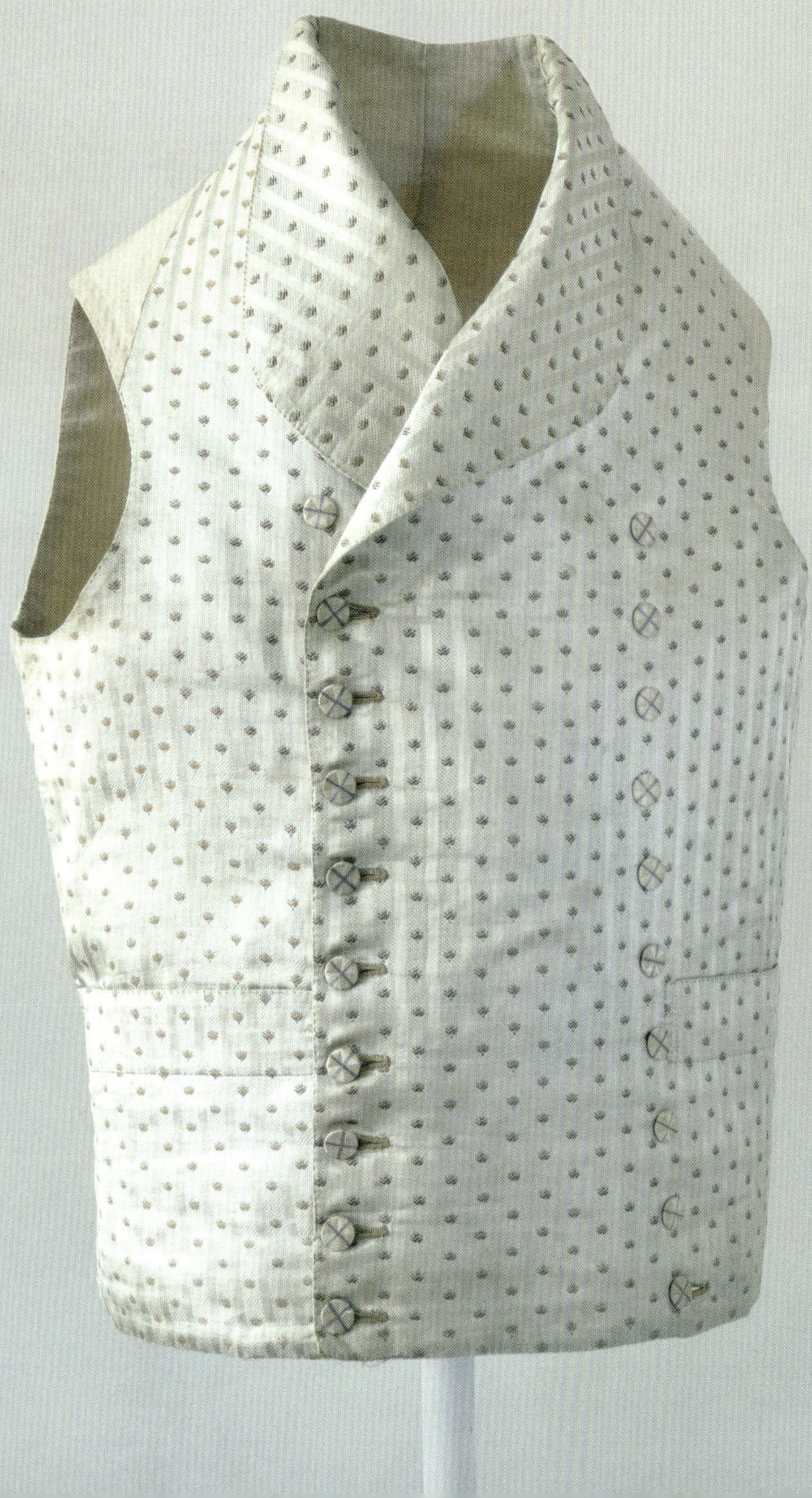

A waistcoat in ivory silk, 1800-1810.
HC.W-10.89-8

The silk has self stripes in contrasting weaves of hopsack and satin, and woven motifs in brown and blue. The waistcoat has a roll collar and two welted pockets. It is double-breasted with ten pairs of buttons but only nine buttonholes on the edge of the left forepart. The buttons are covered with a cross design in blue and pink threads on an ivory ground. There is a button on the bottom corner of the right forepart to fasten through a buttonhole on the left forepart at the bottom of the column of decorative buttons, and this keeps the right forepart in place. The waistcoat is lined in natural heavy cotton which continues up to the top of the collar at the back, and there are triangles of this cotton on the shoulders to economise on the silk. The back is in the same cotton and cut high up at the neck to form the back of the collar; there are two pairs of narrow linen tape ties to adjust the waist.

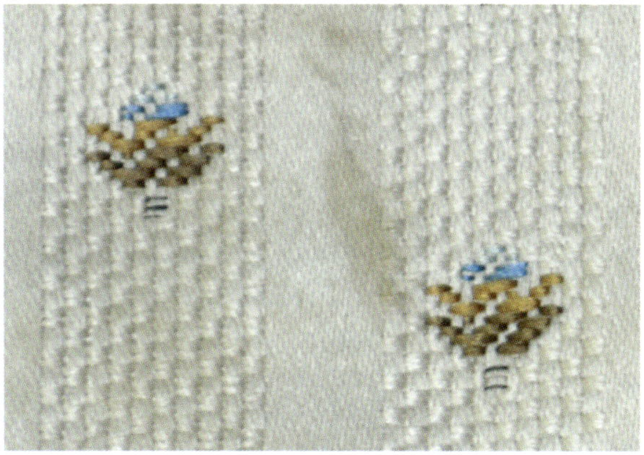

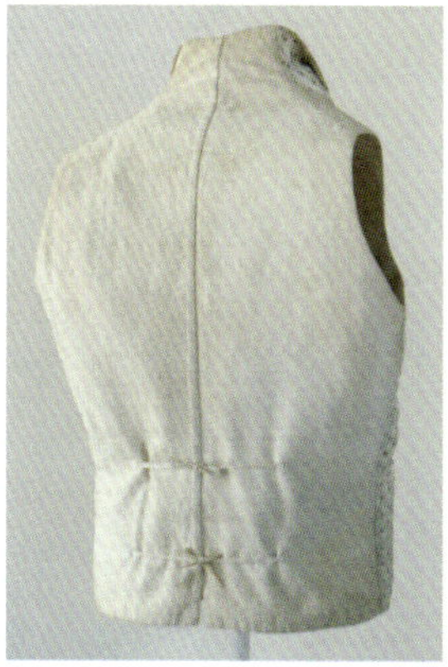

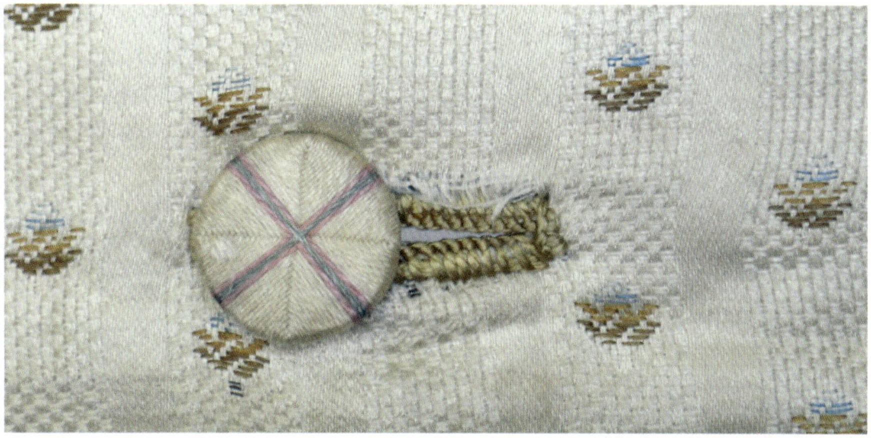

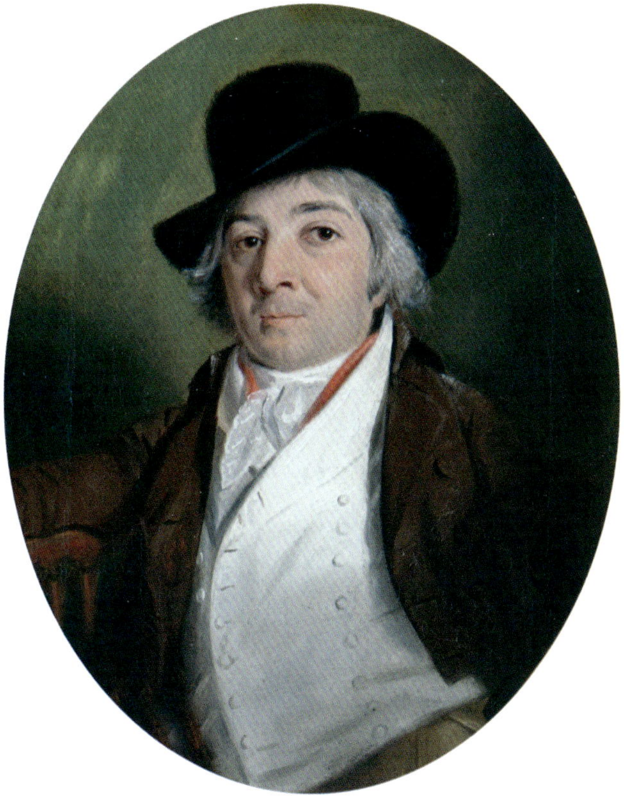

Cremer Cremer by British (English) School, 1800-1805, Felbrigg Hall. © National Trust Images.

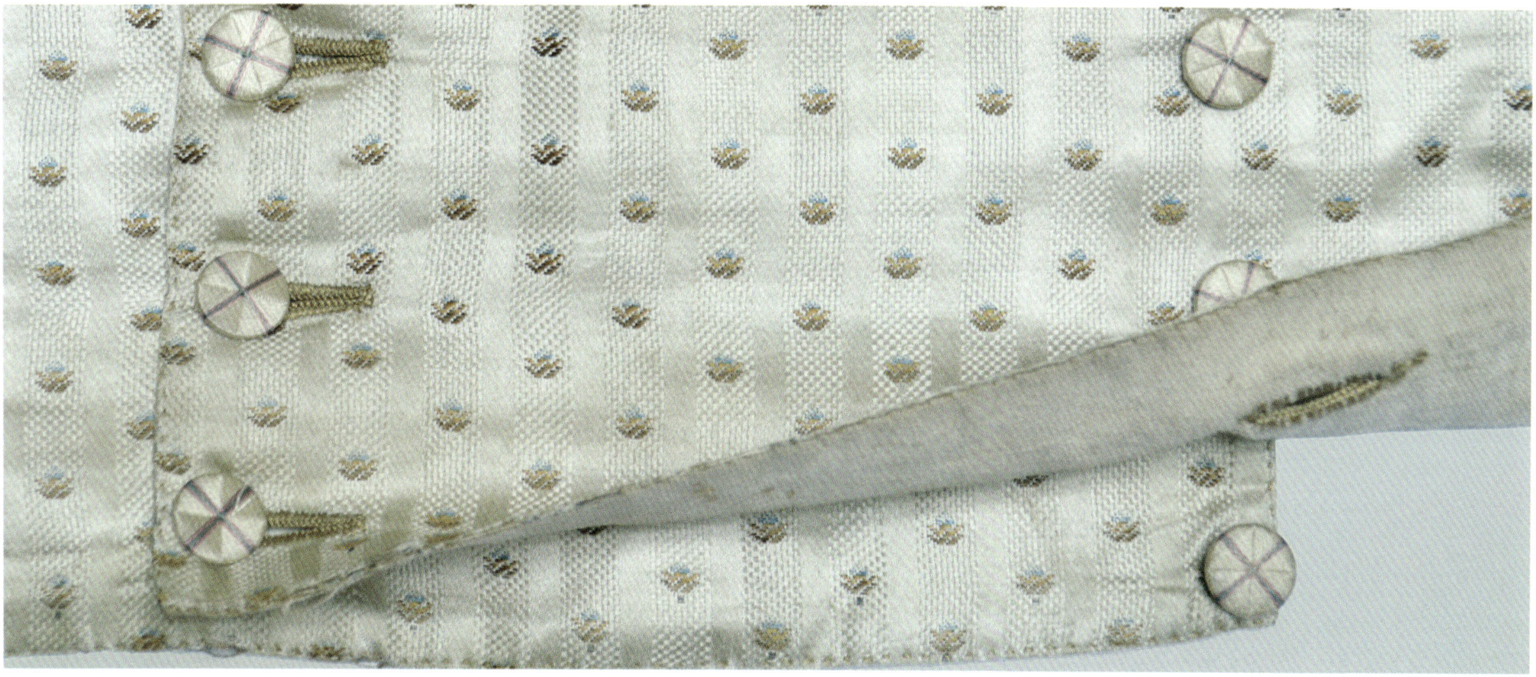

The bottom edge of the front, showing the button on the right forepart to hold it in place.

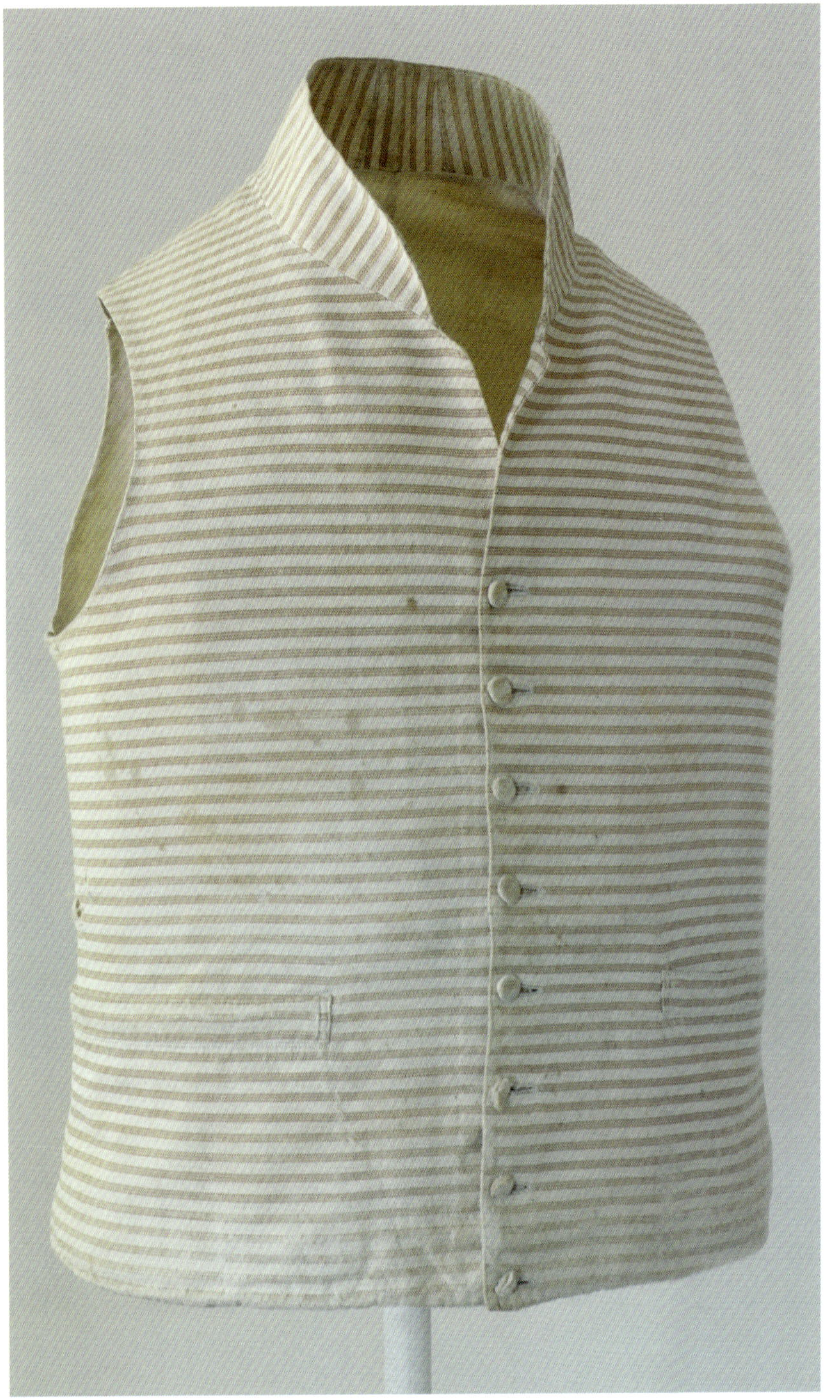

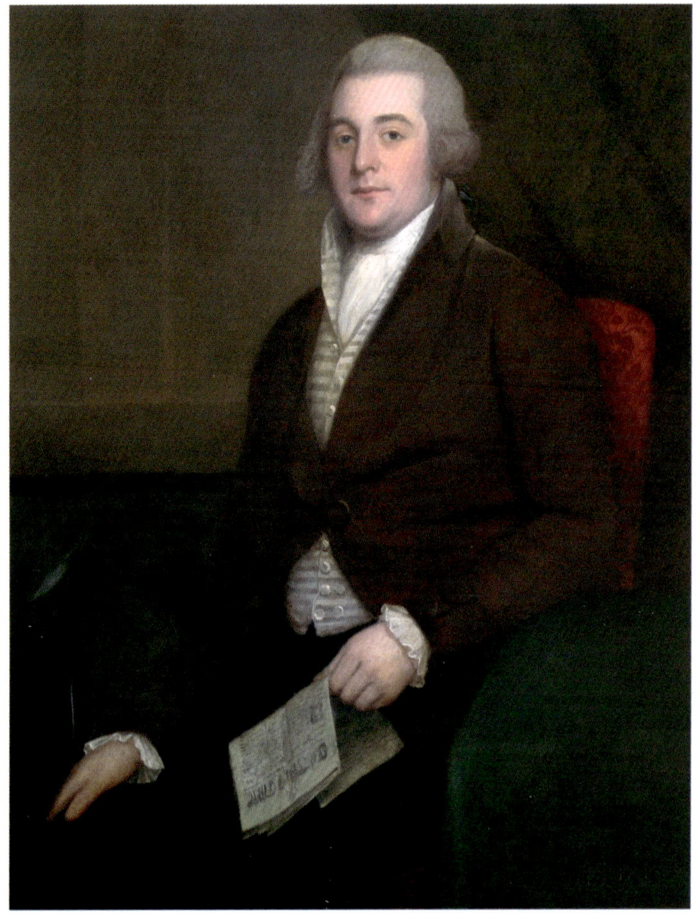

A Painting of a Man Holding a Newspaper by an unknown artist, 1800-1810. Collection of Wokingham Town Council. This is thought to be John Walter, who was owner and editor of *The Times* newspaper, founded by his father.

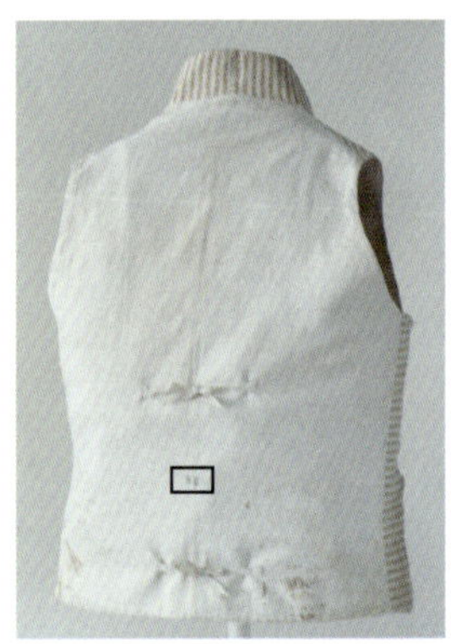

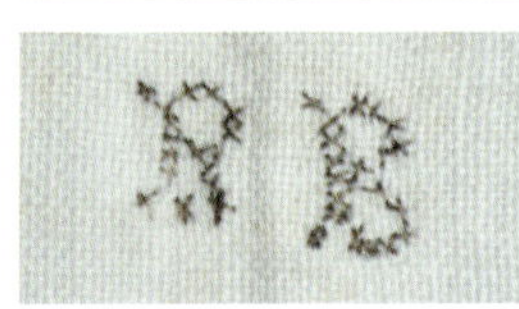

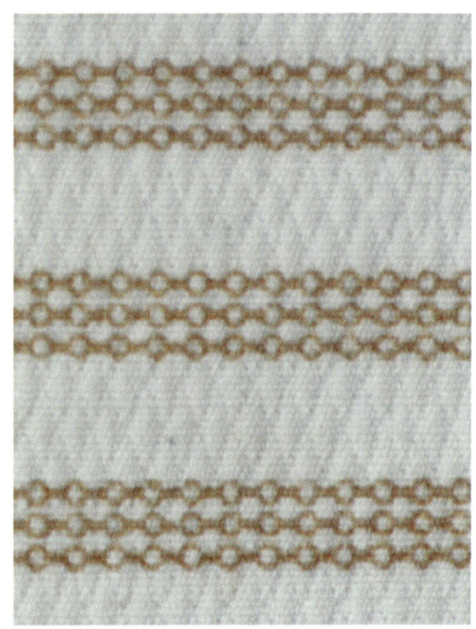

A waistcoat in cotton piqué, 1800-1810. HC.W-11.76-1

The cotton is ivory with printed horizontal stripes in fawn. The lining and back are in white plain cotton with two pairs of cotton tapes on the back, to adjust the size. The lowest three, of the eight self-covered flat buttons, have lost their bone mould middles. There are two welted pockets and a stand collar. On the centre back, between the two sets of ties, the initials R B are embroidered in faded black cotton cross stitch.

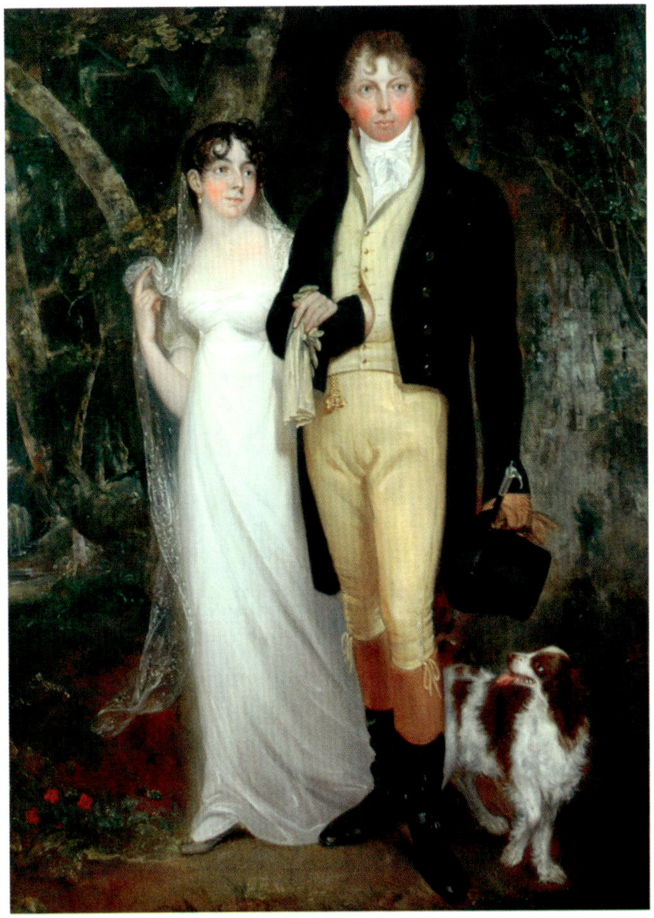

Captain & Mrs Edmund Burnham Pateshall (detail) by William Armfield Hobday, 1810. Image from the Scarborough Collections courtesy of Scarborough Museums Trust.

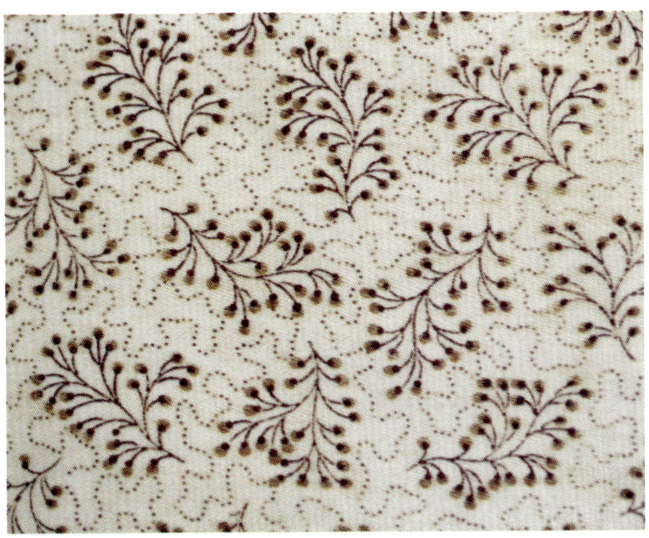

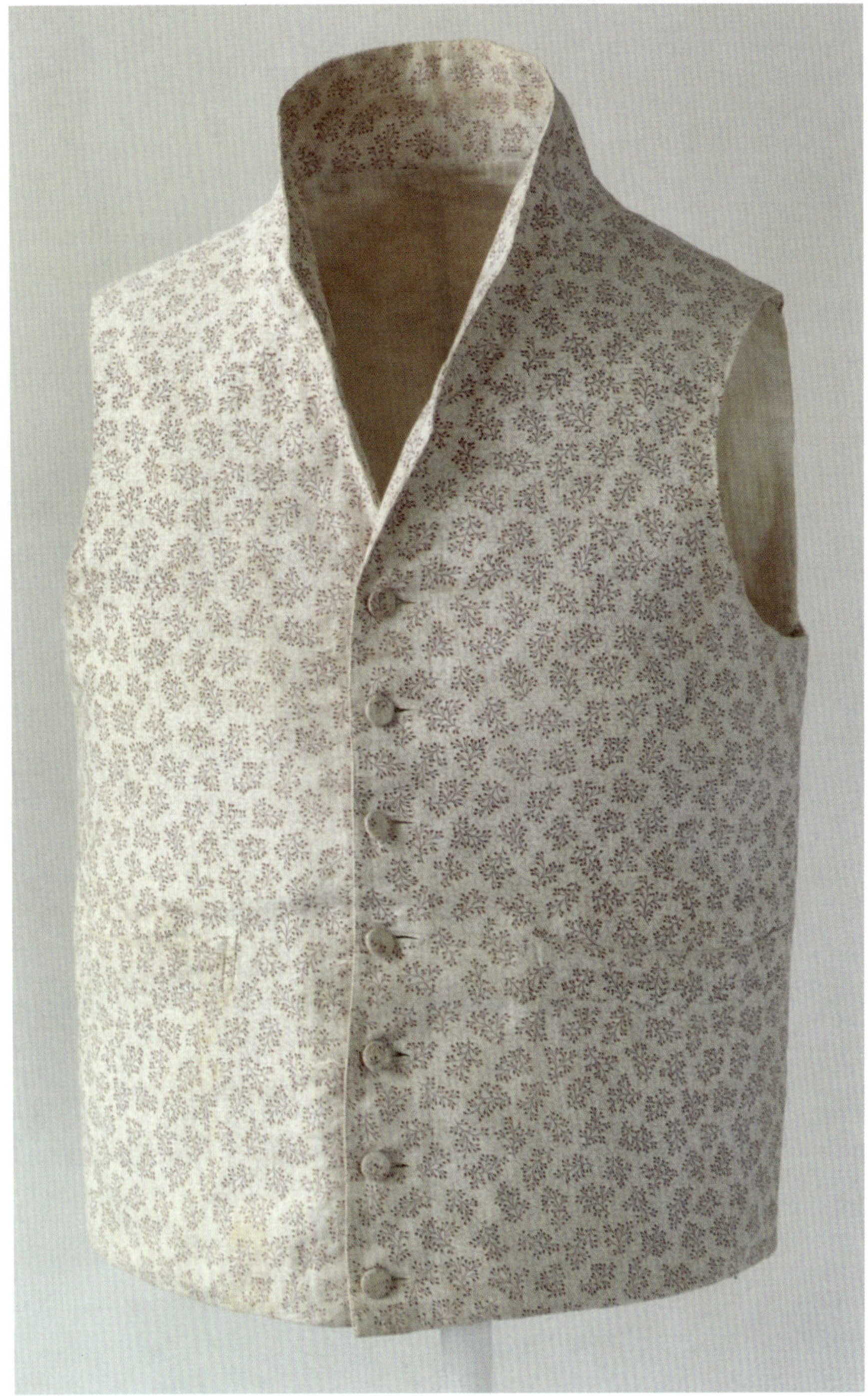

A waistcoat in cream cotton sateen, 1800-1810. HC.W-0.39

The cotton has a printed pattern of sprigs and dotted lines in chocolate and fawn. The lining and back are in white heavy cotton, with two pairs of cotton tape ties on the back to adjust the waist. There are seven self-covered flat buttons, and two welted pockets. The wear on the stand collar suggests that it was worn folded down, at a later date, possibly when the side seams were taken in by 2″ on each side.

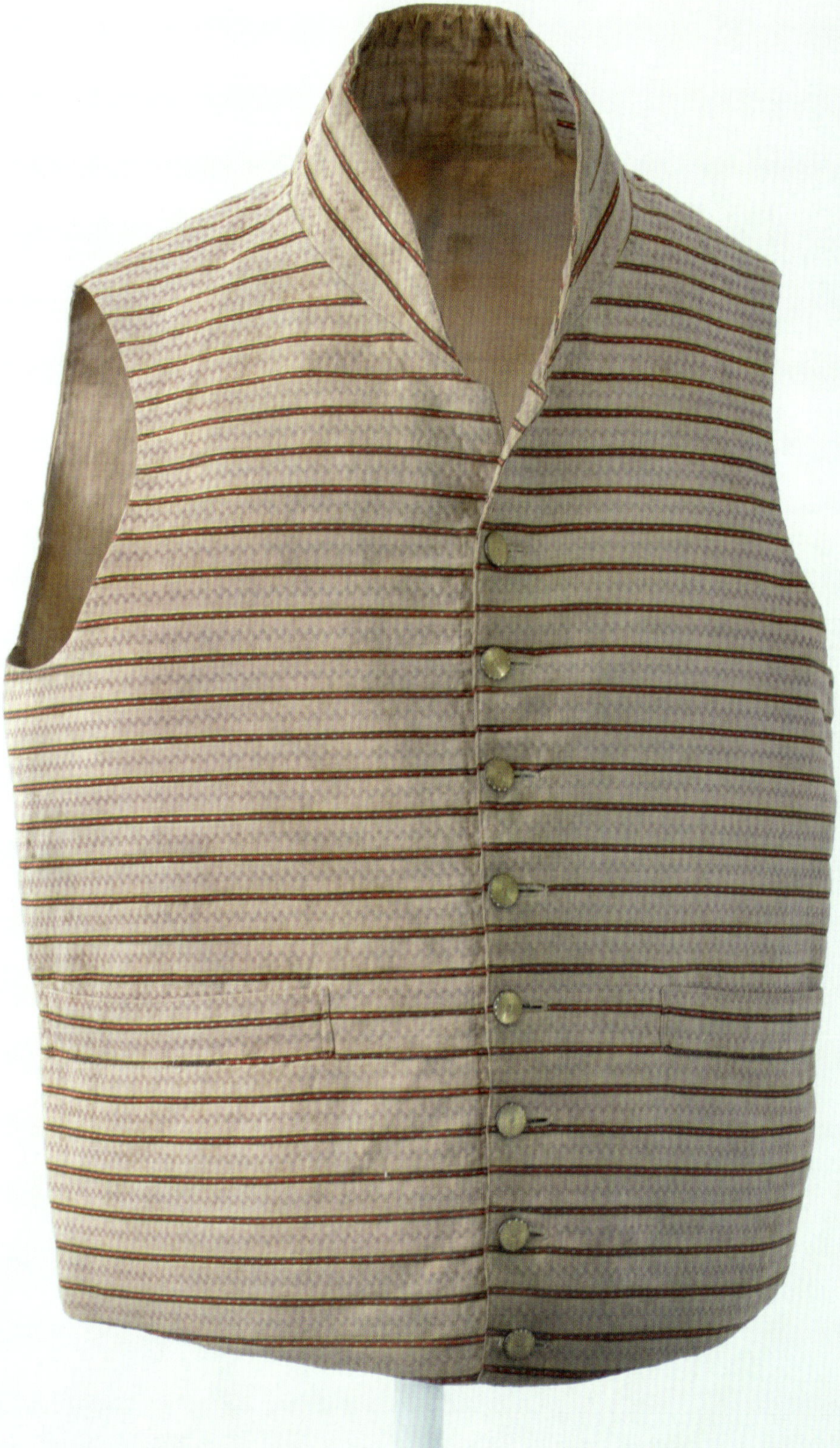

A waistcoat in beige striped wool, 1810-1820.
HC.W-10.89-9

The wool has horizontal stripes of black, red and white, with zig-zag stripes of pink between them. The foreparts are dirty and have faded but the original colours are better preserved on the facings. The waistcoat is lined with cream plain cotton and there is a pocket in the left forepart lining; inside pockets have been found in coats from the late eighteenth century. The back is in the same cream cotton with one pair of cotton tapes to adjust the waist (page 210). There are two welted pockets. The high stand collar has a section of the cotton lining at the centre back which has two rows of running stitches to gather it slightly and hold the collar more closely in to the neck. The eight gilt buttons have an engraved sunburst pattern and inverted scallops round the edge. The words "Standard Orange Gilt" are stamped on the back. Gilt buttons were manufactured in Birmingham from the 1790s and became very popular. There was a regulation about the minimum amount of gold to be used, and various wordings were put on the backs to indicate this. For instance, "Treble gilt" meant that three times the approved amount was there, indicating a better quality.

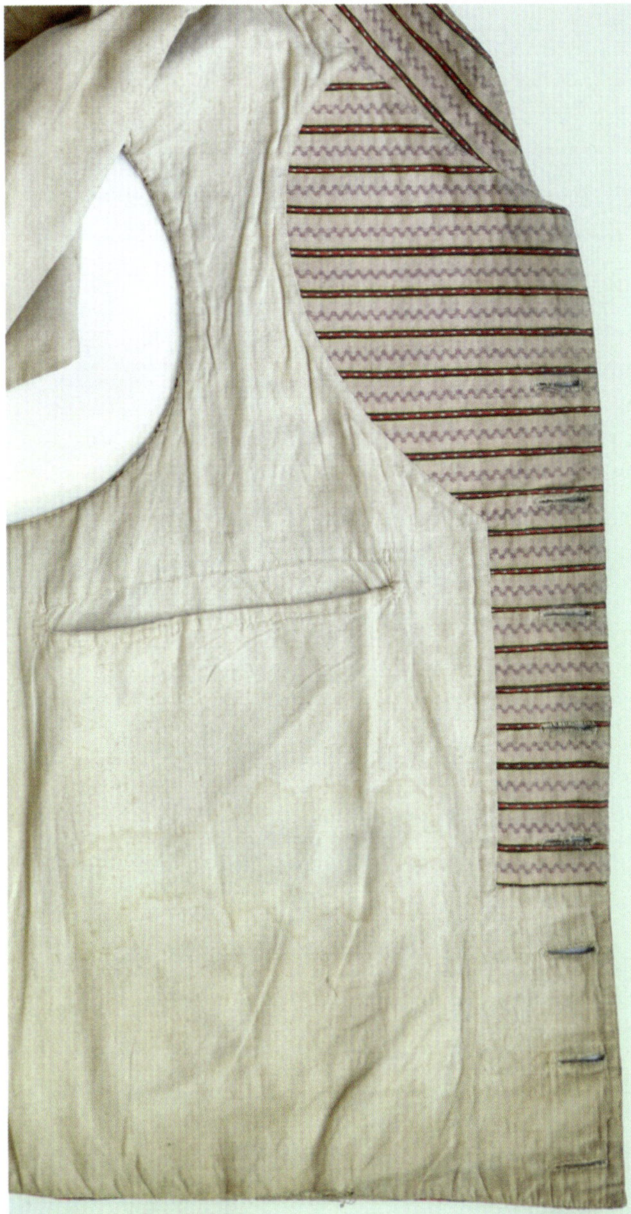

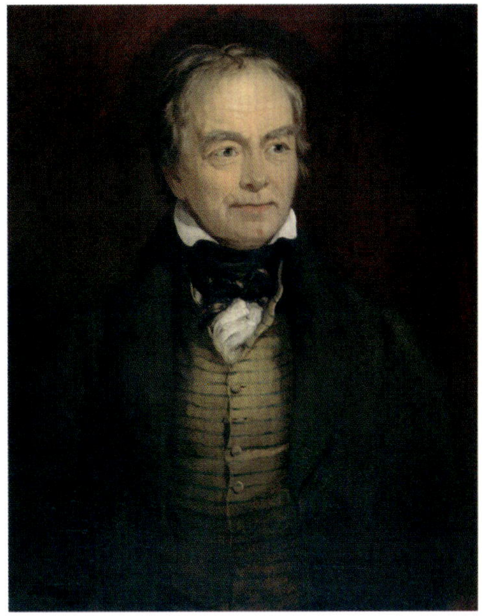

Richard Llwyd by William Jones, 1810. © Amgueddfa Cymru / National Museum of Wales. Llwyd was a noted writer and genealogist, and was known as the Bard of Snowdon.

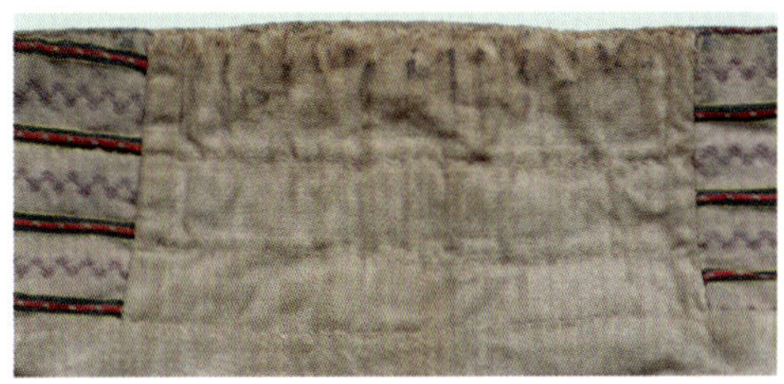

The gathered section inside the back of the collar.

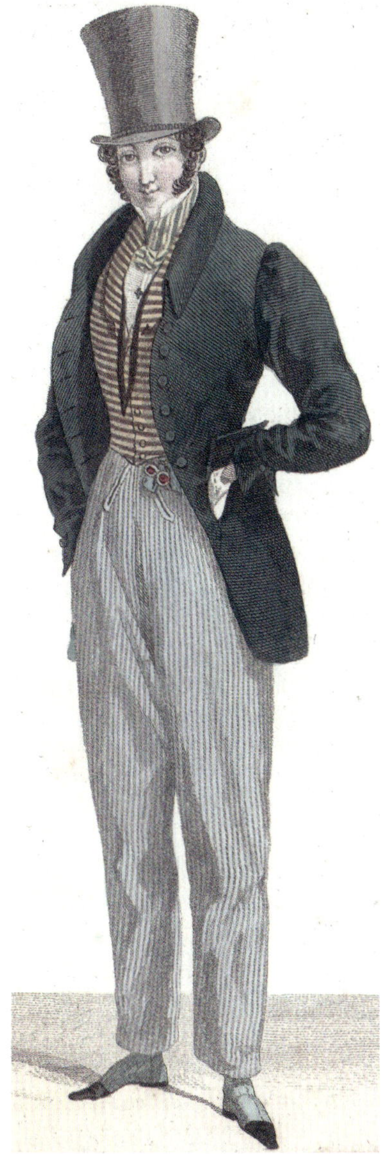

Fashion plate from *Costume Parisien*, 1824.

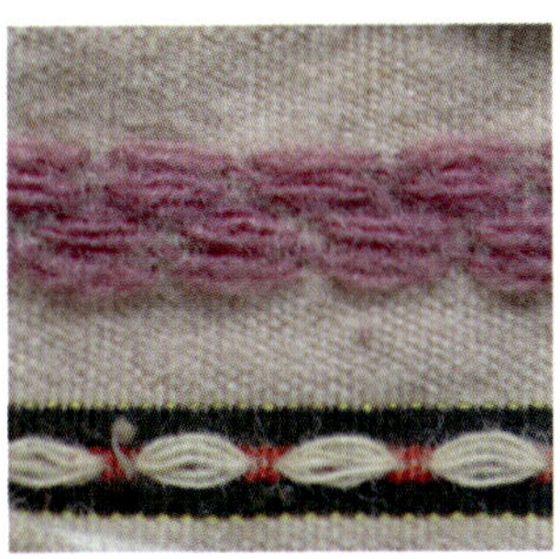

The back of the fabric, where the colour has not faded.

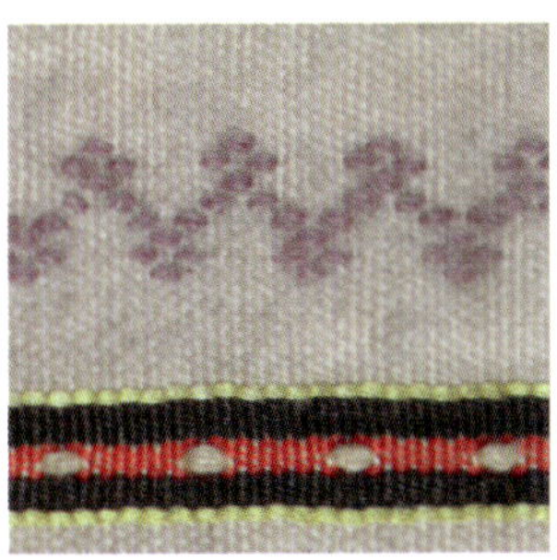

The fabric on the facing is less faded and cleaner.

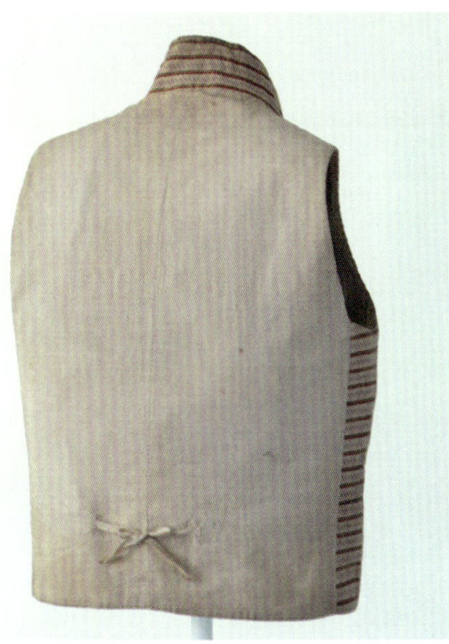

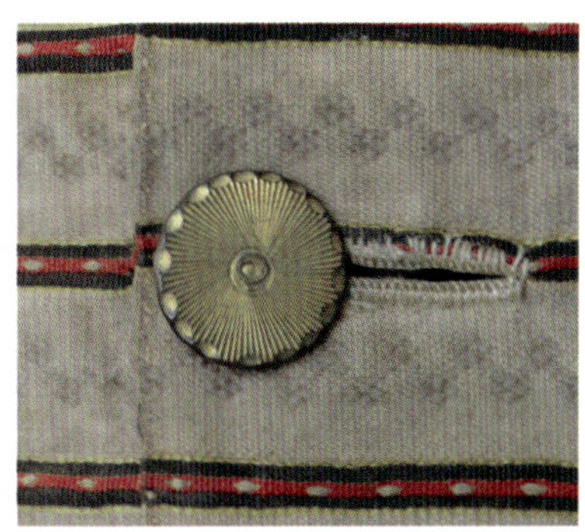

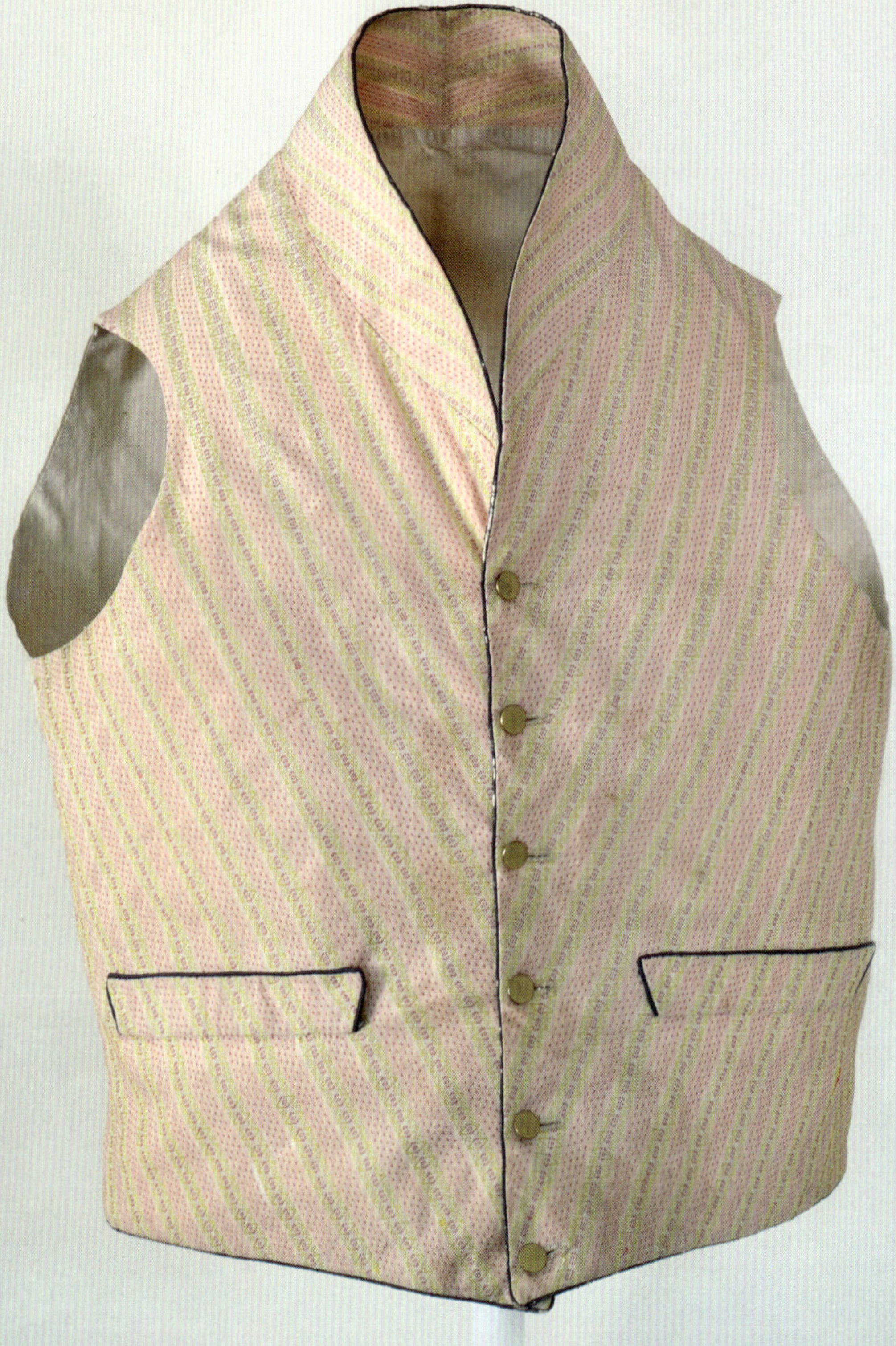

A waistcoat in wool, 1820-1830.
HC.W-10.89-10

The wool has weft stripes of ivory and pink, with a pattern made of broken lines of yellow and red silk. The waistcoat has been cut on the bias of the fabric so that the stripes run diagonally and mitre in the front. It is lined with plain white cotton and the back is in the same cotton with two pairs of cotton tapes to adjust the waist. The foreparts, stand collar and pocket welts are edged with black silk piping, and there are six flat gilt buttons with a textured surface.

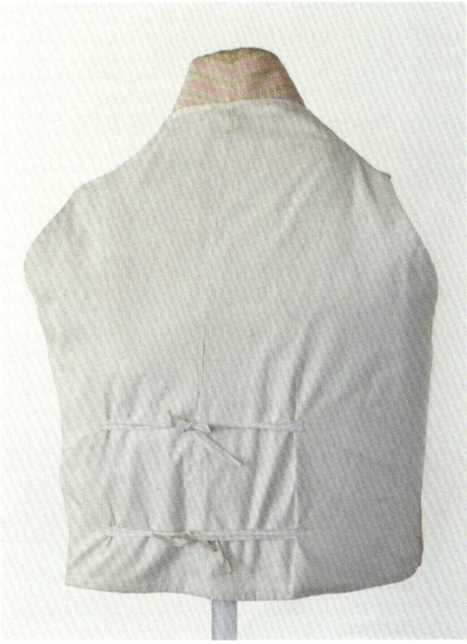

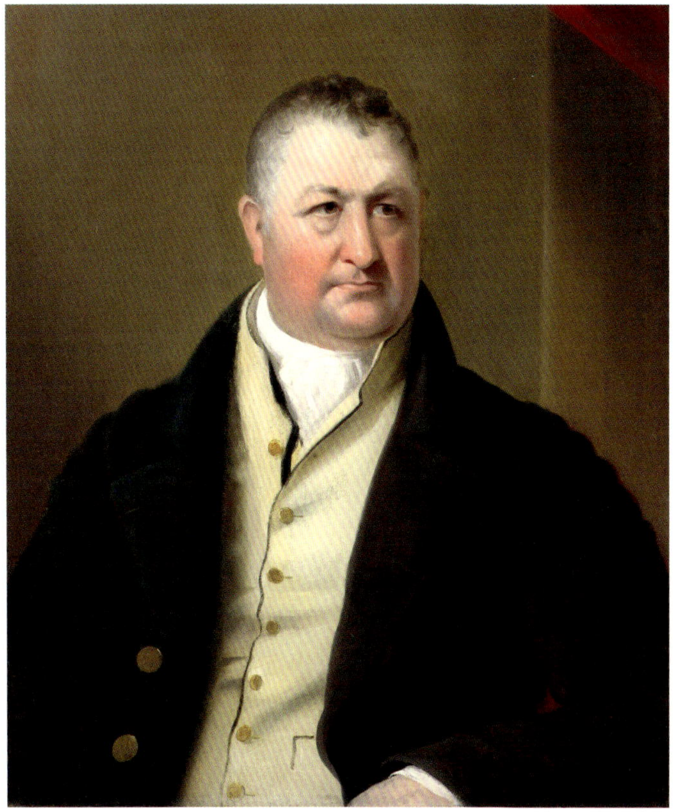

Right: *Samuel Horrocks* by James Lonsdale, 1820. Harris Museum and Art Gallery, Preston. Samuel Horrocks was a successful cotton manufacturer in Preston.

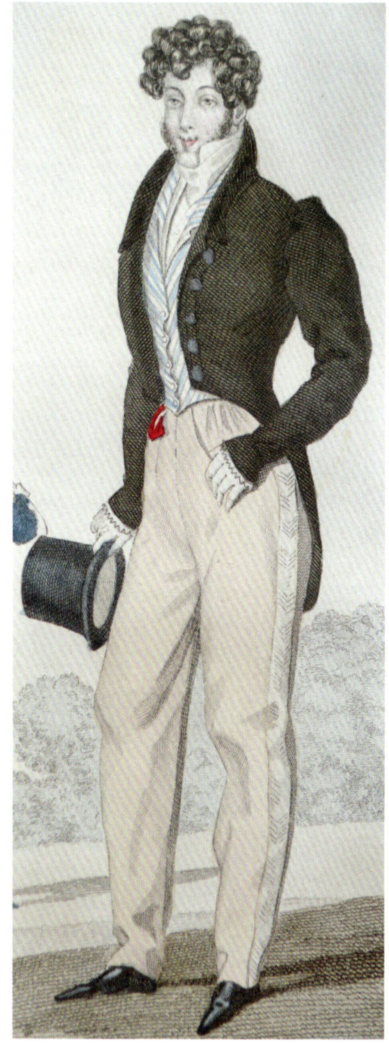

Fashion plate from *Petit Courrier des Dames*, May 1825.

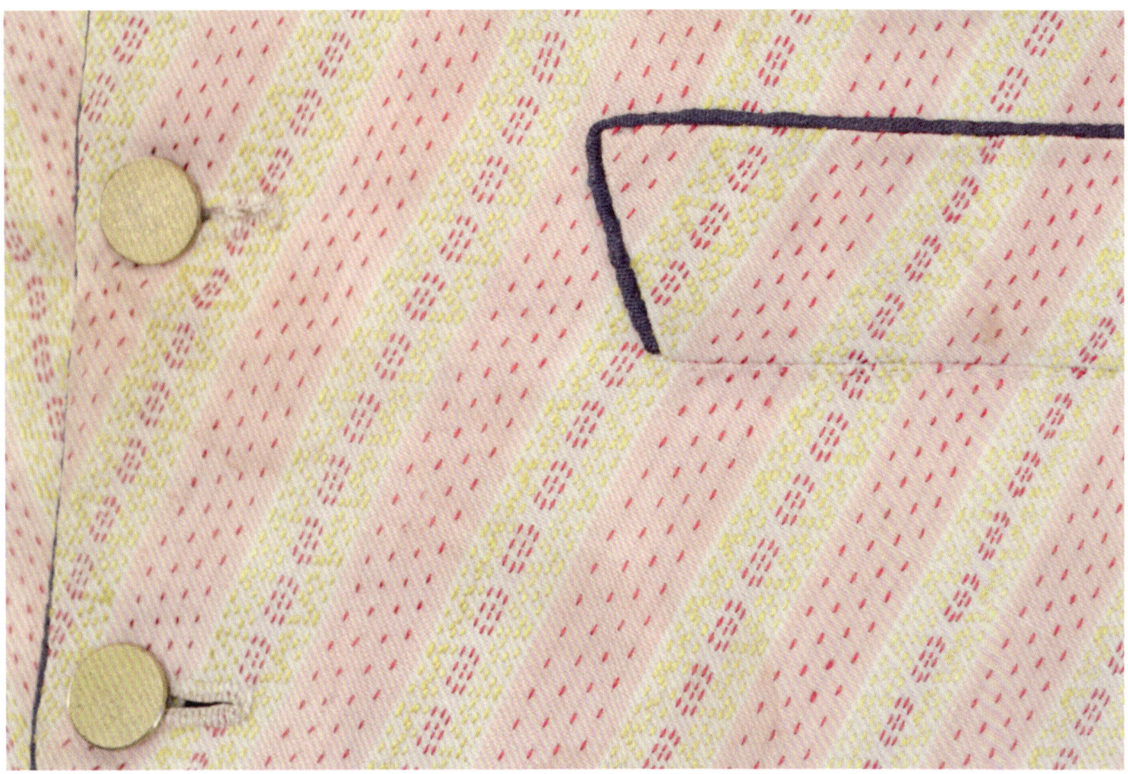

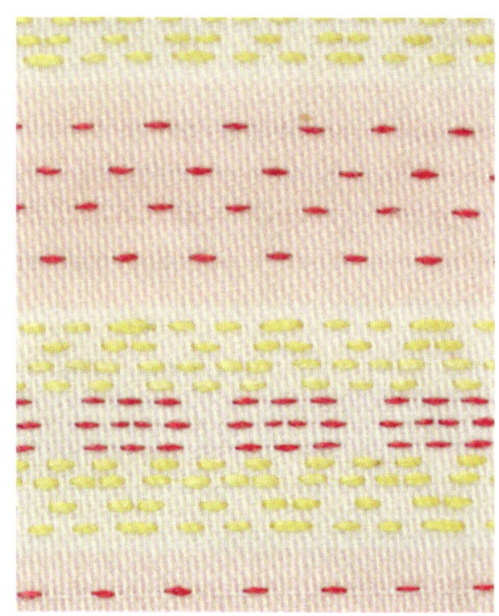

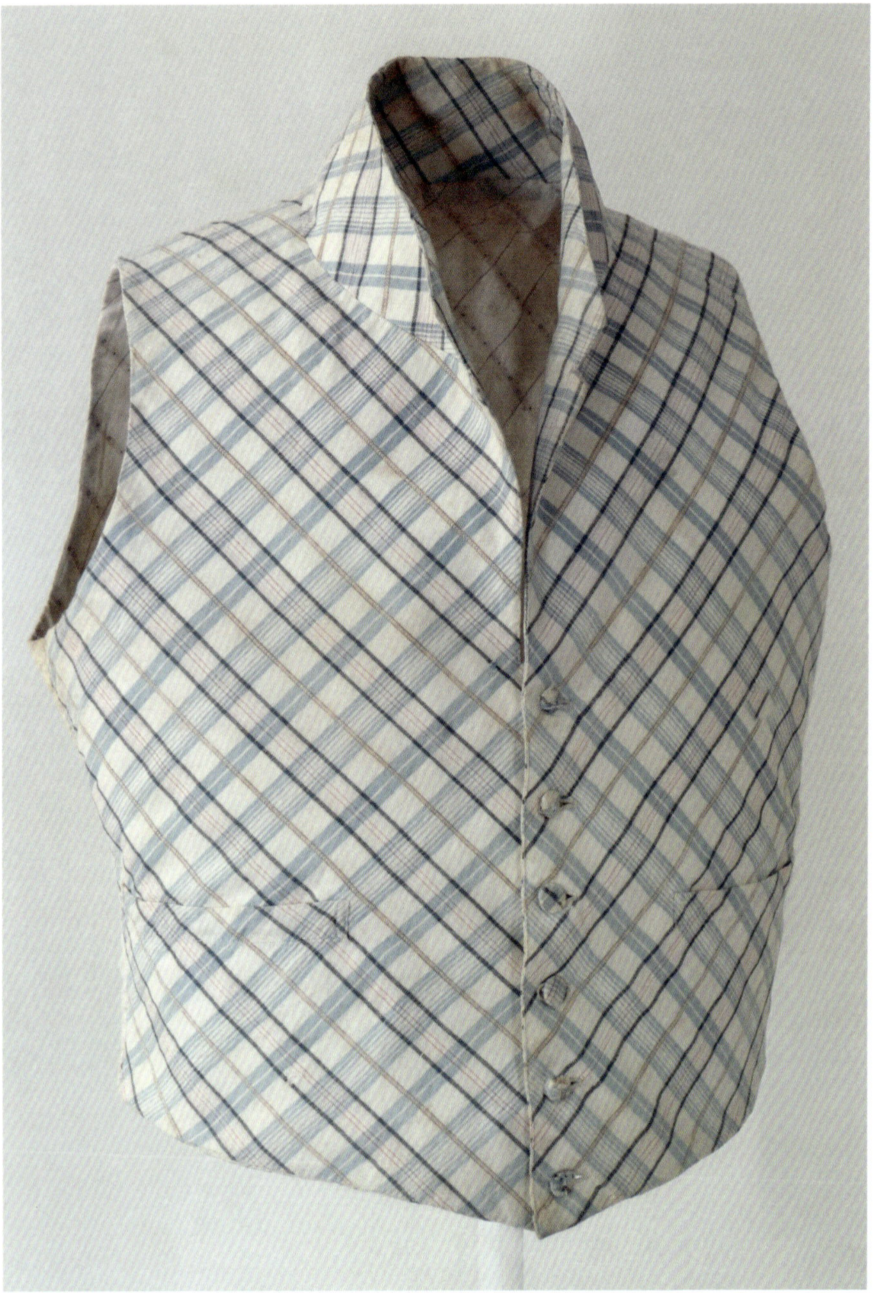

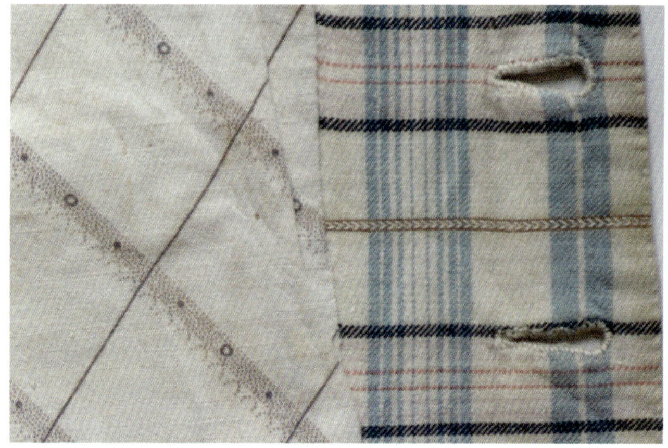

Inside the left forepart; the facing has been cut on the straight of the fabric, and the printed lining can be seen.

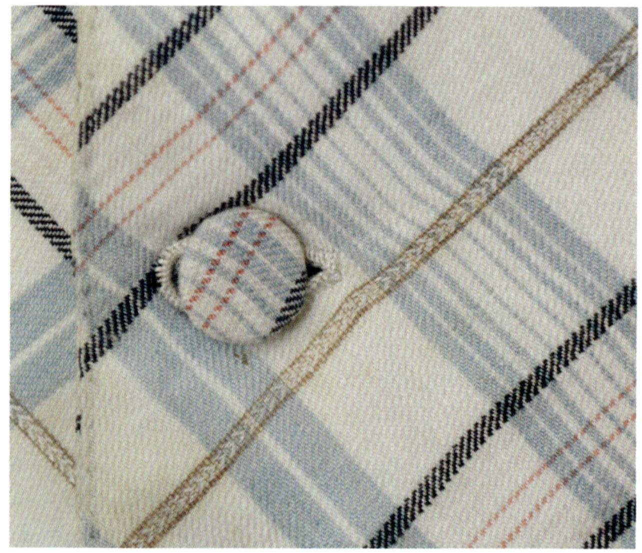

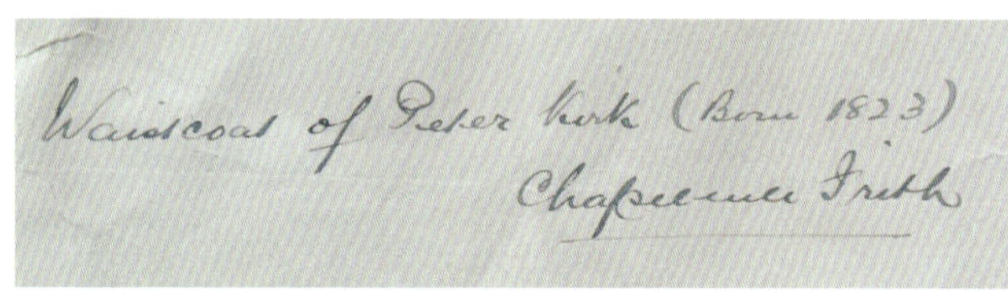

The piece of paper sewn inside the back of the waistcoat.

A waistcoat in checked wool, 1820-1830. HC.W-10.15-4

The wool has a pale blue and white striped warp, with narrow weft stripes of black, red and fawn making the checks; there are chevrons in ivory silk along the middle of the fawn stripe. The waistcoat is cut on the bias of the fabric so that the stripes run diagonally. The lining is in ivory cotton printed in dark mauve with patterned lines crossed by plain ones on the bias, making diagonal checks. The back is in plain white cotton with two pairs of cotton tape ties to adjust the waist. There are six self-covered buttons, two welted pockets and a stand collar. A piece of paper sewn on the inside says: "Waistcoat of Peter Kirk (Born 1823) Chapel en le Frith".

This waistcoat would have been rather old-fashioned by the time this Peter Kirk (1823-1889) was old enough to wear it, so it is possible that it belonged to his father, also Peter Kirk (1782-1848), who was a farmer, in Derbyshire. He married Rachel Thornhill in 1822, and he might have worn this waistcoat for his wedding.

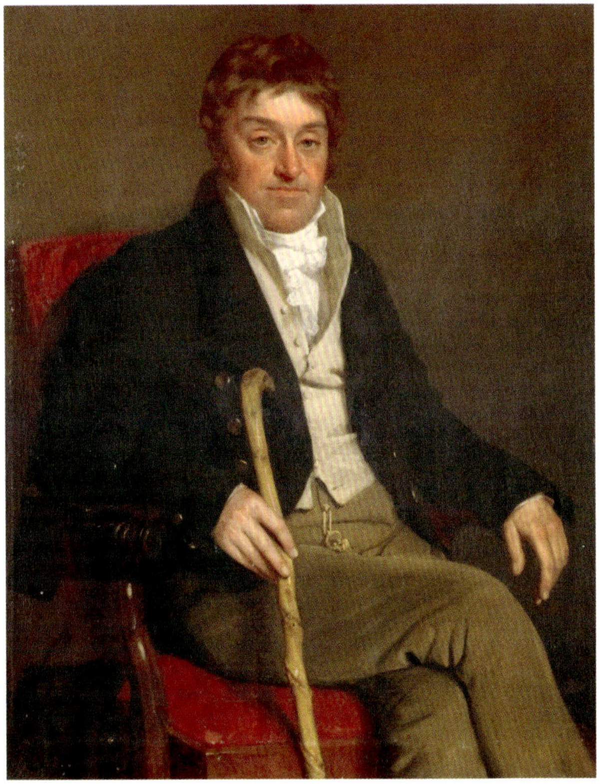

William Metcalfe by George Watson, 1821. © The Hunterian, University of Glasgow 2016.

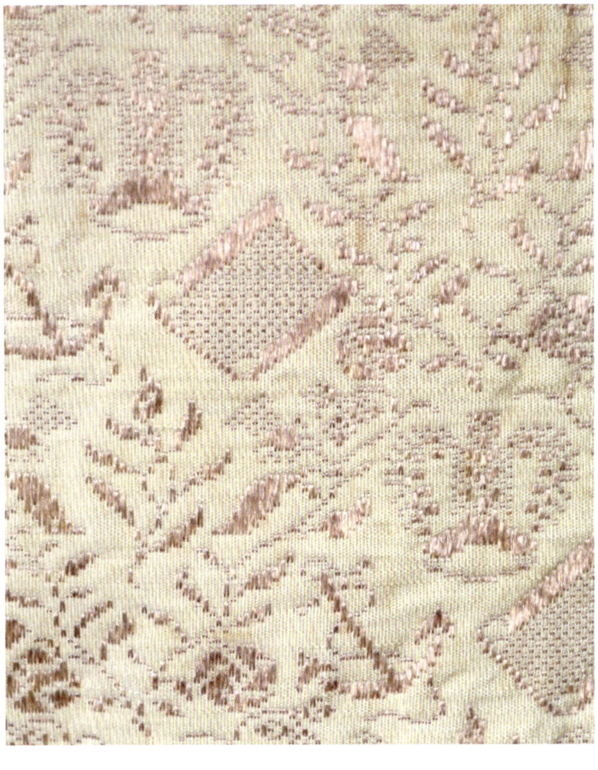

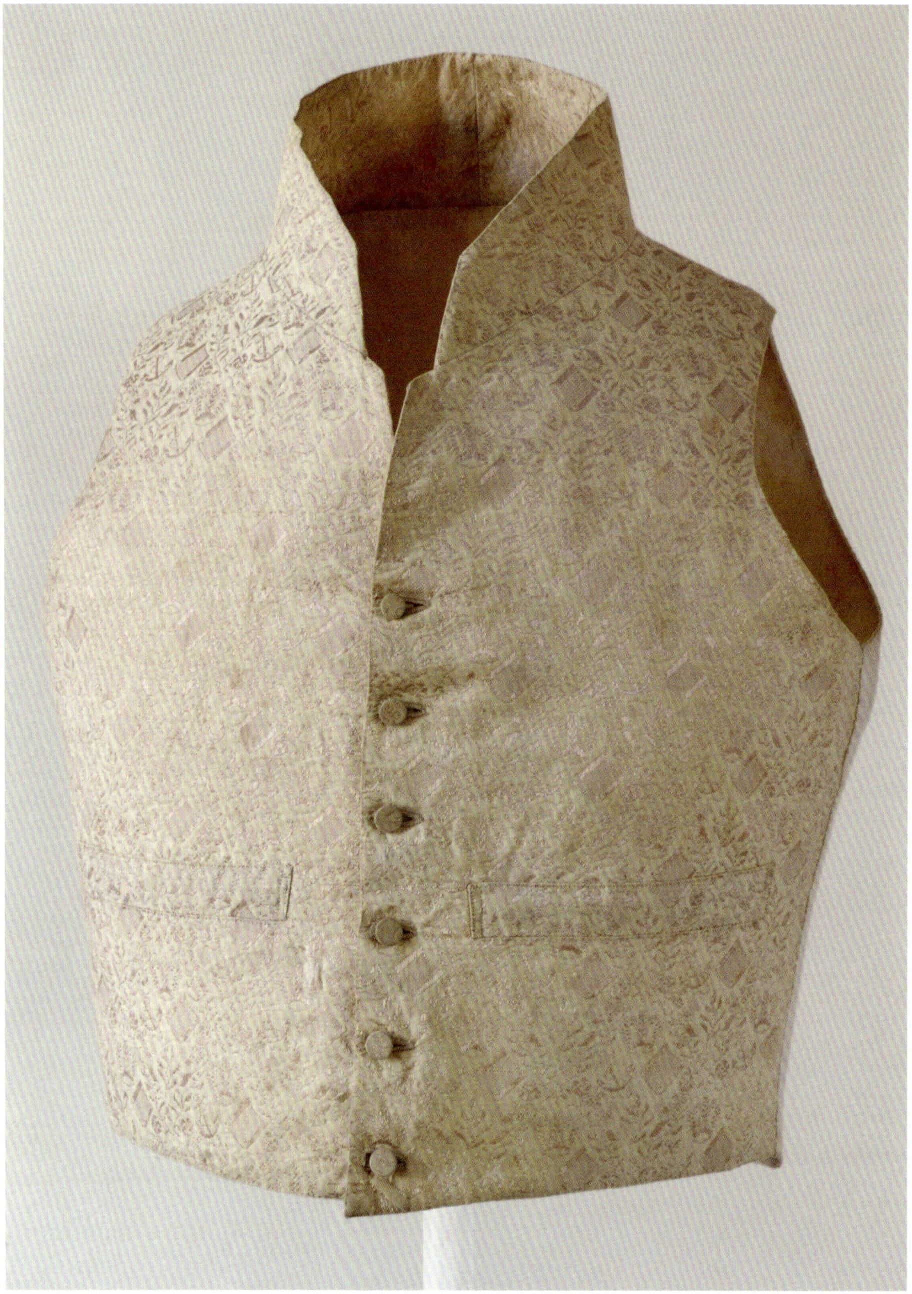

A waistcoat in cream wool, 1820-1830. HC.W-3.88

The wool has a woven pattern in pale pink silk, of crowns, scrolls, anchors and trailing plants, including a rose and a thistle; the significance of the design is not known. The back is in heavy ivory cotton, with no seam in the centre back but a gusset starting 4″ down from the collar and widening to 2$^{1}/_{2}$″ at the hem; there are no waist adjustments. The lining is in the same heavy cotton with a pocket inside the left forepart. The stand collar is 2$^{1}/_{2}$″ deep at the back; there are two welted pockets, and six small self-covered buttons.

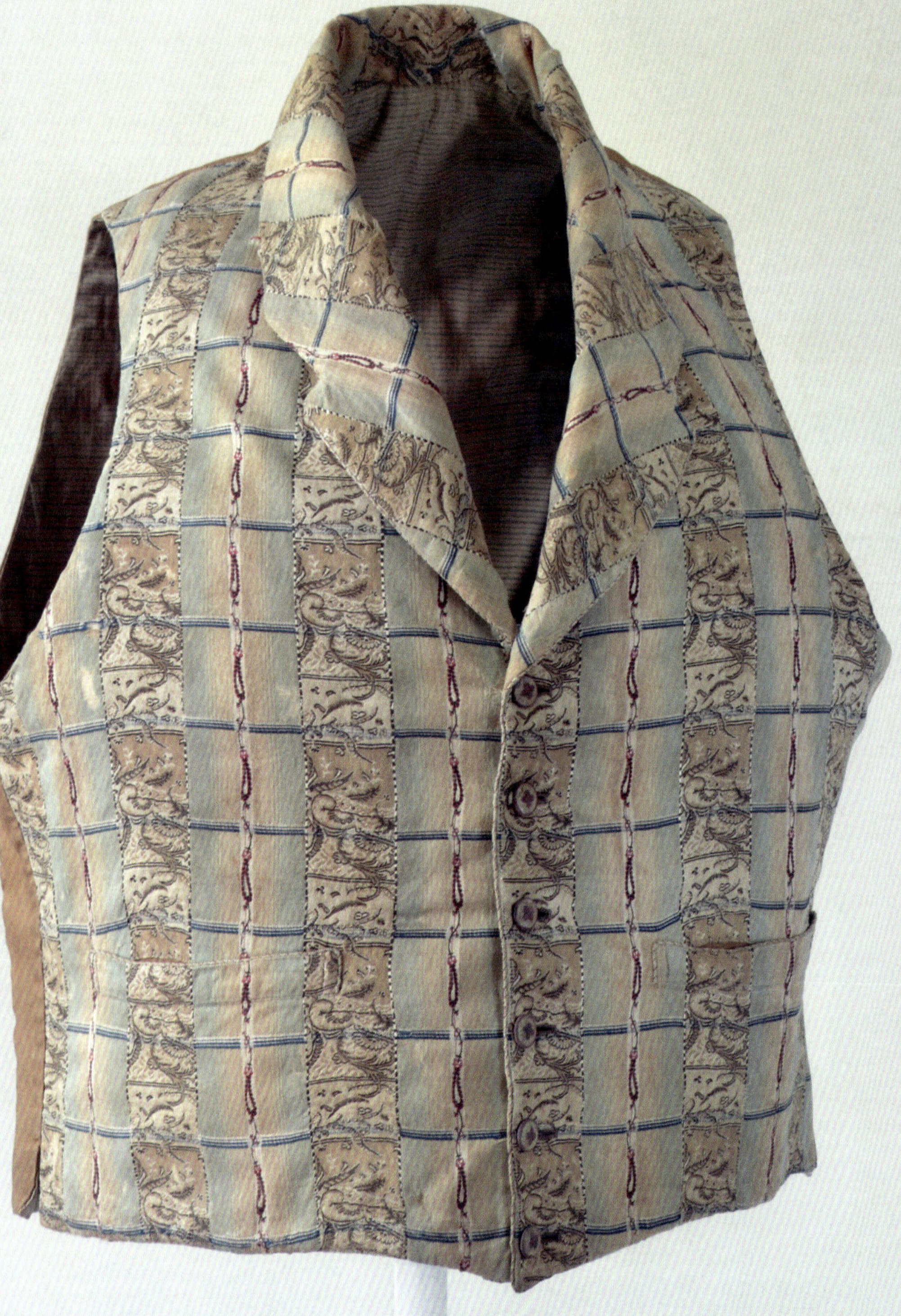

A waistcoat in silk and wool, 1825-1835. HC.W-10.76-2

The warp is ivory silk with narrow stripes of dark blue and ivory. The pattern is formed by pale blue, cream and fawn wool weft stripes, now discoloured, with additional black, ivory and red silk patterning. The waistcoat has been cut sideways across the width of the fabric, so that the patterned stripes run from shoulder to hem. The six buttons are covered in a fabric woven to shape, giving a plum edge and central cross motif on a self-patterned ivory ground. The step-roll collar, foreparts and welted pocket tops are edged with a fine ivory and red silk cord. The lining is cotton, white originally but now very discoloured, with narrow blue printed stripes. The back is ginger cotton twill with a waist adjustment of tabs with boned ends, three pairs of hand-worked eyelets and grey silk narrow ribbon lacing (page 210). The waistcoat has been let out with sections of the back fabric in the side seams and these have a natural linen lining. The side seams have 1 1/4″ openings at their base.

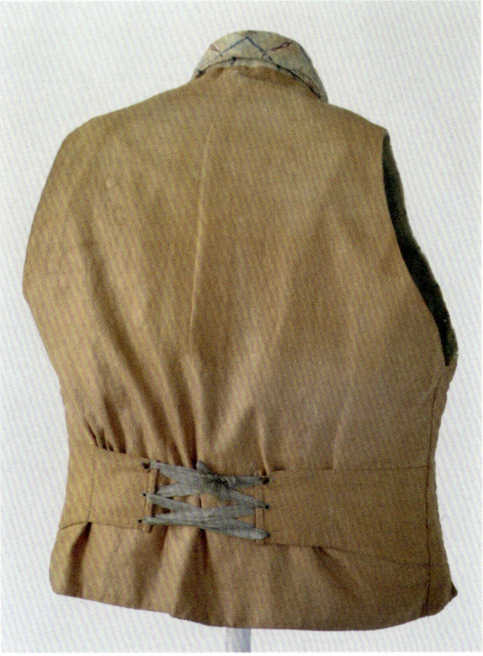

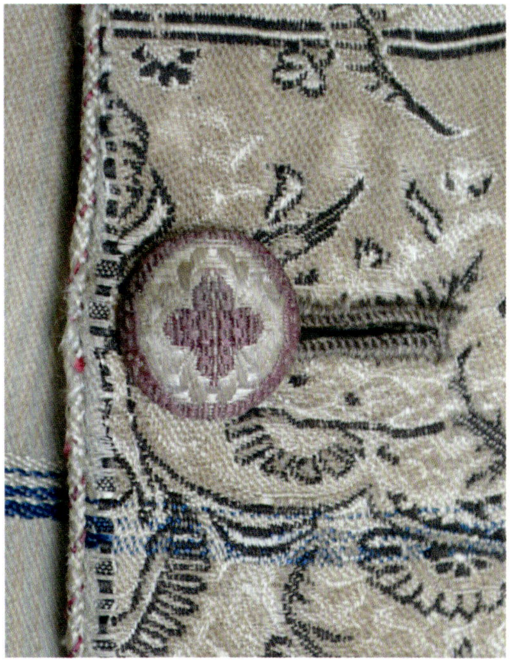

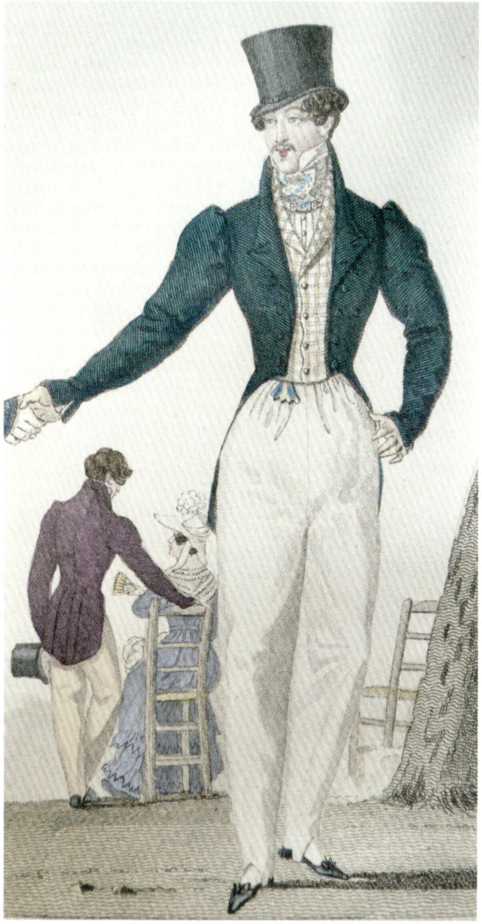

Fashion plate from *Petit Courrier des Dames*, 1825.

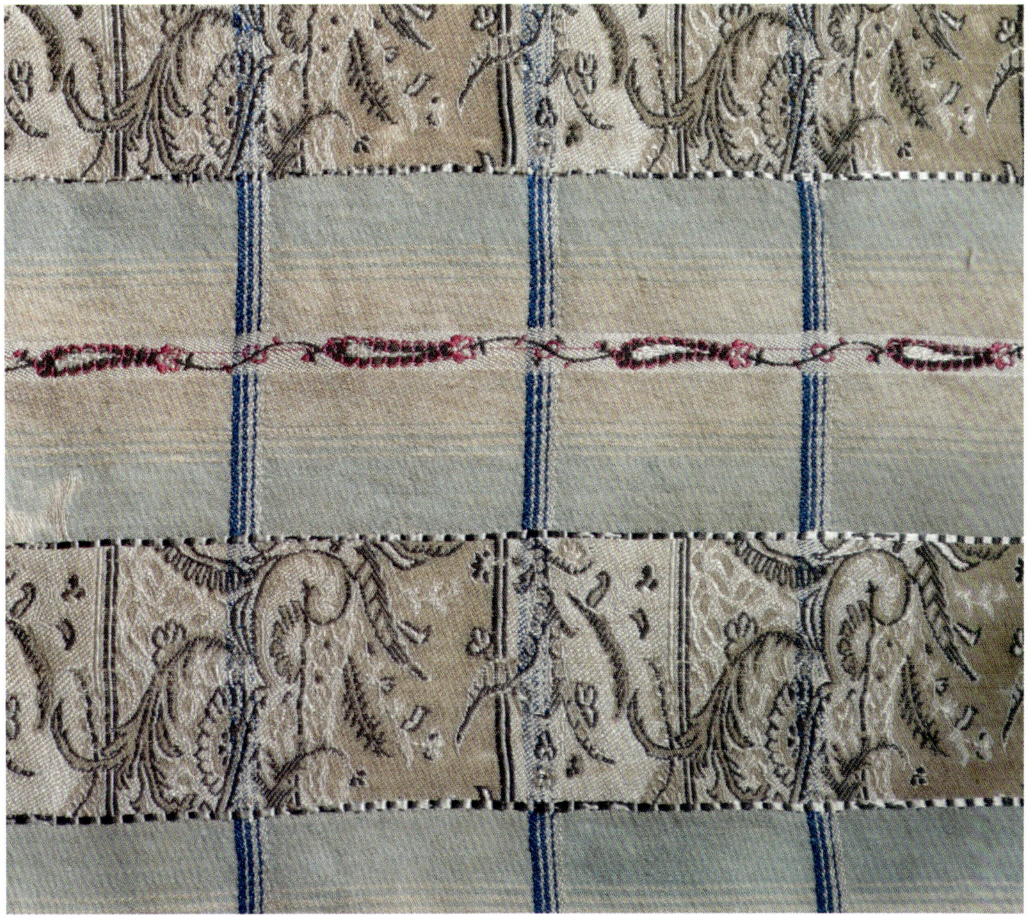

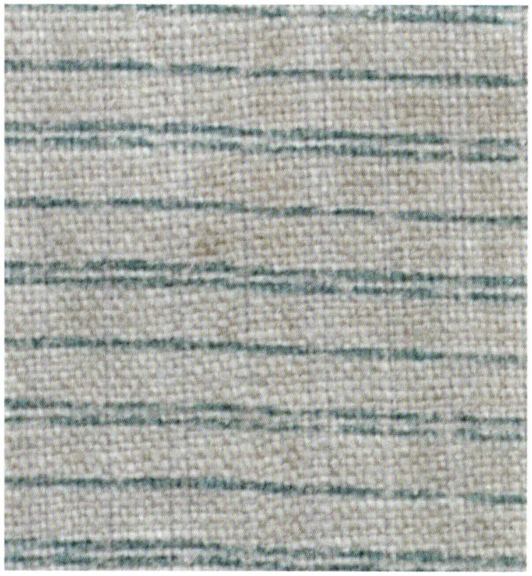

The cotton lining with printed blue stripes.

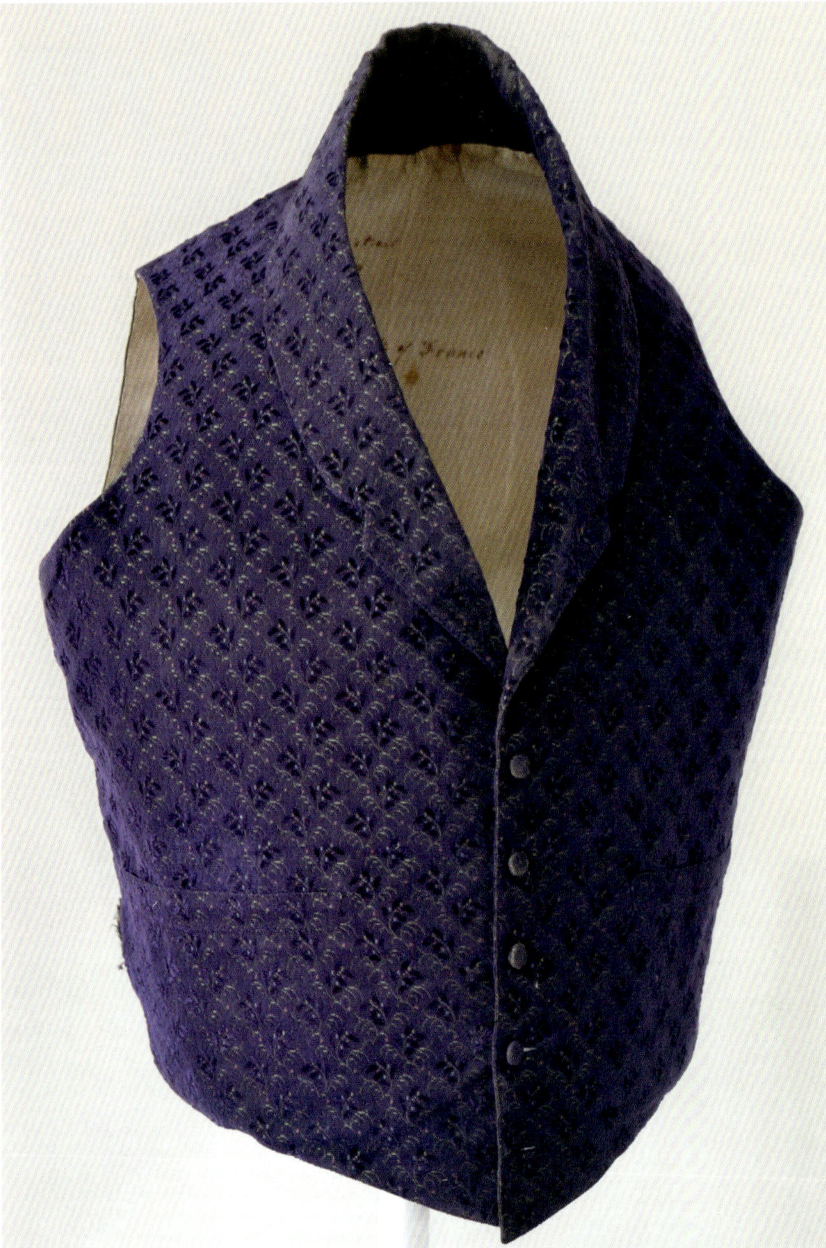

A waistcoat in deep purple silk velvet, 1825-1835. HC.W-2.85-4

The design has leaves in cut velvet on a ground of uncut velvet, with an additional pattern in polychrome silk threads. One of the five self-covered buttons is missing, and the roll collar has a shallow step. The lining is cream cotton and the back is dark brown cotton with a pair of black silk ribbon ties, broken on one side, to adjust the waist, as well as a pair of straps in the same cotton with a buttonhole in the end of one, and three buttons on the other. The lining has a written message in the back which says: "This waistcoat given me by Emily 1829 chosen at Paris by Mademoiselle of France".

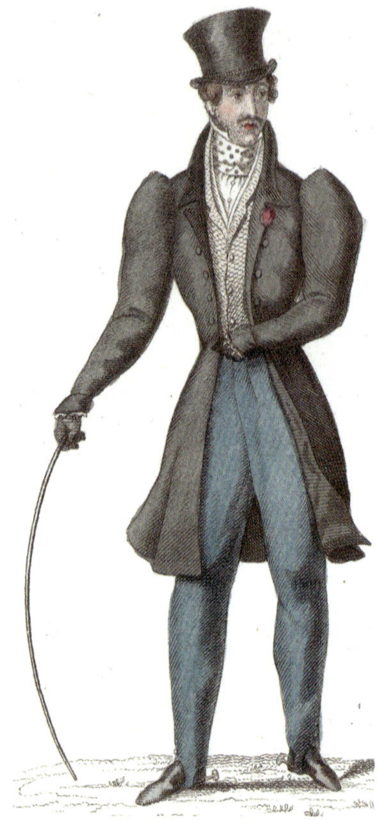

Fashion plate, May 1827.

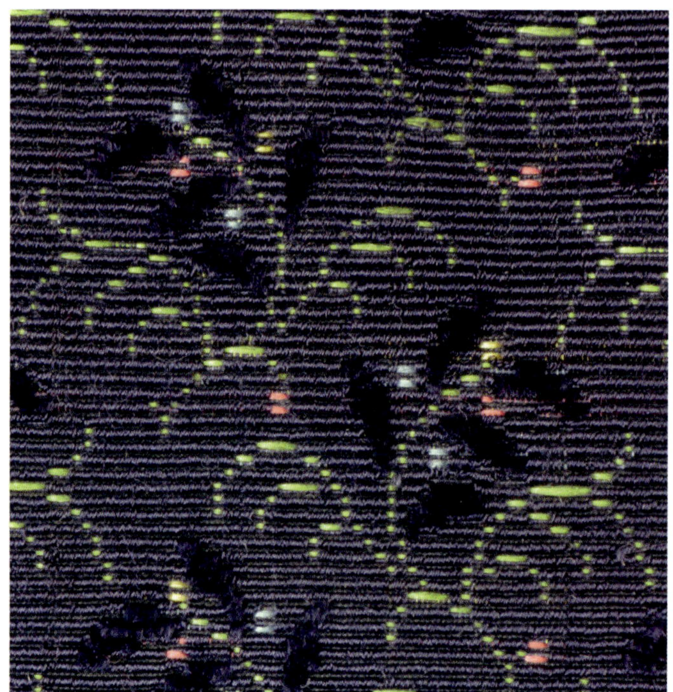

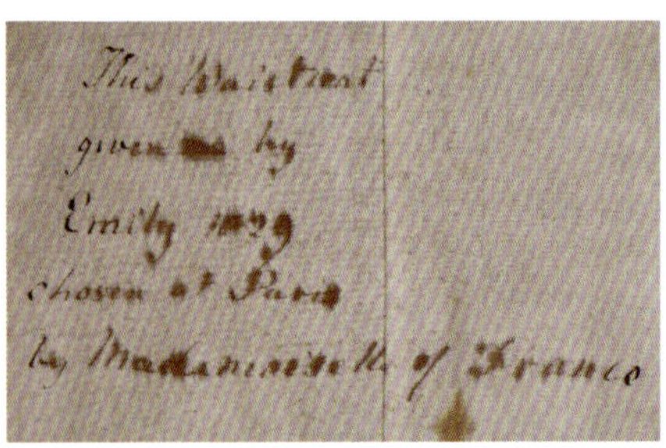

The writing on the back lining.

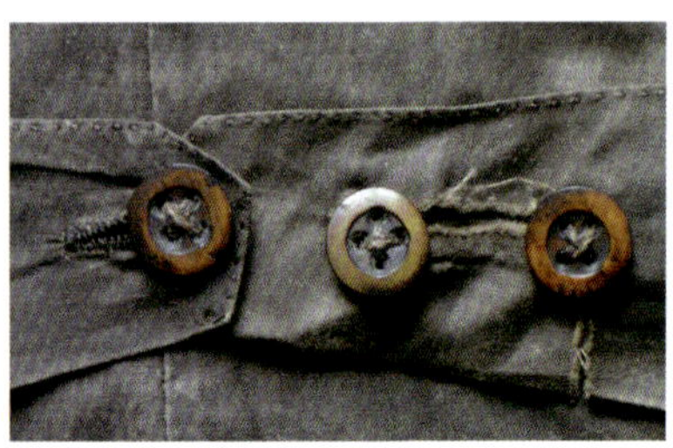

The three buttons on the back waist straps, which are now torn.

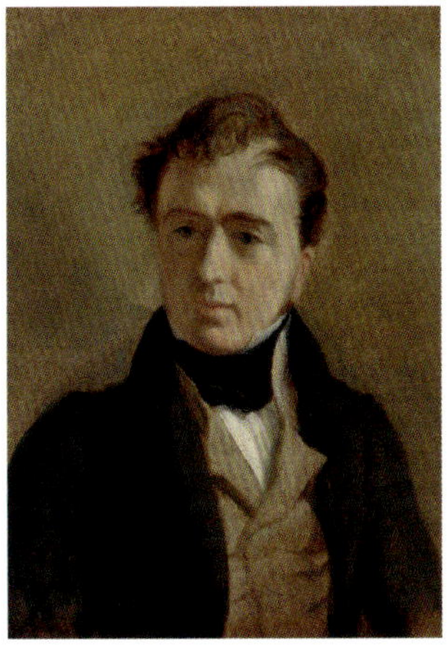

Francis Thornhill Baring, 1st Baron Northbrook by Sir George Hayter, *c.*1833. © National Portrait Gallery, London. Baring (1796-1866) was a member of the banking family; he was M.P. for Portsmouth and held several government offices.

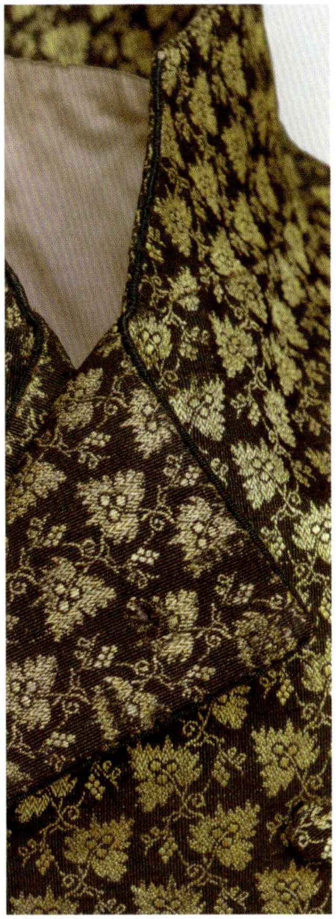

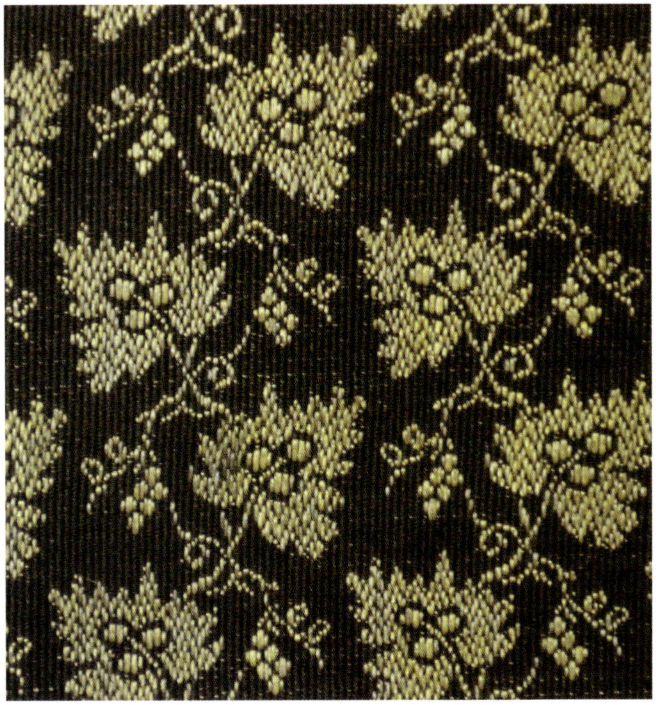

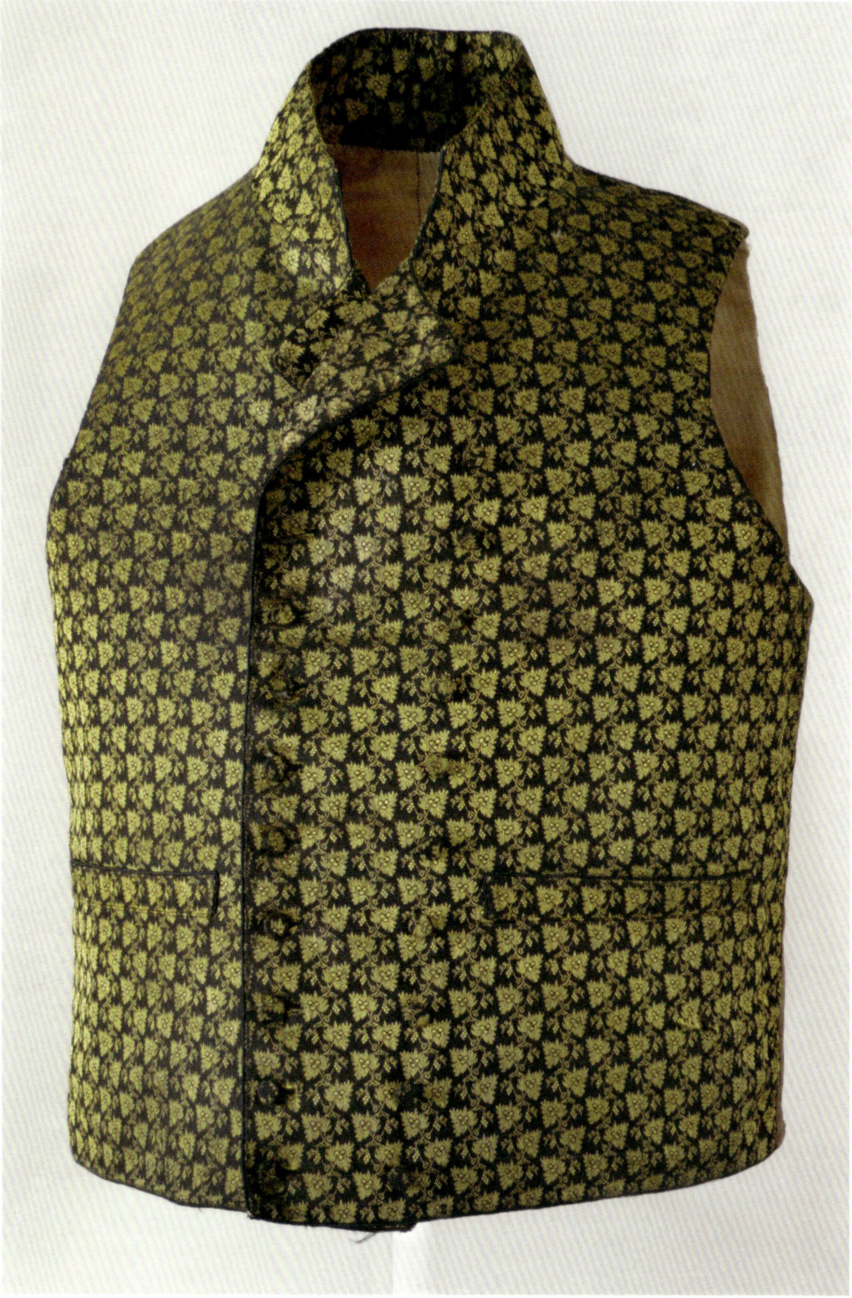

A waistcoat in wool and silk, 1825-1835. HC.W-1.07

The fabric ground is black wool grosgrain with a woven pattern of leaves and stems in yellow silk, and the waistcoat has been cut sideways across the width of the fabric. It is double-breasted with ten pairs of self-covered buttons, and buttonholes on the front edge of each forepart, so it could be buttoned either way; the buttonholes have been mostly unpicked for some reason. It is lined with cream cotton, and the back is in brown linen with a section of a darker brown glazed cotton let in to the centre back, to increase the size. There are two pairs of black cotton tape ties on the back, to adjust the waist. The front edges of the stand collar, the foreparts and the welted pockets are edged with black piping.

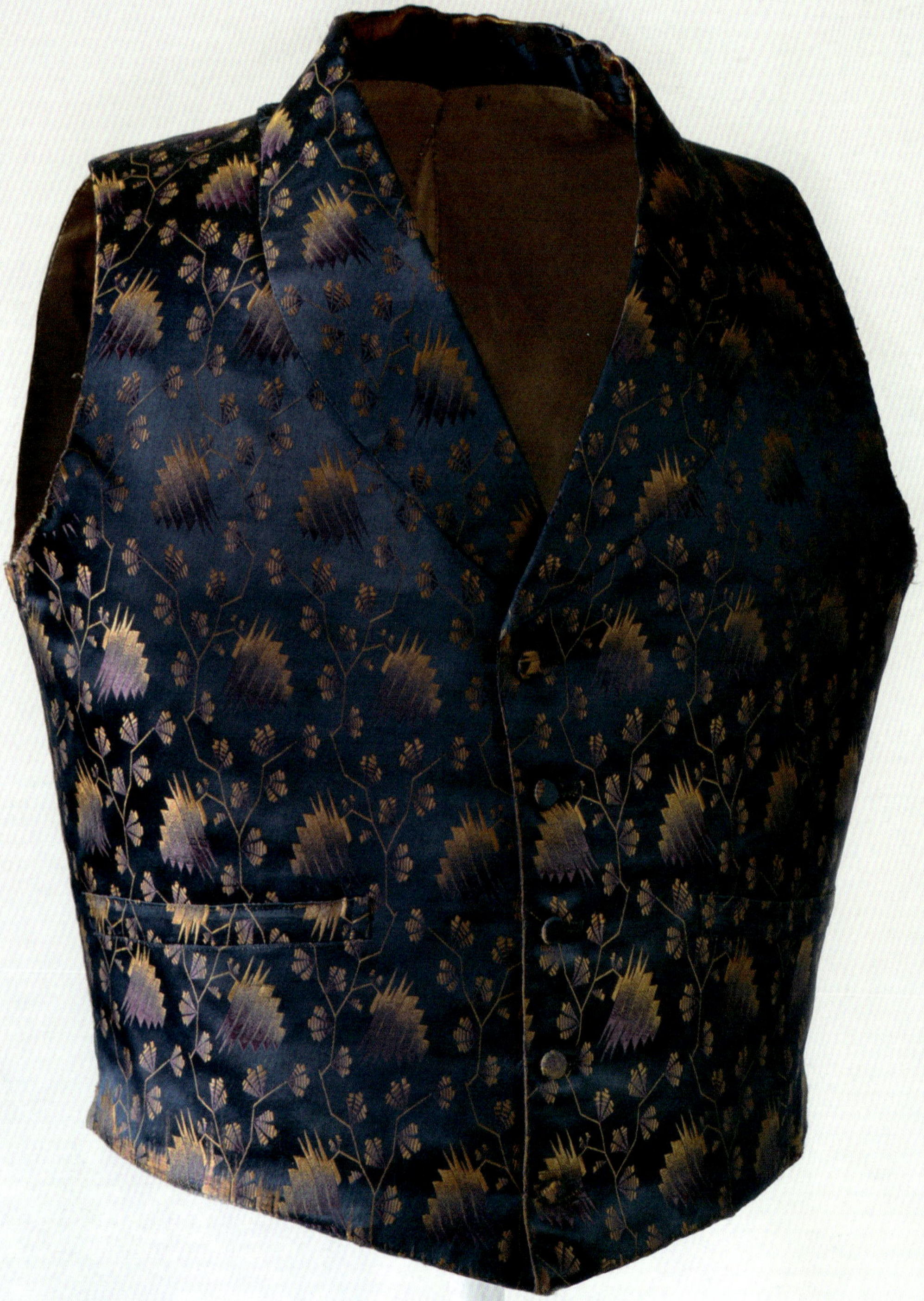

A waistcoat in patterned black silk satin, 1829-1835. HC.W-0.44

The design is of stylised flowers and leaves in brown and purple. This is similar in style to patterns in a sample book of 1829, from a French company, Monterrad et Fils. The waistcoat has a roll collar and five small flat covered buttons; there are two welted pockets. The lining is light brown cotton twill, and the back is in brown silesia, with two pairs of black silk ribbon ties to adjust the waist. A triangular piece of black wool twill has been inserted in the centre back to let out the waistcoat, with a fawn cotton twill insertion in the lining.

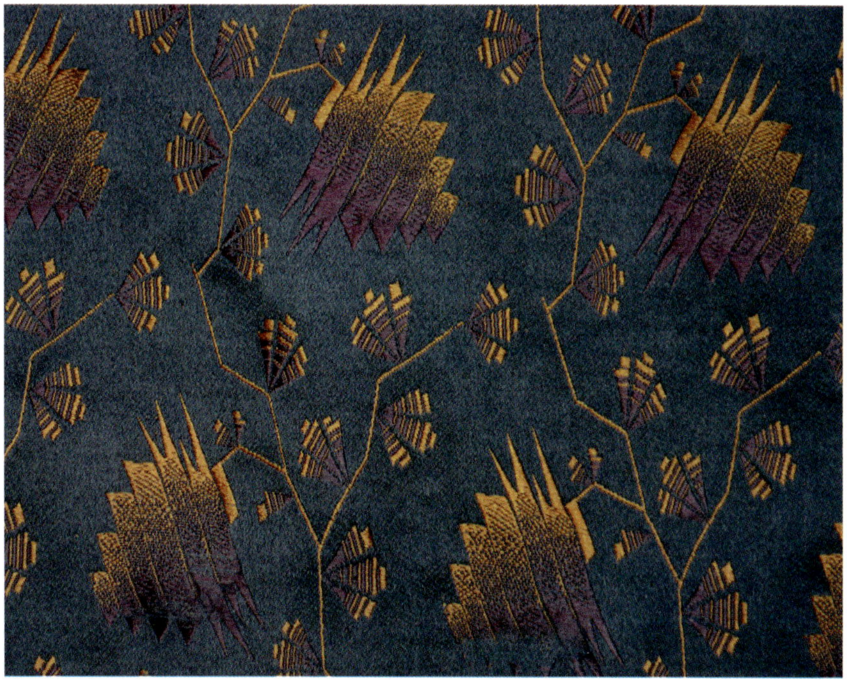

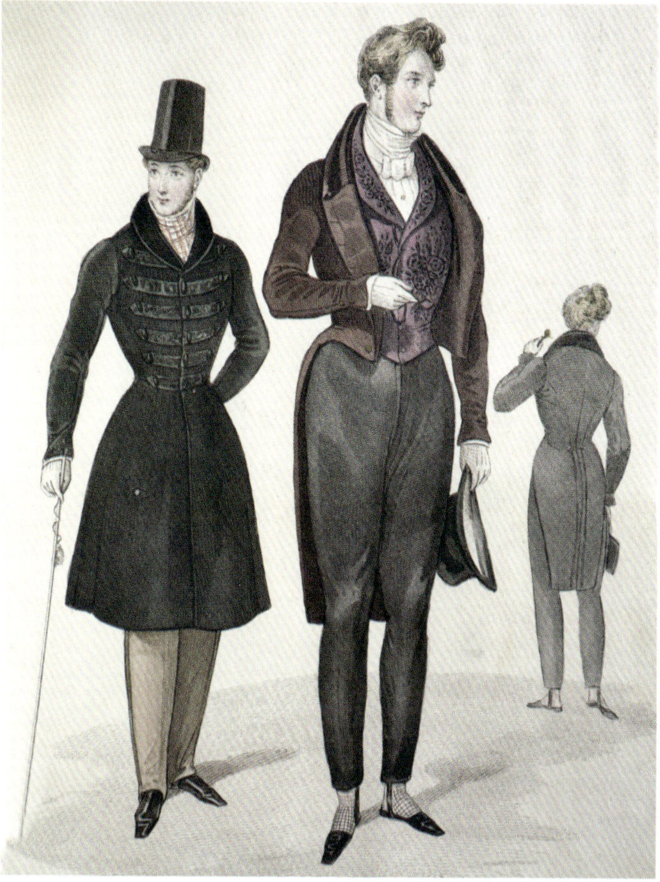

Fashion plate from *Le Follet*, November 1833.

Joseph Monterrad was a prominent merchant in the Lyon silk industry, during the mid-eighteenth century. His son, Sébastien, succeeded him, and by the time his grandson Amédée took over in the early nineteenth century, the company was known as one of the most important silk manufacturers in Lyon.

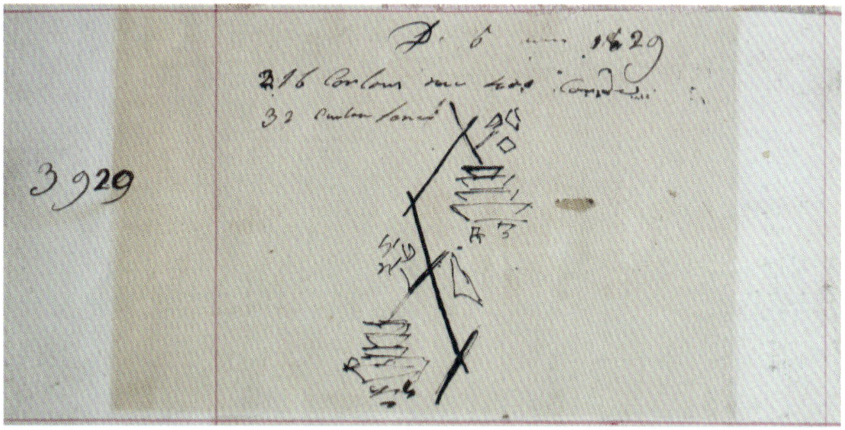

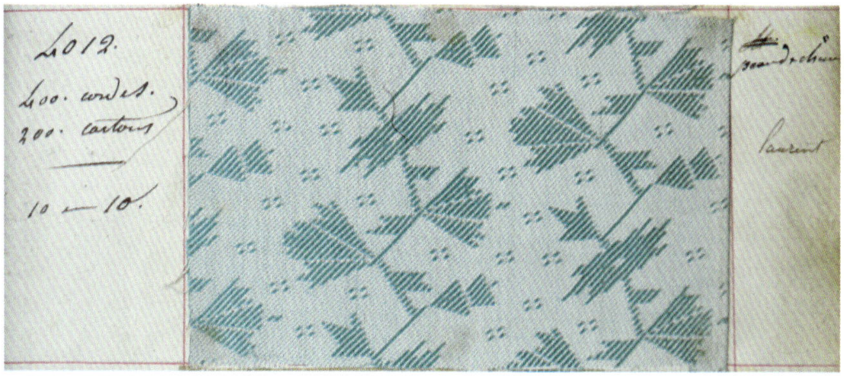

Above and centre: Two patterns from a sample book of Monterrad et Fils, silk merchant-manufacturers of Lyon, France, 1829. The School of Historical Dress.

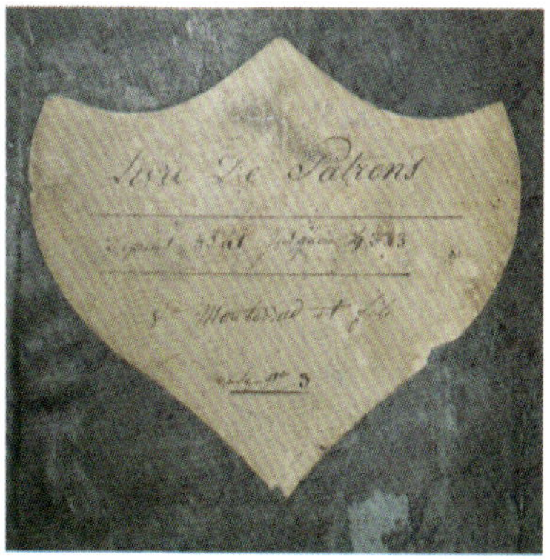

The label on the front cover of the sample book.

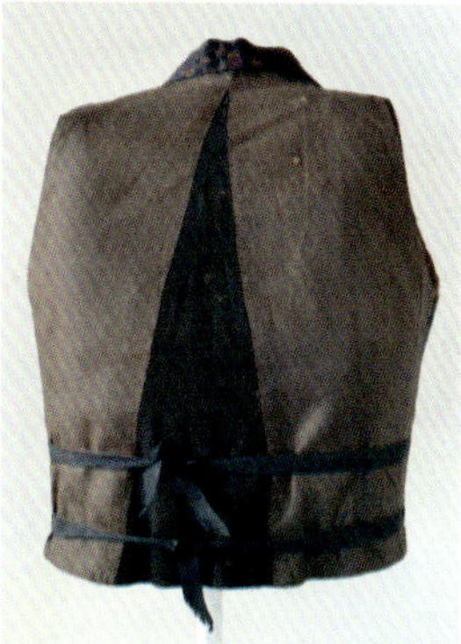

The ties are sewn down for 3″ from each side.

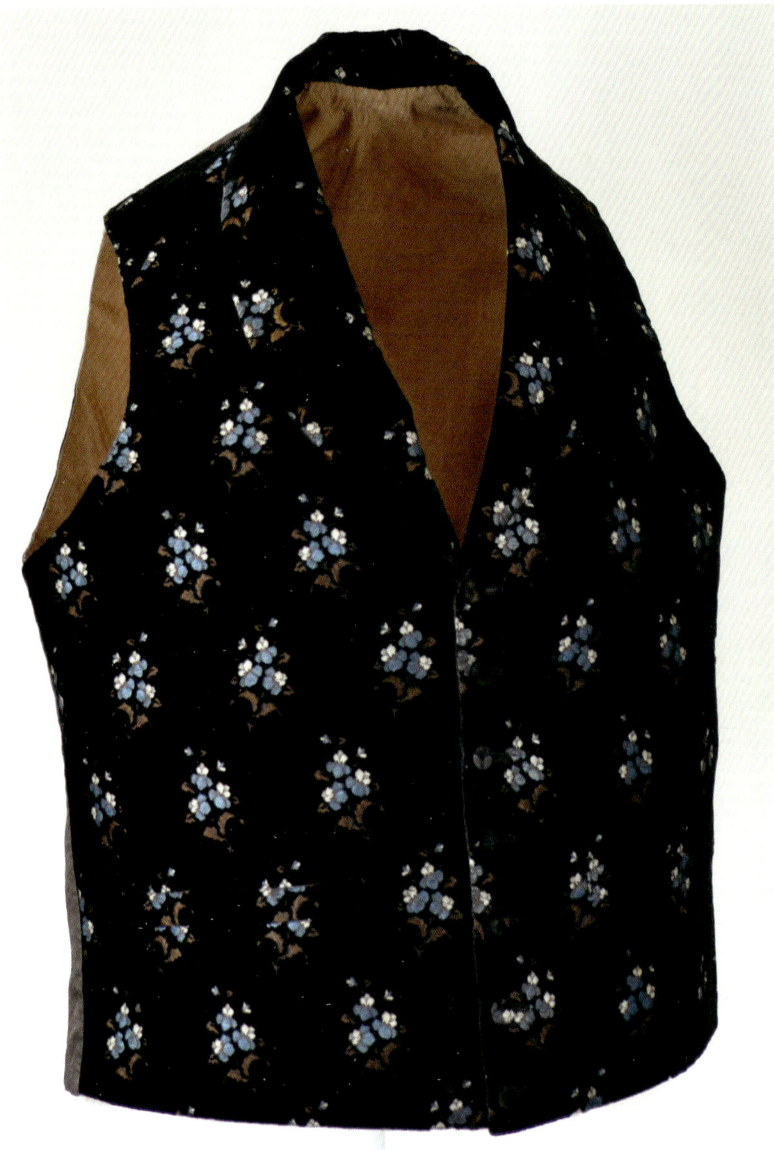

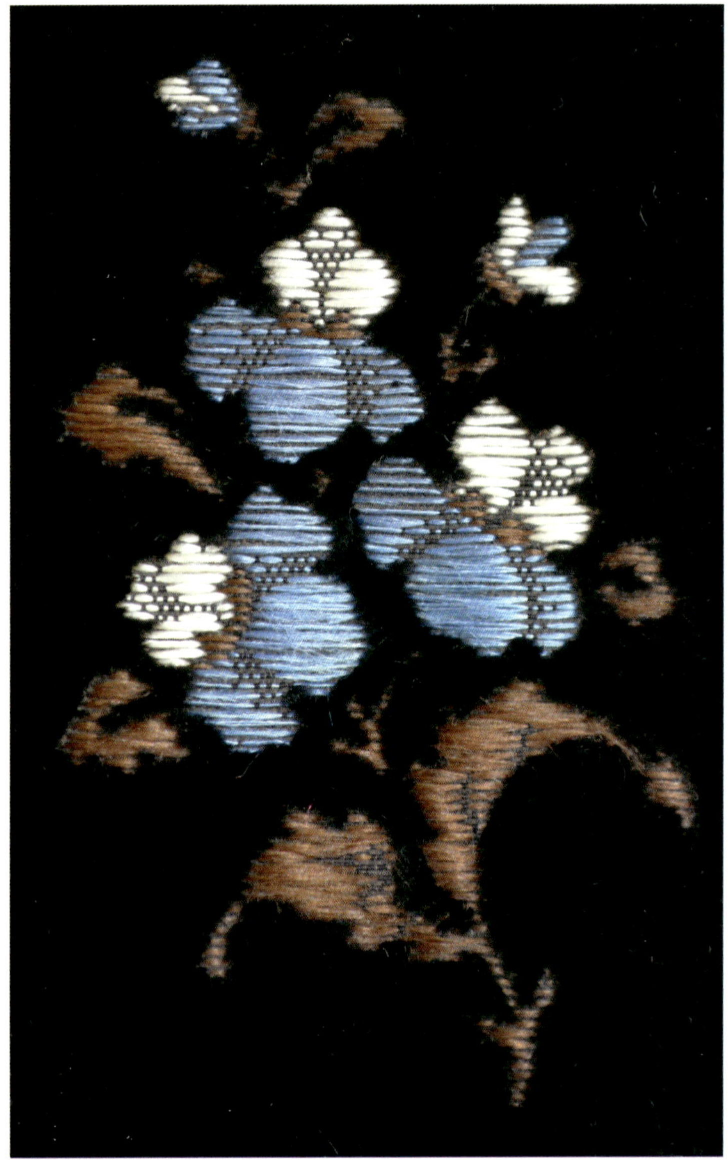

A waistcoat in black silk voided velvet, 1830-1840.
HC.W-7.80

The velvet has a voided pattern of flower sprays woven in blue, brown and white silk. The waistcoat has a roll collar and is lined in light brown cotton twill. The back is in dark brown silesia with two pairs of black silk ribbon ties, now broken, and the forepart hems are faced with the dark brown silesia. There are seven self-covered buttons and two welted pockets.

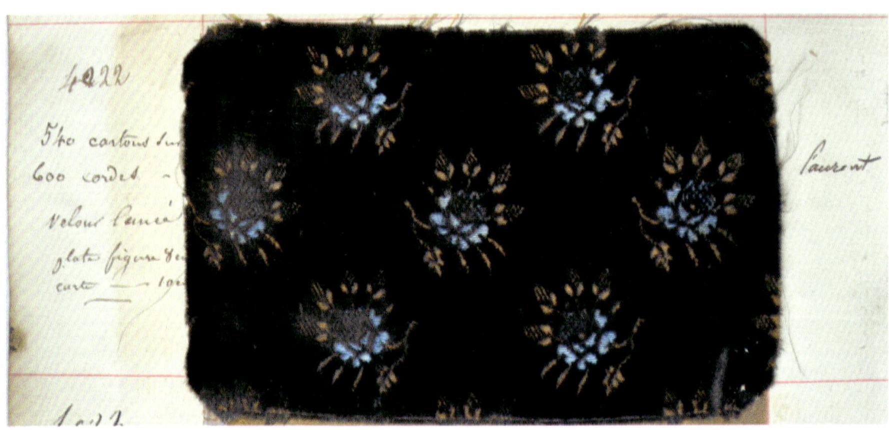

Right: Pattern from a sample book of Monterrad et Fils, silk merchant-manufacturers of Lyon, France, 1829. The School of Historical Dress.

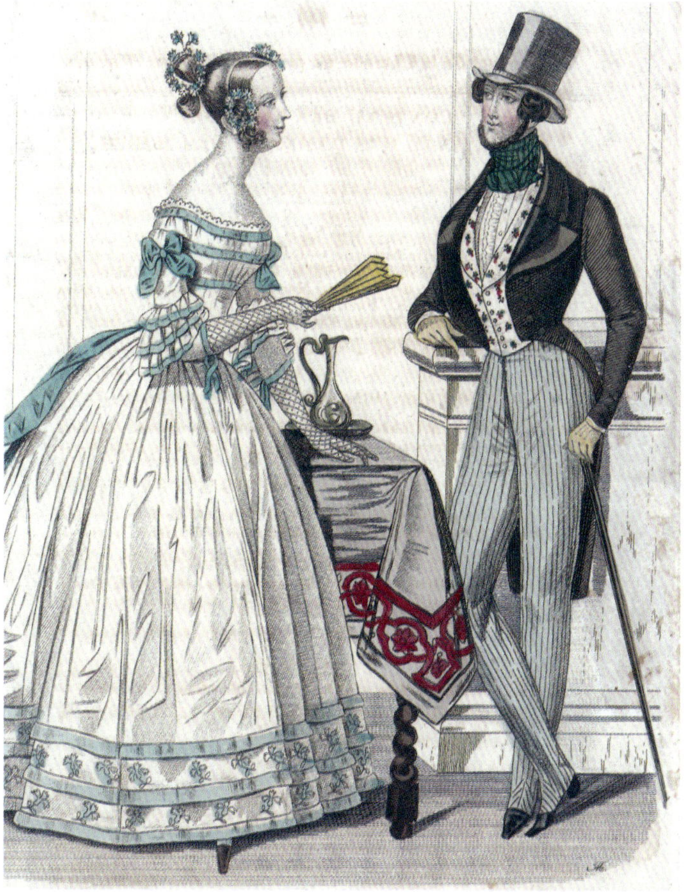

Fashion plate from *Modes de Paris*, 1836.

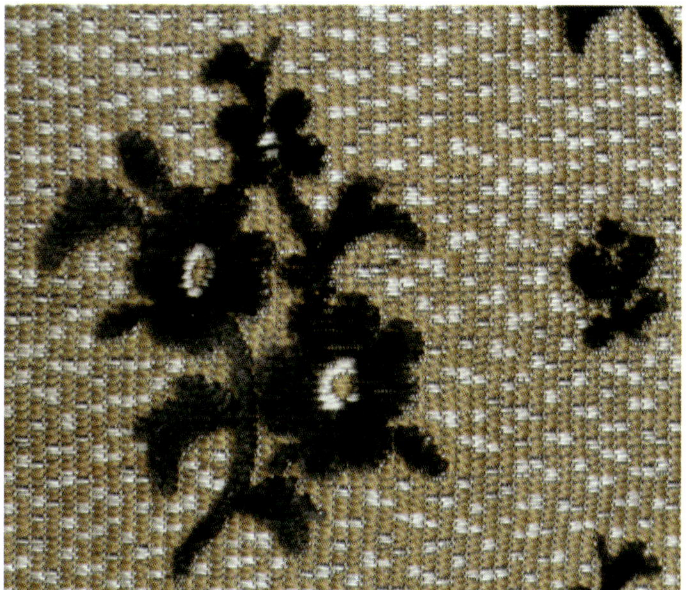

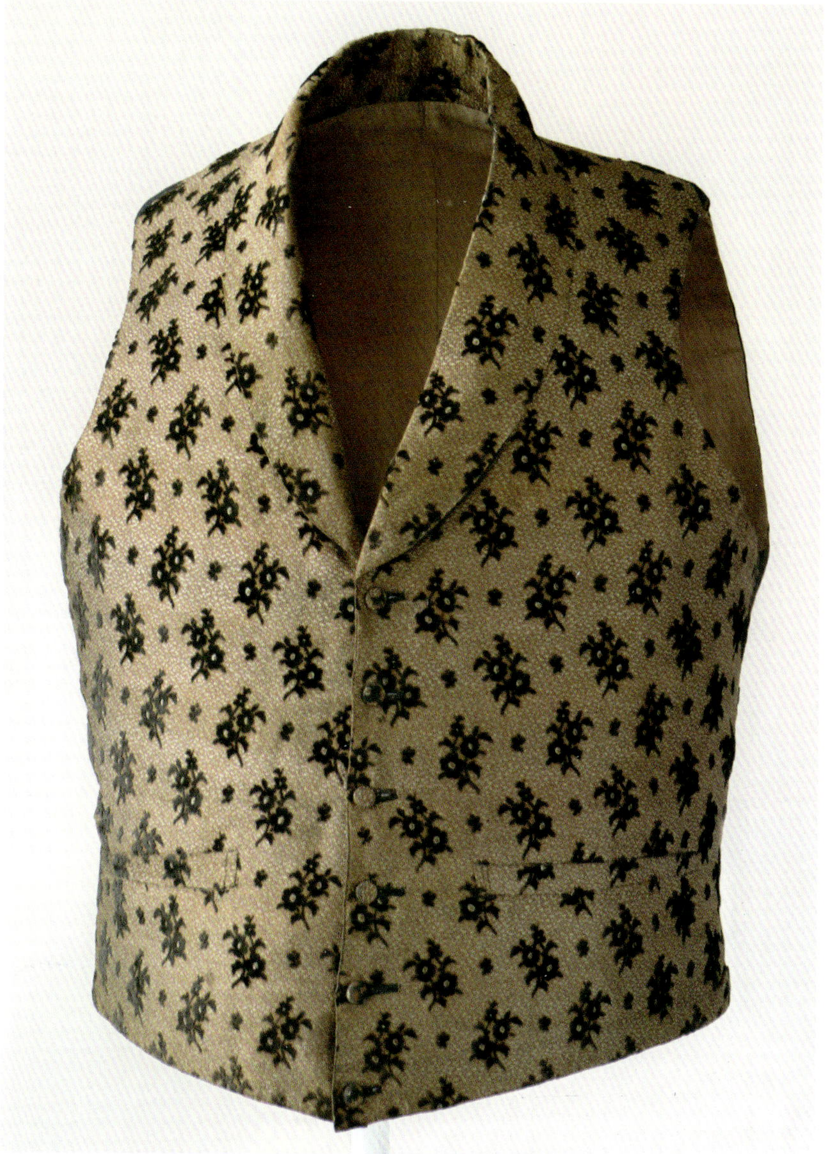

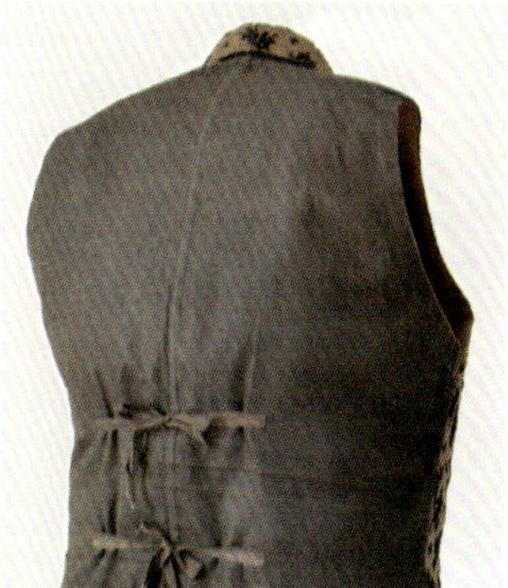

A waistcoat in cinnamon vertically ribbed silk, 1830-1840. HC.W-11.94-1

The pattern of random spots in cream silk gives a speckled effect, and the flower sprays are in dark brown silk velvet. The waistcoat has a roll collar, six self-covered buttons and two welted pockets. It is lined in light brown cotton twill, and the back is in brown cotton twill with two pairs of brown cotton tape ties to adjust the waist. The under collar is in black silk twill and there are small triangles of this let in to the shoulder seams at the top of the armholes, to economise on the patterned silk.

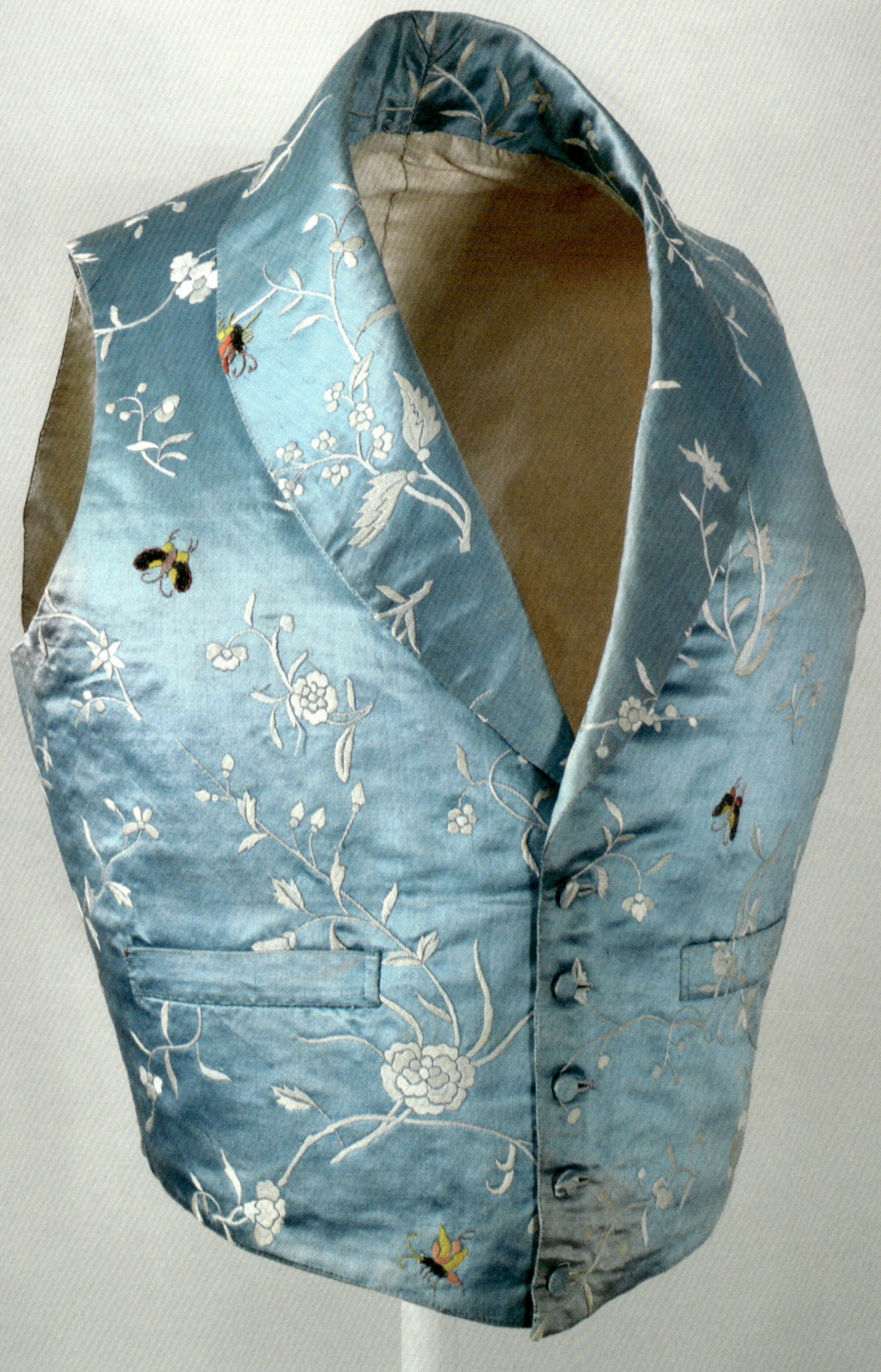

A waistcoat in pale blue silk satin, 1830-1835.
HC.W-1.01

The silk thread embroidery is probably Chinese and shows trailing plants in ivory, and butterflies in colours; this was not done to shape, the waistcoat was cut from a piece of embroidered fabric. It has a roll collar, five covered buttons and two welted pockets. The lining is ivory glazed cotton and the back is in fawn silk twill with a waist adjustment of tabs, with three pairs of hand-worked eyelets and a fawn silk ribbon lacing. The back has a centre seam and the back of the silk twill has been used for the panel on the right, which looks a slightly different shade. There is a loop made of the silk twill inside the base of the right forepart, to fasten on to the top trouser button and secure the waistcoat from riding up.

The waistcoat came with a dress in the same silk with matching embroidery; the colour of the silk here has faded badly in some places.

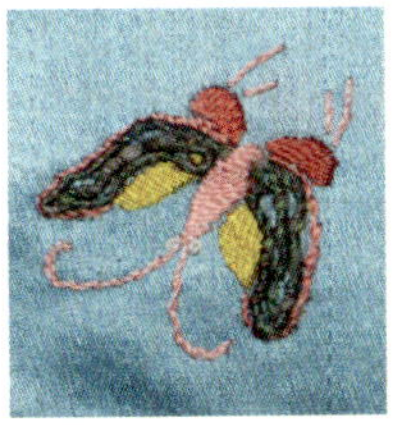
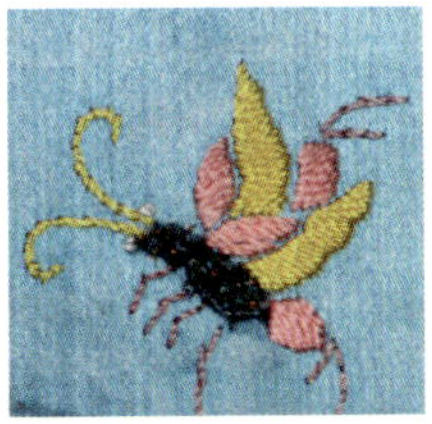
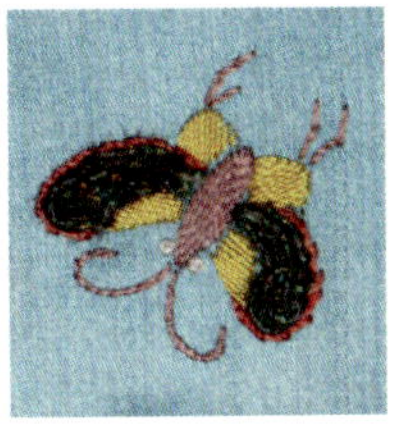
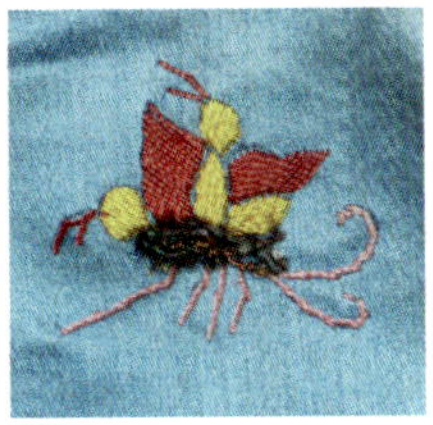
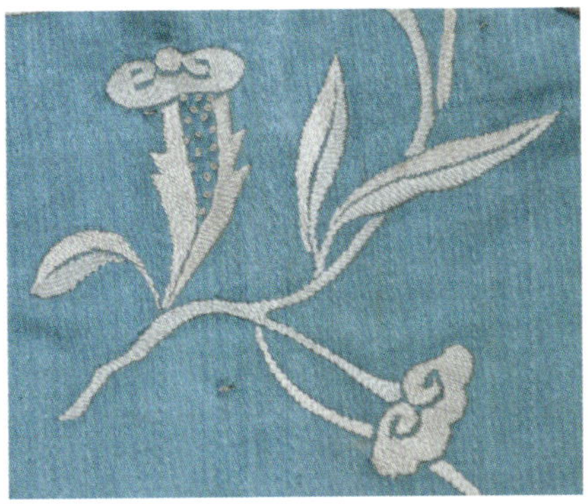
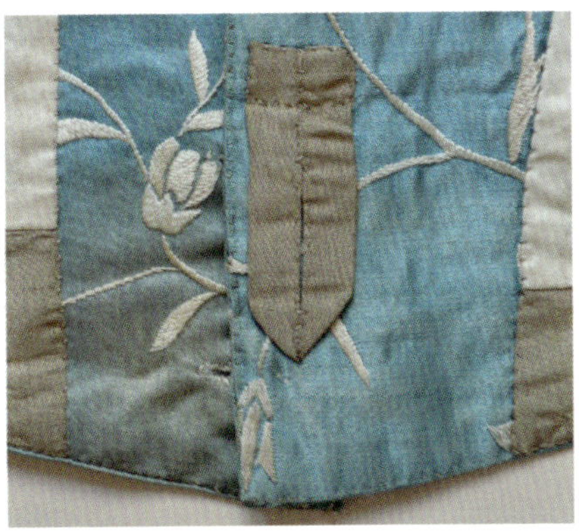

The silk loop inside the base of the right forepart.

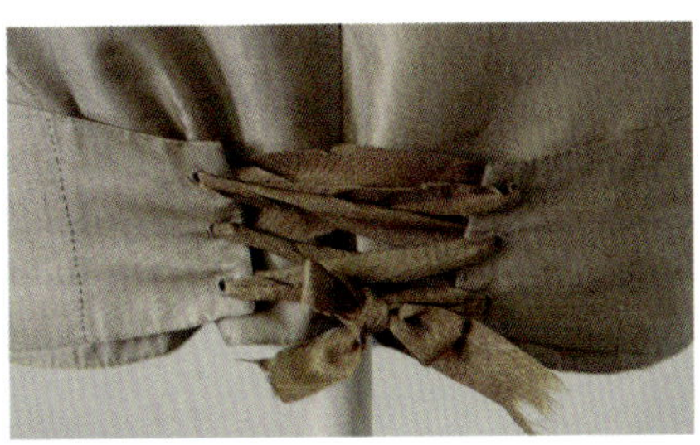

The lacing tabs on the back.

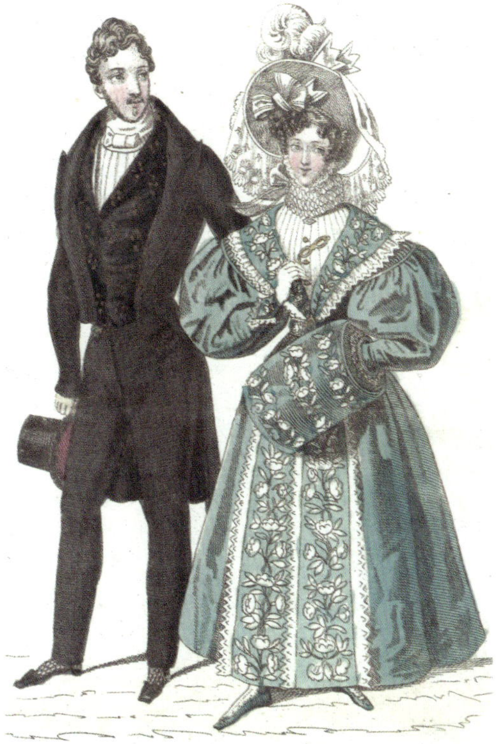

Fashion plate "Moda di Francia", from *Corriere delle Dame*, 1832.

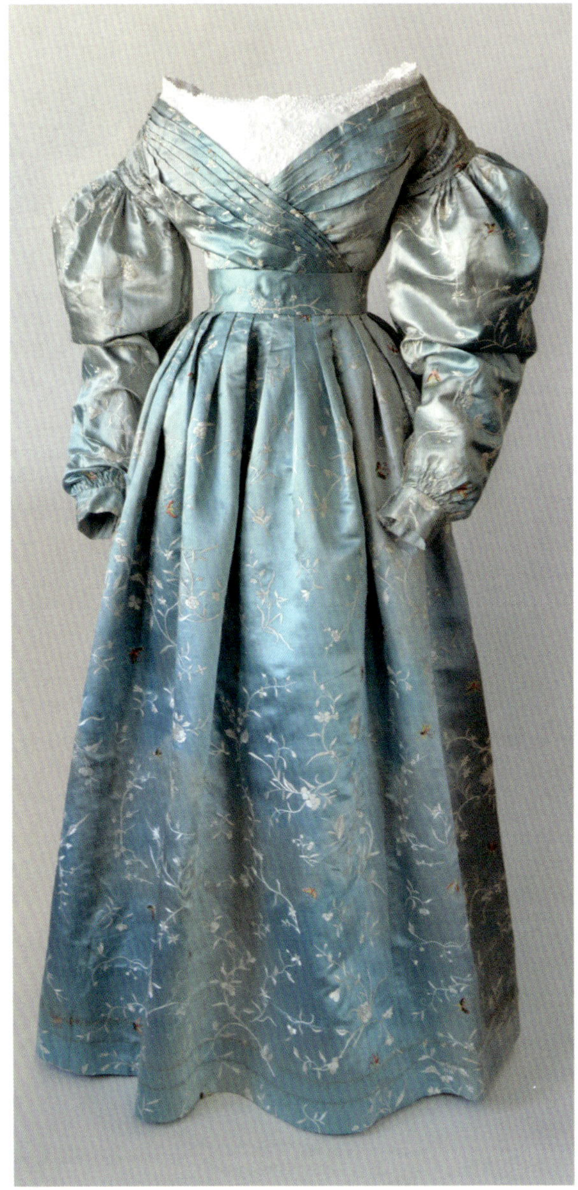

The dress which came with the waistcoat, 1830-1835.
HC.D-1.01

It is in the same pale blue silk satin, and with the same embroidery. Two tucked strips of the fabric cross diagonally across the bodice. The skirt has wide pleats into the waistband, and the pleats at the top of the sleeves are held down by narrow bands; the cuffs are gathered into wristbands. There may have been a separate belt but this is now missing, and the silk is very faded in places. The dress is shown with a white embroidered fine cotton chemisette, or fill-in, at the neck.

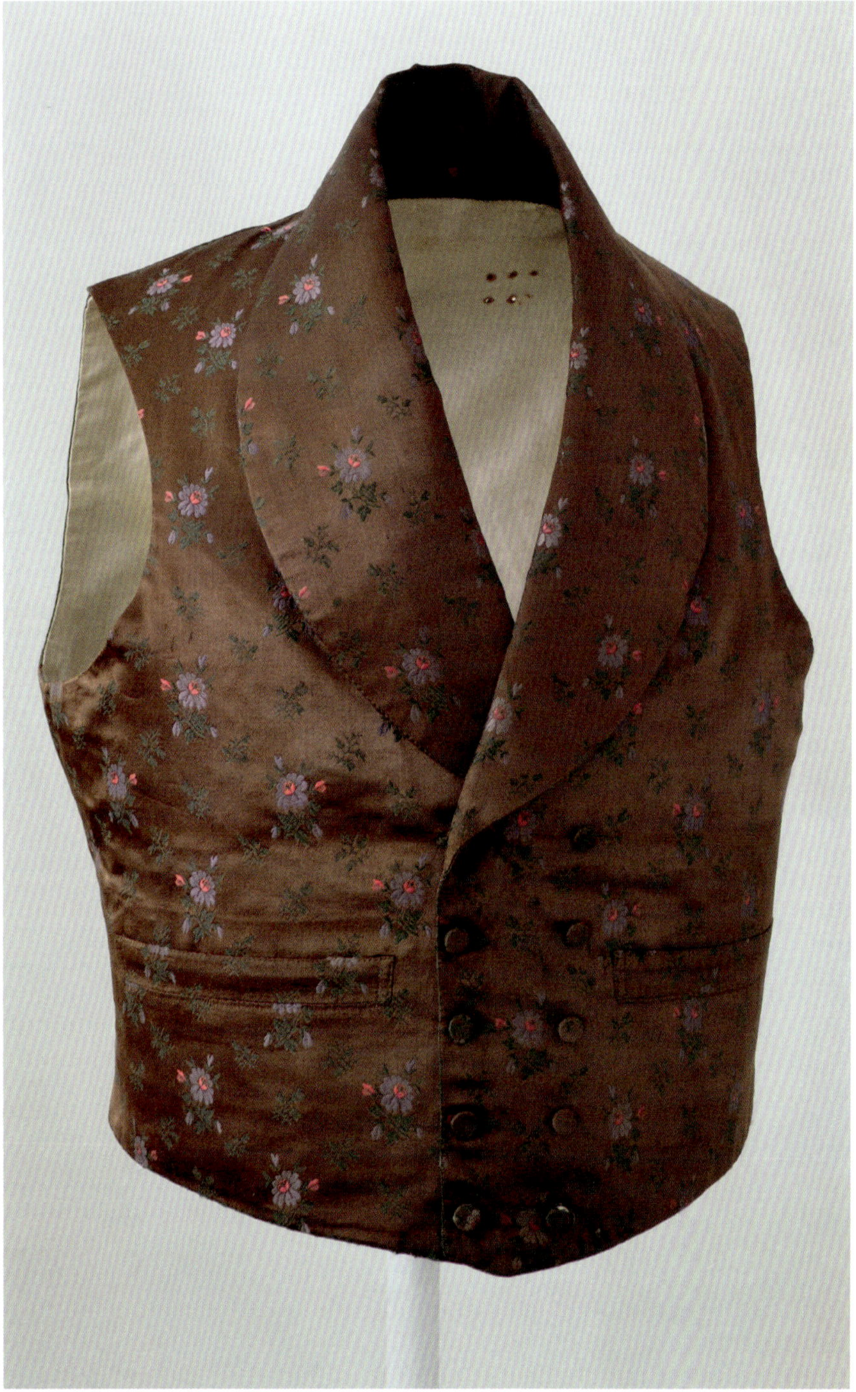

A waistcoat in chestnut silk satin, 1830-1840. HC.W-1.03

The silk has a woven pattern of sprigs with flowers in mauve and pink, and green leaves. The waistcoat is double-breasted with five pairs of self-covered buttons, a roll collar, and welted pockets. The lining is a plain white cotton and the back is dark brown silesia. The back waist adjustment is by two pairs of black cotton tape ties, two of which have broken off short.

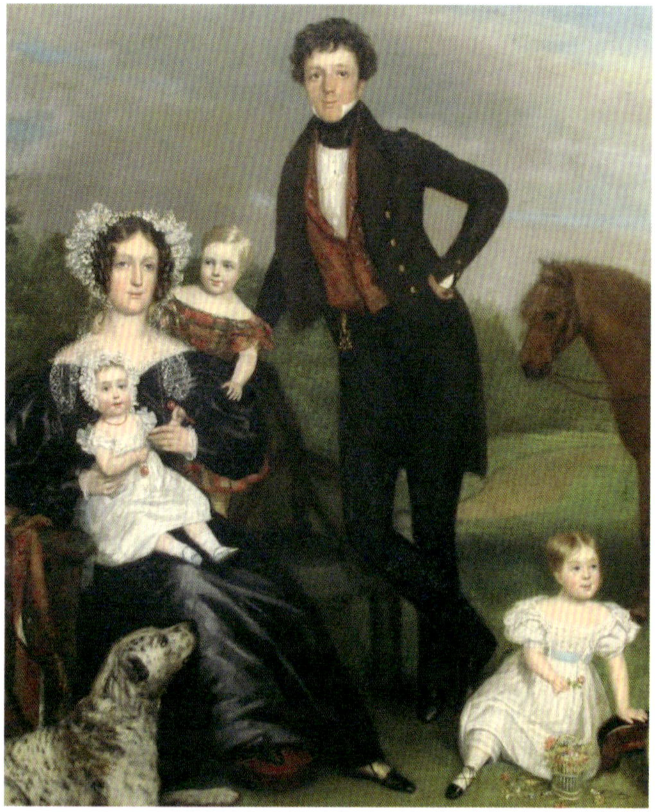

Detail of *The Fenner Family of Hull* by Archibald Archer, 1834. Private Collection.

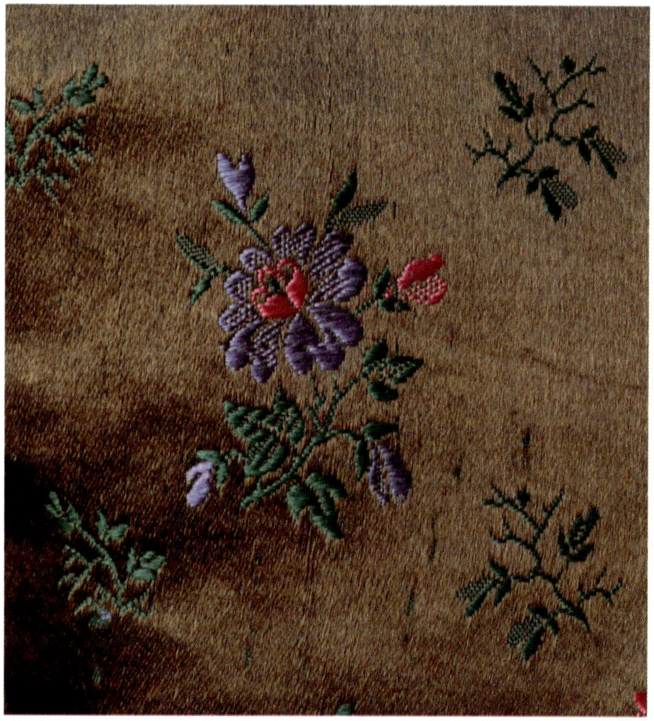

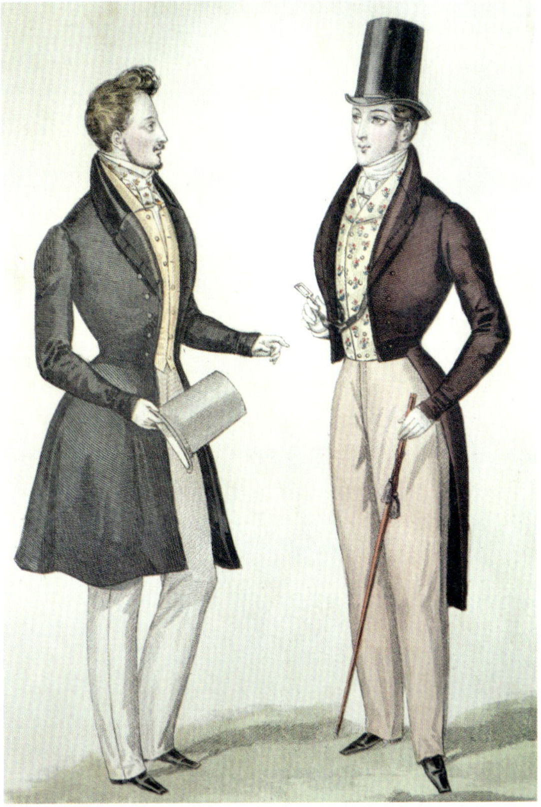

Fashion plate from *Le Follet*, August 1833.

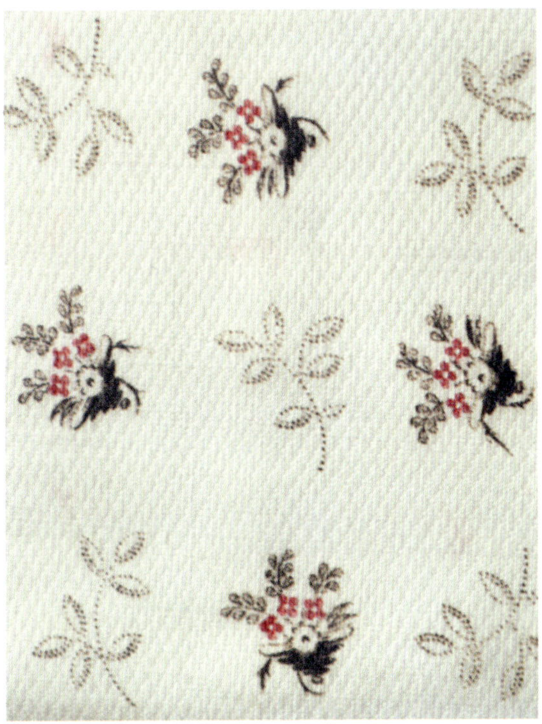

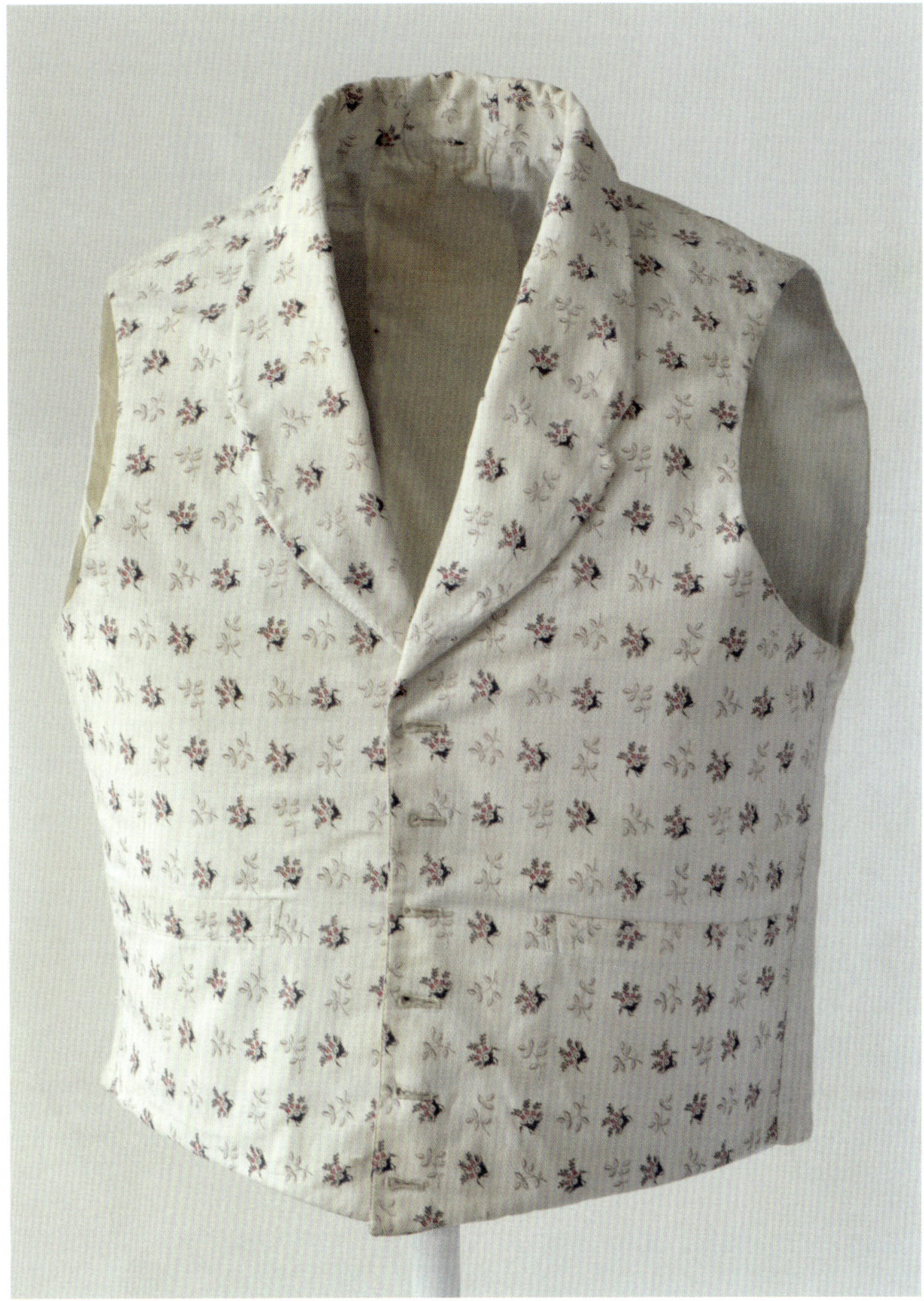

A waistcoat in white cotton marcella, 1830-1840. HC.W-3.16-1

The cotton has a printed pattern of sprigs and leaf sprays in dark brown and crimson. The roll collar has a shallow step and there are two welted pockets; there are six hand-worked eyelet holes for removable buttons, which are missing. The lining and back are in plain white cotton, with two pairs of white cotton tape ties to adjust the waist. The size has been increased by 1″-wide insertions of cotton in the side seams, and a 3″-wide insertion of cotton, unlined, in the centre back, with an extra piece of the printed cotton put in to the back of the collar.

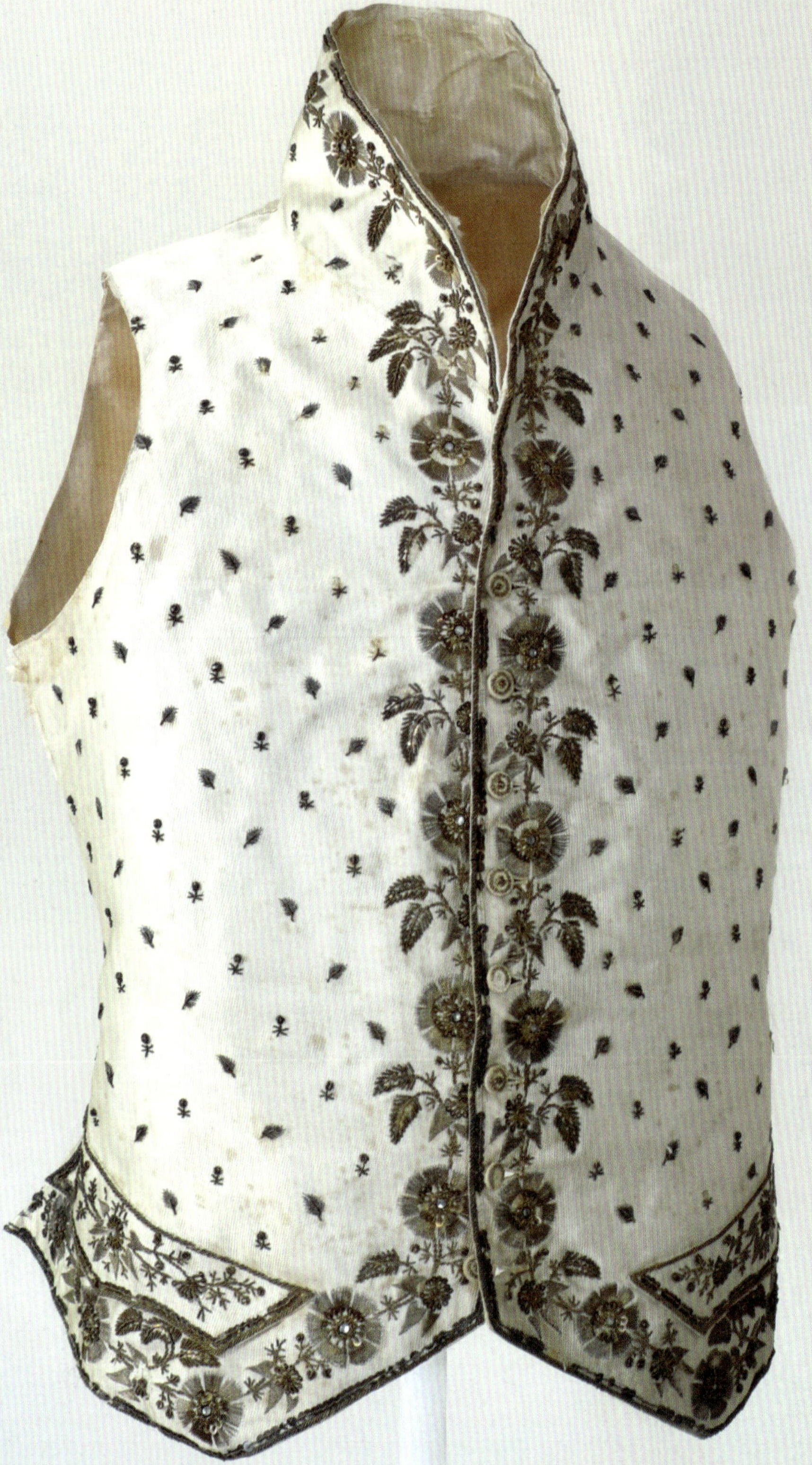

A waistcoat in white silk, 1825-1840.
HC.W-10.11-1

This is a court dress waistcoat in the fossilised style of the late eighteenth century, but with the high stand collar of the early nineteenth century. The silk has a vertical rib weave, and there is embroidery in silver-gilt filé, with purl (page 211) and spangles, on the borders of the foreparts and most of the collar, which has a plain section in the back. The embroidery is also on the pocket flaps, which are decorative only; there are no pockets. The foreparts are scattered with small motifs in silver filé and purl. The waistcoat is lined in plain white cotton and the facings and inside collar are in cream silk with a diagonal rib. The back is in the same silk, with two pairs of ivory silk ribbon ties to adjust the waist. There are eight self-covered buttons with silver gilt purl embroidery. The initials N W are written in ink on the right shoulder of the lining.

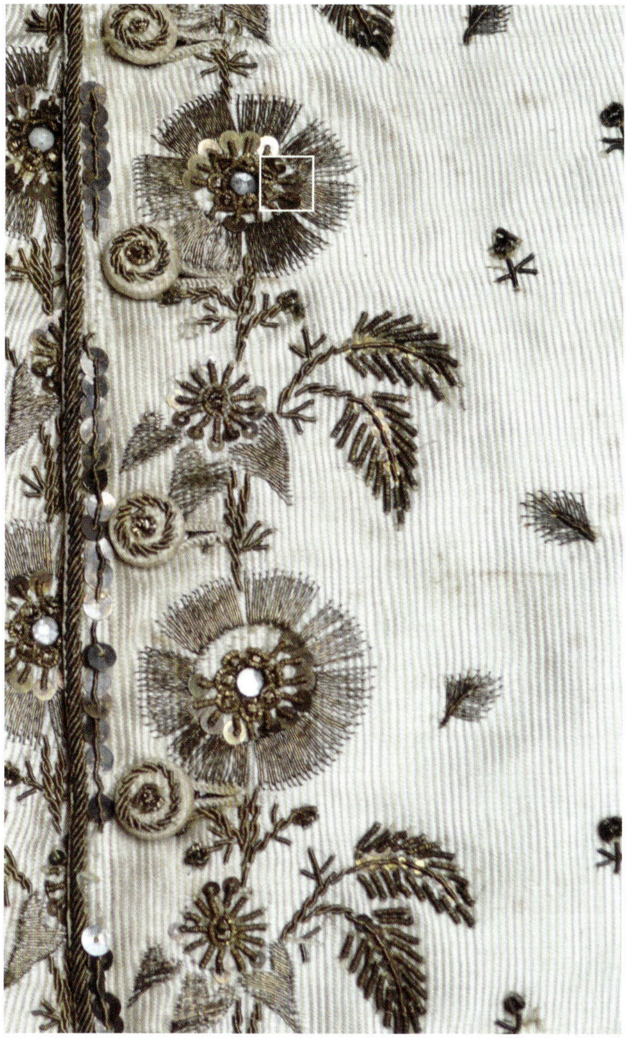

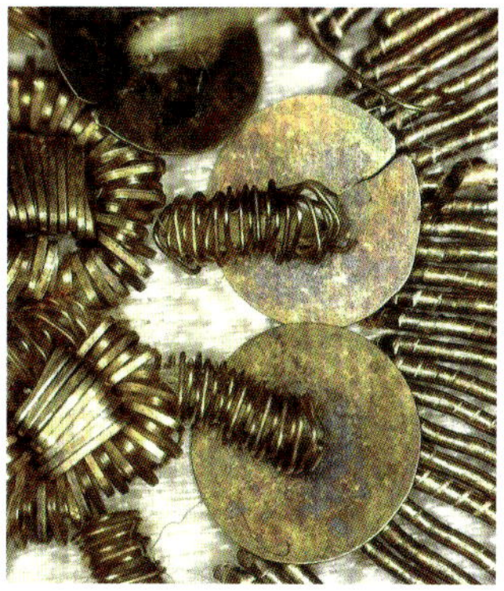

Detail, outlined left, of the silver-gilt filé, purl and spangles in the embroidery.

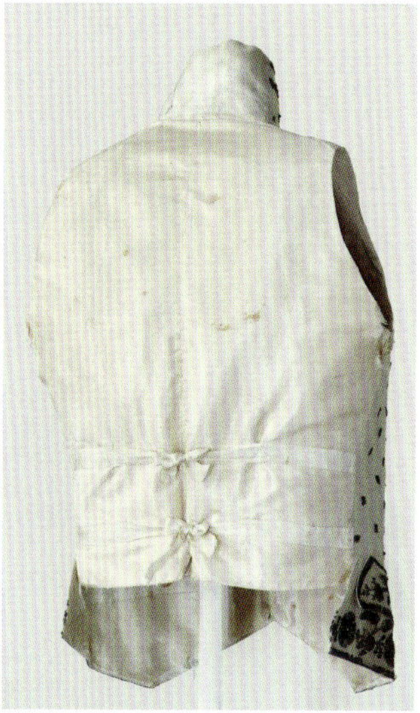

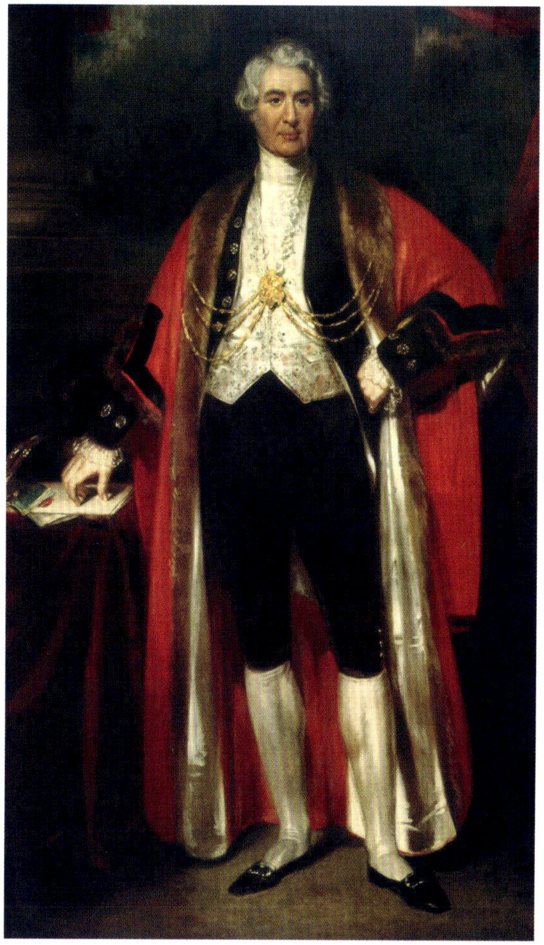

Sir George Carroll by John Wood, 1838, Guildhall Art Gallery, City of London. He is in his robes as a Sherriff of the City of London.

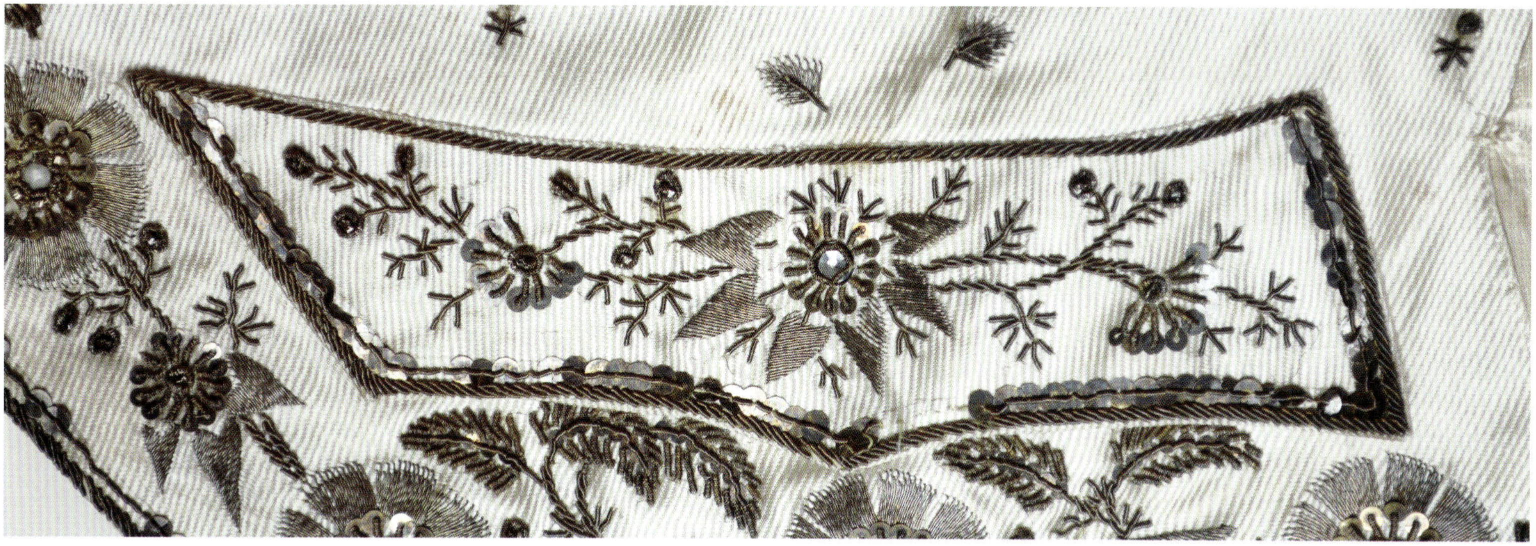

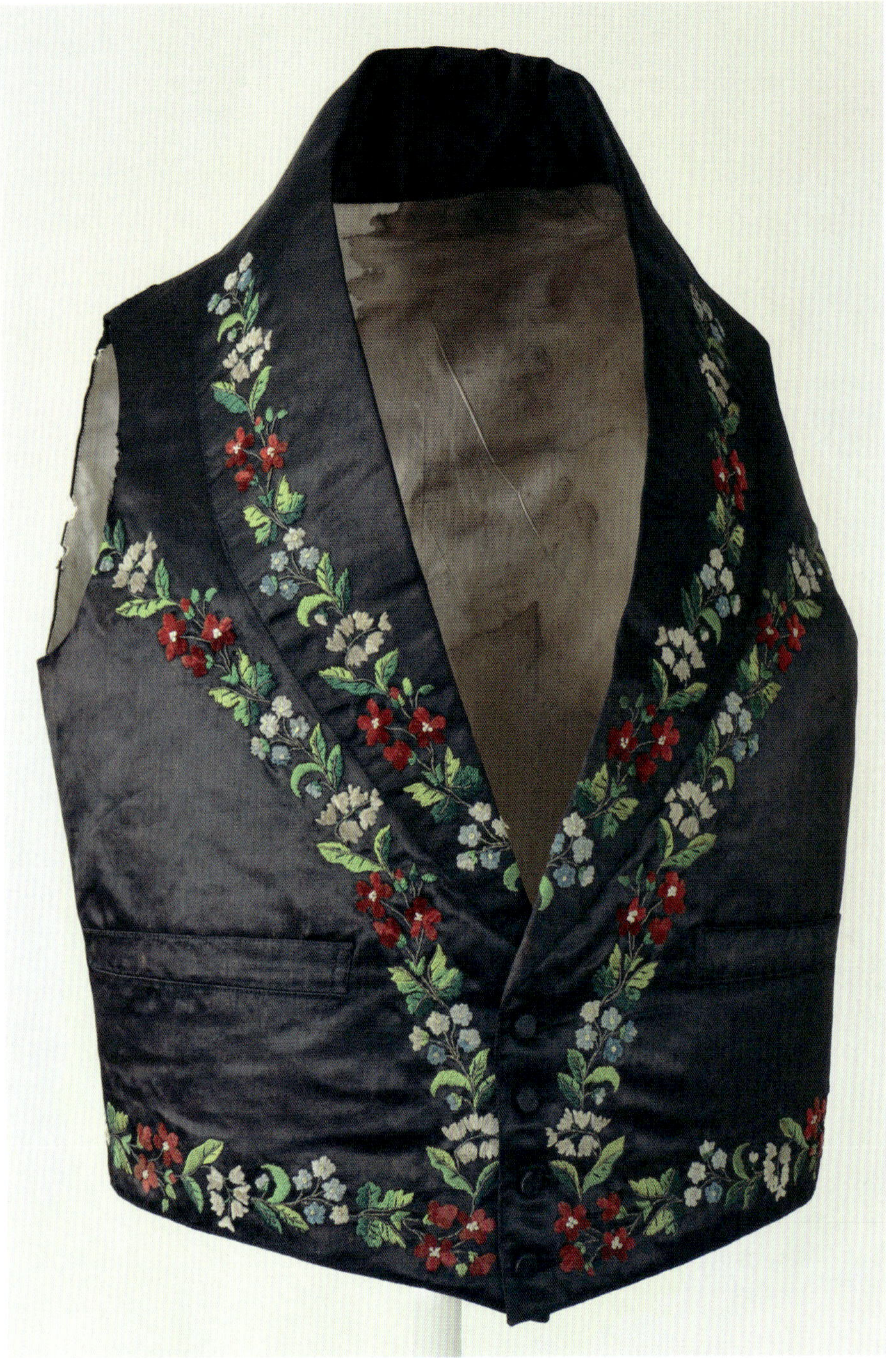

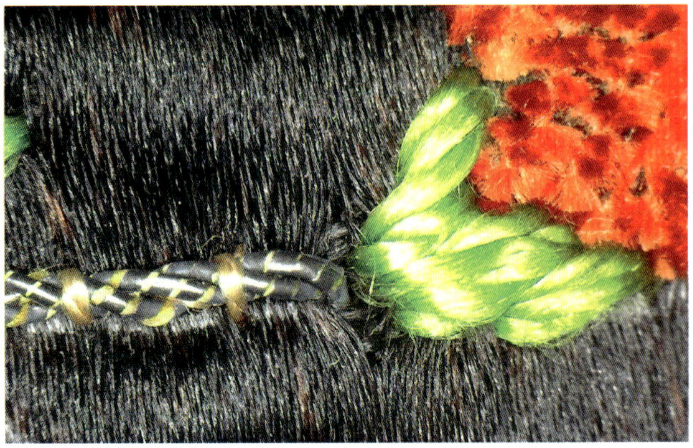

Detail of the silver filé, silk threads and chenille, outlined below.

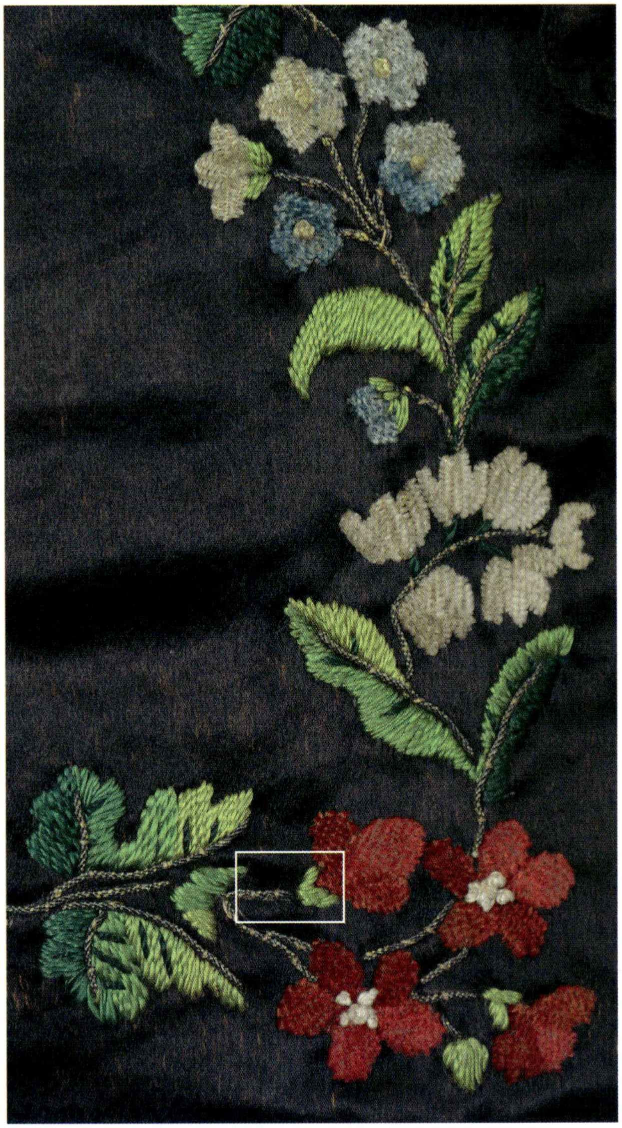

A waistcoat in black silk satin, 1830-1840. HC.W-4.93-1

The embroidery of flowers and leaves is in polychrome silk and chenille threads with couched twisted silver filé threads forming the stems; this decorates the forepart hems and roll collar, and forms curved lines over the chest. The waistcoat is lined with ivory cotton which is badly stained, and the back is dark brown silesia; the two pairs of back waist adjusting tapes have been cut off. There are four small self-covered buttons, and the pocket welts have no decoration.

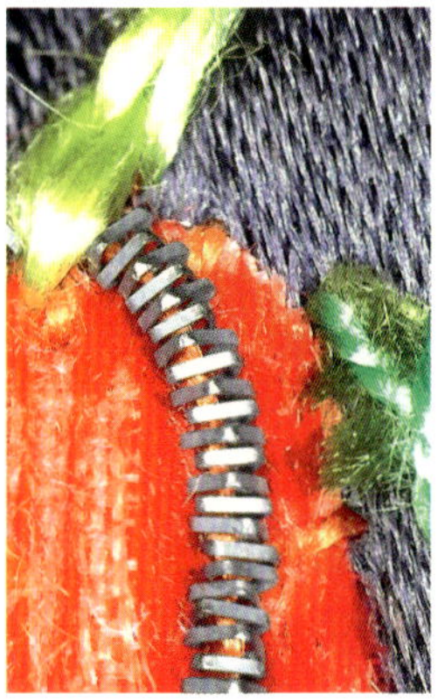

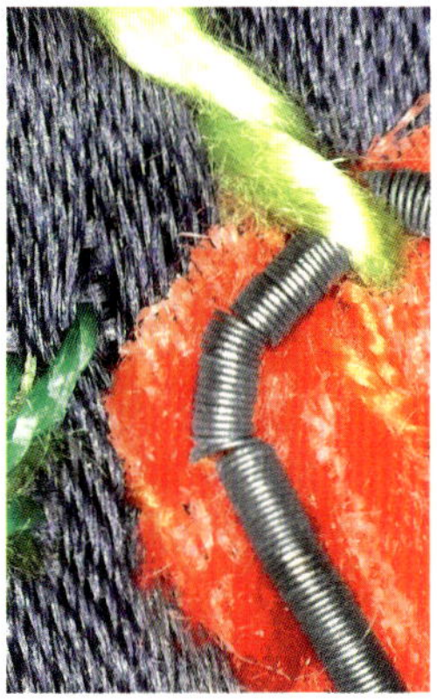

Details of the silver check and purl, outlined below.

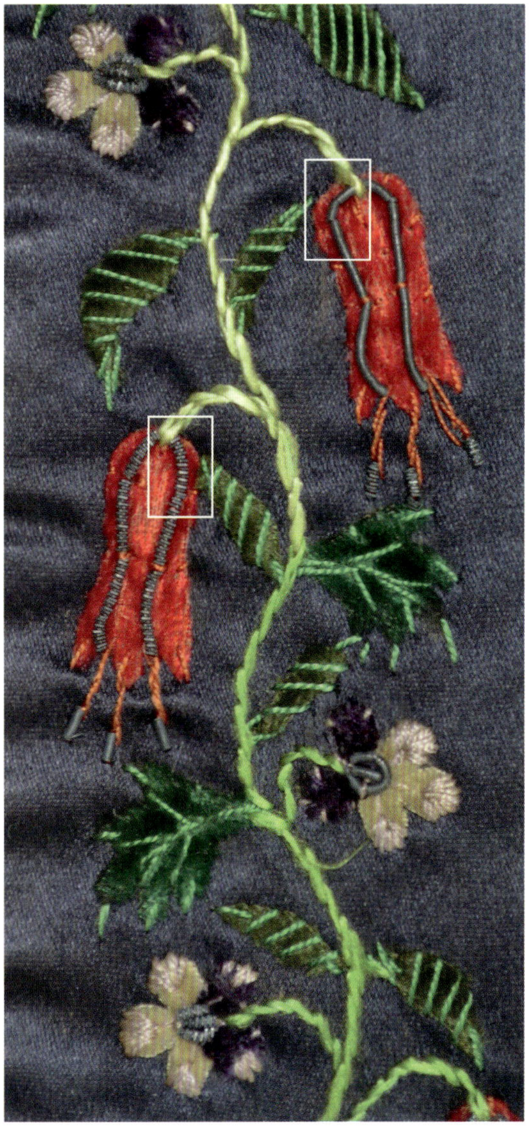

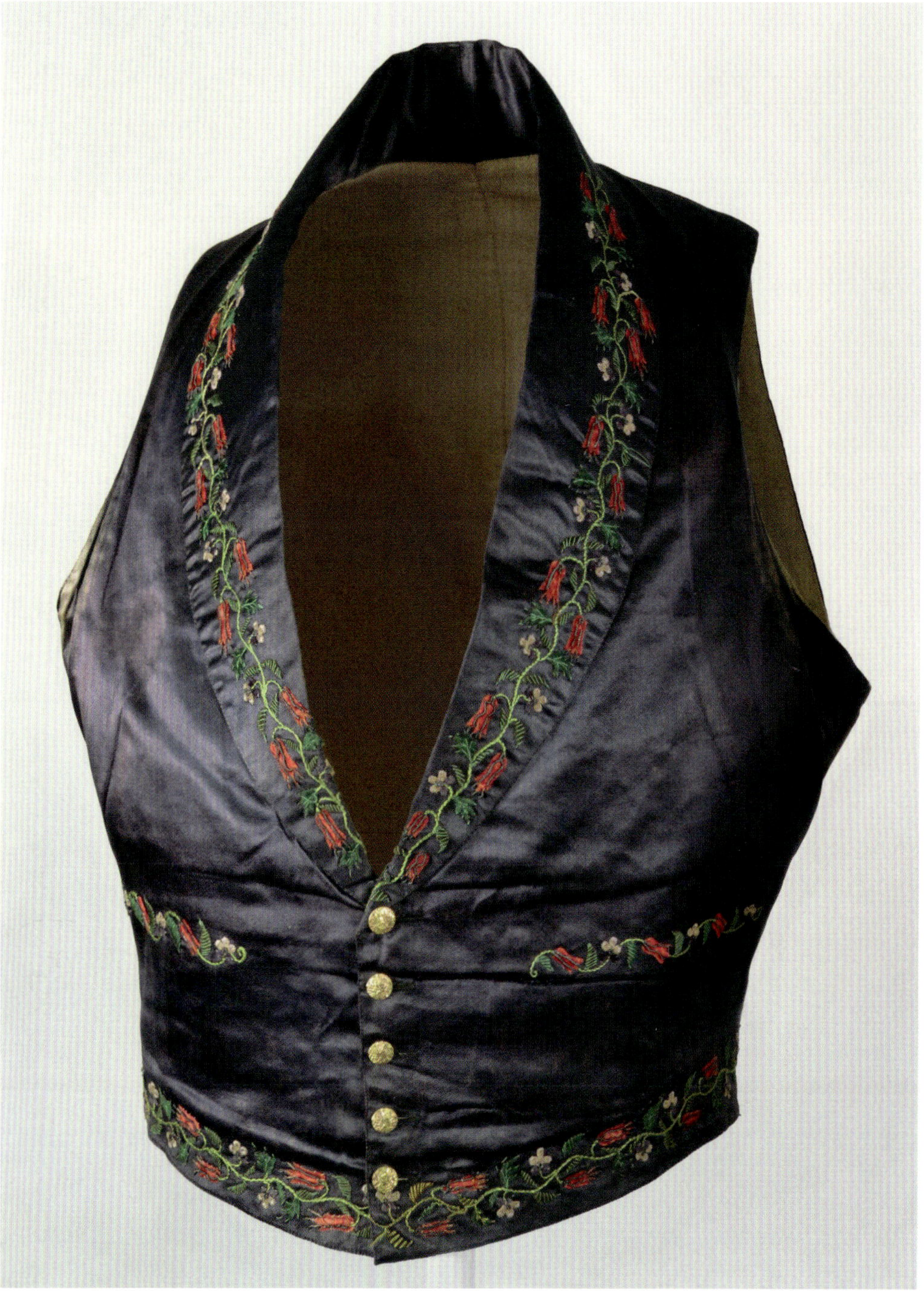

A waistcoat in aubergine silk satin, 1835-1845. HC.W-11.94-2

There is an embroidered trail design on the roll collar and the forepart hems; silk threads are stitched on to pieces of appliquéd velvet which form flowers and leaves, with added silver purl and check. There are no pockets, but there is a strip of embroidery on each forepart where a pocket would be. The waistcoat is lined with gingery cotton twill, and the back is dark brown silesia, with waist adjustments of a pair of tabs with boned ends, three pairs of metal eyelets and black linen tape lacing (page 210). The five gilt buttons may not be original.

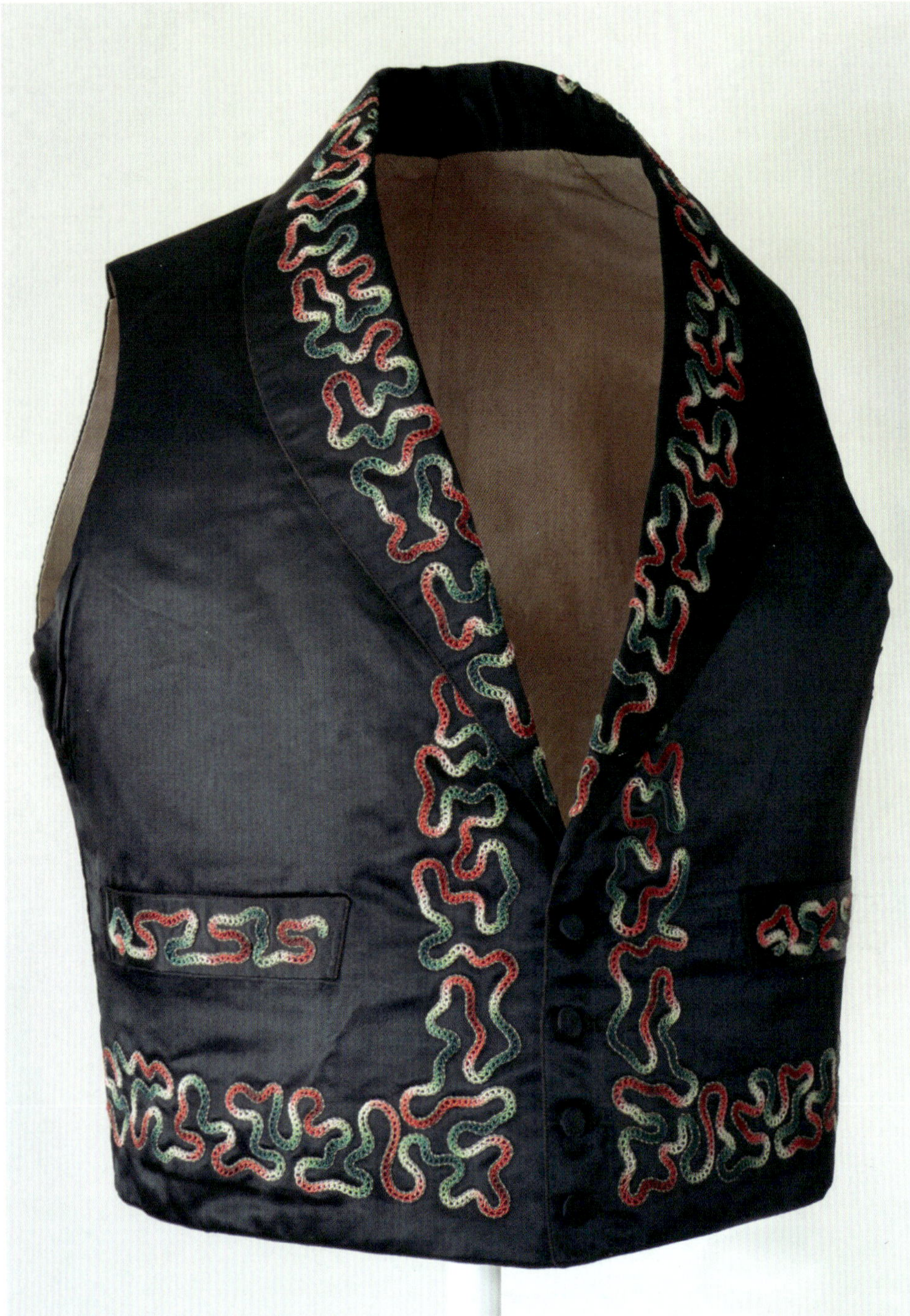

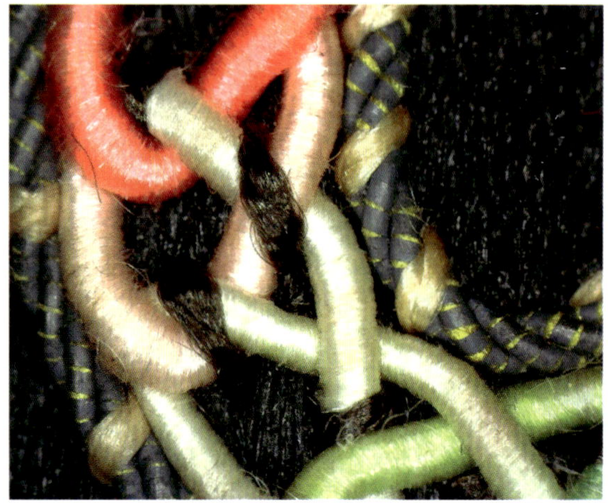

Detail of the gimp and filé thread, outlined below.

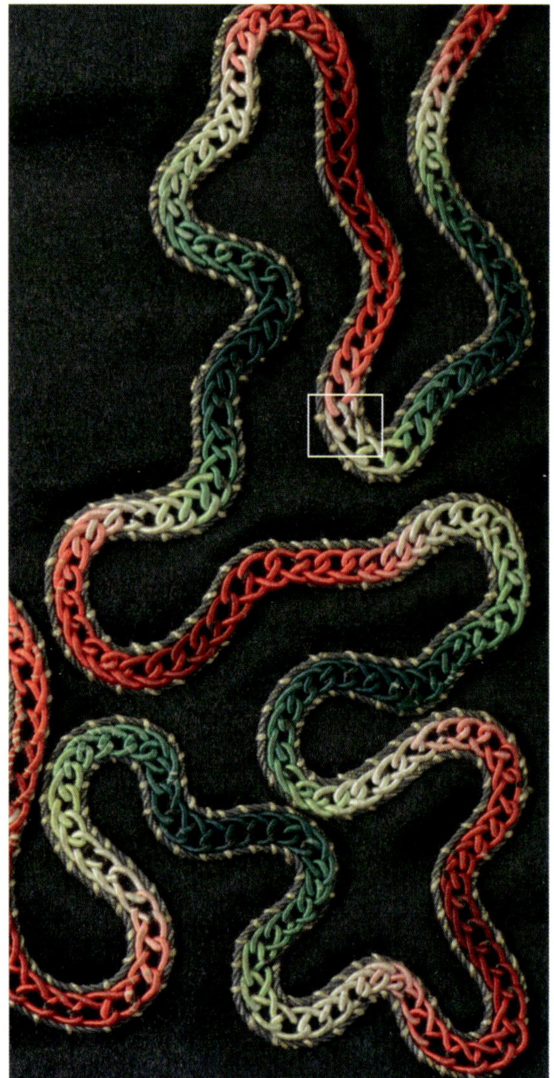

A waistcoat in black silk satin, 1830-1840. HC.W-3.99-2

It has applied decoration bordering the foreparts, and on the roll collar and the welted pockets. This consists of interlaced gimp shaded in red, cream and green, couched in a wiggly pattern, with twisted silver filé threads, now tarnished, on each side. The waistcoat is lined in fawn silk twill, and the back is black silk twill; the waist adjustment is by a pair of tabs with three pairs of metal eyelets, but the lace is missing. There are four self-covered buttons.

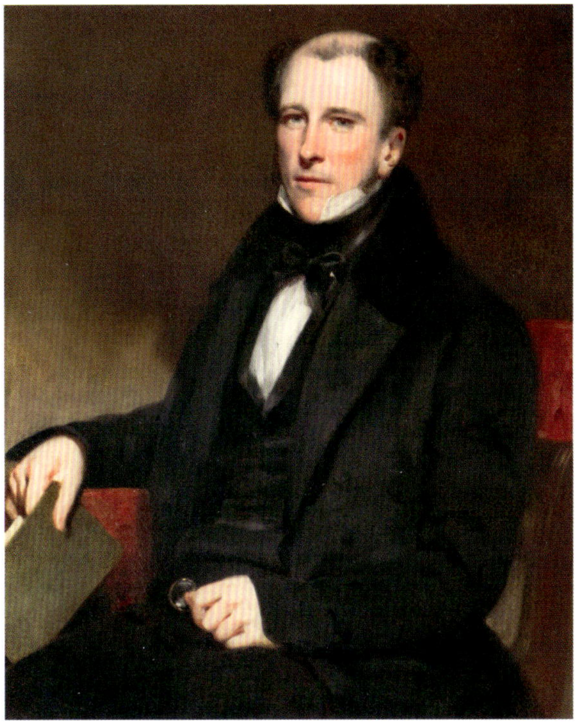

Sir Daniel Keyte Sandford by John Watson Gordon, 1837. © The Hunterian, University of Glasgow 2016. Sandford was Professor of Greek at the University.

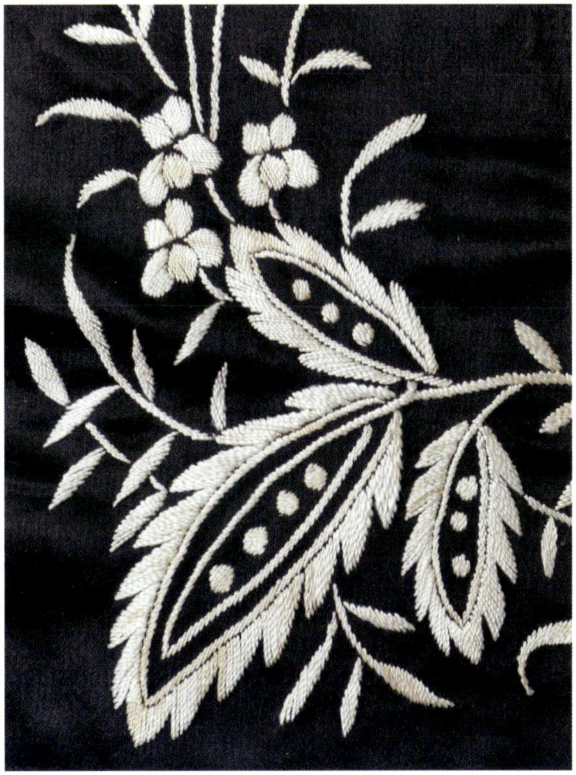

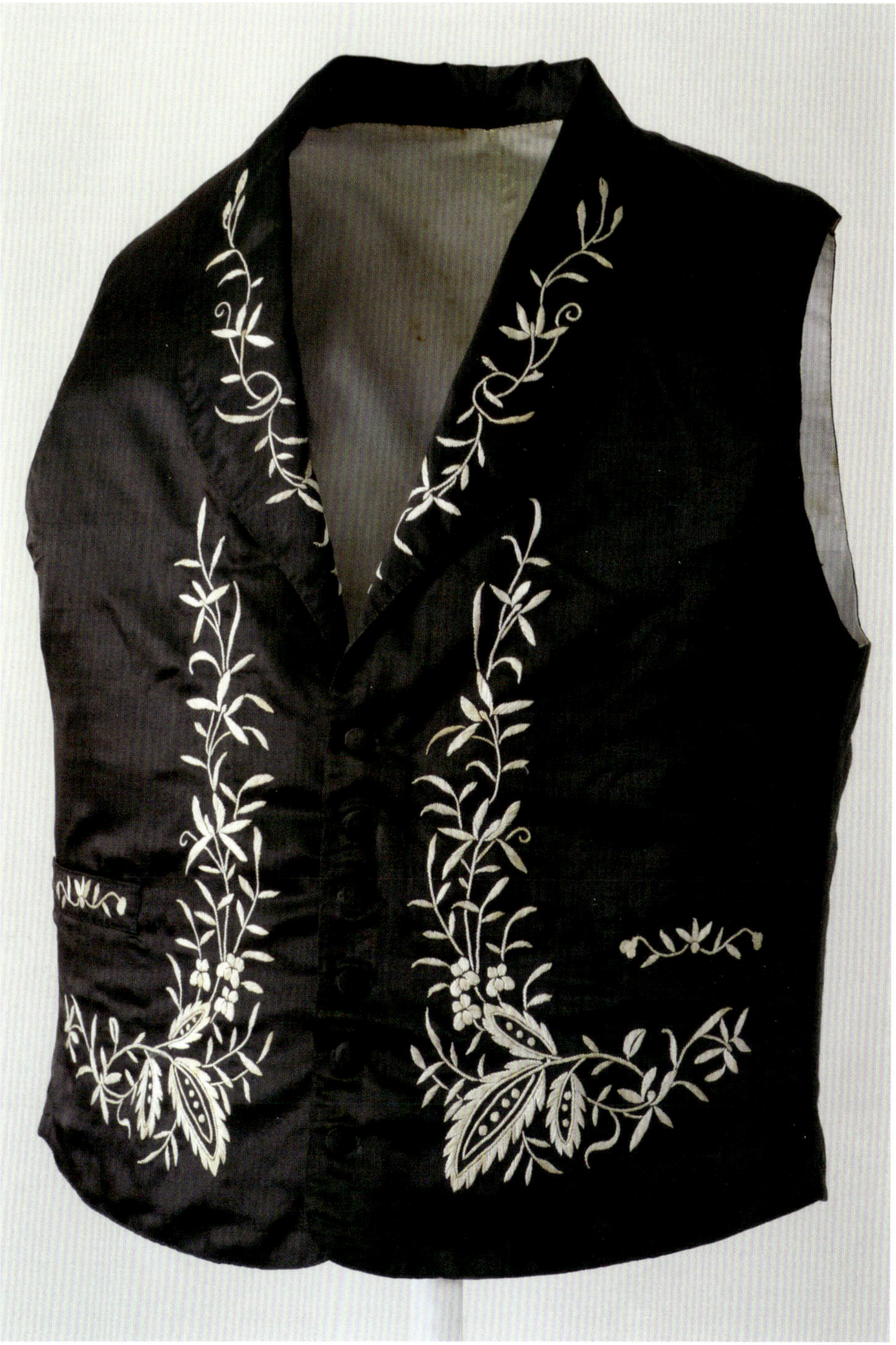

A waistcoat in black silk satin, 1835-1845. HC.W-10.97-1

The foreparts, welted pockets and roll collar have embroidery in ivory silk, possibly Chinese. The waistcoat is lined in plain white cotton and the back is a similar cotton in black; the waist adjustment is by tabs with three pairs of hand-worked eyelets, but the lace is missing. There are six self-covered buttons. The waistcoat is flimsy, with no interlinings in any part, and it may have been made in China, for the European market.

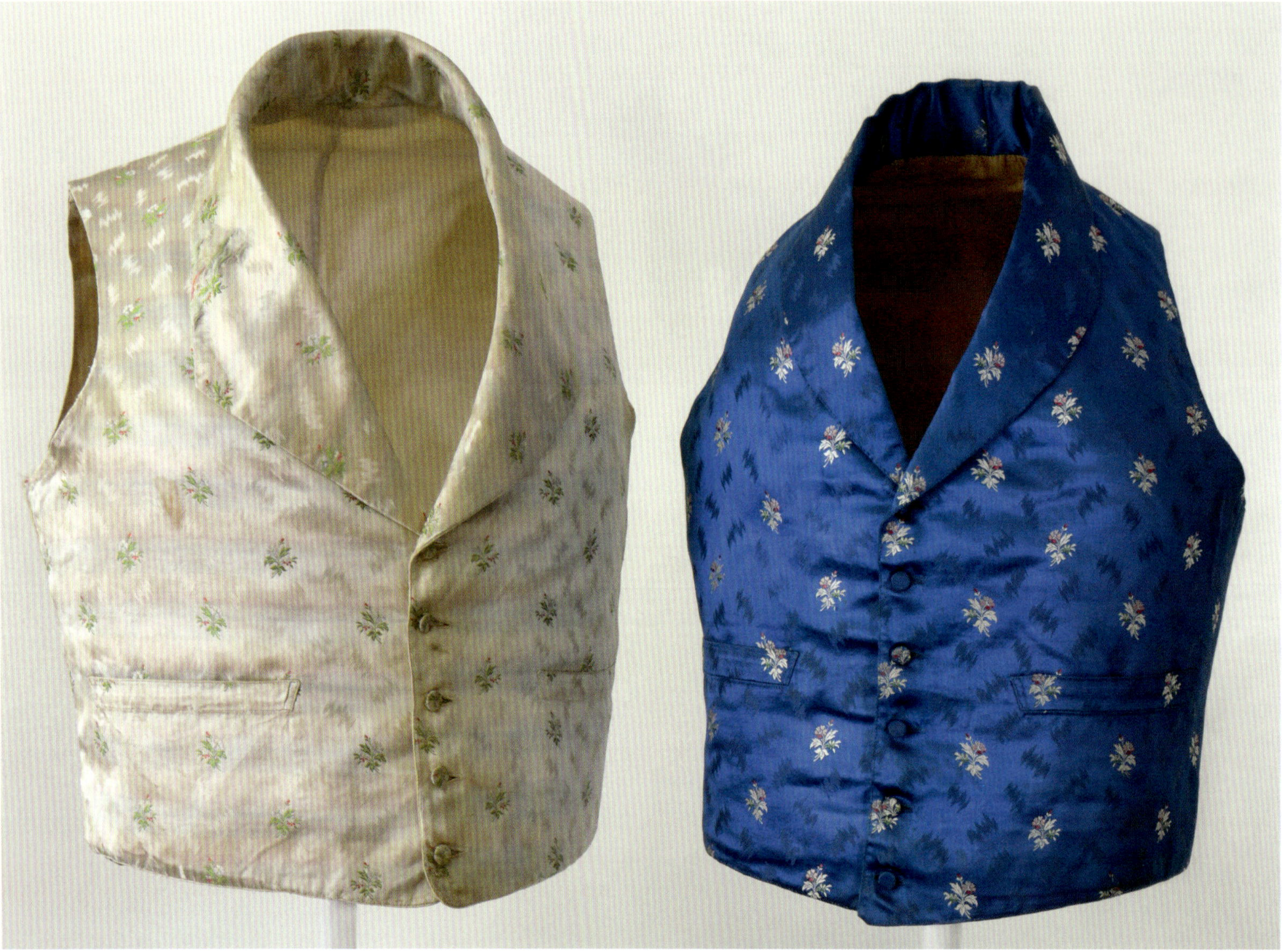

A waistcoat in ivory figured silk satin, 1830-1840. HC.W-1.95-3

The satin has a self pattern, and a sprig with green leaves, and flowers in red and ivory. The waistcoat is lined with plain white cotton; there are five self-covered buttons and two welted pockets; the edge of the roll collar is extended to a shallow point. The back is in cream silk twill with a waist adjustment of tabs with boned ends and three pairs of hand-worked eyelets. The lacing is by three separate ivory silk ribbons, and the middle of each one is stitched to the centre back seam. The forepart hems are faced with ivory leather.

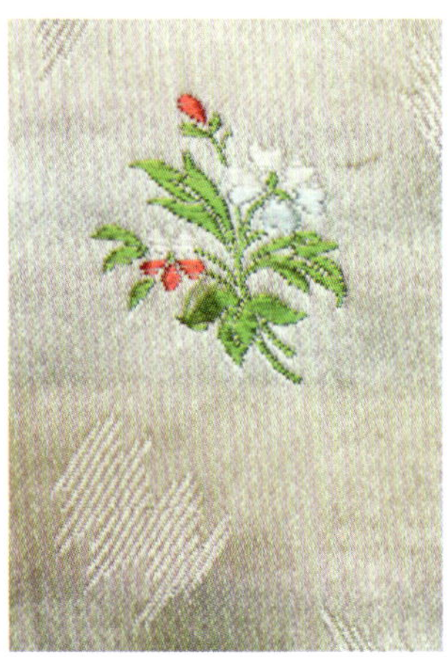

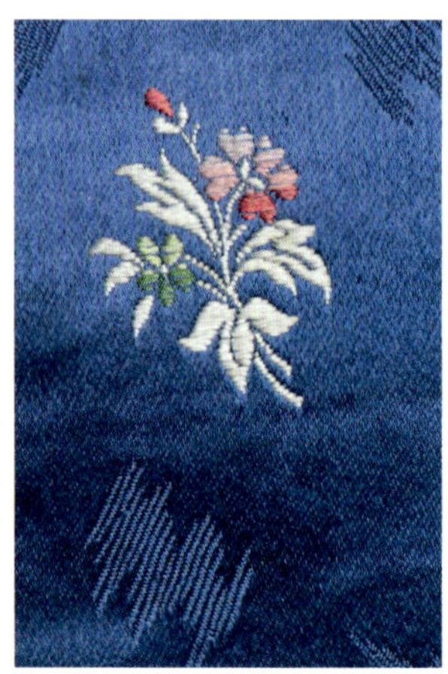

A waistcoat in blue figured silk satin, 1835-1845. HC.W-0.59

This silk is another colourway of the fabric of the waistcoat on the left, with red and pink flowers and white leaves. The waistcoat has a roll collar, six self-covered buttons and two welted pockets. The lining and back are in ginger-coloured cotton twill: the back waist adjustment is by tabs with boned ends and three pairs of brass eyelets for lacing, but the lace is missing. The forepart hems are faced with brown leather.

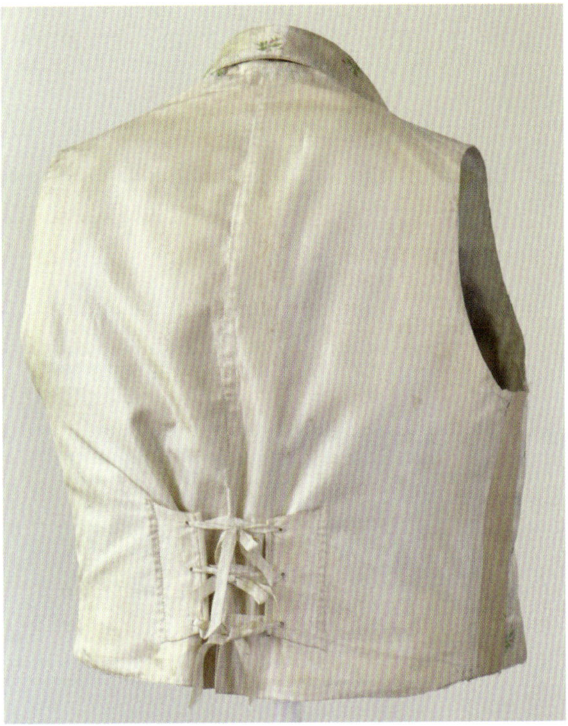

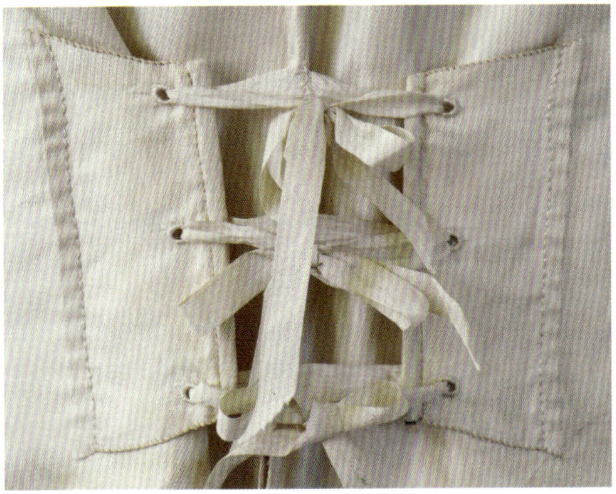

The back waist adjustment with eyelets and silk ribbon lacing on the ivory waistcoat, far left.

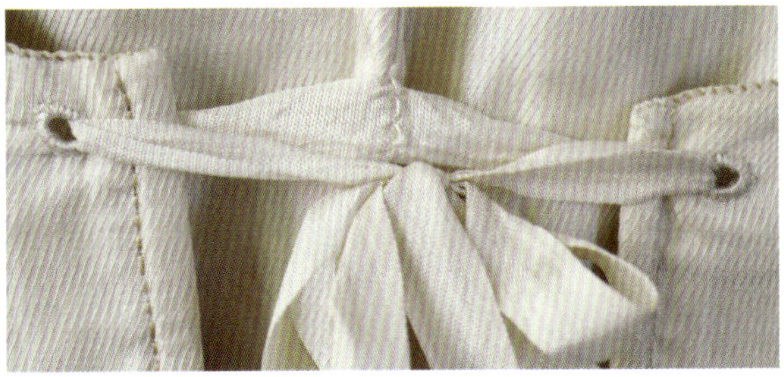

One of the silk lacing ribbons, stitched to the centre back seam.

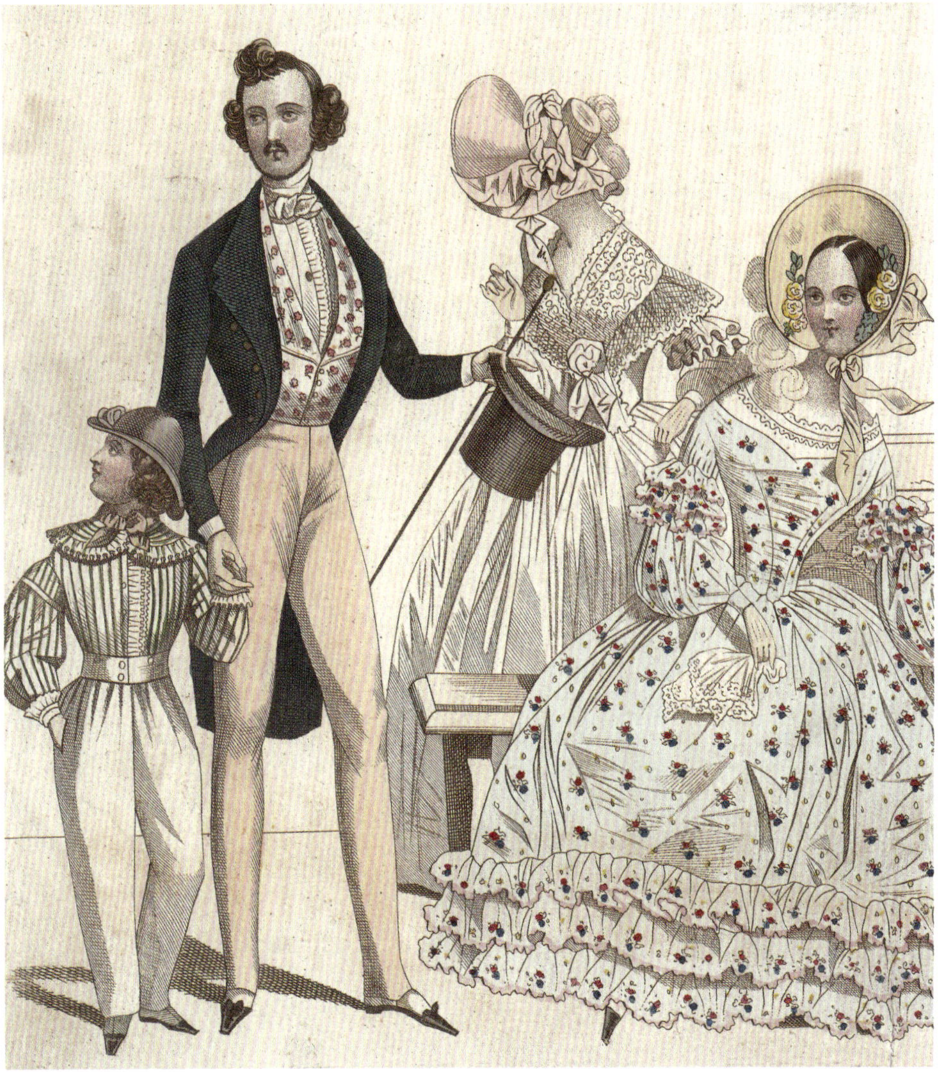

Fashion plate, 1838.

Recent patents announced in the *London Journal of Arts and Sciences* for 1824.

"To Thomas Rogers, of Buckingham Street, Strand, in the county of Middlesex, Esq. for an Improvement on Stays or Bodices, which Improvement is also applicable to Boots. (Sealed 18th March 1823)

"This improvement is a new mode of forming the lace-holes or eyes of stays, corsets, boots, and other articles of dress by means of small round pieces of metal (silver or plated metal is to be preferred) which are perforated in the centre, and otherwise formed by pressure."

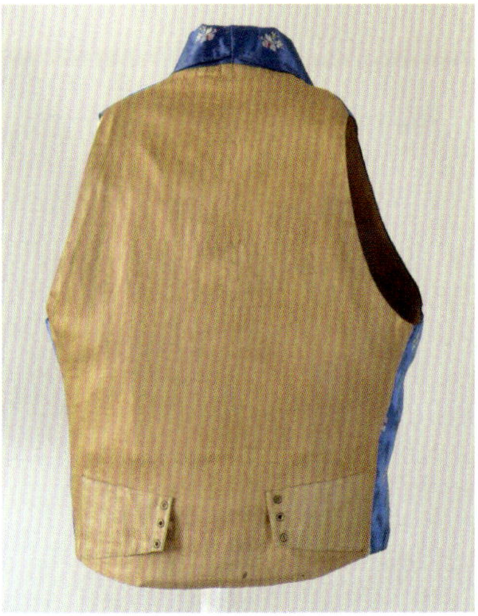

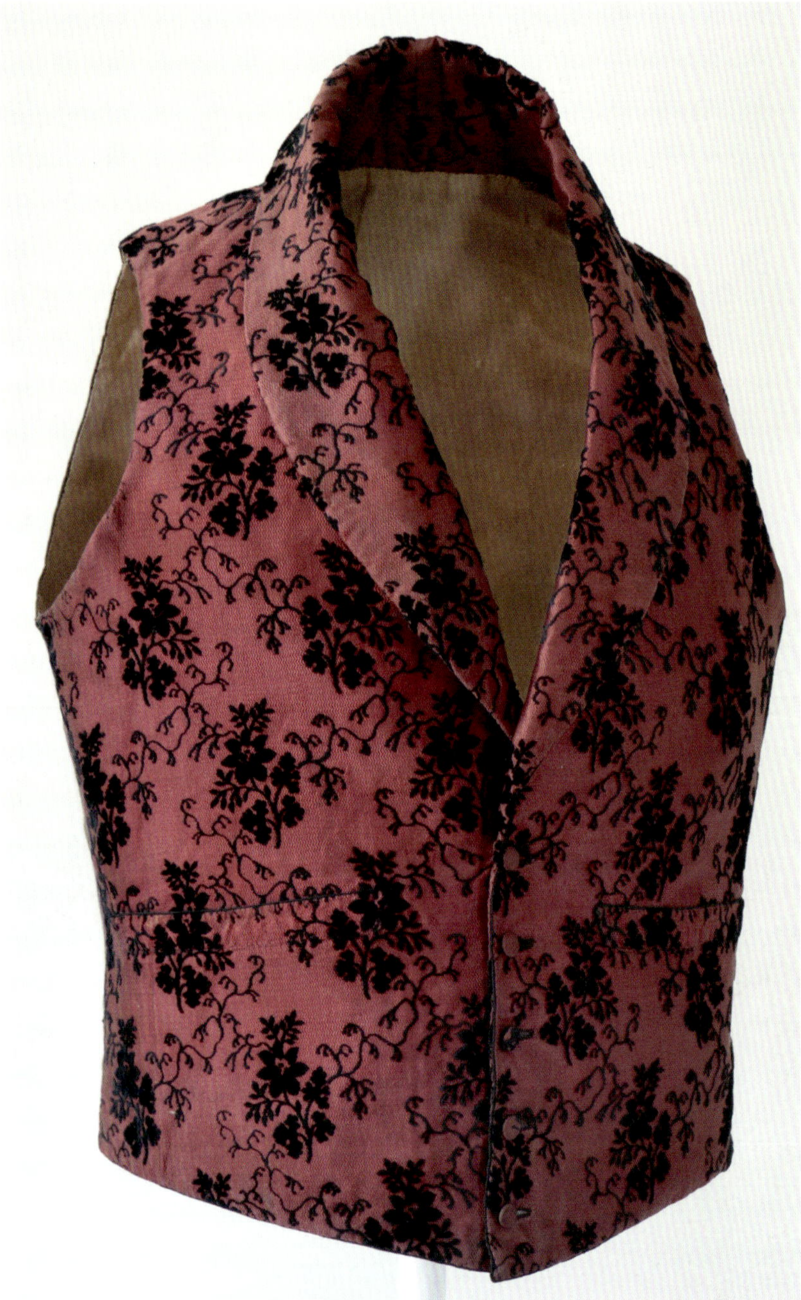

A waistcoat in deep pink silk, 1835-1845. HC.W-1.82

The silk is woven with a vertical zig-zag texture in the ground, and a pattern of black velvet flowers and branches. The waistcoat front edges, hems and welted pocket tops have black silk piping, and there are five self-covered buttons and a roll collar. The lining is fawn cotton twill and the back is dark brown cotton twill with a centre back gusset of black linen. The waist adjustment is a strip of 1¾″ wide elastic, now perished. Elastic was only beginning to be used at this period, and it was not really successful until the discovery of the vulcanising process, in 1844, which made the use of rubber more viable.

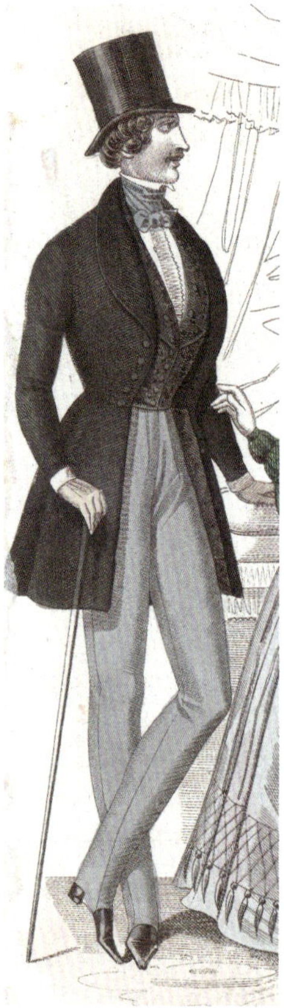

Fashion plate "Moda di Parigi" from *Corriere delle Dame*, 1839.

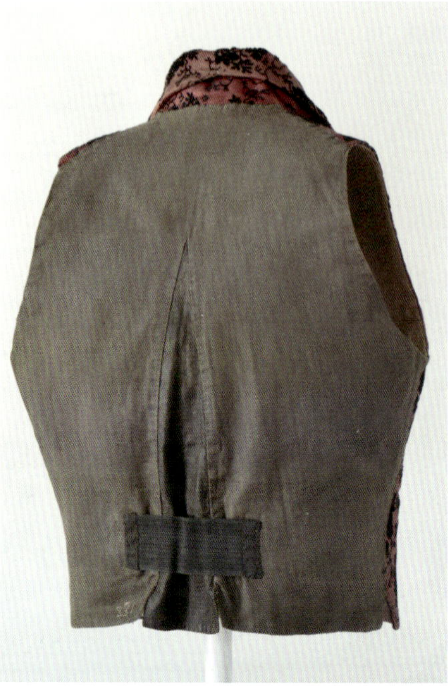

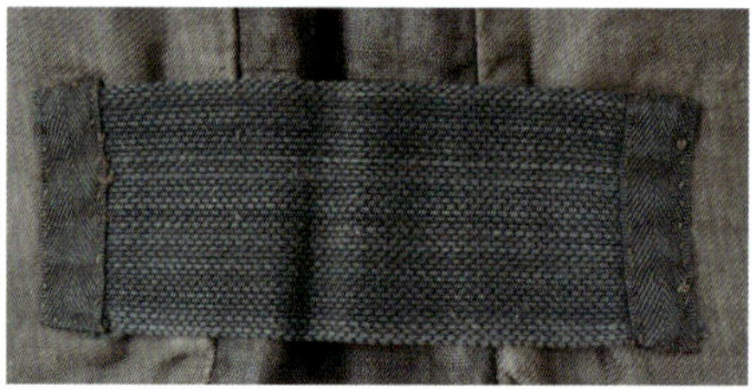

The elastic strip at the back waist.

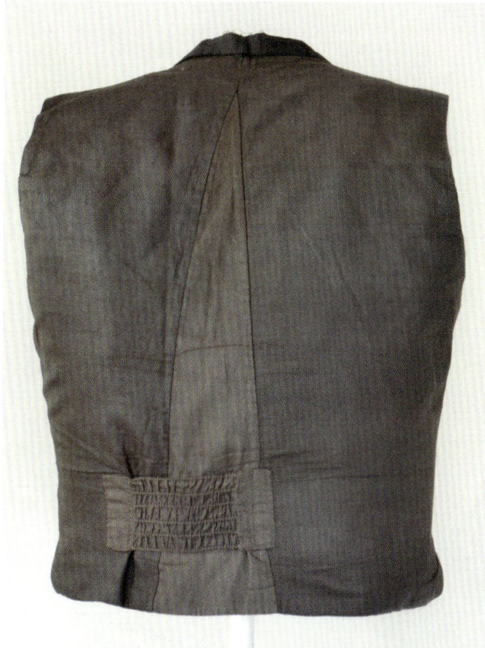

Springs had been used in clothing since the end of the eighteenth century. In 1799 John Foster took out a patent for a "Brace or sling acting by means of a steel spring for suspending breeches, pantaloons or drawers", which included a drawing of the braces. In 1846 James Quantrille registered a design for a "Spring back for waistcoats and trowsers."

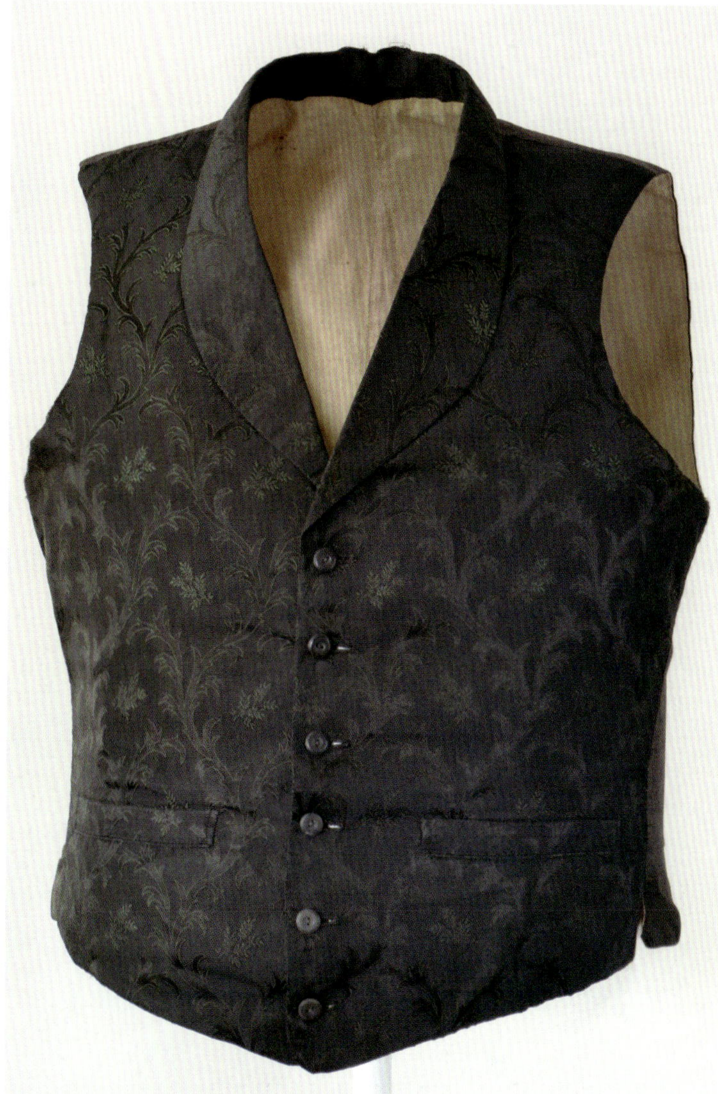

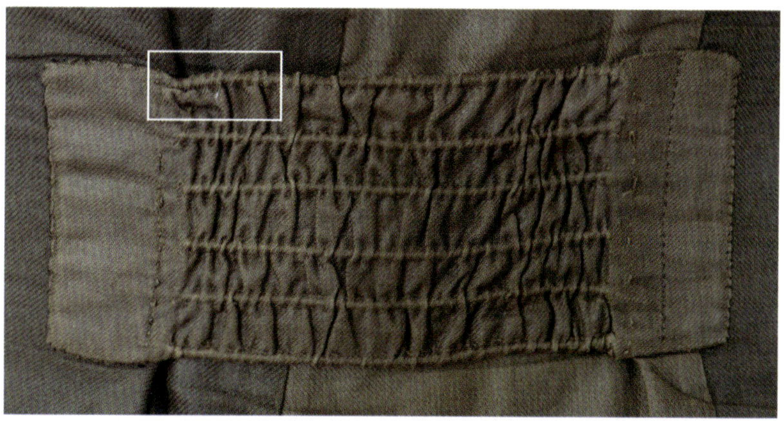

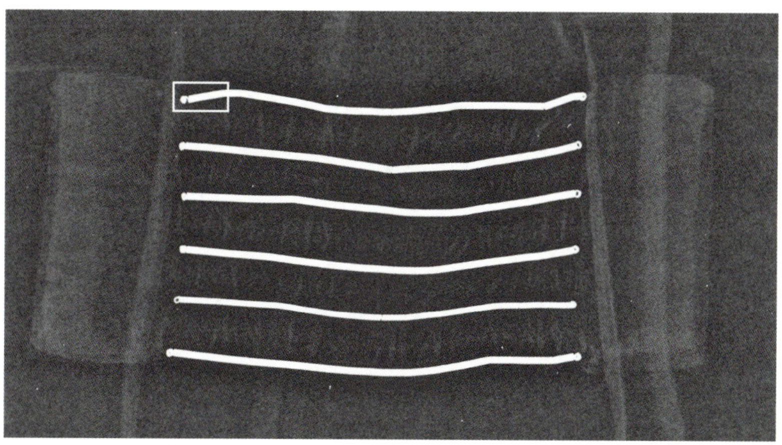

An X-ray image of the panel on the back waist with the steel springs.

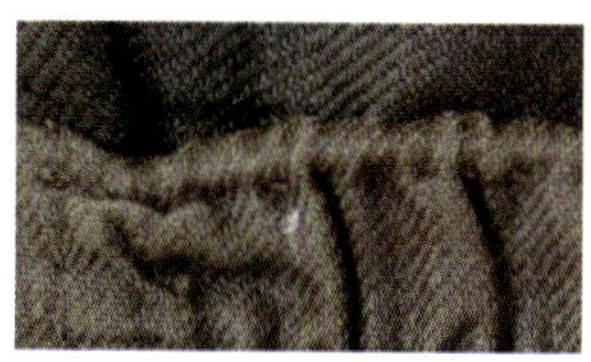

Detail of the end of a spring, outlined above left.

X-ray detail of the end of a spring, outlined left.

A waistcoat in black silk, 1840-1850.
HC.W-4.92

The ground of the silk is grosgrain with a design of branches in satin outlined with dark green silk, and sprays of dark green leaves in the spaces. The waistcoat is lined with cream cotton twill and the back is in dark brown silesia with a gusset in the centre back. The waist adjustment is a set of six steel springs encased in brown cotton. The forepart hems were faced with dark brown leather but only the one on the left side remains. There is a roll collar, and the six black buttons may not be original.

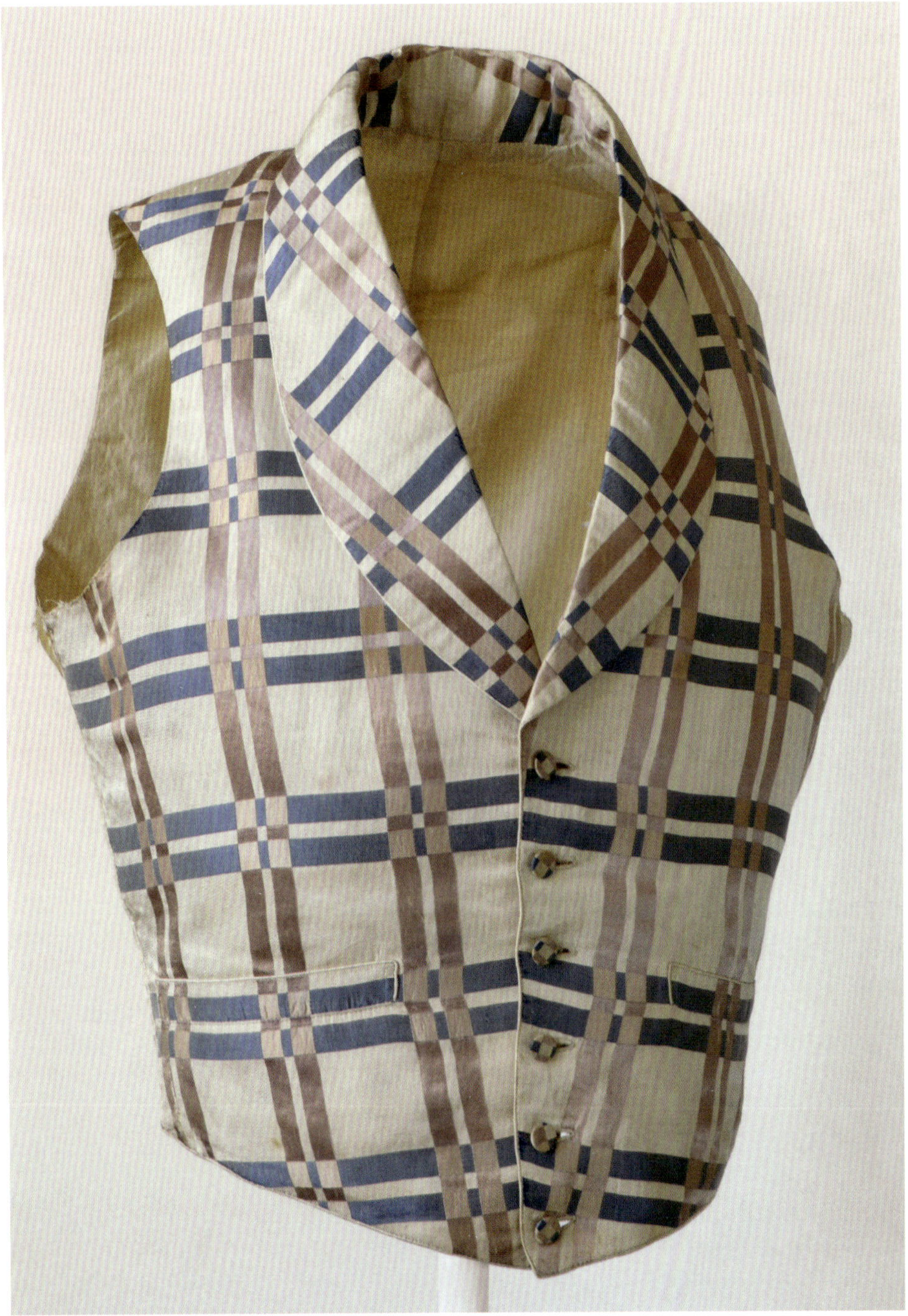

A waistcoat in checked ivory silk grosgrain, 1835-1845. HC.W-9.87

The checks are made by satin stripes in old rose and blue stripes in a twill weave with squares of beige plain weave silk at the intersections. The roll collar, forepart edges and pockets are edged with ivory silk piping, and there are six covered buttons. It is lined in plain white cotton, and the back is ivory silk taffeta. The lacing tabs are white cotton twill which has been covered in the silk taffeta; the ends are boned and have three pairs of metal eyelets, but the lace is missing. The waistcoat has been washed at some point.

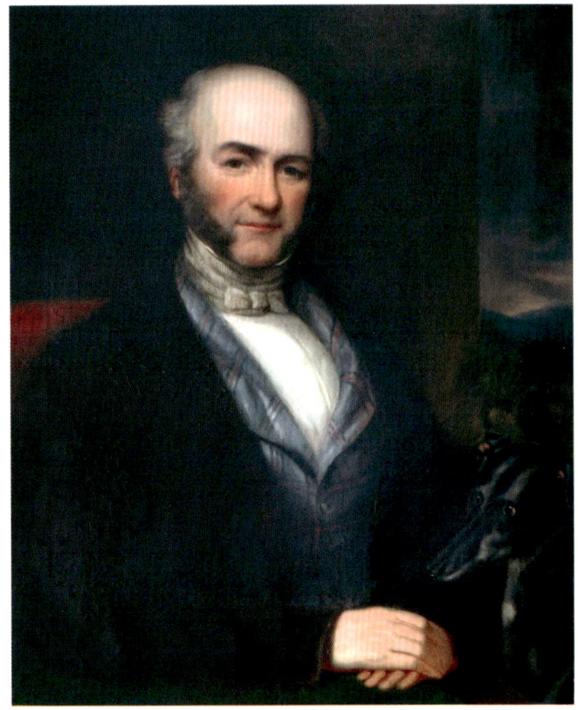

William Bennett by an unknown artist, 1837, Faringdon Library, Oxfordshire. William Bennett (1790-1844) was High Sheriff of Berkshire in 1836.

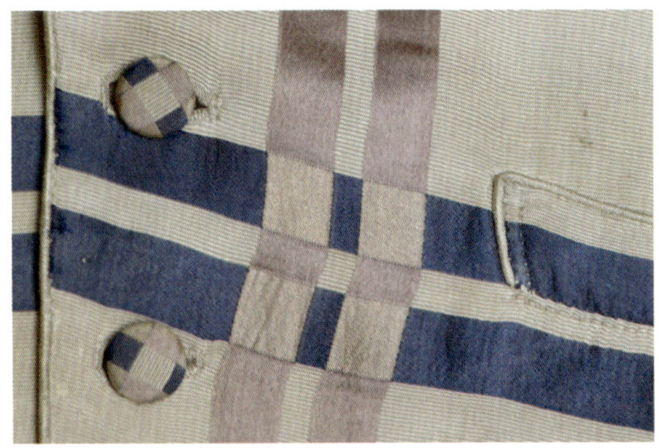

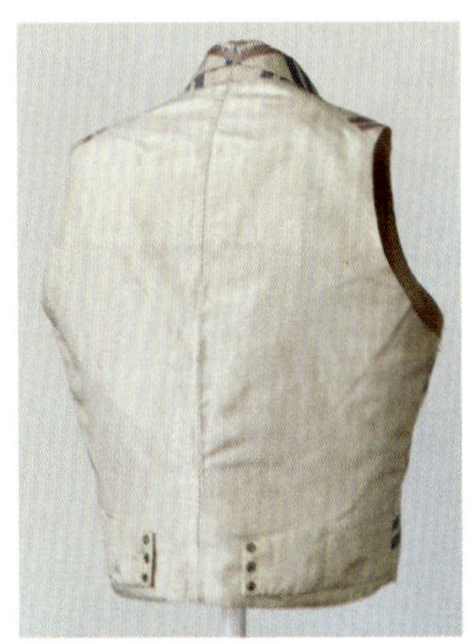

"Little patterns and Scottish checks are considered in good taste for waistcoats; the *Dandys* have adopted little checks or stripes for trousers."
Le Follet, Courrier des Salons, June 1835.

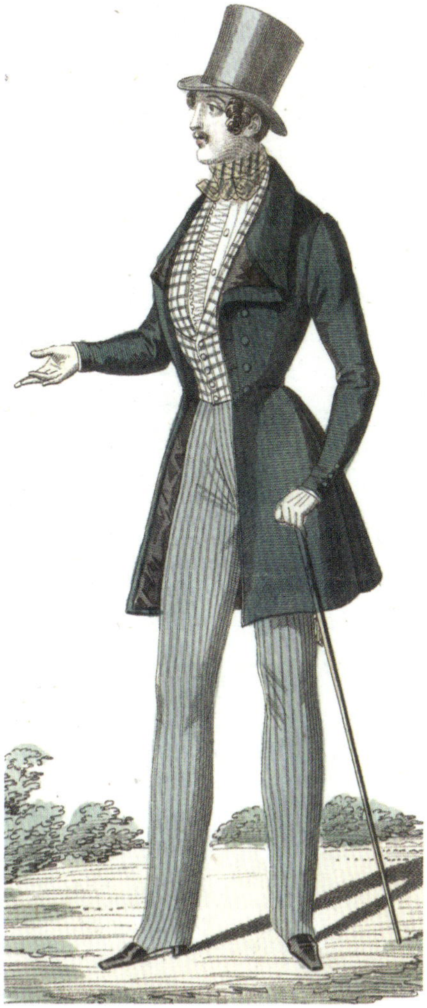

Fashion plate "Moda di Parigi", from *Corriere delle Dame*, 1836.

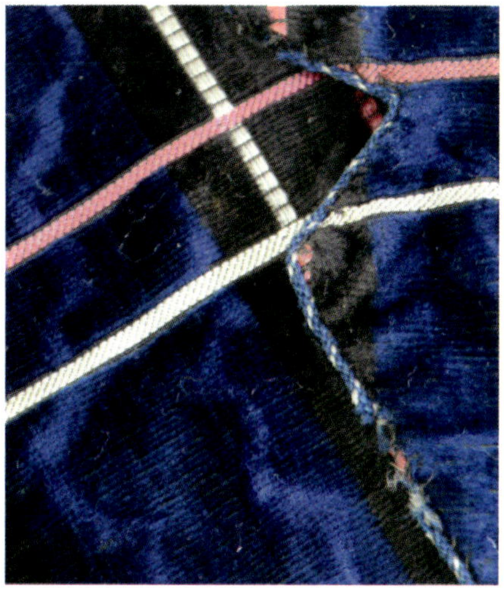

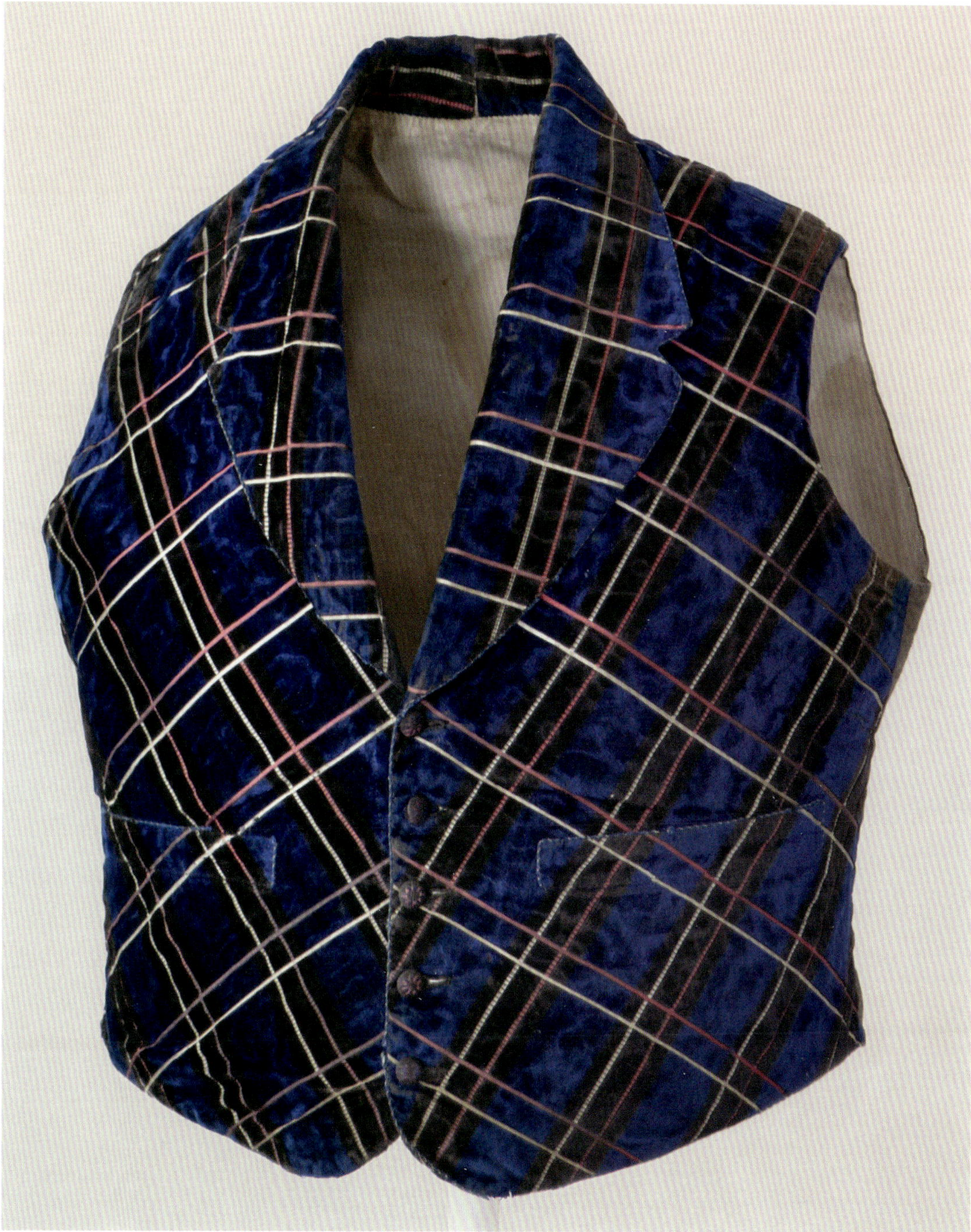

A waistcoat in checked silk velvet, 1835-1845. HC.W-4.95

The checks are made by blue and black warp stripes in the velvet, and pink and white narrow silk warp and weft stripes; the velvet has an impressed moiré pattern. The waistcoat has been cut on the bias so that the checks appear diagonally, and the step-roll collar, front edges and pocket tops are edged with narrow blue and white silk cord. The five buttons are covered in black silk with a pink and blue pattern (page 216), and the lining is beige cotton. The back is in dark brown silesia (back cover) with a waist adjustment of tabs with boned ends, three pairs of brass eyelets and a narrow brown linen lacing tape.

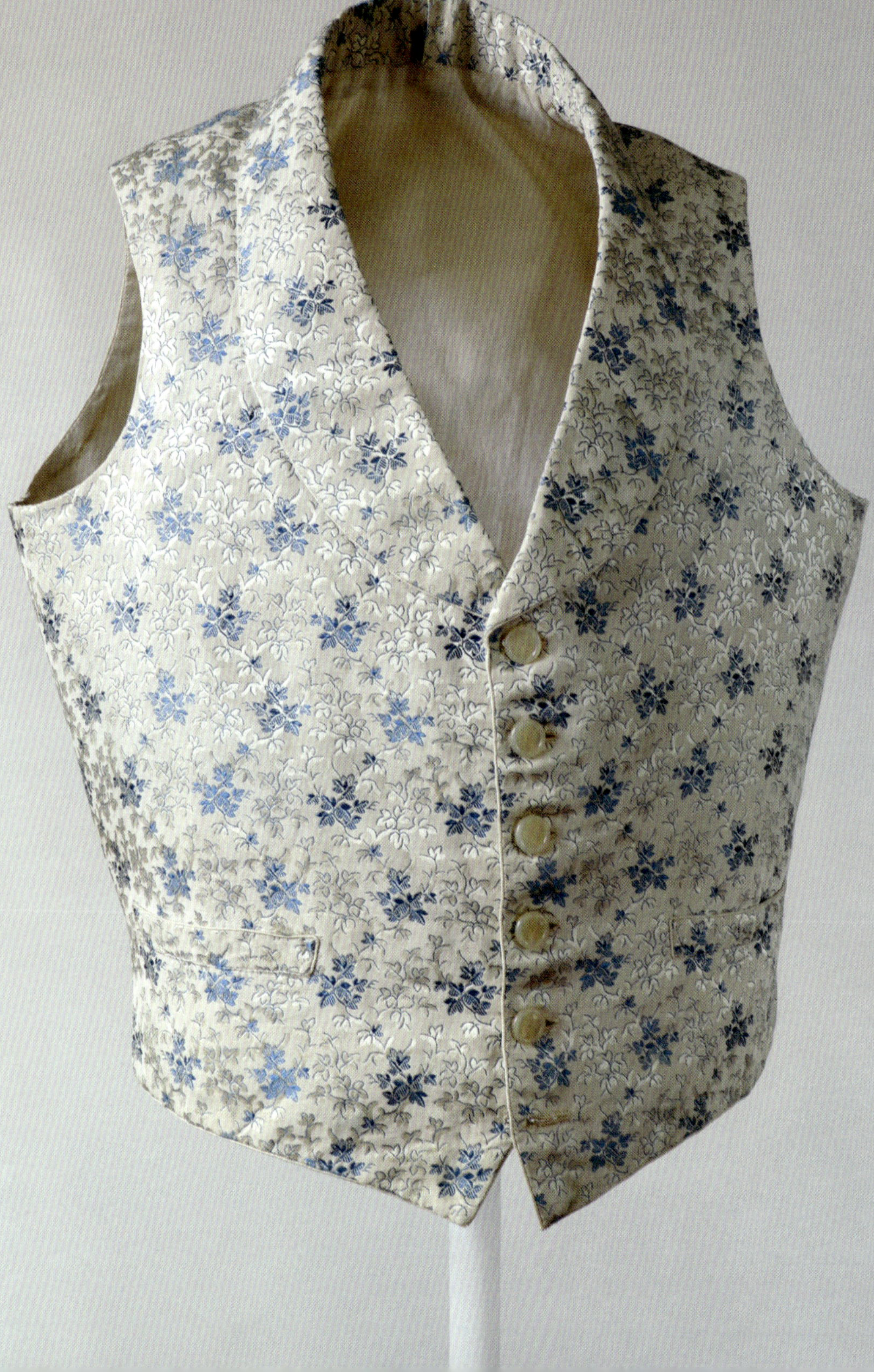

A waistcoat in ivory silk, 1835-1845.
HC.W-3.15-1

The silk has a woven pattern of leaves in dark blue. The waistcoat is single-breasted and has six buttonholes but the five buttons here are not original. The roll collar and the welted pockets are edged with a very fine ivory silk cord. The lining and the back are in white cotton twill, and there are tabs at the back waist with three pairs of metal eyelets for lacing to adjust the size; the lace is missing.

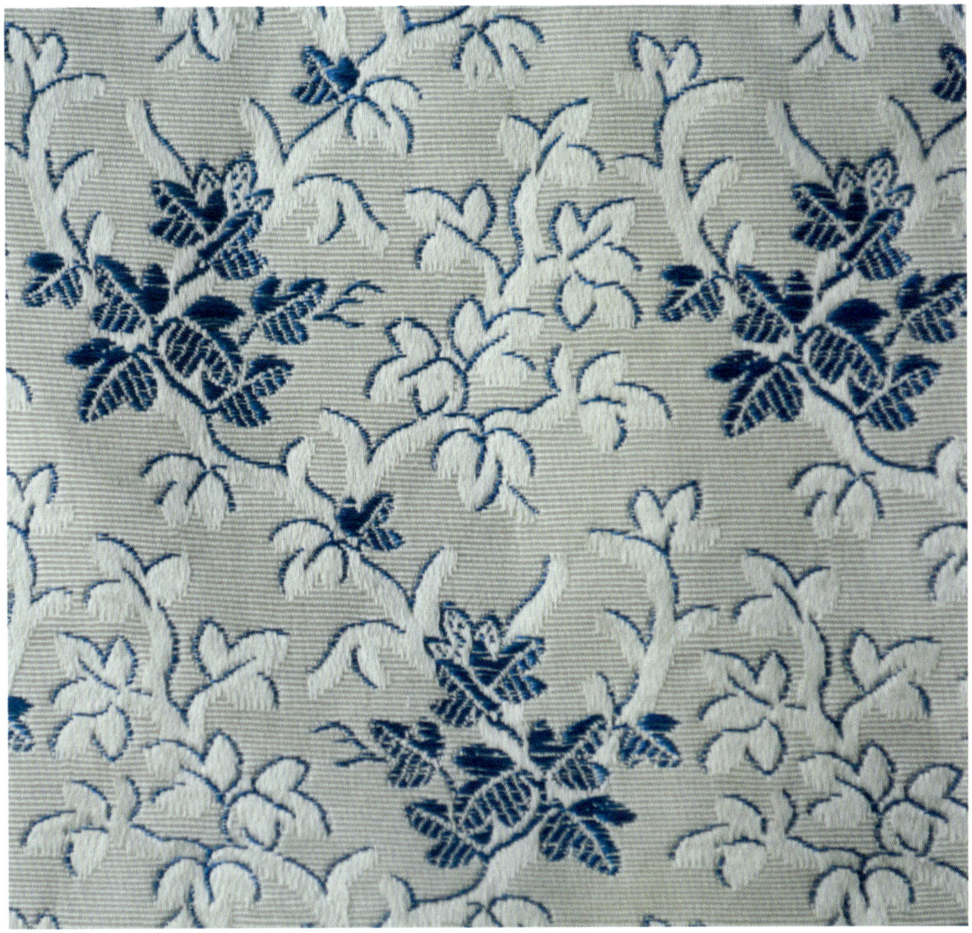

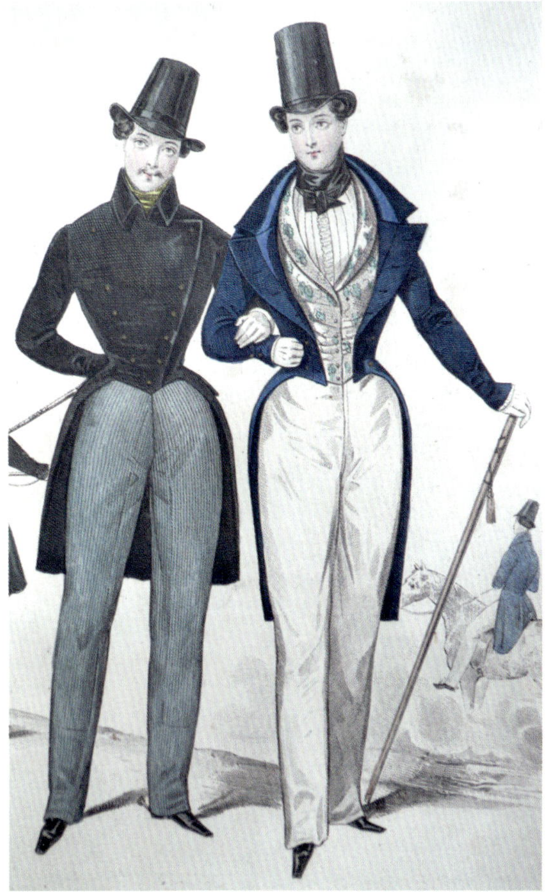

Fashion plate from *Le Follet*, April 1834.

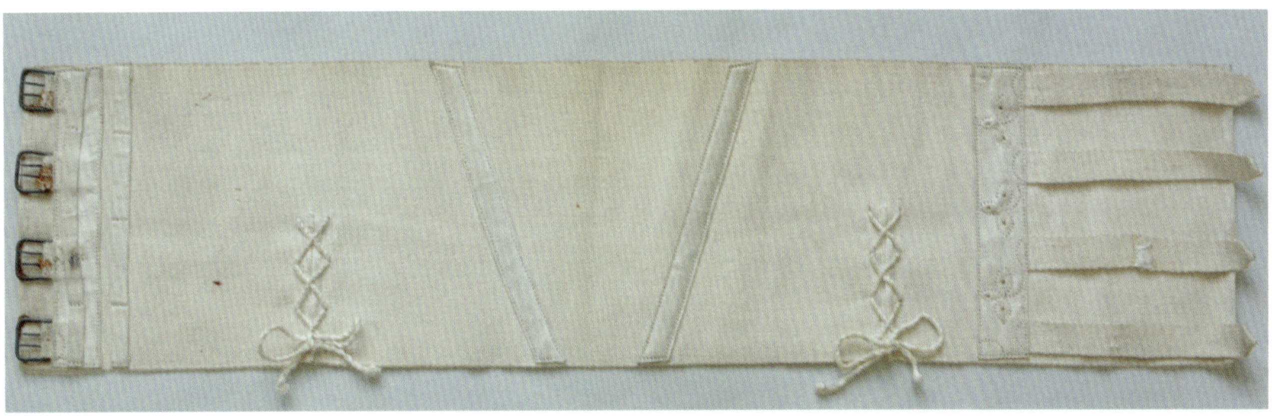

A man's corset or body belt, 1830-1845. HC.U-0.1

It is made from a heavy corded ivory cotton, woven 7½″ wide, and fastened by four webbing straps and buckles; the buckles are quite rusty. A strip of twilled cotton covers the ends of the straps where they are attached to the corset, and this has some decorative stitching. There are openings with cord lacing for adjustments over the hips. The two bones in a V shape at the front are covered in the twilled cotton. This would have been worn in an attempt to achieve the tiny waist fashionable for men at this period.

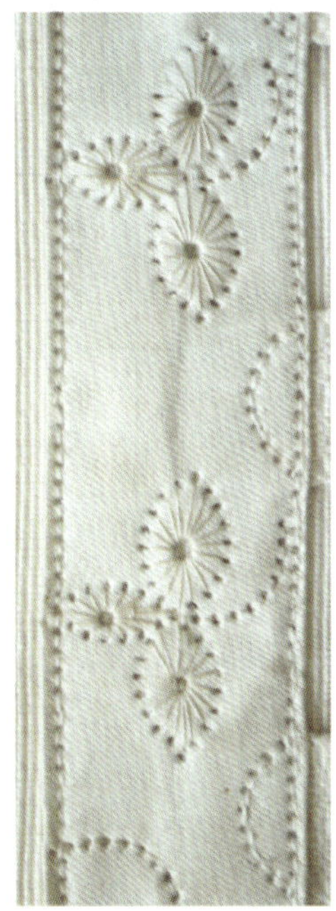

Right: The cotton strip, with decorative stitching, covering where the straps are attached.

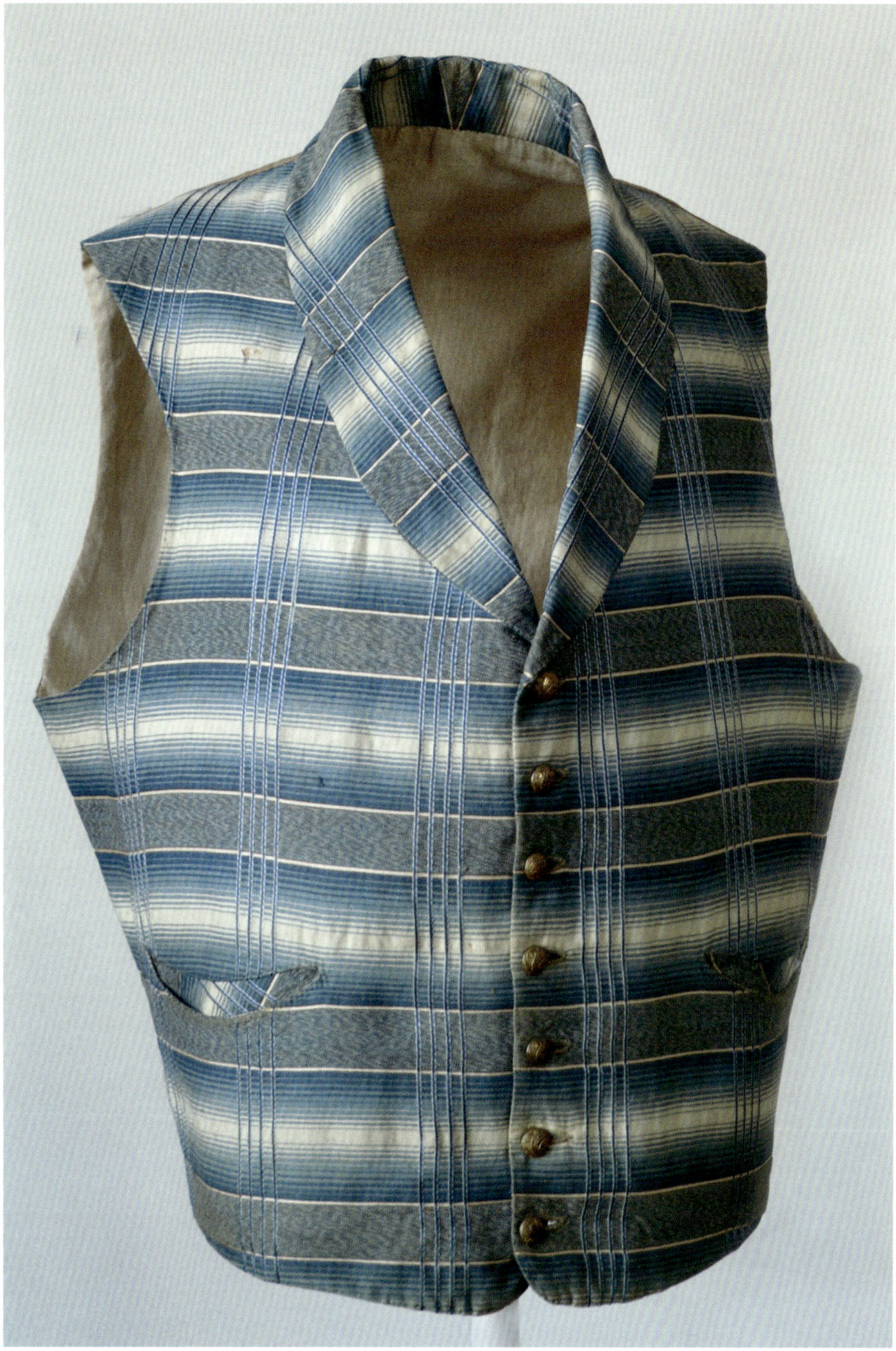

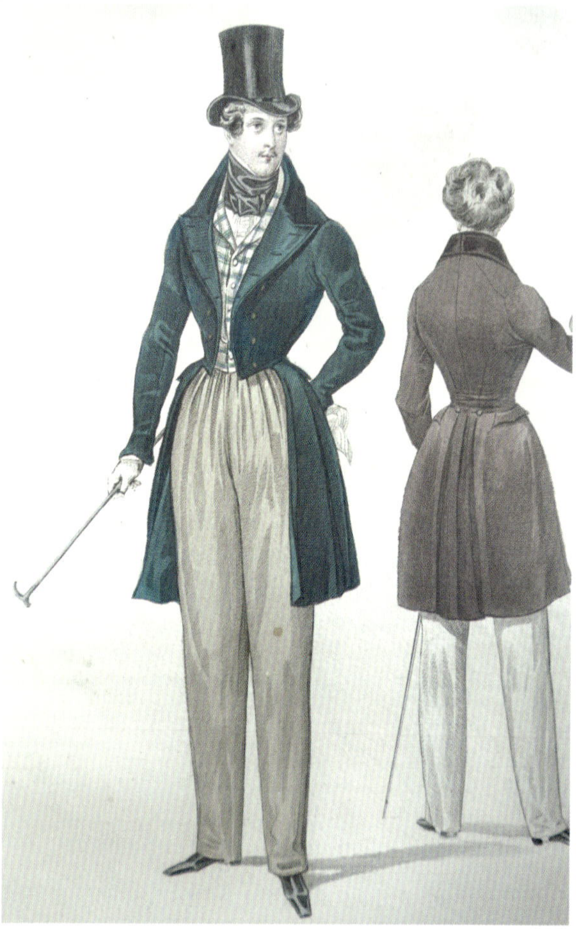

Fashion plate from *Le Follet*, June 1834.

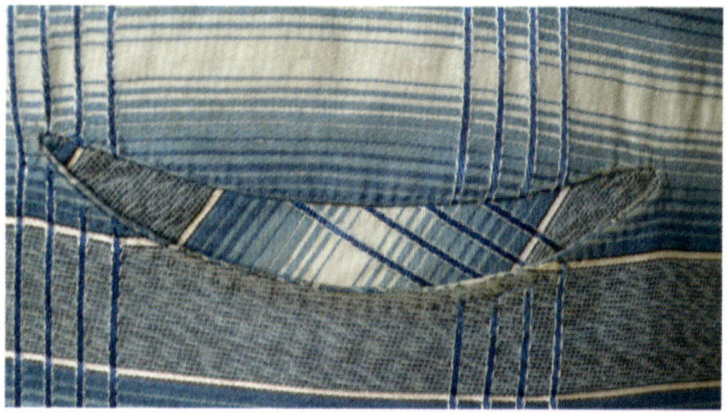

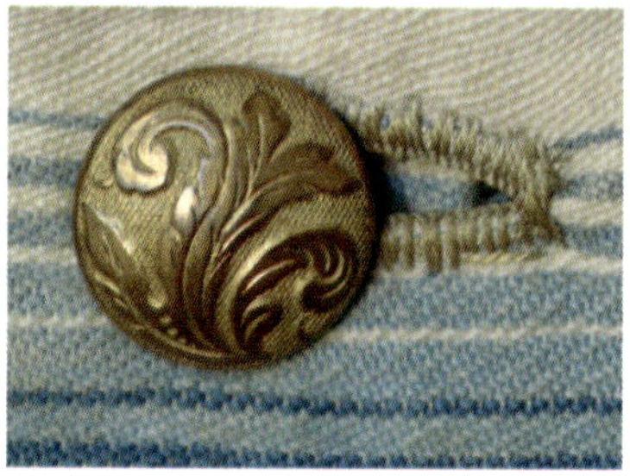

Left: One of the gilt buttons, on the backs of which is stamped "Extra Superior".

A waistcoat in blue and ivory, 1835-1845. HC.W-4.98

This has a silk warp and a wool weft, in a twill weave. The narrow vertical stripes are silk with narrow ivory silk horizontal stripes in the broader striped wool weft. The lining is ivory linen and there is a breast pocket inside the left forepart. The back is light brown cotton twill with two pairs of white linen tape ties to adjust the waist. It has a roll collar, two crescent-shaped pockets with a piped edge and seven gilt buttons with a leaf pattern.

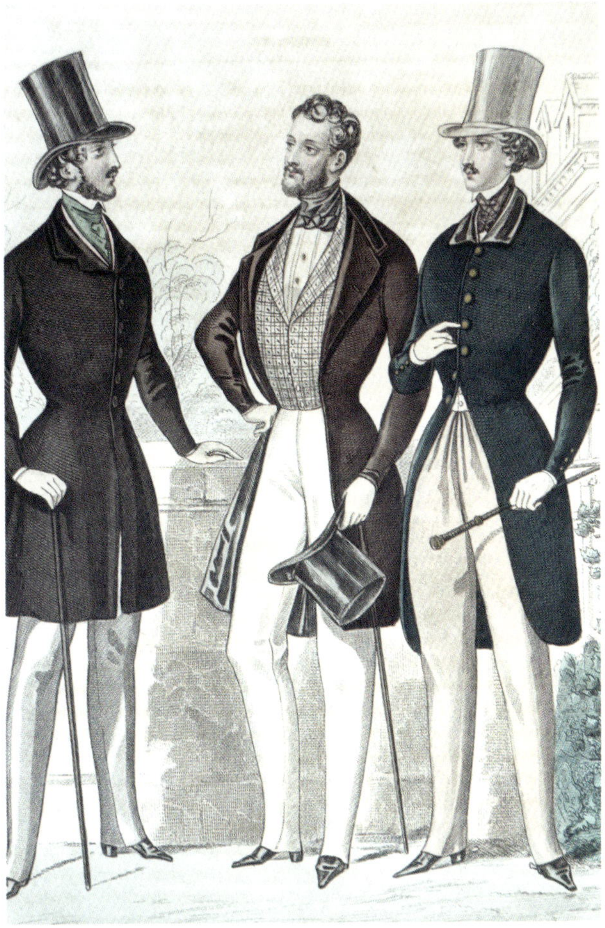

Fashion plate from *Le Follet*, April 1841.

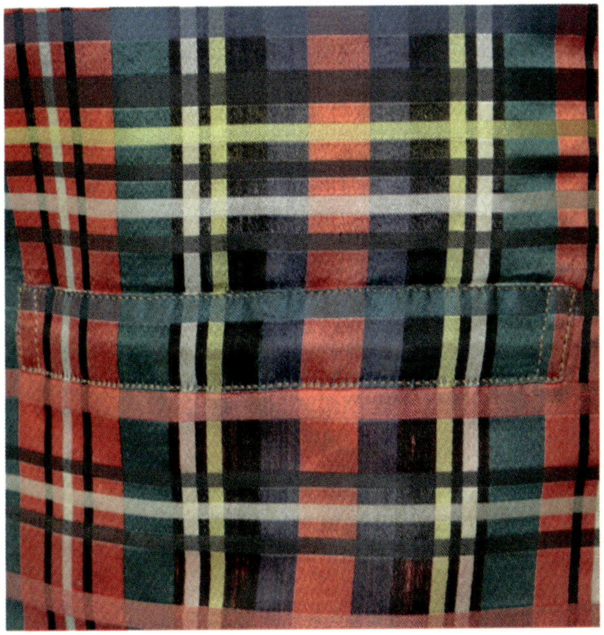

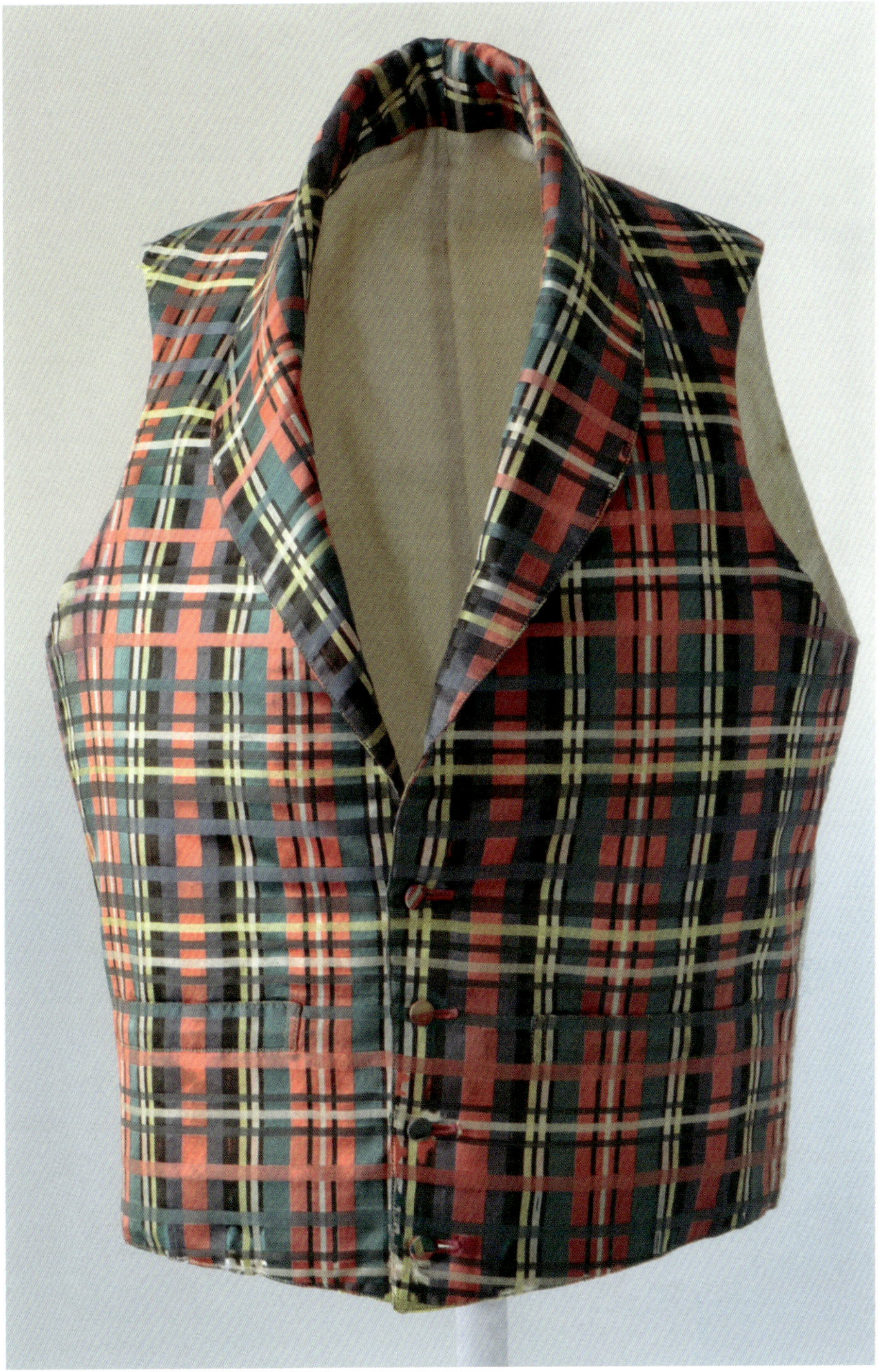

A waistcoat in polychrome checked silk satin, 1835-1845. HC.W-4.84

It has a roll collar, two welted pockets and four self-covered buttons. The lining and back are in white cotton, with a pair of tabs which have boned ends and three pairs of metal eyelets to adjust the waist at the back; the lace is missing.

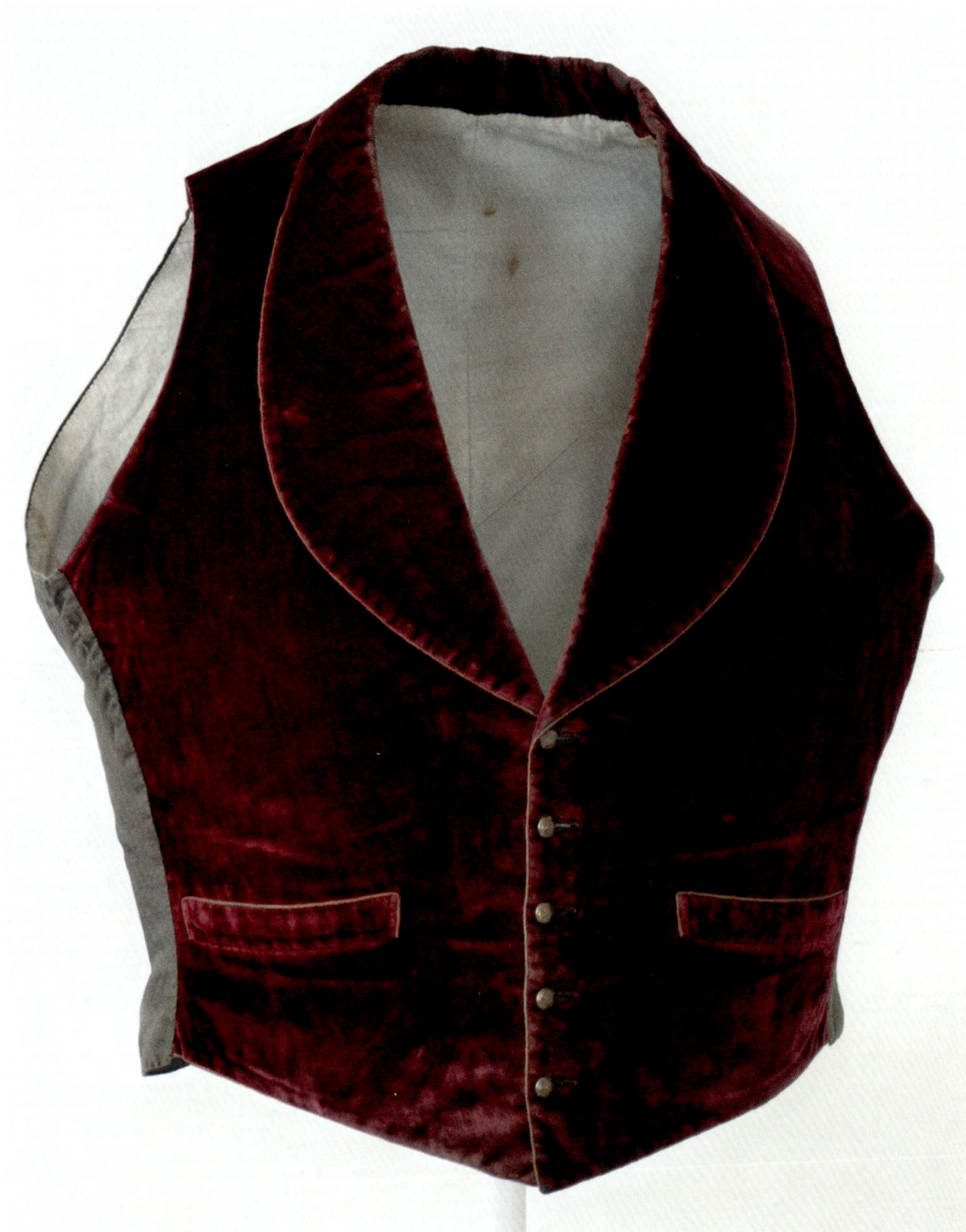

A waistcoat in crimson silk velvet, 1835-1845. HC.W-6.90-2

It has a roll collar and five patterned coppery-metal domed buttons. The foreparts are lined with beige cotton twill and the back with plain white cotton. The back is in dark brown silesia with a small gusset let in to the centre back hem and no waist adjustments; there are fragments of threads on the back where tabs have been unpicked. The edges of the foreparts, welted pockets and the front parts of the collar are piped with deep pink silk; the foreparts have slight padding over the chest. The under collar is in black silk twill and there is a buttonhole in it, each side, to attach to a button on the forepart, to hold down the collar. A loop of dull crimson silk ribbon is sewn inside the right forepart, to attach the top trouser button, and the hems of the foreparts are faced with dark brown leather. The leather was probably to protect the inside of the waistcoat from damage caused by rubbing against the buttons for braces on trousers.

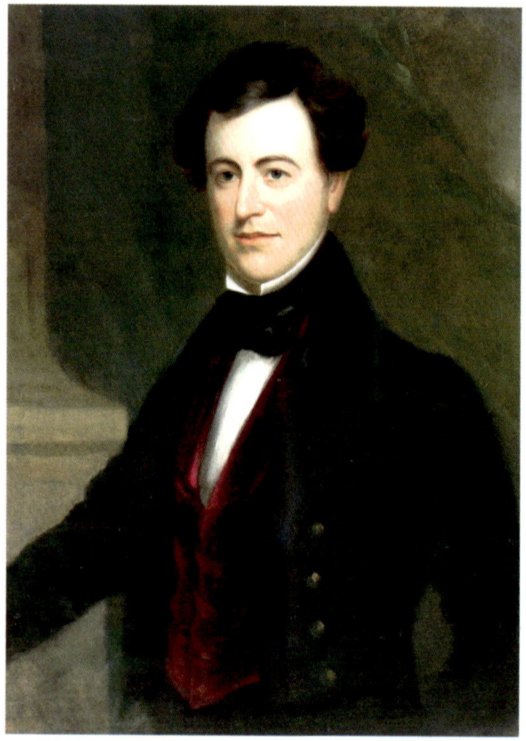

Frederic Thesiger by William Harold Cubley, 1840. National Civil War Centre – Newark Museum.

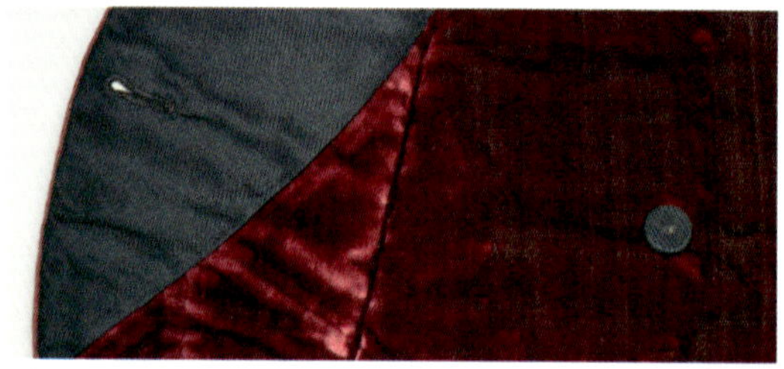

The concealed buttonhole under the collar on the left side, and the button on the forepart.

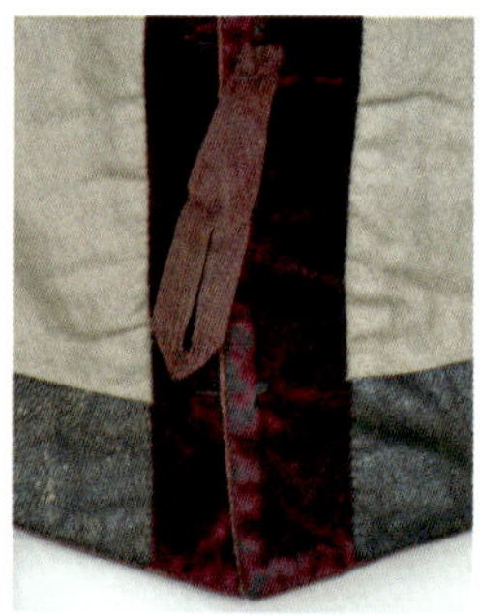

The loop inside the right forepart; the leather hem facings can also be seen.

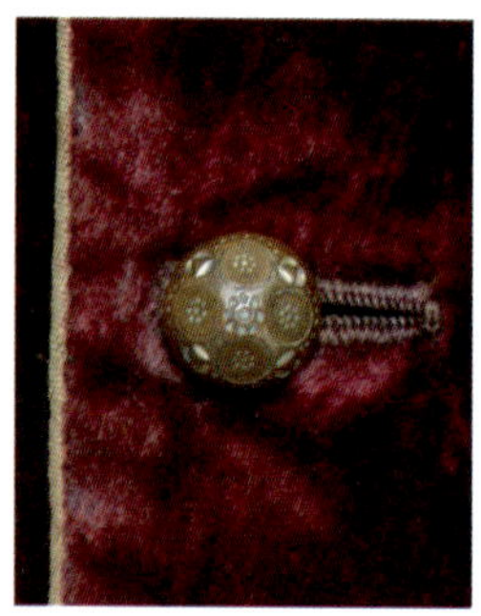

One of the buttons (page 216), showing as well the pink silk piping on the forepart edge.

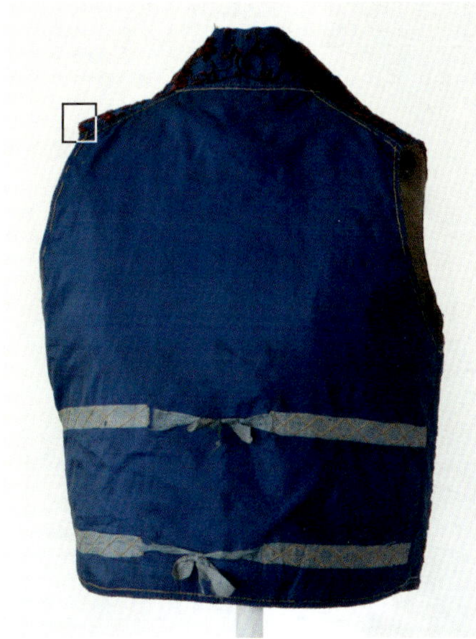

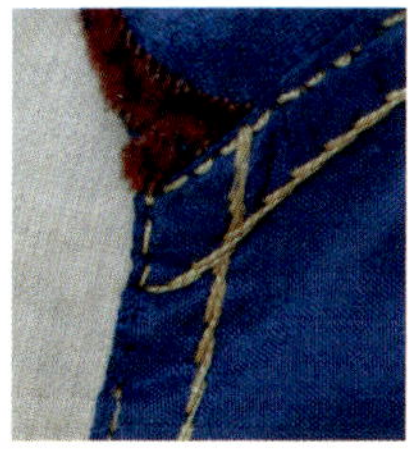

The decorative stitching on the back, outlined left.

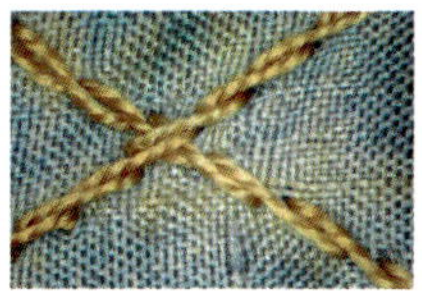

Detail of the stitching outlined below.

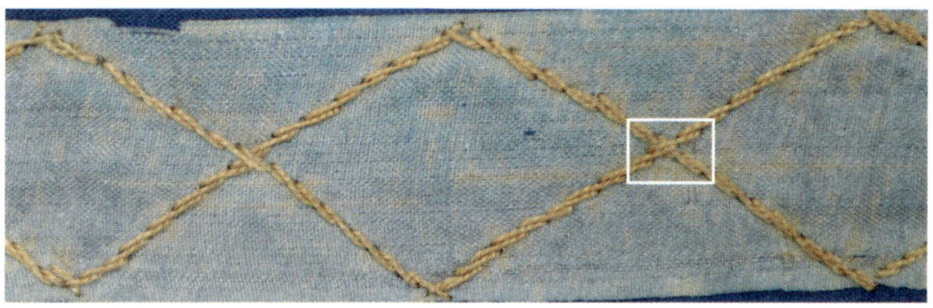

The decorative stitching on the ribbon ties.

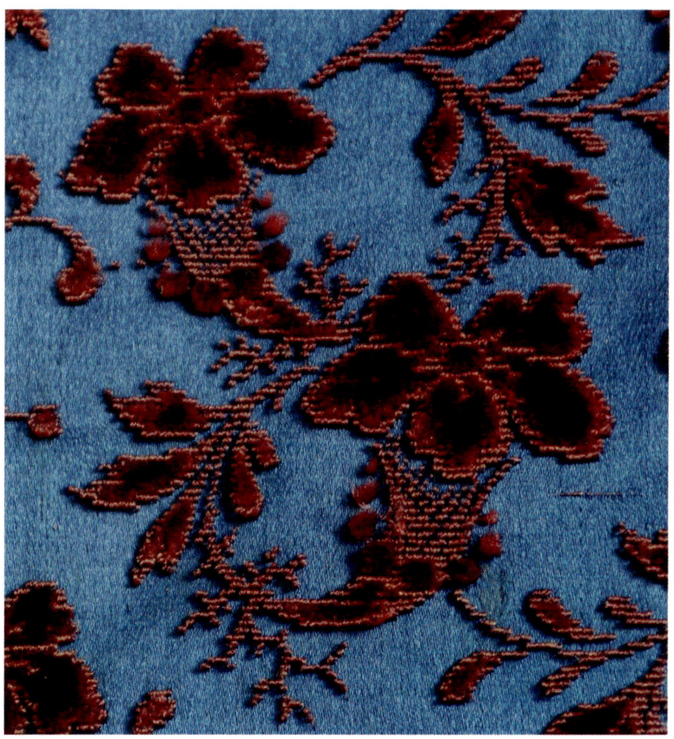

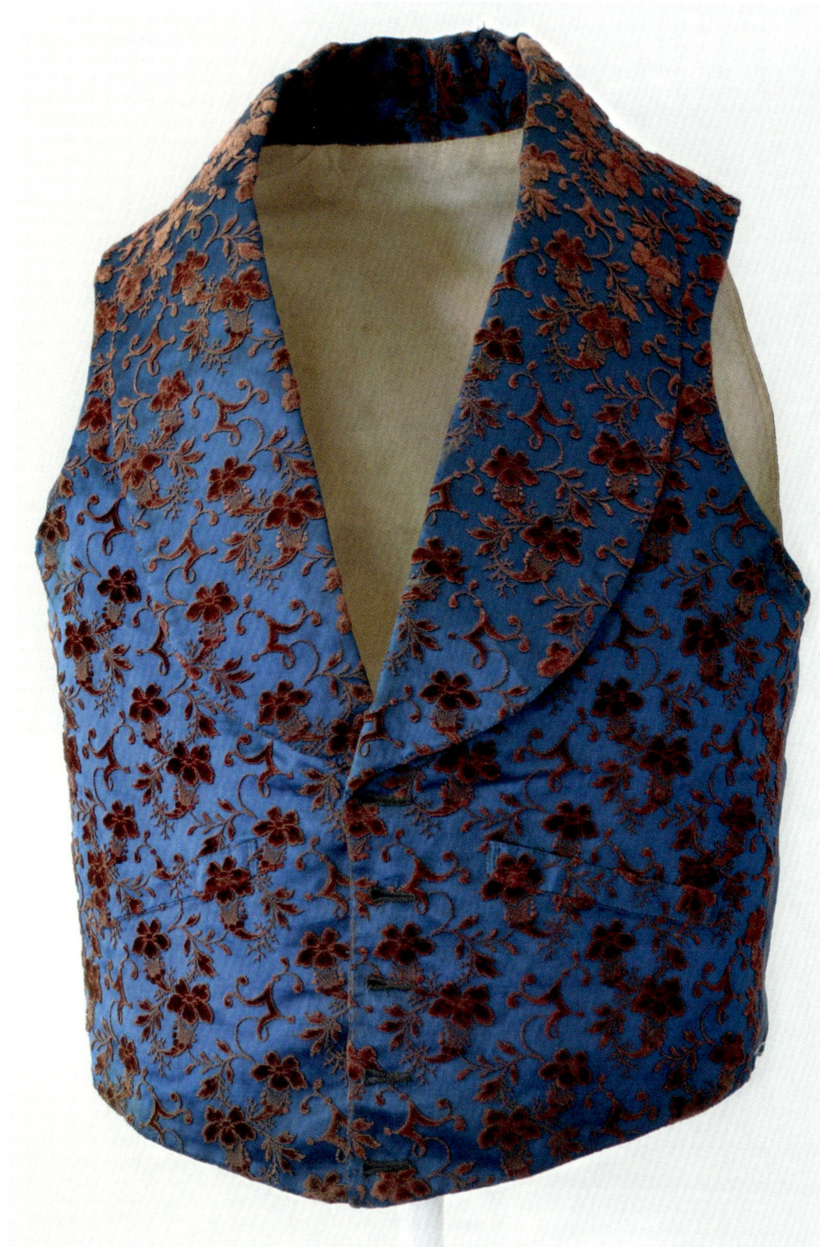

A waistcoat in blue silk satin, 1835-1845. HC.W-12.87

It has a pattern of flowers and scrolly branches in cut and uncut red silk velvet. The waistcoat has a roll collar and five buttonholes, but the buttons are missing; the pocket welts slant up towards the centre. It is lined in plain cream cotton and the back is in blue silk taffeta. The waist adjustment is by two pairs of pale blue silk ribbon ties which are now fragile; they are attached by decorative stitching in fawn twisted silk and the same stitching goes round the edges of the back. There are 2″-wide insertions of the blue taffeta in the side seams and the decorative stitching has been continued in cream silk, on their edges.

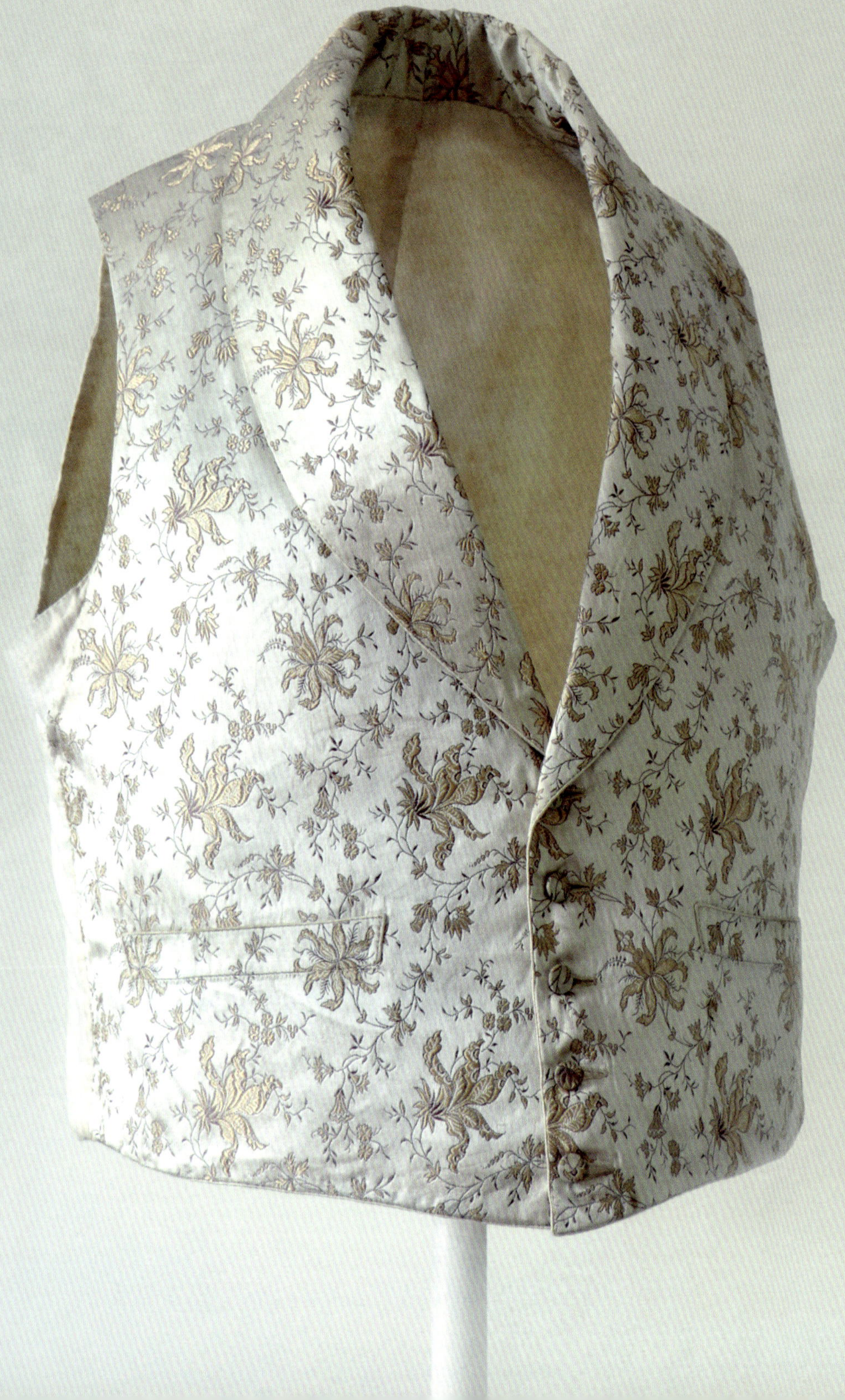

A waistcoat in ivory silk satin, 1835-1845.
HC.W-3.97-2

The silk has a woven pattern of stylised flowers and trailing stems in peach and plum colours. The waistcoat has a narrow ivory silk piping on the edges of the roll collar, the foreparts and the tops of the two welted pockets; there are five covered buttons. The lining and the back are in ivory plain weave cotton, and there is one pair of ivory chevron weave cotton tapes on the back to adjust the waist size. The waistcoat seems to have been altered to fit another wearer; there is an inserted section at the back of the collar, inserted triangles of linen where the shoulder seams meet the collar and pieces of linen added to make the armholes less deep.

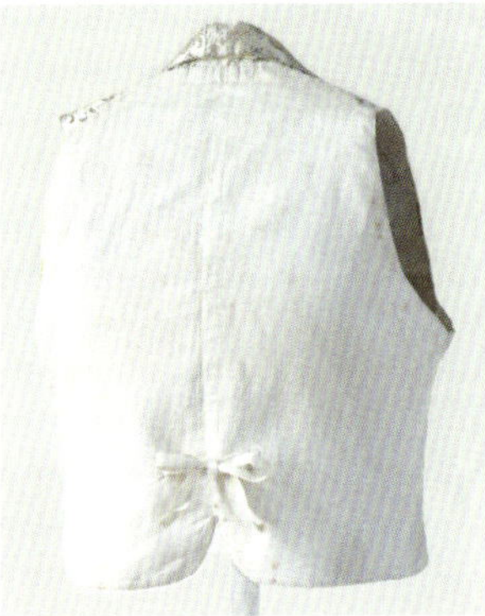

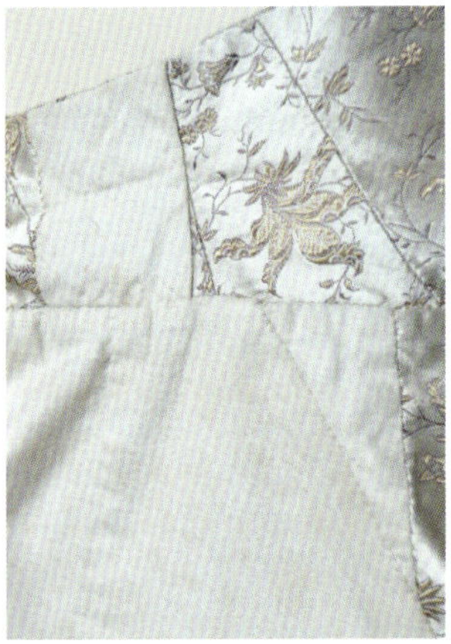

Underneath the collar at the back, showing the piecing and the inserted triangle in the shoulder seam.

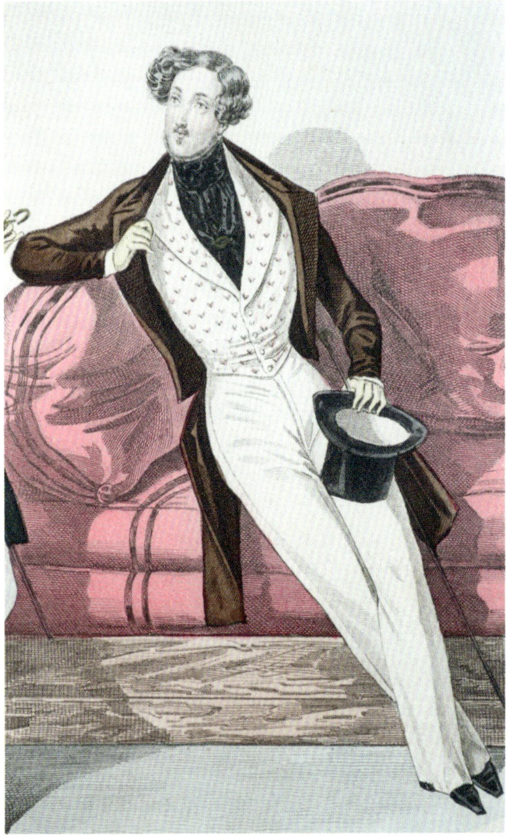

Fashion plate from *Le Follet*, July 1835.

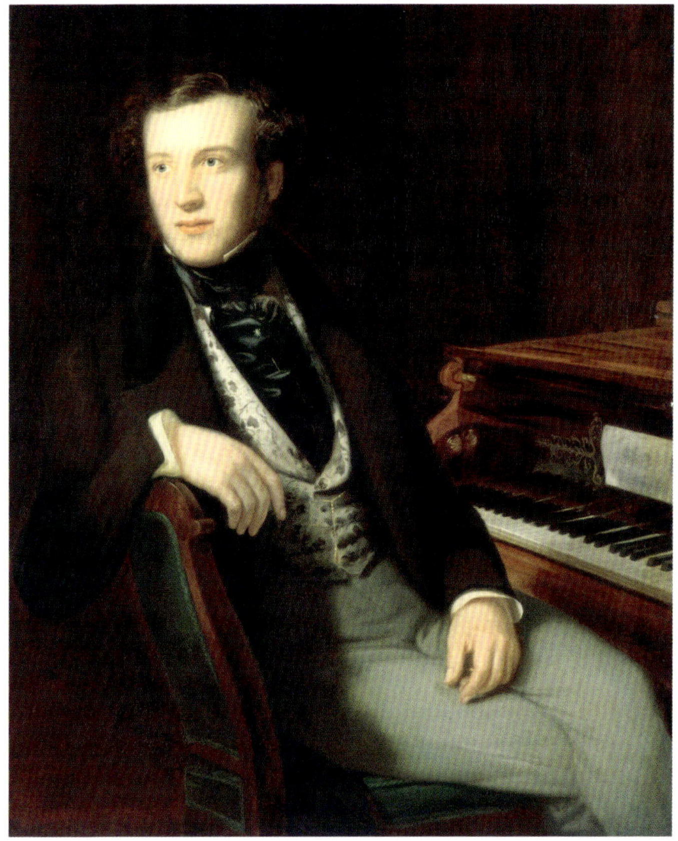

Unknown Man, formerly known as *Michael William Balfe* attributed to Richard Rothwell, 1840. © National Portrait Gallery, London.

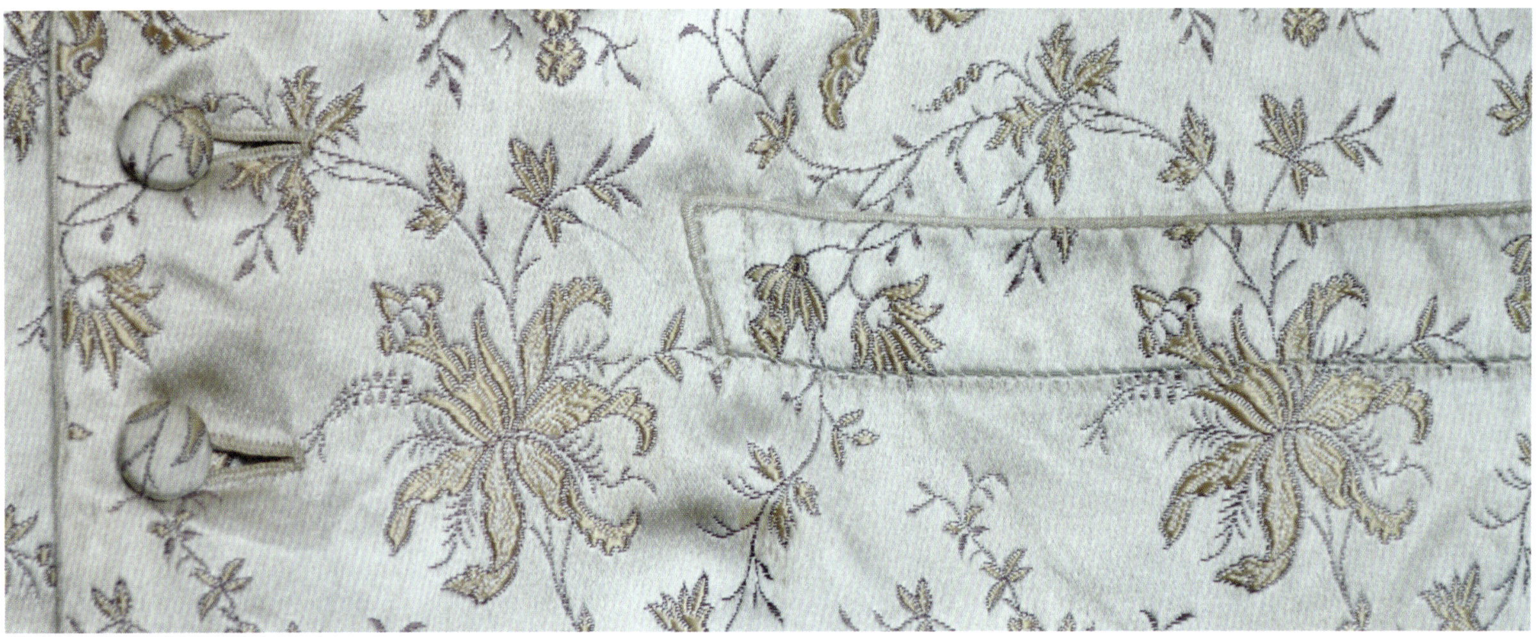

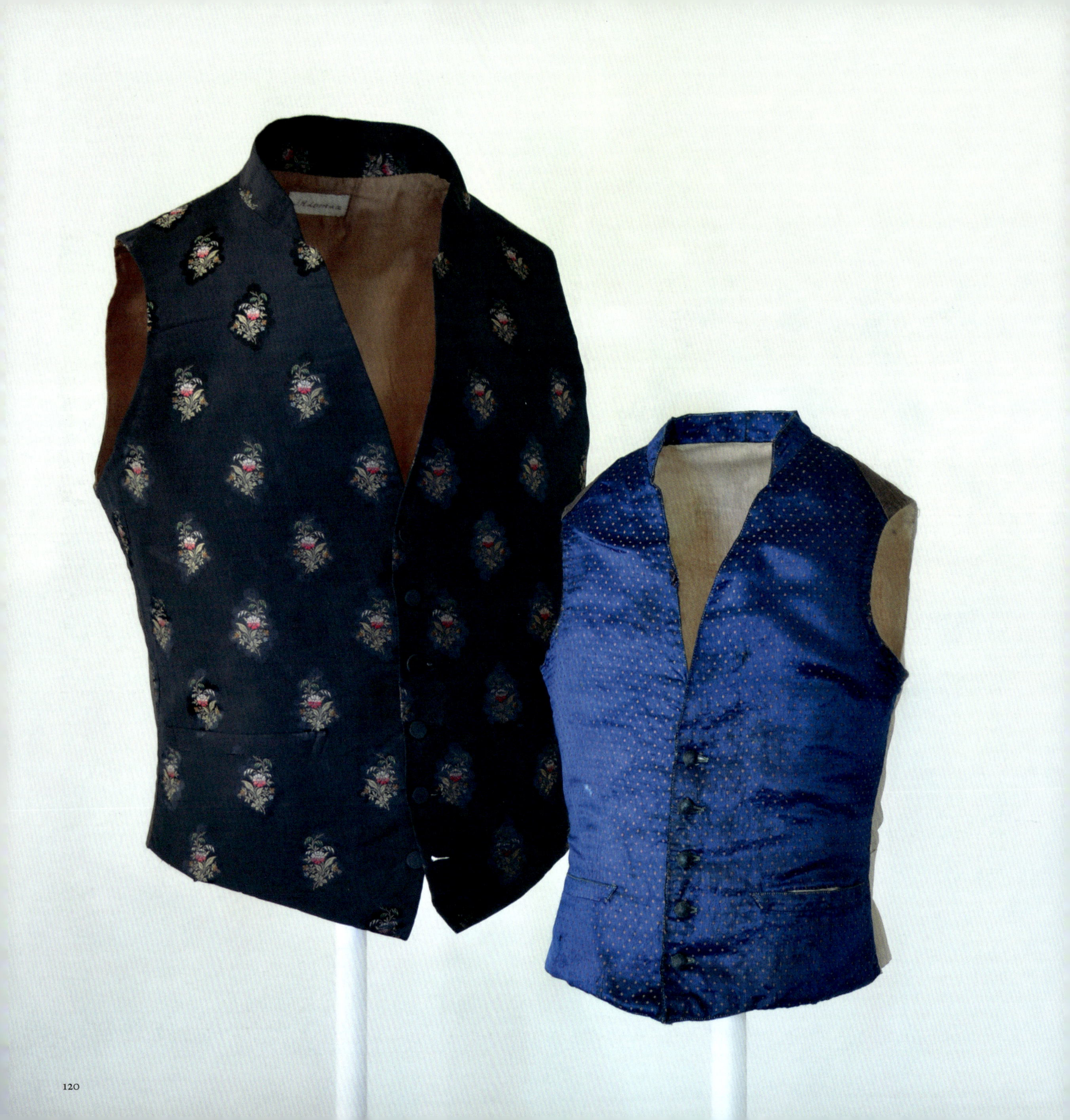

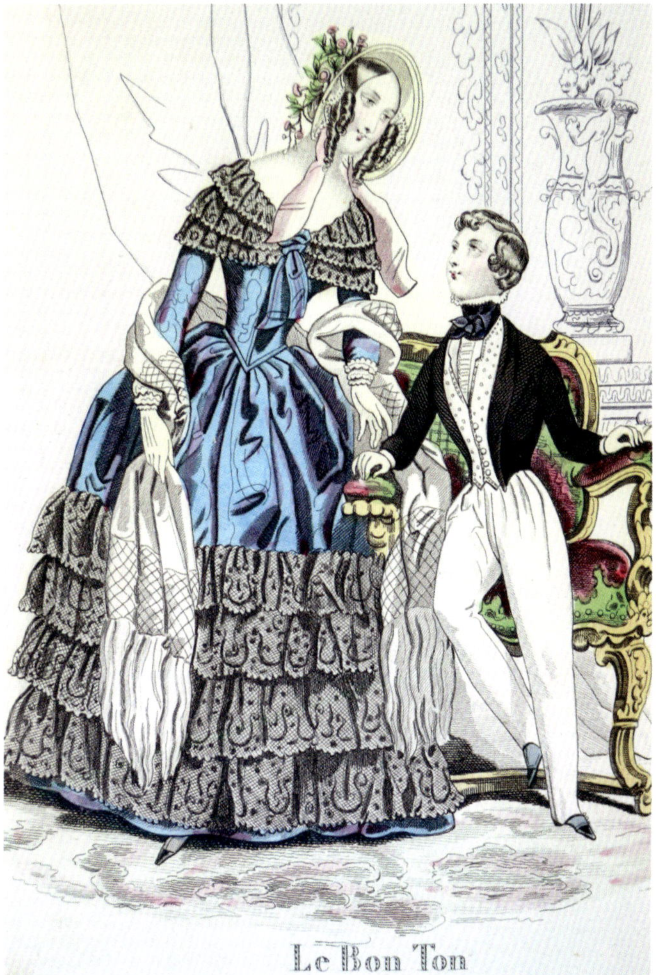

Fashion plate in *Blackwood's Lady's Magazine and Gazette*, 1841.

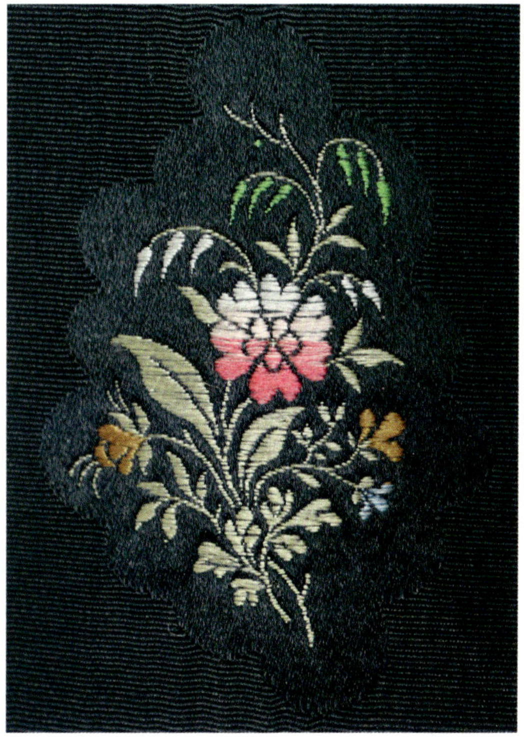

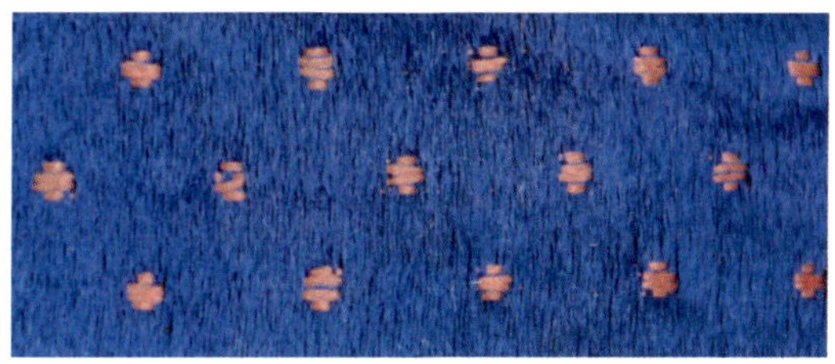

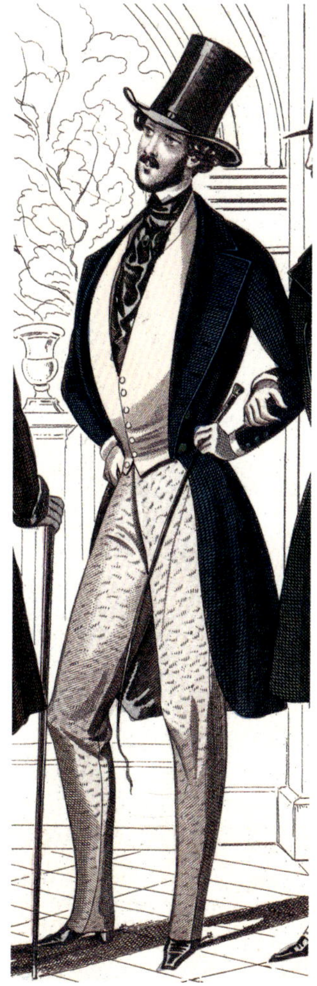

Fashion plate from *Paris Élégant*, 1843.

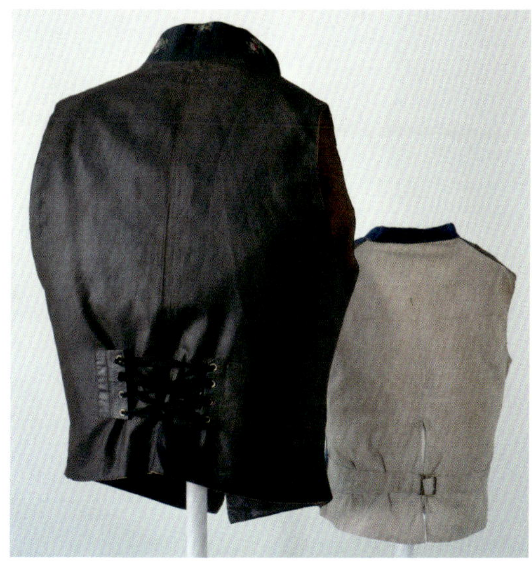

***Opposite, left:* A waistcoat in black silk grosgrain, 1840-1850.** HC.W-5.86

The silk has a woven pattern of polychrome sprays of flowers and leaves on a cloud-shaped satin lozenge. There are six black satin-covered buttons, a stand collar and two welted pockets; the forepart hems are faced with dark brown leather. The lining is ginger-coloured cotton twill and the back is in dark brown silesia with a waist adjustment of tabs with four pairs of metal eyelets and a narrow black cotton ribbon for lacing. A name-tape is sewn inside the back neck, with the name J. A. Lomax written in ink.

***Opposite, right:* A waistcoat, for a boy, in blue silk satin, 1840-1850.** HC.W-10.13

The silk has a woven pattern of pink dots, a stand collar and five thread-covered domed buttons; there are two welted pockets. The foreparts are lined in natural linen and the back is in the same linen, with no lining; the waist adjustment is by a backstrap with a brass buckle (page 210). There are triangles of dark brown linen on each shoulder at the top of the armhole, and there is a 5 1/2″ slit at the bottom of the centre back. At some point a 1 1/2″ tuck had been taken across the shoulder blades, which has now been unpicked.

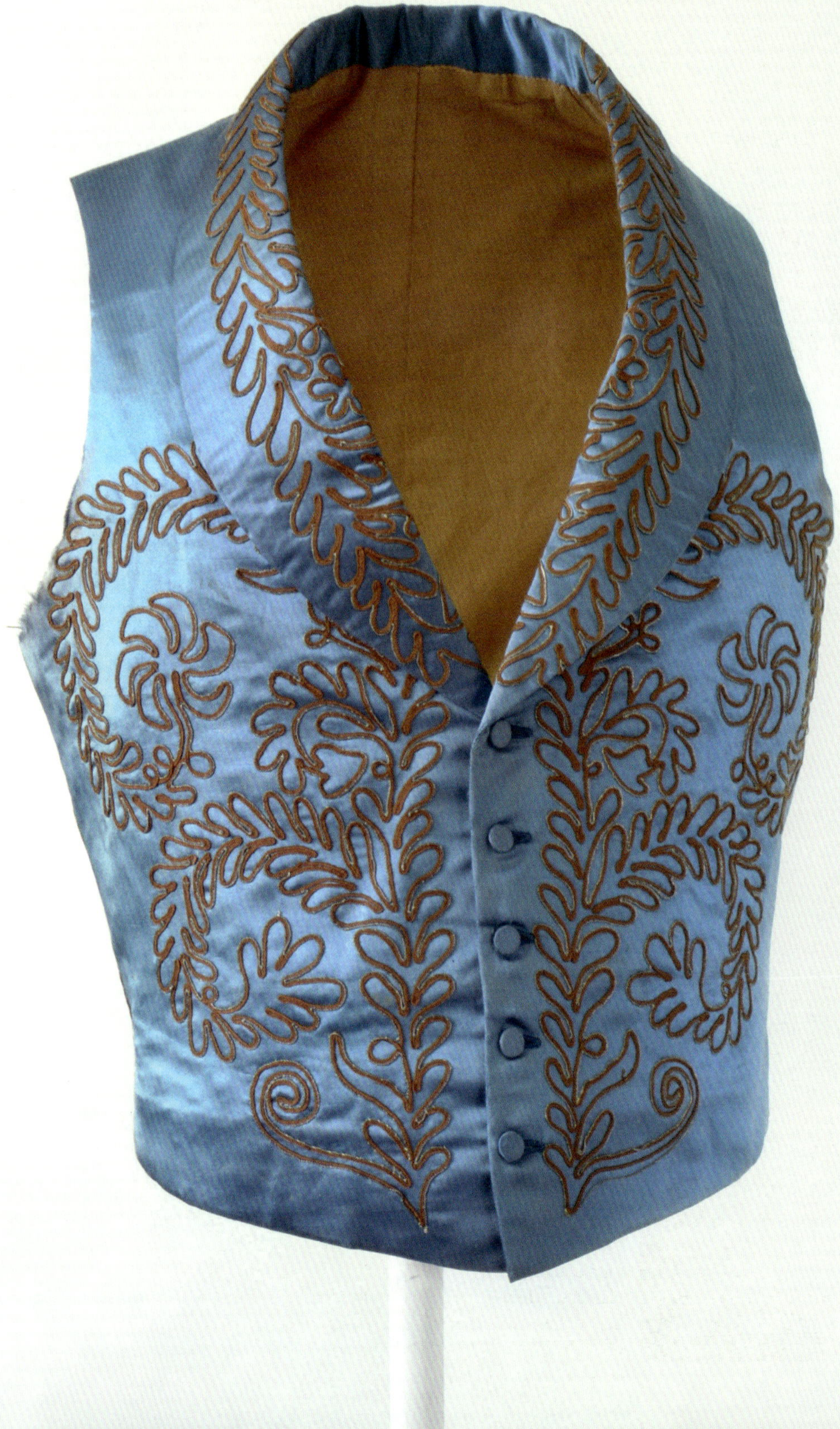

A waistcoat in blue silk satin, 1845-1855.
HC.W-4.15-1

It has a design of loopy-edged leaves made by couched tan-coloured russia braid, or soutache, and a cord of twisted silver filé threads; this covers the foreparts and the roll collar. The five buttons are covered in the blue satin. The back is black cotton twill and the lining is pale tan plain cotton; the forepart hems are faced with dark brown leather. The back waist adjustment is two long tabs with eight pairs of metal eyelets, through which is threaded narrow black elastic, now perished; each end of this is sewn under the tabs, beside the bottom two eyelets. The tabs are marked "Masters's Patent".

A piece of paper came with the waistcoat stating: "Worked by Frances Cathcart for her dear Brother James – he died in India aged 24 – Lt. in the 50th B.A.I."

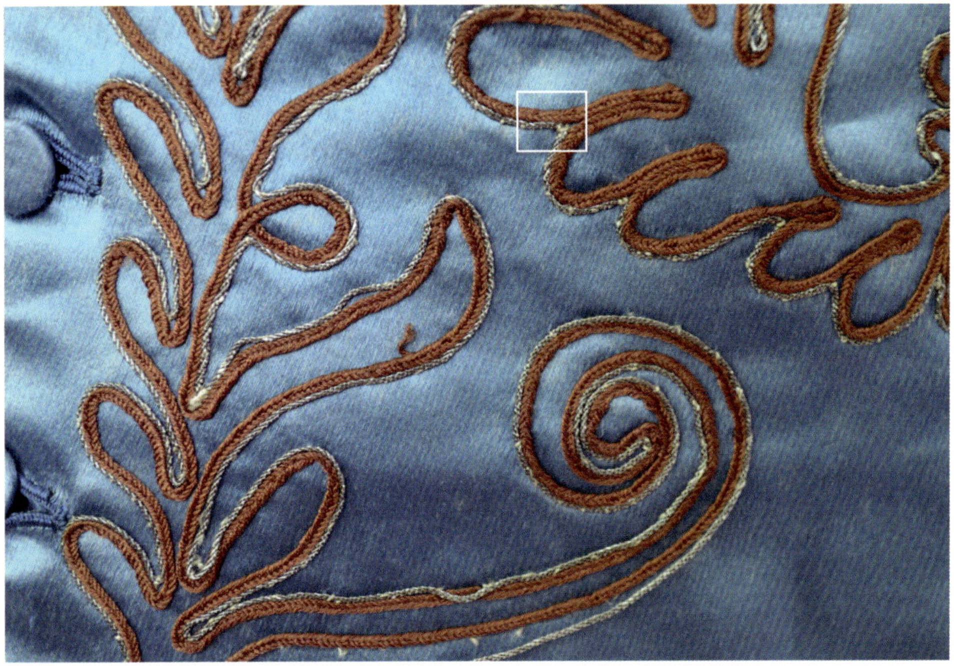

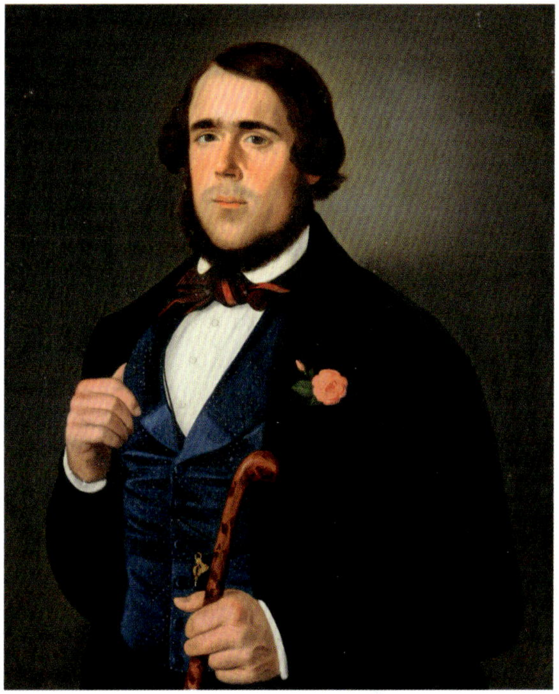

Portrait of a Young Gentleman in a Blue Waistcoat, British School, 1840. Courtesy of the Jersey Heritage Collections.

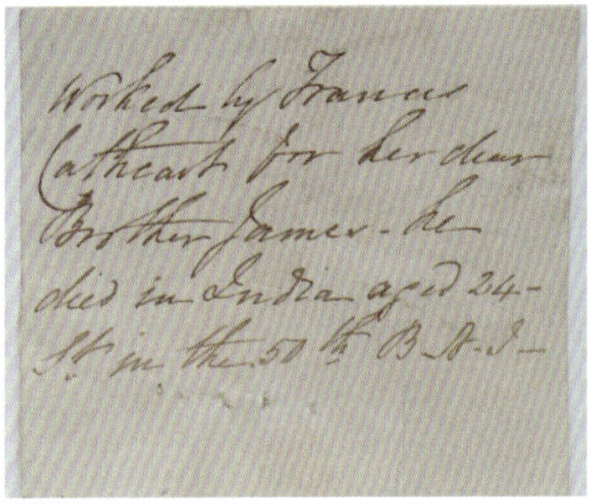
Worked by Frances
Cathcart for her dear
Brother James - he
died in India aged 24 -
Lt in the 50th B.N.I. -

Right: Detail of the embroidery outlined above.

Left: The piece of paper which came with the waistcoat.

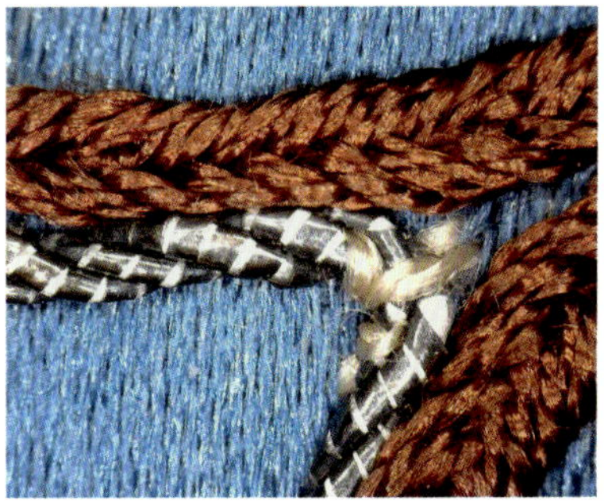

John Masters (1803-1873) applied for this patent when he was living in Leicester; he is described as a retired druggist in the 1851 census. His patent concerned the use of elastic material in clothing, and the elastic connector, described below, was primarily designed to expand the side seams of a waistcoat.

Excerpt from the patent application from John Masters, 31 May 1845.
"... I introduce the elastic connector, consisting of two vertical strips of cloth or other suitable material, which are stitched by their outer edges to the fore and back parts of the waistcoat and furnished on their inner edges with eyelet holes, and laced together by means of an elastic cord, made wholly or in part of caoutchouc [rubber]..., and passed backwards and forwards through the eyelet holes, in the usual way of lacing, the lace being drawn more or less tightly according to the degree of play desired to be given to the waistcoat. A band of the same description as the elastic connector last before described may be applied to the backs of waistcoats in order to give elasticity of the same... Such bands and connectors may be made and sold separately from the waistcoats to which they are to be applied."

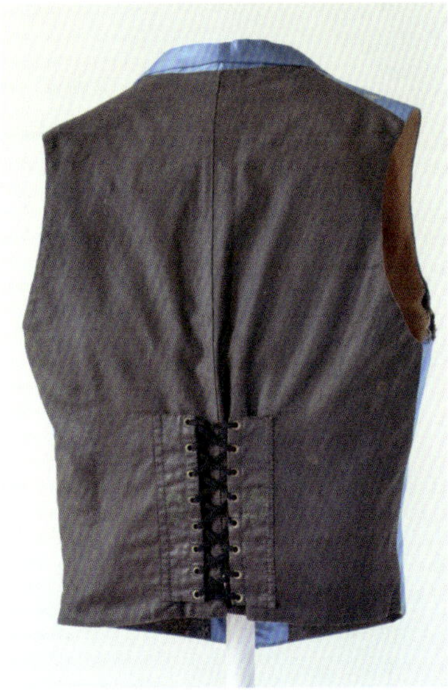

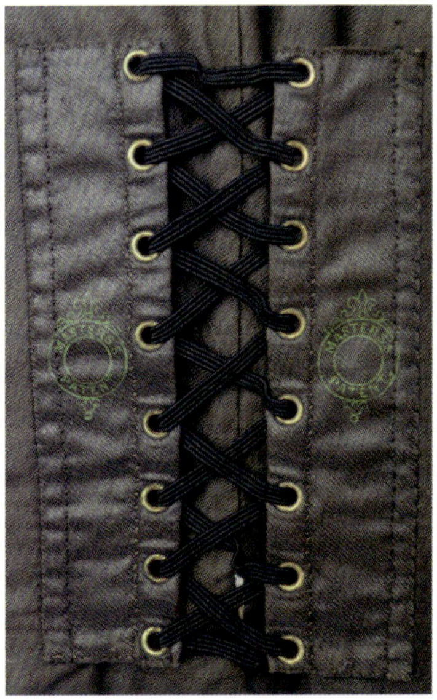

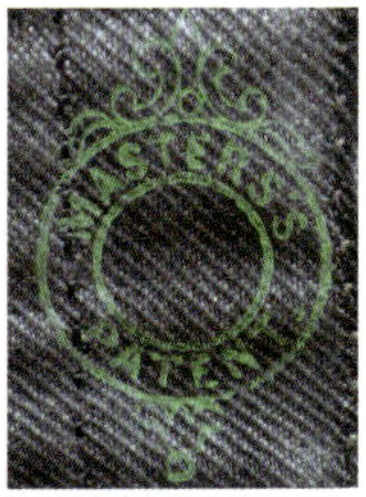

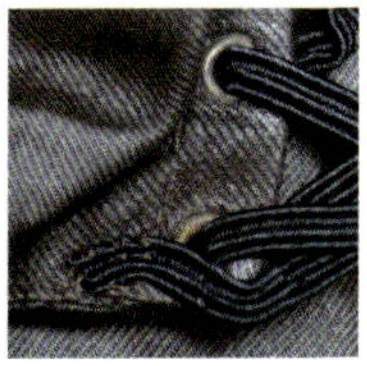

One end of the elastic stitched inside the base of a tab

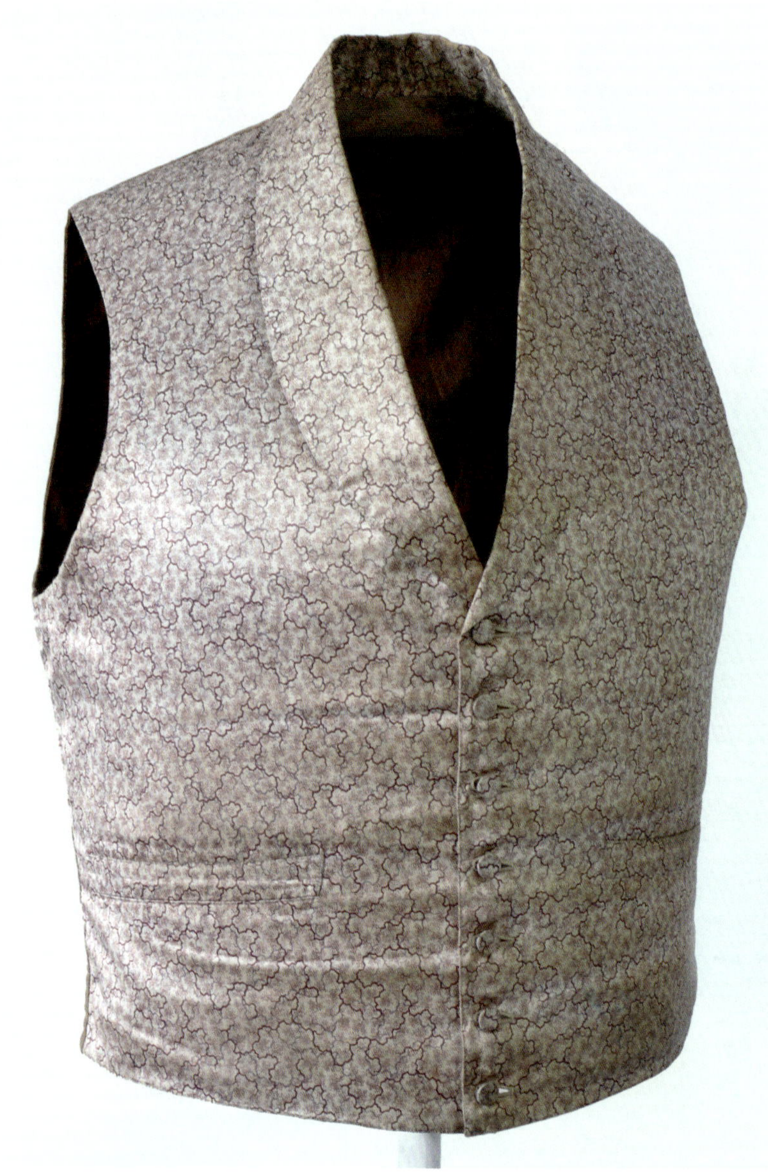

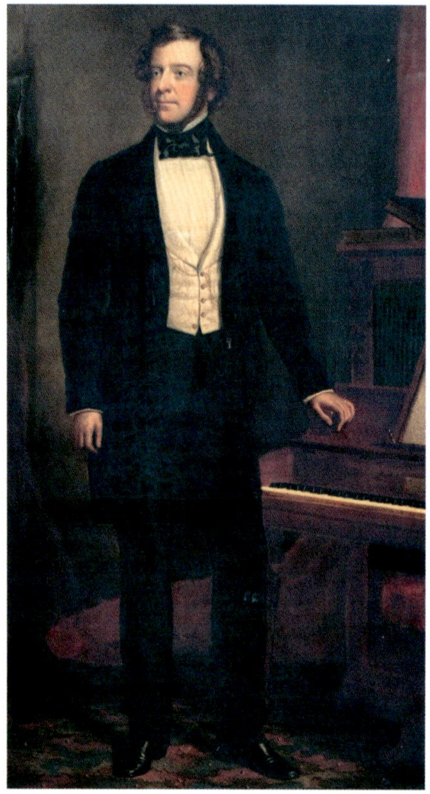

Left: Detail from *John Templeton* by Alexander Keith, 1846. By permission of East Ayrshire Leisure/ East Ayrshire Council. John Templeton (1802-1886) was a tenor, born into a musical family, in Riccarton, Kilmarnock. In the 1820s he moved to London where he had a successful career singing leading roles in opera. He retired in 1852.

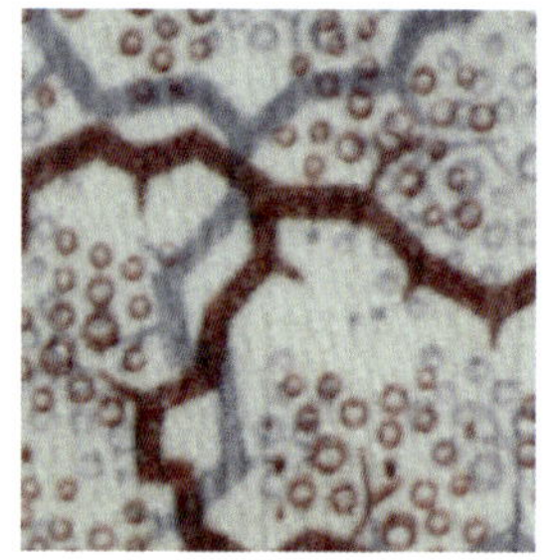

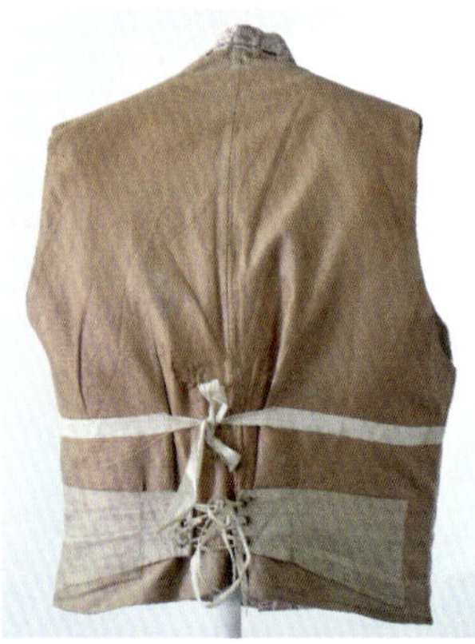

A waistcoat in ivory silk satin, 1840-1850.
HC.W-10.87-1

The pattern is printed in wine with the same pattern printed upside-down in greyish mauve. The waistcoat has a roll collar, welted pockets and seven self-covered buttons. The lining and back are in light brown cotton twill, with two types of waist adjustments: there is a pair of linen tape ties, and a pair of straps, in a lighter brown cotton, with bents in the ends and three pairs of brass eyelets for lacing with a linen tape. The foreparts are creased from wear.

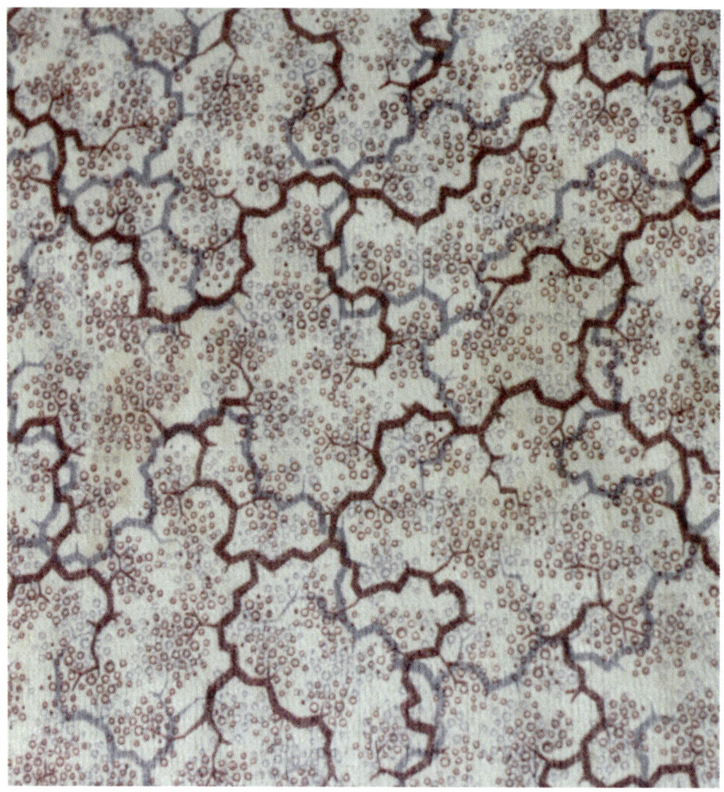

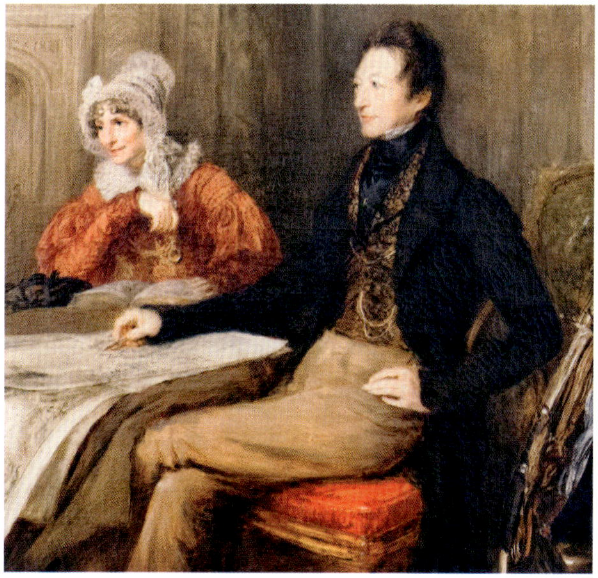

Detail from *General John Le Mesurier and His wife Martha ... at the Handing over of the Island of Alderney* by John Linnell, 1841. Alderney Island Hall.

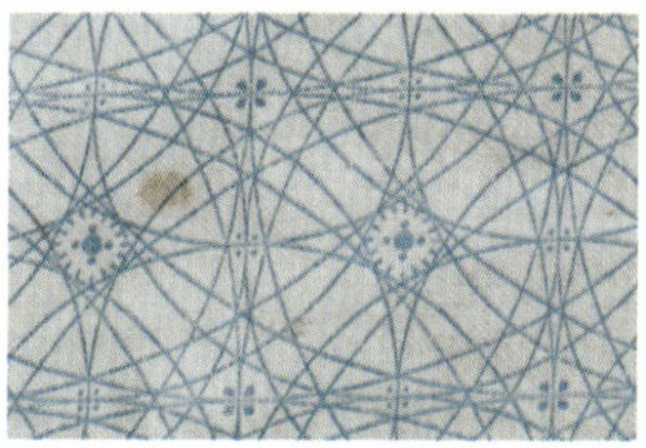

The printed cotton lining of the foreparts.

Around this date, watch chains began to be worn fastened into a buttonhole of the waistcoat, with the watch in one of the pockets, as in the painting, above.

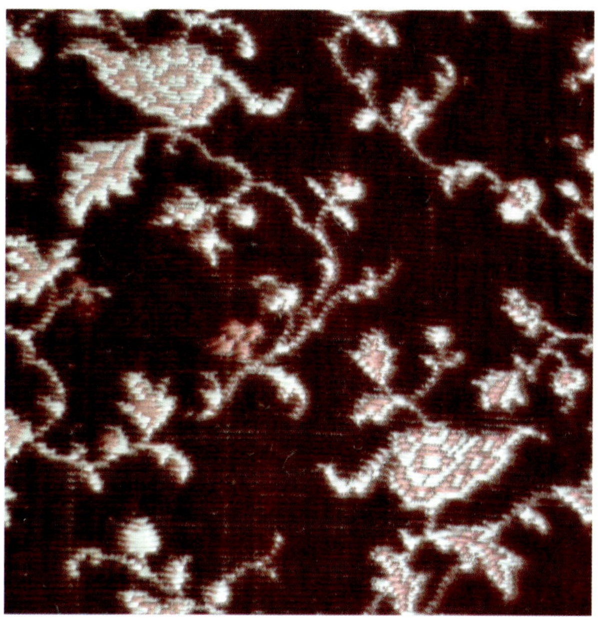

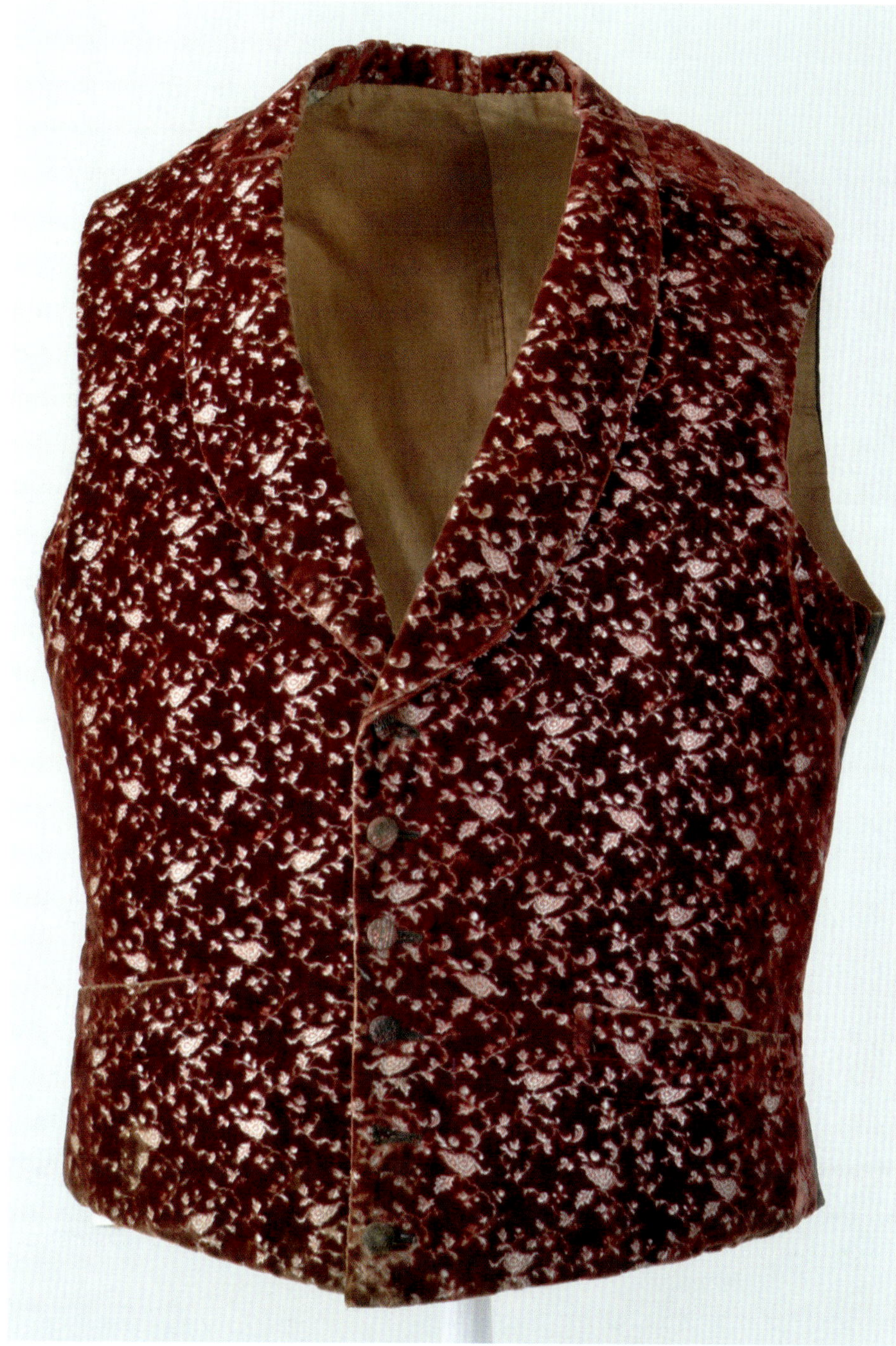

A waistcoat in crimson silk voided velvet, 1845-1855. HC.W-3.15-3

The velvet has a voided leafy pattern in coral and ivory silk. The waistcoat foreparts are lined in ivory cotton twill with a printed pattern of blue curved lines, and the back lining is brown cotton twill. The back is in dark brown silesia with a waist adjustment of tabs with bents in the ends and three pairs of brass eyelets; the narrow black silk ribbon lacing may not be original. The forepart hems have a lining of wine morocco leather, and the buttons are covered in red, white and black patterned silk.

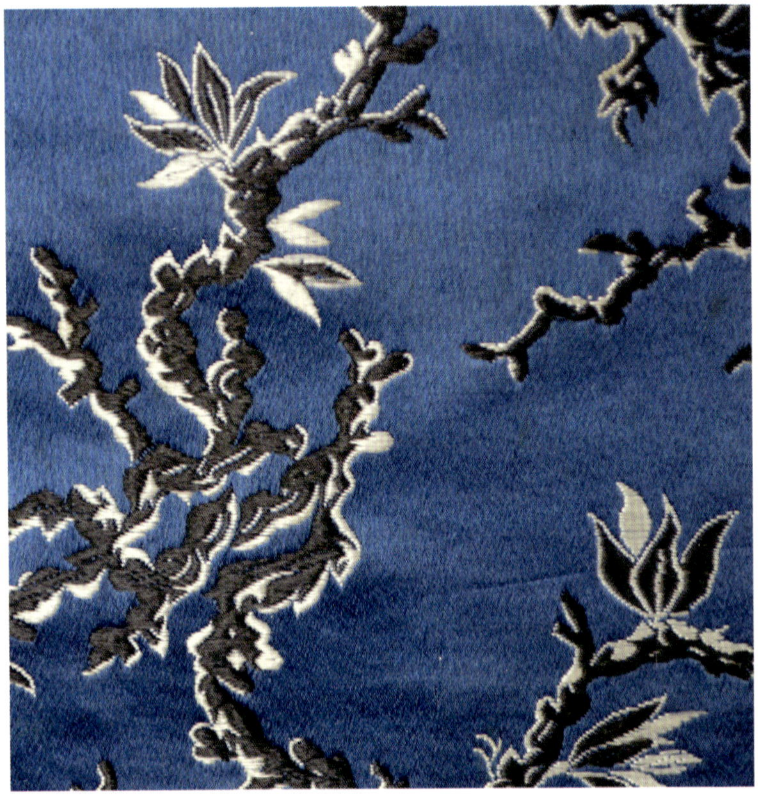

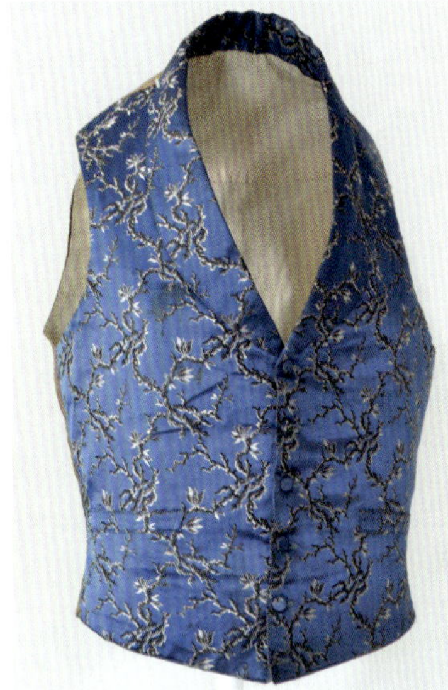

A waistcoat in patterned blue silk satin, 1840-1850. HC.W-0.58

The lining is cream, and the back is brown cotton twill with lacing tabs at the waist. There are six covered buttons and the front hems are faced with red morocco leather.

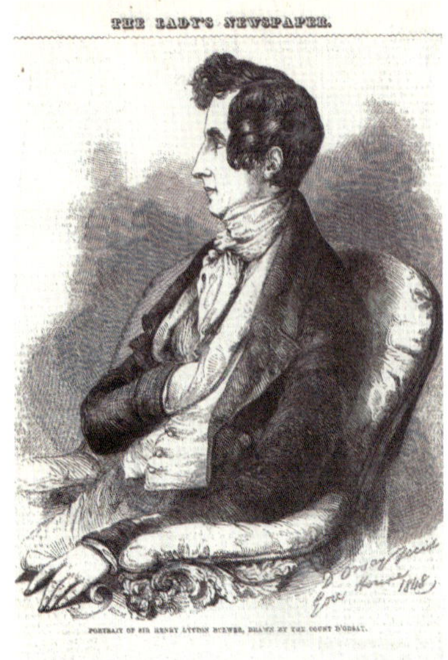

Portrait of Sir Henry Lytton Bulwer, drawn by the Count d'Orsay for *The Lady's Newspaper*, 1848.

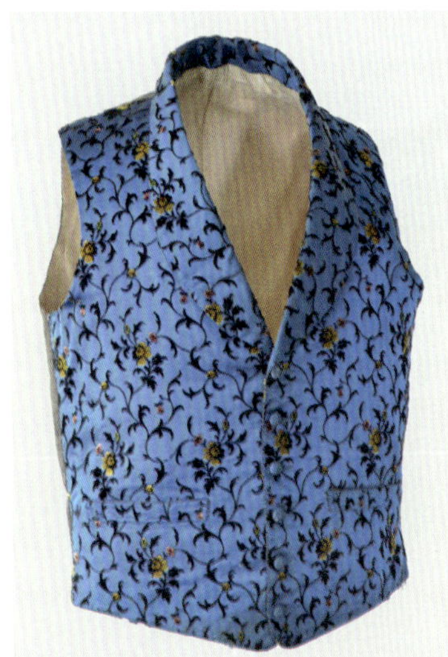

A waistcoat in blue silk satin, 1840-1850. HC.W-2.97

The silk has a trailing pattern in velvet. The lining is fawn cotton twill and the back is dark brown silesia with a backstrap at the waist. The six domed buttons are patterned with blue silk threads.

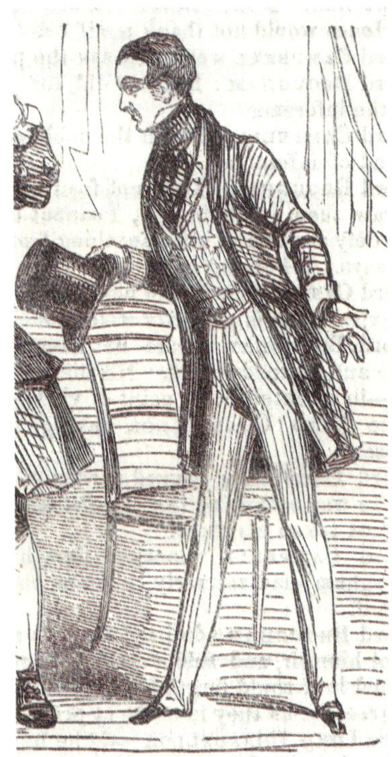

Detail from a cartoon in *Punch*, 1844.

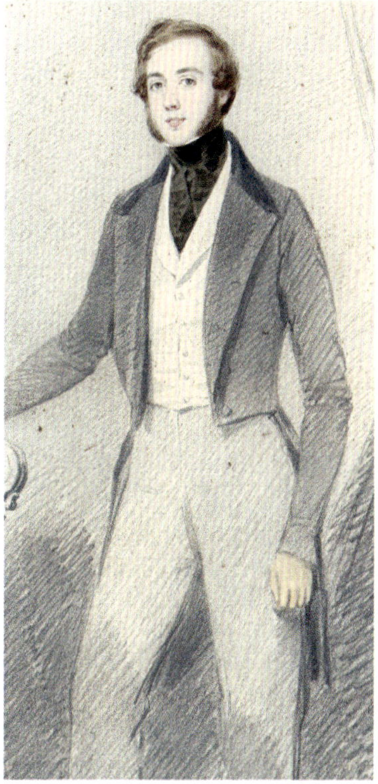

Sketch of an unknown man, 1841.

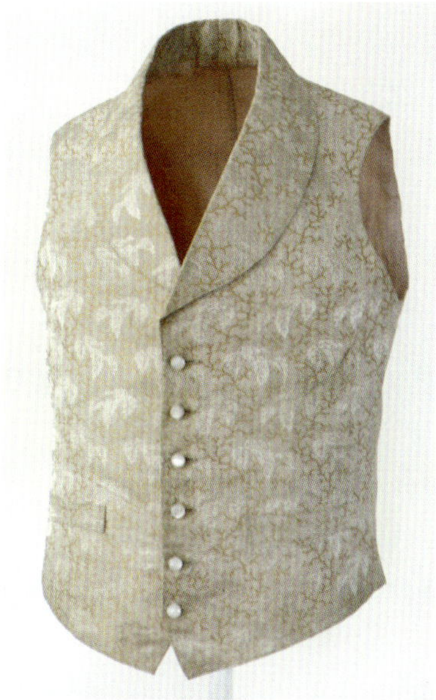

A waistcoat in patterned beige silk, 1840-1855. HC.W-4.89-1

It is lined in pink cotton twill and the back is plain white cotton with two pairs of tape ties. The removable buttons here are replacements.

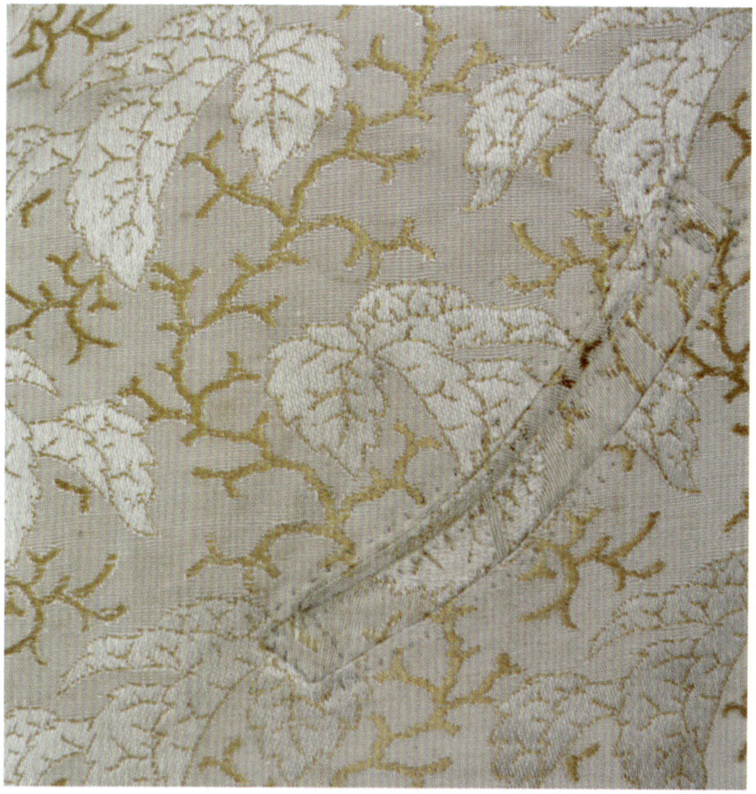

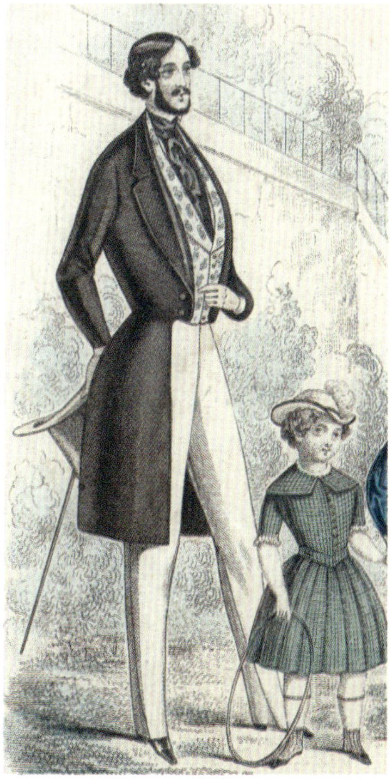

Fashion plate from *Musée des Modes*, 1842.

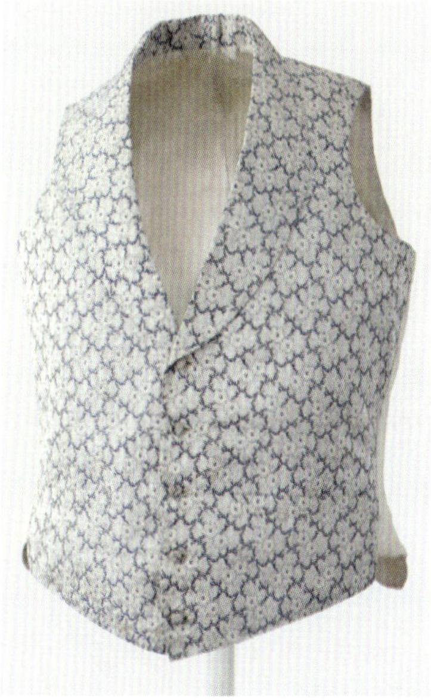

A waistcoat in ivory silk, 1840-1855. HC.W-0.71

The floral pattern in different weaves has twigs in dark blue. The lining and back are plain white cotton, with a backstrap at the waist.

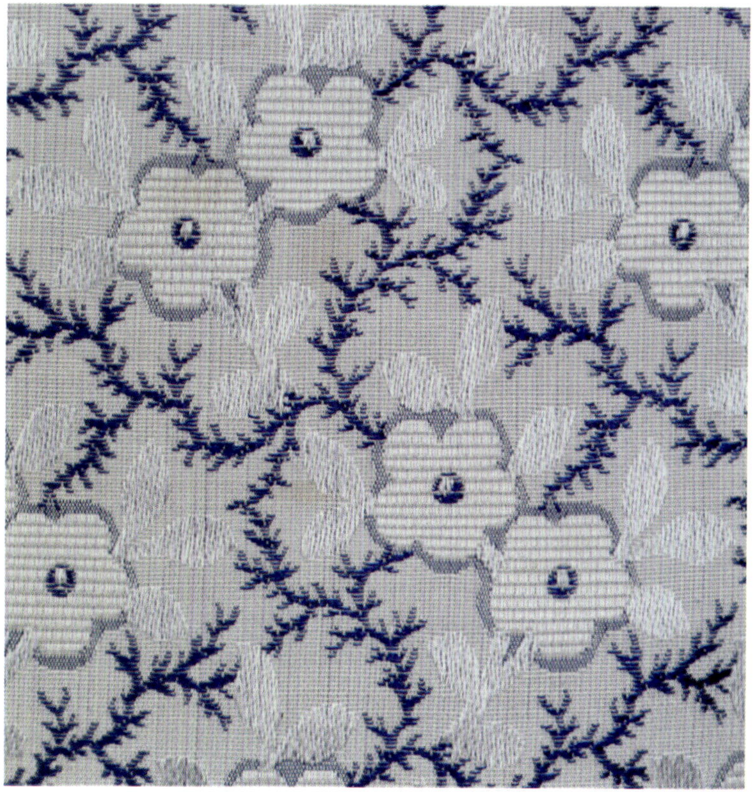

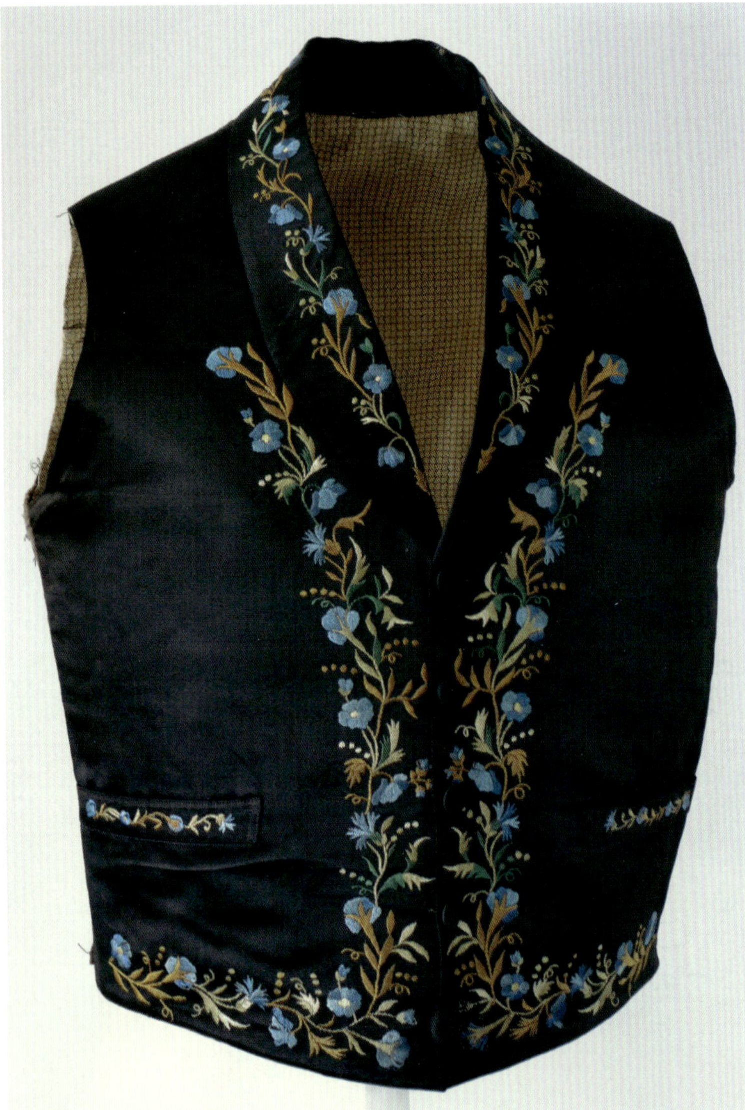

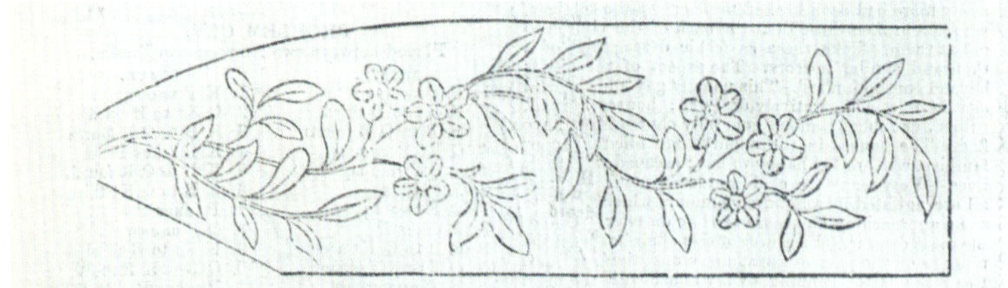

COLLAR FOR WAISTCOAT.

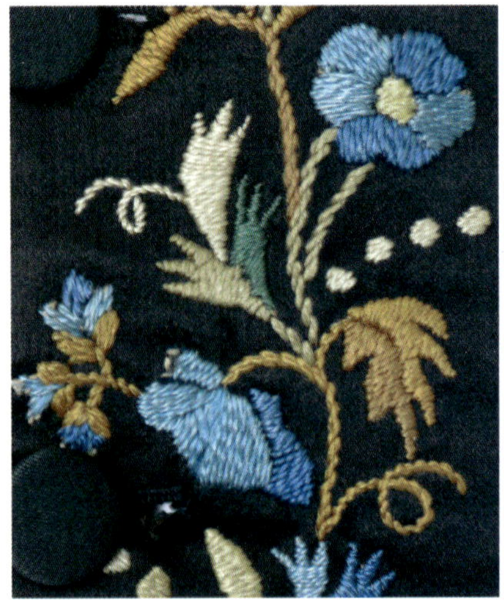

EMBROIDERY.

PATTERN FOR GENTLEMAN'S WAISTCOAT.

Materials—White or black satin, and three shades of green, three of blue, one of yellow, and two of brown Mitorse or Dacca silk.

Having framed the satin, draw the pattern with a crayon, and work in embroidery stitch. The stems are worked with the browns, the leaves with the greens, the flowers with the blues: shading according to taste. Make small dots in the centre with yellow, to form the petals of the flowers.

This pattern is very handsome and effective when worked in tambour, on blue or French-grey cashmere, using sewing silk a shade darker than the material, and a tambour needle No. 18.

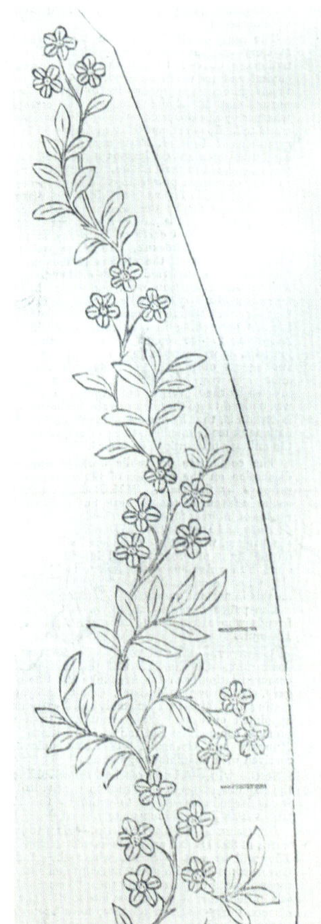

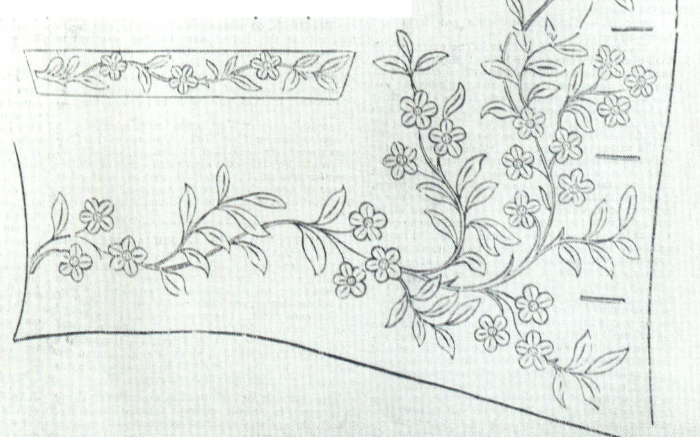

PATTERN FOR GENTLEMAN'S WAISTCOAT.

A waistcoat in black silk satin, 1840-1850. HC.W-3.15-1

It has an embroidered flower trail in blues and light brown silk threads, which decorates the roll collar and welted pockets, and forms a border to the foreparts. The lining is fawn cotton with a printed checked pattern of black and brown lines, and the back is brown silesia with a waist adjustment of tabs with bents on the ends and three pairs of metal eyelets for lacing; the original lace is missing. There are five covered buttons, one of them a replacement, and the forepart hems have a brown leather facing. The waistcoat has been altered and mended for theatrical use in the late twentieth century.

Right: An embroidery pattern for a waistcoat published in *The Lady's Newspaper*, 1848. The collar pattern is at the top and the instructions are in the centre.

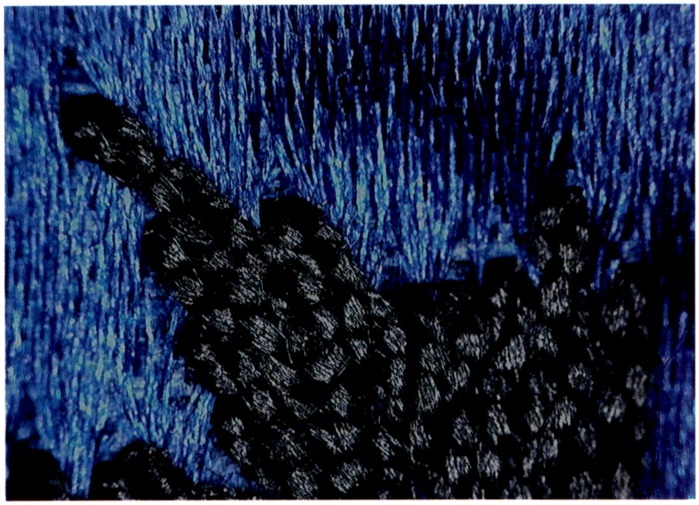

Detail of the embroidery, outlined below.

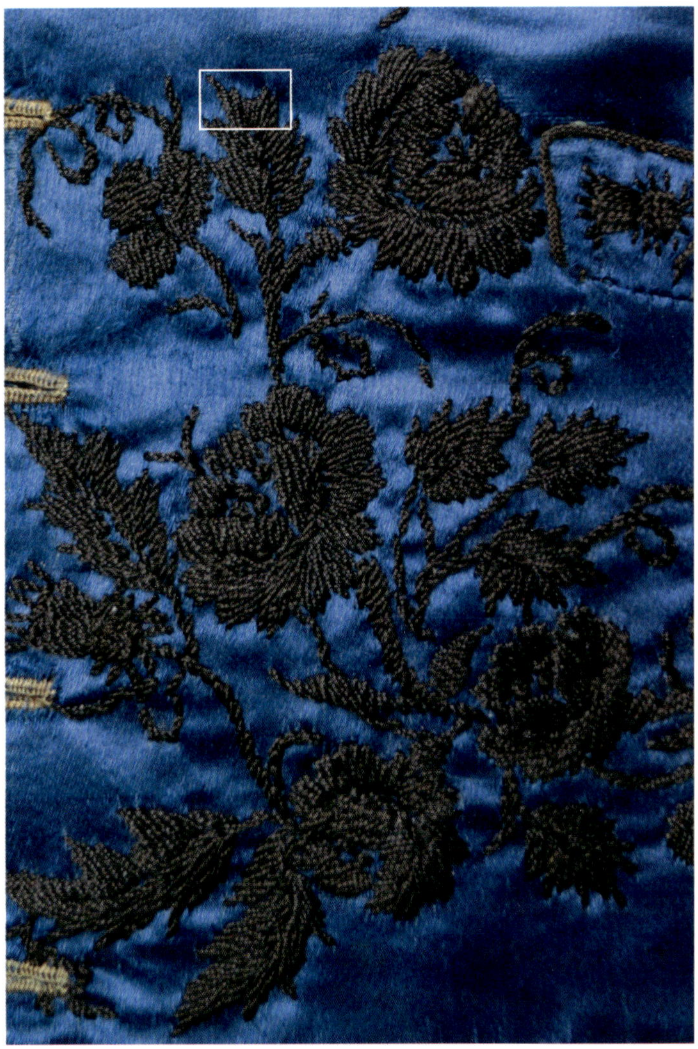

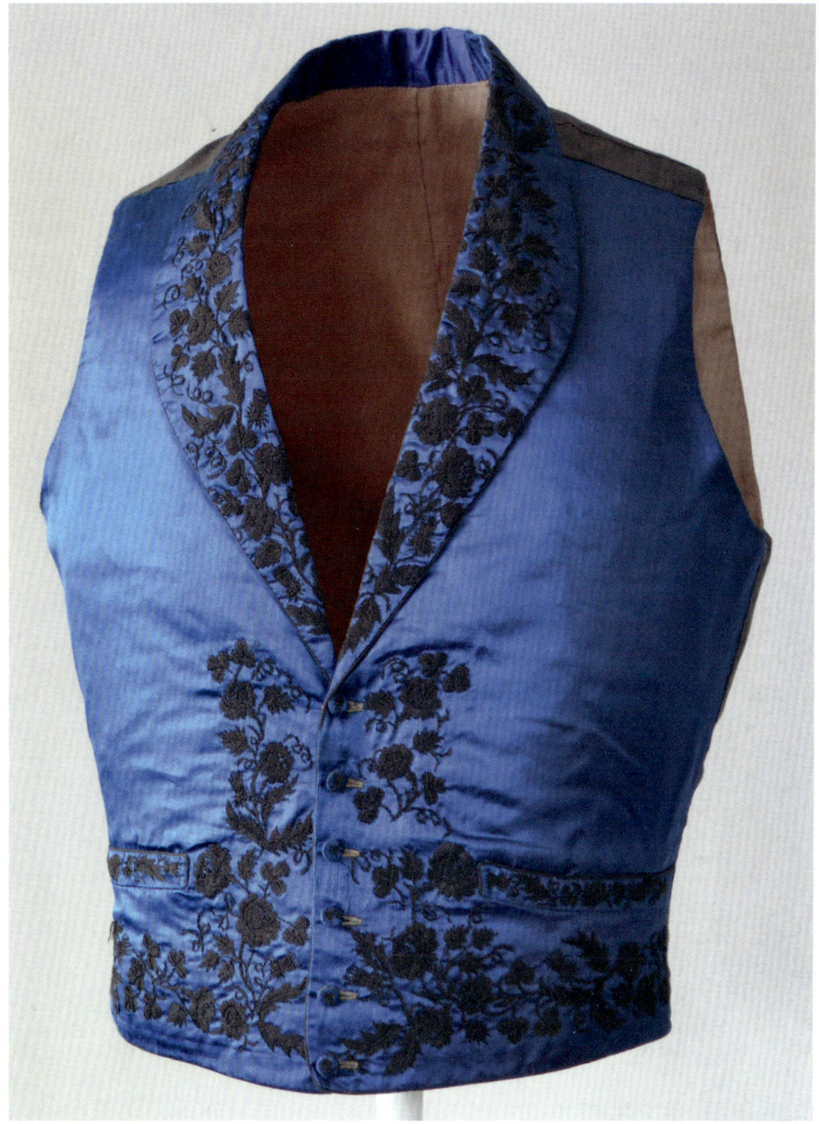

A waistcoat in blue silk satin, 1840-1850. HC.W-11.80

It has embroidery in a thick twisted black silk cord forming a pattern of flowers, leaves and stems on the foreparts, roll collar and welted pockets. The lining is a ginger-coloured cotton twill, and the back is dark brown silesia, with no waist adjustments. The six buttonholes are worked in fawn silk and the buttons are covered in the satin, with a motif in the black silk cord embroidered on each one. The hems of the foreparts are faced with black leather, which, unusually, extends up the front edges behind the buttonholes and buttons. The pocket tops, front edges and collar are edged with a fine black silk cord, to resemble piping.

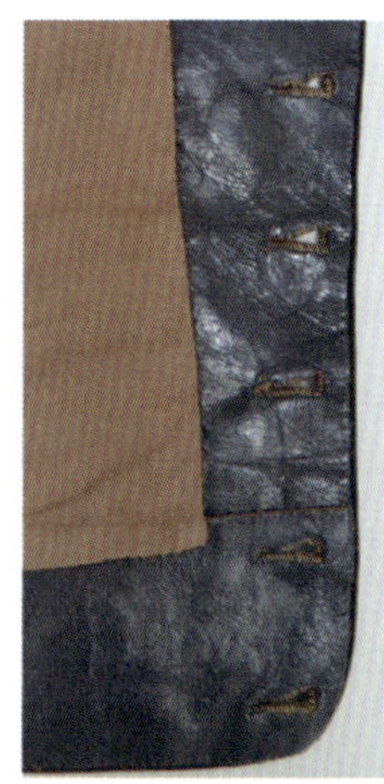

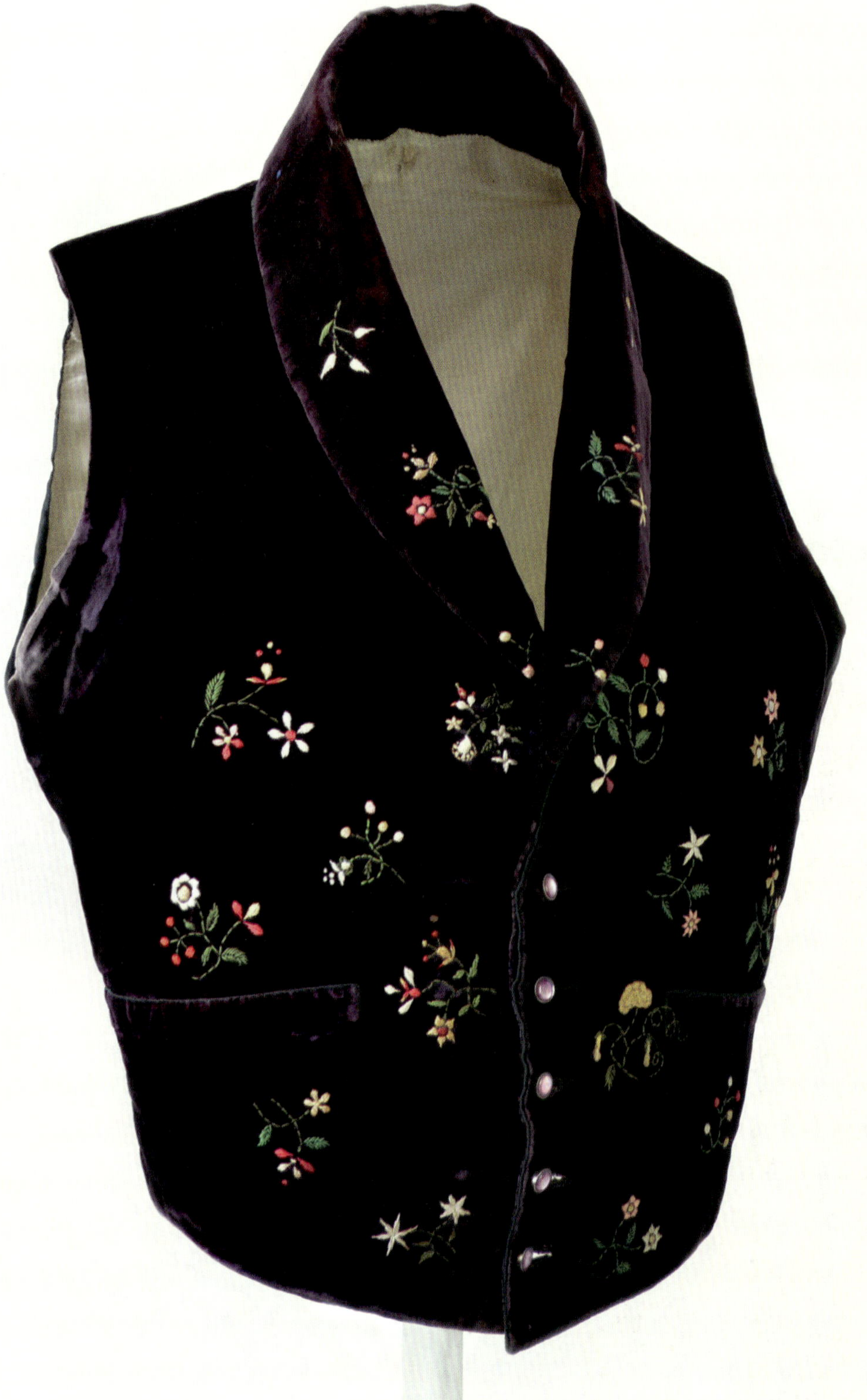

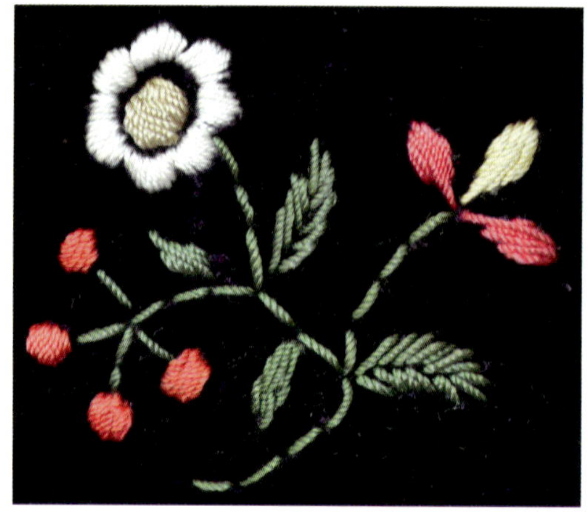

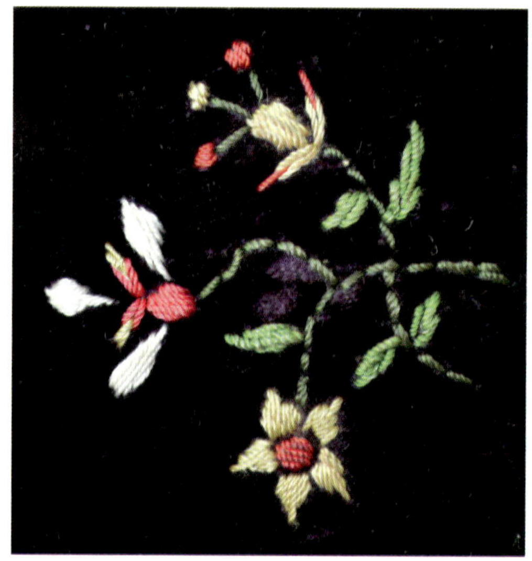

A waistcoat in deep purple silk velvet, 1835-1845.
HC.W-6.88-1

It has embroidered flower sprays in polychrome silk threads. They are all different, and the design and embroidery were probably not professionally done. There are five holes for removable buttons but the originals are missing and the ones here are replacements. It has a roll collar and two welted pockets. The lining is ivory silk which is left open along the right front edge and secured by a button to enable the fastenings of the removable buttons to be reached. The back is in black silk twill with a pair of black silk ribbon ties and a pair of straps, with a buttonhole in the end of one; the button is missing from the other strap. The waistcoat is well worn, so whoever it was made for must have appreciated the embroiderer's efforts.

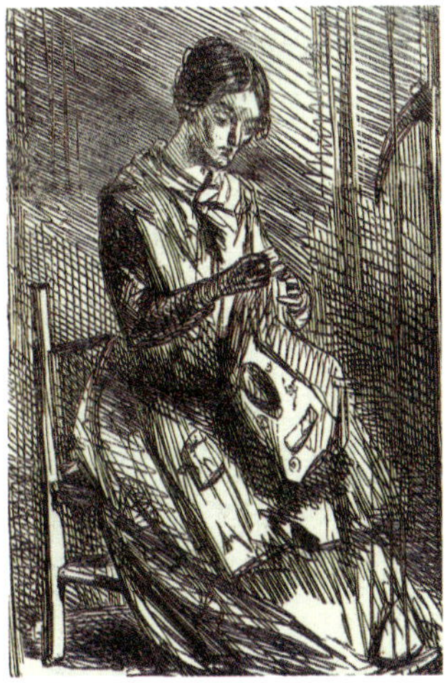

Detail from a cartoon in *Punch*, 1850.

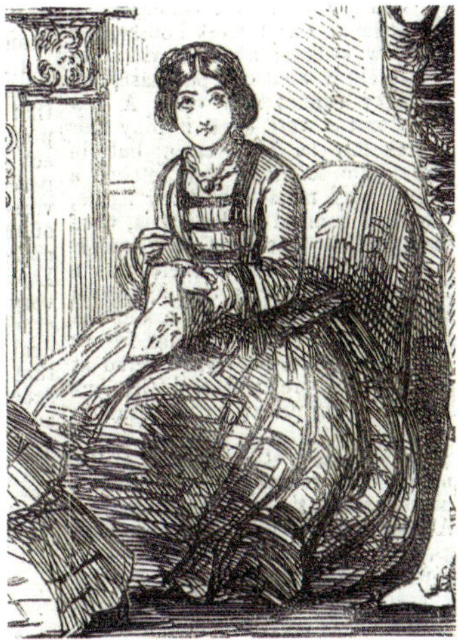

Detail from a cartoon in *Punch*, 1855.

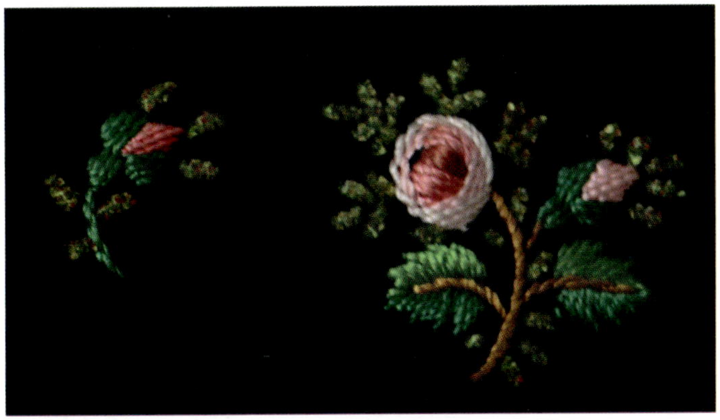

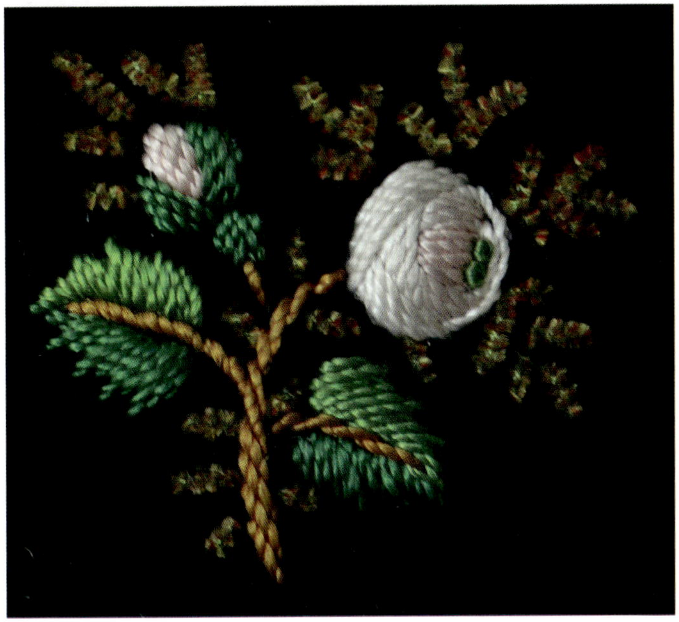

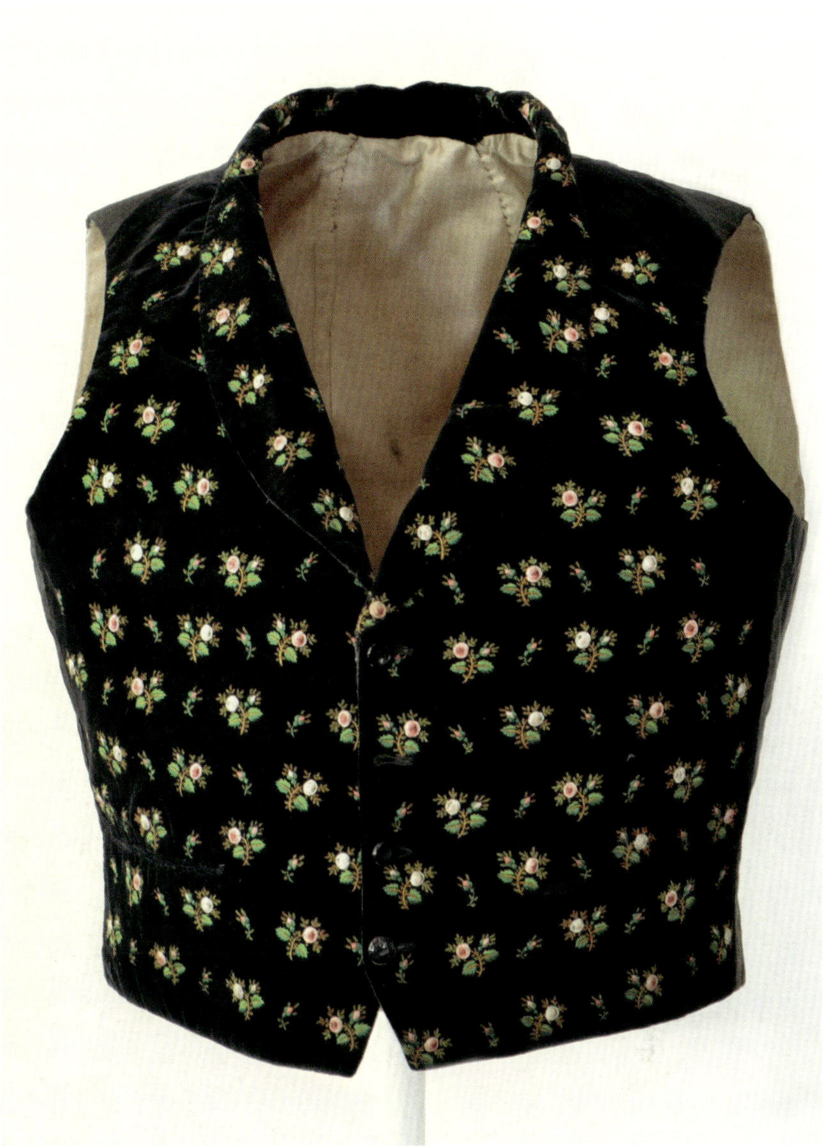

A waistcoat in black silk velvet, 1840-1860. HC.W-11.96-1

It has embroidery in silk threads of pink and peach rose sprigs with green leaves and brown chenille twigs. The work is very organised and neatly done, and was probably professional. The waistcoat is lined in fawn cotton sateen and the back is in dark brown silesia with a backstrap and a black metal buckle (page 210) to adjust the waist. The back has a wide section let in, to make the waistcoat a much bigger size, and one of the straps has an added extension. The roll collar has an inset piece of black velvet at the back, to make that wider as well. There are four eyelets down the edge of the right forepart, for removable buttons; the three here are all different and probably none are original. The edges of the foreparts are faced with black silk taffeta, and there are triangles of this on the shoulders at the top of the armholes and in the side seams, to economise on the velvet.

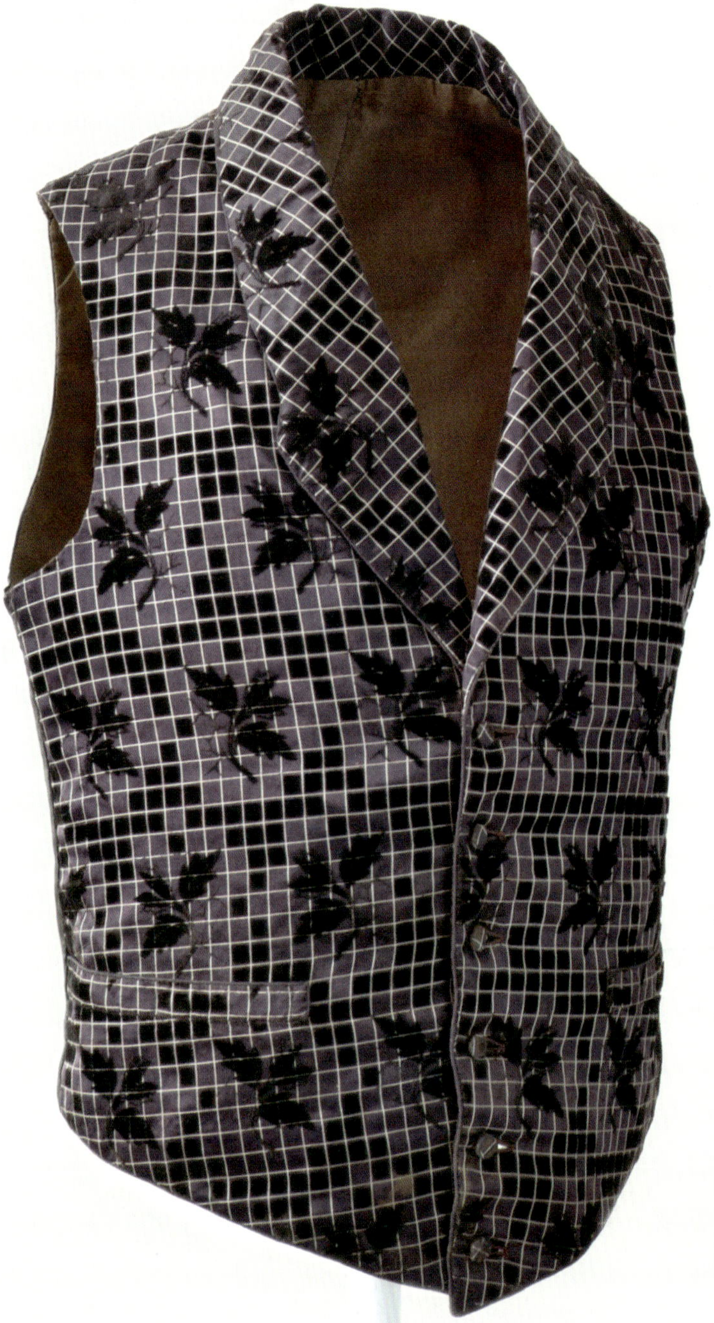

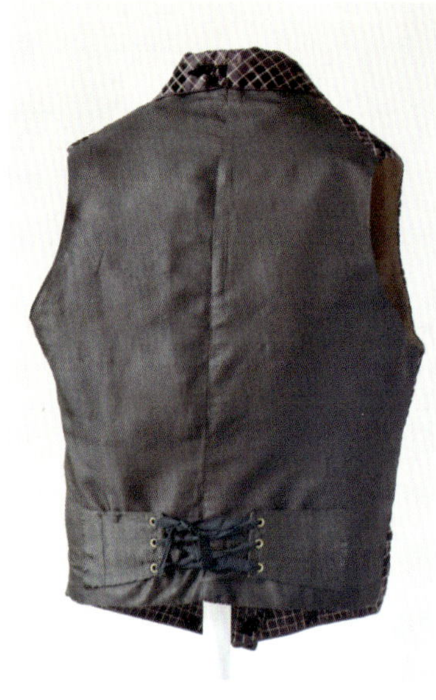

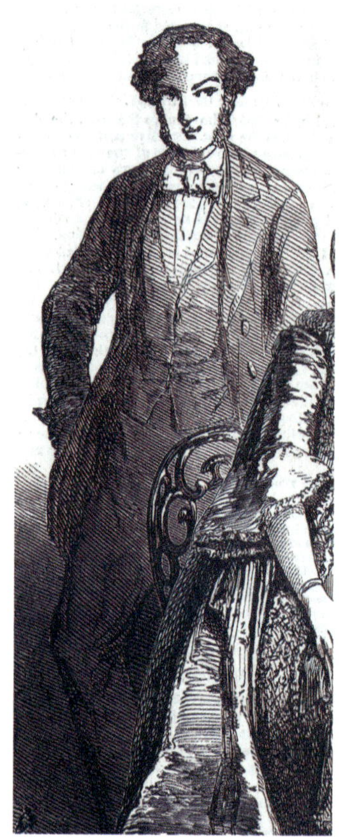

Detail from a drawing in *The Illustrated London News*, 1849.

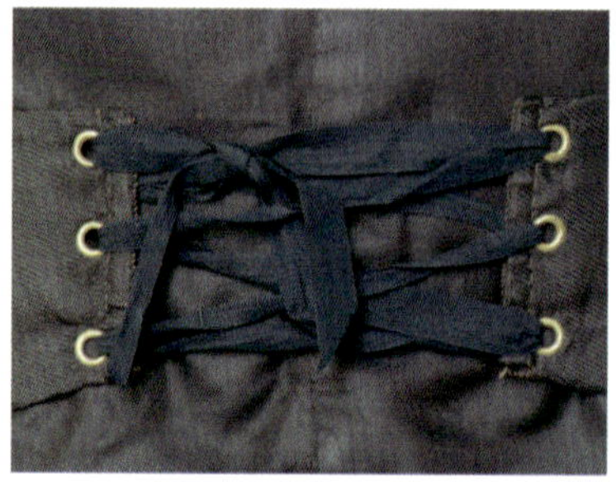

A waistcoat in dull mauve silk satin, 1845-1855. HC.W-6.04

The white window-pane checks have some squares filled in with black silk velvet, which also forms leaf sprays. The waistcoat is lined in brown cotton twill, and the back is brownish-black silk twill with a pair of tabs with boned ends, three pairs of metal eyelets and narrow black silk ribbon lacing to adjust the waist. There are six self-covered buttons, two welted pockets and a step-roll collar.

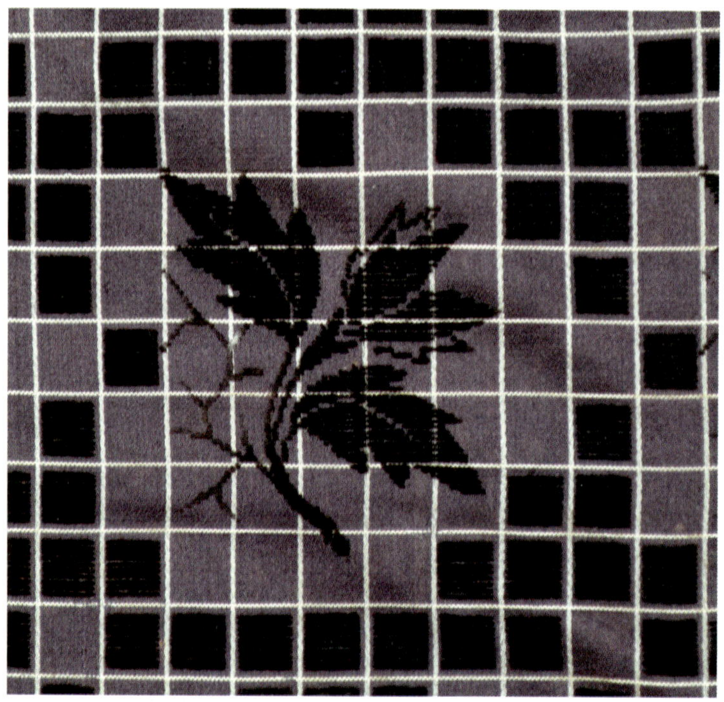

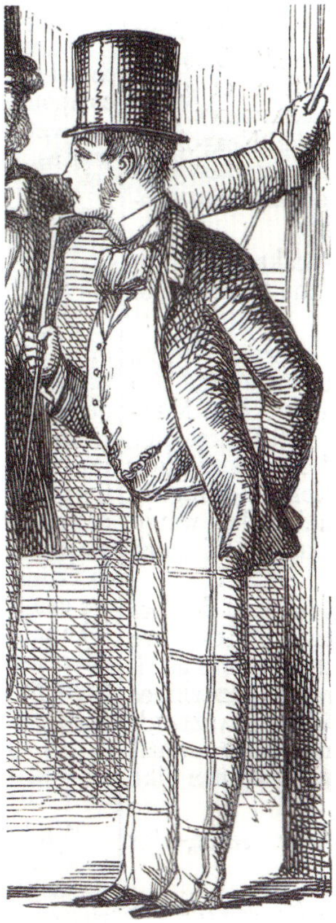

Detail from a cartoon in *Punch*, 1851.

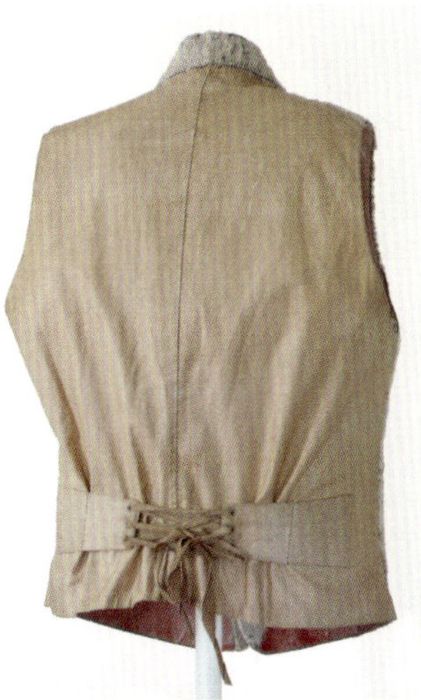

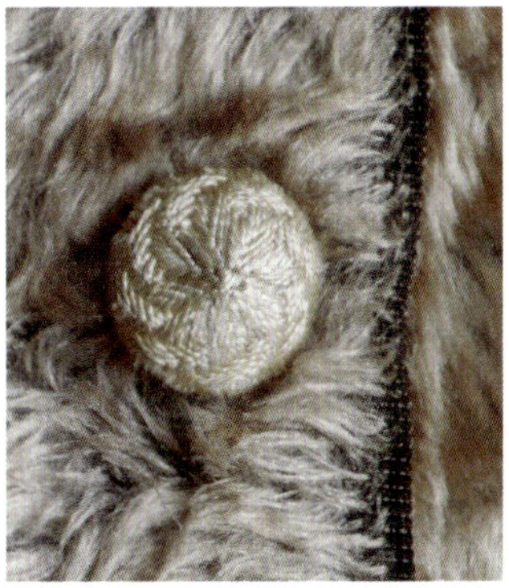

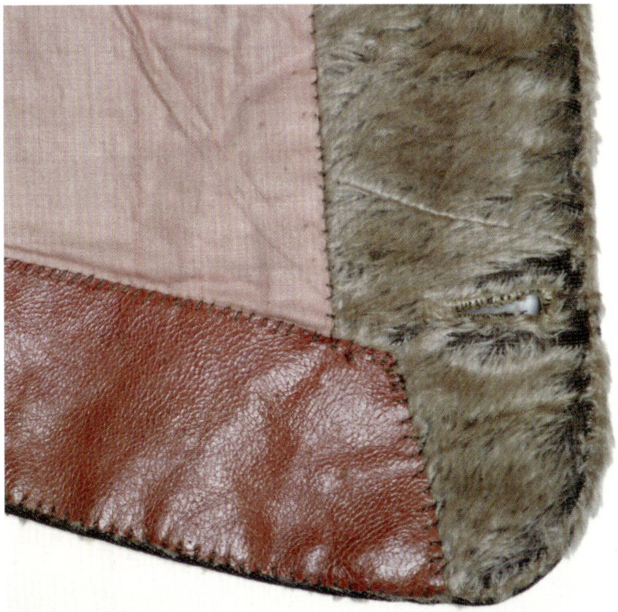

The front edge of the hem of the left forepart, showing the leather facing.

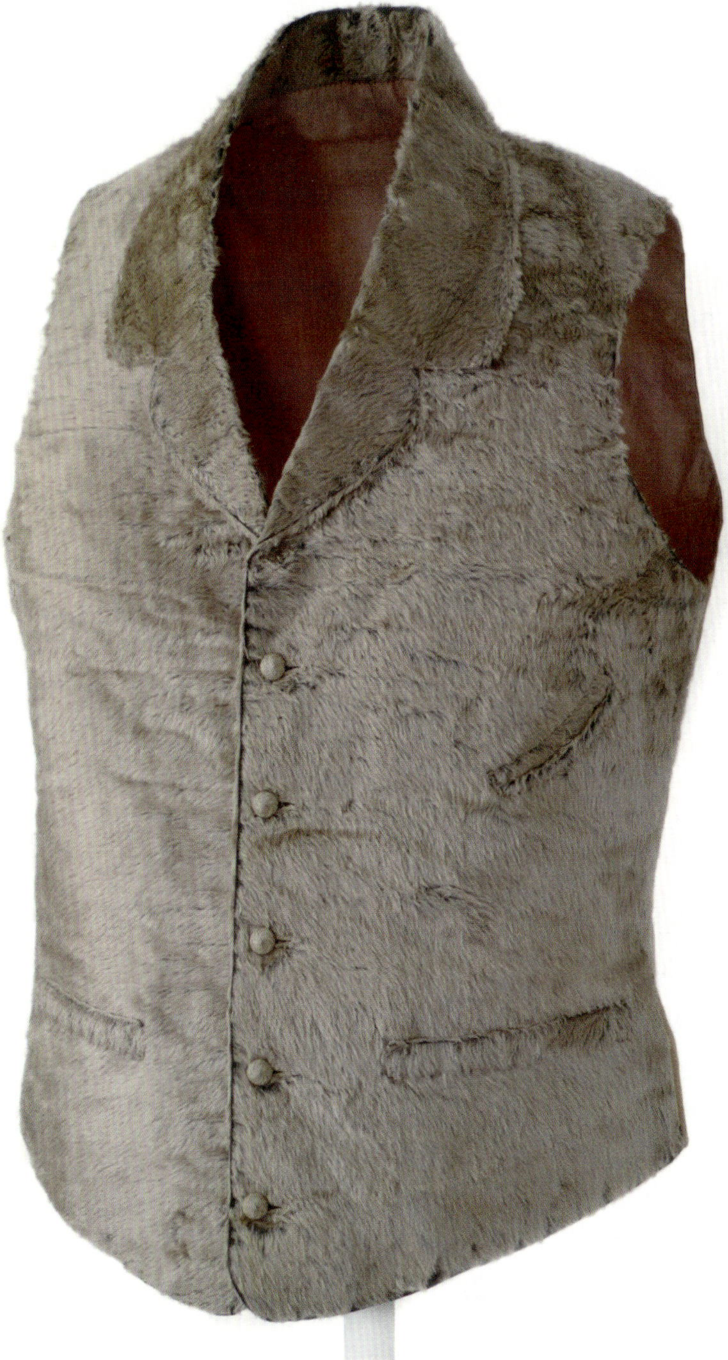

A waistcoat in beige silk shag, 1845-1855. HC.W-4.13-2

The step-roll collar has rounded points; there are six ivory thread-covered buttons, two welted pockets and a crescent-shaped breast pocket on the left forepart. The lining is plain pink cotton, and the back is in fawn cotton twill with a pair of tabs with boned ends and three pairs of brass eyelets; the fawn cotton lacing tape here may not be original. The hems of the foreparts are faced with coral pink leather.

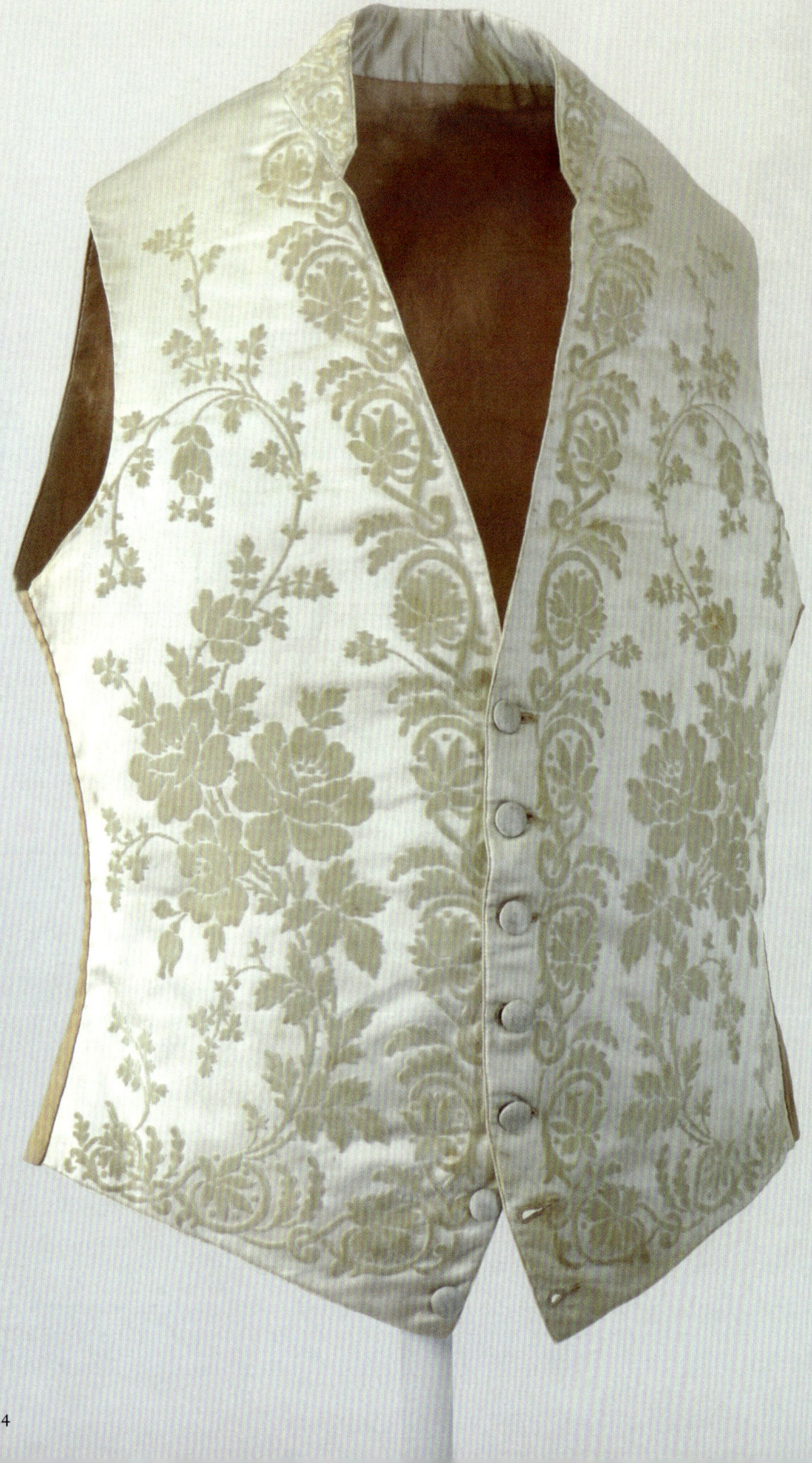

A waistcoat in cream silk satin, 1845-1855.
HC.W-11.81-1

It has a floral design in cream silk velvet woven to the shape of the foreparts and the stand collar. The lining and back are in fawn cotton twill, and the back waist adjustment is by two pairs of white cotton tapes, which was an old-fashioned method by this date. There is padding over the chest between the front and the lining, and seven self-covered buttons; there are no pockets.

Waistcoats made from fabric woven to shape in this style were around as early as 1833. The French fashion magazine *Le Follet* has an account of a Parisian tailor who had commissioned something similar. It is described as a type of waistcoat for evenings and balls, "made in Lyon from designs composed by one of our most stylish artists, which will, without doubt, be in great demand. Nothing can equal the richness and elegance of these waistcoats, of which the ground is satin with a single bouquet brocaded in velvet, starting at the hem and rising all over the body of the waistcoat in a most graceful development; a garland in velvet, echoing the main bouquet, winds smoothly round the shawl [roll collar] or collar, and altogether gives a rich and pleasing look."

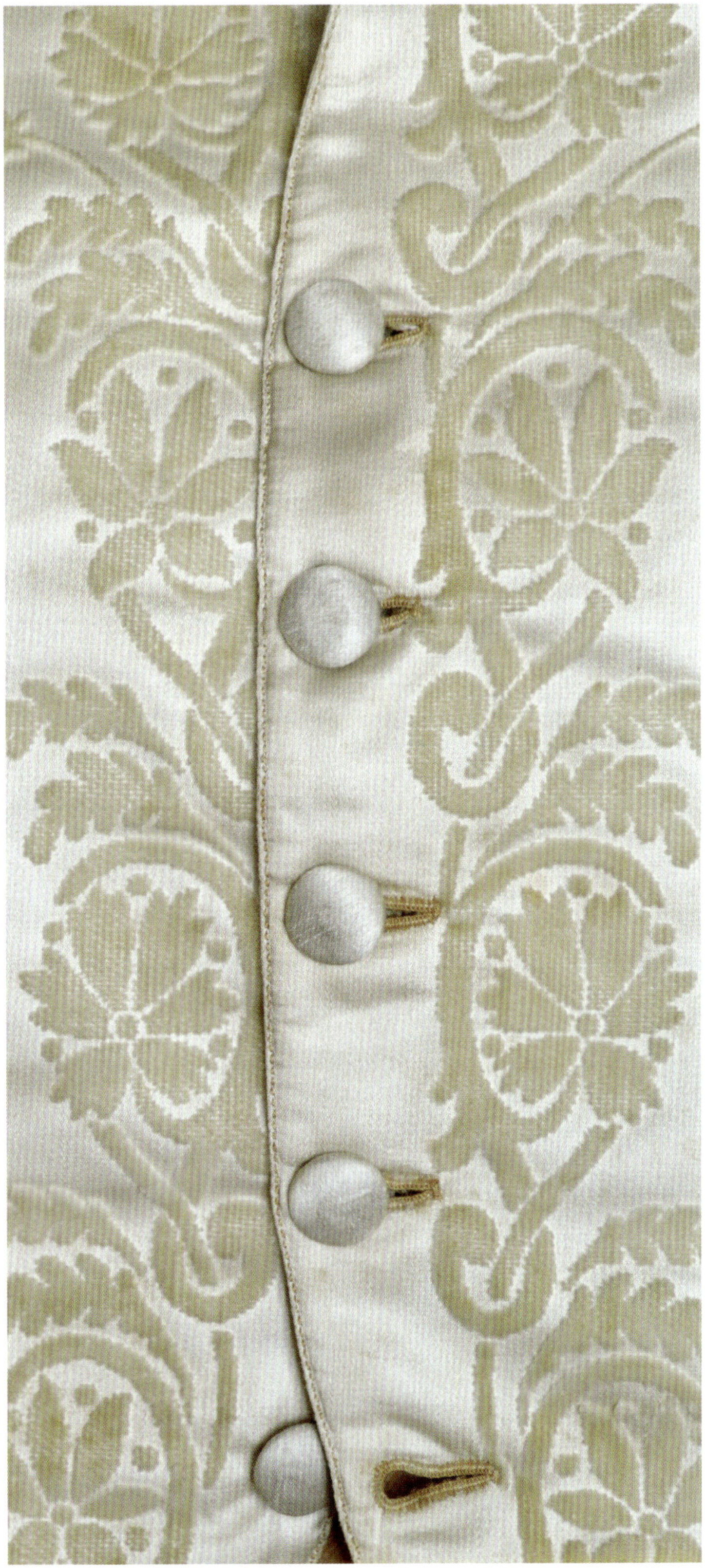

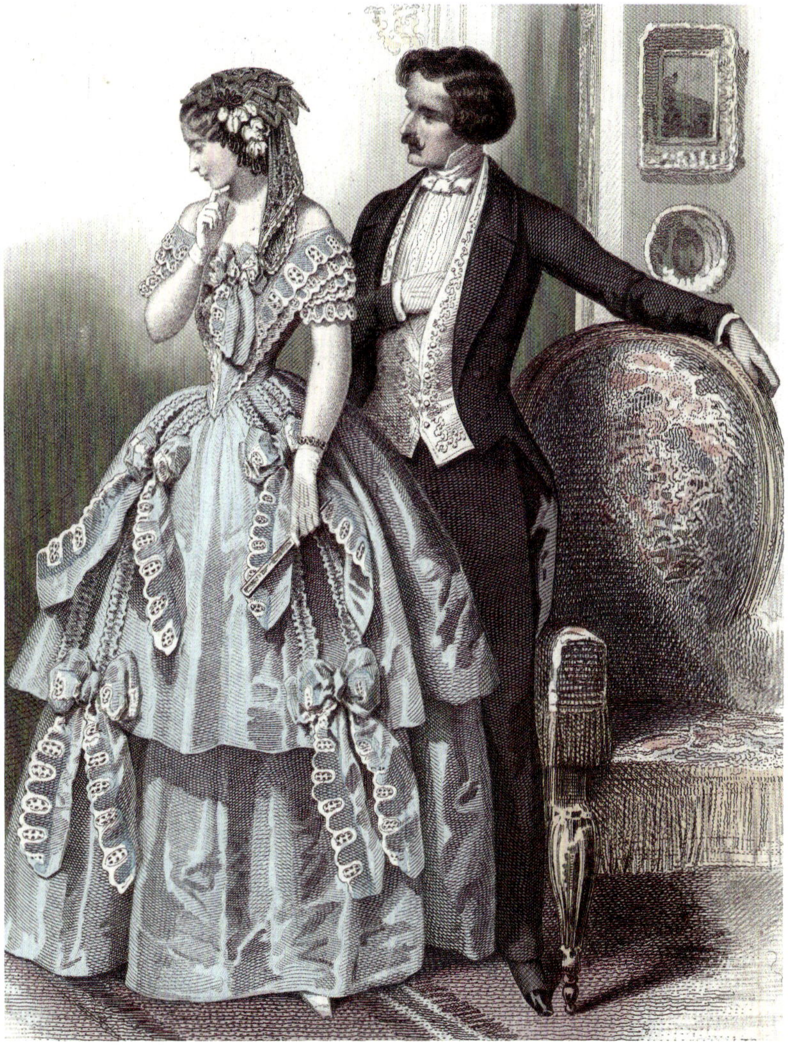

Fashion plate from *Les Modes Parisiennes*, 1850.

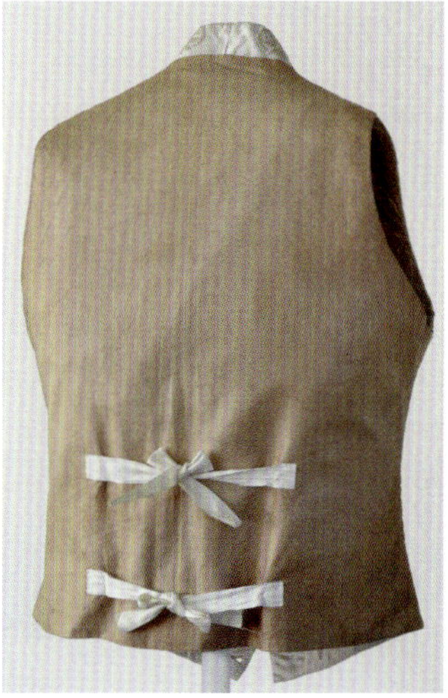

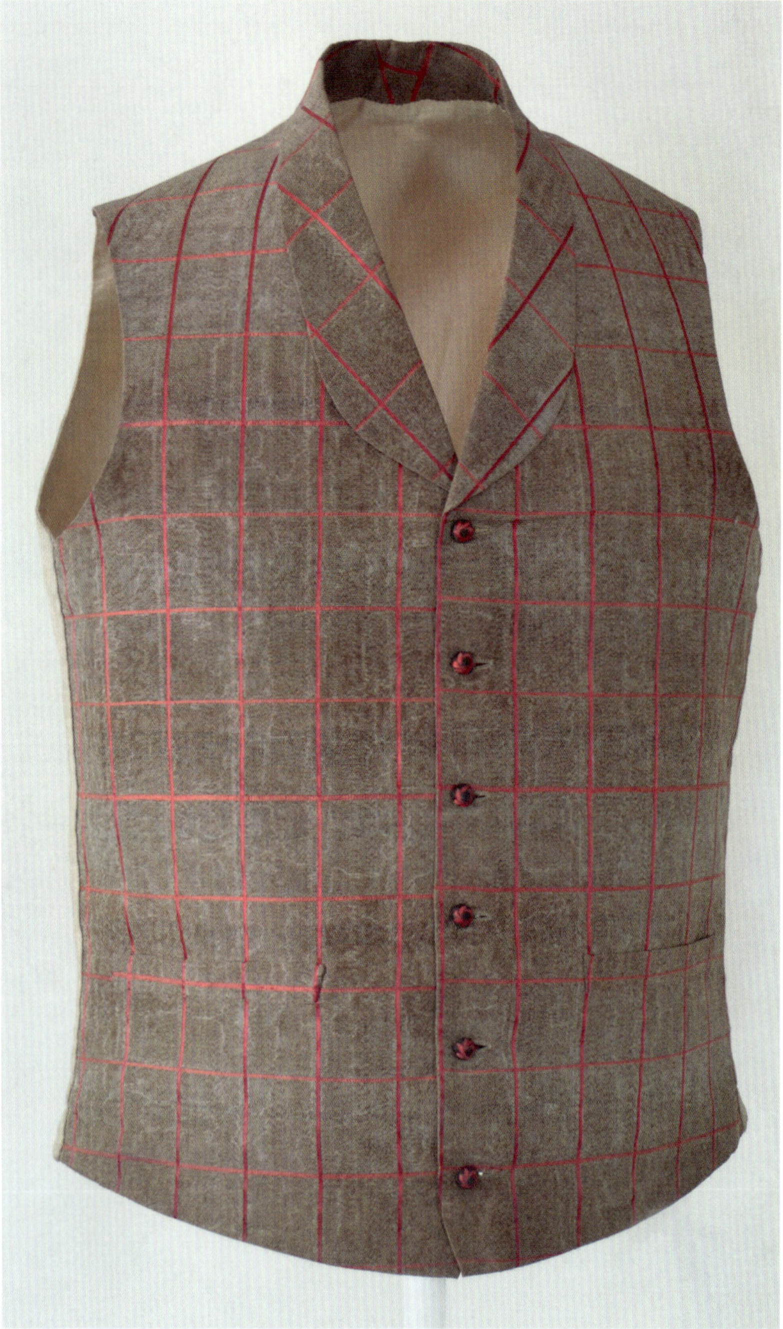

A waistcoat in silk and wool moiré, 1850-1860. HC.W-1.92

This has a silk warp in brown and ivory threads producing a speckled effect when woven and covering the worsted weft. There are vertical and horizontal lines in cherry red silk, forming a window-pane check. The waistcoat has a roll collar and two welted pockets. It is lined in cream cotton twill with a large pocket in the lining of the left forepart; the back is in beige cotton twill with a backstrap in a darker shade to adjust the waist. The six domed buttons are covered in black silk with a woven flower motif in cherry red.

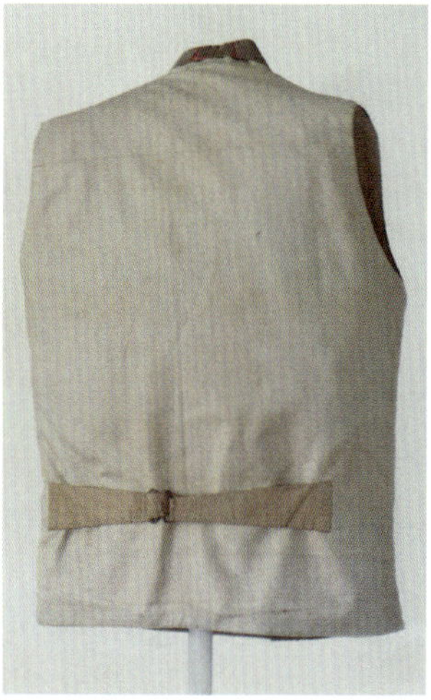

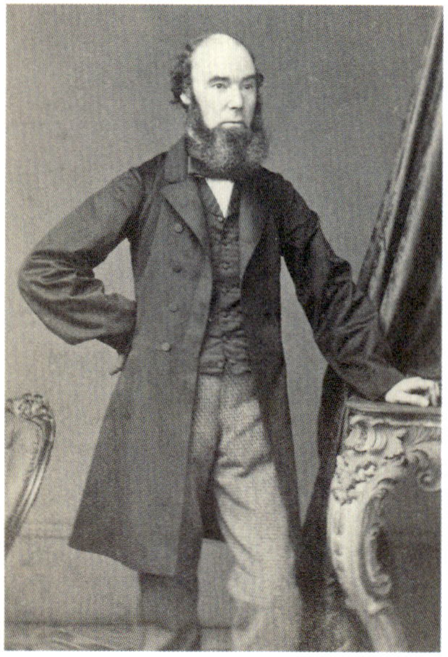

Right: Unknown man, *c.*1860.

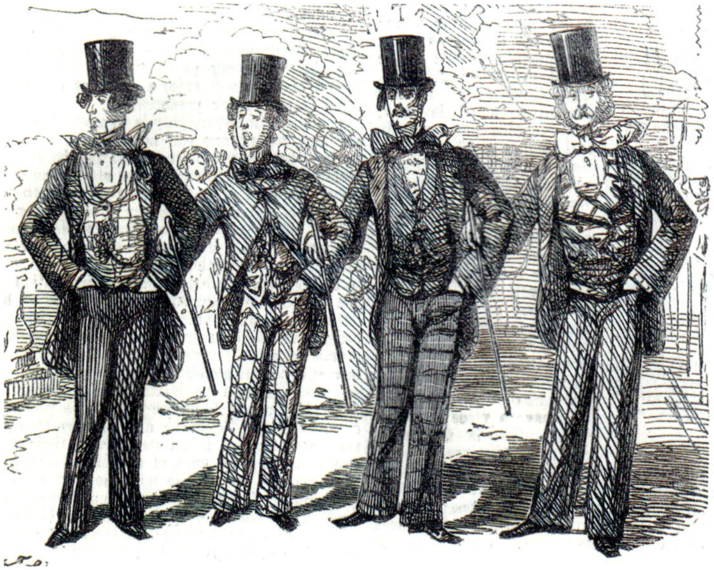

Detail from a cartoon in *Punch*, 1850.

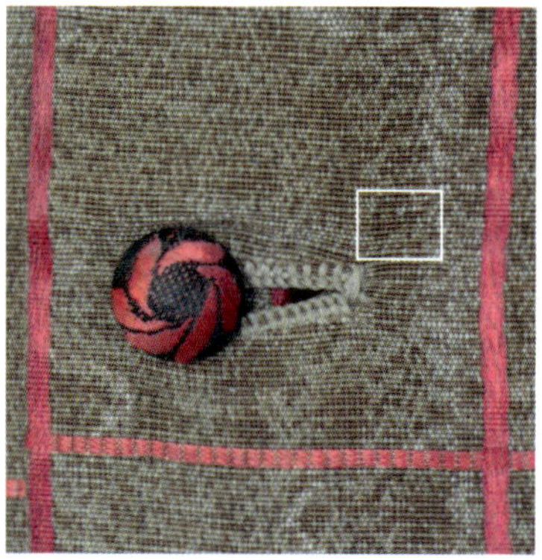

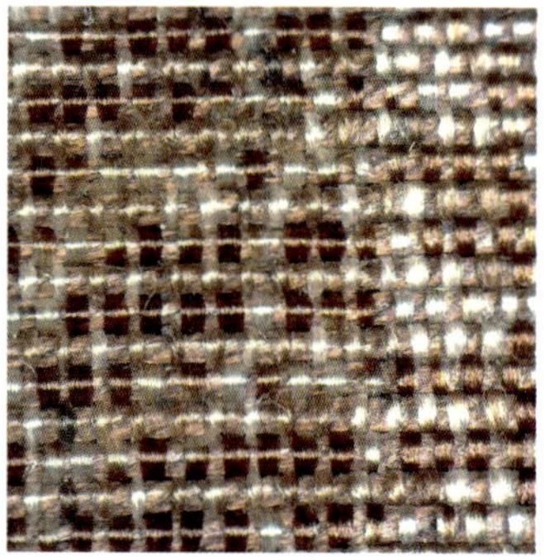

Detail of the fabric outlined left.

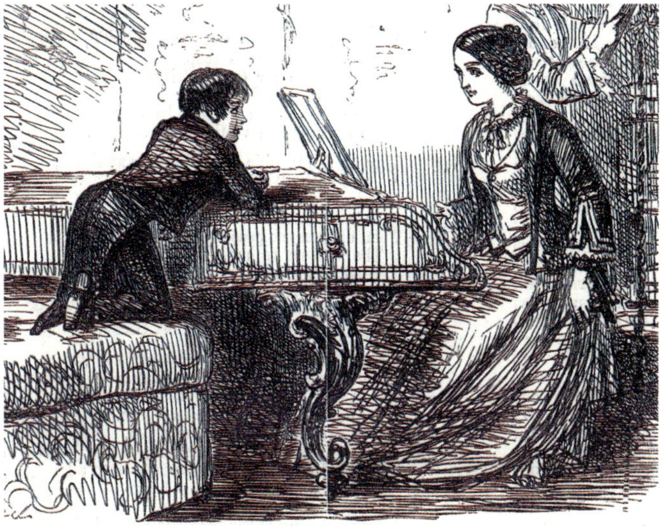

Gus (who is always so full of his nonsense). "DASH MY BUTTONS, ELLEN ! THAT'S A STUNNING WAISTCOAT. I WISH YOU'D GIVE US YOUR TAILOR'S ADDRESS !"

Detail from a cartoon in *Punch*, 1852.

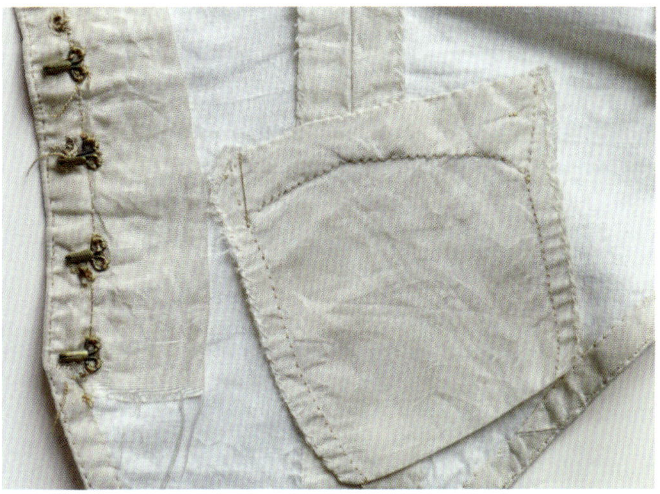

Inside the bottom of the right front, showing the pocket bag, the hooks and the eyelets for the removable buttons.

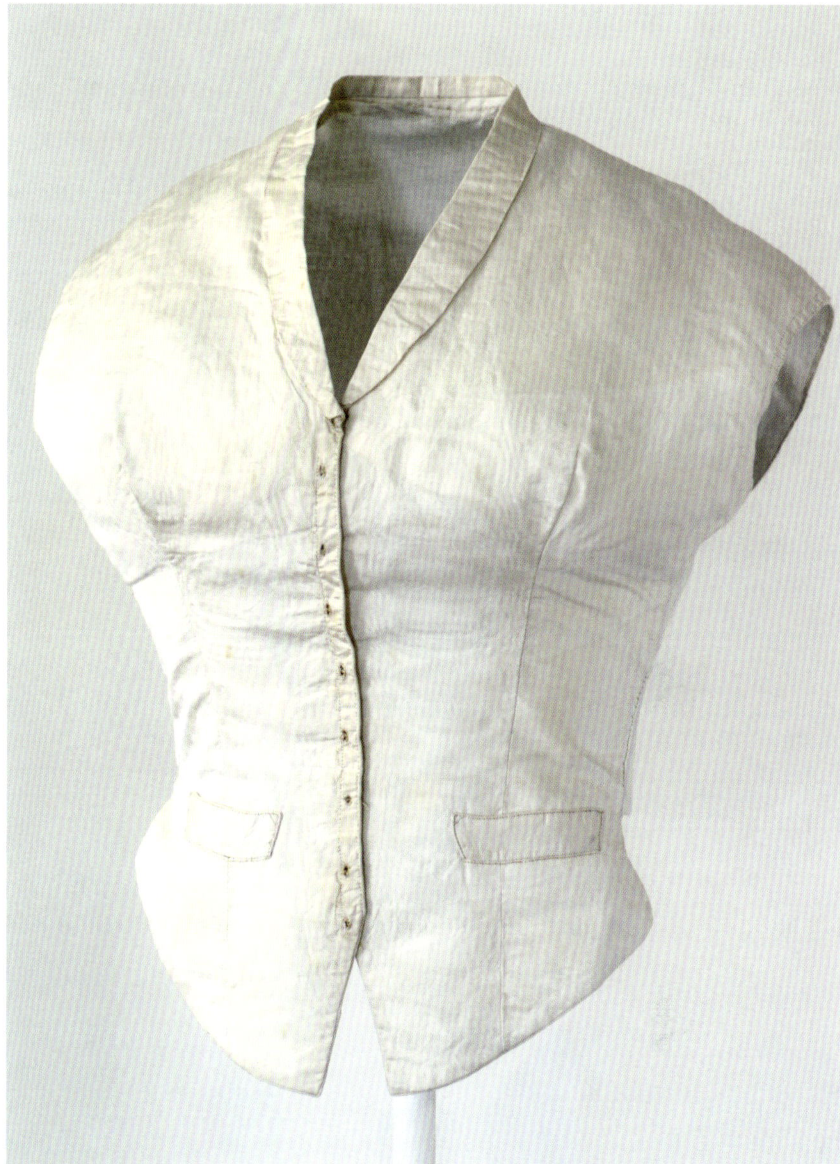

A woman's waistcoat in ivory silk moiré, 1850-1855. HC.W-10.15-2

The moiré is mounted on ivory linen, and the back is plain white cotton with tabs, with three pairs of metal eyelets and narrow white cotton tape lacing to adjust the waist. The waistcoat has a narrow roll collar, two welted pockets and it is unlined. The front fastens with hooks and worked loops, and there are worked eyelets for removable decorative buttons.

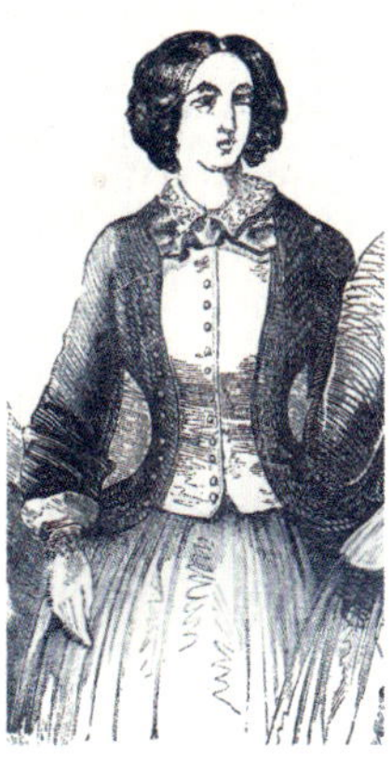

THE VEST.

Fig. 1. Front of vest.

Fig. 2. Back of ditto.

A. and B. Gussets.

Join *a* to *a*, *b* to *b*, *c* to *c*, *d* to *d*. The *d* at back (fig. 2), when joined to *d* at side (fig. 1), leaves a lappet to fall over the hip.

B, in fig. 1, represents a plain line, which is to be cut up to the highest point. Close the open seam thus made down to the narrow part, only leaving room for gusset-piece marked B, which should be inserted where its corresponding letter stands. Gusset A to form the fulness over the hip.

Instructions for the pattern for a waistcoat from *The Englishwoman's Domestic Magazine*, 1852.

Left: A drawing showing the finished waistcoat.
Right: The pattern for the waistcoat.

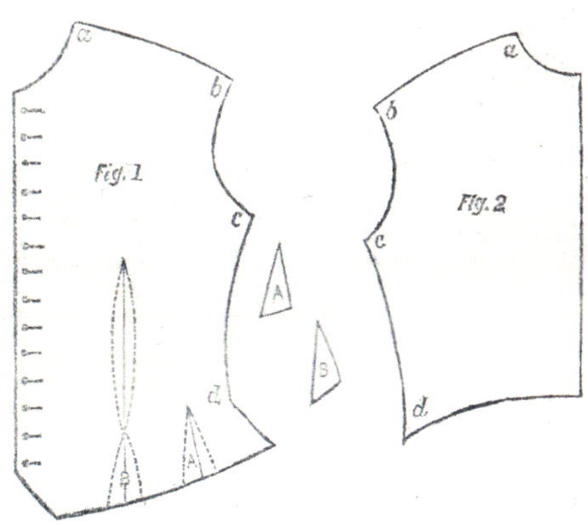

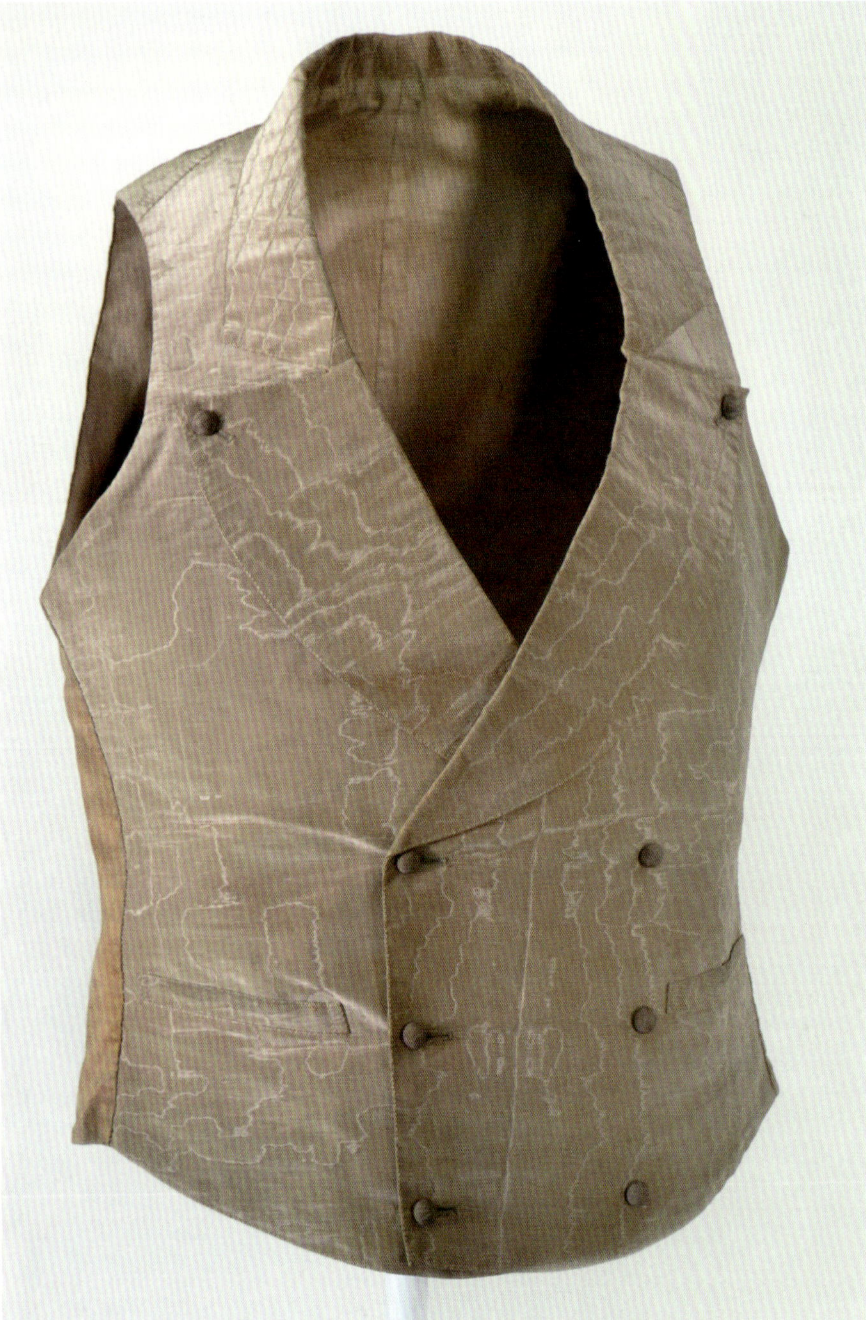

A waistcoat in fawn silk moiré, 1850-1860. HC.W-3.96

It is double-breasted, with three buttonholes on the edge of each forepart. There are three pairs of domed self-covered buttons, and a buttonhole at the tip of each wide, curved lapel fastened to a button on the forepart. It is lined in fawn cotton twill and the back is in pale ginger cotton twill with a backstrap to adjust the waist (page 210). The forepart hems are faced with fawn leather. The moiré pattern has been formed by folding the fabric lengthwise before putting it through heated rollers which flatten the fabric unevenly, giving a watered effect; the pattern can be seen to be mirrored across the fold line in the centre front.

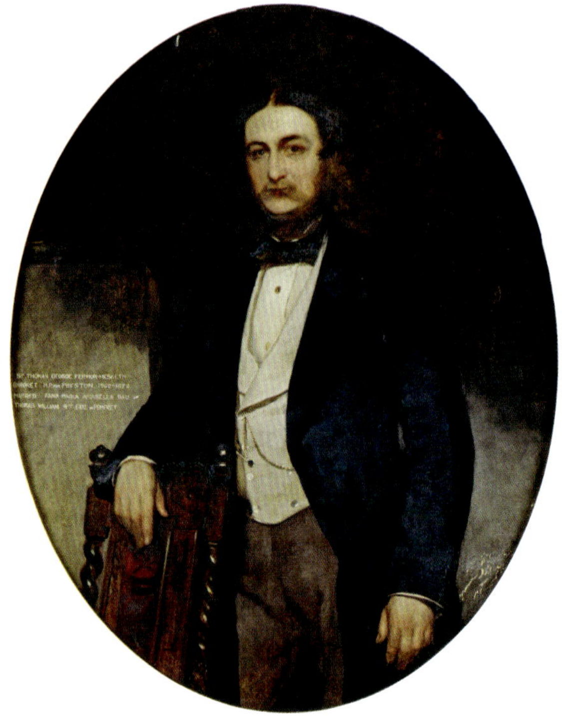

Sir Thomas George Fermor-Hesketh, 5th Baronet Hesketh of Rufford by G. Williams, 1854, Rufford Old Hall. © National Trust Images / John Hammond.

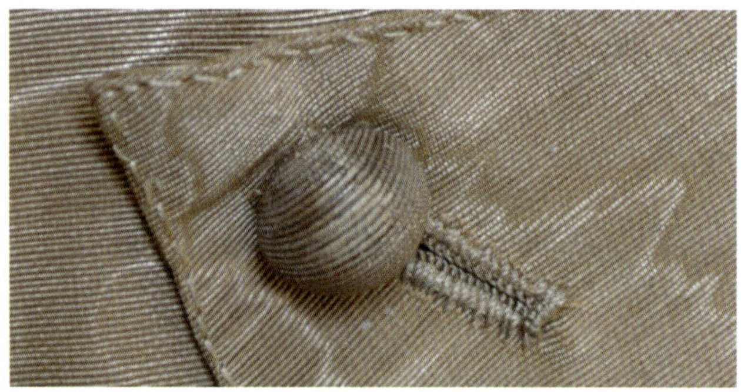

The button at the tip of one of the lapels.

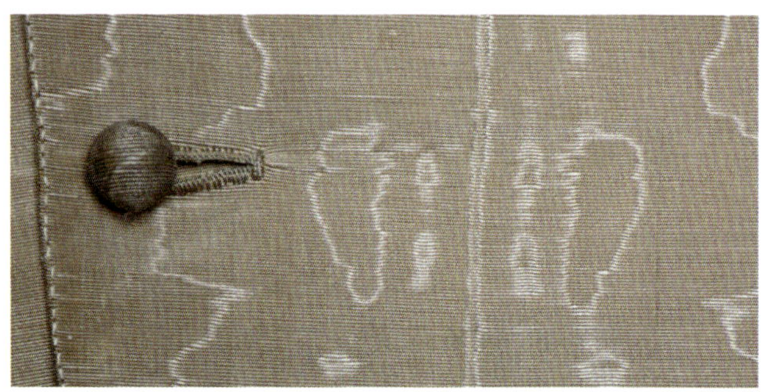

The moiré pattern mirrored over the centre crease of the fabric in the middle of the left forepart.

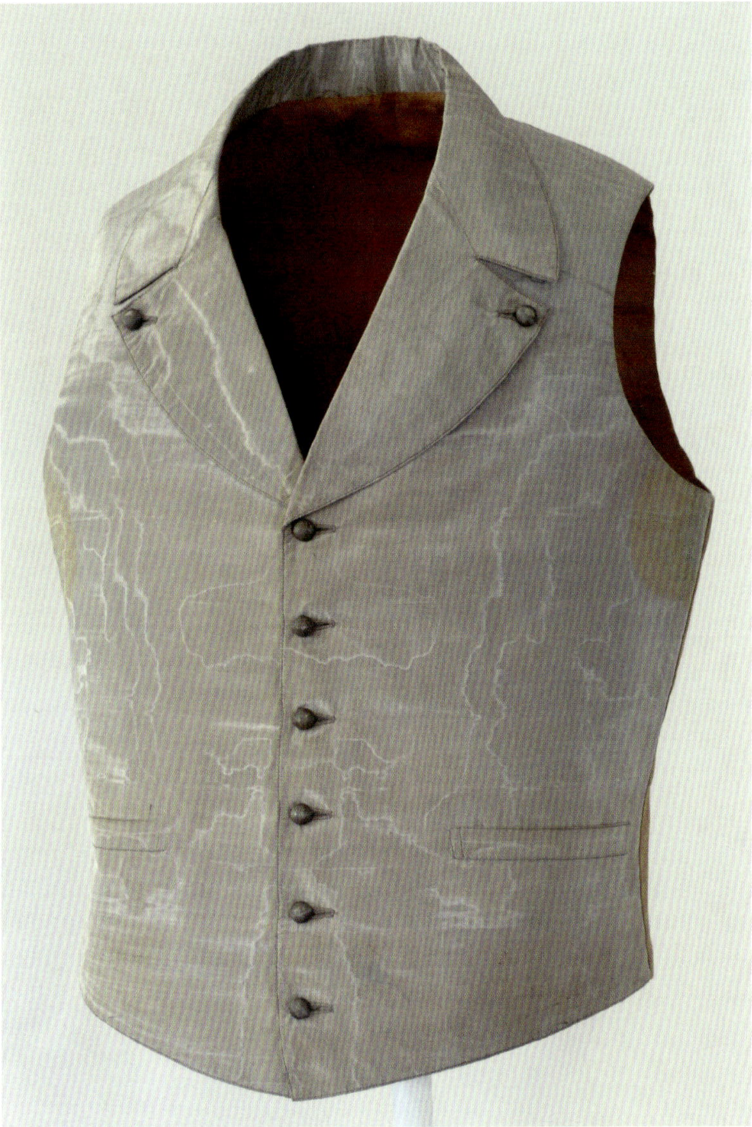

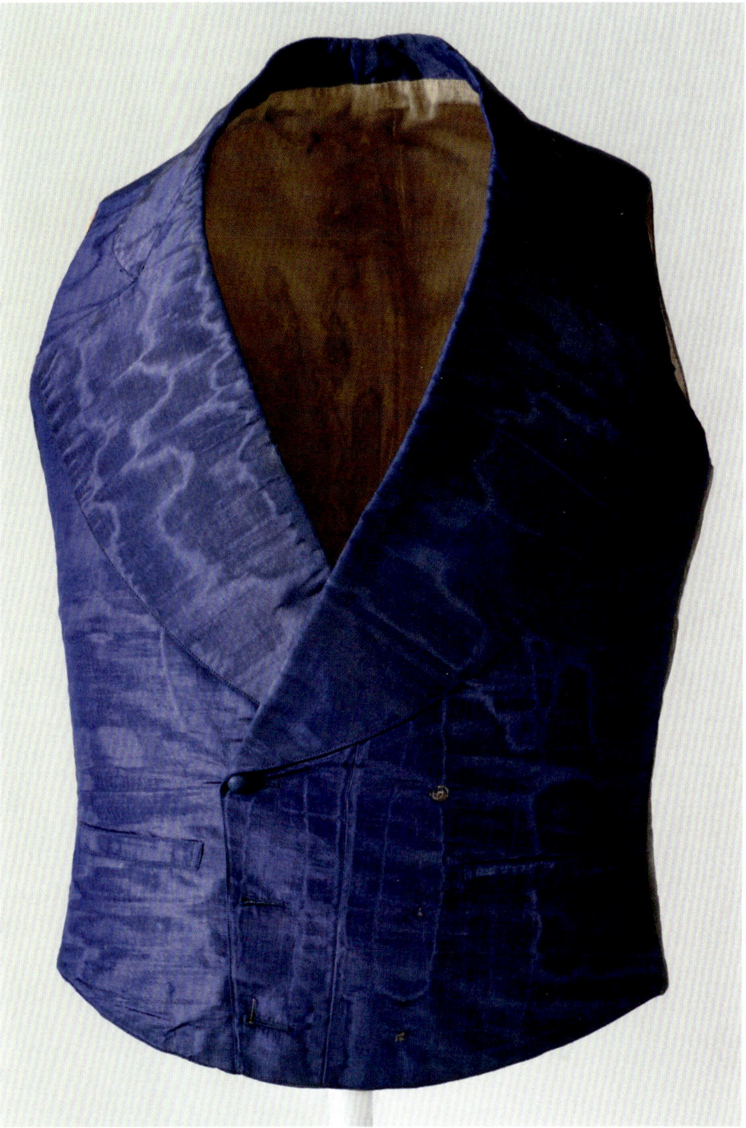

A waistcoat in dove grey silk moiré, 1845-1855. HC.W-0.74

It is single-breasted with six covered domed buttons. The curved lapels of the step collar have buttoned-down points, and there is a concealed button at the neck under the right lapel, on which the left lapel could be fastened when folded over, closing the waistcoat up to the neck. The lining and the back are in ginger-coloured cot cotton on twill, and there are two pairs of cotton chevron weave tape ties at the back to adjust the waist, an old-fashioned method by this date.

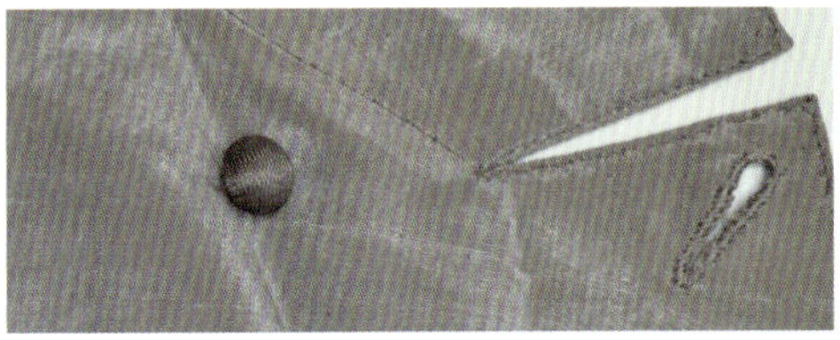

Left: The button at the neck, under the right lapel.

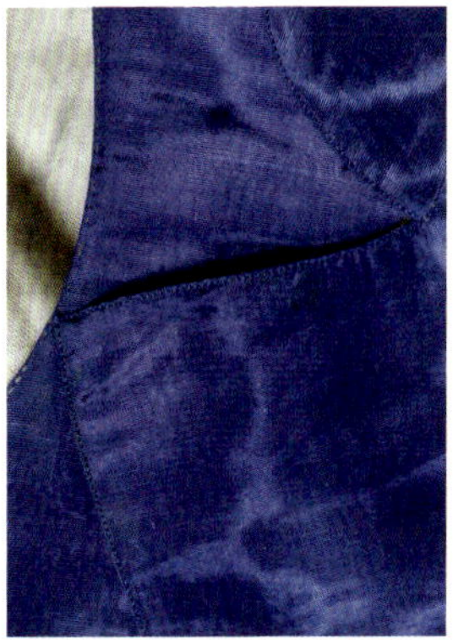

The tip of the right lapel, stitched to the armhole.

A waistcoat in blue silk moiré, 1850-1860. HC.W-6.13-2

It is double-breasted with very wide, curved lapels, whose tips are stitched to the edges of the armholes; the collar has rounded ends. Only one covered domed button survives out of the three original pairs, and there are three buttonholes on the front edge of each forepart, but no sign of any buttons on the inside to fasten the right front edge. The lining is fawn cotton twill and is badly stained with watermarks. The back is in brown silesia with a backstrap to adjust the waist. The forepart hems have a fawn leather facing, now fragile.

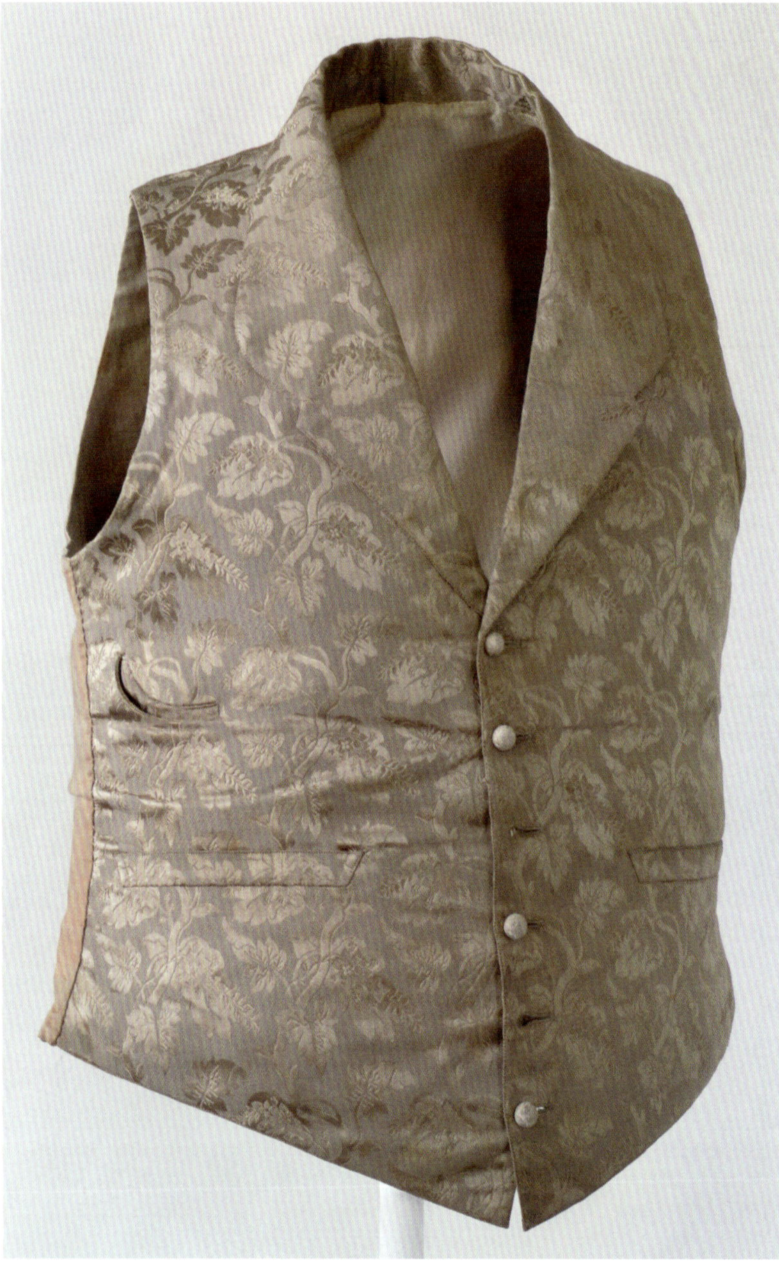

A waistcoat in light brown silk, 1845-1855. HC.W-7.89-1

The silk has a woven self pattern of leaves and branches. The waistcoat is lined with cream cotton in a zig-zag weave, with a pocket inside the left forepart, and the back is in ginger cotton twill. It has a step-roll collar, and six domed buttons covered in a beige silk woven to shape; two of these are missing. The forepart hems are faced with fawn leather, and there are two welted pockets and a curved breast pocket on the right forepart. The waist adjustment at the back is by a pair of tabs, each with a piece of shaped metal on the end, containing three eyelets for lacing; the lace is narrow beige silk satin ribbon, now fragile, and may not be original.

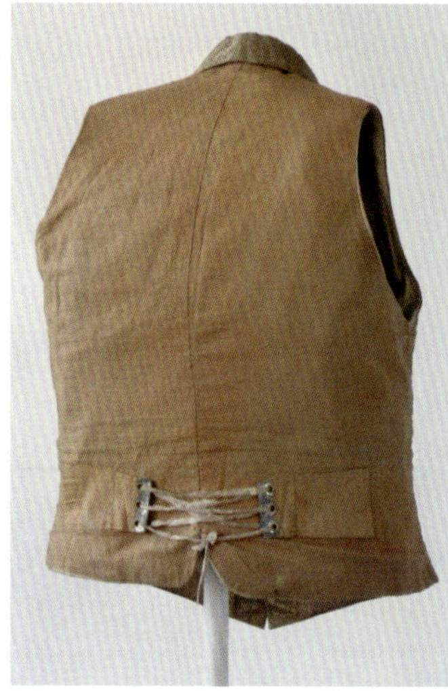

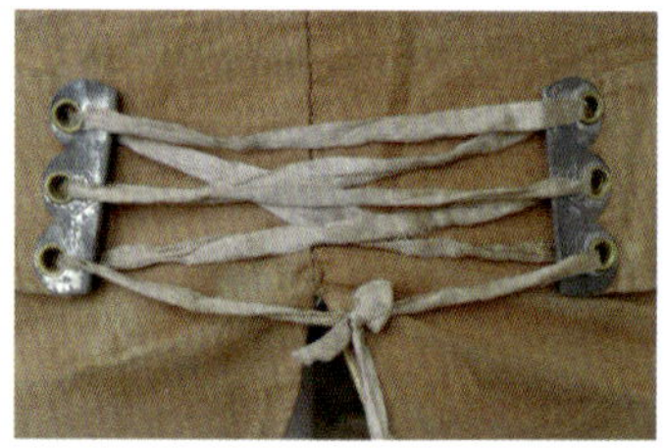

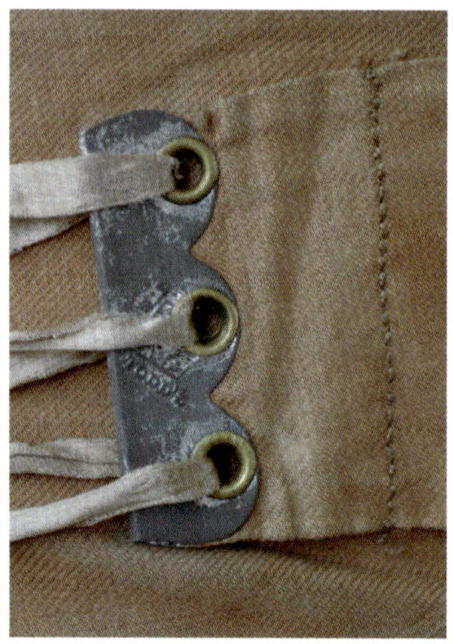

This design of a "Metal Eyelet Fastener" was registered in 1844, by Joseph and Thomas Todd, of 3, Melbourne Place, Edinburgh. The diamond mark for registered designs is stamped on it, partly obscured by one of the eyelets. The chromium plating is wearing off in places.

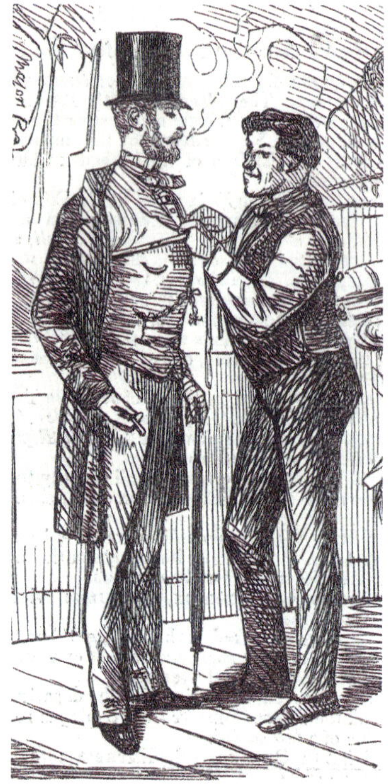

Detail from a cartoon in *Punch*, 1855.

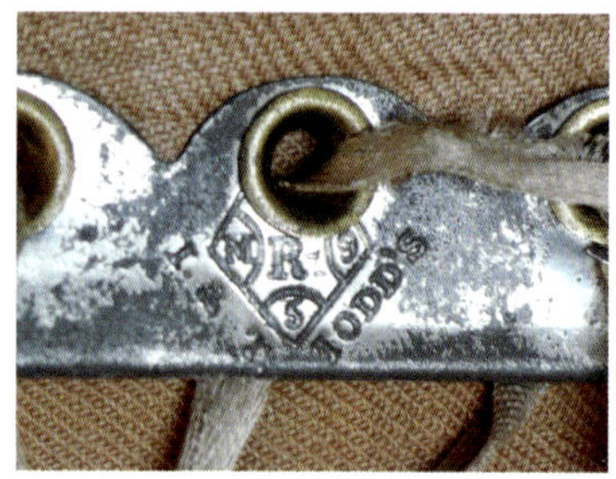

The system for registering designs was set up in 1839, for ornamental or decorative designs, and from 1843 for non-ornamental or useful designs. This item was classed as useful. Diamond marks were issued with a registration number by the Patent Office when a design was registered, between 1842 and 1883. The diamond mark has letters and numbers in its corners, which indicate the date of registering and the class of material used.

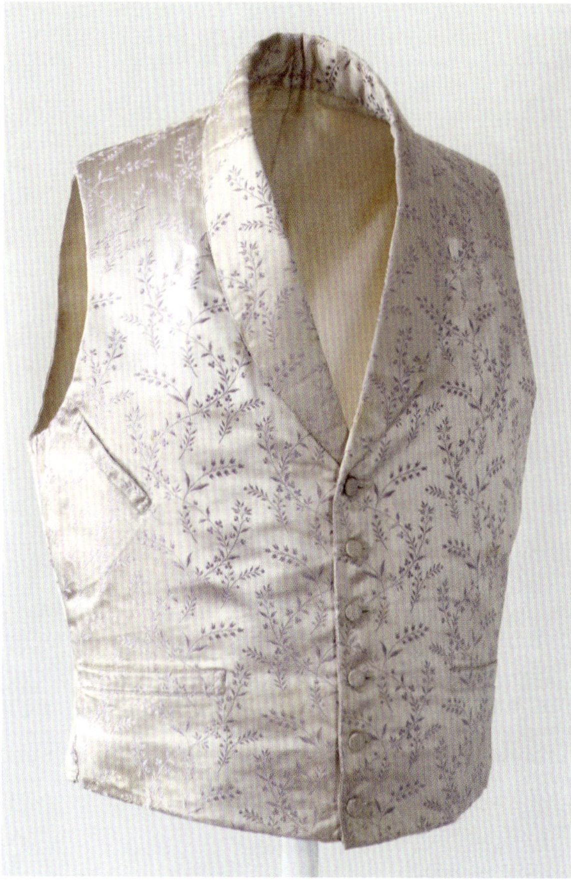

A waistcoat in ivory silk, 1845-1850. HC.W-4.90

The silk has a woven leafy pattern in lilac silk. The waistcoat has a roll collar and six covered buttons; there are two welted pockets and a similar slanted breast pocket. The lining and the back are in white cotton twill, and the forepart hems are faced with fawn leather. The waist adjustment is a pair of tabs with boned ends, three pairs of metal eyelets and a linen tape for lacing. The right-hand tab has the label of Welch & Margetson printed on it.

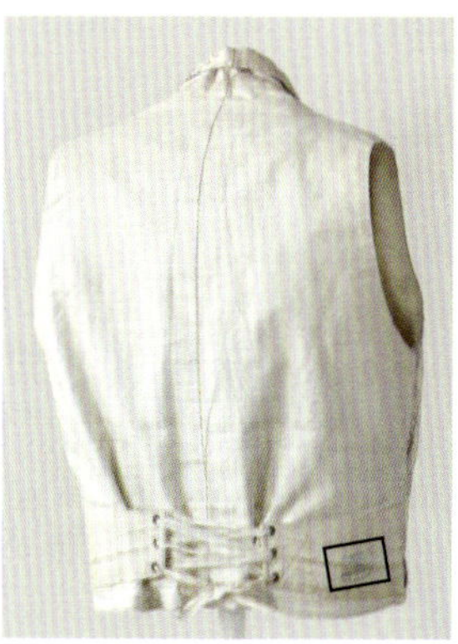

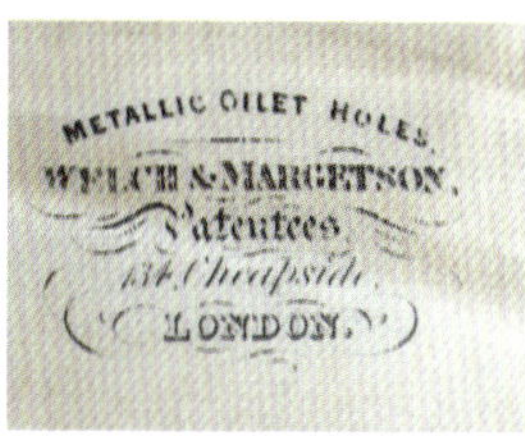

The Welch & Margetson label outlined left; it appears upside-down, so the tabs must have been sewn on upside-down.

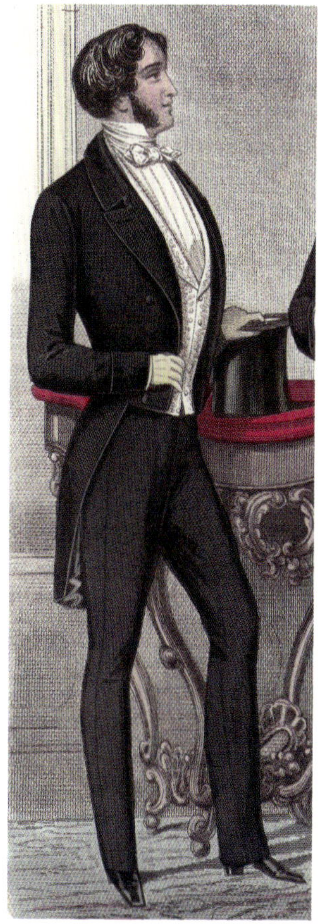

Fashion plate from the *Gentleman's Magazine*, 1852.

Welch & Margetson were known for their high-quality menswear, particularly shirts and neckwear. Joseph James Welch was taken on as an apprentice, around 1825, by Sarah Coulsell, the widow of a glove and brace manufacturer in Farringdon Street, in the City of London. In 1831 she re-married, and in 1832 she sold the business to Welch, who was joined by her brother, John Stewart Margetson.

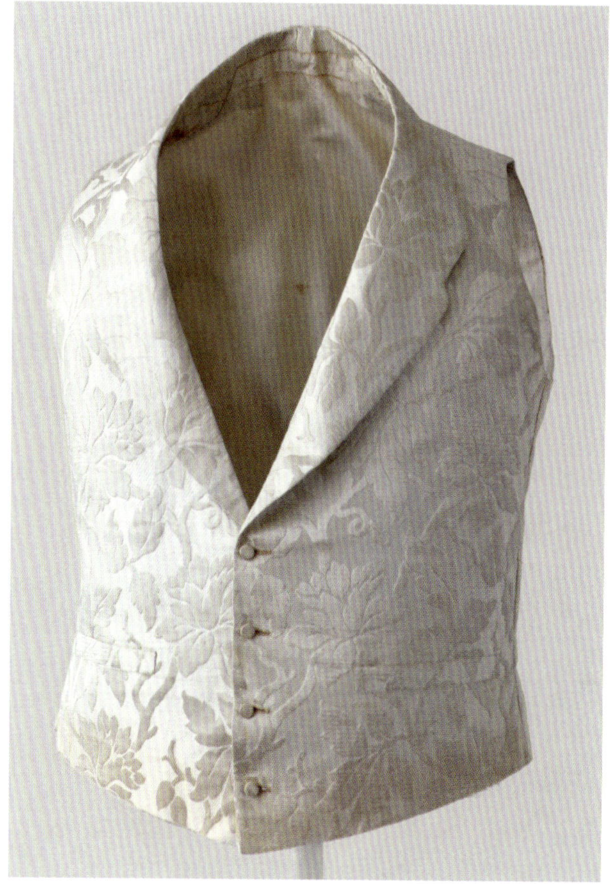

A waistcoat in ivory silk, 1850-1860. HC.W-5.05-2

The silk has a large leafy pattern in satin on a twill ground. The waistcoat has a step-roll collar, four self-covered buttons and two welted pockets. The lining and back are in plain white cotton, and the forepart hems are faced with white leather. It has two types of waist adjustment: there is a pair of cotton tape ties, and a pair of white cotton twill tabs with boned ends and three pairs of metals eyelets; the original lace is missing. The right-hand tab has the label of Welch & Margetson printed on it.

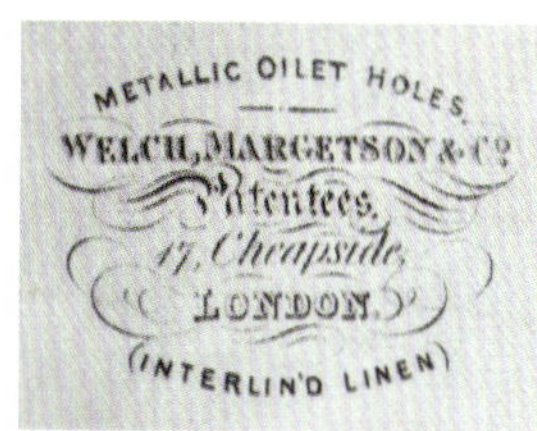

The Welch & Margetson label, outlined right; it too appears upside-down, so the tabs must have been sewn on upside-down.

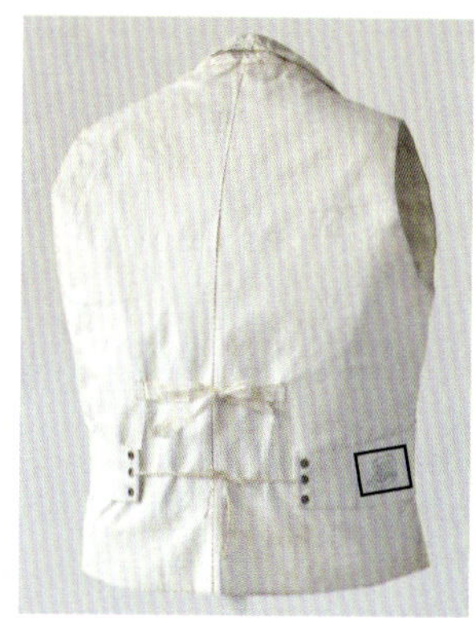

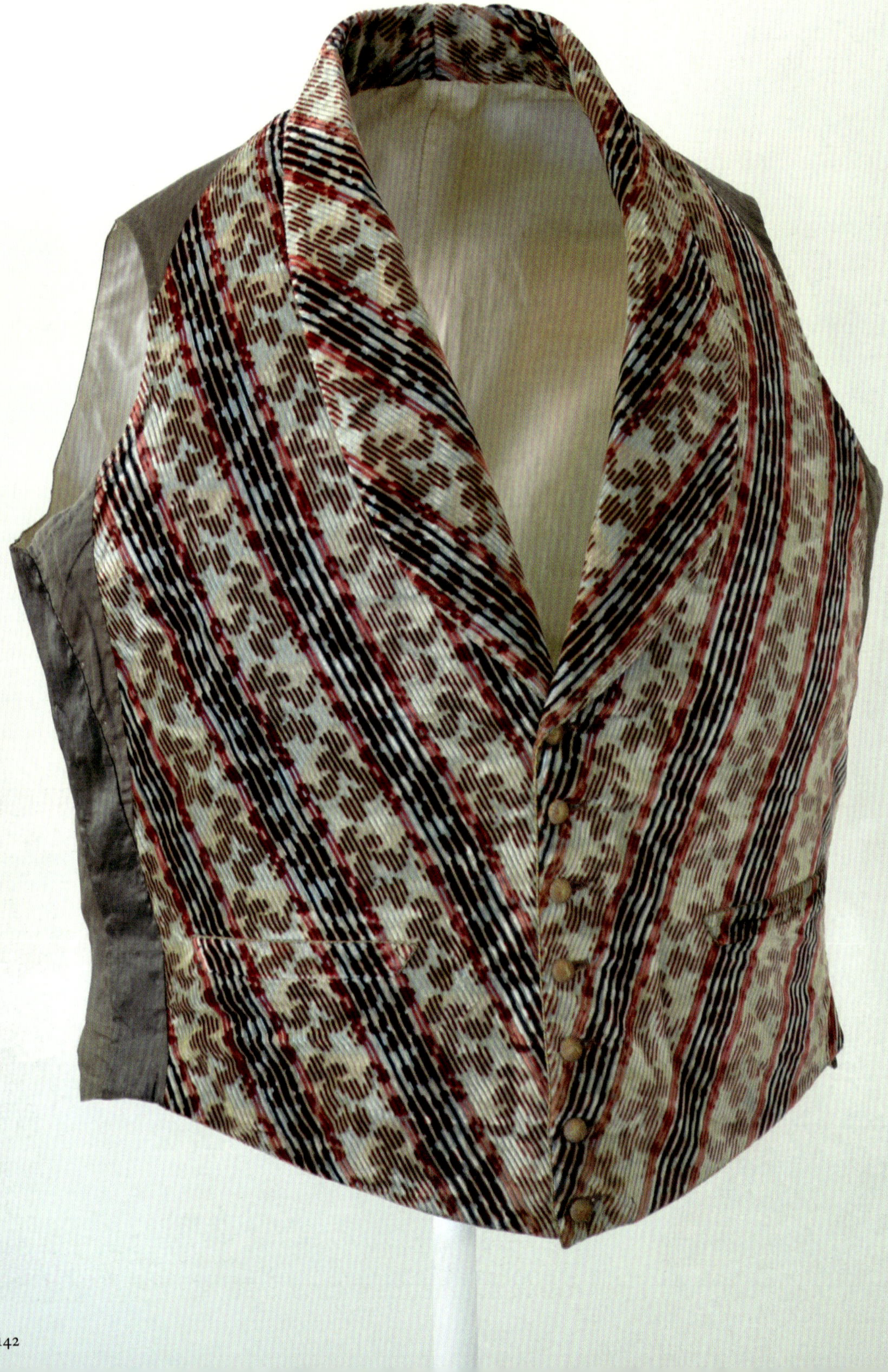

A waistcoat in silk voided velvet, 1845-1855. HC.W-12.00-1

The velvet has very narrow stripes of ivory, red, wine and black, with voided stripes of pale blue and peach. The waistcoat has been cut on the bias of the velvet so that the stripes mitre down the front. It is lined in plain white cotton, and the back is in brown glazed cotton with a backstrap to adjust the waist. The seven small domed buttons are covered in red, fawn and blue threads. There are triangles of the back fabric inserted on the shoulders and at the base of the armholes, which would have economised on the velvet, and the 2″ insertions of a dark brown cotton at each side seam increased the size. There is slight padding over the chest, and the roll collar, fronts and welted pocket tops are edged with fawn, pale blue and black fine silk cord.

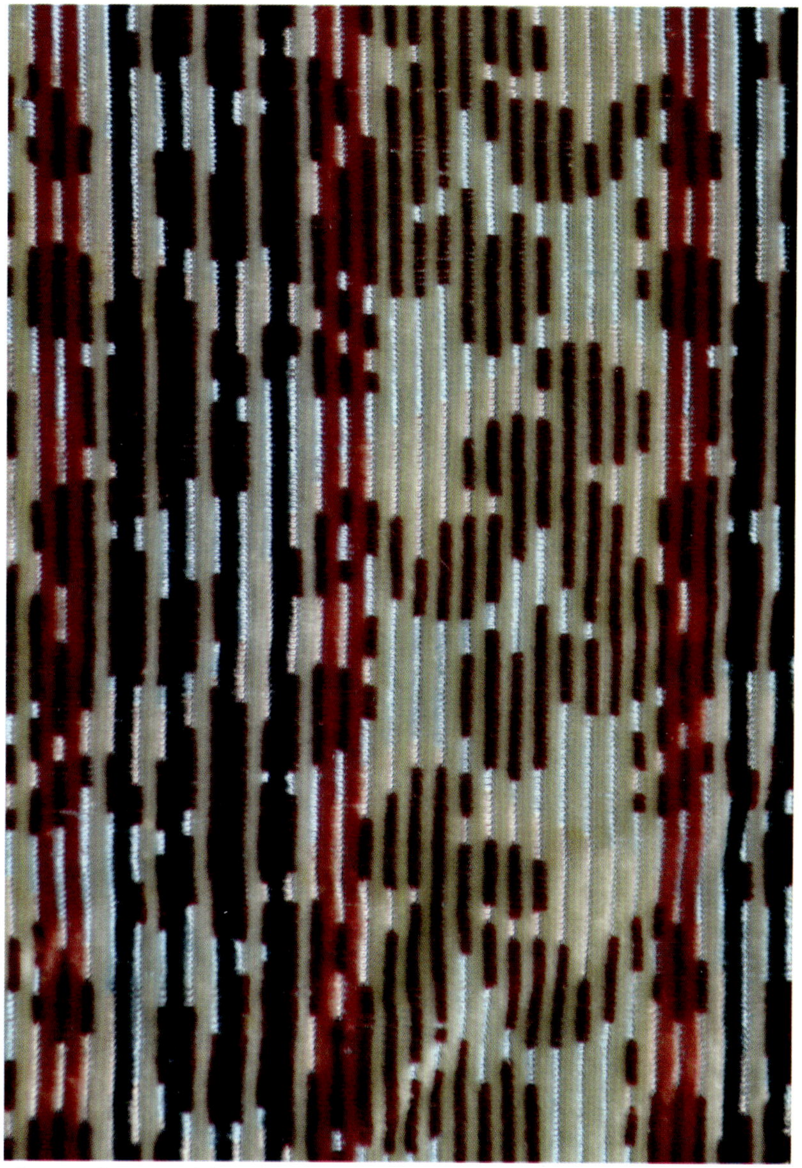

The straight grain of the velvet.

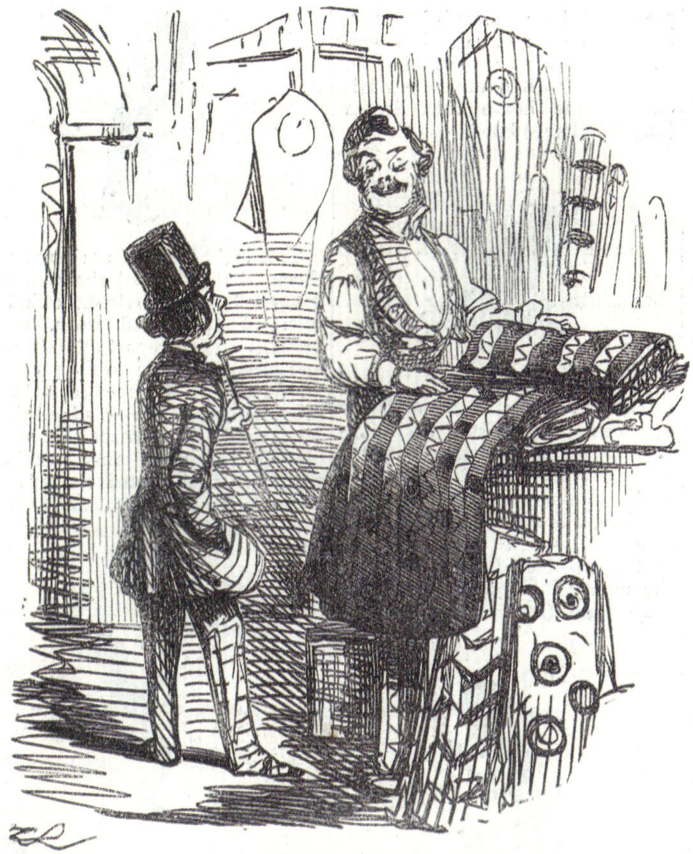

Cartoon in *Punch* 1846.

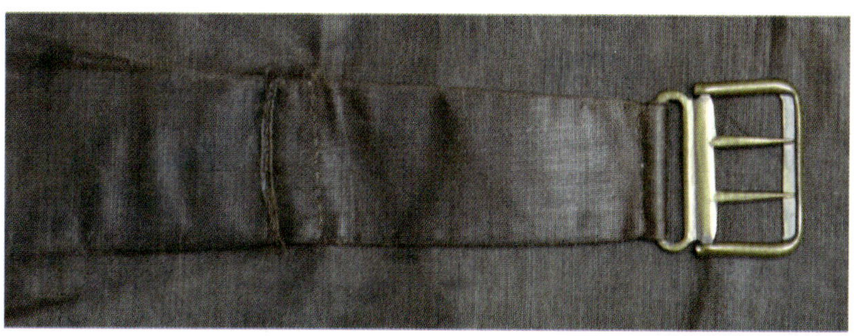

The end of one half of the backstrap, with its brass buckle. The other end has been inserted through a slit in the back fabric, so that it lies between the back and the lining, and is sewn into the side seam.

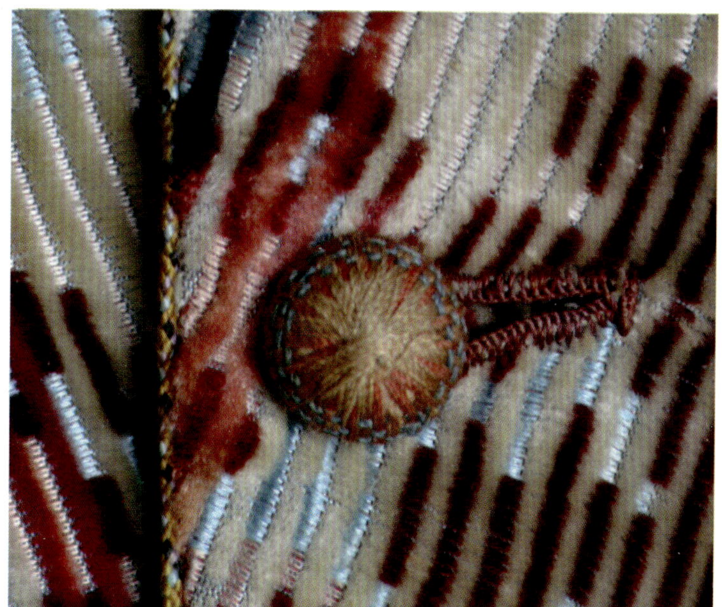

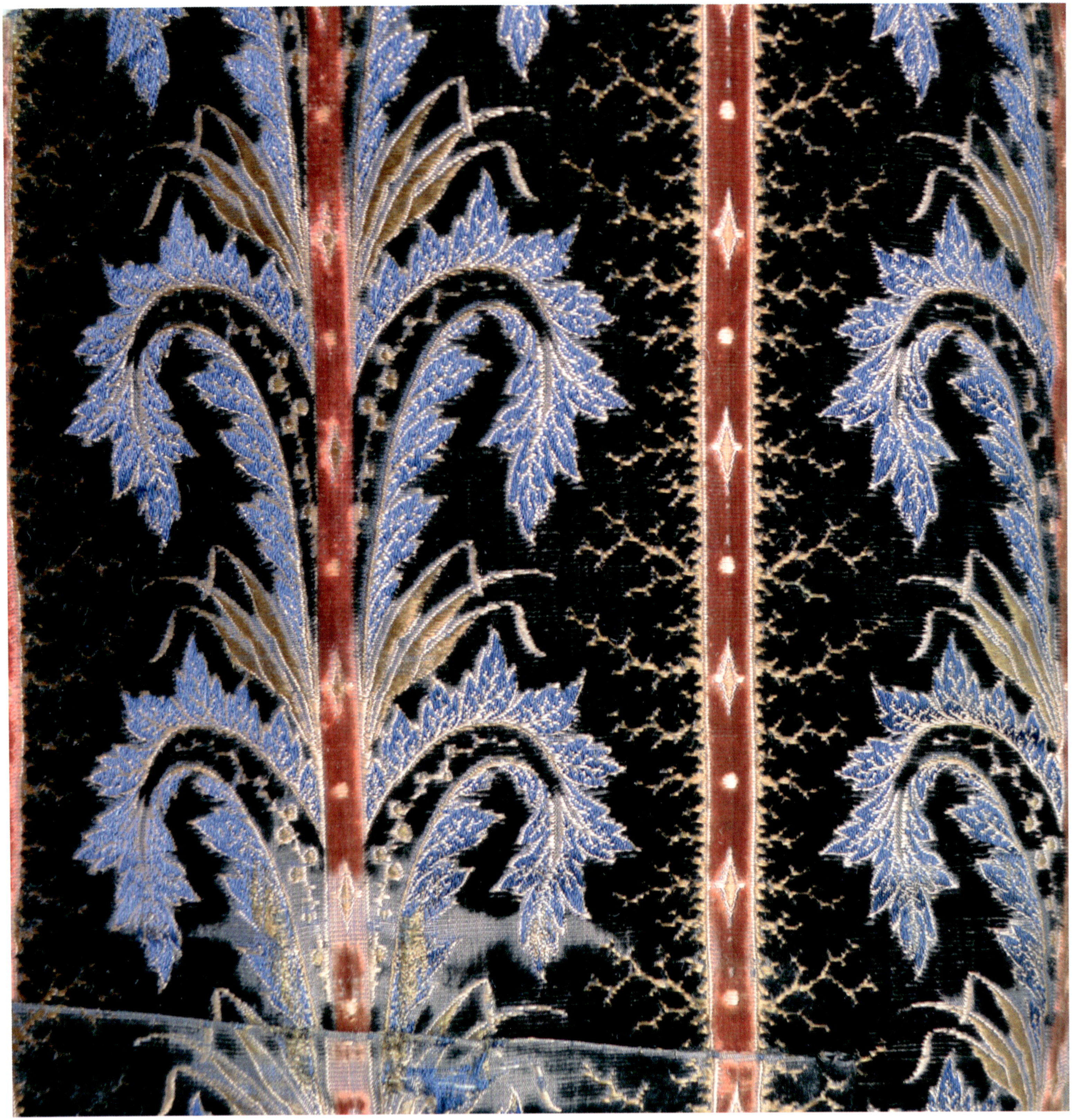

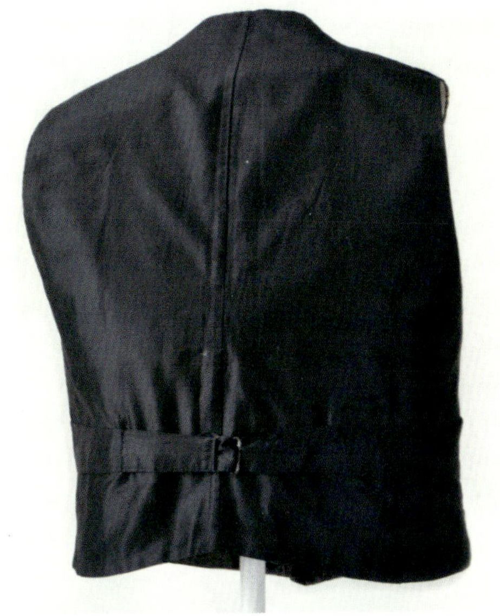

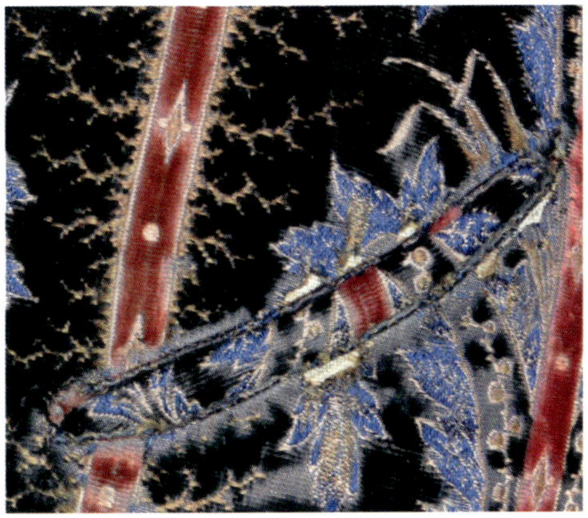

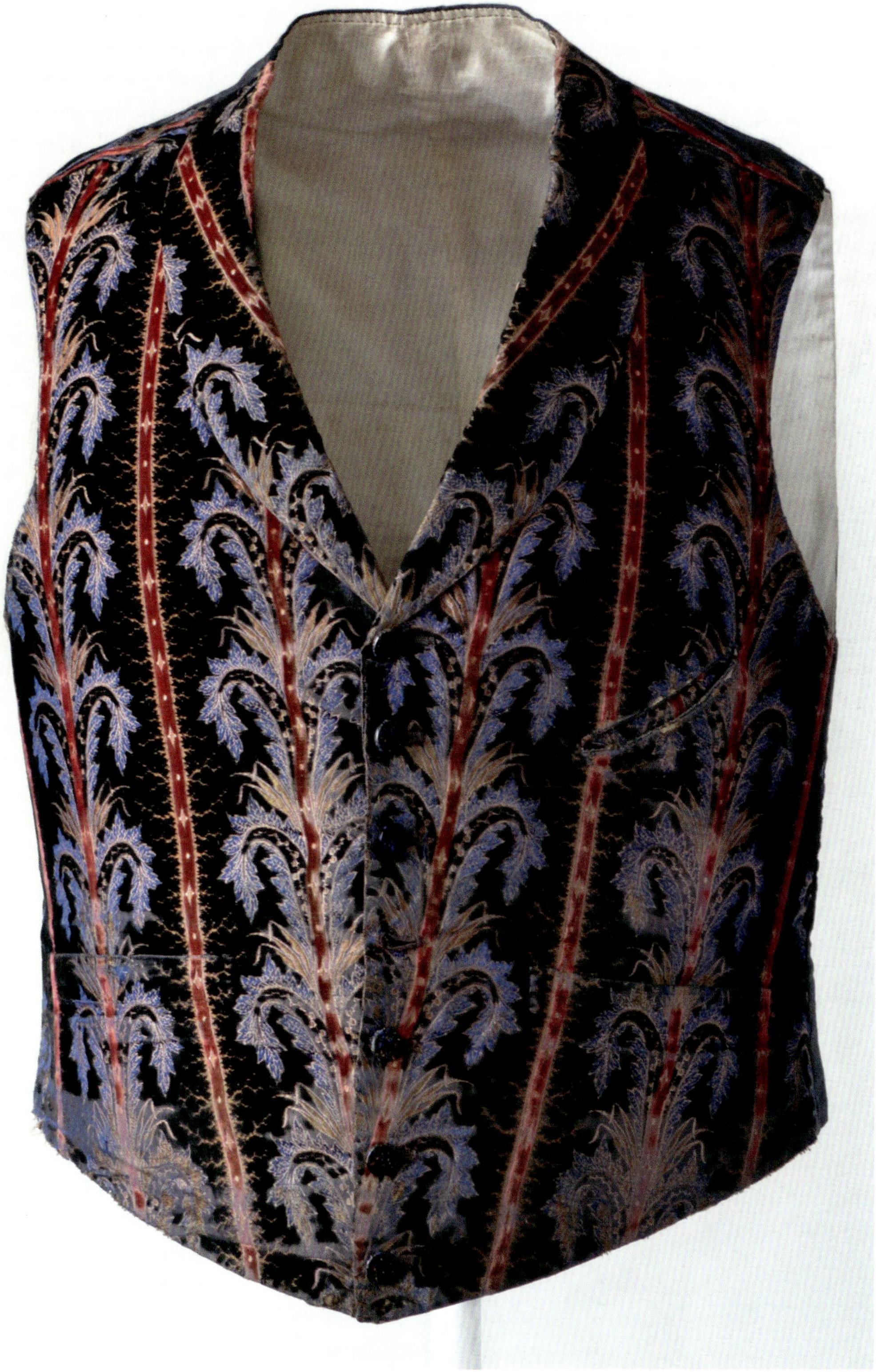

A waistcoat in voided silk velvet, 1845-1855.
HC.W-11.76-6

The velvet ground is black with narrow brick-coloured stripes, and a pattern of stylised leaves and twigs in peach and blue silk. There are two welted pockets and a crescent-shaped breast pocket on the left forepart. The waistcoat is lined in plain cream cotton and the back is in black cotton sateen with a backstrap and a black metal buckle as a waist adjustment. The buttons are black glass discs with irregular blue spots and sparkly gold bits in them, mounted on brass shanks; one of the seven is missing. The lining, back and buttons may be replacements from later in the nineteenth century.

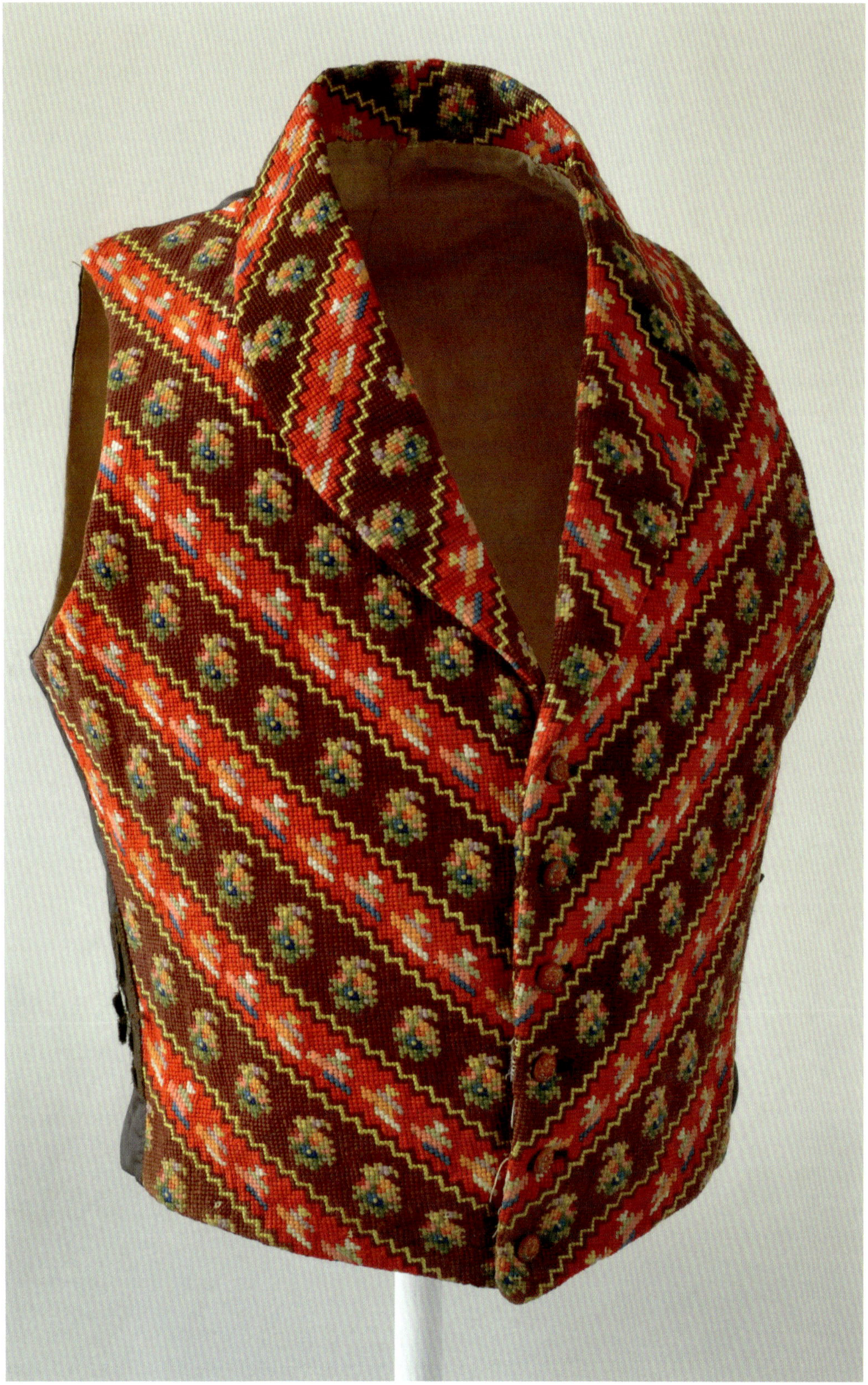

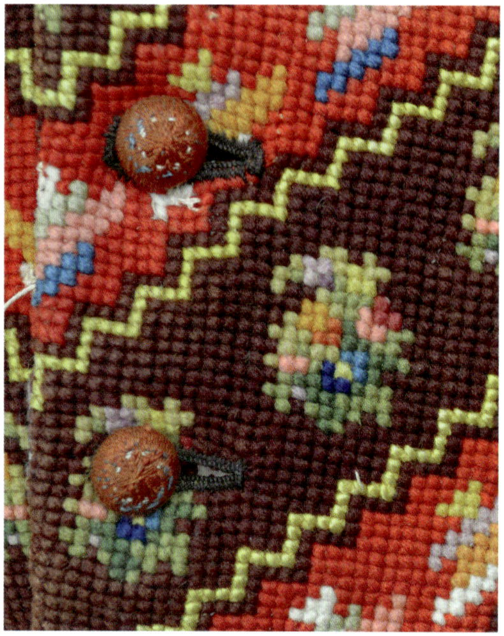

A waistcoat in Berlin woolwork, 1850-1860.
HC.W-4.11

It is worked in cross stitch on canvas, in polychrome Berlin wool, making a pattern of diagonal stripes, each decorated with motifs; the yellow zig-zag lines are in silk. The waistcoat has a roll collar and no pockets. It is lined with fawn cotton twill, and the back has been replaced with a modern man-made fabric, although the original waist adjustment tabs have been sewn back on to it. They are in dark brown silesia, probably the same as the original back fabric; the end of one is missing, and the other has a bent at the end, and three metal eyelets for lacing. The six shallow domed buttons are covered in red silk threads in a star pattern, over blue and ivory threads (page 216).

Berlin wool was a fine dyed worsted wool for knitting and embroidery, and worsted embroidery was known as Berlin work. It came from Germany and was a popular pastime from the 1830s until the 1880s when changing tastes led to its waning. Ladies' magazines published patterns for articles of clothing and other household items, often accompanied by details of where the necessary materials could be obtained.

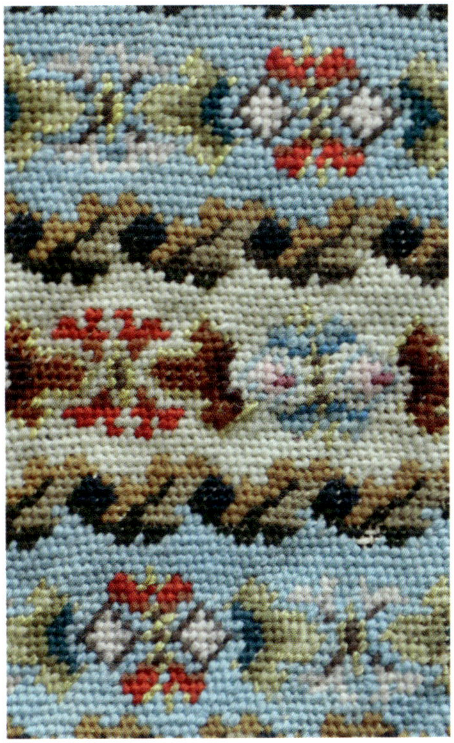

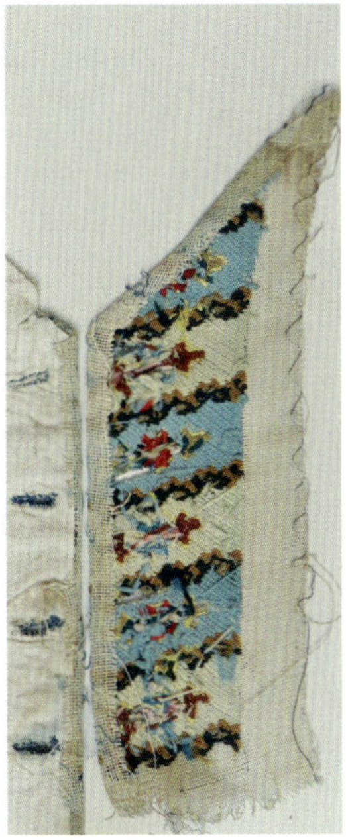

The back of the facing and the top front edge of the forepart.

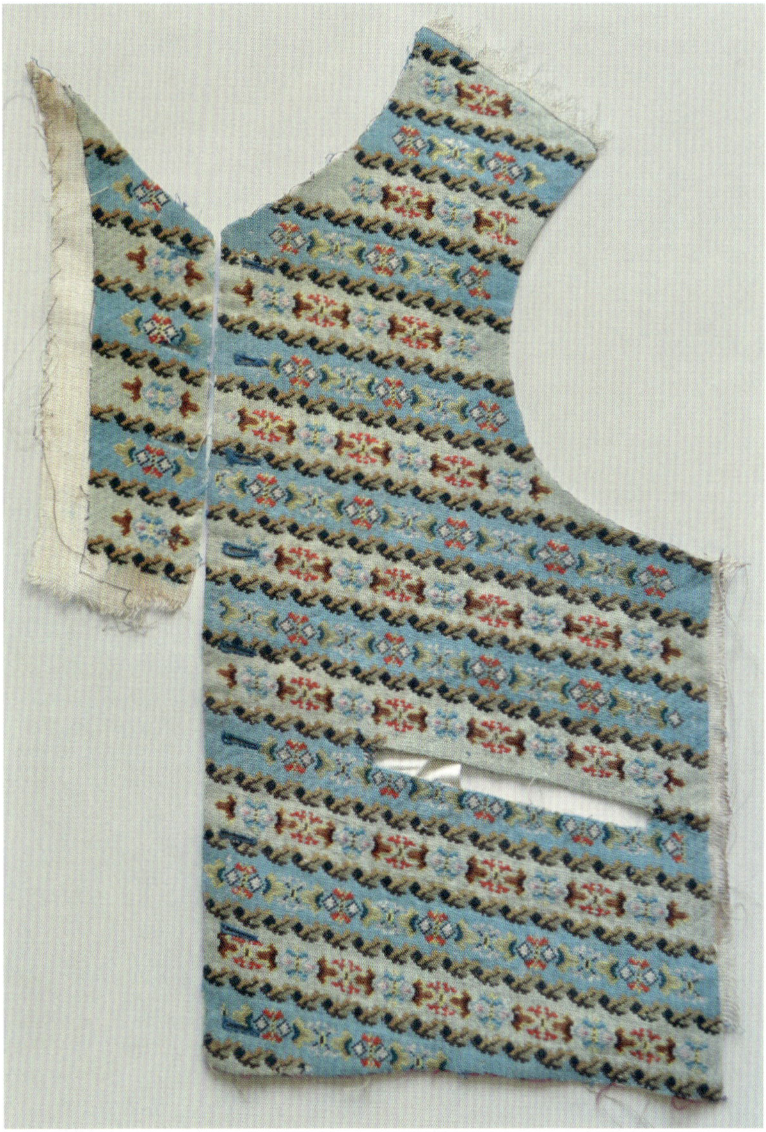

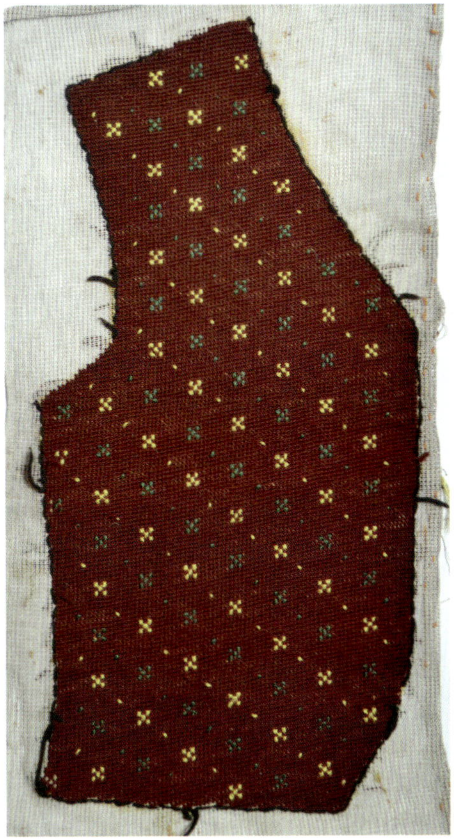

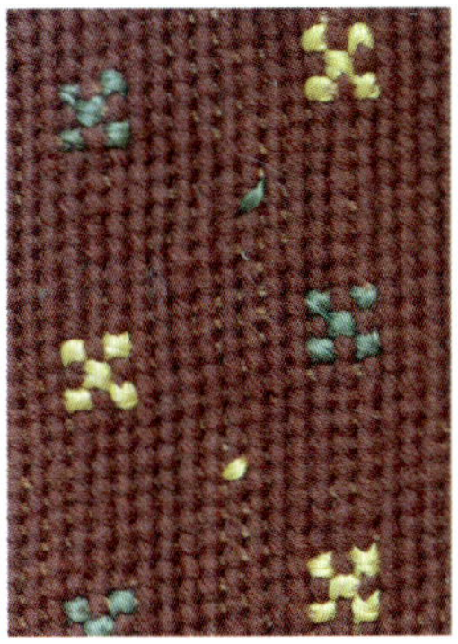

Left: **One of a pair of panels of Berlin woolwork on canvas, 1850-1865.** HC.W-7.82

This is for the right forepart of a waistcoat and has not been made up. It is in brown wool with cross motifs and dots in yellow and turquoise silk. The canvas is off-grain, causing the pattern to slope upwards.

Pieces of a waistcoat in Berlin woolwork, 1850-1860. HC.W-8.82

The left forepart is shown here with a section of the facing. They are worked in cross stitch on canvas, and have been assembled and unpicked. The canvas is very off-grain, causing the pattern to slope upwards. The buttonholes have been worked and a hole cut for a pocket. The front edge of the forepart, behind the buttonholes, is backed on plain white cotton.

The supplier recommended by *The Englishwoman's Domestic Magazine* was "Mrs. Wilcockson, 44, Goodge-street, Tottenham-court-road, London". Emma Wilcockson (1829-1871) was listed in the 1851 census as a dressmaker, but branched out into supplying all the materials for working these embroideries as well as everything else needed for the finished article. She was born Emma Kyte in Suffolk and her family moved to London, where in 1849 she married Herbert Wilcockson, a printer.

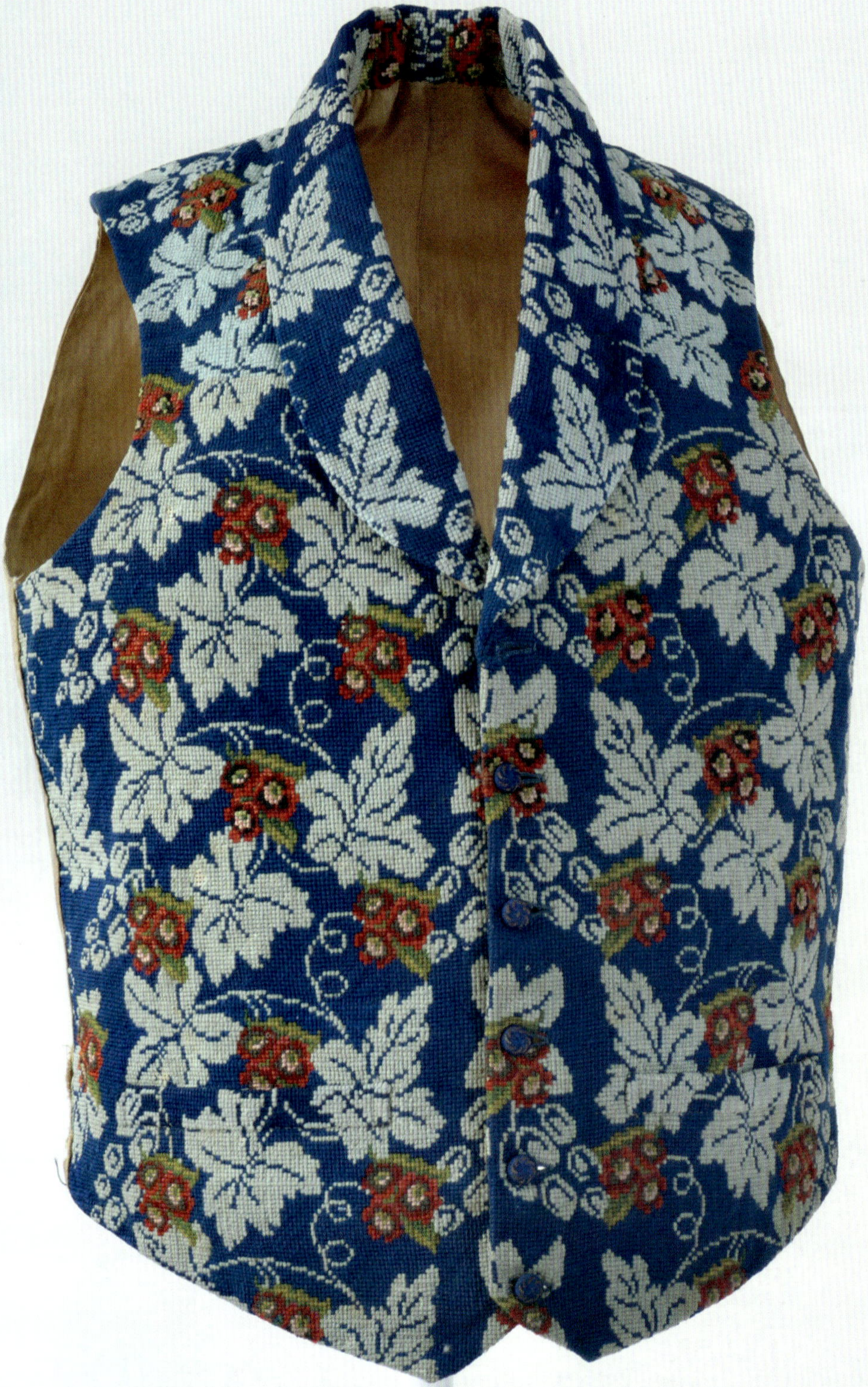

A waistcoat in Berlin woolwork, 1850-1860.
HC.W-12.00-3

The design of polychrome flowers and white leaves on a blue ground is worked in cross stitch on canvas, mostly with Berlin wool but the light red and peach colours are in silk thread. The waistcoat has a roll collar, two welted pockets, and the six shallow domed buttons are covered in dark blue and pink silk threads in a whorl pattern. The lining and back are in fawn cotton twill with a pair of tabs, with bents in the ends and three pairs of metal eyelets for lacing, to adjust the waist; the lace is missing.

Worsted embroidery, known as Berlin work, came from Germany; it was a popular pastime in the middle years of the nineteenth century. Ladies' magazines published patterns for it, often accompanied by details of where the necessary materials could be obtained.

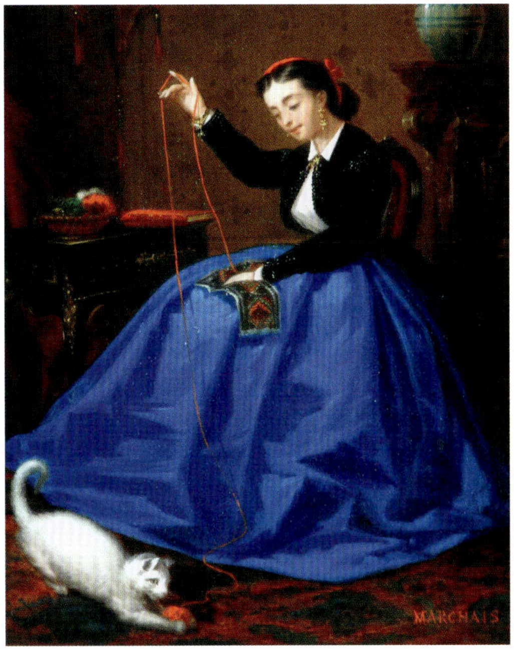

Detail from *Girl in a Blue Skirt, Sewing* by J. B. Marchais, 1860s. The Bowes Museum, Barnard Castle, County Durham.

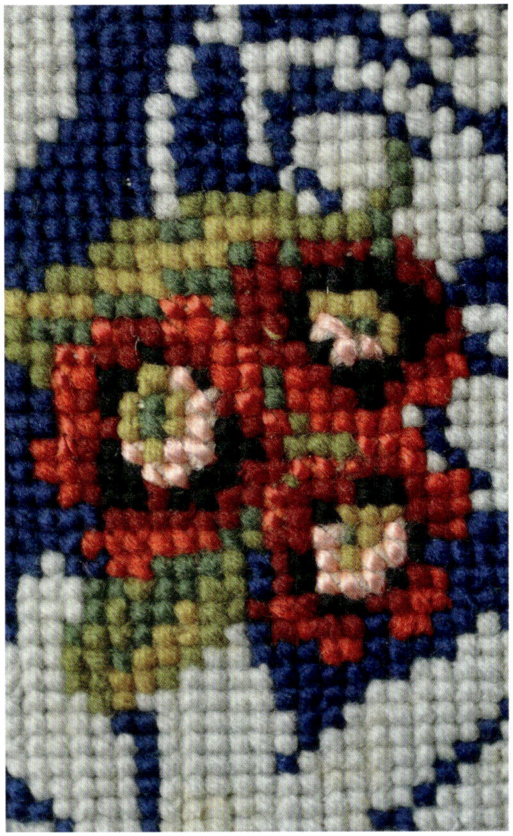

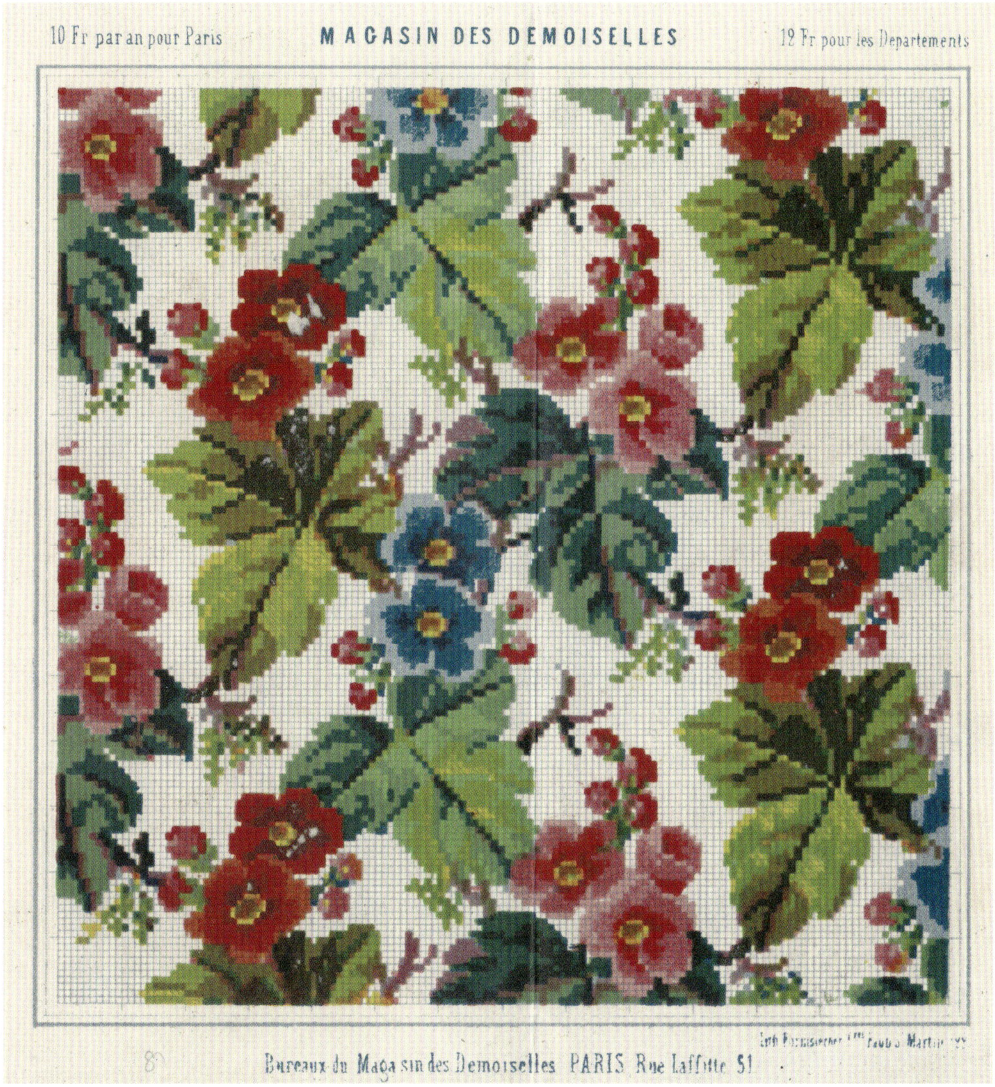

A pattern for Berlin woolwork embroidery published in *Magasin des Demoiselles*, *c*.1855.

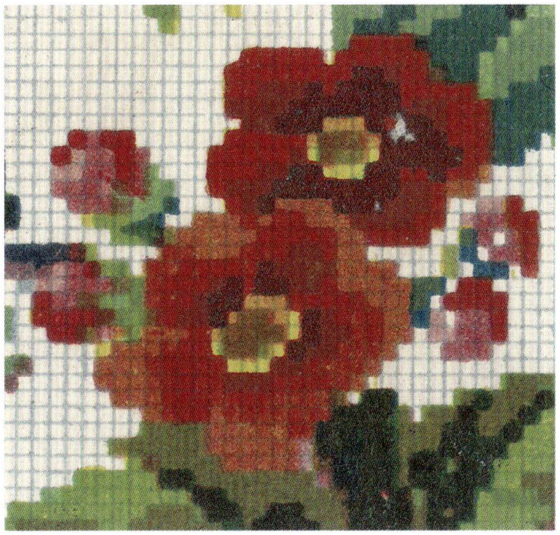

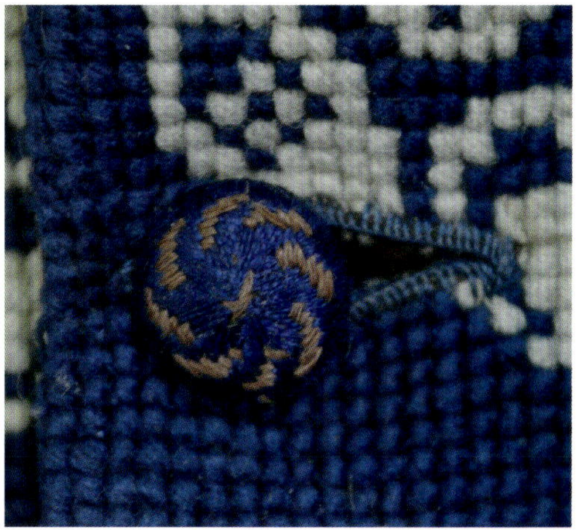

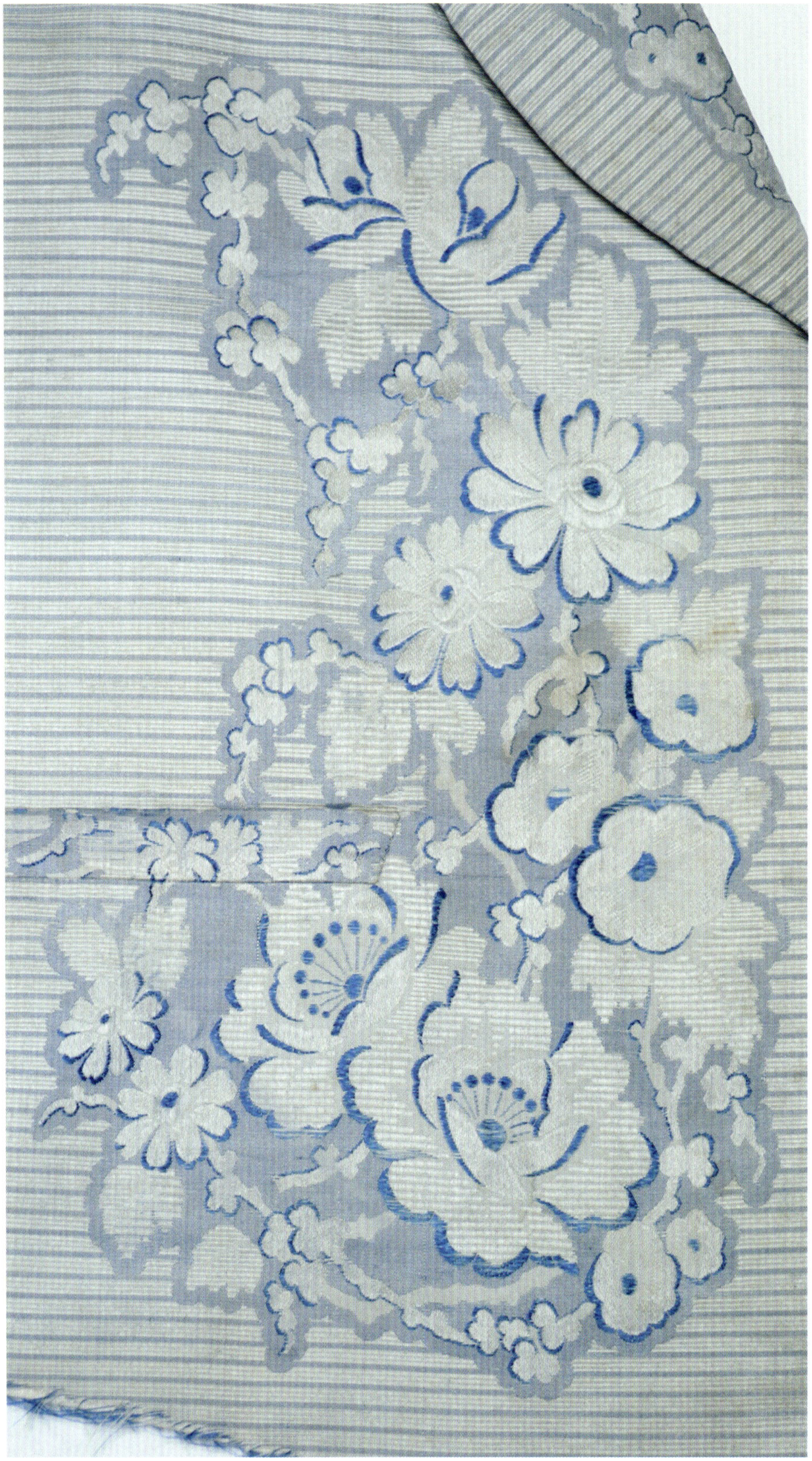

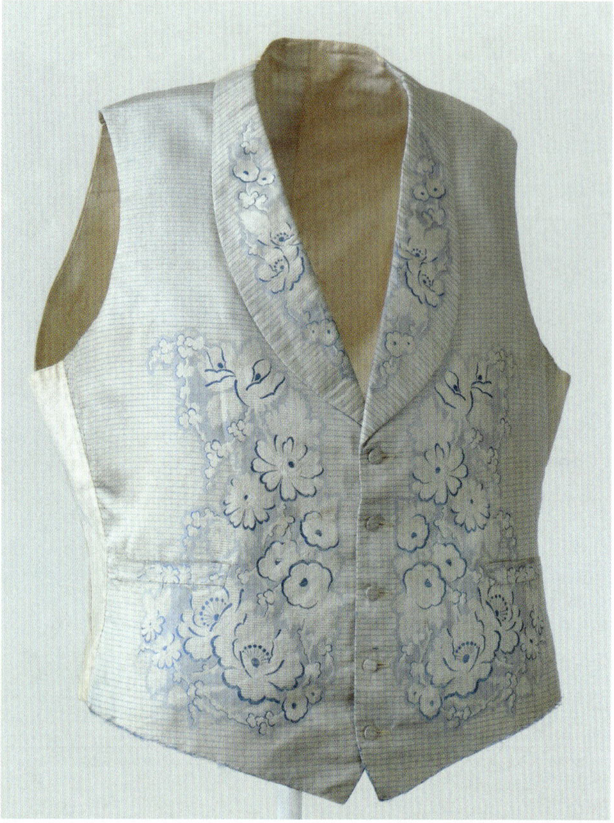

A waistcoat in white and blue silk, 1850-1860.
HC.W-0.68

The silk has horizontal stripes and a large floral motif woven to shape on the foreparts and the roll collar; the collar does not extend round the back neck. There are five flat covered buttons, and the lining and back are in white cotton twill; there were originally three pairs of ivory silk ribbon ties to adjust the waist at the back, but one pair is missing. The hems of the foreparts are faced with fawn leather, and the side seams have 3″ strips of plain white cotton let in, widening to 3¼″ at the waist.

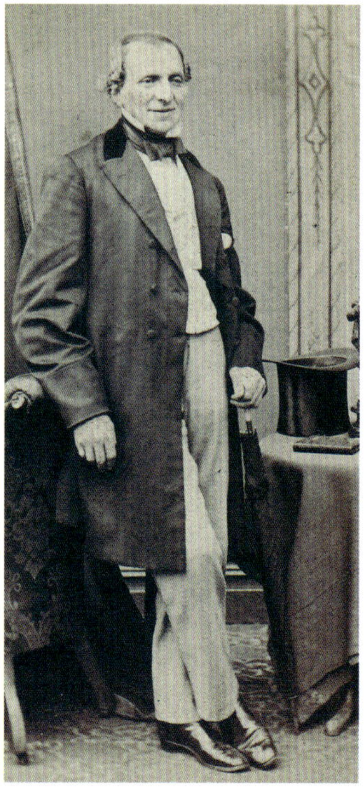

Unknown man, *c.*1860.

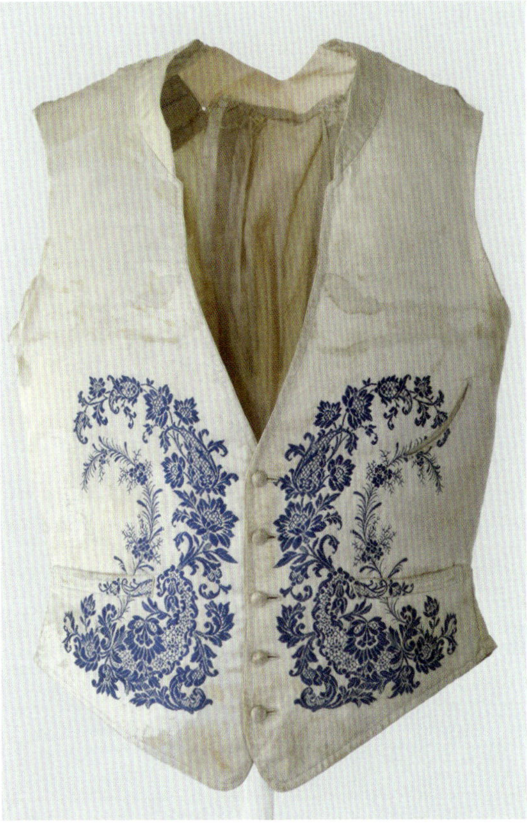

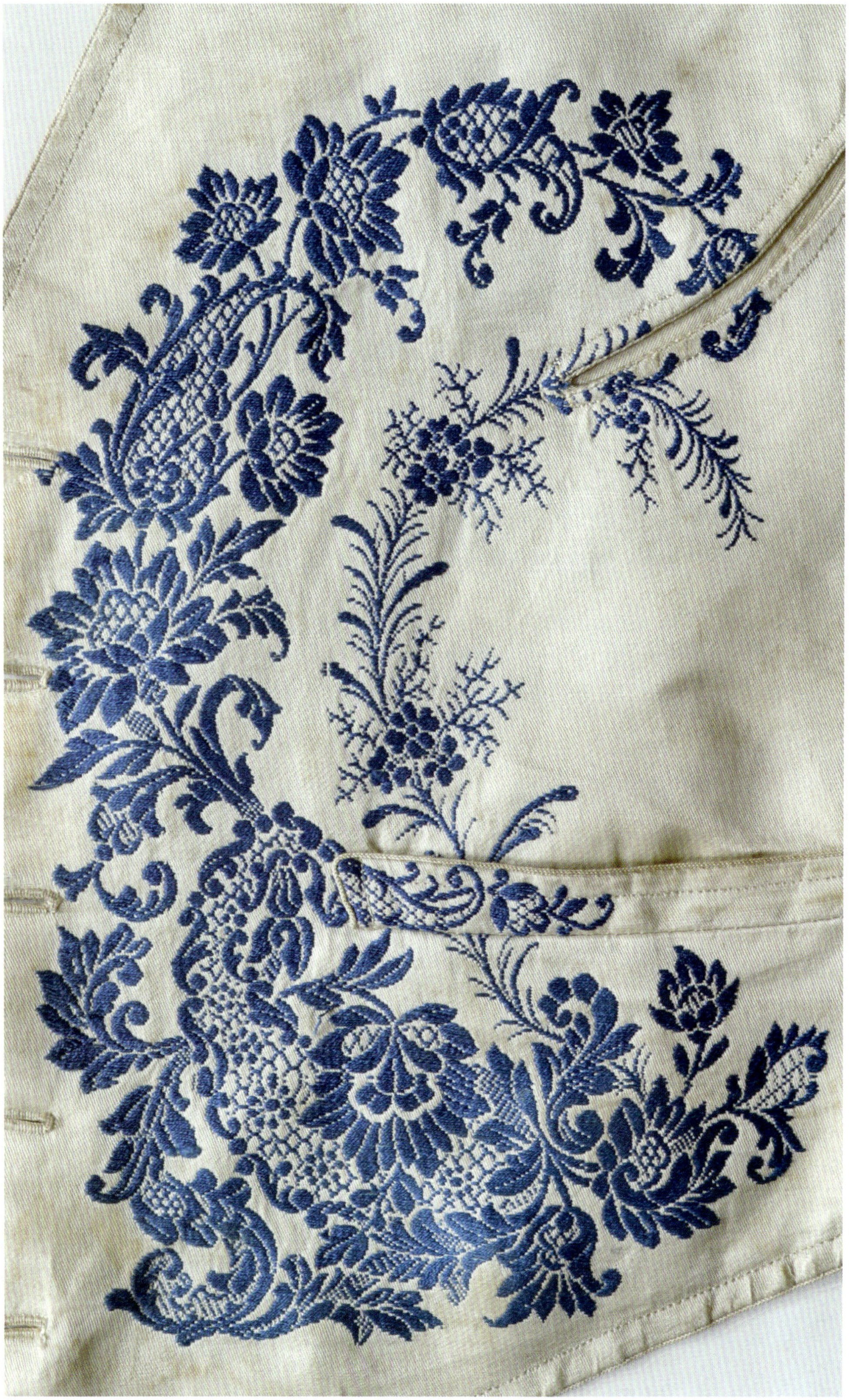

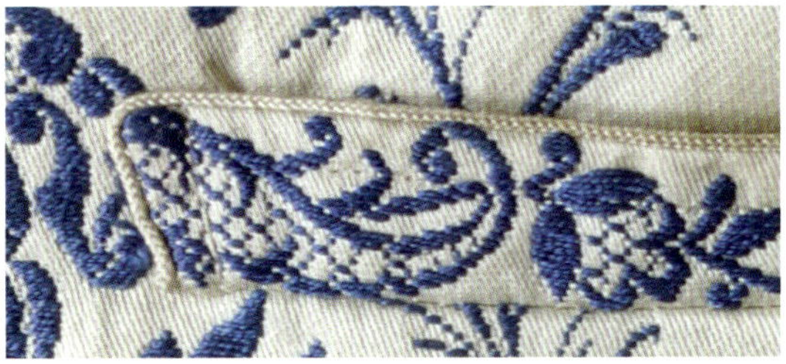

A waistcoat in ivory silk twill, 1850-1860. HC.W-0.98

It has a large flowery paisley shape woven in dark blue silk on each forepart. The foreparts, stand collar and pockets have a row of stitching 1/4″ in from their edges and a fine ivory silk cord on the edge; there is slight padding over the chest. The lining and back are in plain white cotton, with a backstrap and a white metal buckle (page 210) to adjust the waist. The five shallow domed buttons are covered in a patterned silk woven to shape (page 216), and the forepart hems are faced with fawn leather. The waistcoat has been very much altered in the late twentieth century, with pieces of cotton inserted at the shoulders, in the centre back and in the back of the collar.

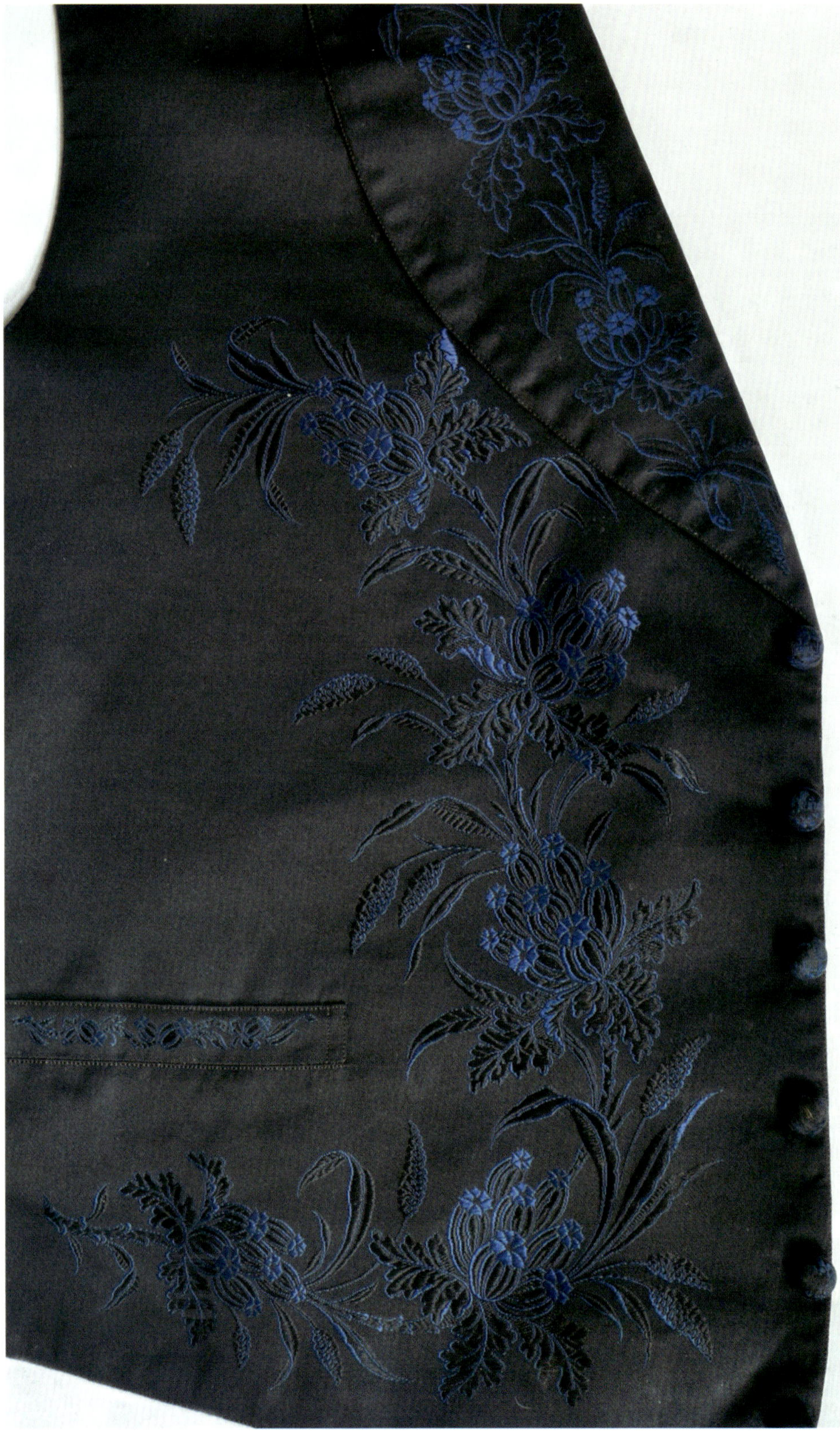

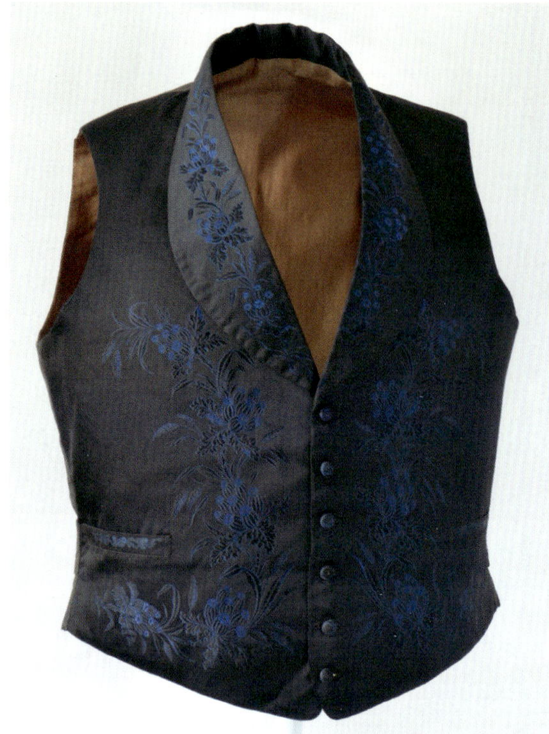

A waistcoat in black silk satin, 1850-1860. HC.W-12.99

The silk has a floral pattern in black and blue, woven to shape, on the foreparts, roll collar and welted pockets. The lining is ginger cotton twill, and the back is in dark brown silesia with a backstrap to adjust the waist. The six domed covered buttons have a blue woven motif on them (page 216).

Right: *James East Oldaker* by Marshall, 1851. Privately owned. James East Oldaker was an estate agent in Ilford.

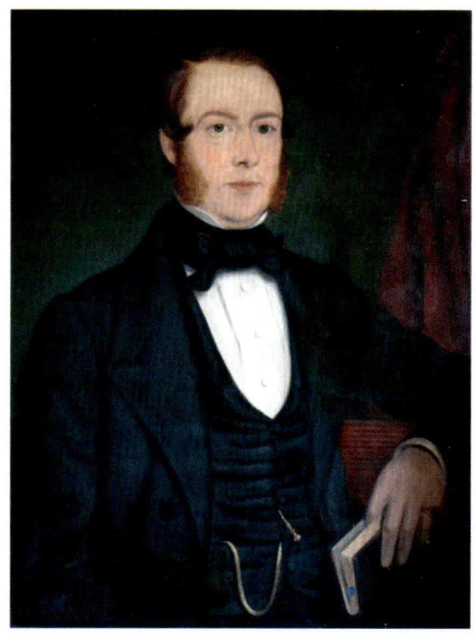

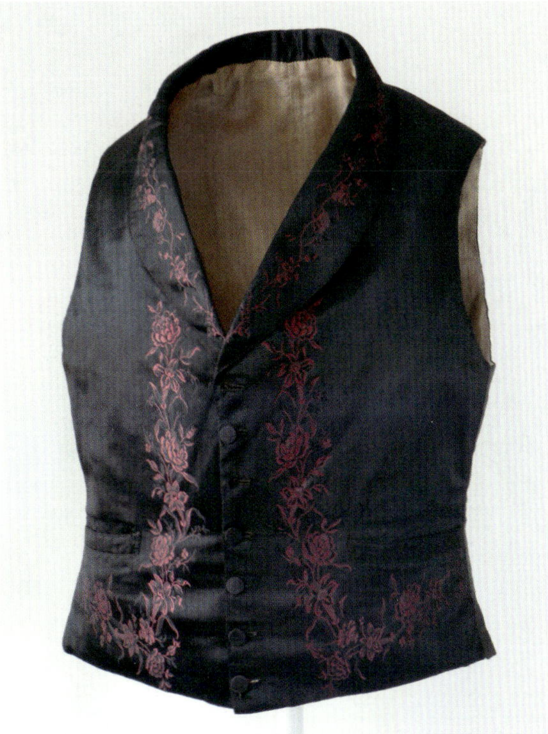

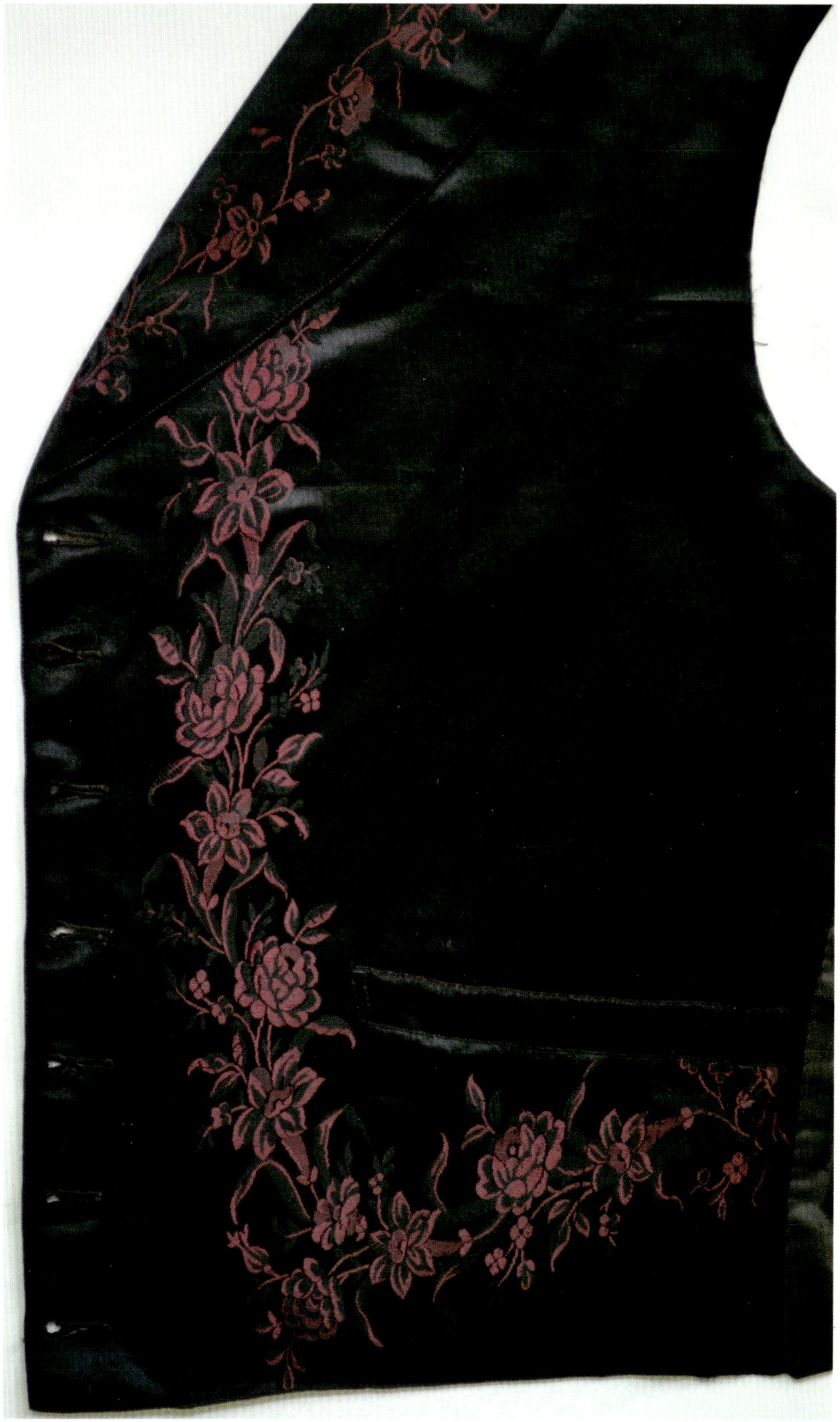

A waistcoat in black silk satin, 1850-1860. HC.W-8.00

The silk has a floral pattern in black and pink, woven to shape on the foreparts and roll collar. The lining is fawn cotton twill, and the back is in dark brown silesia with a backstrap and a black metal buckle to adjust the waist. Two of the seven flat self-covered buttons are missing. The hems of the foreparts are faced with dark brown leather.

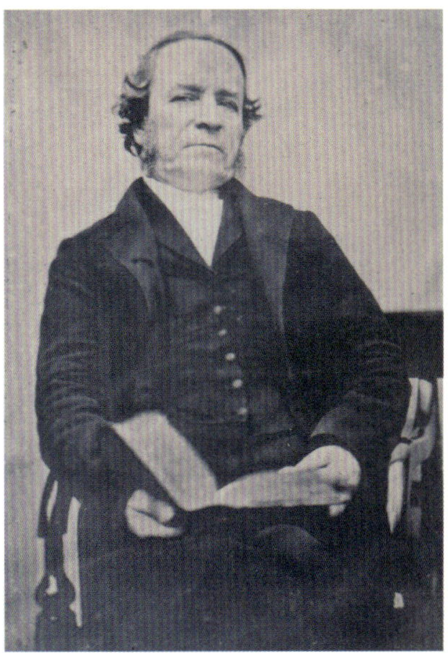

Left: Unknown man, *c.*1860.

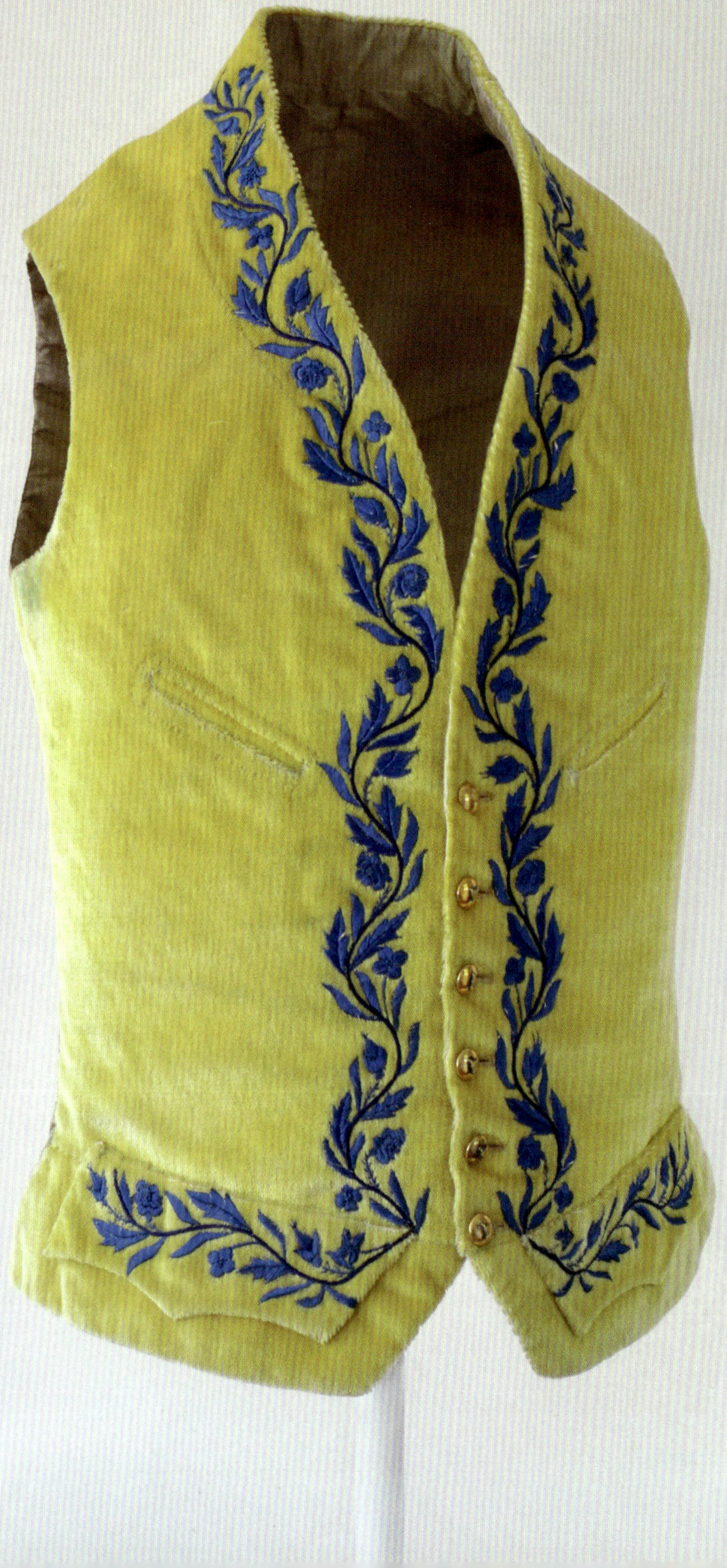

A waistcoat in yellow silk plush, 1850-1860.
HC.W-12.01

This is a hunting waistcoat and it has blue silk embroidery on the front part of the stand collar and the front edge of the foreparts; this has been worked over card which holds it above the pile of the plush. The pocket flaps are embroidered as well, and the pockets open at the top of the flaps instead of underneath them; there are also two slanting breast pockets. The front edges are faced with beige silk velvet, and there is a loop of cream silk ribbon inside the waist of the right forepart to attach to the top trouser button and prevent the waistcoat from riding up.
The lining and back are in stone-coloured silk twill; the back seam is open, with cream silk ribbon, now fragile, laced through hand-sewn eyelet holes, over a wide gusset of the silk.
The waistcoat is padded throughout. The six brass domed buttons have a fox's head on them and were made by Jennens & Co. whose name is stamped on the back.

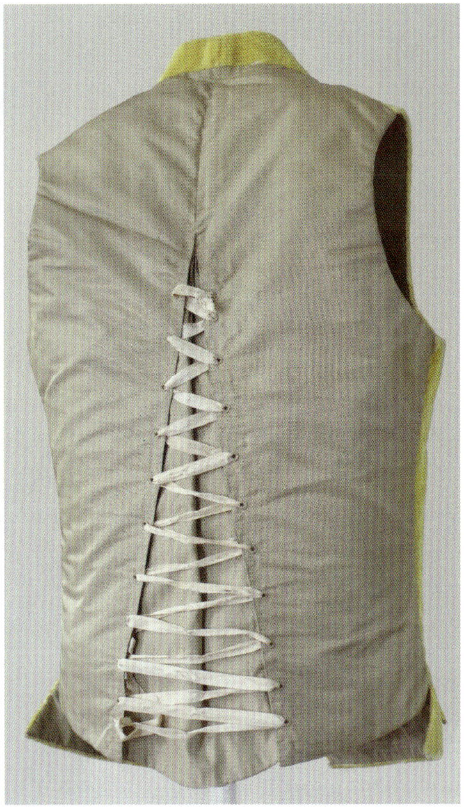

The lacing is not tightened because of the fragility of the ribbon.

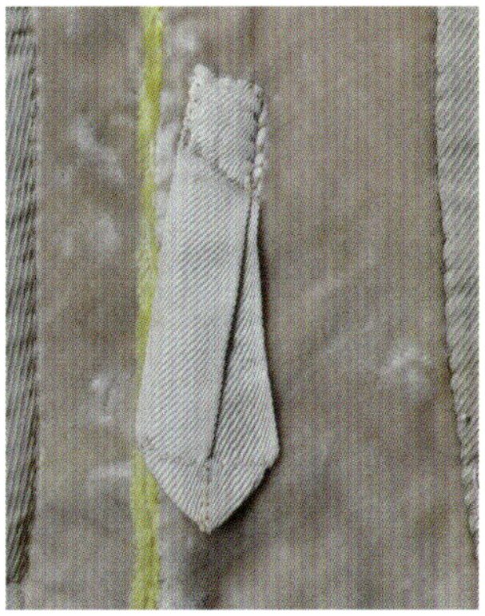

The ribbon loop at the waist inside the right forepart.

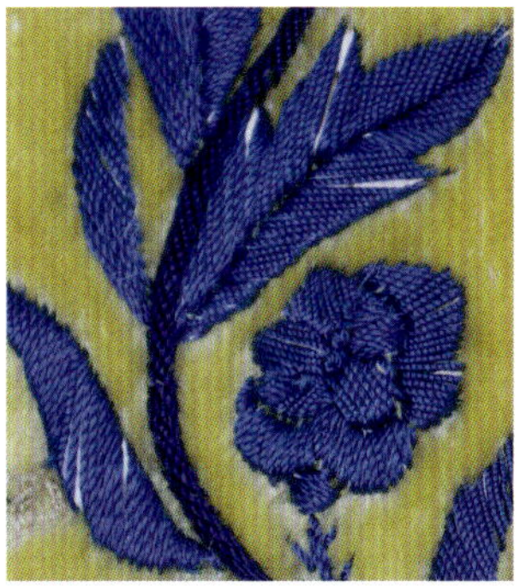

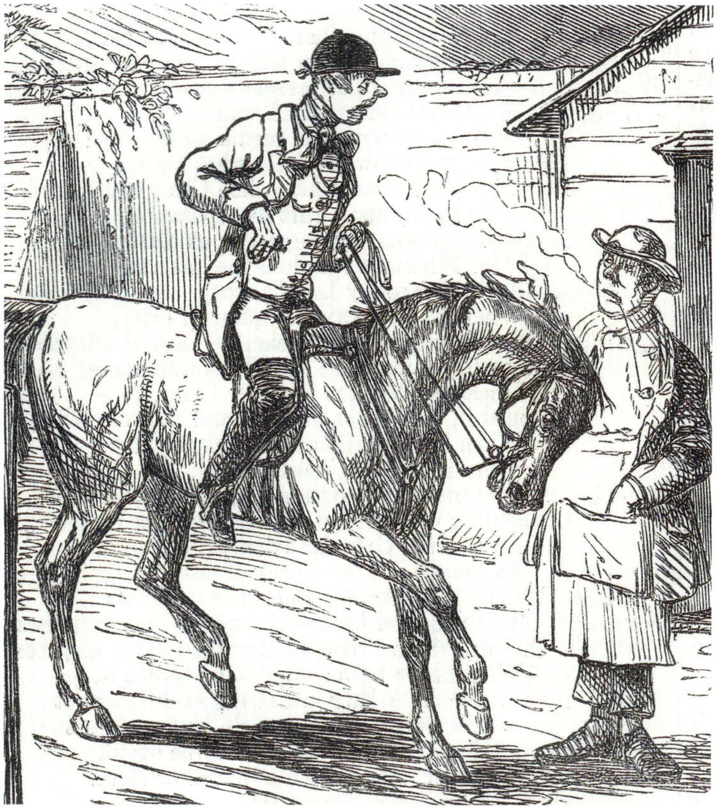

Detail from a cartoon in *Punch*, 1851.

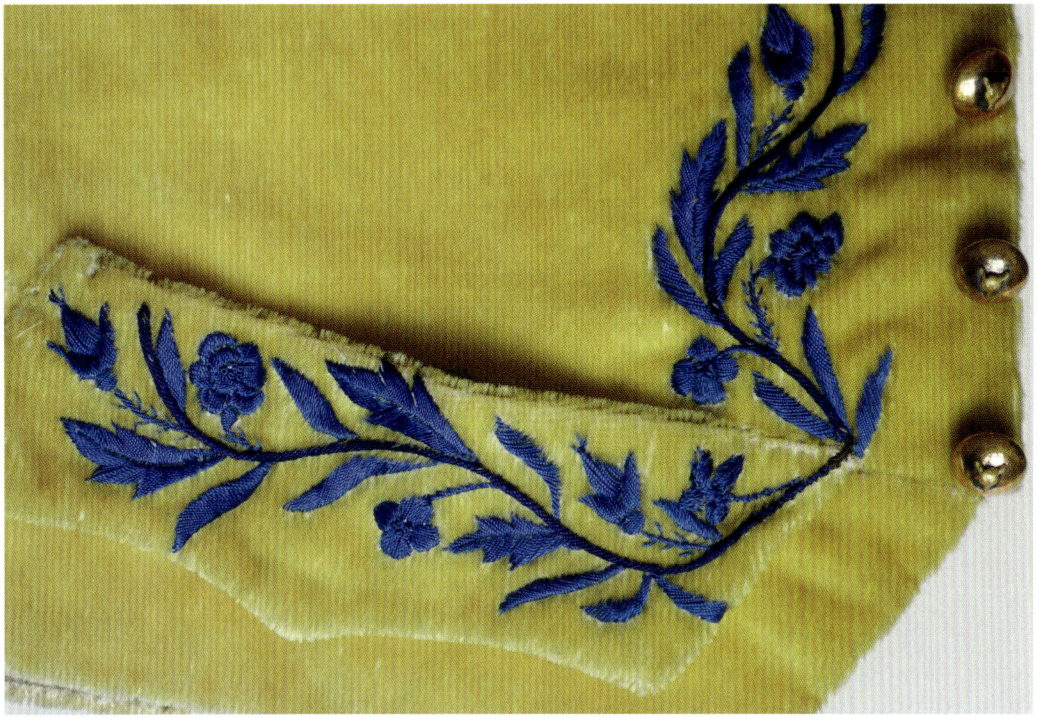

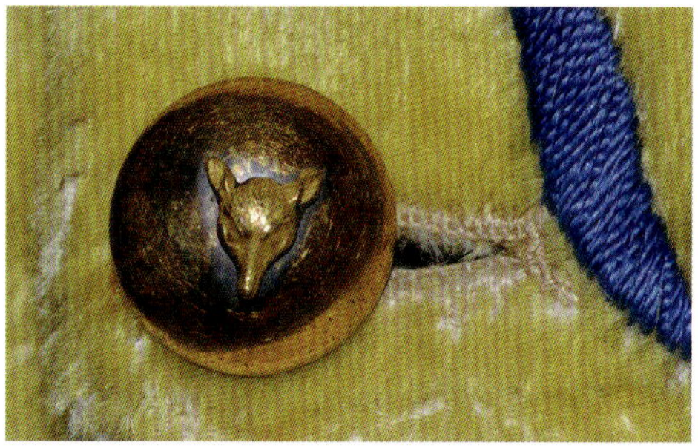

One of the brass buttons with a fox's head made by Jennens & Co.

Jennens & Co. was founded around 1760, as Makers of Military Accoutrements, gathering royal warrants during the nineteenth century. The firm made all kinds of uniform ornaments out of silver and other metals for military and many other uses, such as court dress, livery and hunting. Although the company was based in London, the work was produced in Birmingham.

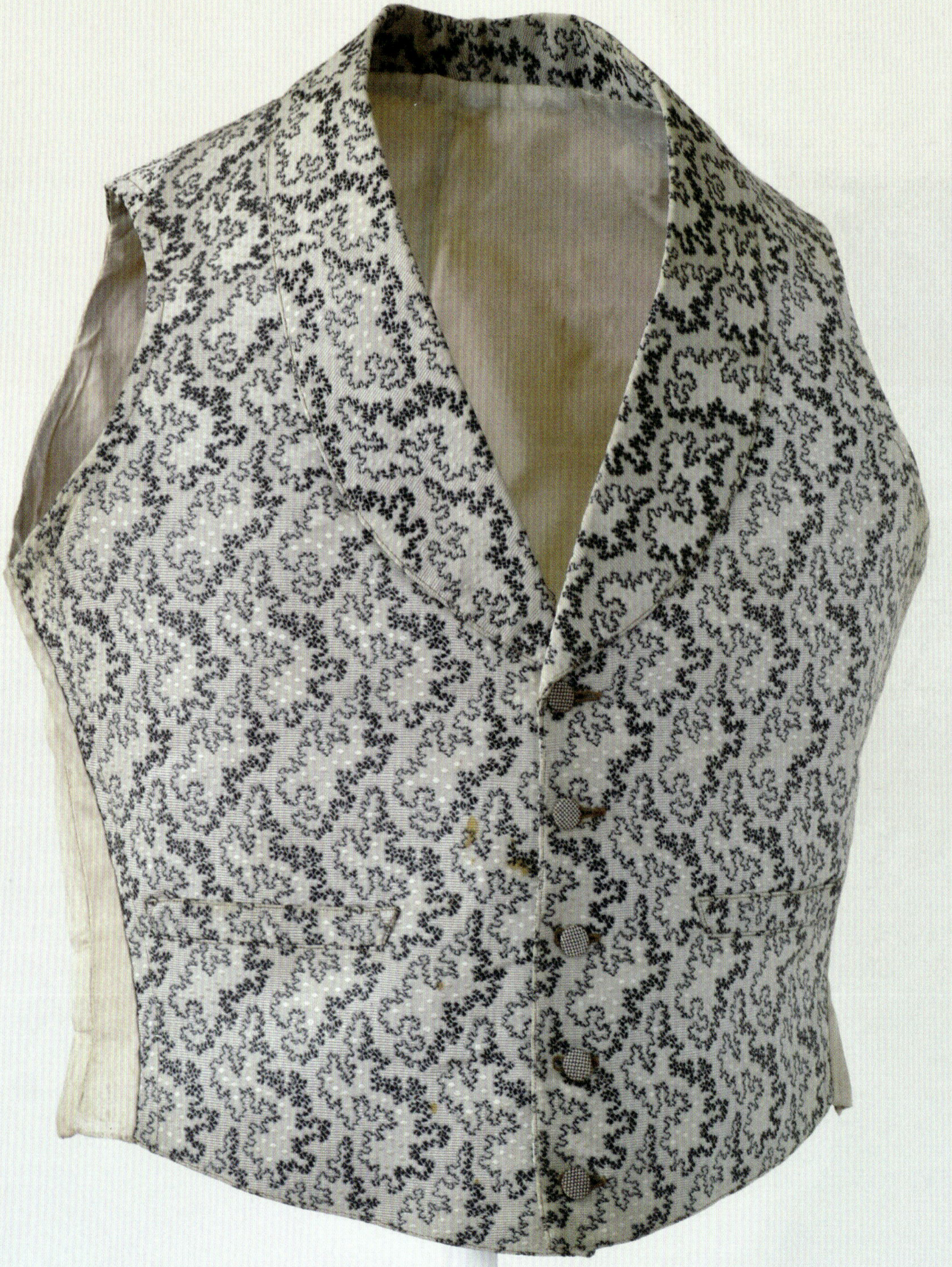

A waistcoat in ivory silk, 1850-1860.
HC.W-12.00-2

The silk has a squiggly pattern in dark blue on an ivory ground of different weaves. The waistcoat has a roll collar and two welted pockets. The five buttons are covered in silk with a tiny check pattern in ivory and dark brown, and the buttonholes are worked in brown silk. It is lined in plain white cotton, and the back is in cream silesia with a backstrap and a brass buckle to adjust the waist. The centre back seam has an inverted V-shape opening at the base, and there are two small gussets in the back hem towards the sides. The side seams have strips of 1″ let in, widening to 1½″ at the waist, to increase the size.

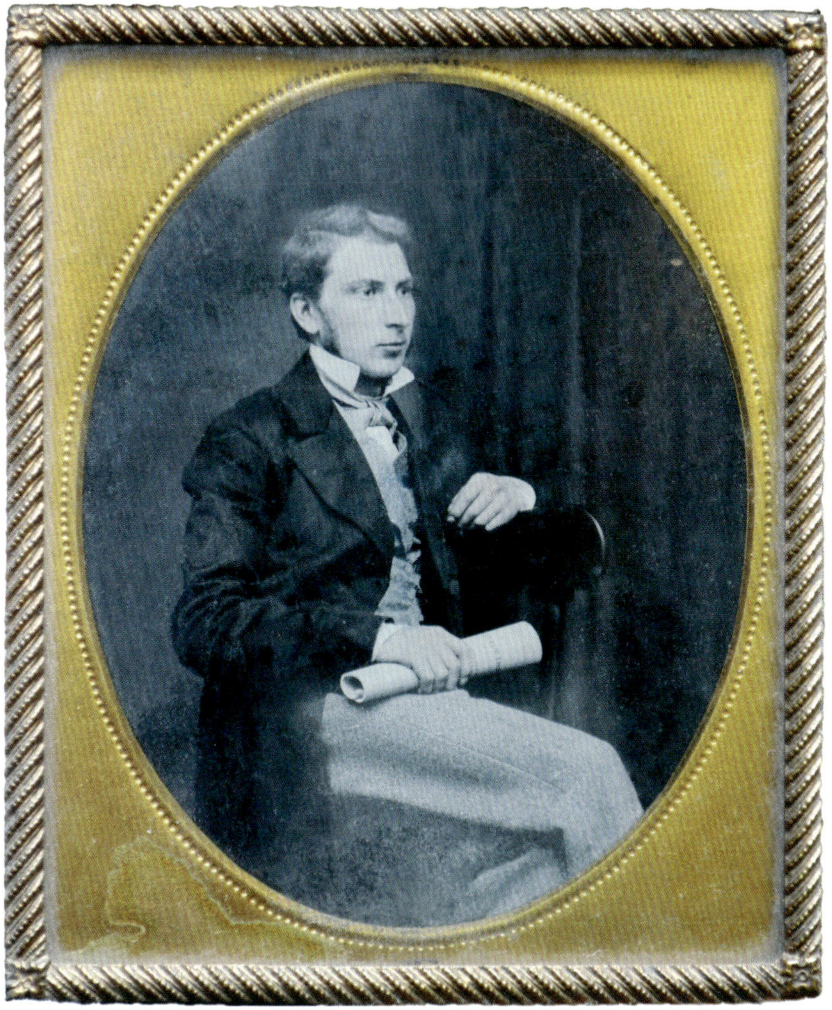

John Perrin Hopkins, a shopkeeper, *c.*1855. This is an ambrotype, one of the early forms of photograph.

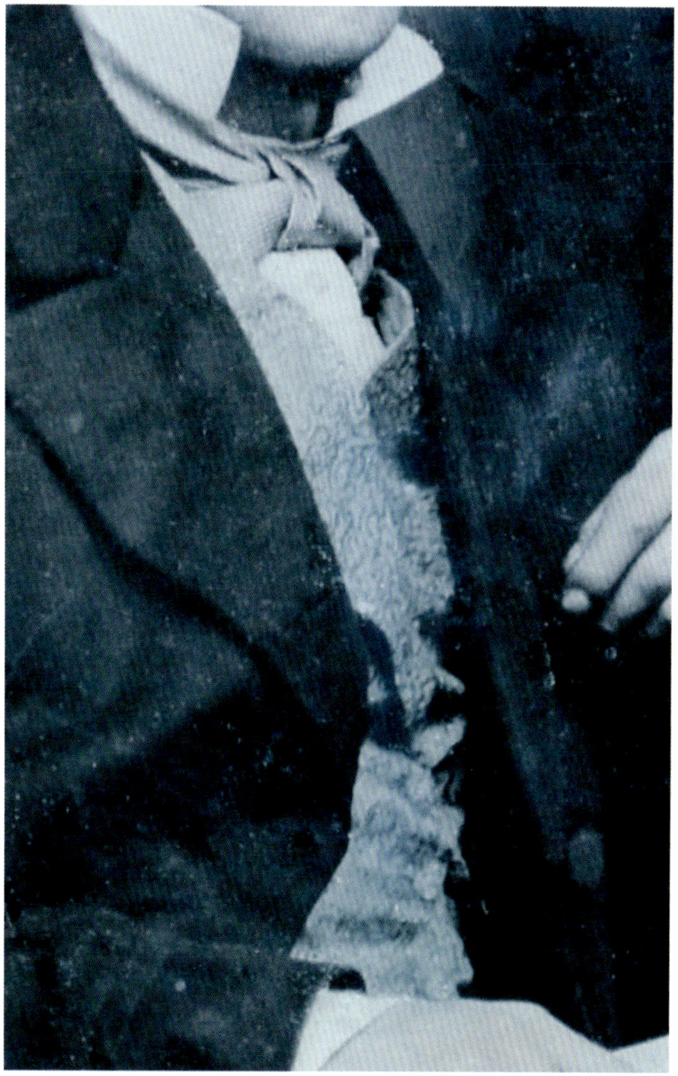

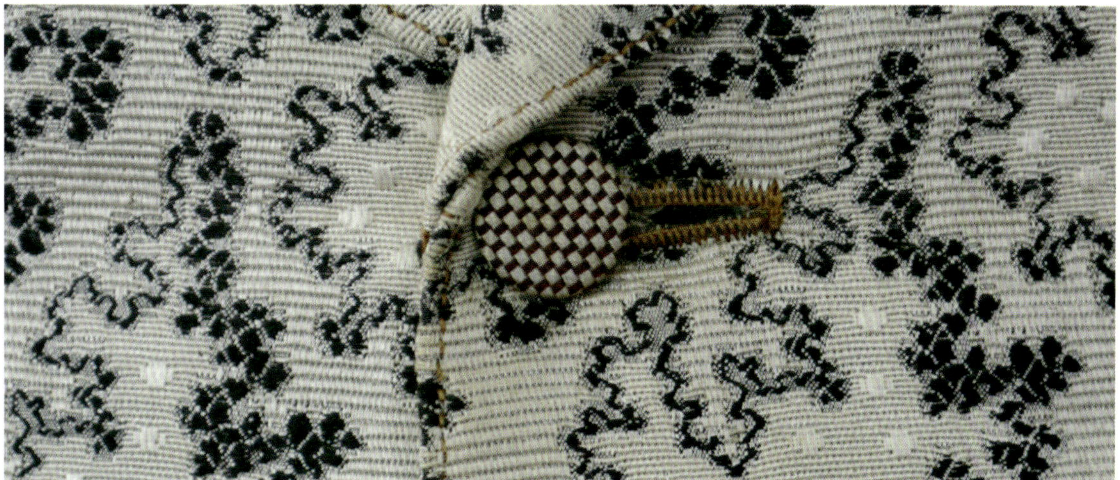

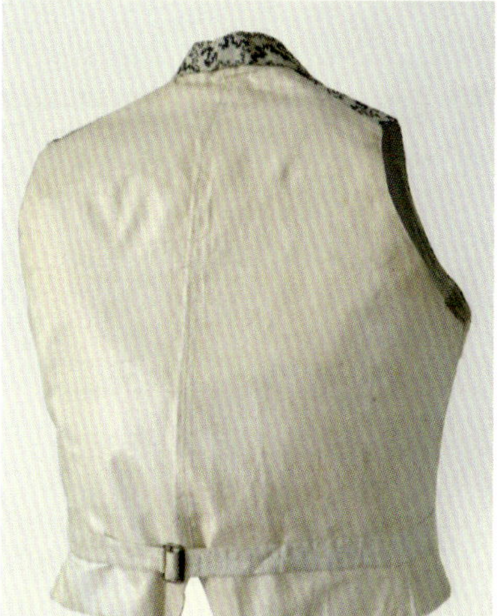

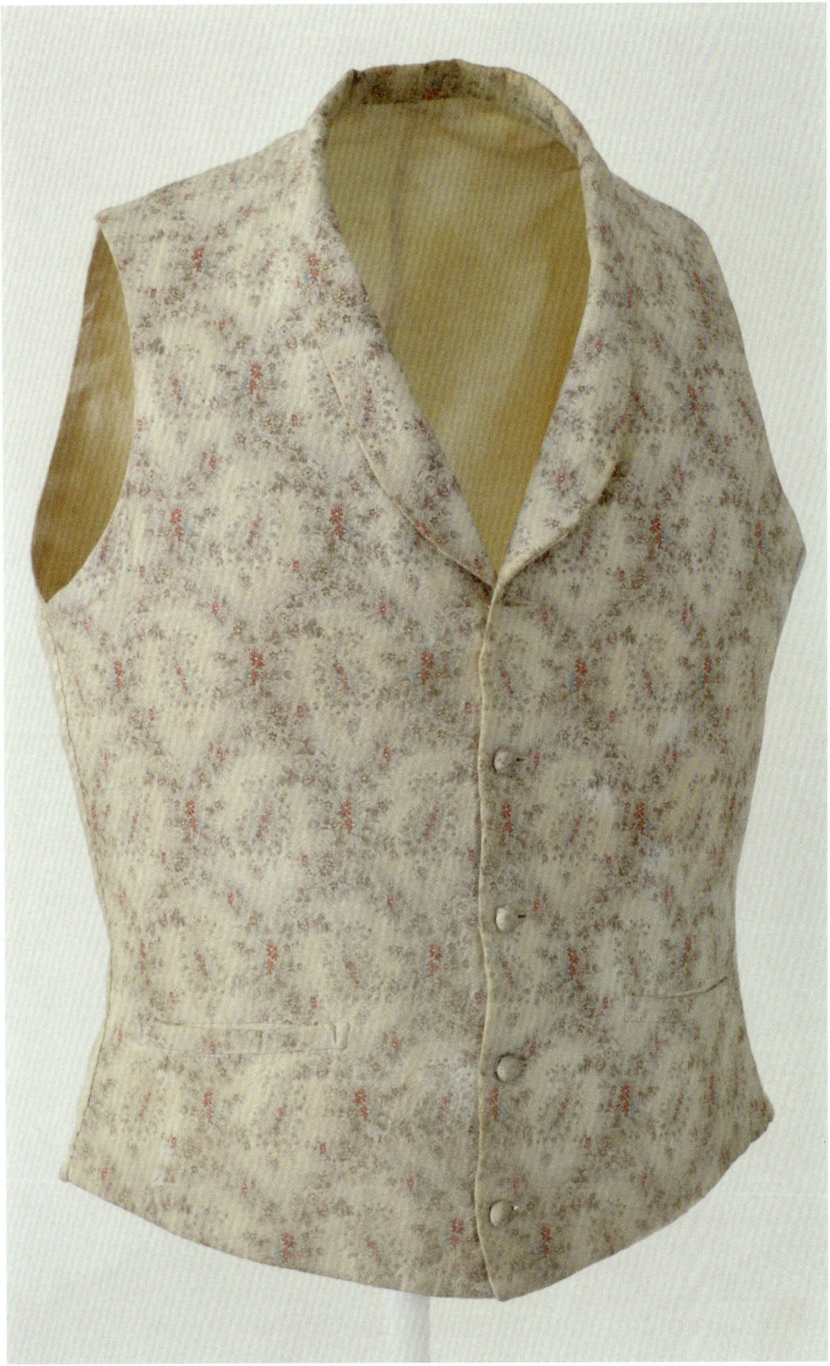

A waistcoat in cream cotton, 1850-1860. HC.W-1.95-4

The cotton has a woven pattern of paisley shapes with a trellis of flowers and leaves in light brown, pinks and pale blue. The waistcoat has been cut sideways, across the width of the fabric. It has a roll collar and one of the five self-covered domed buttons is missing. The lining and back are in plain white cotton, with a backstrap and a pale metal buckle to adjust the waist. The back hem curves up towards the centre back seam. There are two welted pockets.

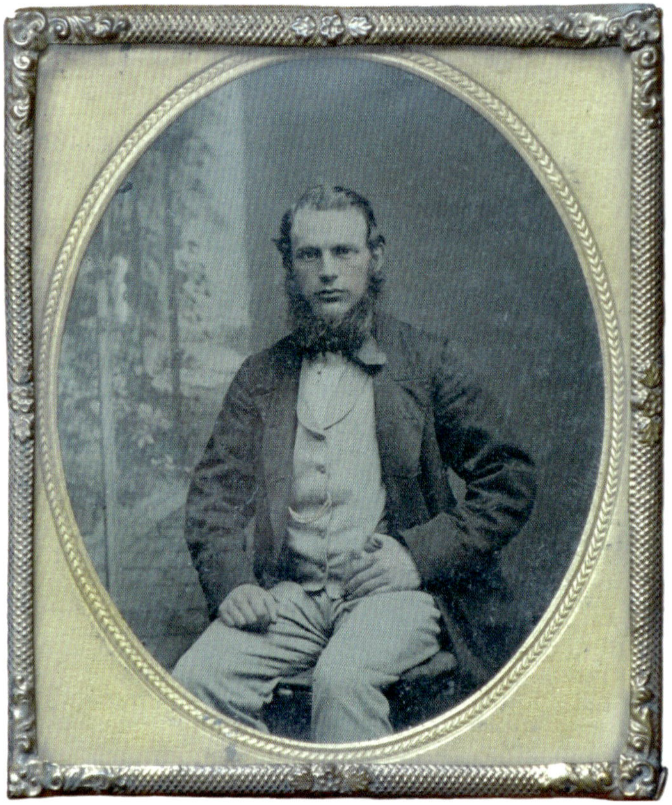

An ambrotype of an unknown man, 1855-1860.

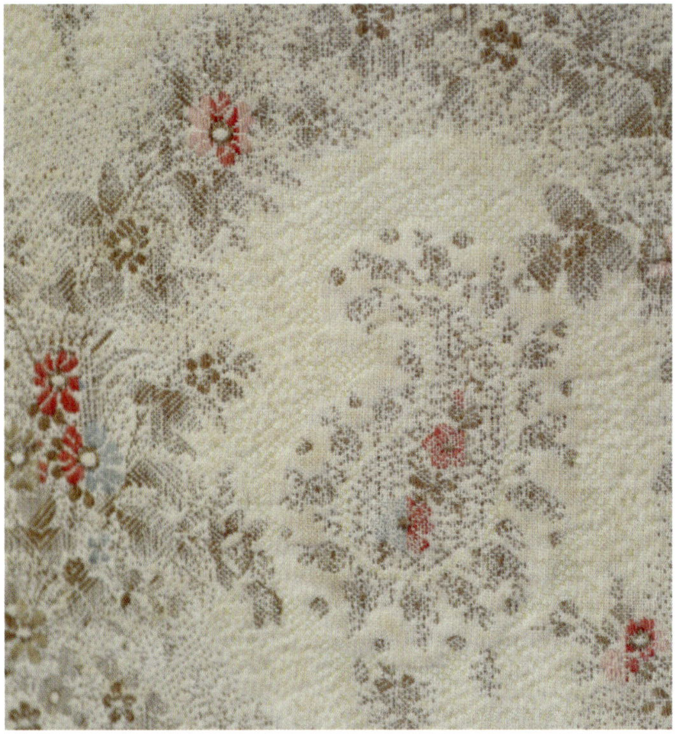

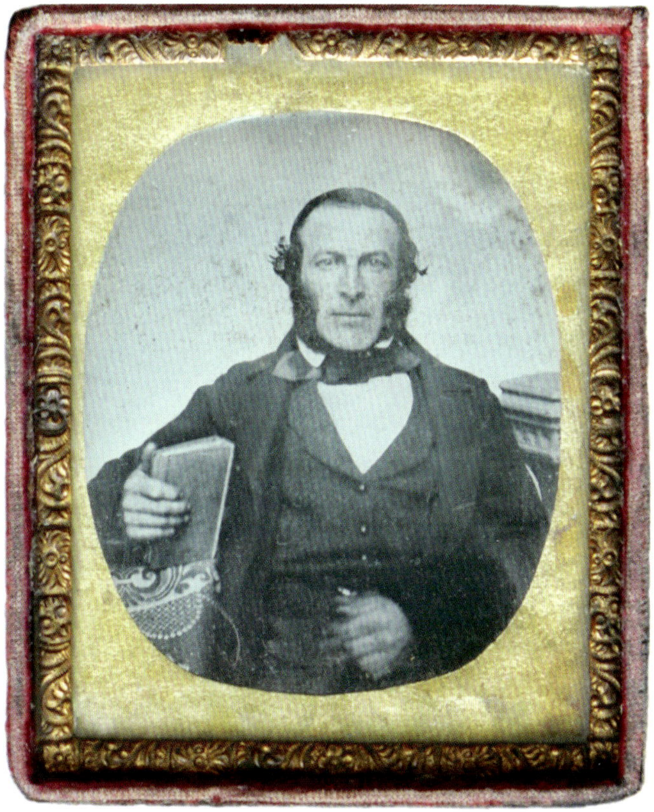

An ambrotype of an unknown man, 1855-1860.

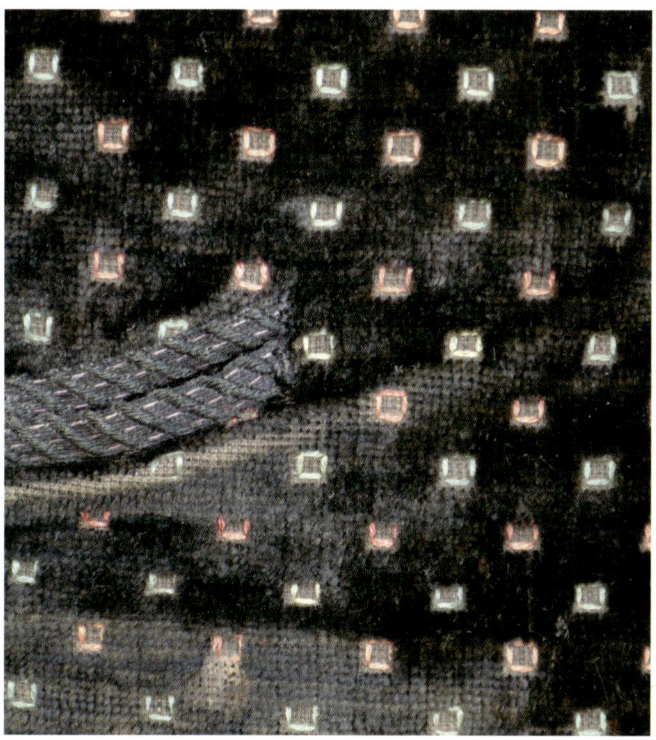

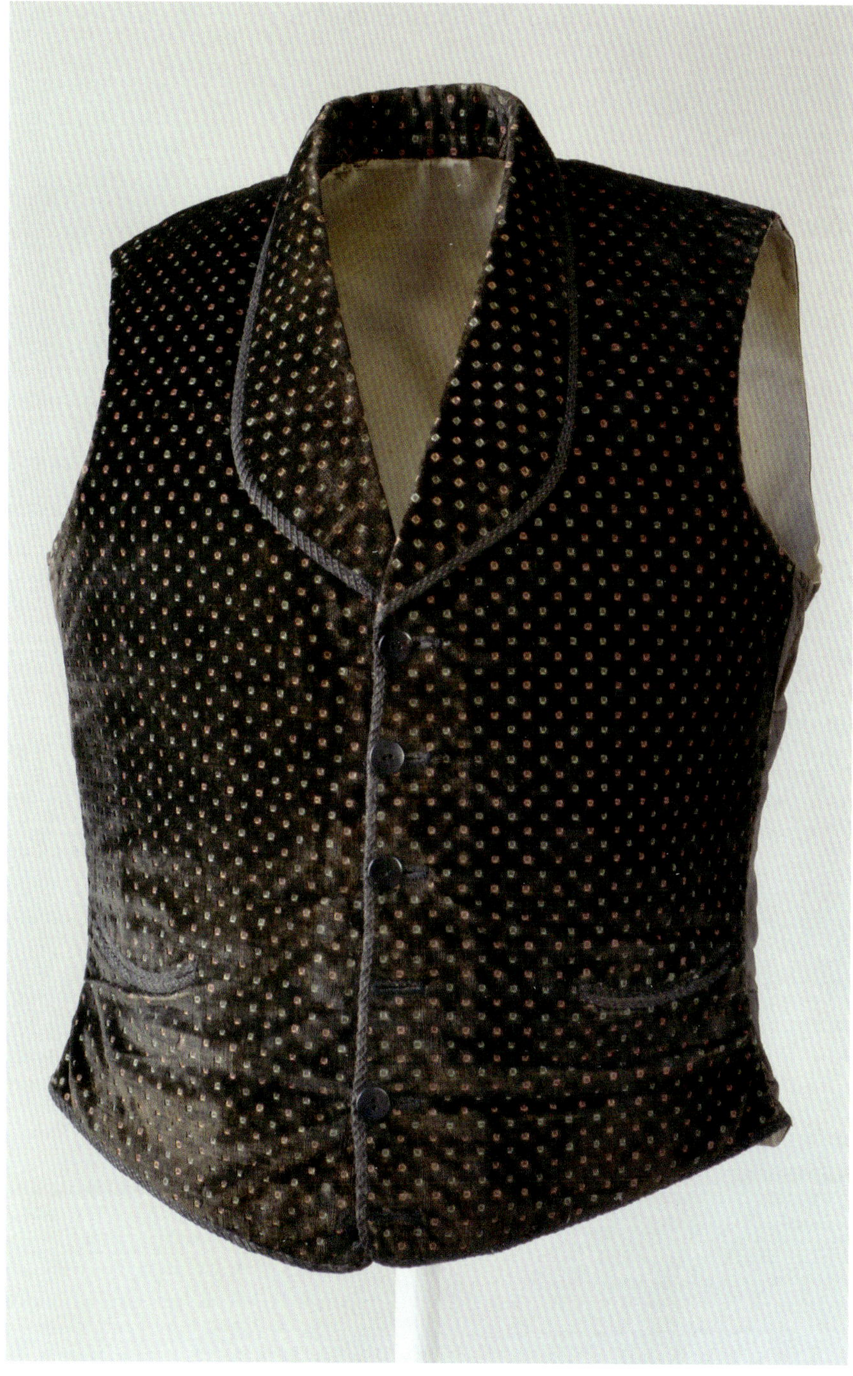

A waistcoat in dark brown voided silk velvet, 1855-1870. HC.W-12.07-1

The velvet has voided square spots outlined in pink and pale green silk. The waistcoat is lined in beige cotton twill with a fine white diagonal stripe, and the back is in dark brown glazed cotton with a backstrap and a black metal buckle to adjust the waist. The foreparts, the curved pockets and the roll collar are edged with black braid which has raised diagonal cords and pink single-thread broken stripes. Two of the six black lacquered wooden buttons are missing.

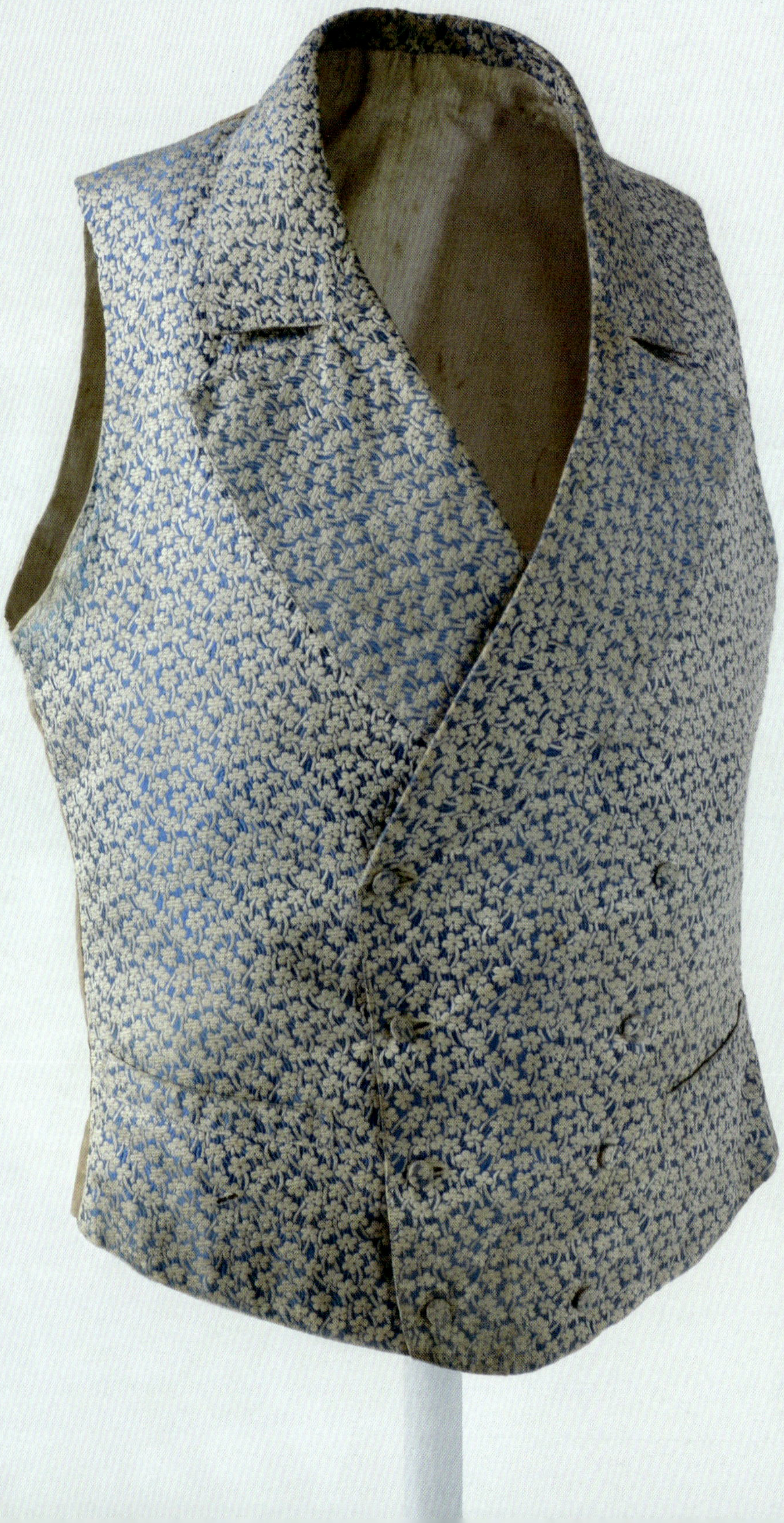

A waistcoat in blue and white silk, 1850-1865.
HC.W-2.95

The silk has a stylised floral woven pattern. The waistcoat is double-breasted with four sets of self-covered buttons, and a step collar with curved lapels which have rounded ends; there is slight padding over the chest. The lining is plain white cotton, and the back is in fawn cotton twill, with a backstrap and a buckle to adjust the waist. There are buttonholes on the edge of each forepart and two brass buttons on the inside of the left forepart to keep the right forepart in place. The forepart hems are faced with fawn leather. The inside brass buttons carry the name J. C. Haisom, who is probably the tailor who made the waistcoat.

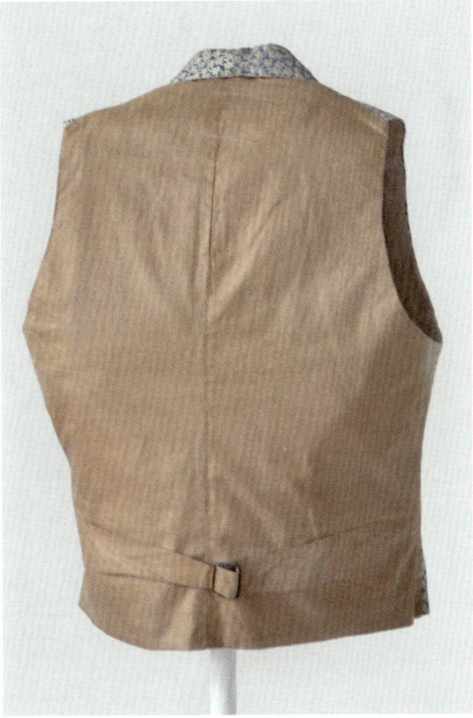

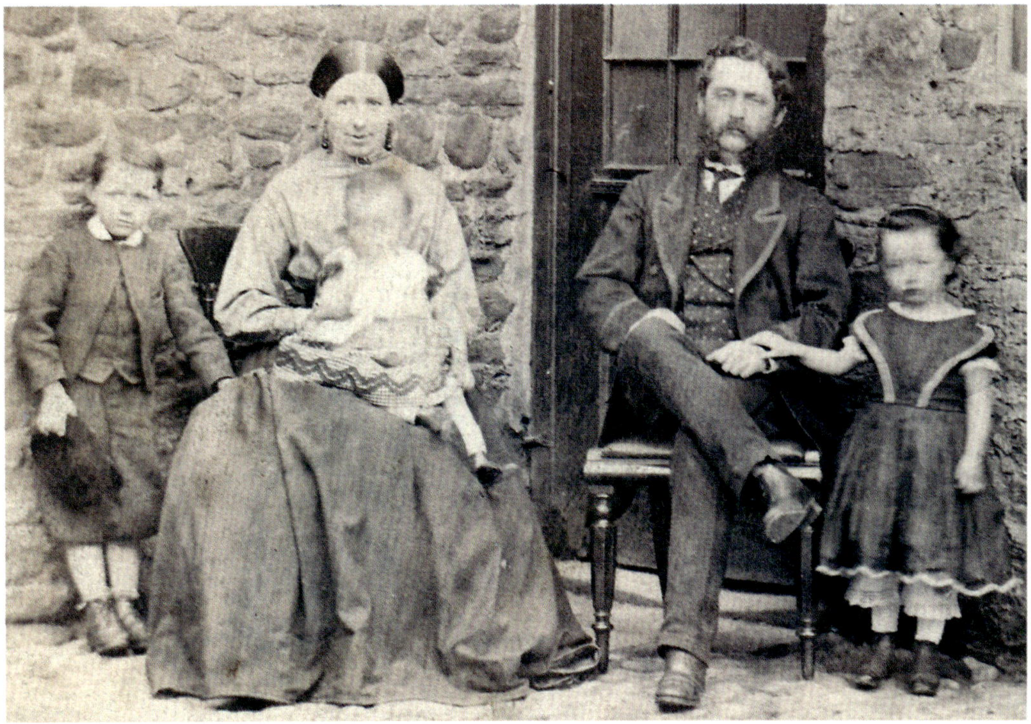

Unknown family, *c.*1860.

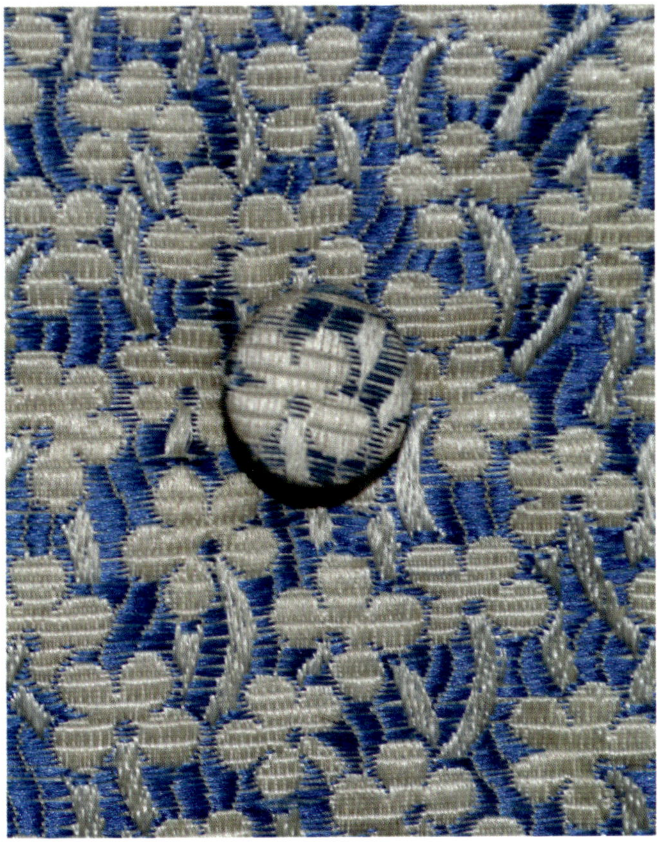

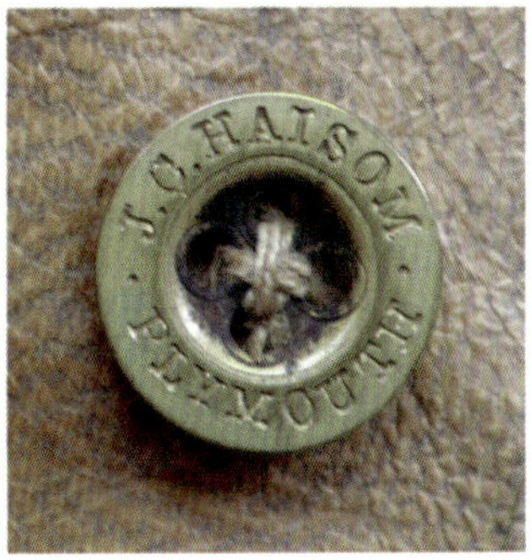

The brass button on the leather facing to the hem of the left forepart; the tailor's name can be seen on it.

James Charles Haisom (1820-1866) was a master tailor in Plymouth by 1861. He was well enough established to get his name stamped on his brass buttons.

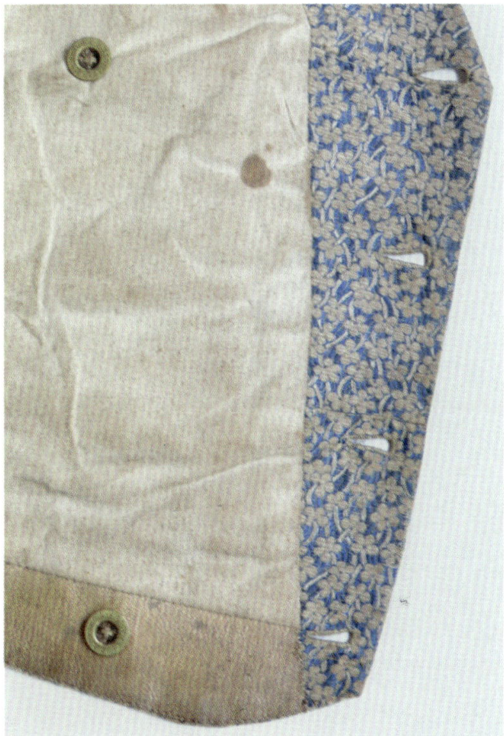

Inside the left forepart, showing the brass buttons which secure the right forepart in place, and the fawn leather facing to the hem.

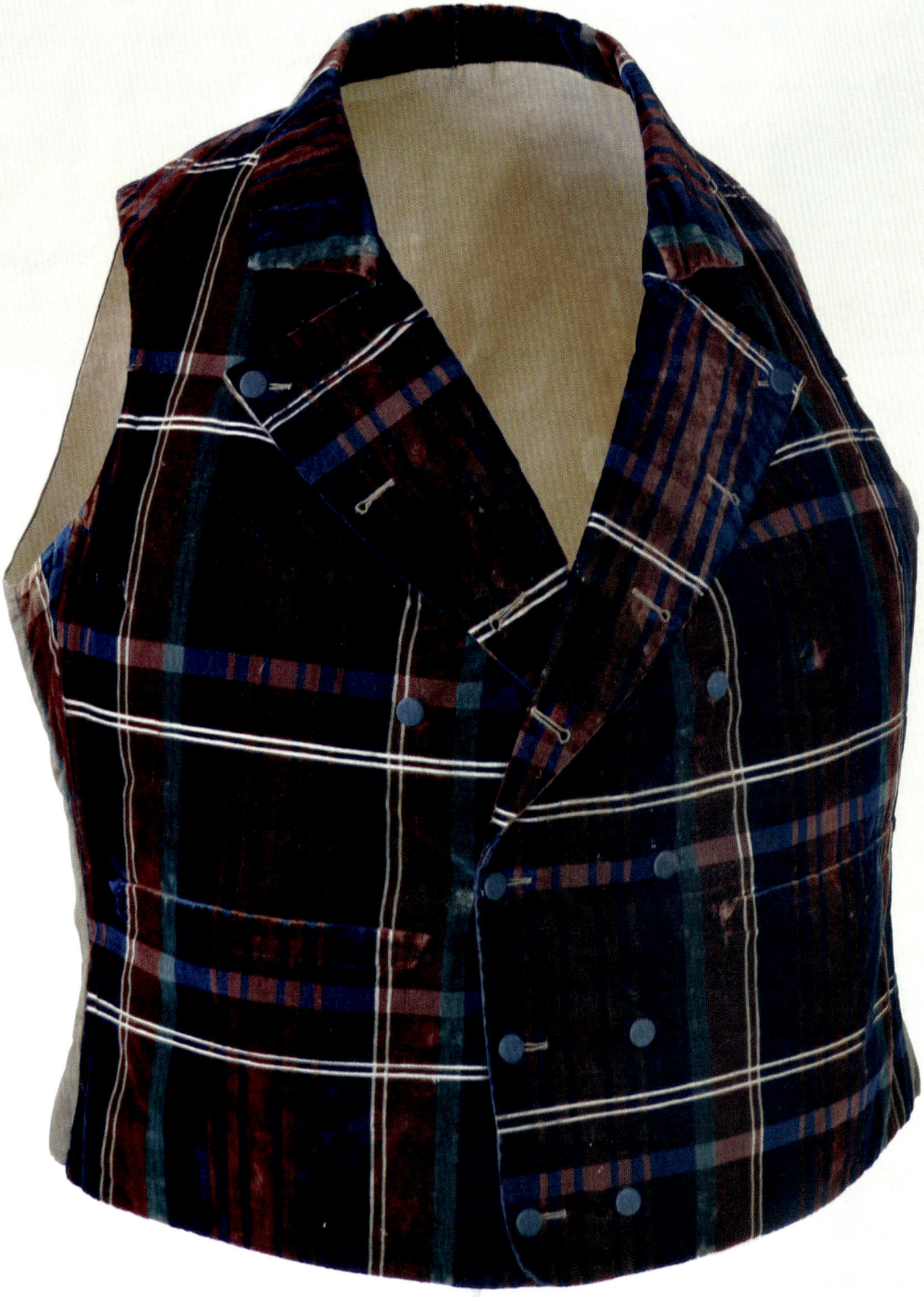

A waistcoat in silk velvet, 1850-1865.
HC.W-12.07-2

The velvet has warp stripes of dark blue, chocolate and teal, with a narrow white double stripe. In the weft there are narrow double stripes in white silk, and stripes of uncut velvet which contrast with the cut pile, and create a check pattern. The waistcoat has a step collar and two welted pockets. It is double-breasted with six pairs of buttons covered in dark blue silk twill; these go right up under the lapels, so that a lapel could be folded across and the waistcoat buttoned up to the neck, with an extra button under the collar of the right forepart for this. There are seven buttonholes on the edge of each forepart, so the waistcoat could be buttoned either way, and the top hole fastens the point of each lapel on to a button on the forepart. The lining is fawn cotton twill, and the back is in brown silesia with a backstrap and a black metal buckle to adjust the waist. There is a small gusset each side in the back hem, and small darts in each forepart at the armhole; the forepart hems are faced with brown leather.

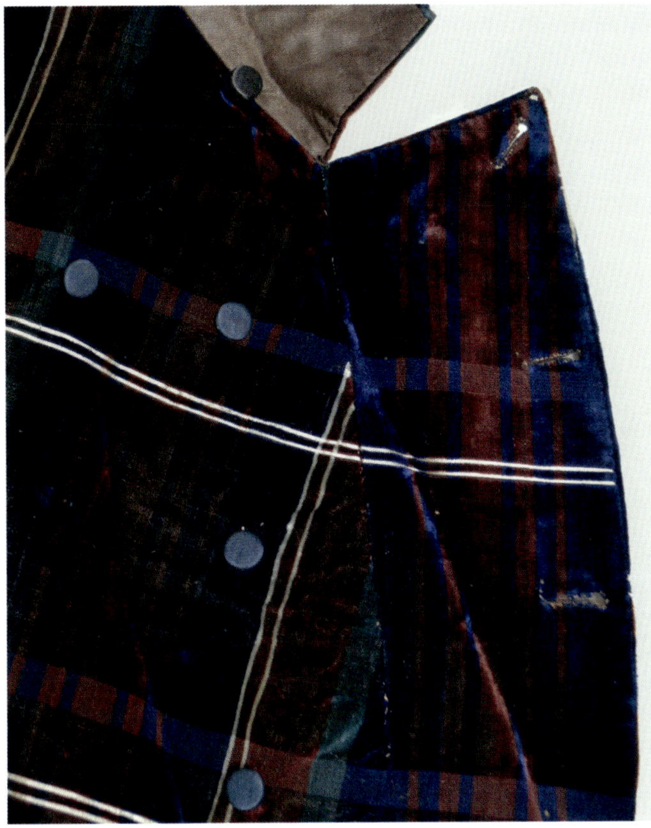

Under the right lapel, showing the buttons for the waistcoat to be closed up to the neck, and the button on the forepart to hold down the point of the lapel.

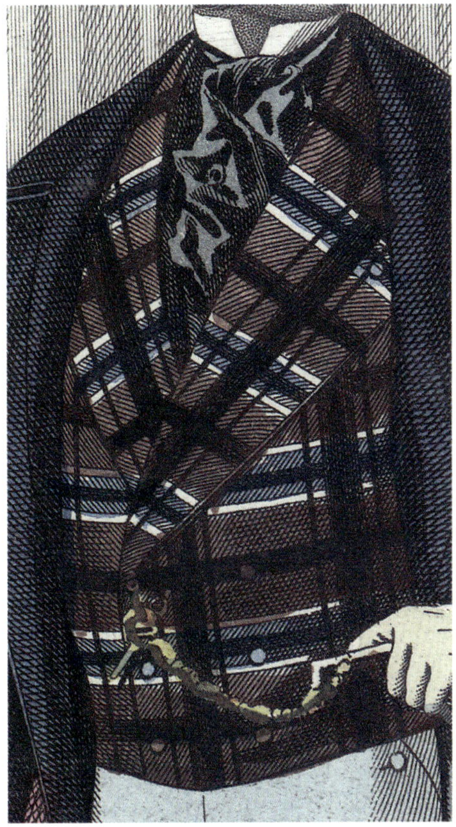

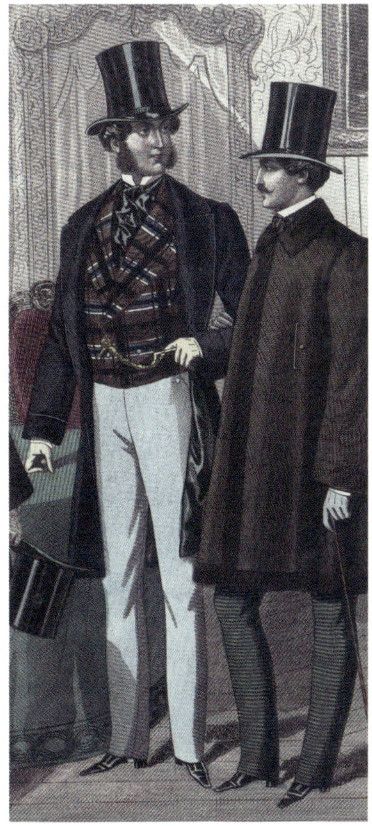

Fashion plate from *L'Élégant*, 1856.

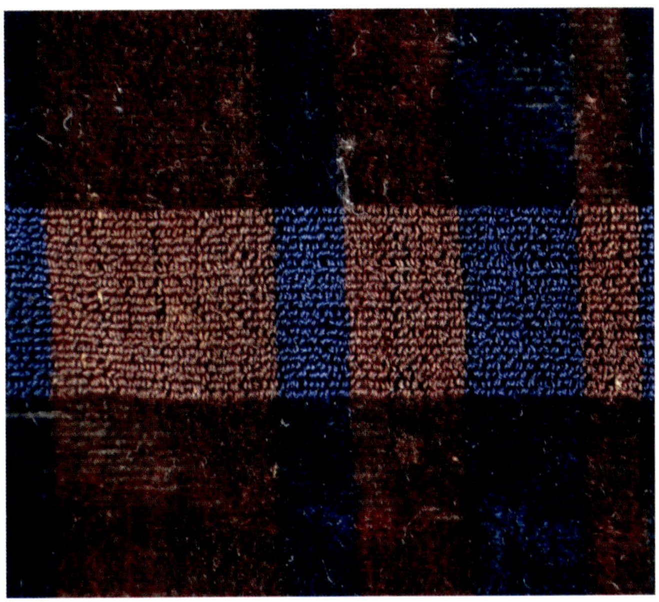

Detail of the velvet, showing the loops of the uncut pile contrasting with the area of cut pile.

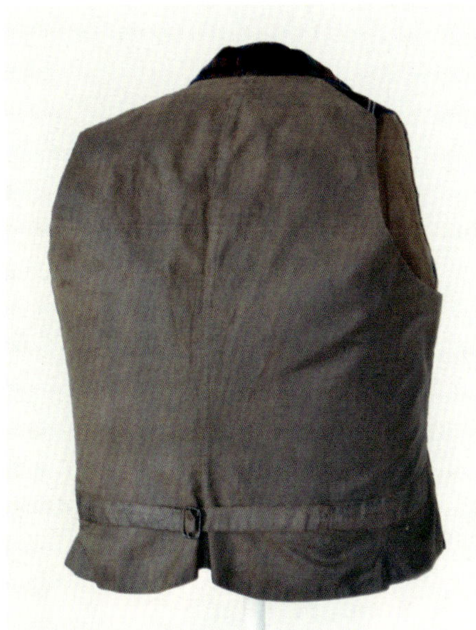

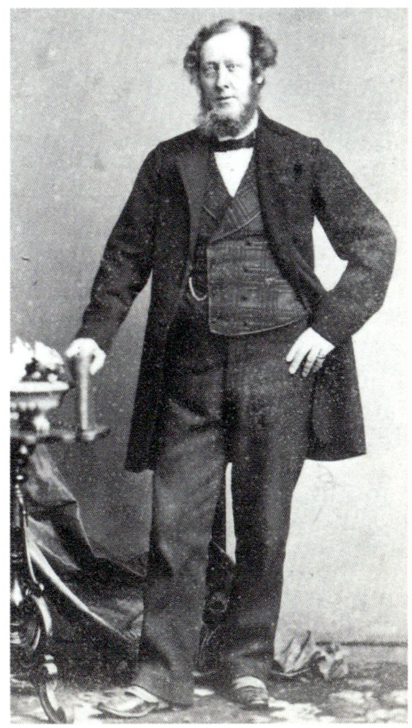

Unknown man, 1855-1865.

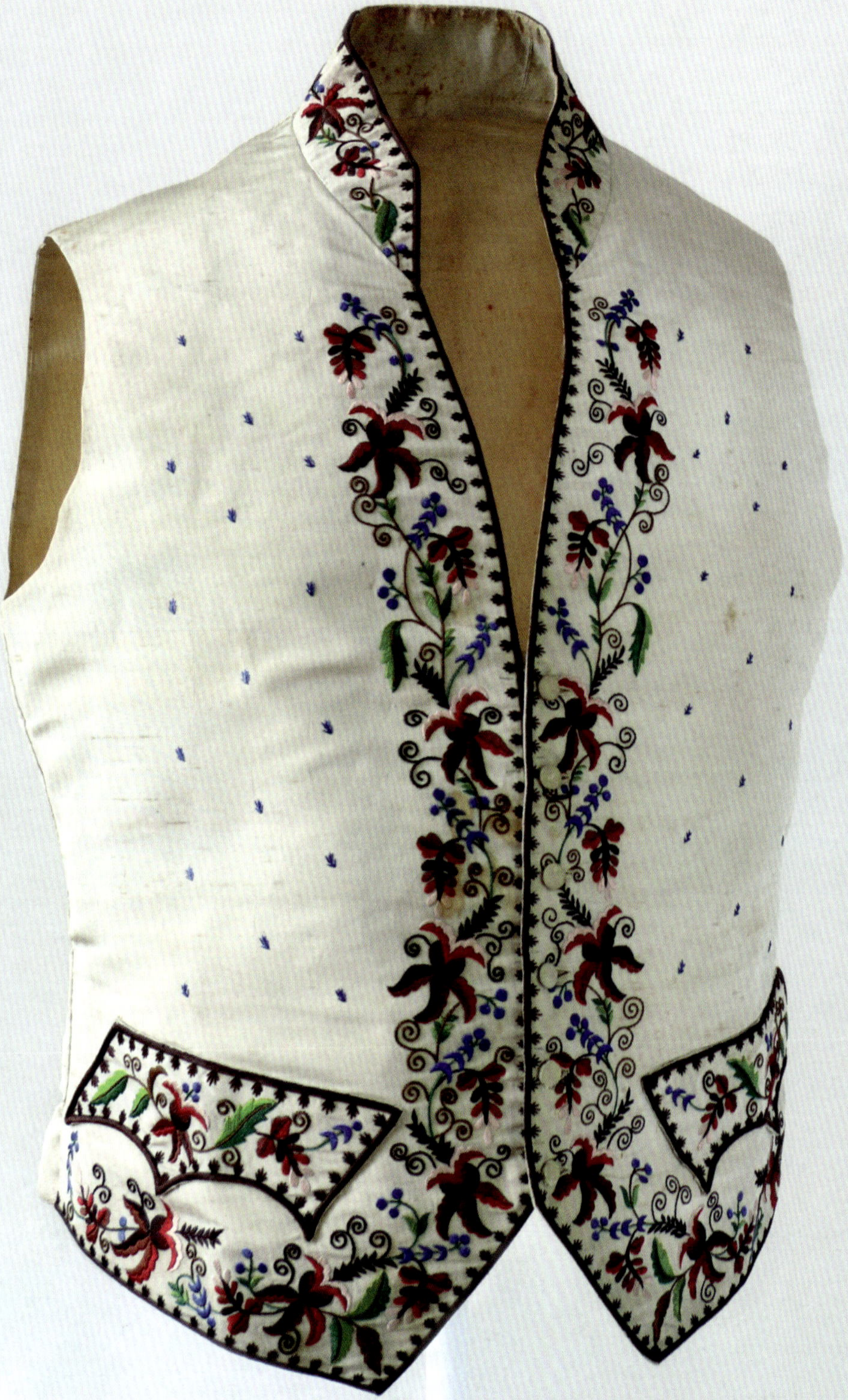

A waistcoat in cream silk grosgrain, 1850-1870. HC.W-6.09

This was worn with court dress, and the style has fossilised from the eighteenth century. The foreparts are bordered with polychrome embroidery of stylised flowers, and this also decorates the stand collar and pocket flaps, which are merely decorative; there are no pockets. There is a small extension to the front edge of the right forepart for the six self-covered buttons, so that when they are done up the embroidery on the foreparts should meet edge to edge. The waistcoat is lined with cream cotton twill, and the back is in cream silk faille with a backstrap and a brass buckle to adjust the waist. There are small gussets in the back hem, towards the sides, and the centre back seam is open for 3″ from the bottom.

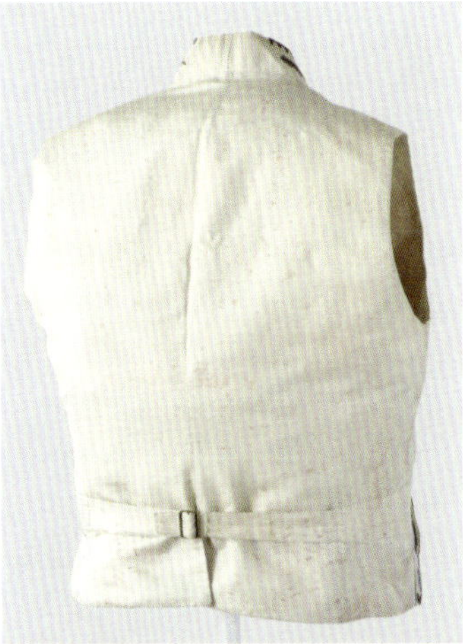

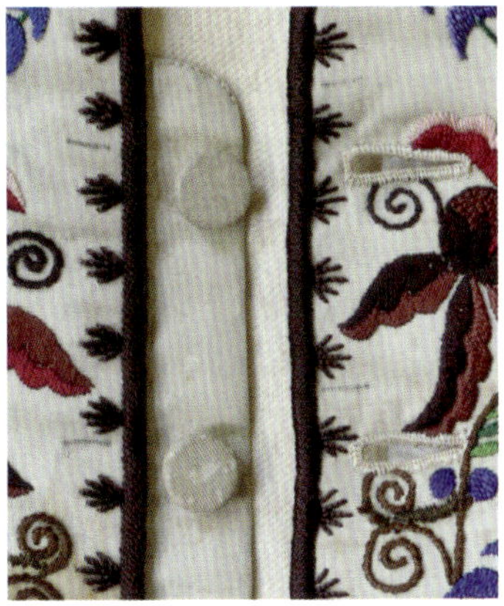

The extension on the front edge of the right forepart for the buttons.

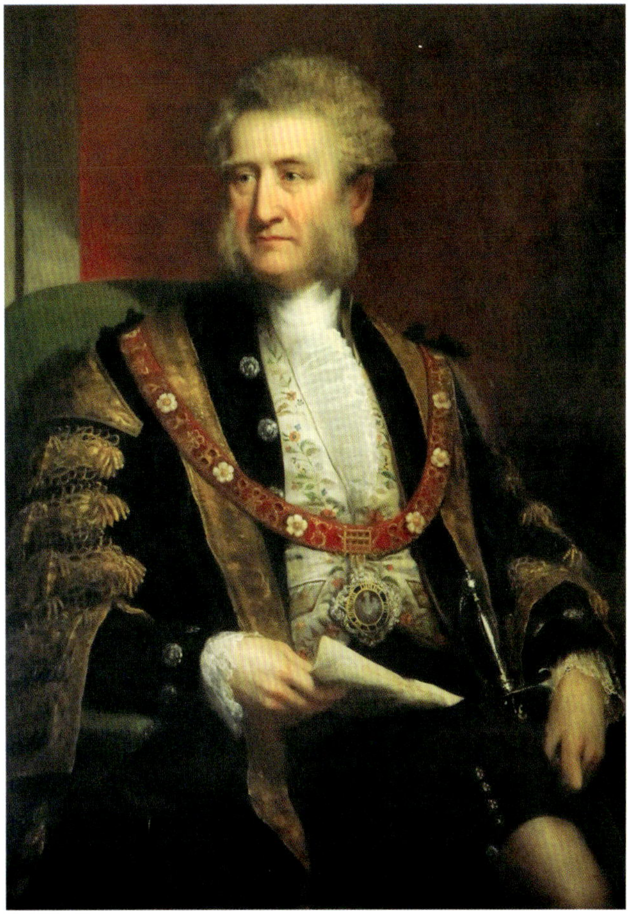

Sir Robert Carden by an unknown painter, 1857, Cutlers Hall, London. He was Master of the Worshipful Company of Cutlers three times, and Lord Mayor of London in 1857. A stockbroker by profession, he was a magistrate and a noted philanthropist.

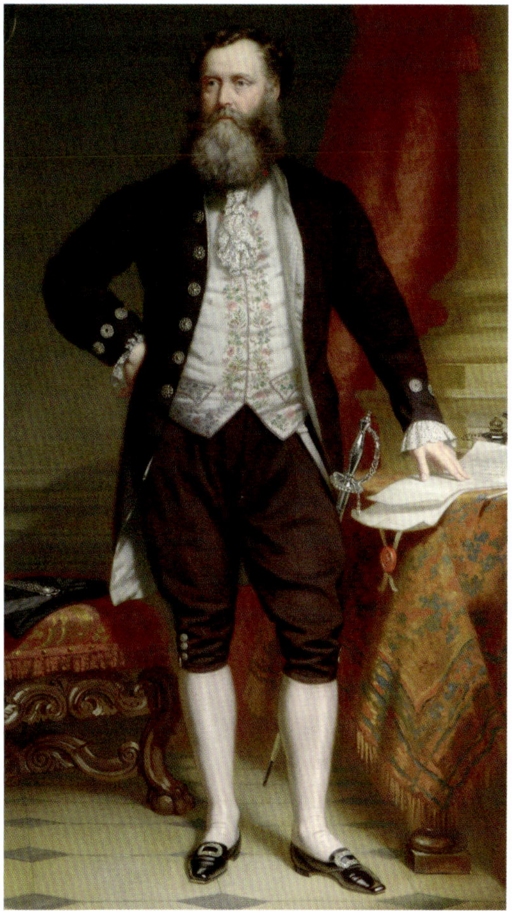

John Ralph Shaw (detail) by John Lucas, 1864, Williamson Art Gallery & Museum, Birkenhead; Wirral Museums Service. Shaw owned the Arrowe Park Estate in Cheshire and was a magistrate.

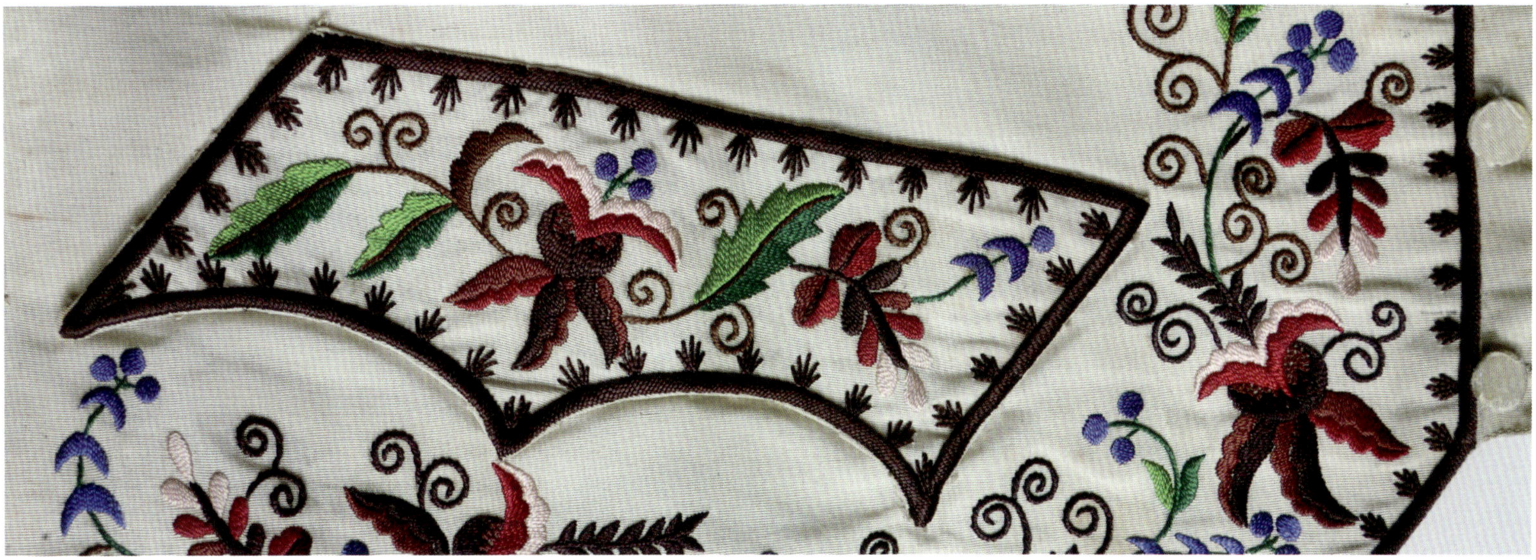

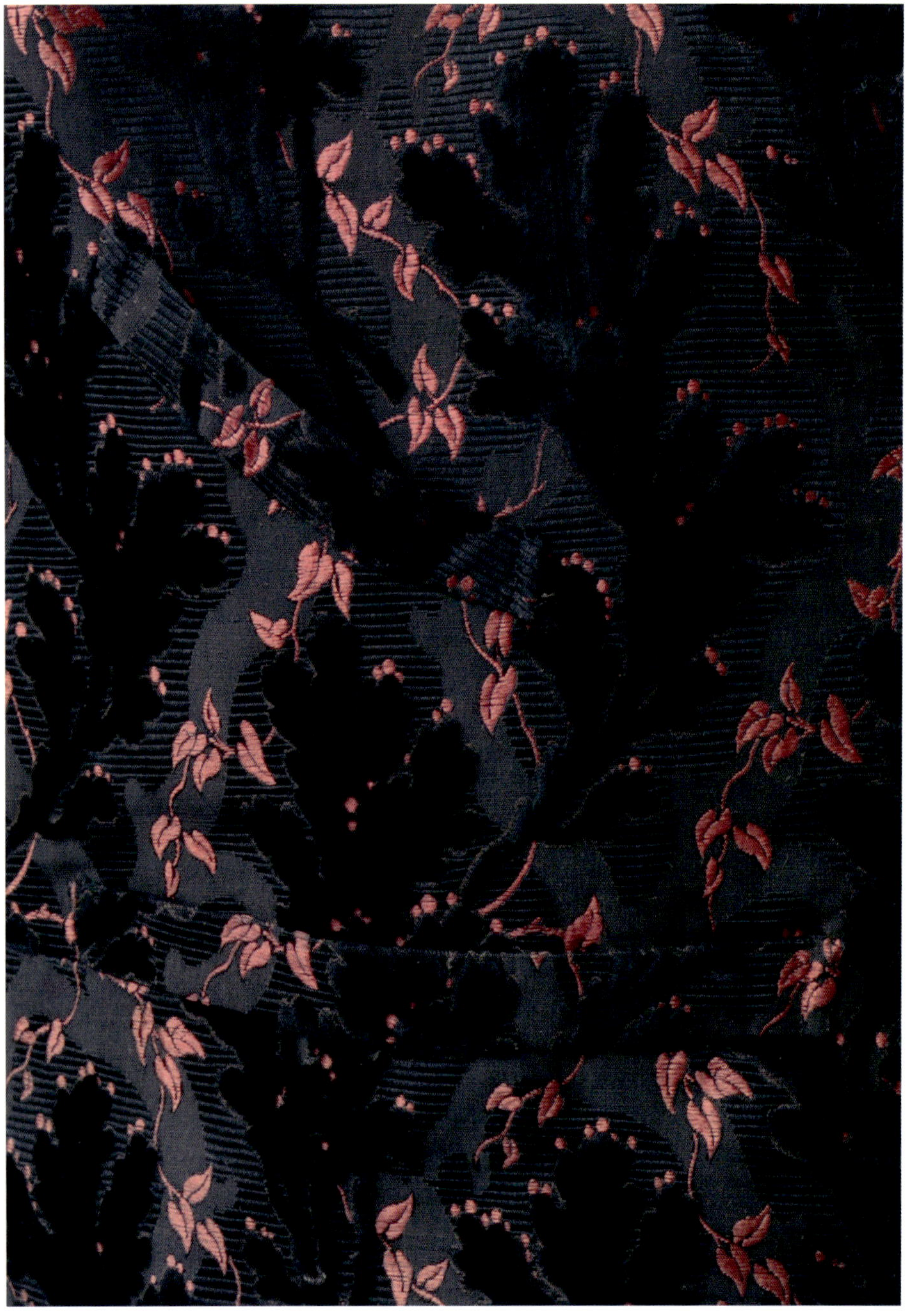

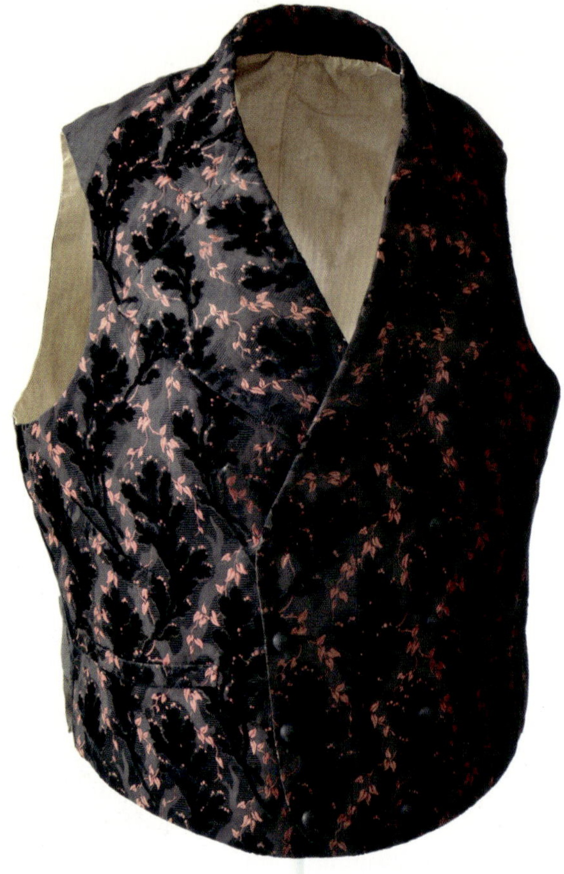

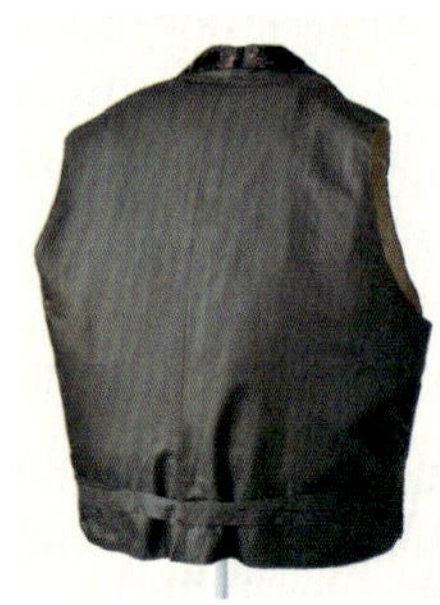

A waistcoat in black silk, 1850-1865. HC.W-3.94

The silk has a pattern of trailing leaves in pink silk, and seaweed shapes in black silk velvet. The waistcoat is double-breasted with four pairs of black silk-covered domed buttons, and buttonholes on the edge of each forepart; there is a seam down each centre front. A metal button on the inside hem of the left forepart fastens through the lowest buttonhole on the right forepart to keep it in place, and the forepart hems are faced with brown leather. The tips of the wide lapels of the step-roll collar are stitched down to the foreparts, which have slight padding over the chest; there are two welted pockets and a slanting breast pocket on the right side. The lining is ivory glazed cotton and the back is in black silk twill with a backstrap and a buckle, now broken, to adjust the waist. There are triangles of the silk twill inserted in the shoulder seams, to economise on the waistcoat fabric.

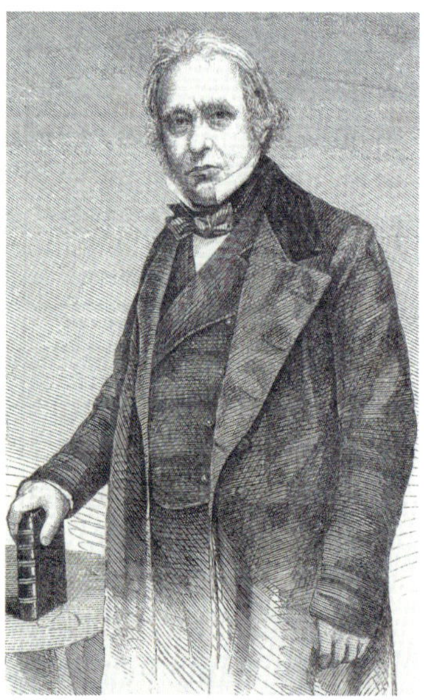

Lord Macaulay, a drawing in *The Illustrated London News*, 1860.

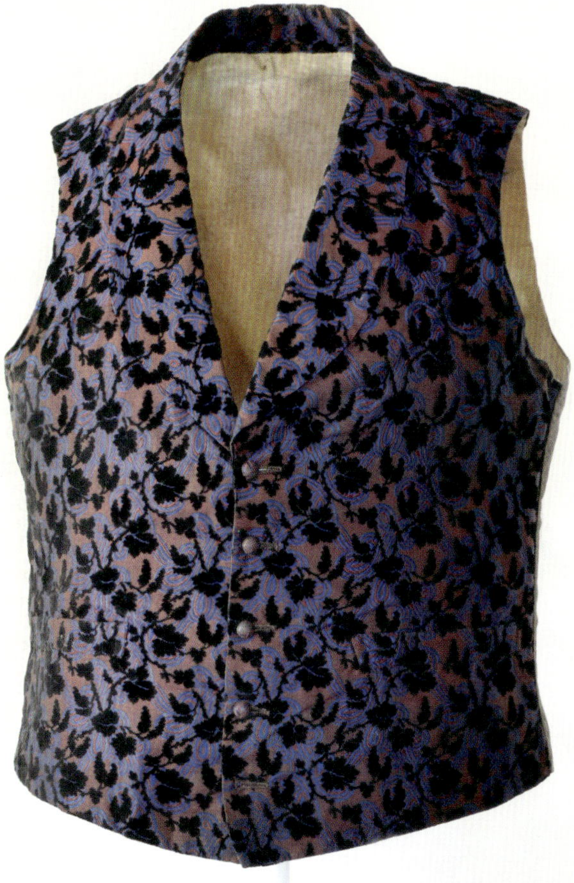

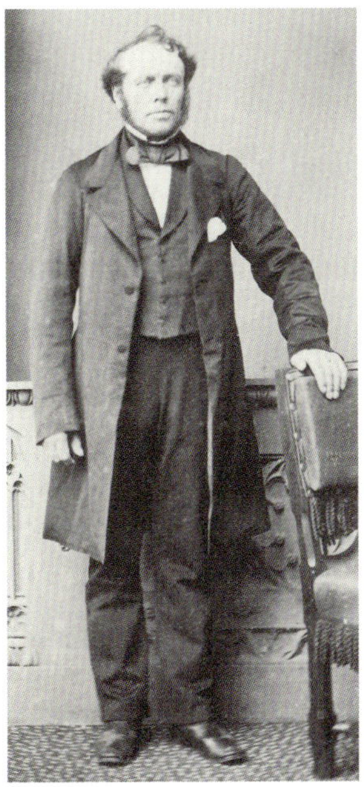

Unknown man, *c.*1860.

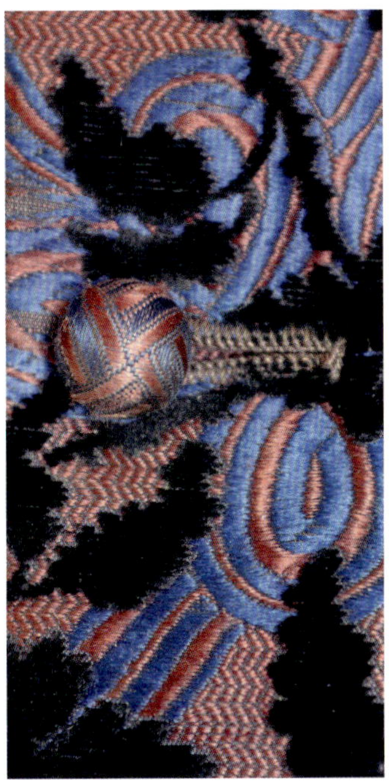

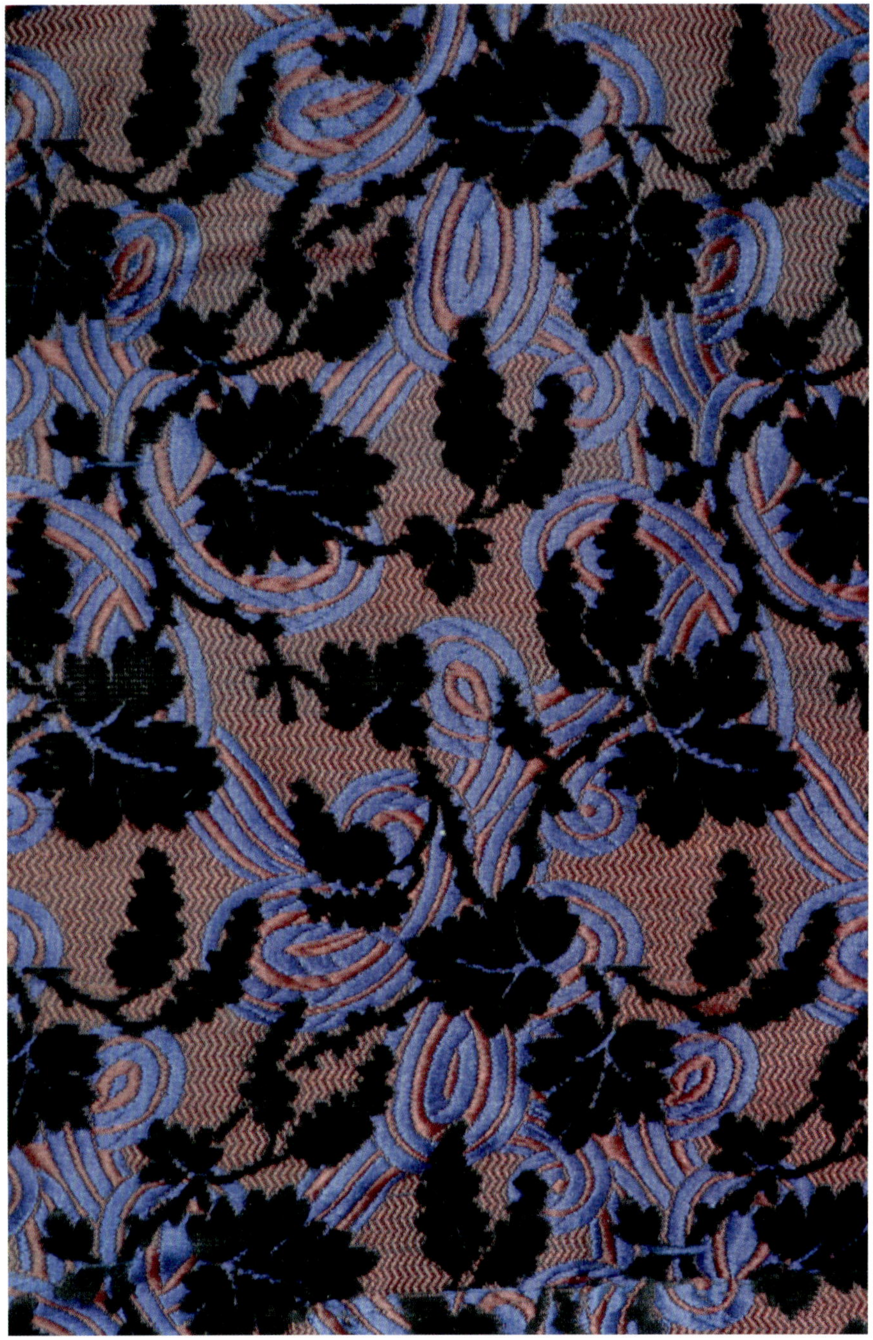

A waistcoat in silk, 1850-1865. HC.W-10.97-2

The silk has a deep pink ground woven in a zig-zag pattern, with a pattern of loops in blue and deep pink silk, and leaves and branches in black silk velvet. The waistcoat has a roll collar and is lined with fawn cotton twill; the back is in dark brown silesia. A pair of straps is sewn on the back at the waist and the ends of these originally had a black material sewn on, which is now stiff and brittle and has mostly broken off. The domed buttons are covered in a deep pink and blue silk woven in a geometric pattern, and one of the five is missing. There are two welted pockets.

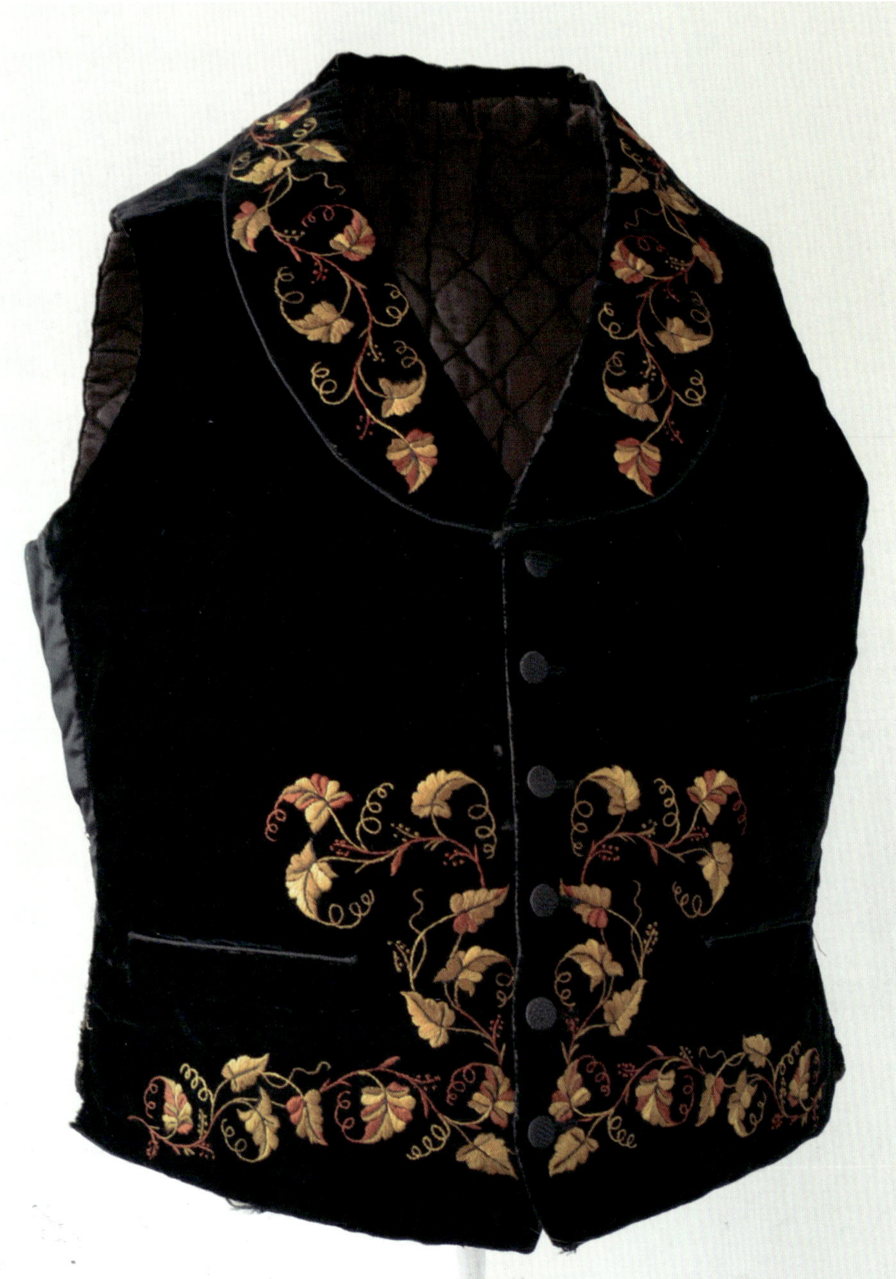

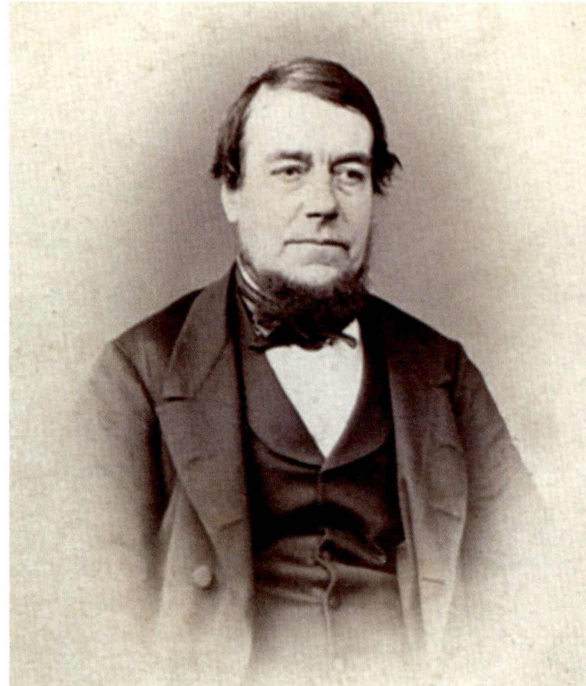

Thomas Herbert (1811-1876), a manufacturer of scales and weighing machines in London, *c.*1870.

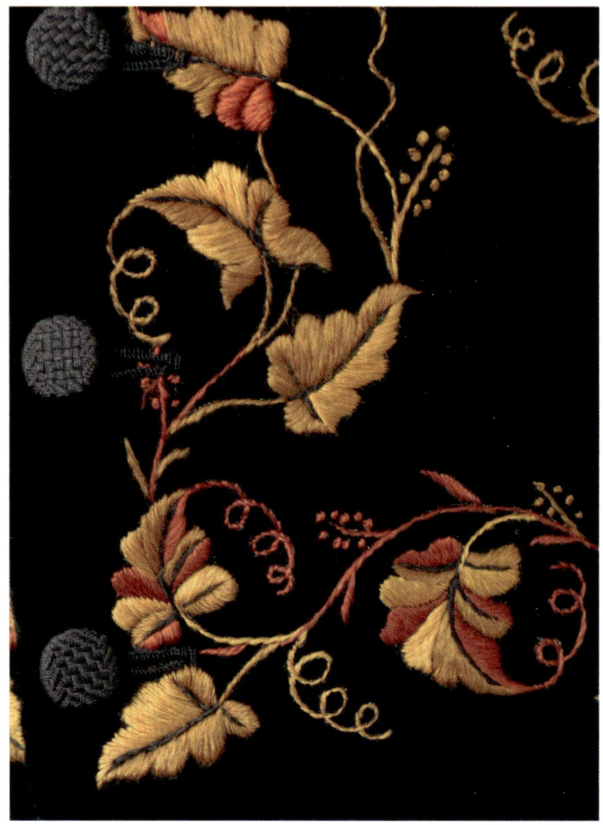

A waistcoat in black silk velvet, 1865-1875. HC.W-7.94

It has embroidery of trailing leaves in cinnamon, rust and brown silk threads, on the lower part of the foreparts and the roll collar. The waistcoat has a quilted lining in brown diagonally ribbed silk; the back is in silk and cotton satin, and there are gussets of this in the side seams, to increase the size. The six buttons are covered in black silk threads with a woven geometric pattern, and there are three welted pockets. The collar, forepart hems and pocket tops are edged with fine black silk cord, which is also on the front edge of the right forepart but missing on the left one. The collar does not extend round the back of the neck, where there is a narrow band of plain black velvet.

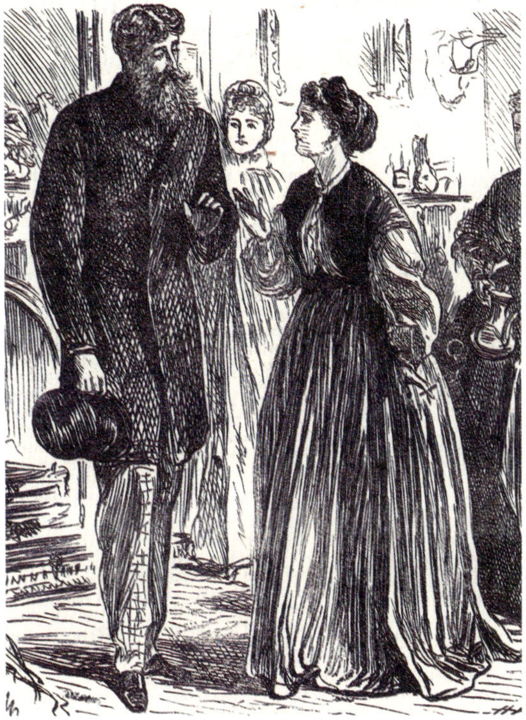

Detail from a cartoon in *Punch*, 1865.

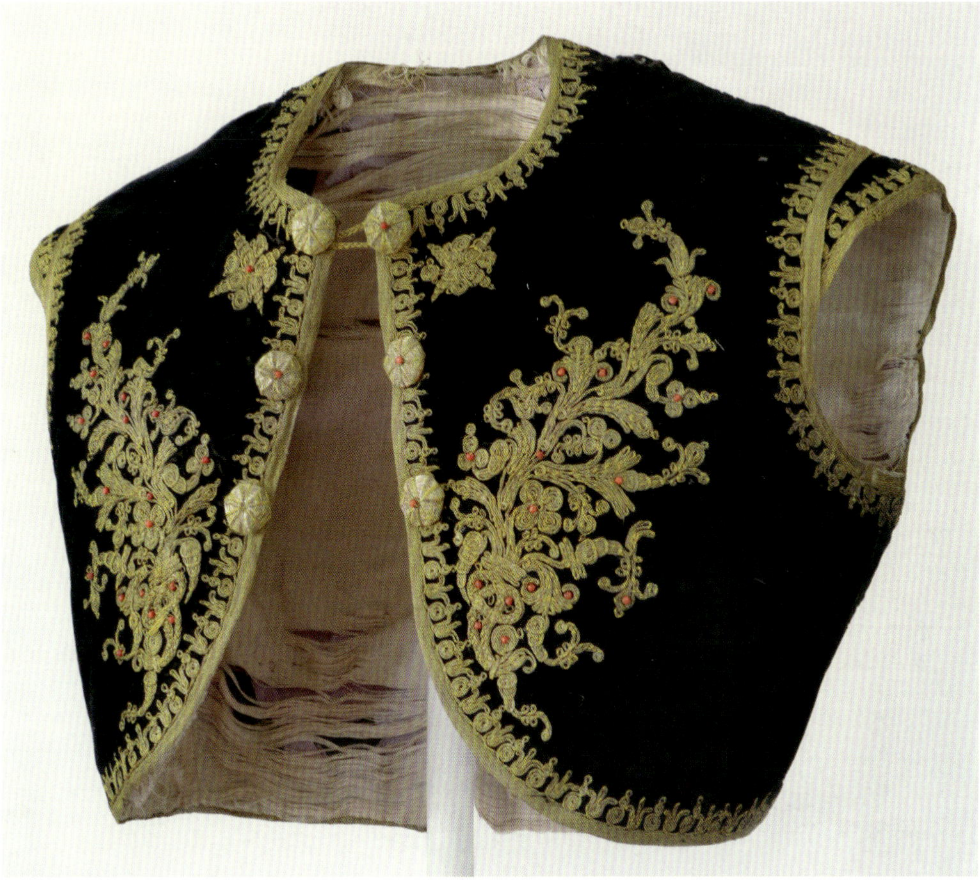

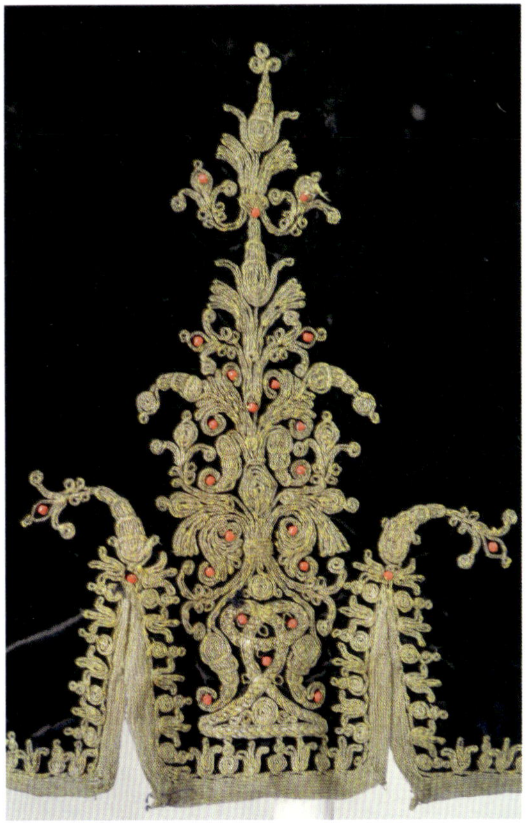

A bolero waistcoat in black velvet, 1860-1870. HC.W-8.74

This is probably Turkish and is similar in style to the zouave jackets, popular with women in the 1860s. The edges of the bolero are covered in flat gold braid, with a border of embroidery in gold thread, which also forms motifs on the fronts and back, with added coral beads. The fastening is by a loop of gold braid which joins the top pair of the three pairs of buttons. The lining is ivory silk/cotton satin, which is now shredded.

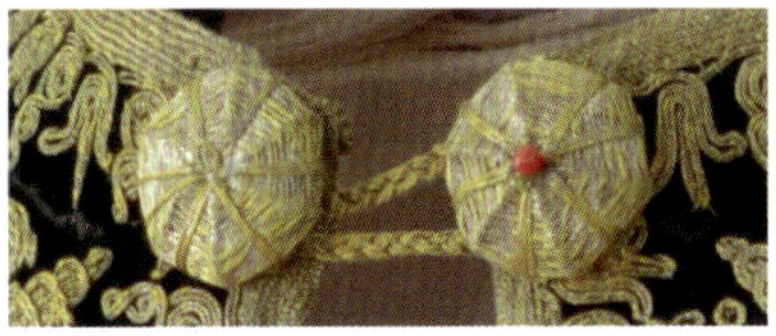

The fastening at the neck; one button has lost its coral bead.

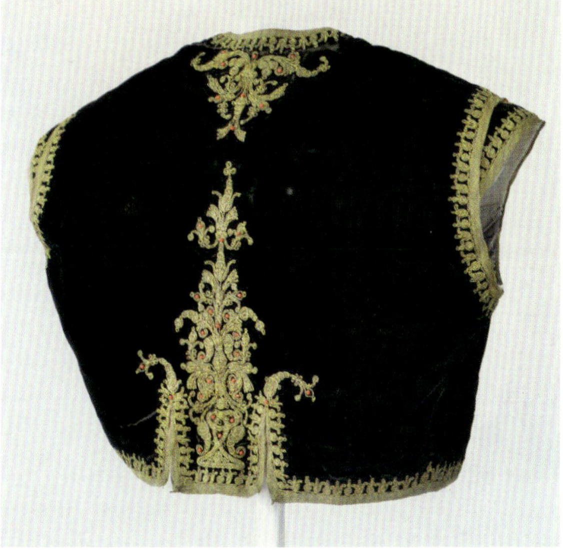

Zouave jackets were copied from the uniform of French-Algerian soldiers and based on their traditional dress.

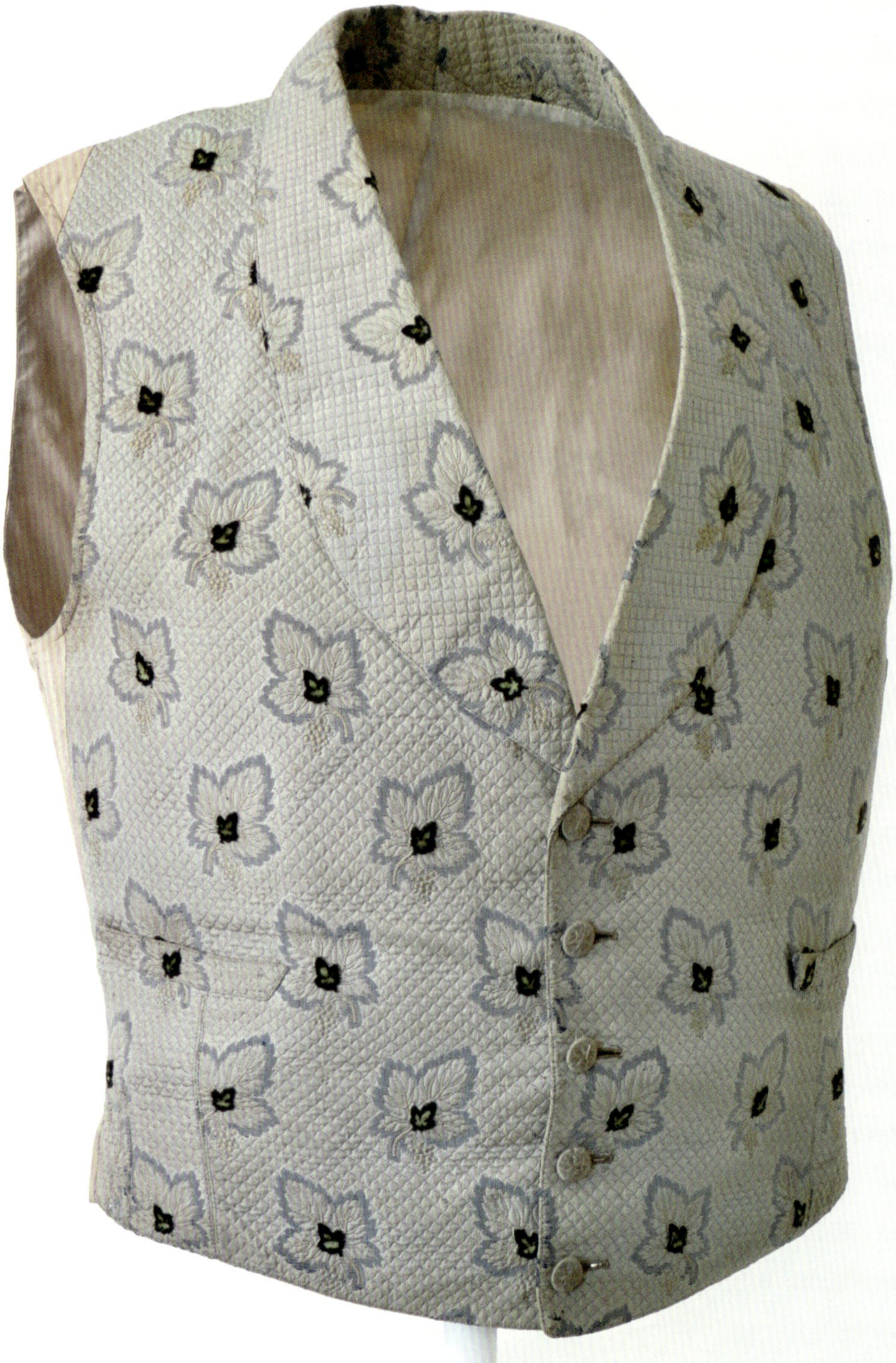

A waistcoat in pale grey silk matelassé, 1865-1875.
HC.W-9.01

The silk has a design of vine leaves outlined in blue with black and green velvet middles, and a bunch of grapes in beige silk. The waistcoat has a roll collar and five buttons covered in beige silk threads in a star pattern. The lining is white glazed cotton and the back is beige glazed cotton with a backstrap and a brass buckle to adjust the waist. There are small gussets towards each side in the back hem, and a small gusset at the side of each forepart hem as well as a dart in the hem running up to the welted pocket. There are also small darts in each armhole and under the collar running into the neck. The triangles of the lining fabric at the shoulders and in the side seams would have economised on the waistcoat fabric.

A piece of paper found in one of the pockets says that it was the waistcoat of Monsieur Achille Dècle, former mayor of Neuville-de-Poitou.

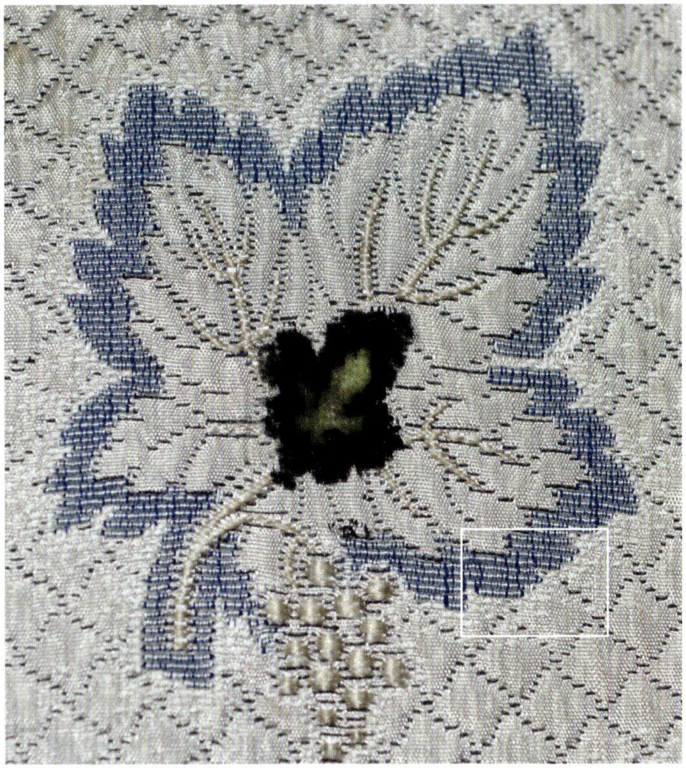

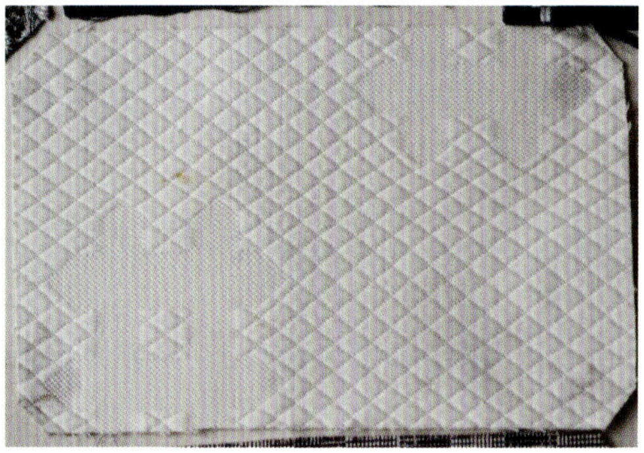

Pattern from a French sample book, 1869.
The School of Historical Dress.

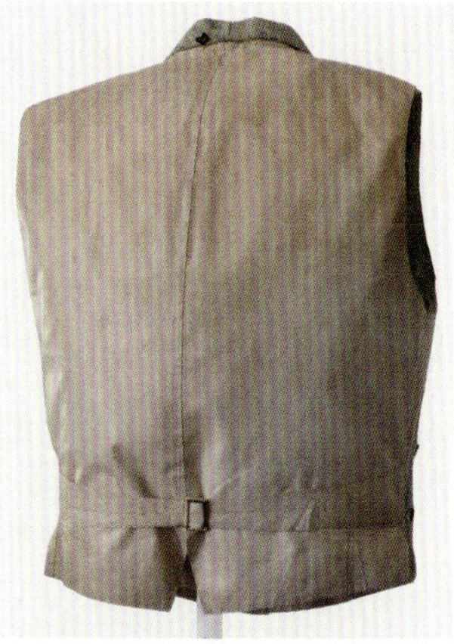

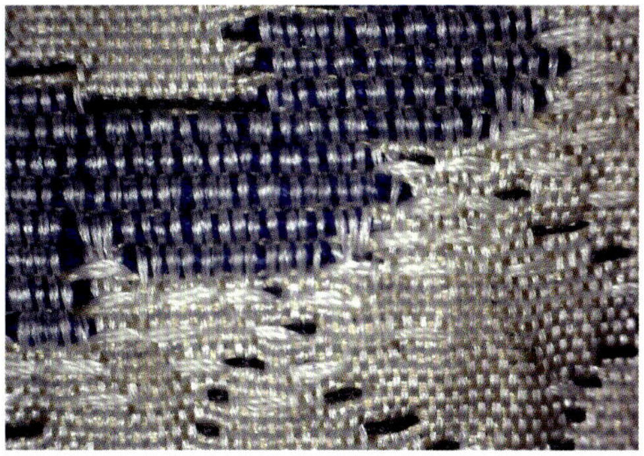

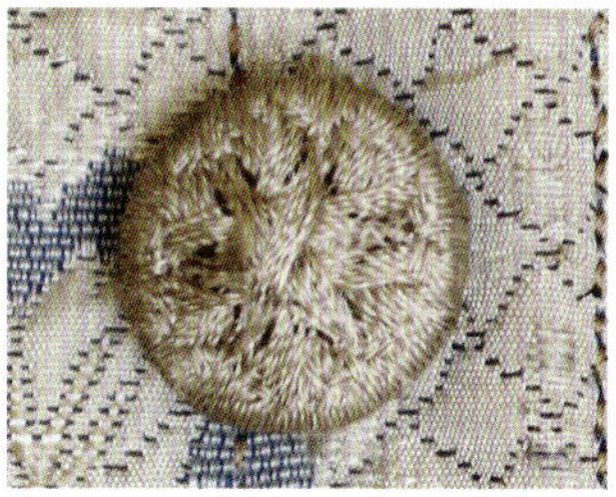

Left: Detail of the fabric, outlined far left.

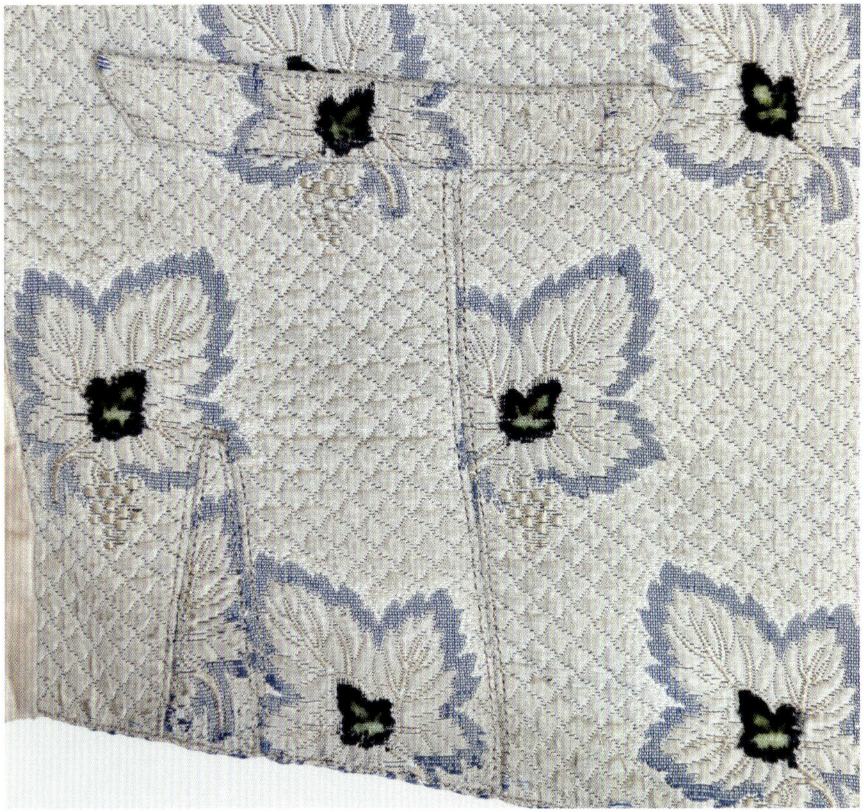

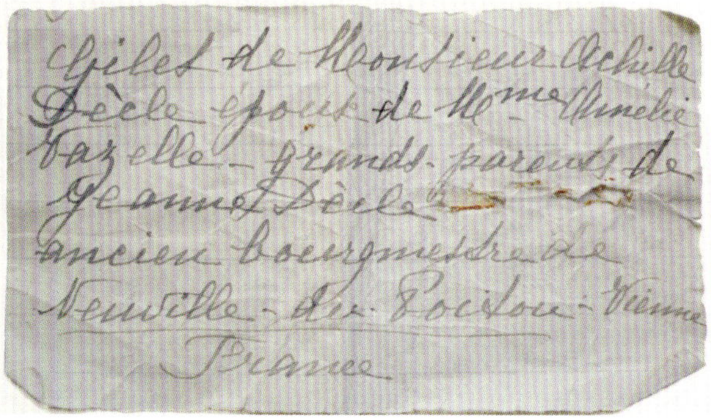

Gilet de Monsieur Achille
Dècle époux de Mme Amélie
Vazelle grands parents de
Jeanne Dècle
ancien bourgmestre de
Neuville du Poitou - Vienne
France

The piece of paper found in one of the pockets, which reads: "Gilet de Monsieur Achille Dècle époux de Mme Amélie Vazelle - Grands-parents de Jeanne Dècle. Ancien bourgmestre de Neuville-de-Poitou-Vienne. France."

Achille Théodore Dècle was born in 1828 in Poitiers, the son of a gardener. In 1852 he married Radegonde *Emélie* Vazelle, daughter of a fabric merchant in Neuville-de-Poitou, and they moved in with her parents, as was traditional. He prospered, becoming a banker and a land-owner, and from 1866 until 1878 he was mayor of the town, overseeing the completion and inauguration of the new town hall. His son, the father of Jeanne Dècle, settled in Belgium, where the word for mayor is *bourgmestre*

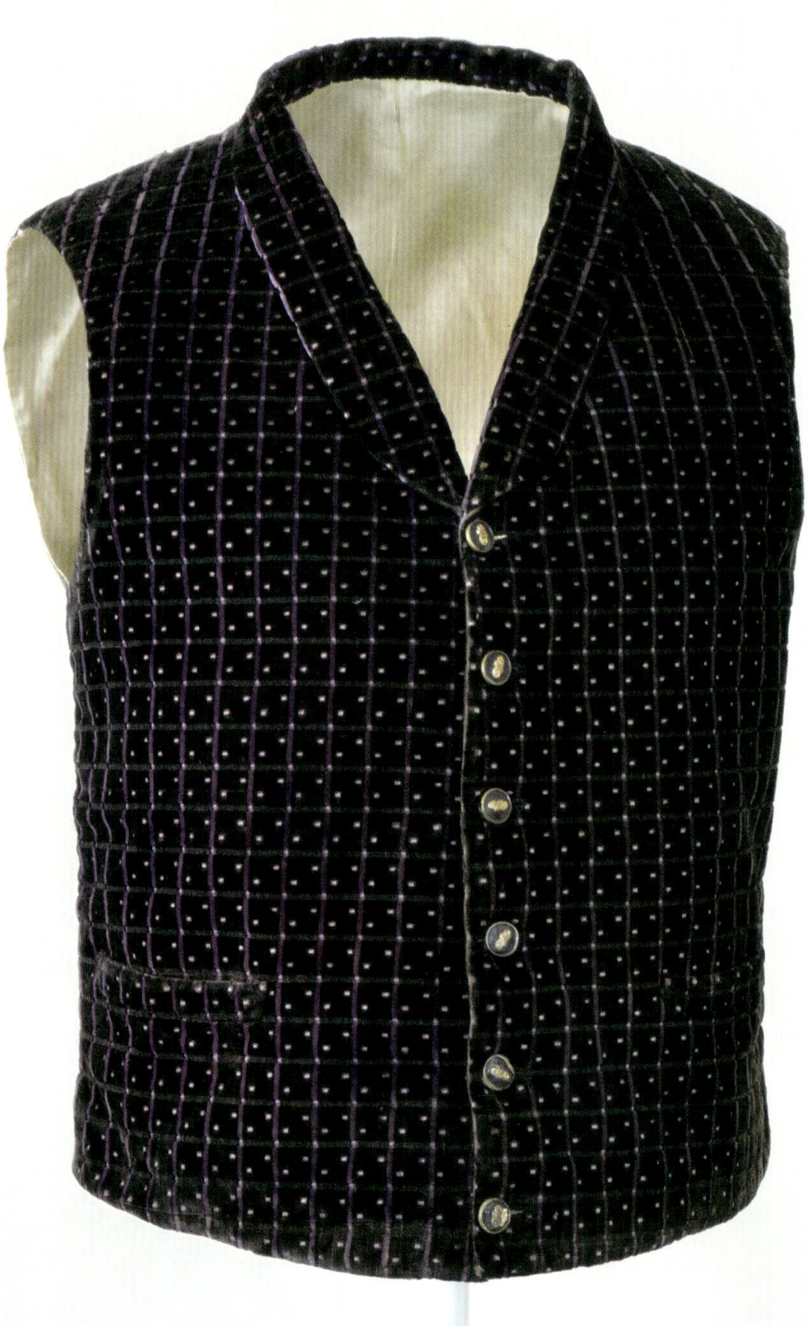

A waistcoat in silk voided velvet, 1865-1875. HC.W-3.99-5

The velvet has narrow mauve vertical stripes with black silk narrow horizontal stripes forming a check pattern; there are spots in lilac silk. The waistcoat has a roll collar, and two welted pockets; it is lined in glazed cotton twill which is pale yellow for the foreparts and cream in the back. The back is in dark brown silesia with a backstrap to adjust the waist; the prongs of the buckle are missing. The buttons are black with gilt rims and a gilt motif in the middle. The side seams have been crudely taken in with 1/2″ tucks.

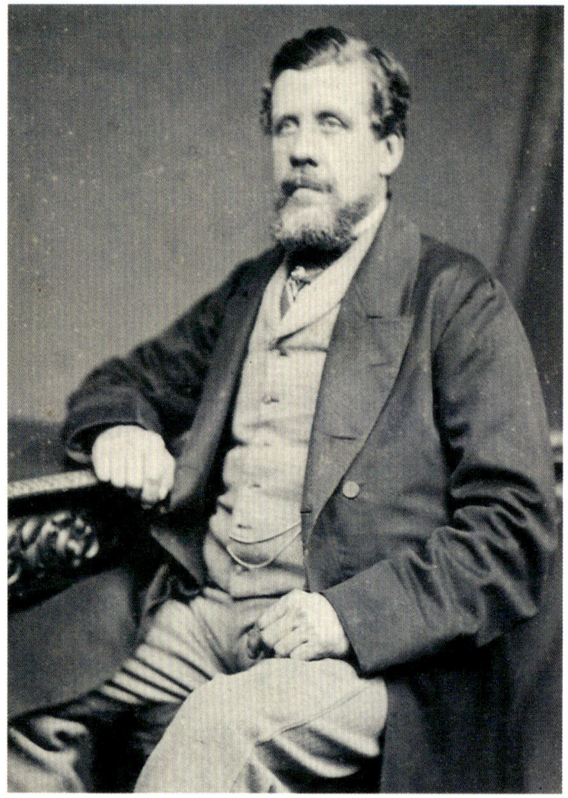

Samuel Draper, a coachsmith and livery stables keeper in London, 1870.

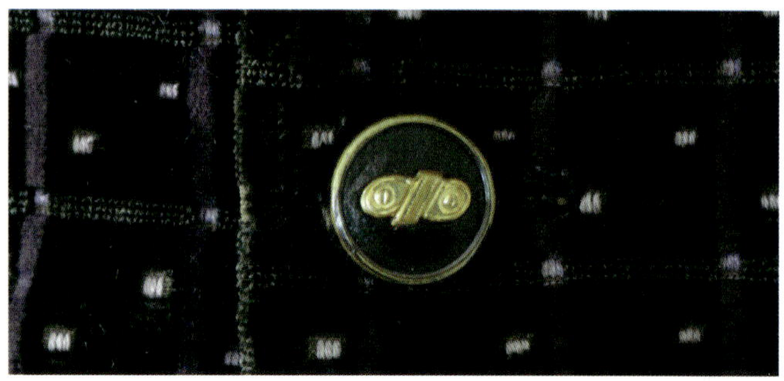

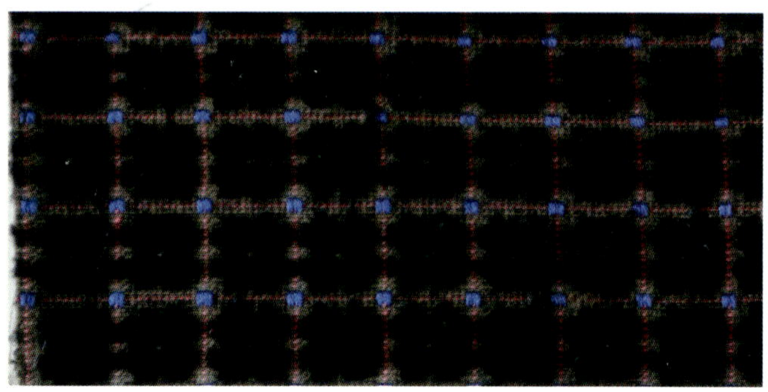

Pattern of a voided velvet from a French sample book, 1869. The School of Historical Dress.

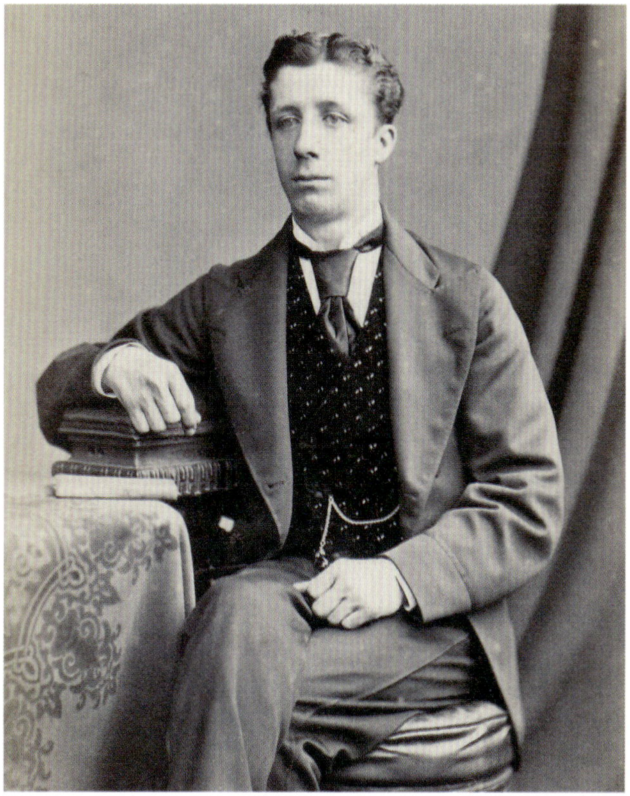

Samuel Draper (junior), livery stables keeper in London, 1870.

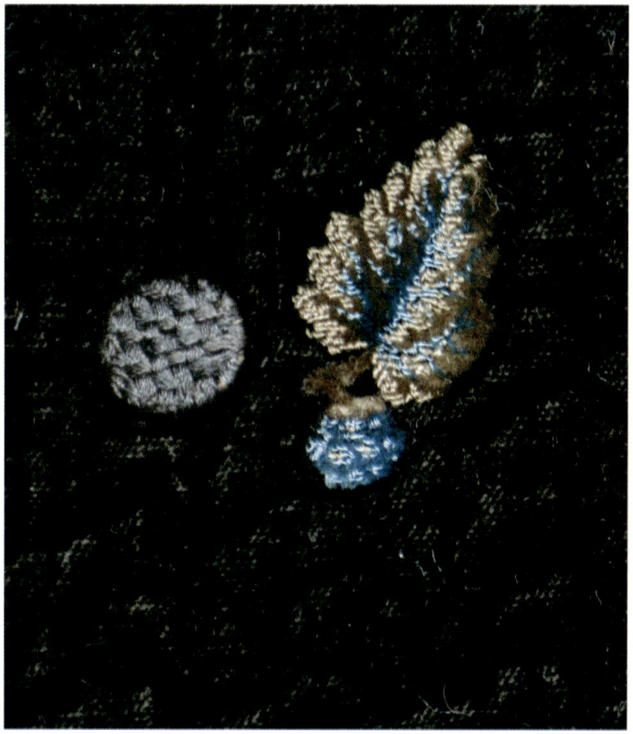

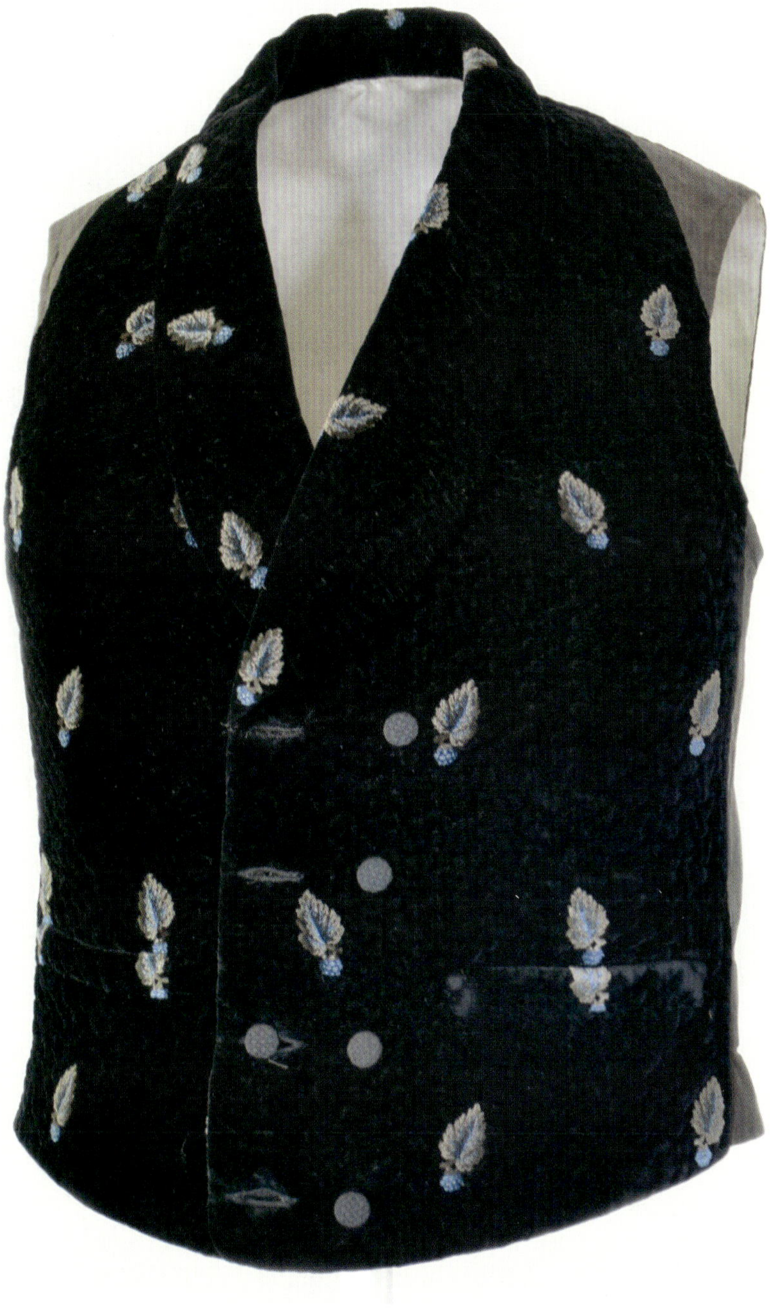

A waistcoat in black silk velvet, 1865-1875. HC.W-10.03-1

The velvet is woven with a quilted effect, and there are scattered woven leaf motifs in brown velvet and loops of blue and beige silk. The waistcoat has a roll collar and two welted pockets. It is double-breasted with four pairs of black buttons covered in thread woven in a check pattern; three of the buttons have disintegrated (page 211). It is lined in ivory silesia and the back is in brown silesia with a backstrap and a brass buckle (page 210) to adjust the waist. There are triangles of the back fabric on the shoulders and in the side seams under the armholes, to save on the velvet.

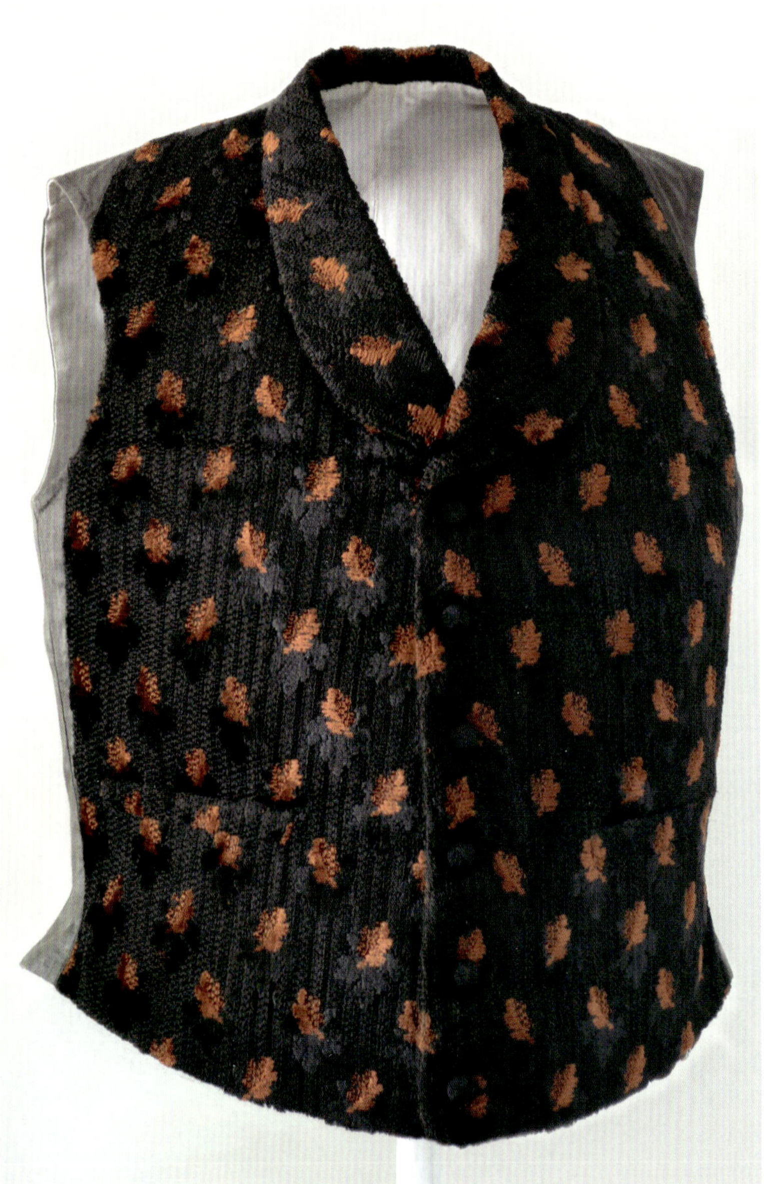

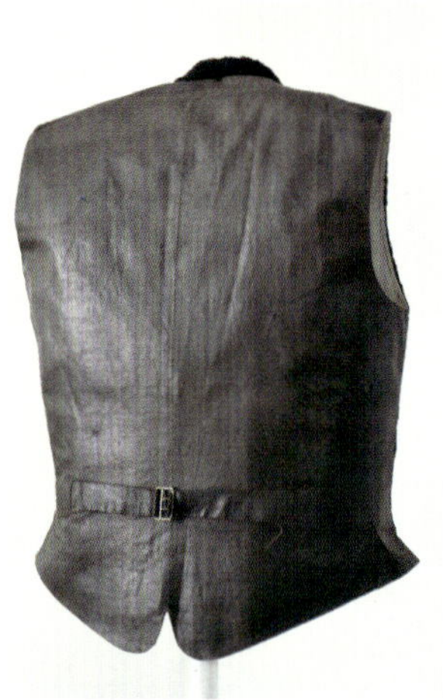

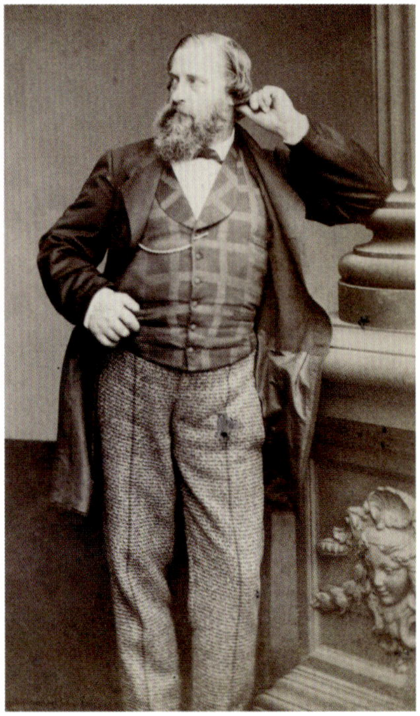

Julius Lucius Brenchley, photographed by Antoine Samuel Adam-Saloman, 1862. Brenchley (1816-1873) travelled the world for much of his life and collected many artefacts which he sent back to his home town, Maidstone, Kent, where they are now on display.

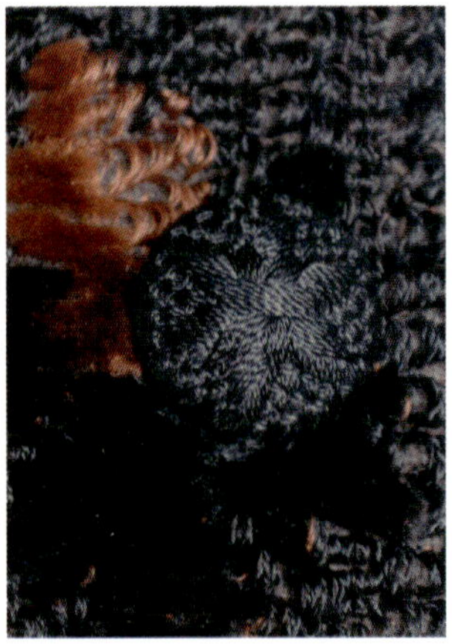

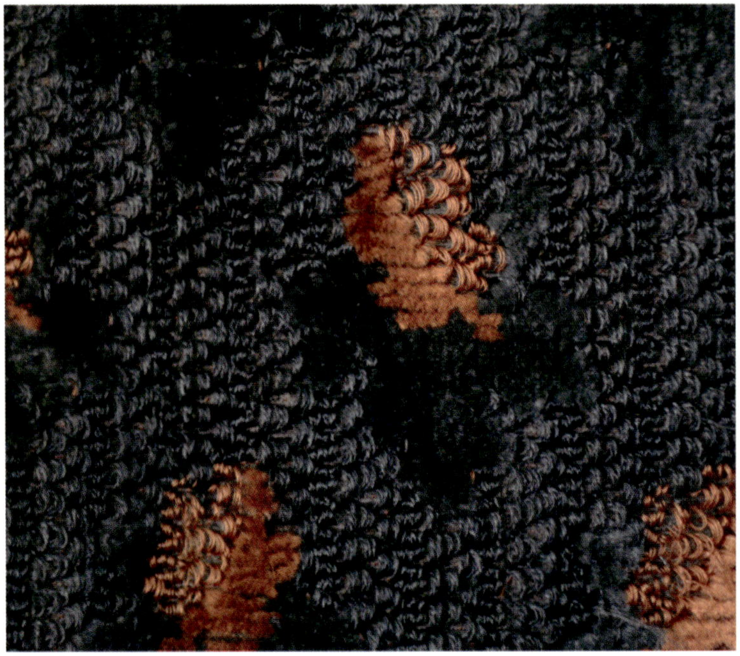

A waistcoat in black silk pile fabric, 1860-1875. HC.W-10.03-2

The ground of the silk is formed of stripes in a looped weave, with a leafy pattern in black and tan velvet. The waistcoat has a roll collar and two welted pockets; it is lined with white glazed cotton and the back is in dark brown glazed cotton with a backstrap and a brass buckle to adjust the waist size. The dark brown glazed cotton also lines the front hems. There are small gussets at each side of the back hem, which curves up in the centre to the back seam, and there are gussets of the back fabric in the side seams under the armholes and at the top, on the shoulders. This was a way of economising on the main fabric, and would not be seen when a jacket was worn. The six shallow domed buttons are covered in black silk thread in a geometric pattern.

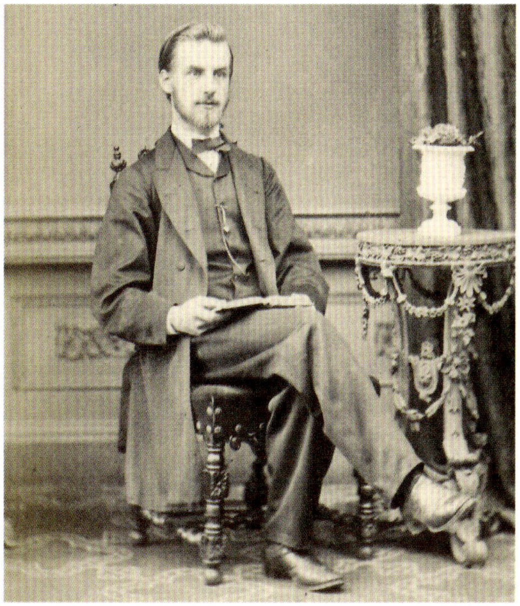

Unknown man, 1865-1875.

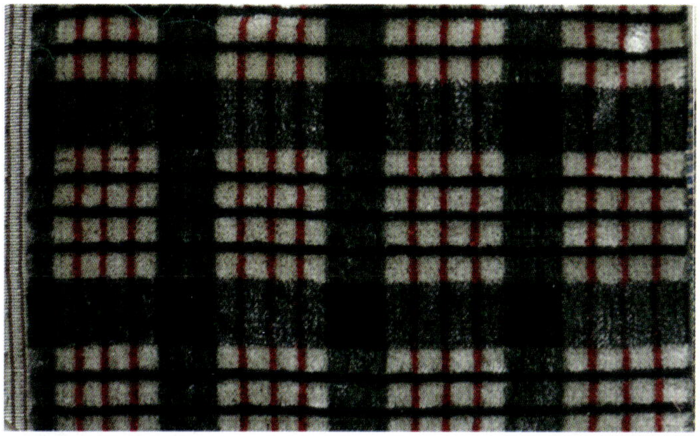

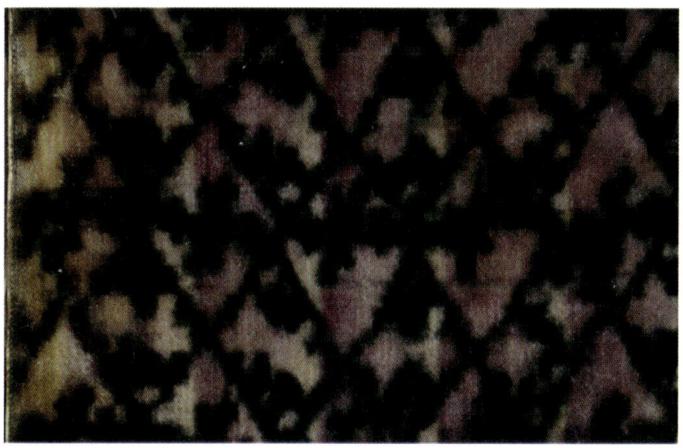

Two samples of silk velvet with woven patterns from a French sample book, 1869. The School of Historical Dress.

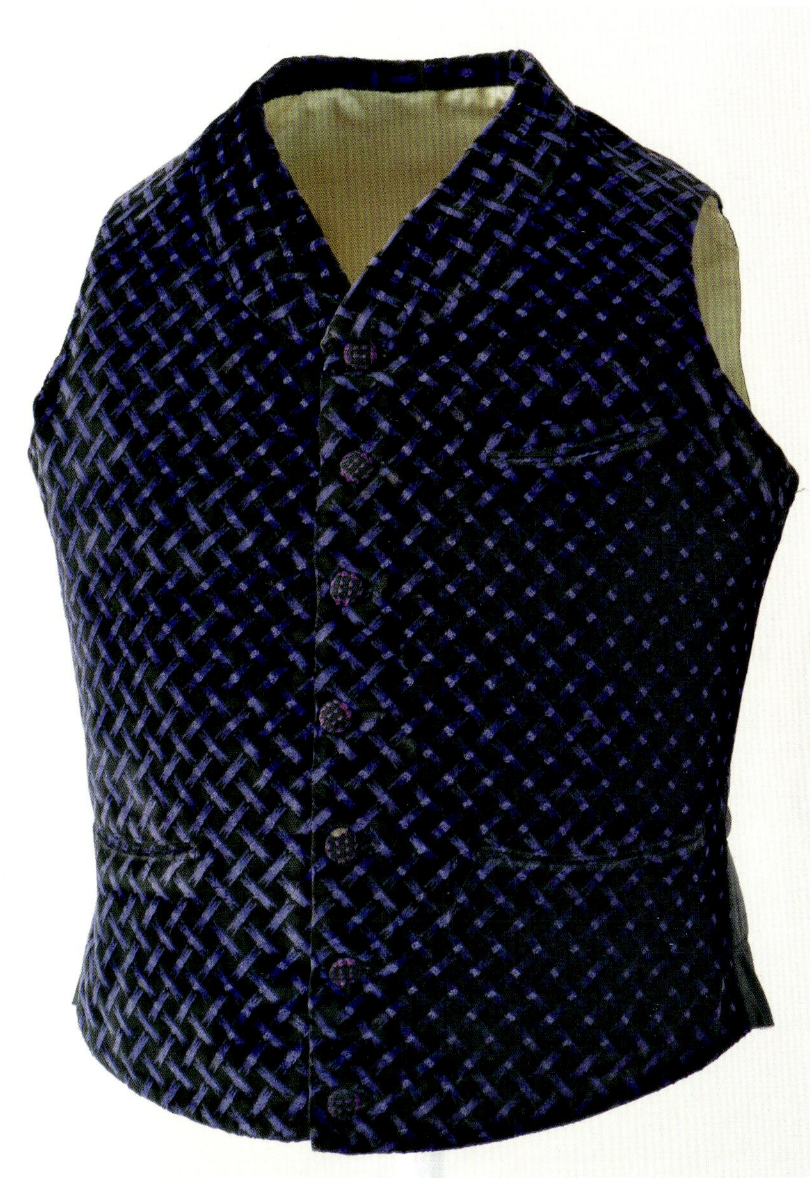

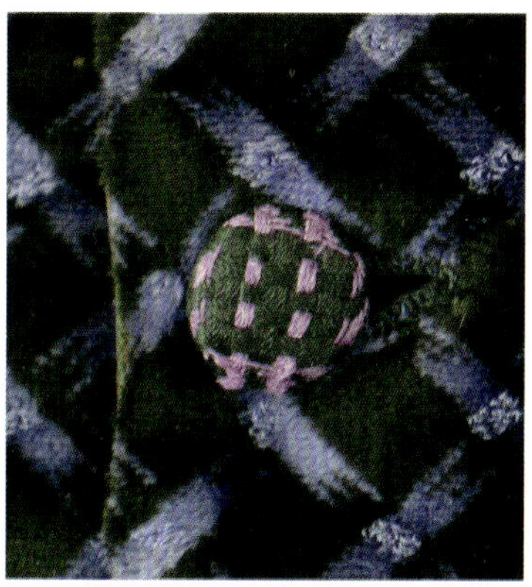

A waistcoat in patterned silk velvet, 1865-1875. HC.W-3.99-3

The velvet is black with a woven pattern of violet diagonal checks in a trompe l'œil effect. The seven buttons are covered in black and magenta silk threads woven in a check pattern. The waistcoat is lined in cream glazed cotton twill and the back is a black plain weave glazed cotton. The backstrap has a brass buckle, and the edges of the three pockets are bound in the silk velvet.

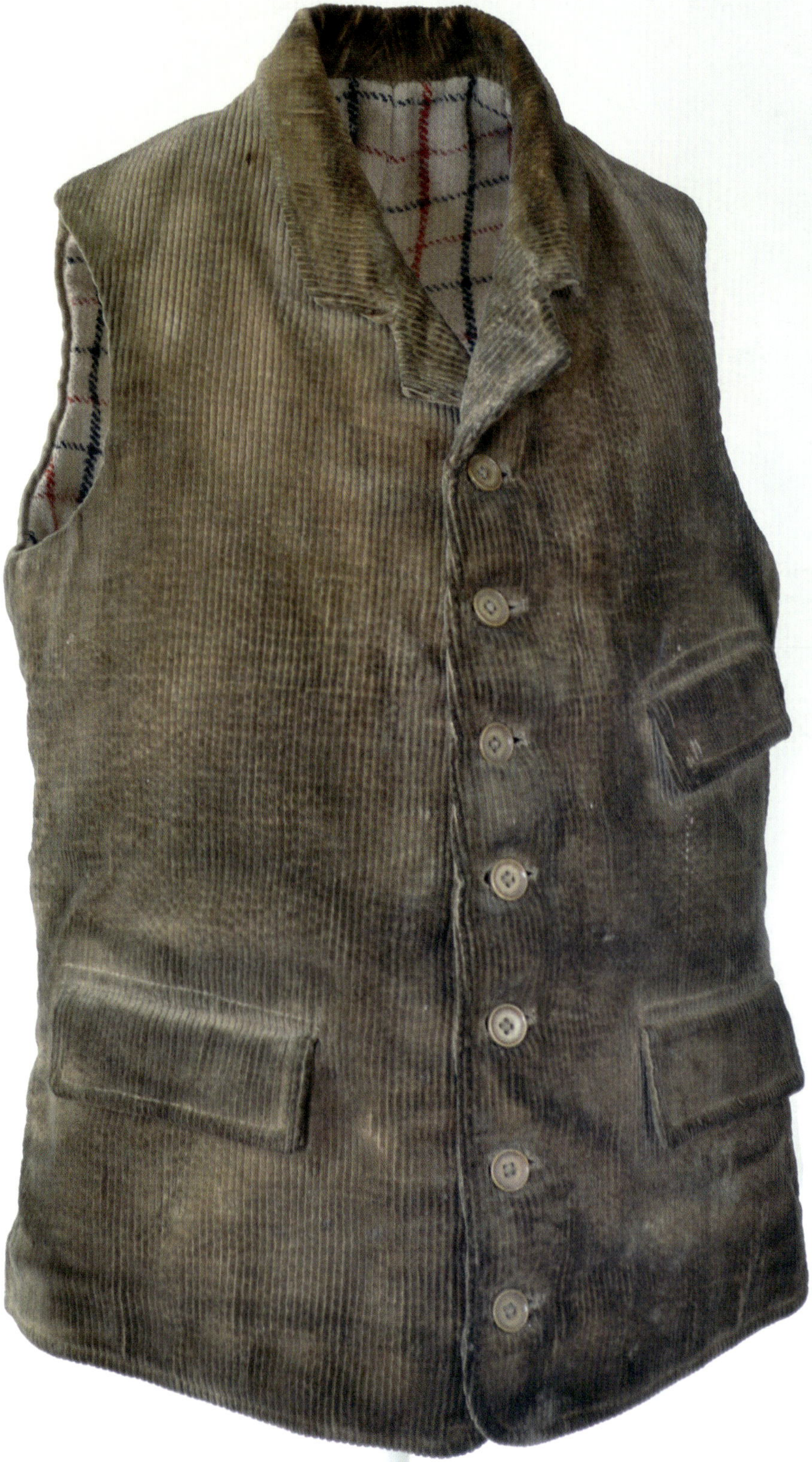

A waistcoat in light brown cotton corduroy, 1870-1900. HC.W-11.86-1

It is lined in white wool tweed with window-pane checks in red and black, and the back is in fawn heavy cotton sateen. There are seven fawn buttons, and three pockets with flaps. The side seams are open for 2½″ at the bottom, with a stitched reinforcement at the top of the opening to prevent the seam from splitting. It is very well worn and grubby, and the original colour can be seen on the corduroy where the pocket flaps have covered it.

It came with matching trousers, shown on the right; they have a fall front, which was very old-fashioned by this date. They are cleaner at the top, where they were covered by the waistcoat, and also below the knees, where they would have been covered by gaiters.

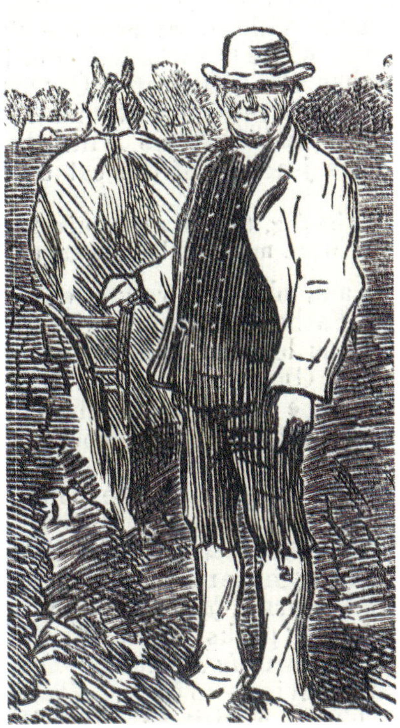

Detail from a cartoon in *Punch*, 1879.

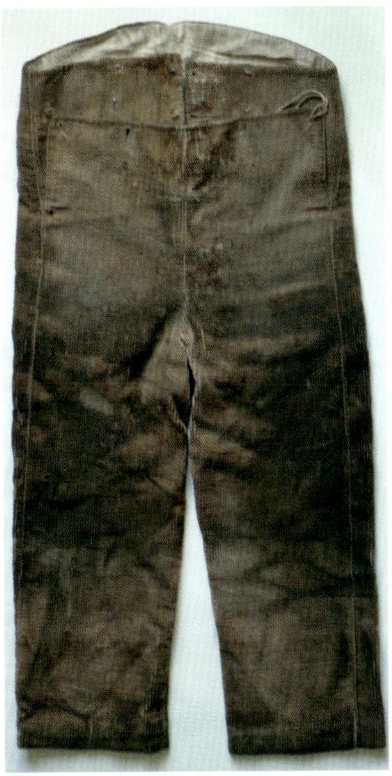

The trousers that came with the waistcoat. HC.W-11.86-2

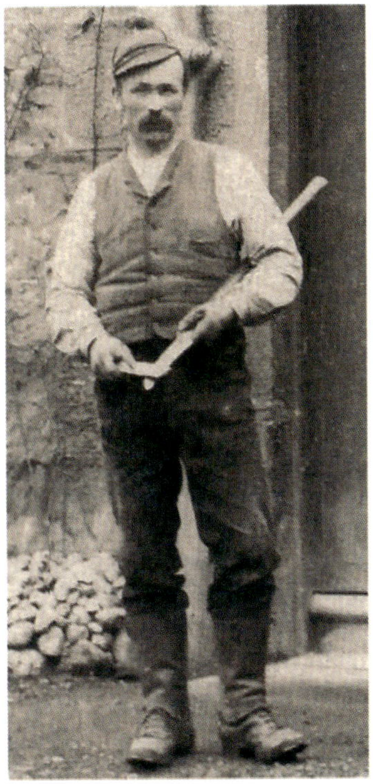

Unknown man, 1890-1900.

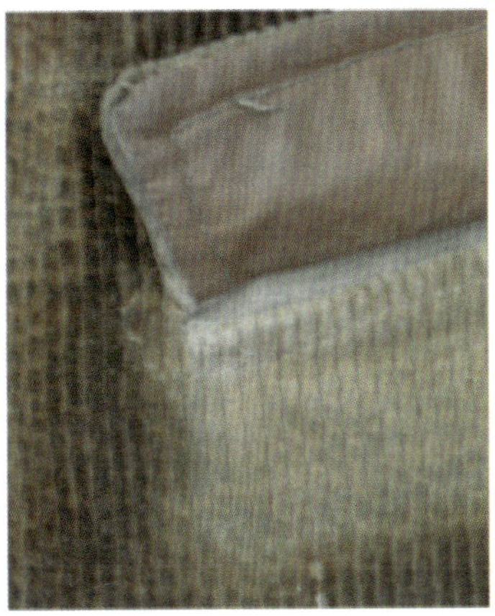

Underneath one of the pocket flaps, where the original colour of the corduroy can be seen.

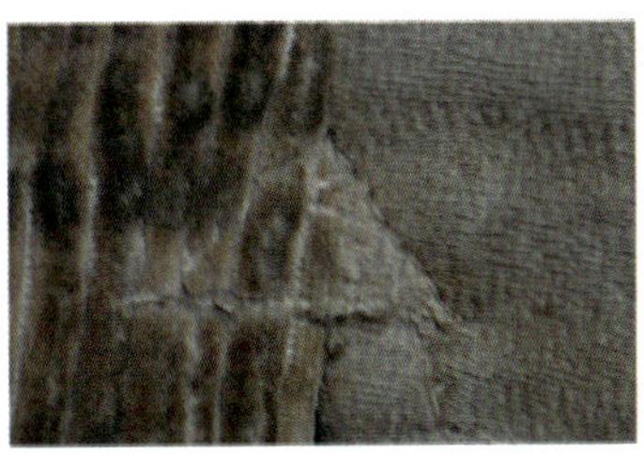

The stitched reinforcement at the bottom of a side seam.

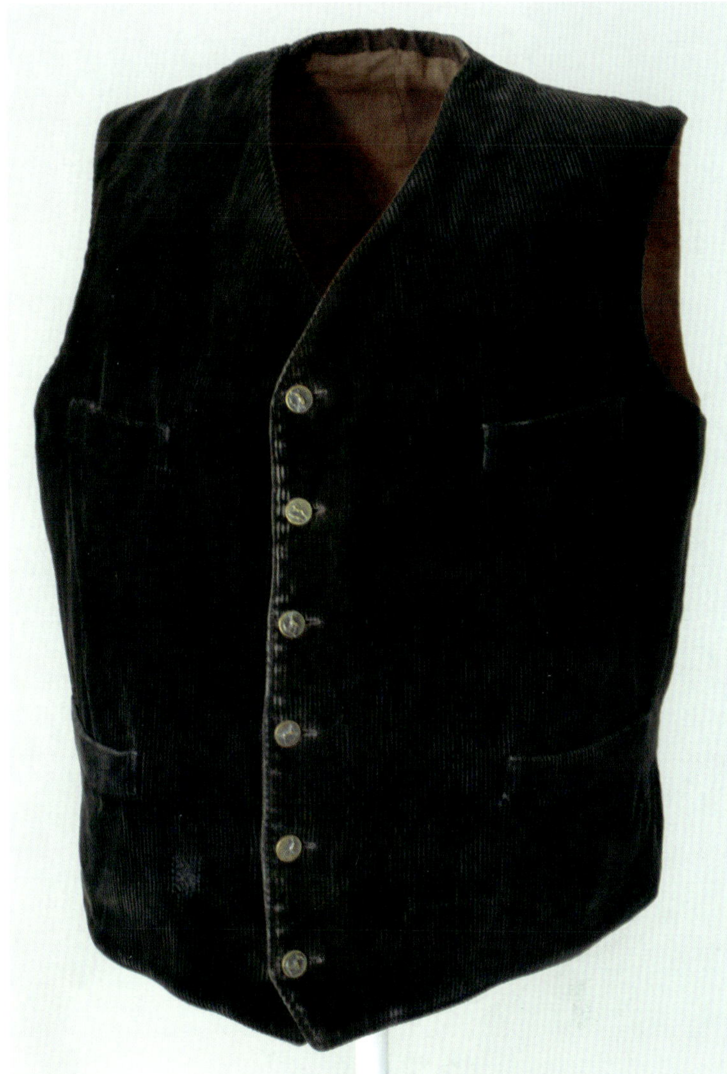

A waistcoat in black cotton corduroy, 1890-1910. HC.W-6.15

It is probably French and the six brass buttons have animals on them which suggests that it was worn for hunting. There are four welted pockets. It is lined in brown cotton sateen with a large pocket inside the left forepart. The back is in black cotton sateen with a narrow band of the corduroy at the back neck, and there is a backstrap to adjust the waist. The waistcoat has been well worn and is darned in places.

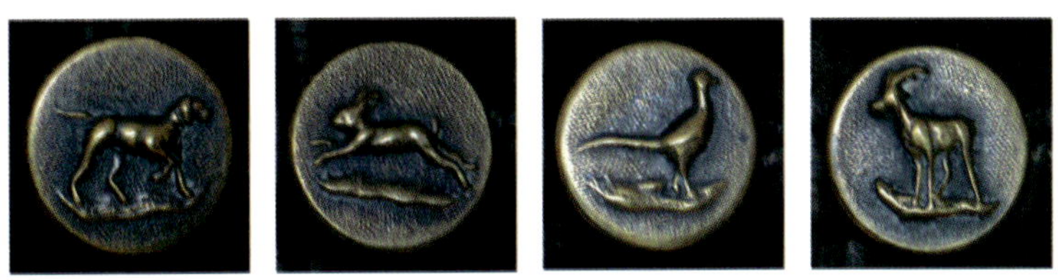

Four of the buttons with their animal motifs.

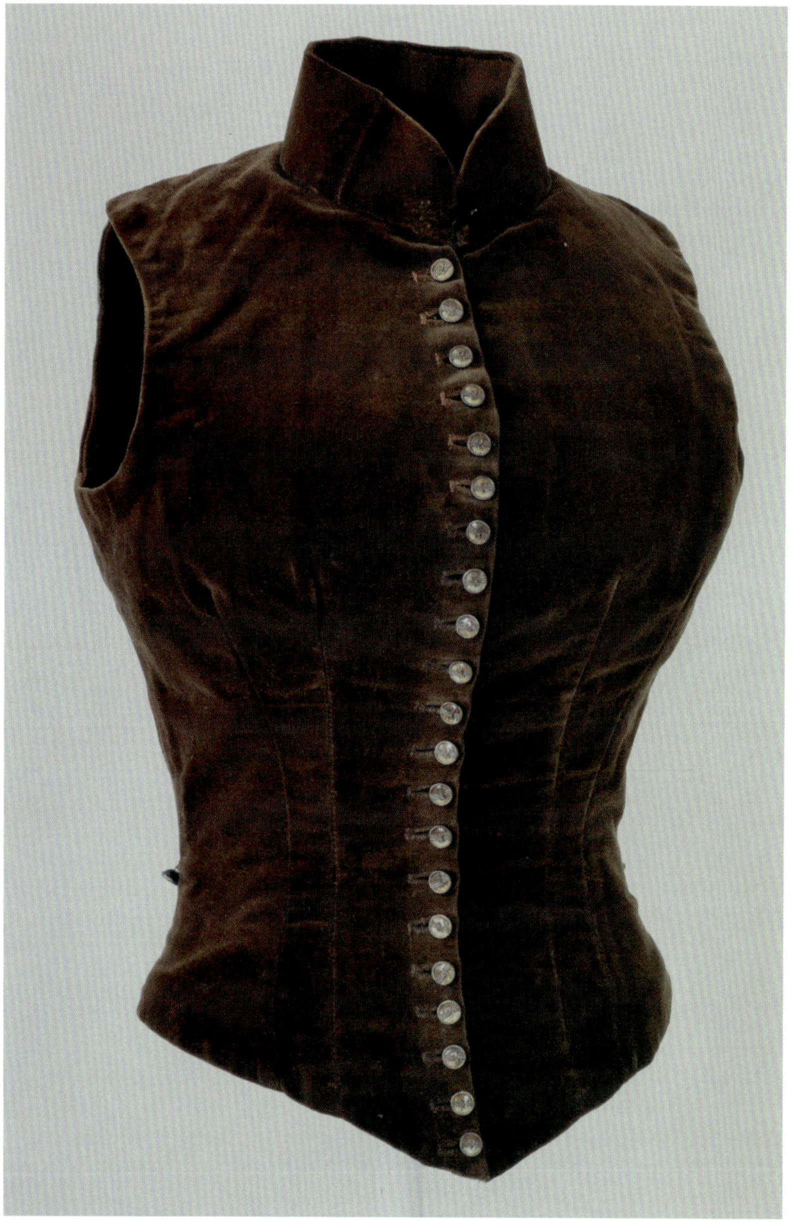

A woman's waistcoat in brown cotton velveteen, 1880-1890. HC.W-0.97

It is unlined and the velveteen is mounted on a plain grey cotton which also forms the back, with a small yoke of velveteen at the back neck; a tuck taken right down the centre back is slashed at the waist to allow for the curve. The hem, armholes and collar are faced with brown wool which has a diagonal rib. There are sections of the brown wool inserted in the side seams, and a watch pocket of the wool inside the right front edge, level with the fifth button down. The side seams are boned, as is one of the darts on each side of the centre front. The twenty-one buttons are copper-coloured metal with a buckle motif on a mottled ground; there is also a button at the waist of each side seam, probably to attach to the inside of a jacket worn over the top. Marks at the front of the collar indicate that a brooch was worn at the neck.

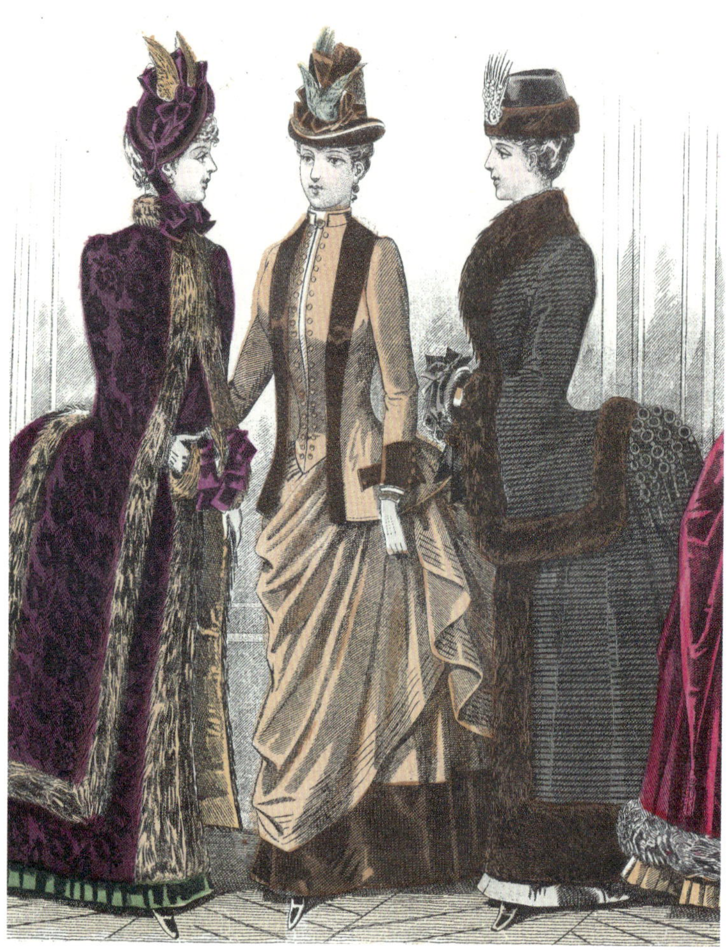

Fashion plate from *The Young Ladies' Journal*, 1886.

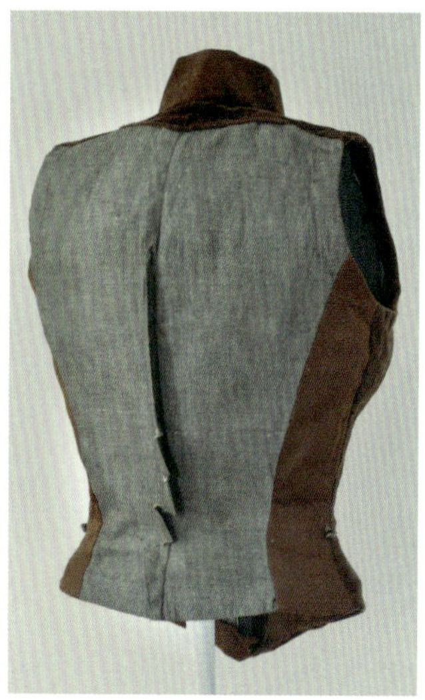

The back, showing the tuck taken down the centre.

"Waistcoats continue to remain in fashion, and are not only useful adjuncts to a toilette, but are also very becoming, especially to stout persons, for whom full chemisettes and blouses are too thick-looking. White waistcoats braided with narrow gold cord are remarkably pretty and elegant for visiting, and all dresses intended for society wear, whether for day or evening." *The Ladies' Treasury*, 1885.

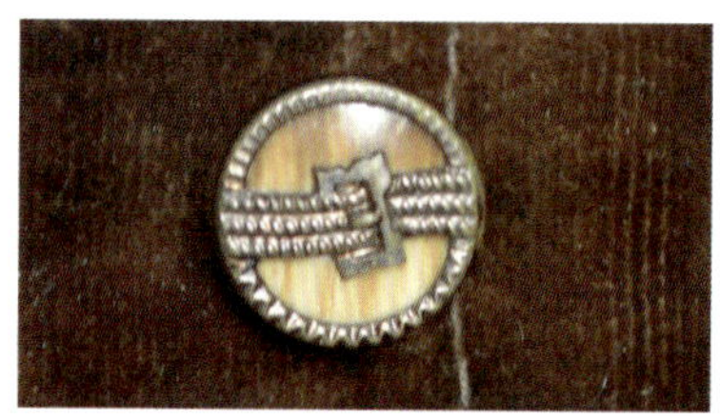

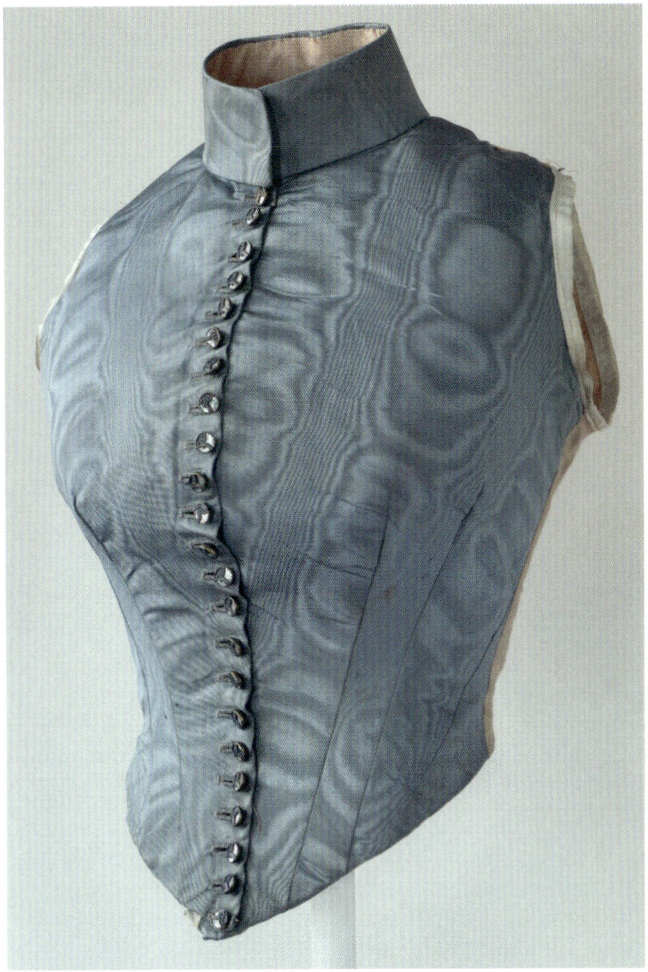

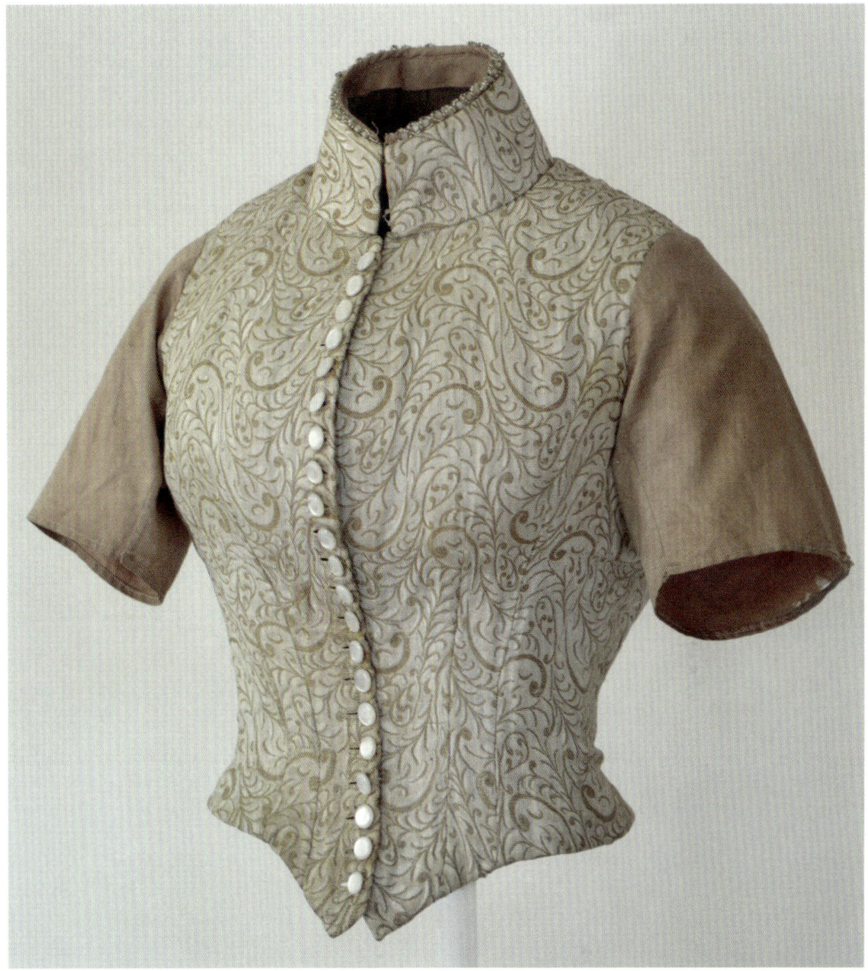

A woman's waistcoat in grey silk moiré, 1885-1895. HC.W-9.82

It is unlined and the moiré is mounted on fawn cotton sateen, which also forms the back. The left front edge and the darts are boned. The armholes are edged with ivory silk ribbon which also edges the left front edge, and faces the hem. The twenty-three buttons have metal openwork on a pearl ground. There is padding over the bust.

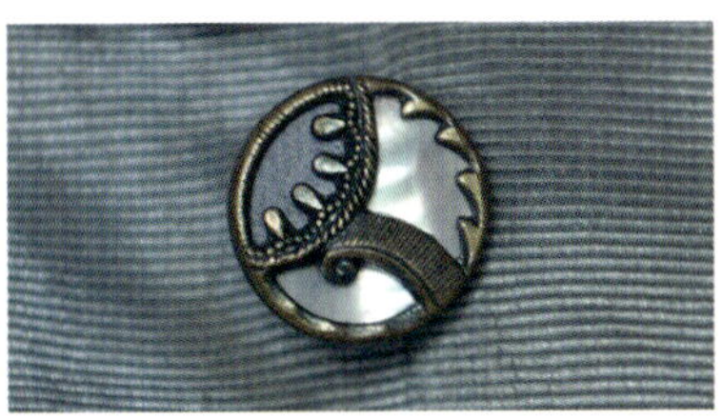

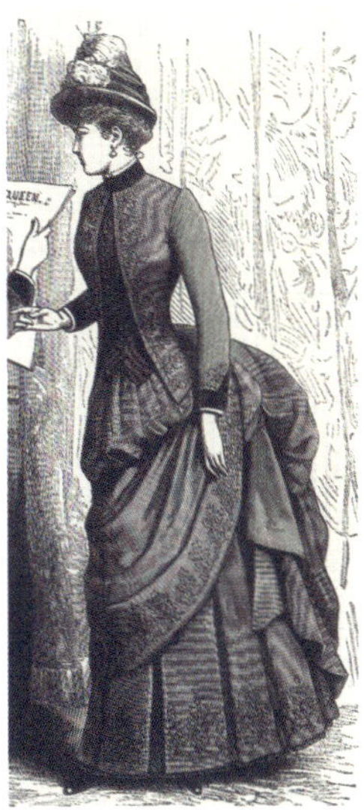

Fashion drawing from *The Queen*, 1885.

A woman's waistcoat in patterned beige cotton satin, 1885-1895. HC.W-0.83

The pattern is woven in ivory silk and a filé thread of copper wound round yellow cotton, giving a gold effect. The waistcoat is unlined and the foreparts are mounted on fawn cotton sateen; this also forms the back and short sleeves, which would not have been seen. The stand collar is lined with the sateen, and edged with a strip of pearly glass beads surrounded by wavy rows of smaller silver beads. The edge of the right forepart is faced with beige silk ribbon, which also faces the forepart hems. There is a hand-worked oval eyelet, 1/2″ deep, each side of the back waist, maybe for a tape on a jacket to pass through, to hold it in place over the waistcoat. There is padding over the bust, and twenty-one pearl buttons.

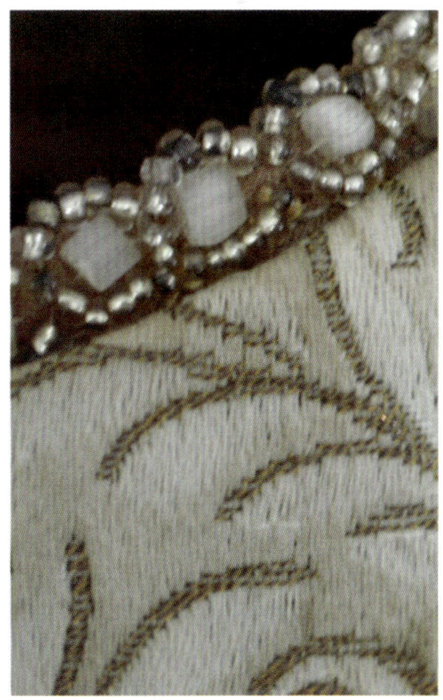

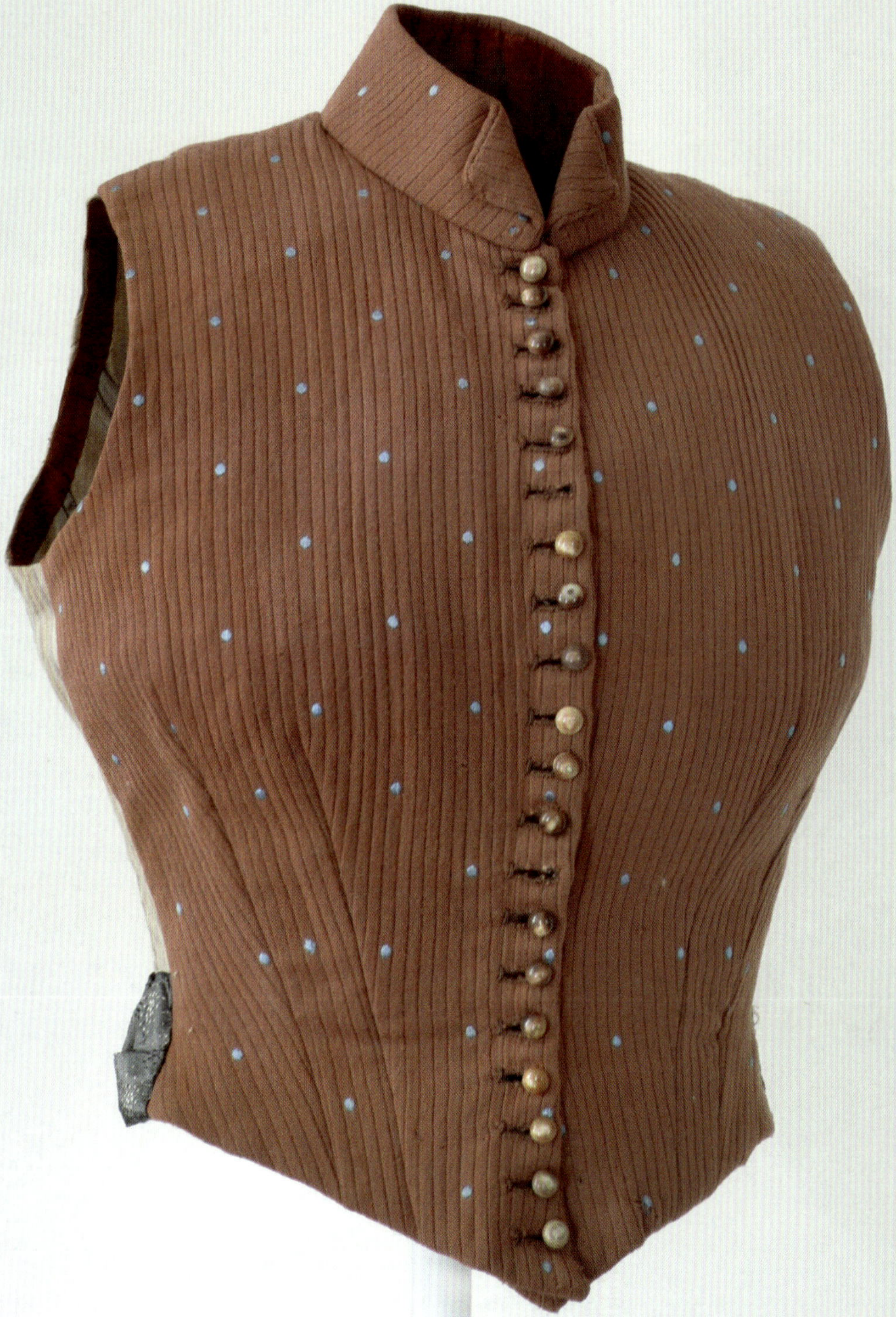

A woman's waistcoat in tan ribbed wool, 1885-1895. HC.W-1.75

The wool has woven spots of blue silk and is mounted on ivory cotton satin which has printed stripes of pale grey and black; this cotton is also used for the back, and the waistcoat is unlined. The stand collar is stiffened and the front corners are folded back to make a wing collar; two of the twenty brown marbled buttons are missing. The waistcoat is heavily boned with a bone on the left front edge under the buttons, three bones in each forepart, one on each side seam and one in the centre back. The front edges are faced with dark brown silk ribbon, and the armholes bound with tan silk ribbon, which also covers the bones. The forepart hems are faced with chestnut-coloured silk, which also covers the inside of the collar. There is a watch pocket in tan silk taffeta sewn inside the edge of the left forepart, near the top, and a cut in that edge at the waist to allow it to curve in. A length of the tan silk ribbon is sewn on to the bone cover at the centre back, to tie round the waist, and a hook is sewn over that to attach to a loop on the waistband of a skirt; both of these hold the waistcoat in place. A piece of 3″-wide grey silk ribbon, with a pattern of black and white spots, goes round the back waist with a tuck, and is sewn to each side seam; a short bone at the centre back is sewn to the back fabric. This ribbon is probably not original.

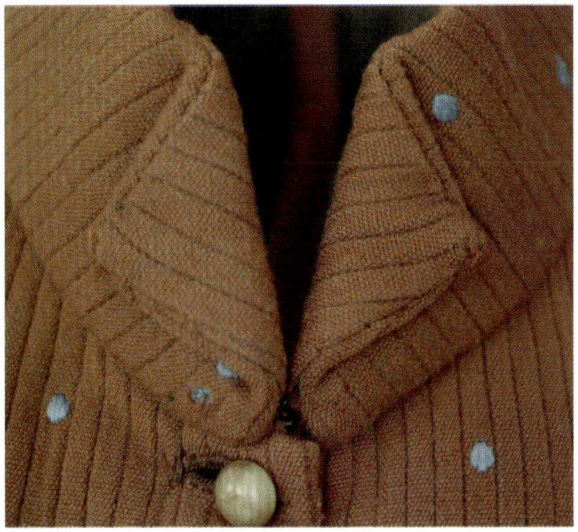

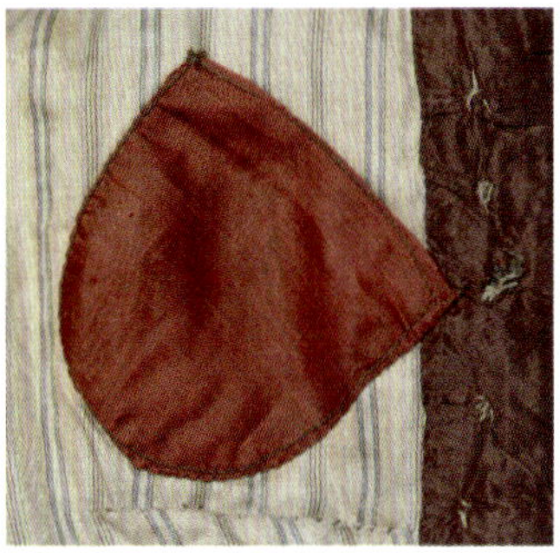

Left: The watch pocket, inside the left front edge.

Right: The back, showing the grey silk ribbon with its centre back bone.

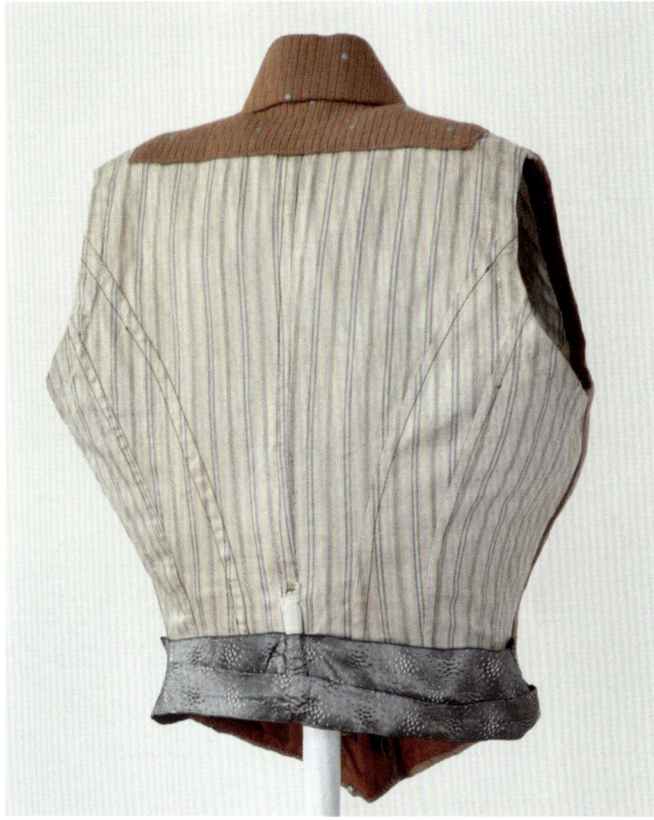

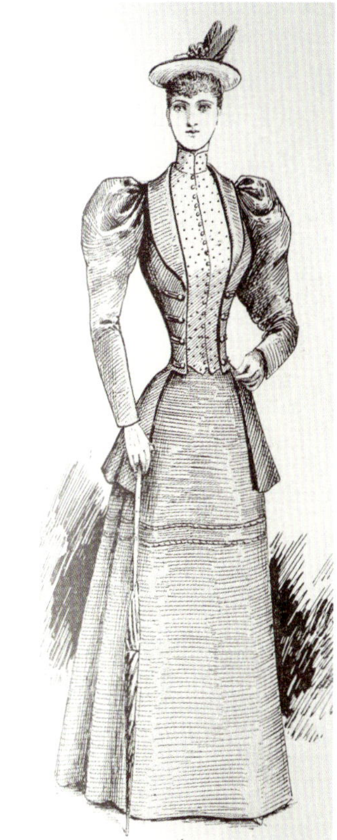

Fashion drawing from *The Queen*, August 1893.

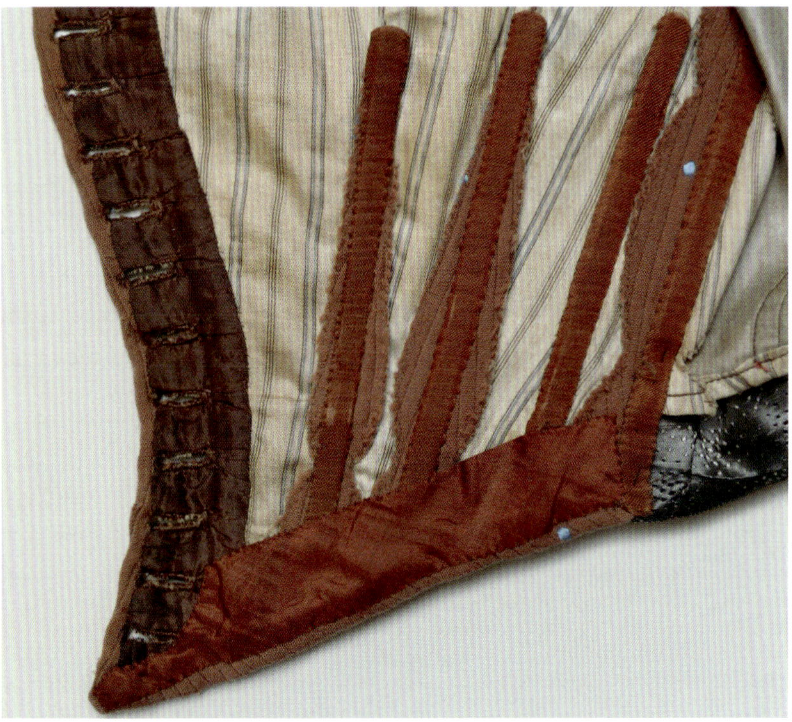

Inside the right forepart, showing the boning.

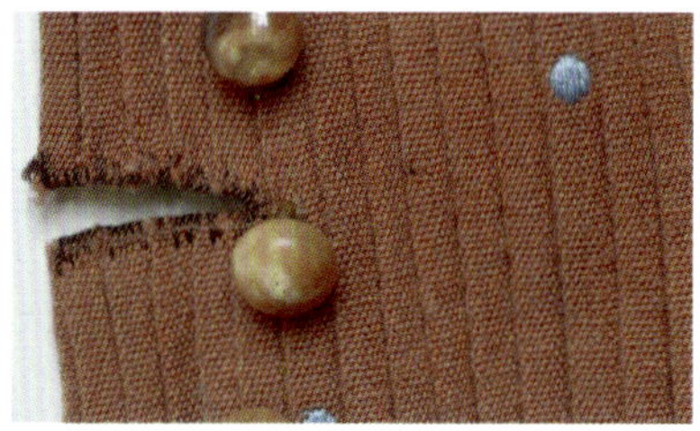

The cut at the waist of the left forepart to allow for the curve of the edge.

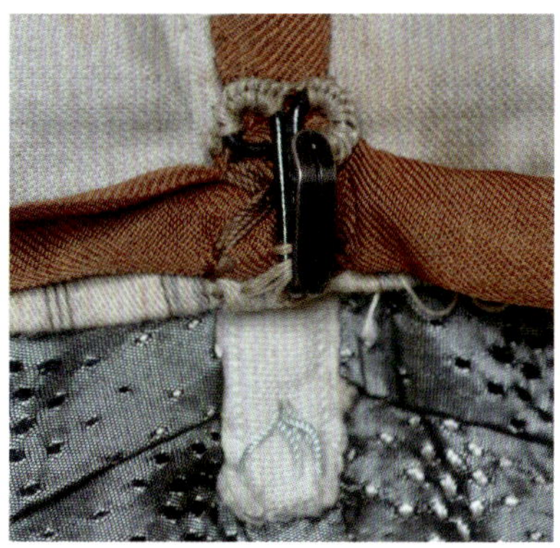

The hook inside the back waist, sewn over the ribbon tie.

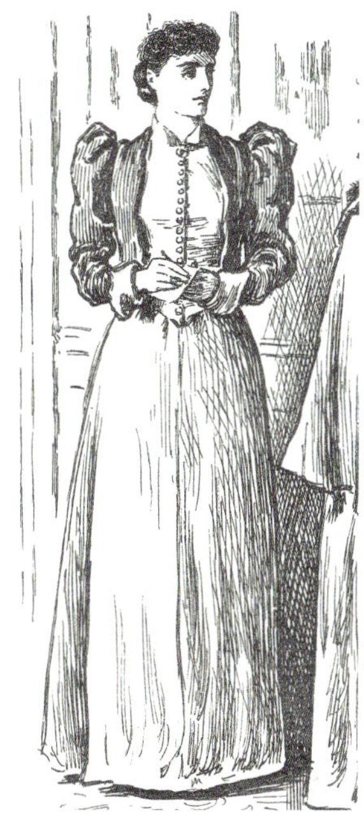

Detail from a cartoon in *Punch*, 1893.

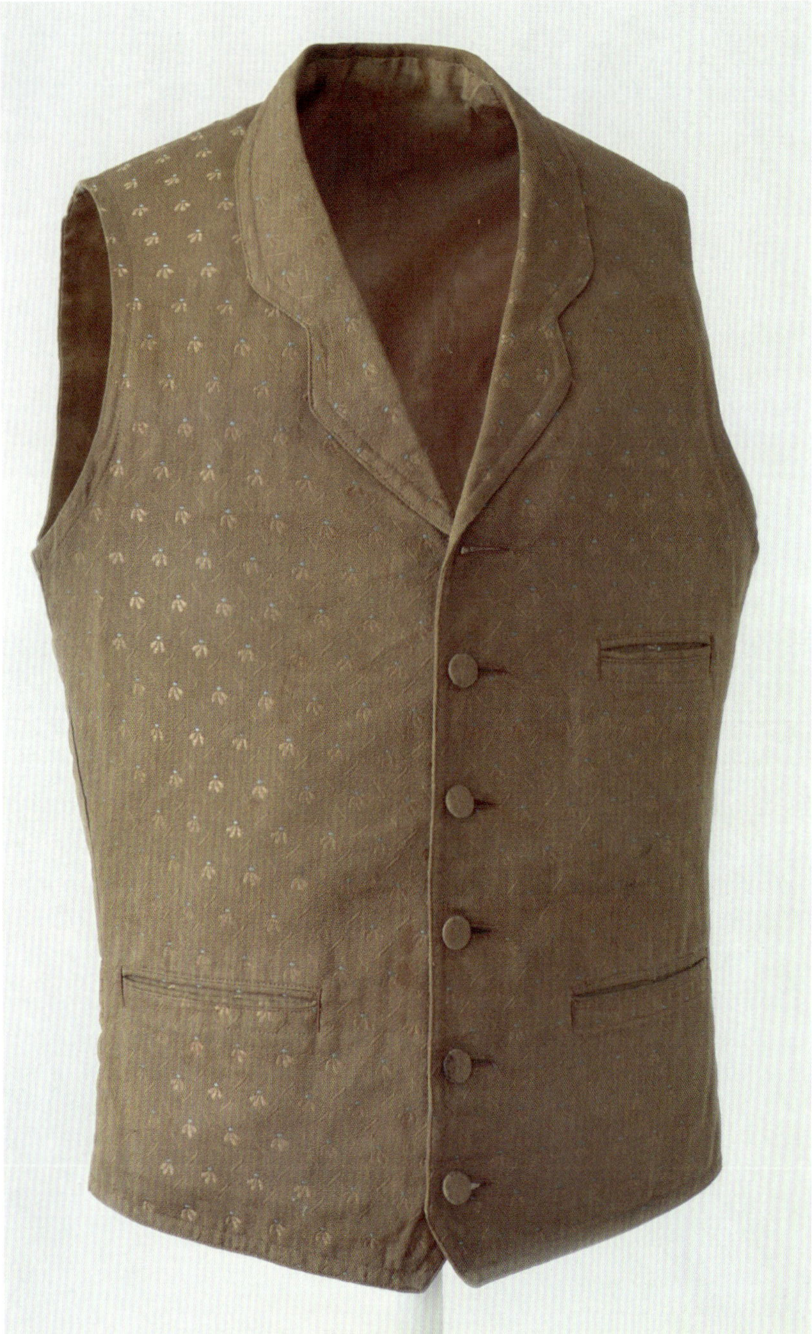

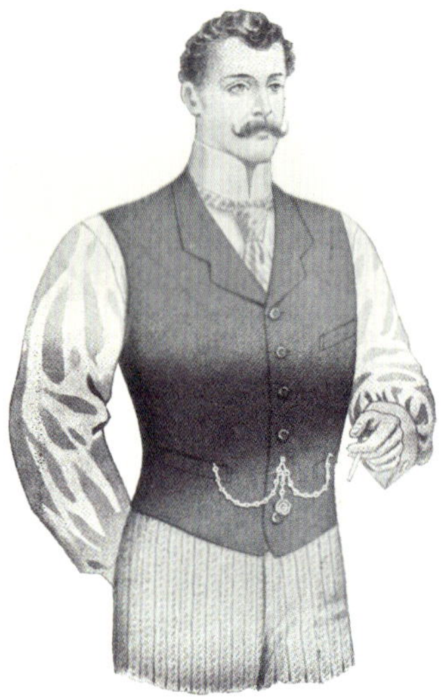

Fashion plate from *The Tailor and Cutter*, 1898.

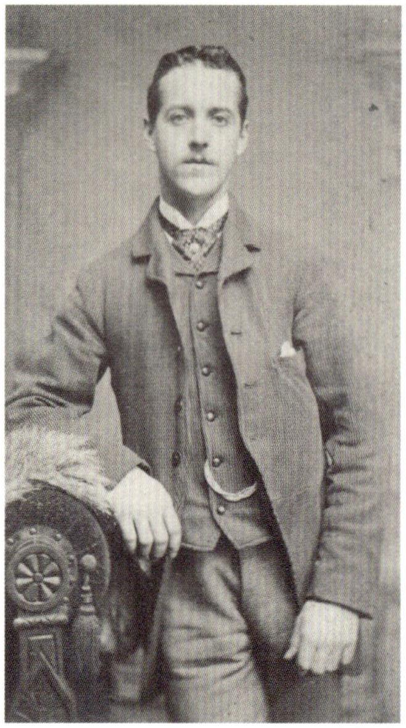

Unknown man, 1890s.

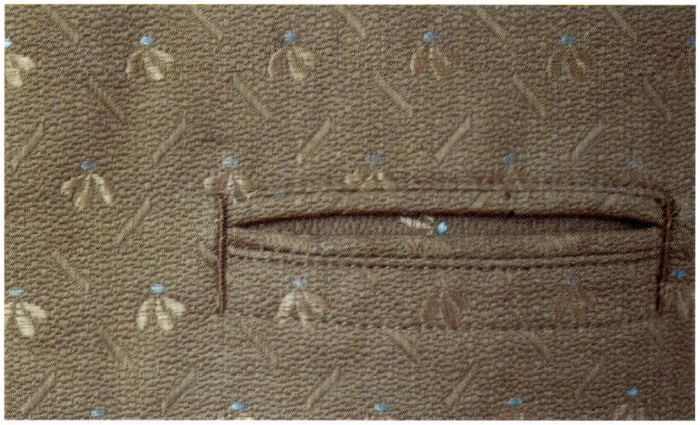

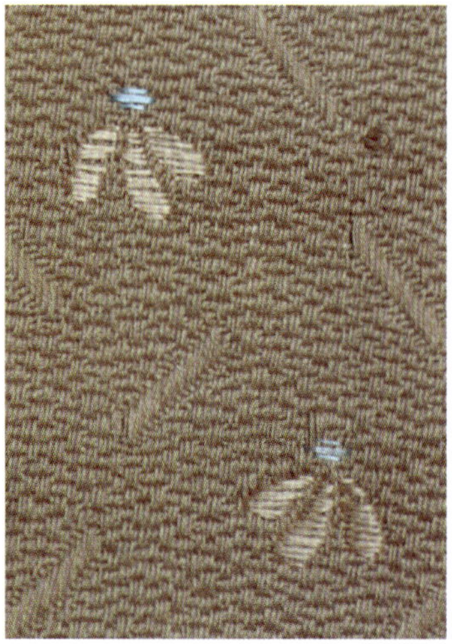

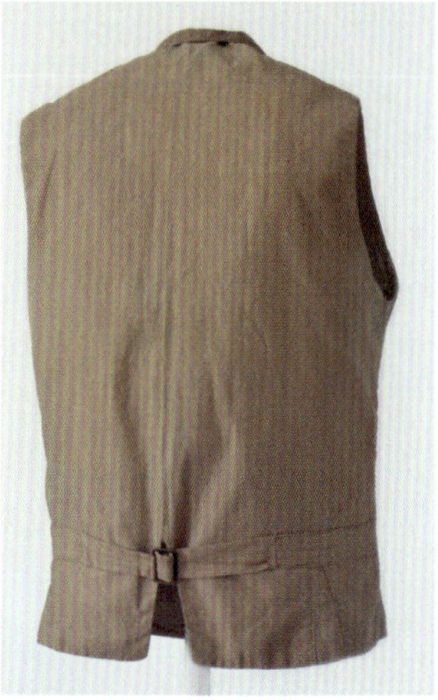

A waistcoat in light brown cotton, 1885-1900. HC.W-3.03-3

The cotton has a self pattern and scattered sprigs in matching silk with pale blue dots. The waistcoat has a step-roll collar, and one of the six self-covered buttons is missing. The lining is fawn cotton twill and the back is in fawn cotton sateen with a backstrap and a copper-plated buckle to adjust the waist. There are gussets each side in the back hem. The foreparts are top-stitched all round, 1/4″ in from the edge, and there is top-stitching round the three pockets which are edged with narrow welts.

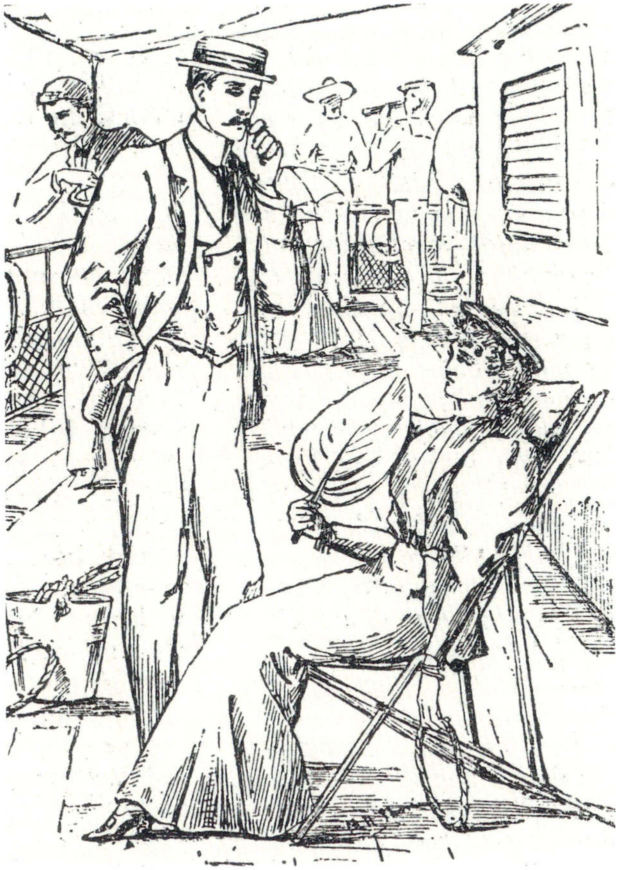

Illustration in *Home Chat*, June 1895.

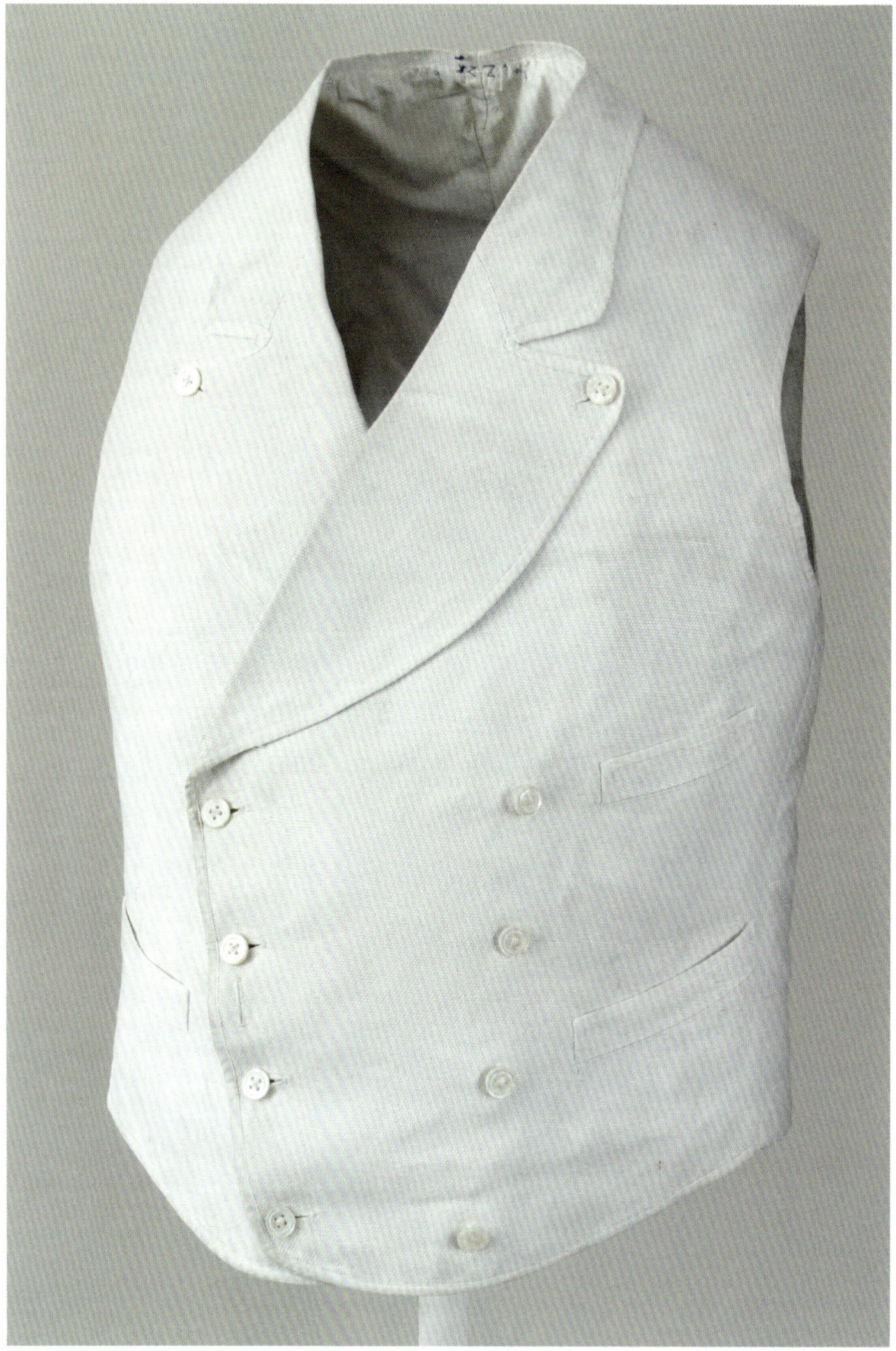

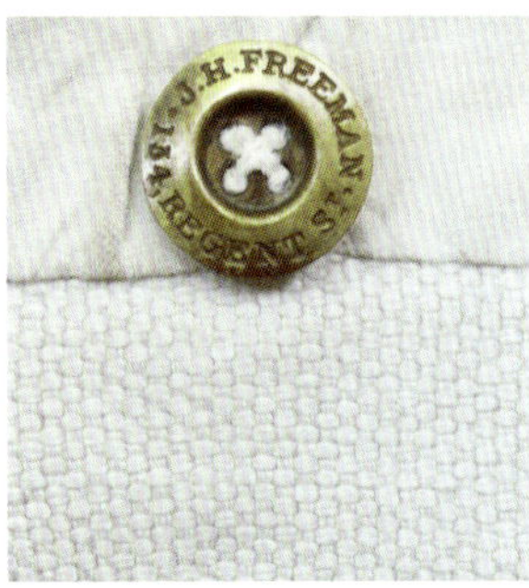

The lower of the two brass inside buttons.

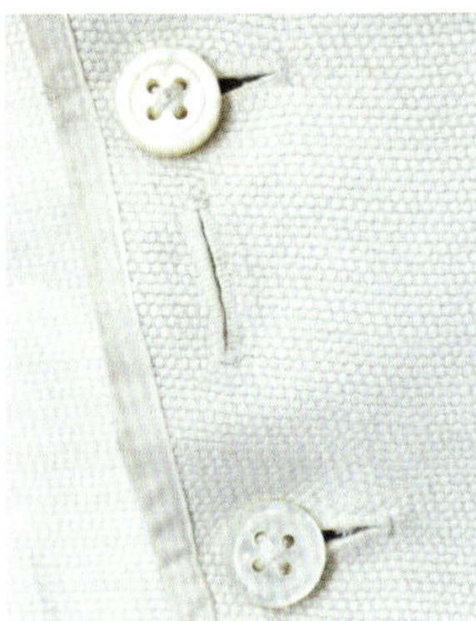

The vertical buttonhole for a watch chain.

Joseph Henry Freeman (1815-1888), the son of an excise officer, was a tailor at 134, Regent Street, London. His son (1845-1918), with the same name, continued the business.

A waistcoat in white cotton hopsack, 1890-1900. HC.W-11.76-5

It is double-breasted with four pairs of pearl buttons, and the end of each curved lapel is buttoned on to its forepart. There is a vertical buttonhole between the middle two buttonholes for attaching a watch chain. The edges of the foreparts and the three welted pockets are bound with white cotton braid, and the lining and back are in plain white cotton, with a backstrap and a brass buckle. The back fabric is stitched over the lower edge of the back of the collar. Two brass buttons on the inside of the left forepart fasten on to the buttonholes on the edge of the right forepart and hold it in place. It was made by J. H. Freeman, whose name is on the brass inside buttons.

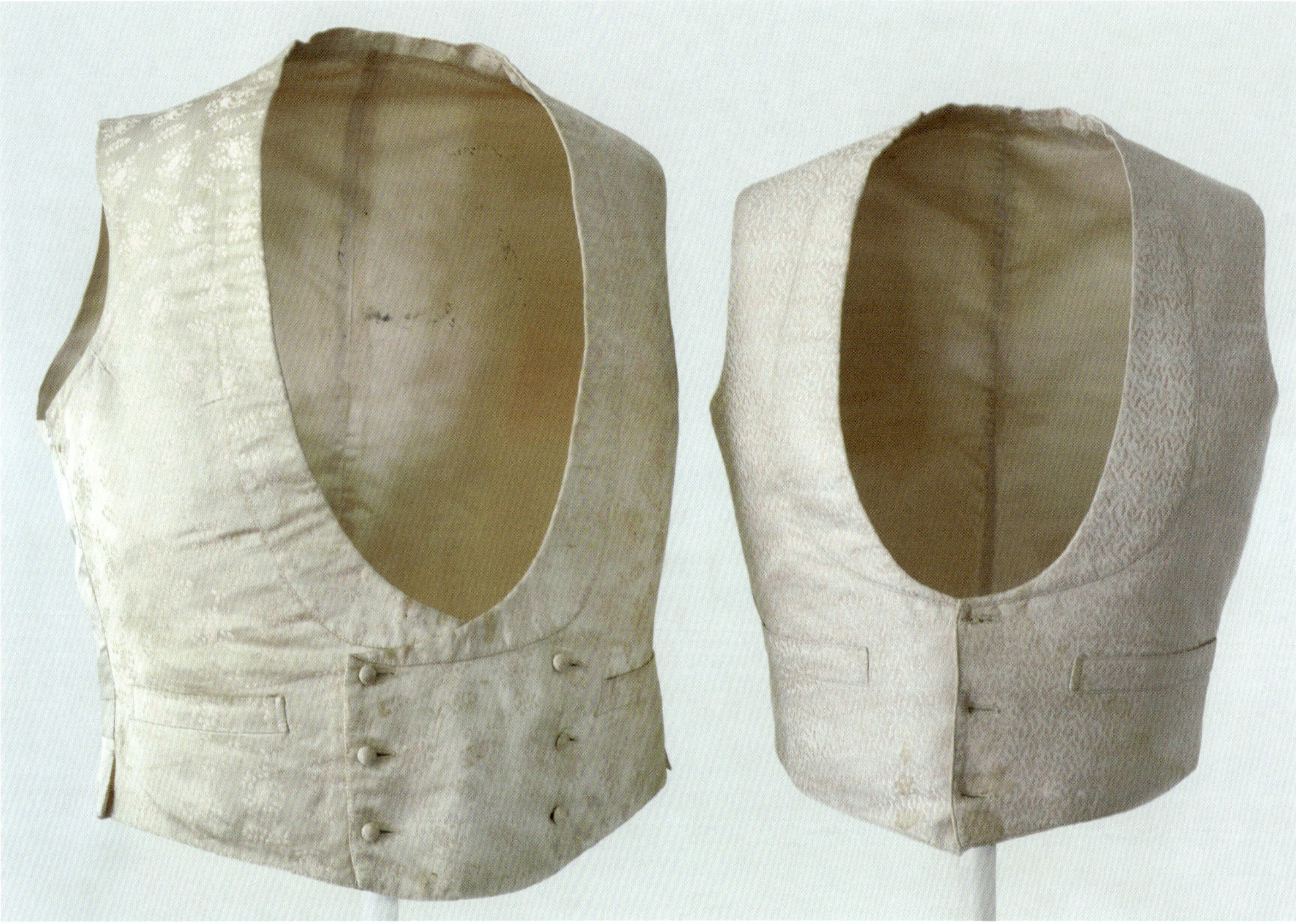

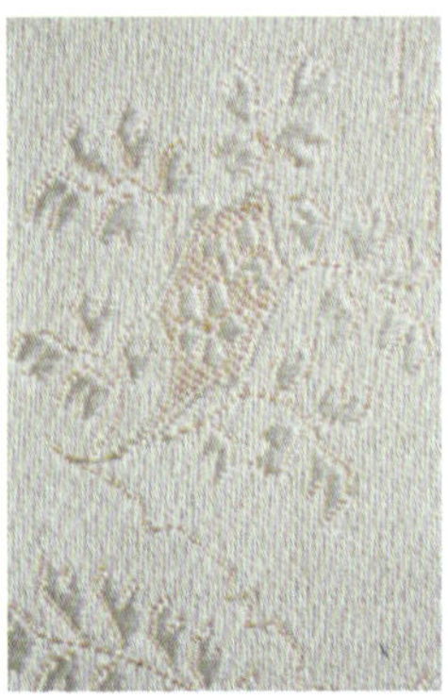

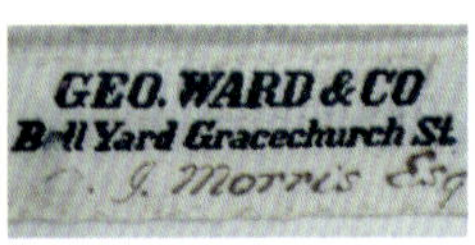

An evening waistcoat in cream silk satin, 1890-1900. HC.W-0.93

The silk has a pale pink woven pattern. The waistcoat is double-breasted with two rows of buttonholes, those on the left fastening buttons on the edge of the right forepart; the domed covered buttons are removable. The roll collar stops at the shoulders and its edges are stitched down to the foreparts. A narrow strip of the silk goes round the back neck, and the lining and back are in cream silk satin, with a backstrap and a brass buckle. The back hem has two small gussets each side of the waist, and there is a small dart in each armhole.

The label, below left, says that it was made by Geo. Ward & Co. for C. J. Morris Esq.; this was possibly Charles James Morris, who was a barrister.

An evening waistcoat in ivory silk twill, 1897. HC.W-3.97-6

The silk has a pale pink woven pattern. The waistcoat is single-breasted and the buttons are missing; the roll collar stops at the shoulders and its edges are stitched down to the foreparts. A narrow strip of the silk goes round the back neck, and the lining and back are in ivory silk satin. The backstrap has a pale metal buckle, and a label sewn inside.

The label, below right, says that it was made by J. B. Johnstone, London and Dublin, for E. H. B. Lacon Esq. in 1897. This was Sir Edmund Beecroft Heathcote Lacon (1878-1911), who inherited his title in 1899.

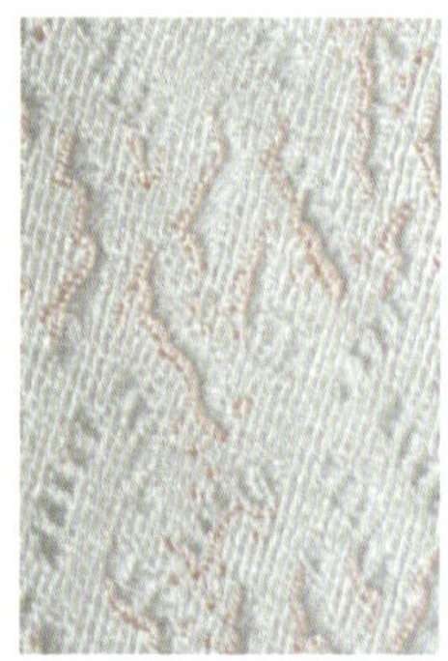

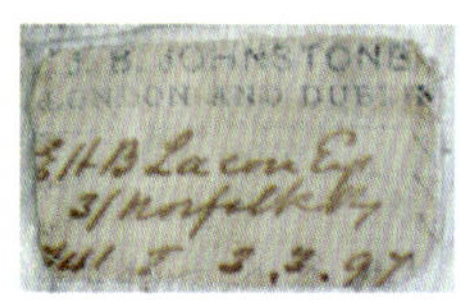

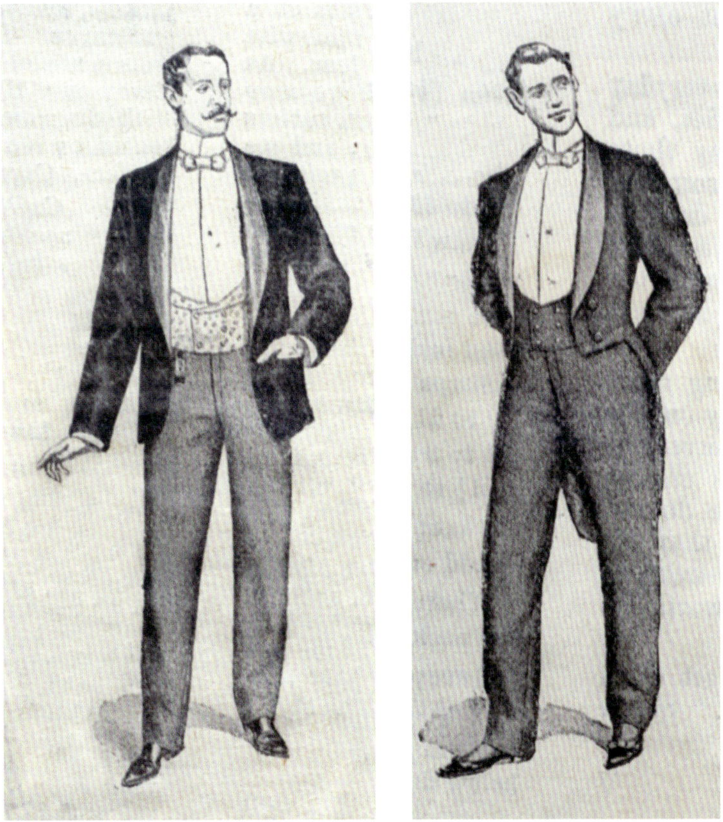

Fashion drawings from *The Tailor and Cutter*, 1898.

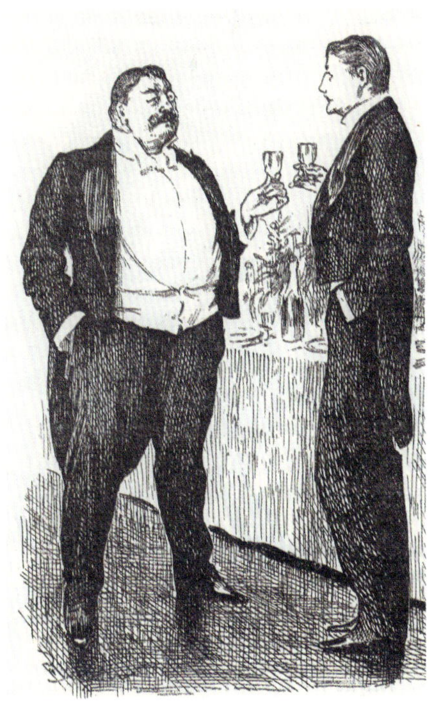

Detail from a cartoon in *Punch*, 1894.

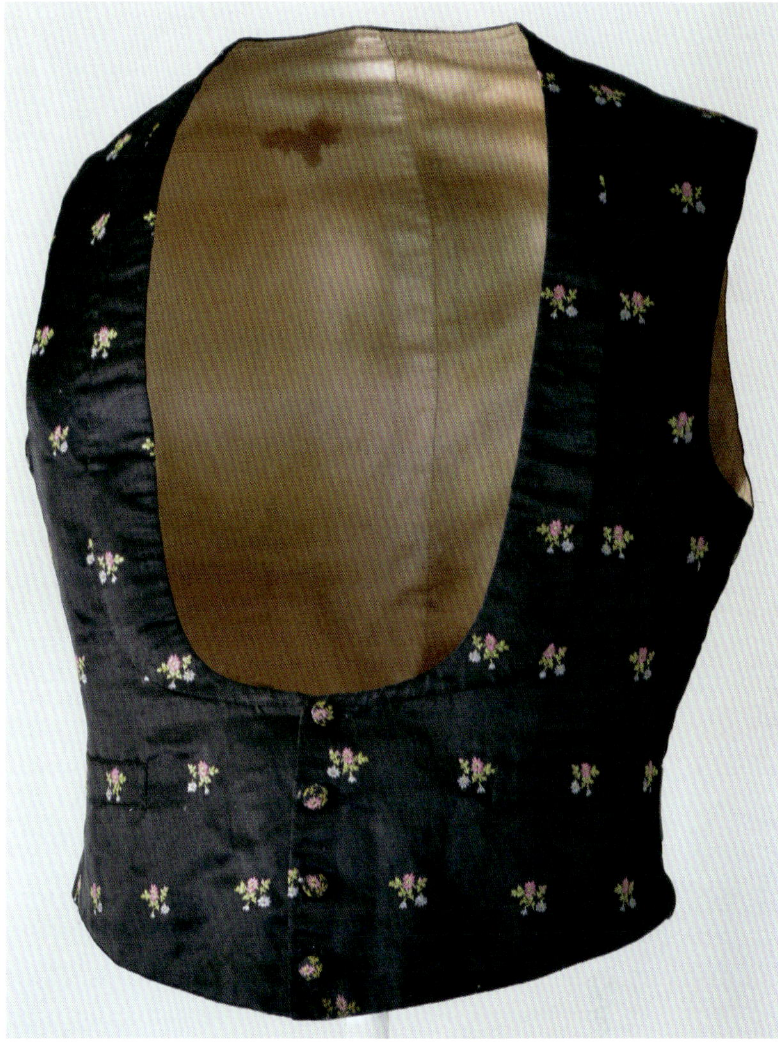

An evening waistcoat in black silk satin, 1895-1900. HC.W-11.06

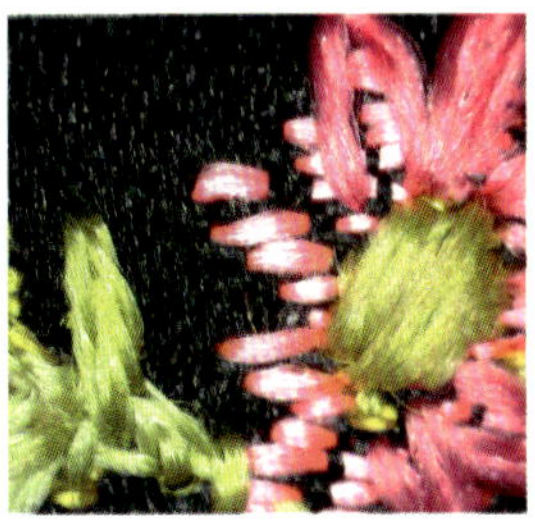

Detail of the motif outlined below. The pink horizontal lines are woven, and the others are embroidered.

An evening waistcoat in black silk satin, 1895-1900. HC.W-11.06

It has a pattern of sprigs of pink and lilac flowers with green leaves, which are woven and then embroidered over the top. A few sprigs round the edges and those on the four buttons have not been over-embroidered. The waistcoat is lined in fawn cotton satin, and the back is in black silk satin with a backstrap to adjust the waist. The roll collar stops at the shoulders and its edges are stitched down where they curve towards the centre.

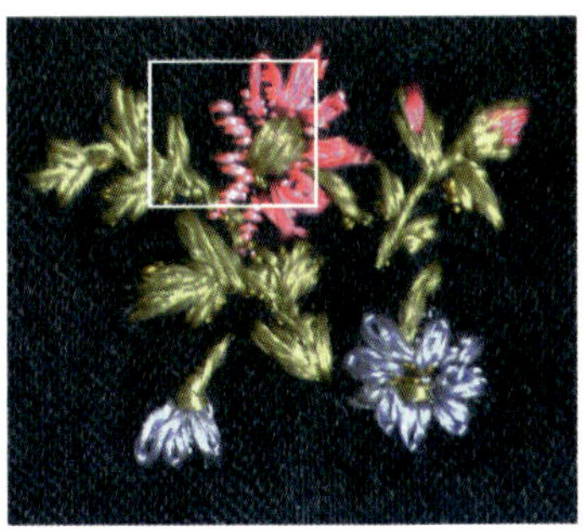

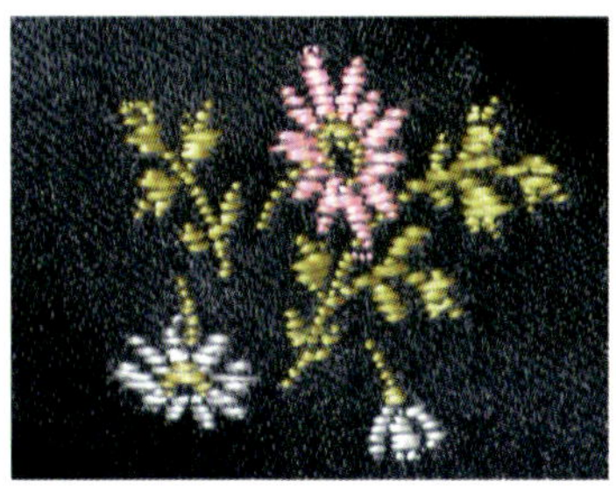

A woven sprig.

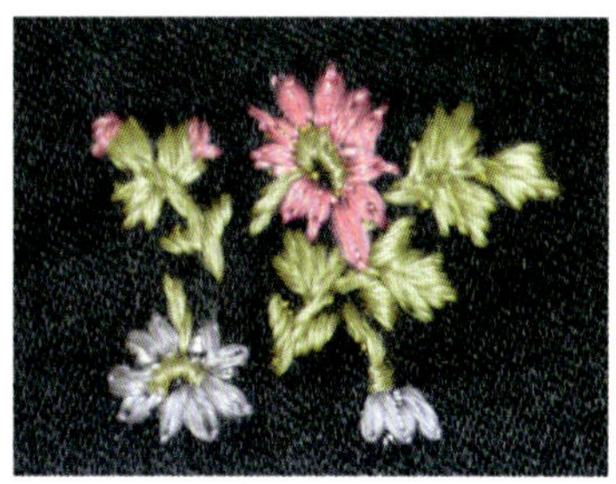

An over-embroidered sprig.

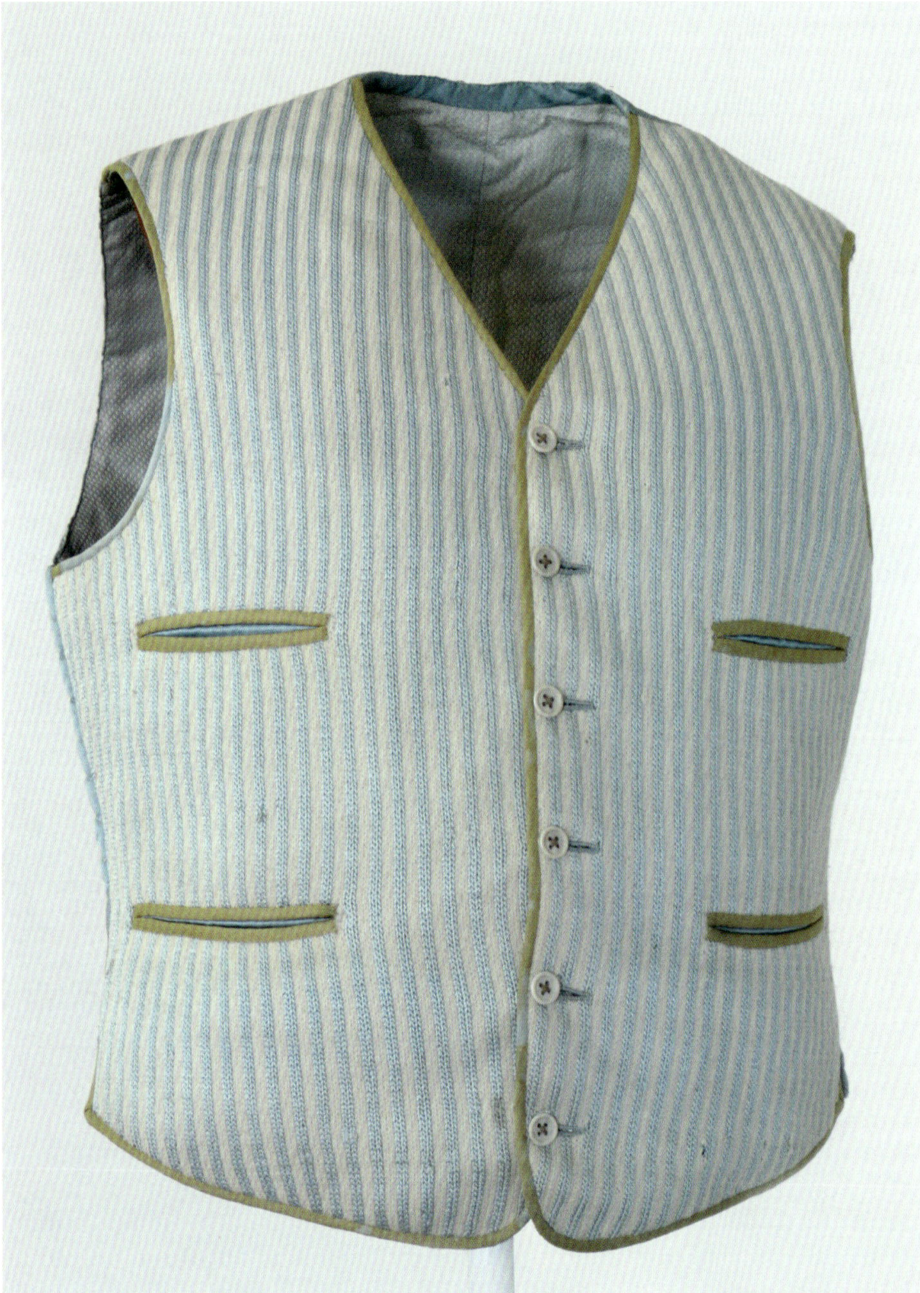

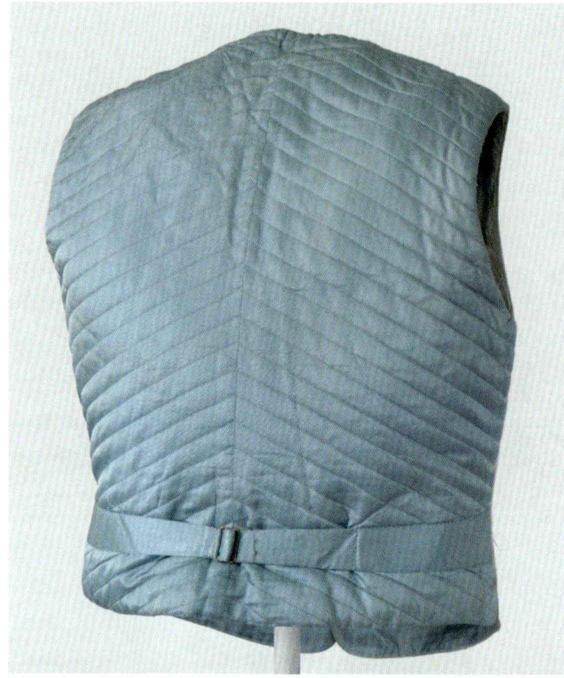

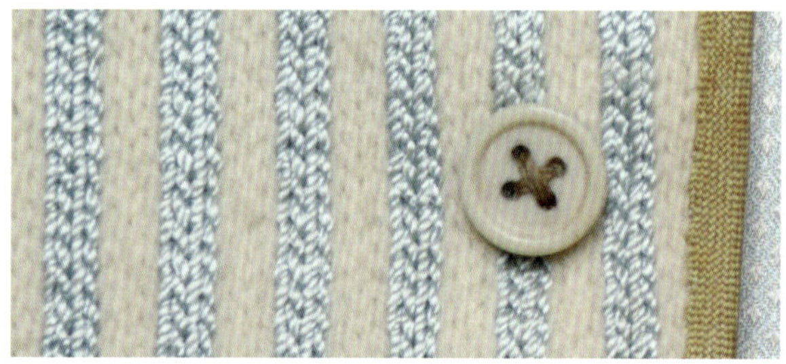

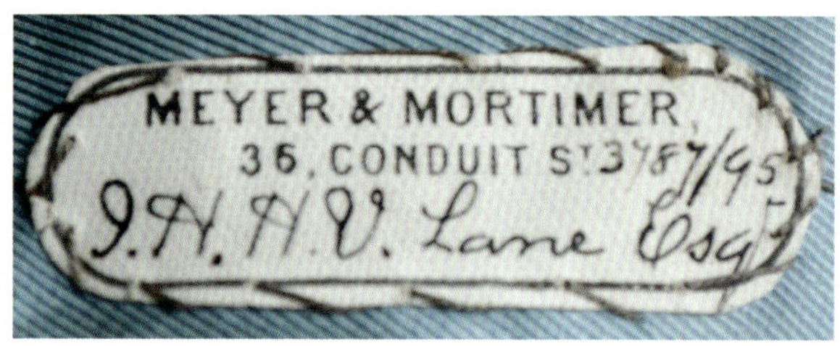

A waistcoat in ivory wool, 1895. HC.W-2.85-1

The foreparts are hand-knitted with stripes of pale blue silk. The edges of the foreparts and the pockets are bound with khaki silk plaited braid and there are six vegetable ivory buttons (page 211). It is lined with pale blue silk which has a tiny ivory diamond pattern, and the quilted back is in pale blue silk twill with a backstrap and a brass buckle to adjust the waist. It was made for John Henry Hervey Vincent Lane by Meyer & Mortimer, whose label is sewn inside one of the straps.

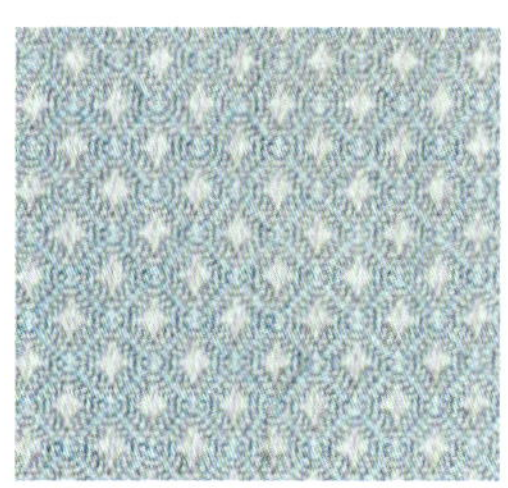

The figured silk lining.

Jonathan Meyer, from Austria, established a tailoring business in Conduit Street, London, in the 1790s. He flourished, making clothes for the Prince Regent and Beau Brummell among many others, and received his first royal warrant in 1820. At the same time, the Mortimer family, in Edinburgh, was specialising in military outfitting, and in the 1830s they merged, forming the company Meyer & Mortimer. The original premises in Conduit Street were bombed in the Second World War, but the firm continues to this day in Sackville Street.

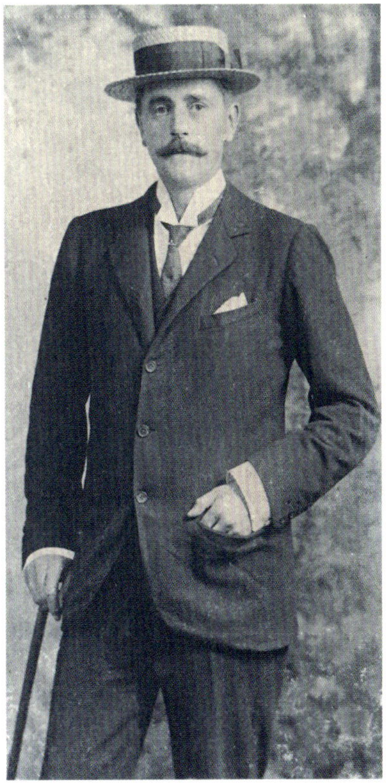

John Henry Hervey Vincent Lane (1867-1917).

Known as "Harry" in his family, John was the last of the line of Lanes who lived at the manor of Kings Bromley in Staffordshire, where they farmed and also managed the village. They came to the estate as a result of their ancestor, Jane Lane, saving the life of the future King Charles II, by smuggling him off the battlefield of Worcester, dressed as her servant, in 1651.

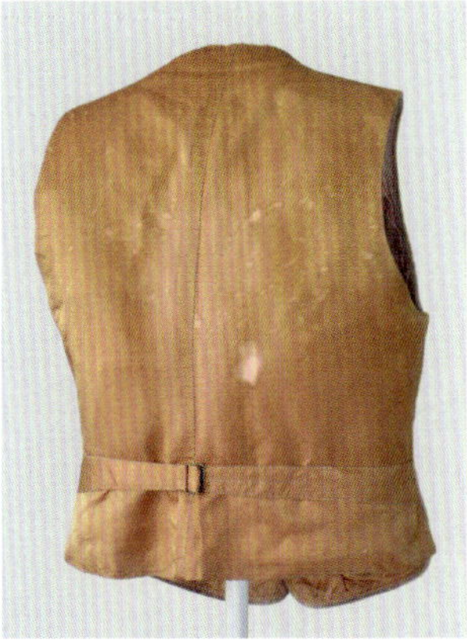

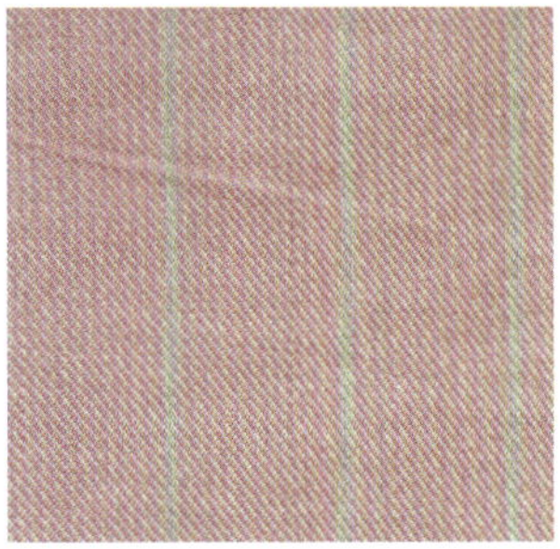

The striped silk twill lining.

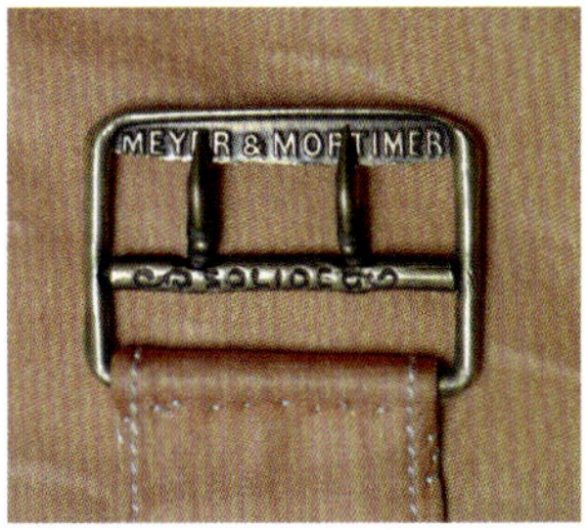

The buckle on the backstrap.

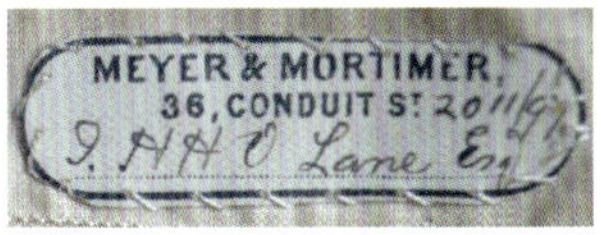

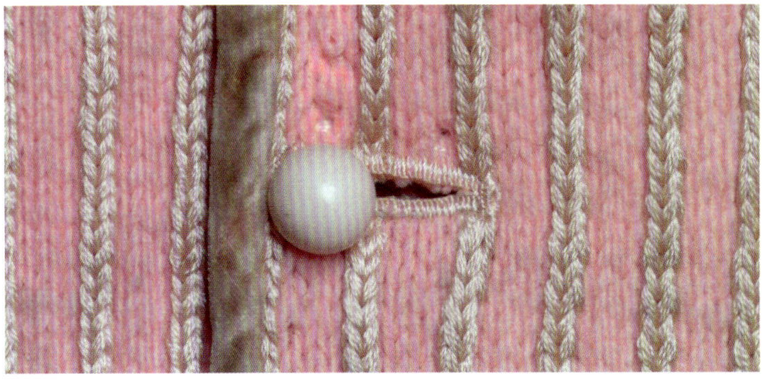

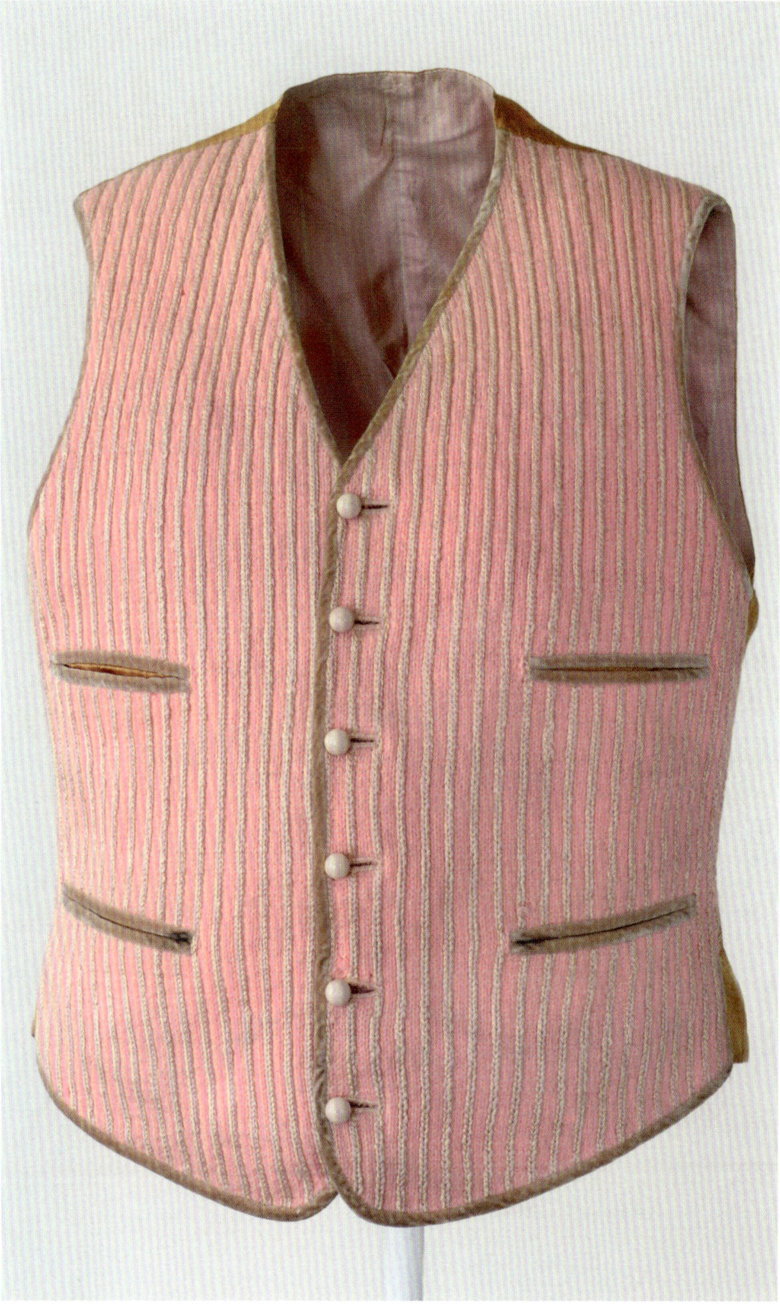

A waistcoat in pink wool, 1897. HC.W-2.85-2

It is hand-knitted with stripes of peach-coloured silk. The edges of the foreparts and the pockets are bound with beige silk velvet and there are six pale pink highly domed vegetable ivory buttons The lining is pink silk twill with an ivory stripe, and the back is in cinnamon silk satin with a backstrap and a brass buckle to adjust the waist. Marks from a watch chain can be seen on the corners of the lower pockets. It was made for John Henry Hervey Vincent Lane by Meyer & Mortimer, whose label is sewn on the inside of one of the straps; their name also appears on the buckle at the back.

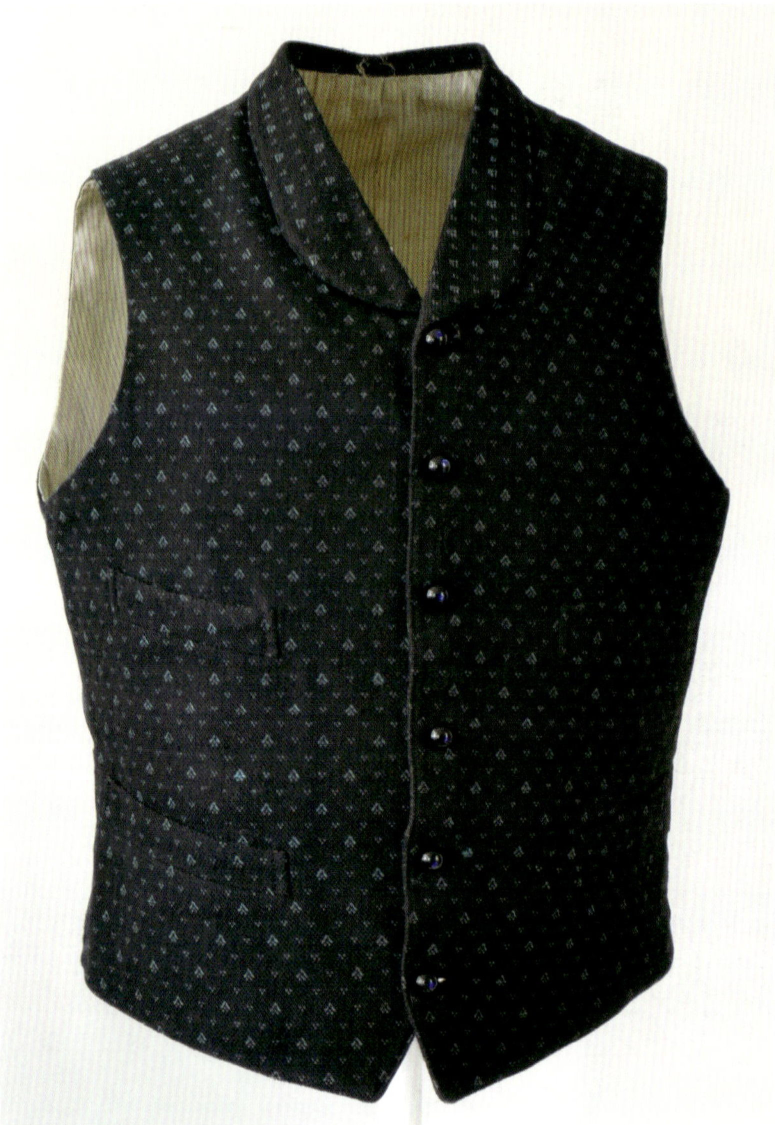

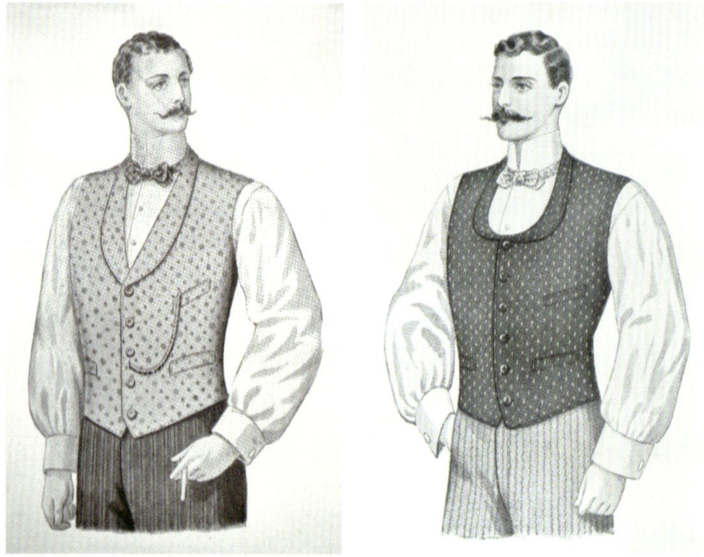

Fashion drawings from *The Tailor and Cutter*, 1898.

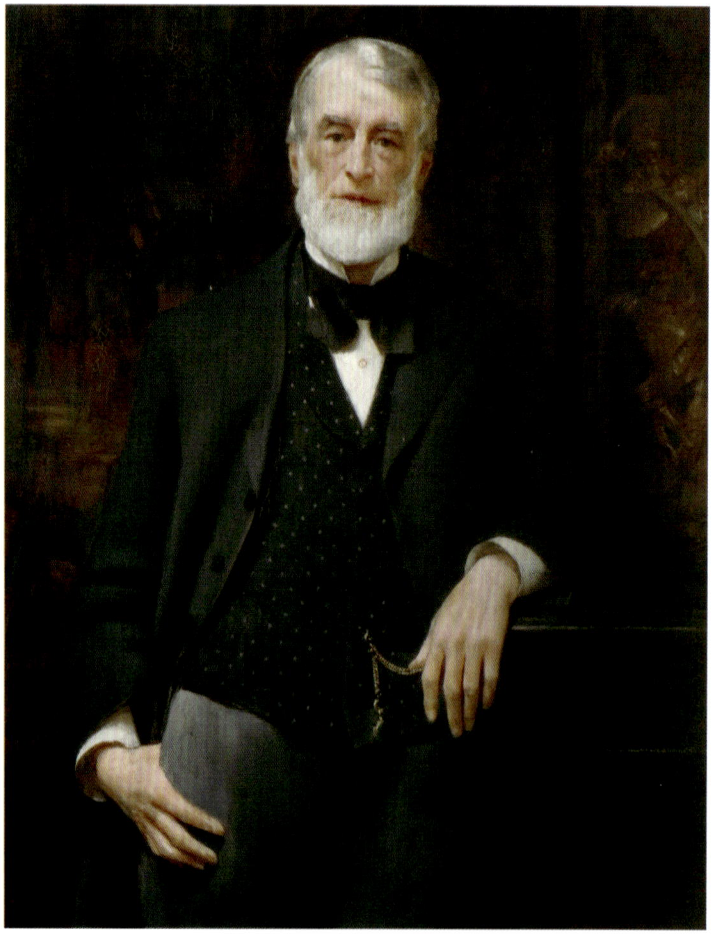

Alderman George Ridgway by Edwin Arthur Ward, 1898. Image courtesy of The Potteries Museum & Art Gallery, Stoke-on-Trent.

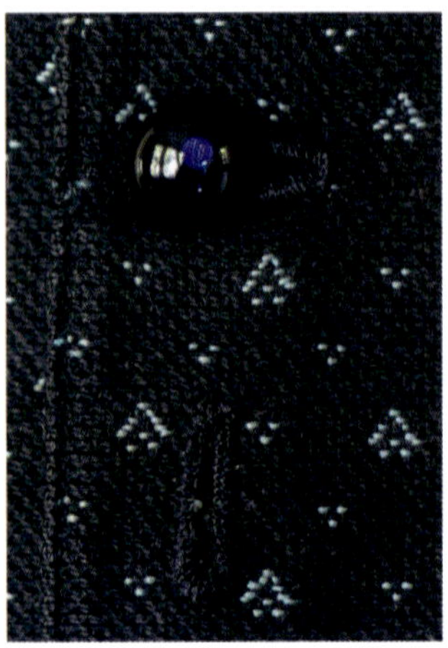

A waistcoat in black wool hopsack, 1890-1900. HC.W-9.15-1

The wool has a woven pattern of dots arranged in groups, in blue silk. The six removable buttons are black glass balls with a blue spot at the top. The lining is ivory cotton satin with a narrow pale blue printed stripe, and the back is in black silk twill with a backstrap and a black metal buckle to adjust the waist (page 210); the back fabric is stitched over the lower edge of the back of the collar. There is a vertical buttonhole, between the second and third buttonholes down from the top, to attach a watch chain.

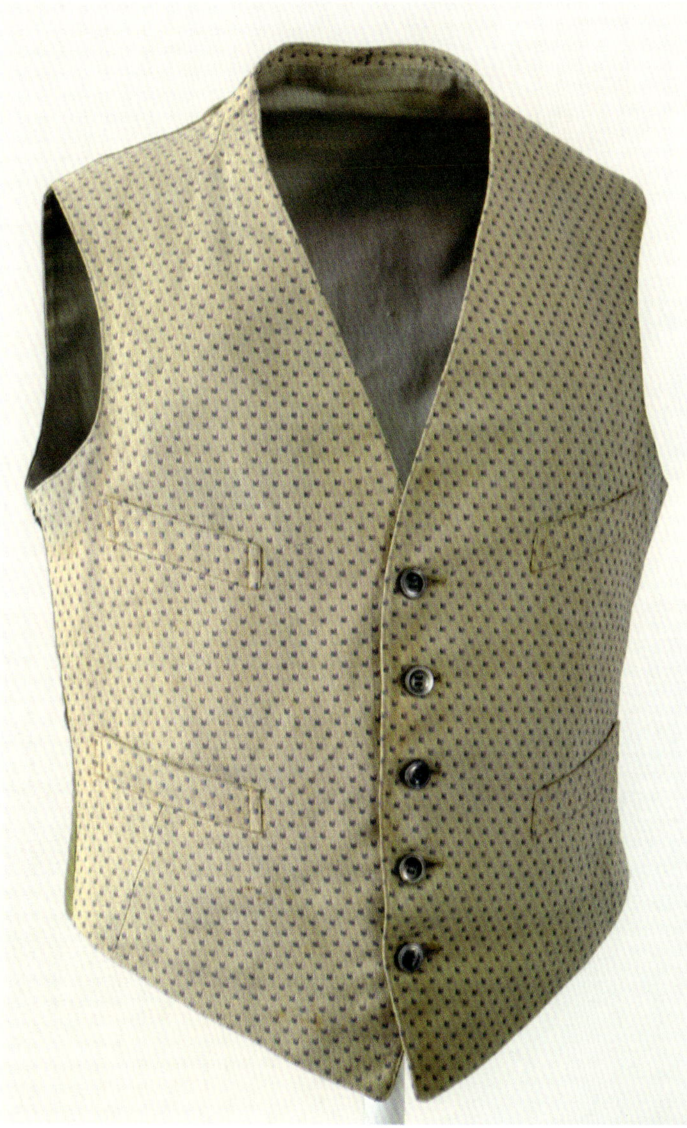

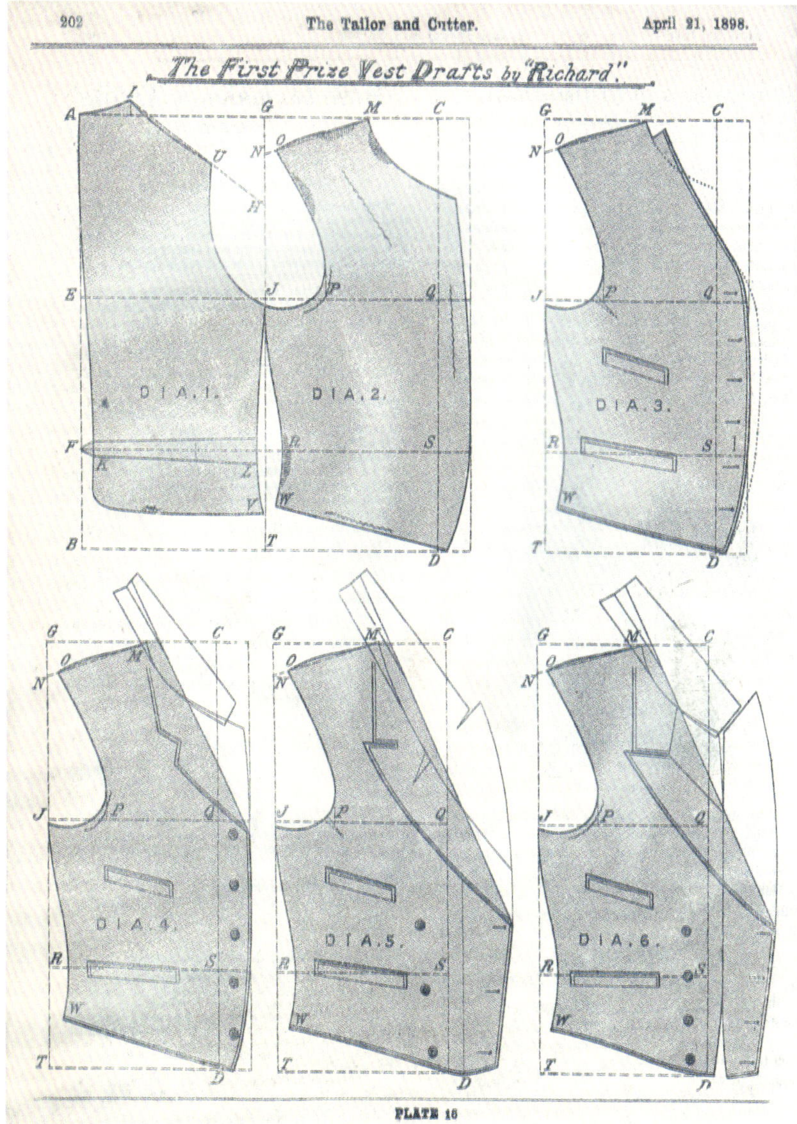

A waistcoat in fawn silk hopsack, 1890-1900. HC.W-3,15-2

The silk has a pattern of tiny squares diagonally divided in blue and mauve. The five buttons are dark pearl (page 216). The lining is pale grey silk twill with a printed very fine black diagonal line, and the back is in khaki-coloured cotton sateen, with a backstrap and a black metal buckle to adjust the waist. There is no collar, but a band round the back of the neck is sewn into a V-shaped notch at the top of the foreparts.

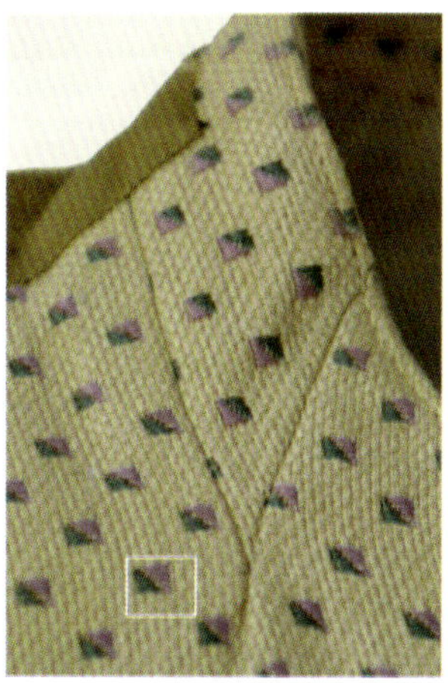

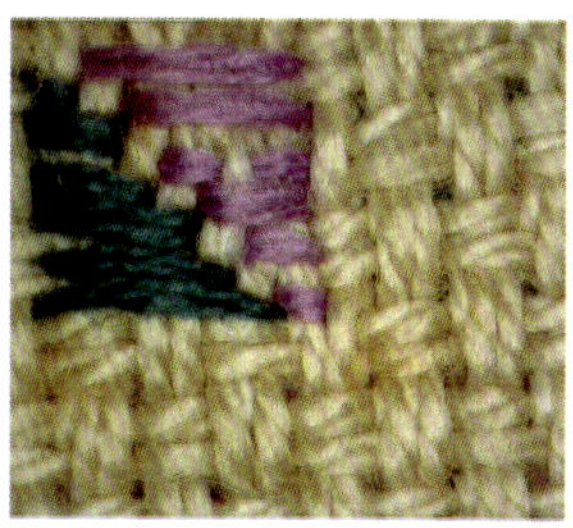

Above: Detail of the fabric, outlined on the left.

Right and top right: Articles in *The Tailor and Cutter* 1898.

Fancy Vests.

Now that it is fashionable for coats to be worn open fancy vests are once more a feature of gent's dress. These are made both in S.B. and D.B. styles. Of the step-roll and no-collar types tastes are pretty well divided, though, for Summer vests, the latter style is thinner, and, in the case of washing vests, much easier to get up.

Many exceedingly neat and stylish materials are being shown for these garments. Spotted cords and Cashmeres are much worn. Fancy silks are all the rage with Frock suits, and when cut in D.B. form are very dressy.

We think it is well for the bespoke tailor to cultivate this class of trade; it is a splendid opportunity for the introduction of a little brightness into the suit, and so livening up the complete outfit.

A marked feature in these vests is the buttons; stone, onyx, fancy glass, &c., are amongst the materials used.

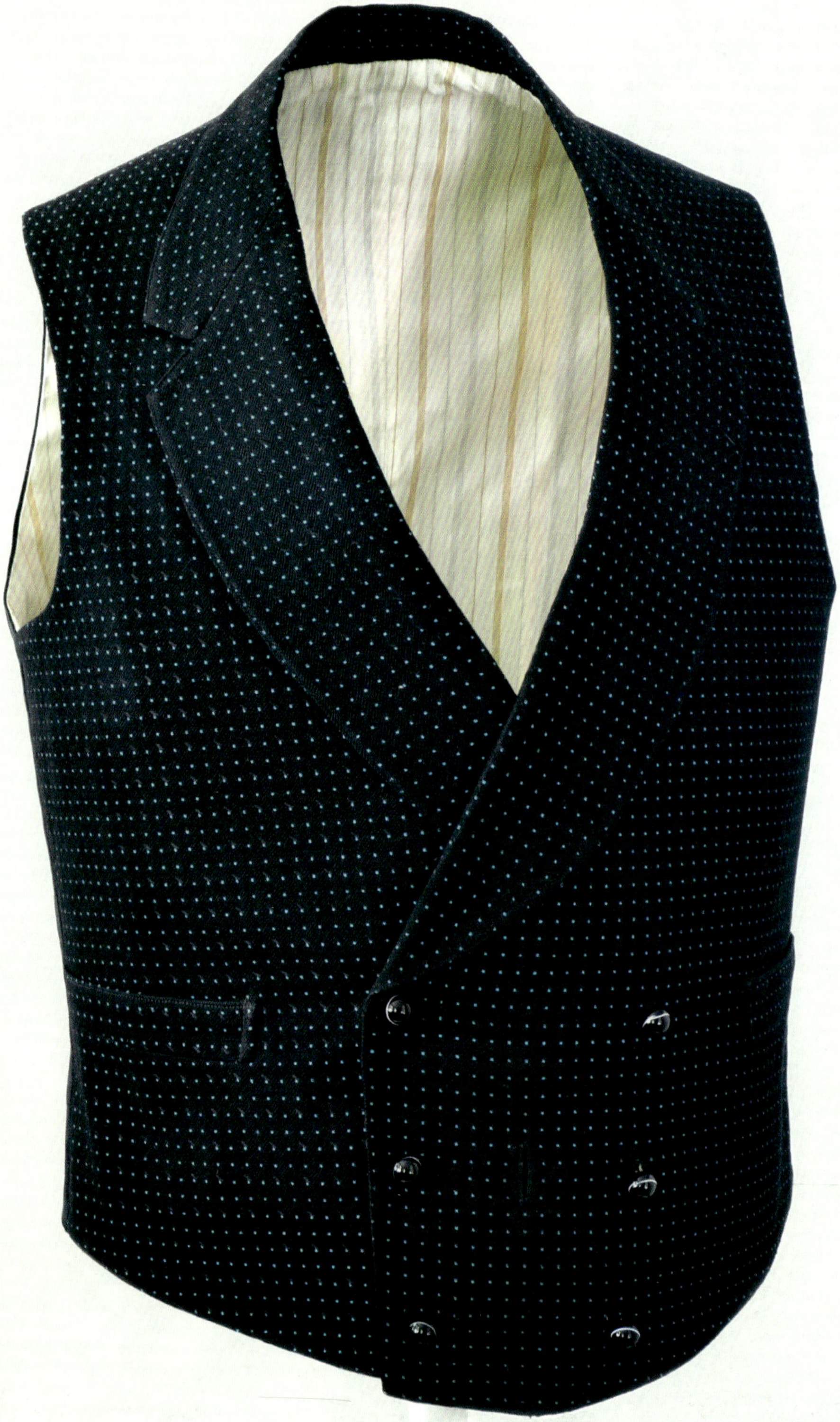

A waistcoat of black wool, 1895-1910. HC.W-5.97-3

The wool is in a herringbone weave with a pattern of dots in pale blue and black silk. The waistcoat has a step collar and two welted pockets. It is double-breasted with three pairs of onyx ball buttons, which are removable and secured on the inside with split pins (page 211). There is a vertical buttonhole in the centre, between the middle pair of buttons, for a watch chain to be attached. The back is black cotton sateen and the lining is ivory cotton sateen with printed stripes of pale orange and grey; there is a backstrap with a black buckle to adjust the waist.

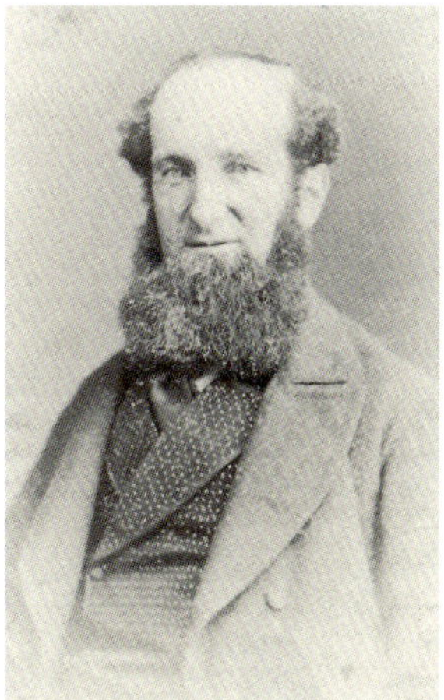

Unknown man, 1885-1895.

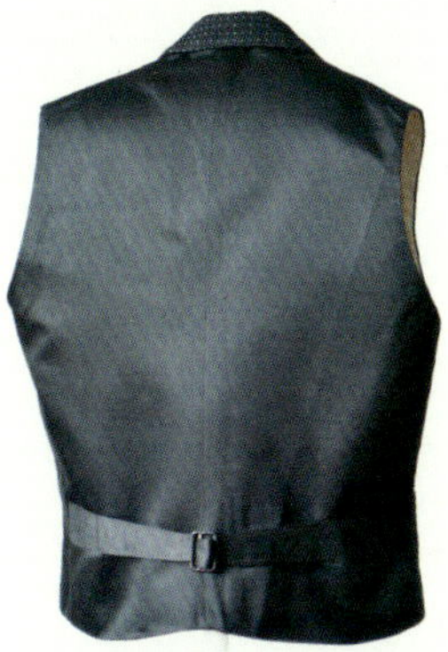

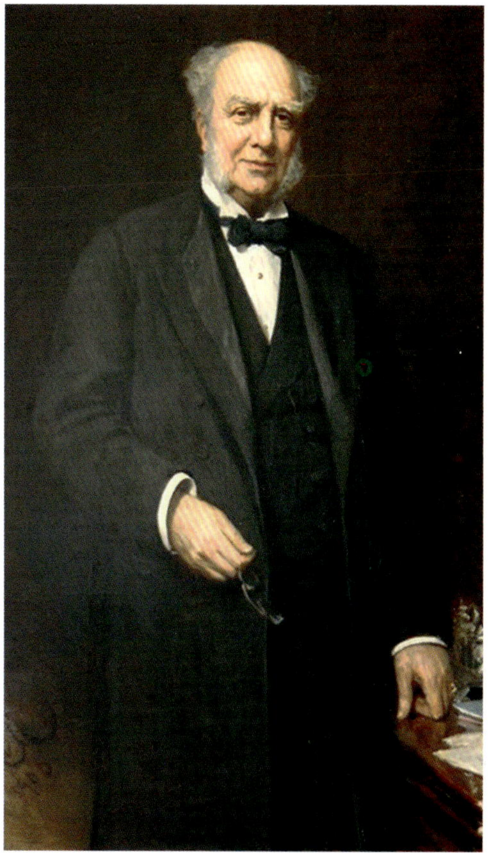

Portrait of an Unknown Gentleman by Hubert von Herkomer, 1906, the Institute Building in Caernarfon.

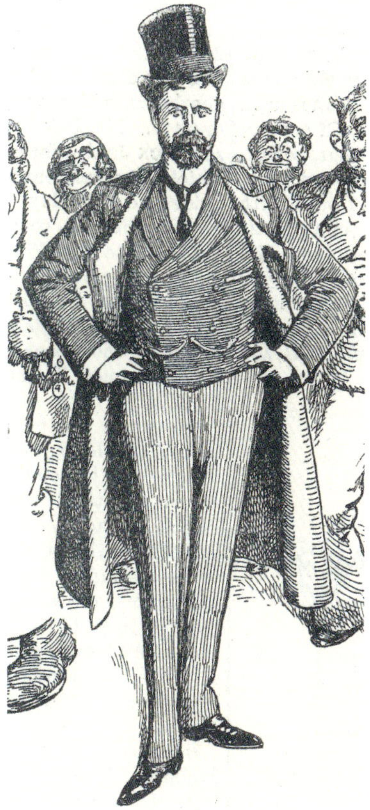

Detail from a cartoon in *Punch*, 1901.

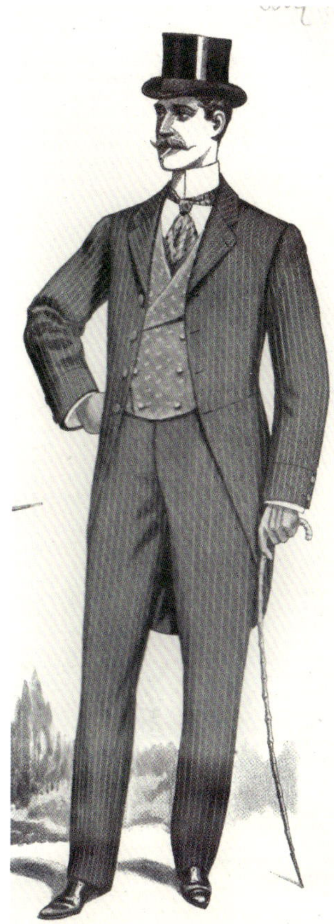

Fashion drawing from *The Tailor and Cutter*, 1898.

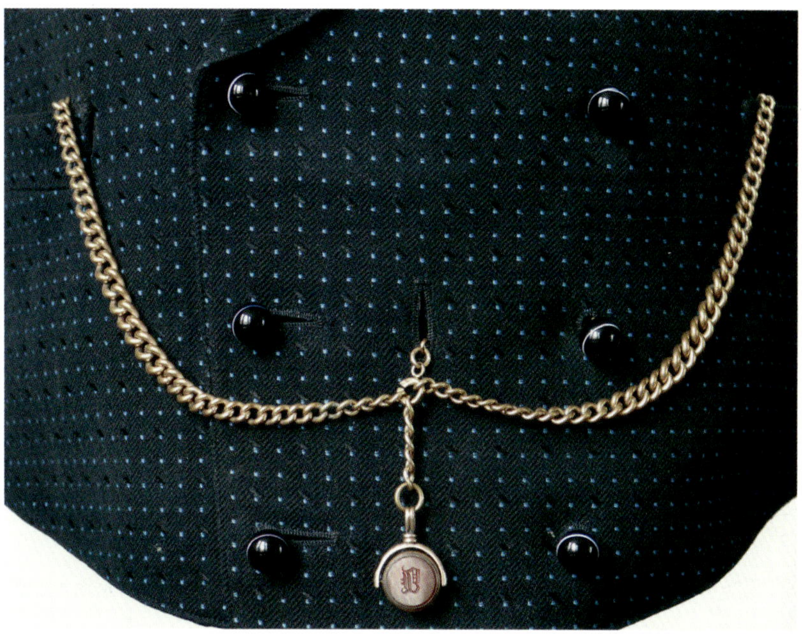

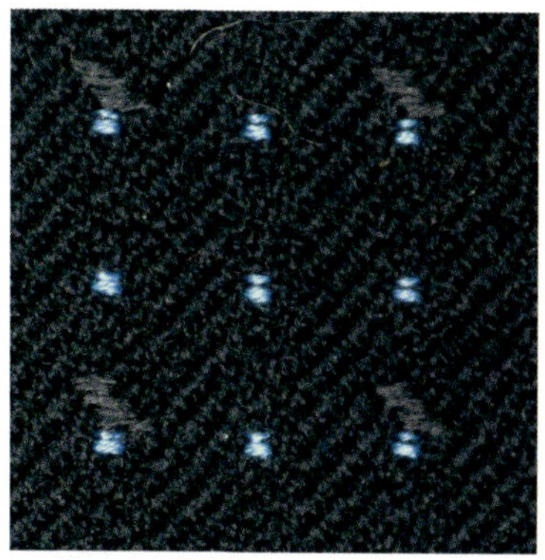

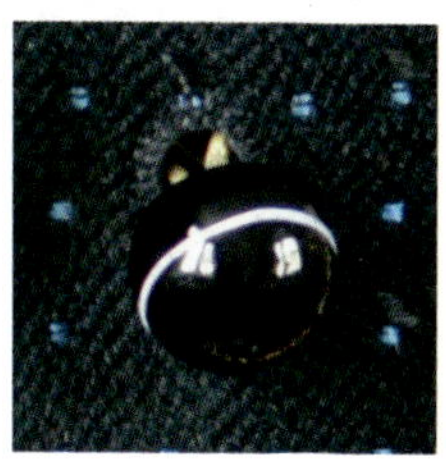

Right: A selection of onyx and other removable ball buttons.

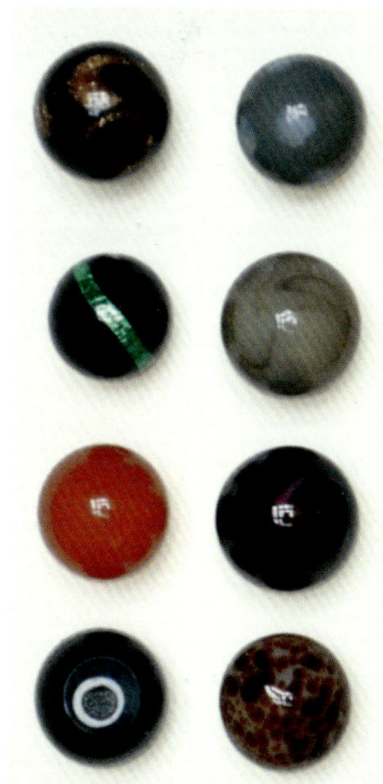

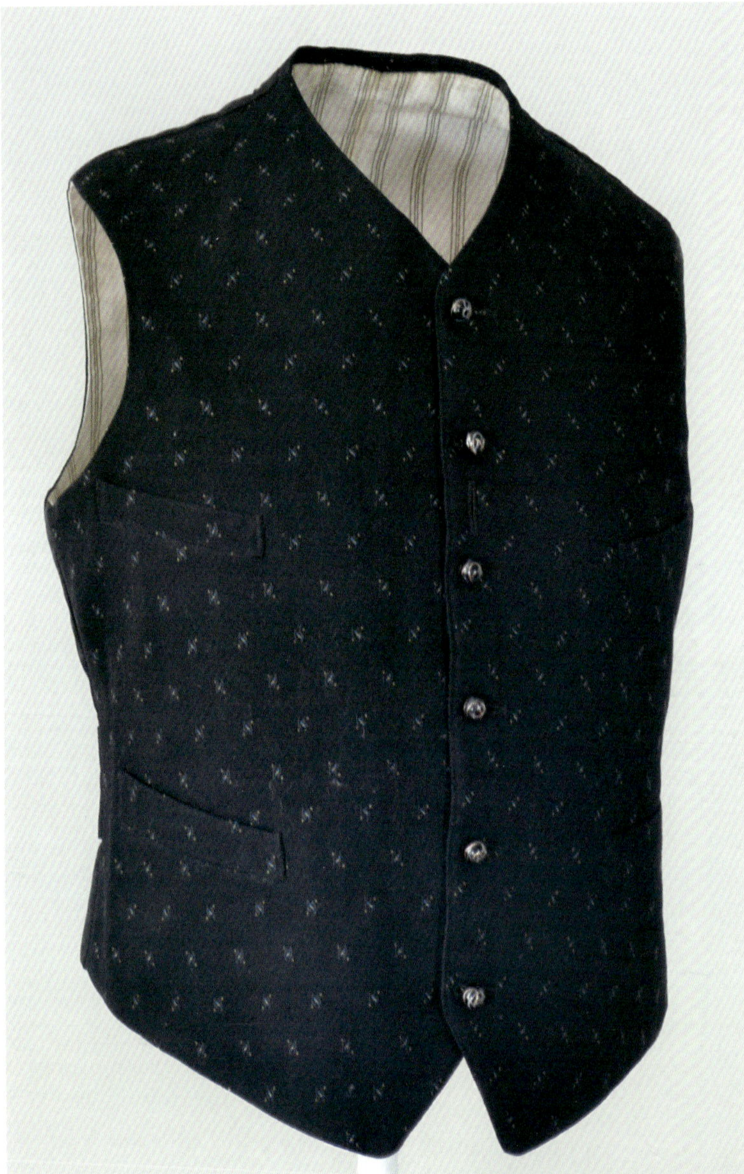

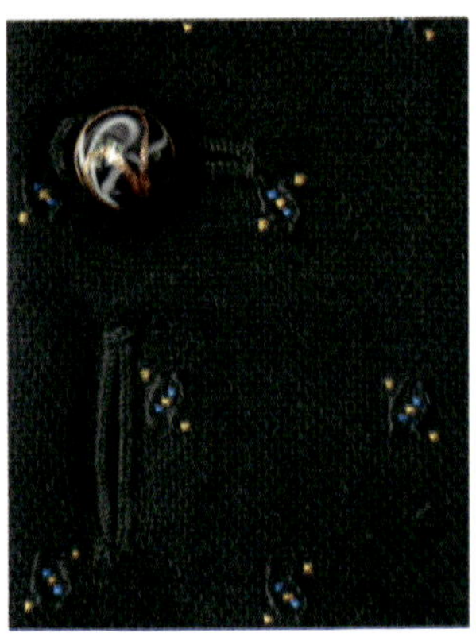

A waistcoat in black wool hopsack, 1895-1910. HC.W-7.89-4

The wool has a woven pattern in silk of blue and yellow dots in a black oblong. The removable ball buttons are black glass with a swirly pattern in grey and gold (page 216). The lining is ivory cotton sateen with narrow brown printed stripes, and the back is black cotton satin with a backstrap and a black buckle to adjust the waist. There is a vertical buttonhole to attach a watch chain.

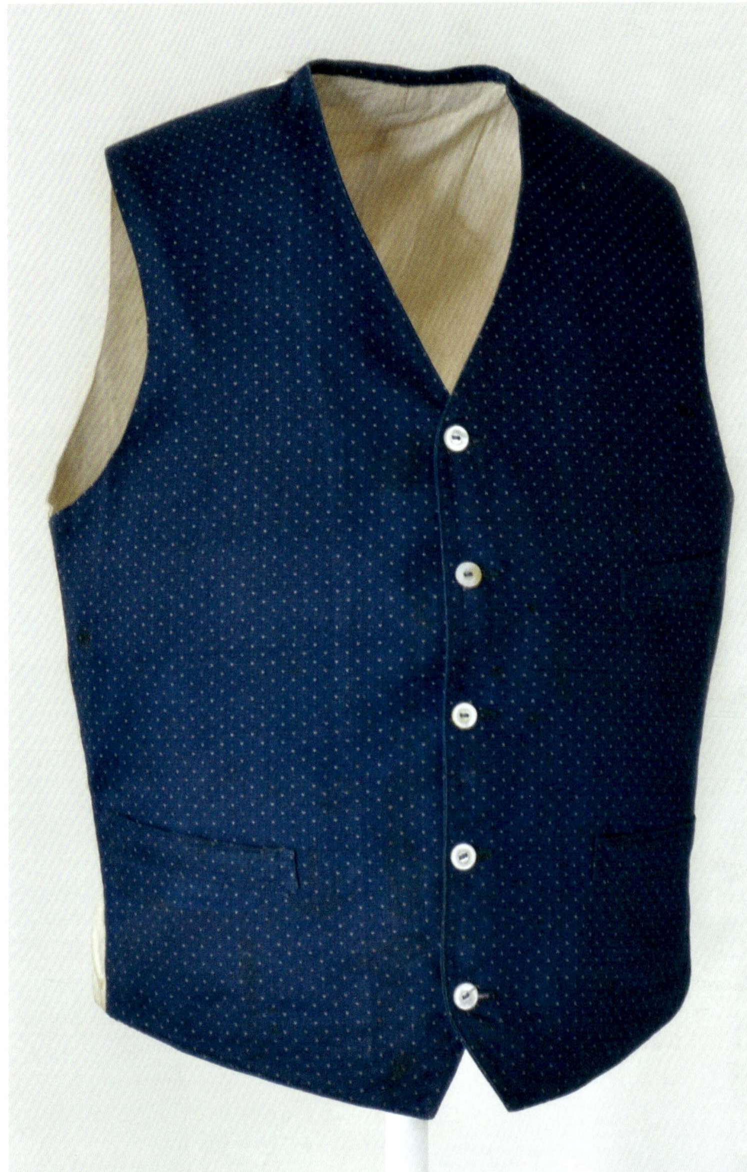

A waistcoat in dark blue cotton, 1895-1910. HC.W-5.94

The cotton has a woven pattern of self and ivory spots, and there are five pearl buttons. The lining and the back are in plain white cotton, and the waist adjustment is by a backstrap with a metal buckle which is removable; the strap to hold the buckle has a buttonhole at the end, which passes through the buckle and is fastened by a linen button.

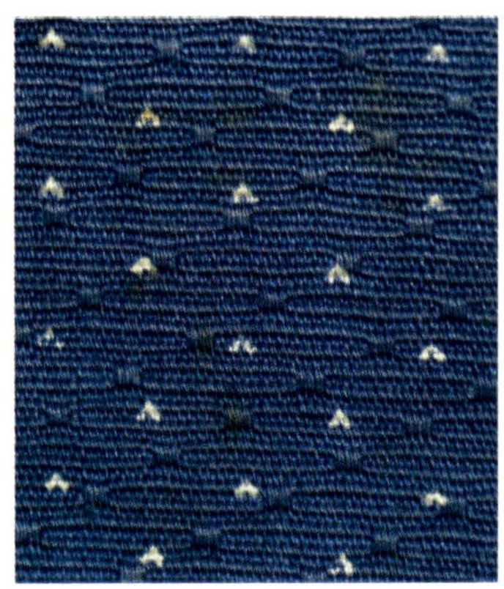

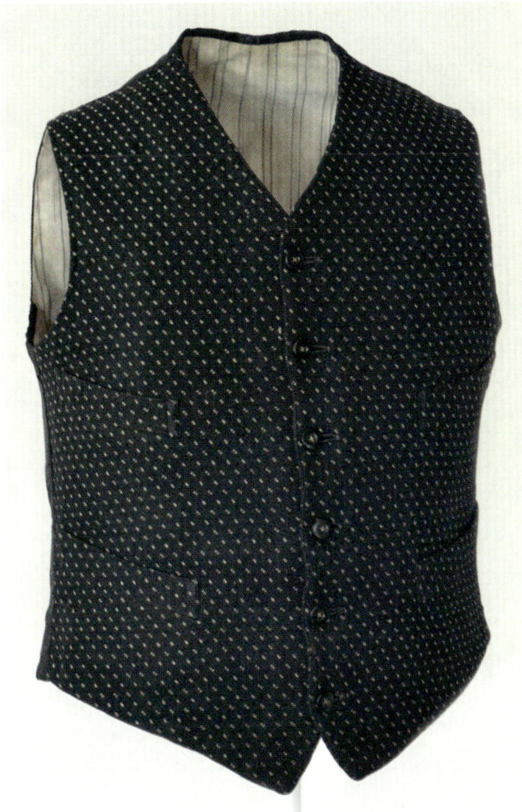

***Left:* A waistcoat in black wool twill, 1895-1910.** HC.W-0.88

The wool has a woven pattern of double dots in ivory. The six removable buttons are black vegetable ivory with a gilt cross in the centre to resemble stitching. The lining is ivory cotton sateen with double black broken stripes, and the back is in black silk twill with a backstrap and a black metal buckle to adjust the waist.

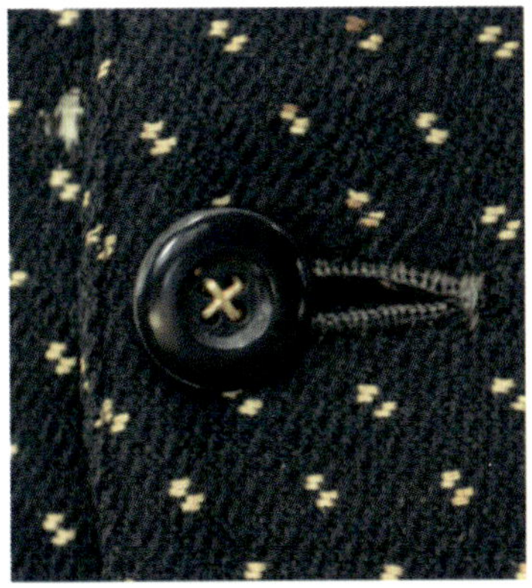

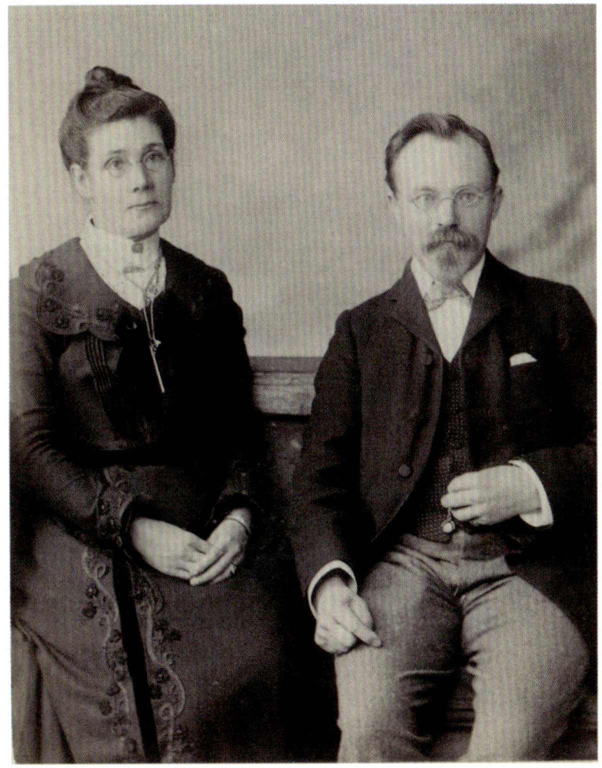

Edmund Cole, a master printer in London, and his wife, Ellen, *c.*1900.

Right: Edwin Russell (1863-1922) at his tailoring business at 85, Rectory Grove, Clapham, London, *c.*1900. His father, George Russell (1825-1898) was listed as a journeyman tailor in central London in the 1851 census; he established his own business in Clapham in 1852, and advertised it as "From Jermyn St." over the door. Jermyn Street has been a centre for fashionable menswear since Charles II authorised Henry Jermyn, Earl of St. Albans, to develop the area in 1664.

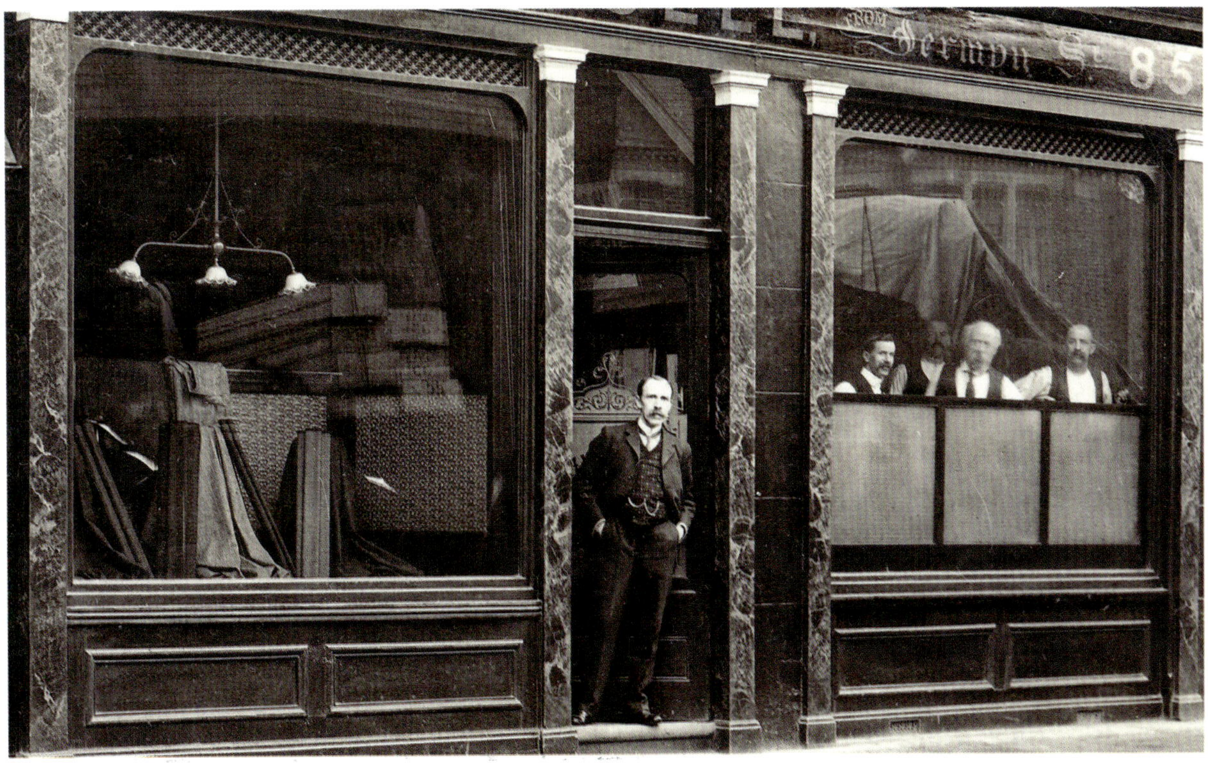

Edmund Cole, pictured above right, lived less than a mile away, and the families knew each other; it is possible that Edmund Cole was a customer of Edwin Russell's tailoring business.

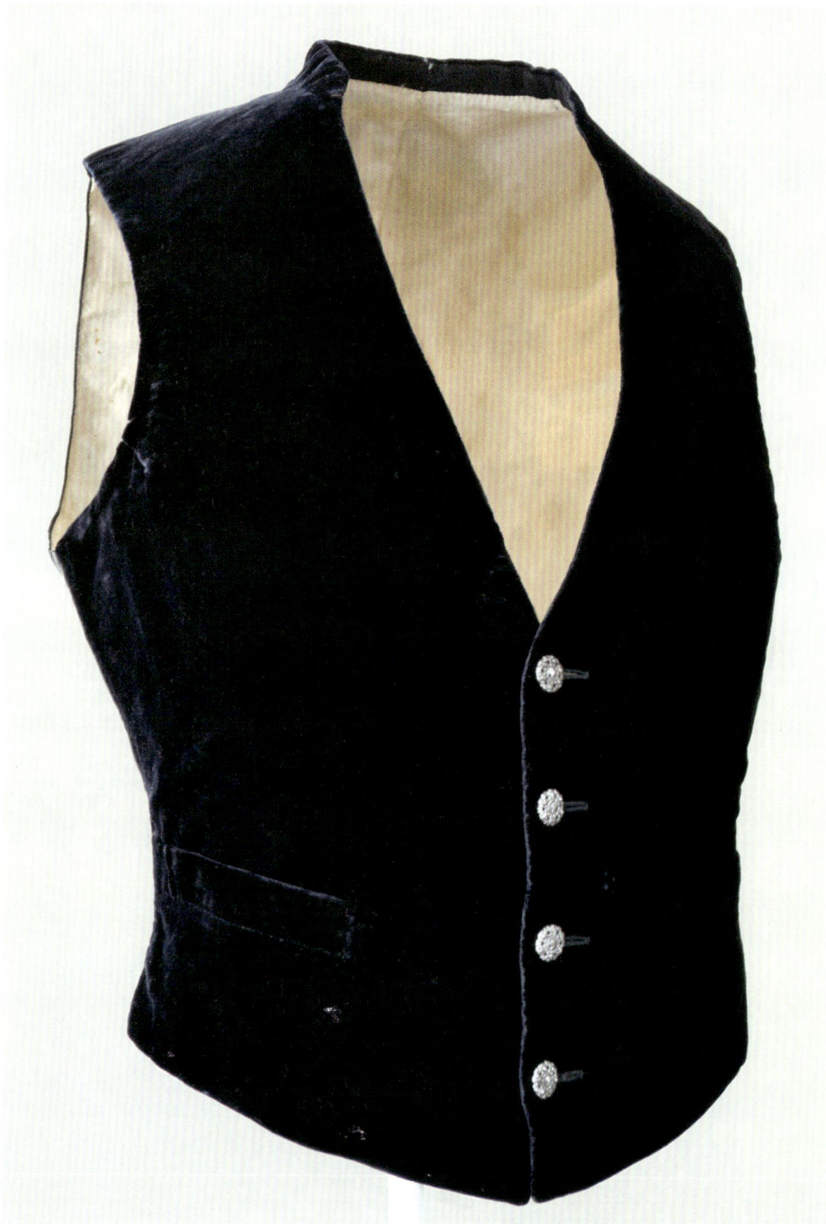

A waistcoat in black velvet, 1900-1910.
HC.W-5.74

This is part of a court dress suit, and has a small stand collar and four cut-steel buttons. The lining is plain cream cotton and the back is in black silk satin with a backstrap and a brass buckle to adjust the waist. The tailor's label (right) is on the inside of one of the straps; it says William Scott, 2, Lower Sackville St., Dublin, and Scott, Dublin is embossed on the buckle. It was made for Captain Verschoyle.

Captain Frederick Thomas Verschoyle (1853-1936) was a career soldier and a magistrate for County Limerick, Ireland.

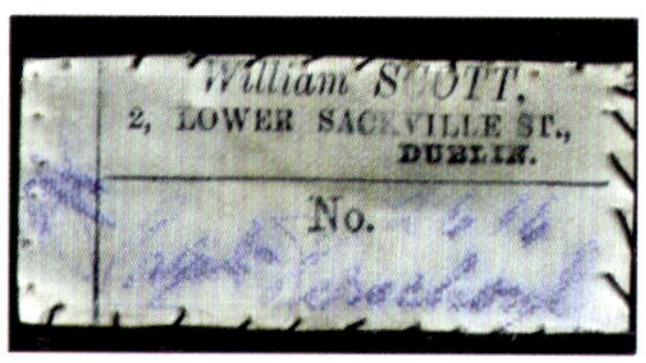

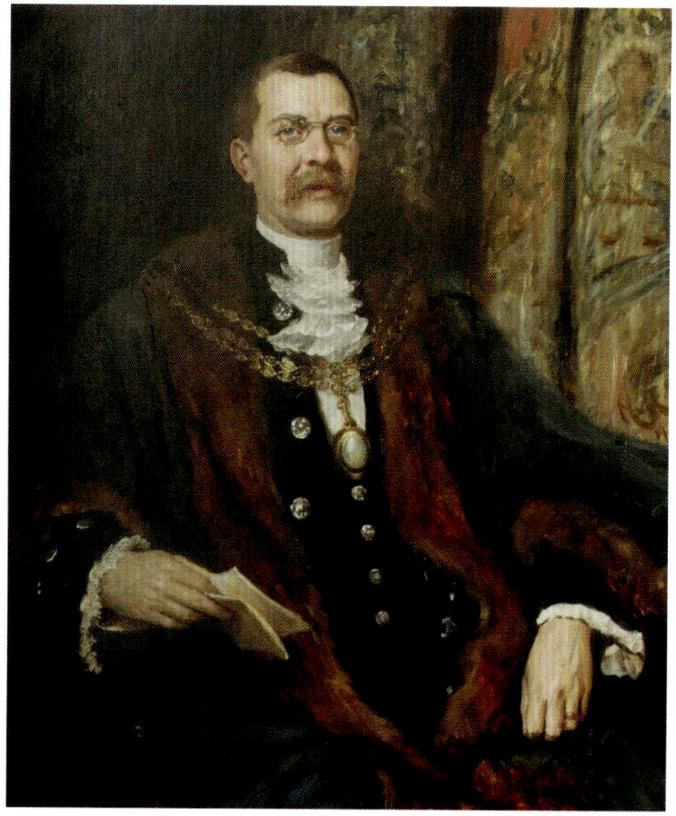

Alderman Sir George Hussey by Hubert von Herkomer, 1901
Southampton City Art Gallery, Hampshire, U.K.

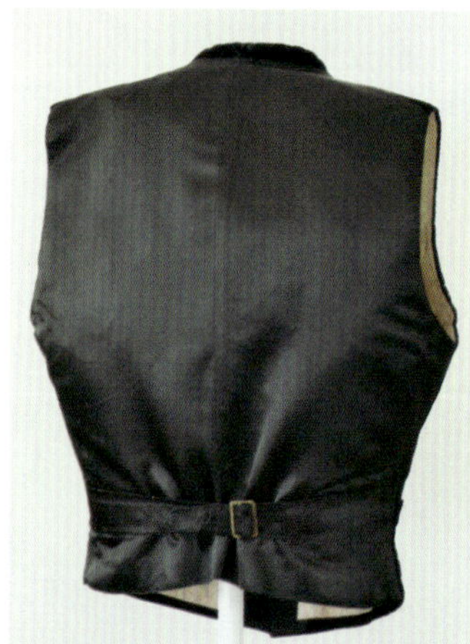

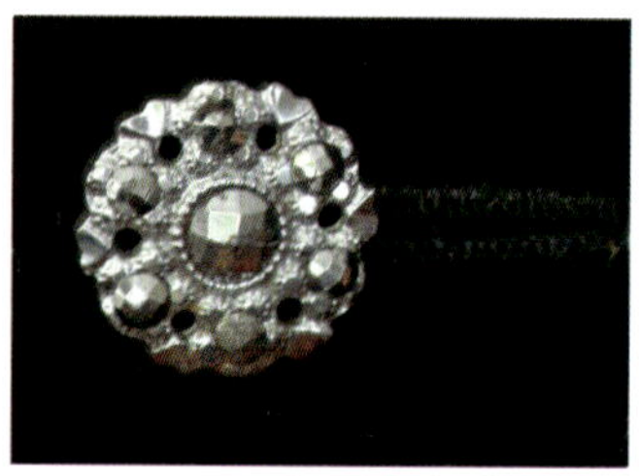

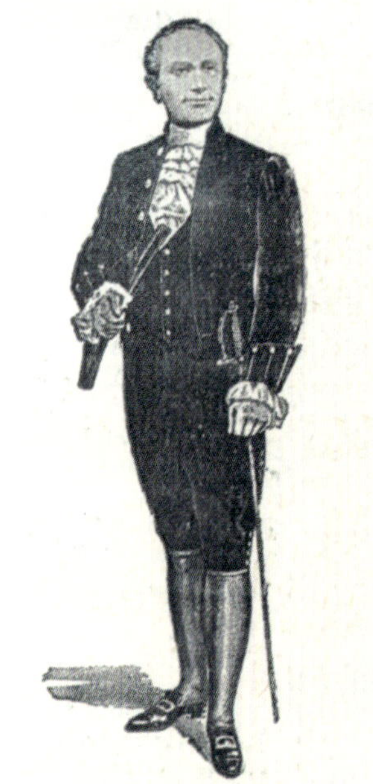

Illustration of court dress in *The Tailor and Cutter*, 1898.

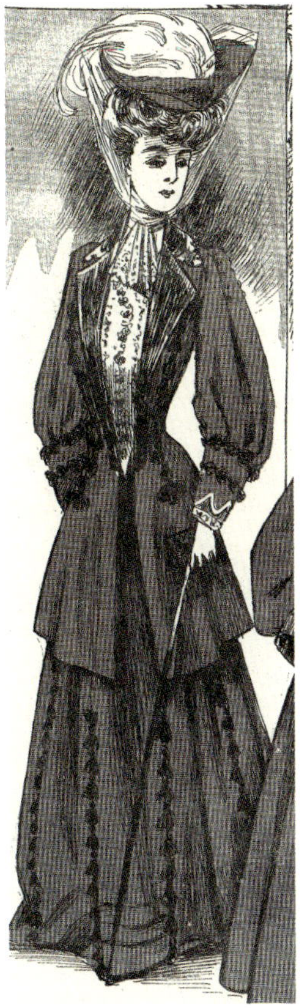

Fashion drawing in *Femina*, 1904.

"A charming plan for these vests which are now so fashionable is to make them of any old embroidery which one may have at hand." Article in *The Lady's World*, 1908.

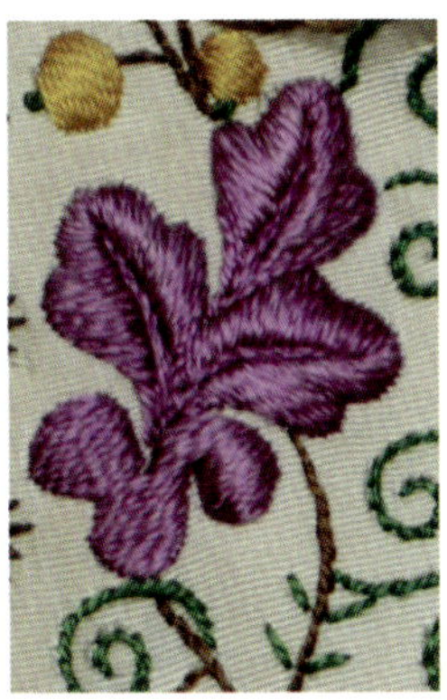

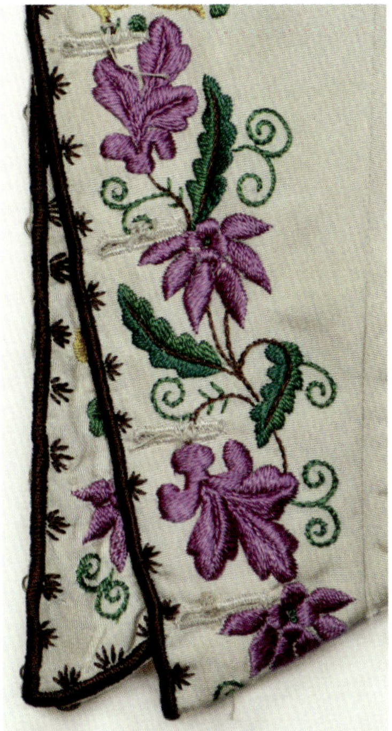

The bottom of the left front edge, with the inserted piece; the sewn-up original buttonholes can be seen.

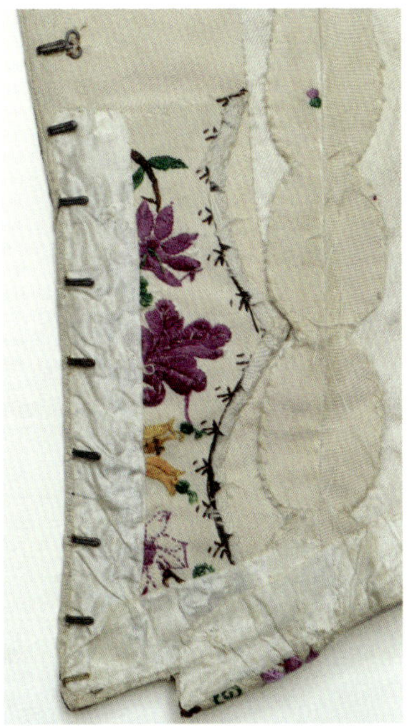

Inside the right front edge, showing the original pocket flap, sewn on to show at the front waist.

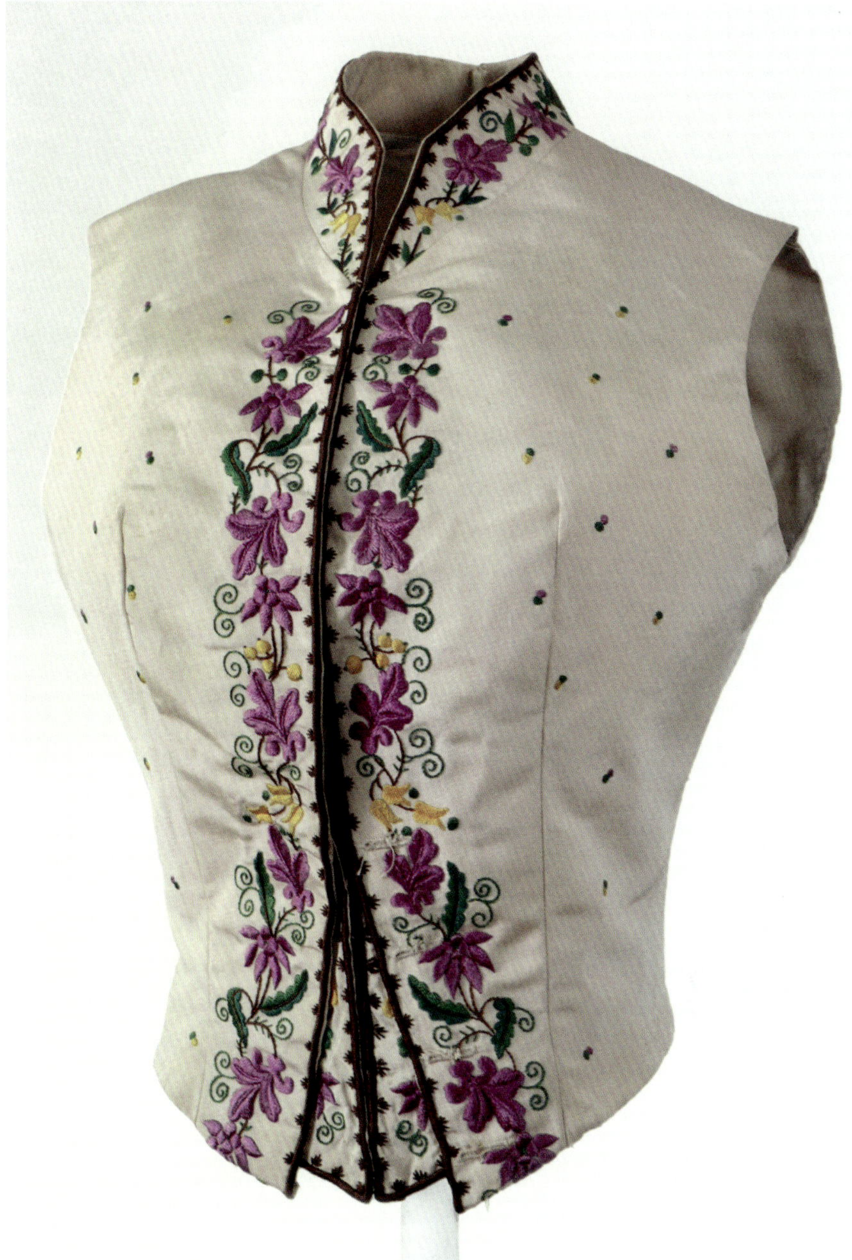

A woman's waistcoat in cream silk faille, 1900-1910. HC.W-0.83

It has been made out of a man's court dress waistcoat from the mid-nineteenth century; the regulations for court dress changed to a plainer style at the end of the 1860s, and this is an example of re-cycling. The waistcoat has been shortened and the four original buttonholes have been sewn up; the foreparts are now fastened by hooks and eyes, which go right up to the stand collar. The inserted pieces at the waist are made from the pocket flaps of the original waistcoat, sewn on to the inside front edges. There are darts in the front, from the waist to the bust, and the side seams are boned, as is the left front edge. The back and the lining are in white silk twill.

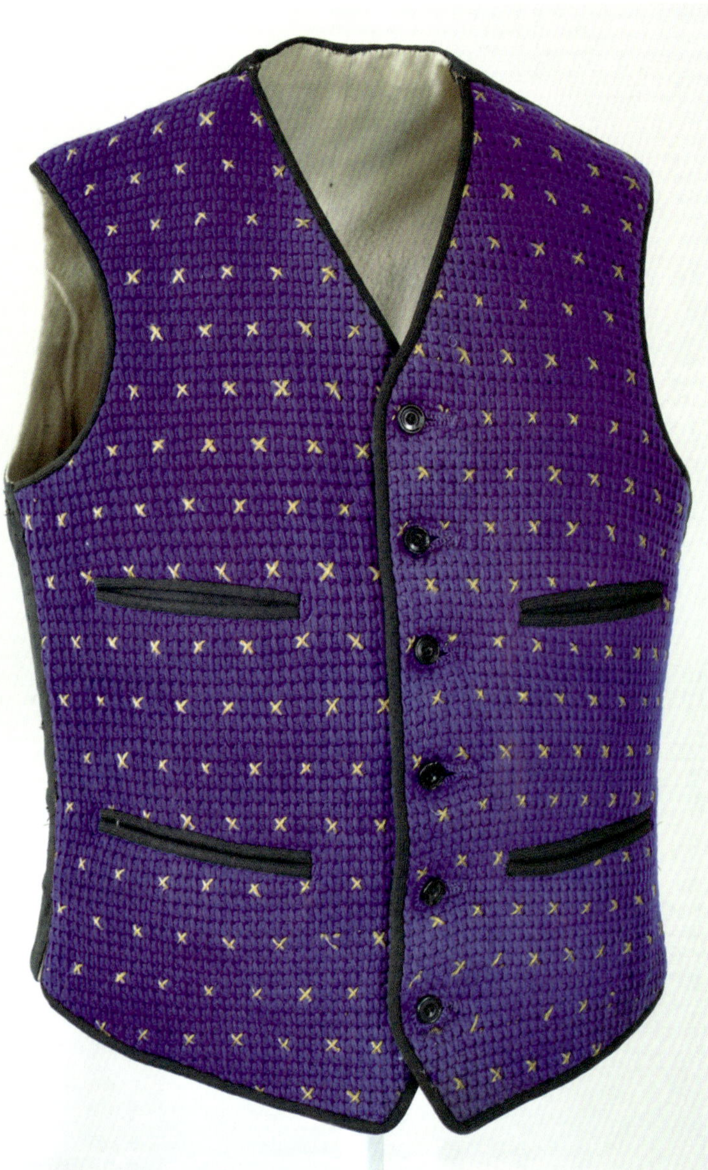

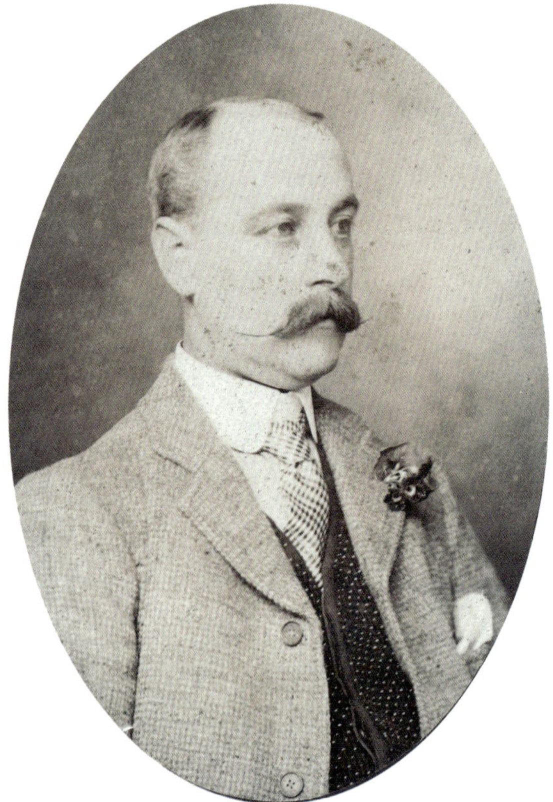

Unknown man, 1895-1905.

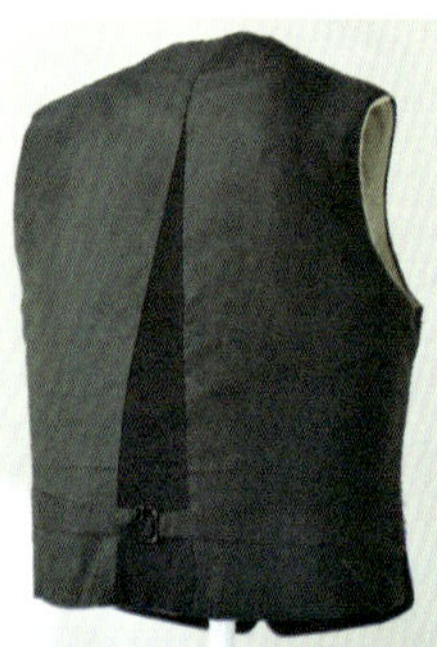

No. XLVII.

GENTLEMAN'S TRICÔT WAIST-COAT IN WOOL AND SILK.

Materials:—1 lb. 8-thread Berlin Wool (a dark colour), 2 doz. skeins Pearsall's Washing Filoselle, Red, or any bright colour. Tricot Hook, No. 6.

THIS well-known stitch is one of the best for gentlemen's waistcoats, and the simplest method is to work a straight piece of tricôt of the required length and width. This should be afterwards cut and shaped by a tailor, who makes the proper incisions for the pockets.

Make a chain of 63 (more or less, according to the width required, but this is a good average number). Proceed to work in tricôt two pieces the required size. When these are finished, work in Filoselle, with a wool needle, a twisted stitch over the upright bars, passing the needle in a slanting direction from right to left under each bar.

N.B.—An experienced worker may prefer to cut out a waistcoat pattern of the required size in thick brown paper, and shape her work to it by increasing and decreasing in the ordinary way. This will take rather less wool.

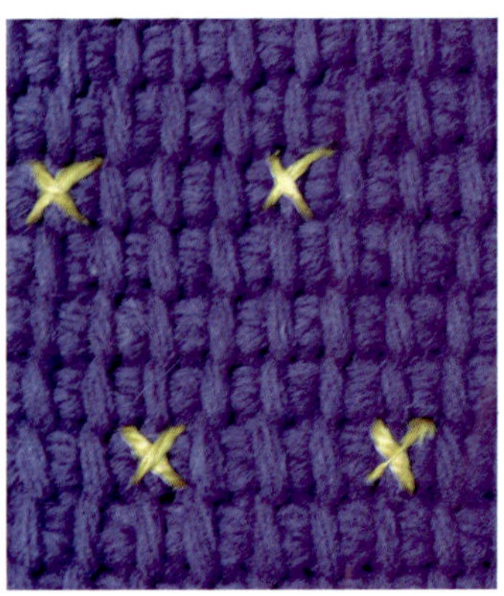

A waistcoat in violet wool, 1895-1910.
HC.W-5.88

The foreparts are made of tricot crochet with added crosses in yellow silk. The edges and pockets are bound with black silk plaited braid, and there are six black buttons. It is lined in cream wool, and the back is in black cotton sateen with a backstrap to adjust the waist. There is a gusset of black cotton satin in the centre back seam which has grey wool in the lining.

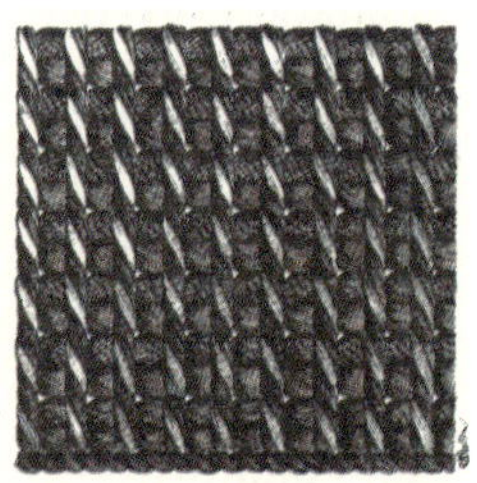

No. XLVII.

Illustration of the tricot in the instructions on the right.

Instructions for a tricot waistcoat in *Pearsall's Illustrated Handbook for Knitting in Silks*, 1902.

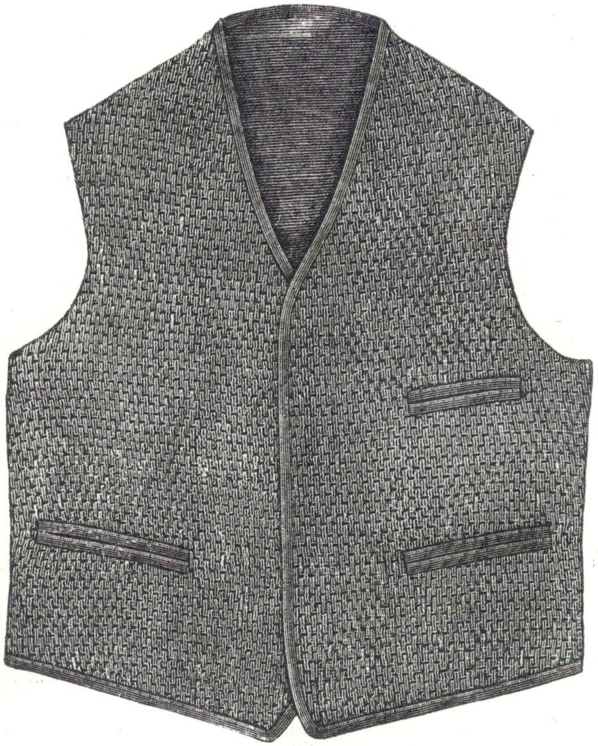

Gentleman's Waistcoat.

In Plain Knitting, with Embroidered Silk Spots.

Our engraving represents a waistcoat that anyone may quickly and easily make, as far as the knitting is concerned, for it is accomplished entirely in plain garter stitch, the effect of which is ultimately enriched by a multitude of tiny silk spots embroidered upon the fronts over every fourth stitch of the knitting, thus greatly adding to the beauty of the work, and making a really handsome waistcoat.

Materials required: From 12 ozs. to 14 ozs. of single Berlin wool, grey, tan colour, or brown, as preferred, and three long bone knitting needles No. 11, or if a loose knitter No. 12, or for an outside waistcoat No. 10; ½ oz. ball of bright blue knitting silk and crewel needle; 3 yards of striped linen twill for lining, 1 yard of sateen to face the fronts, and to make pockets and the band to place on the back to draw in the waist; 3 yards of silk braid for binding; six bone or smoked pearl buttons, and a skein of purse twist for working six buttonholes. But unless quite competent to complete the waistcoat creditably it will be best to send the knitting to a tailor to be made up, and he will find lining and other small belongings, and cut pocket holes, and finish the article far more skilfully and fashionably than it could possibly be if home made.

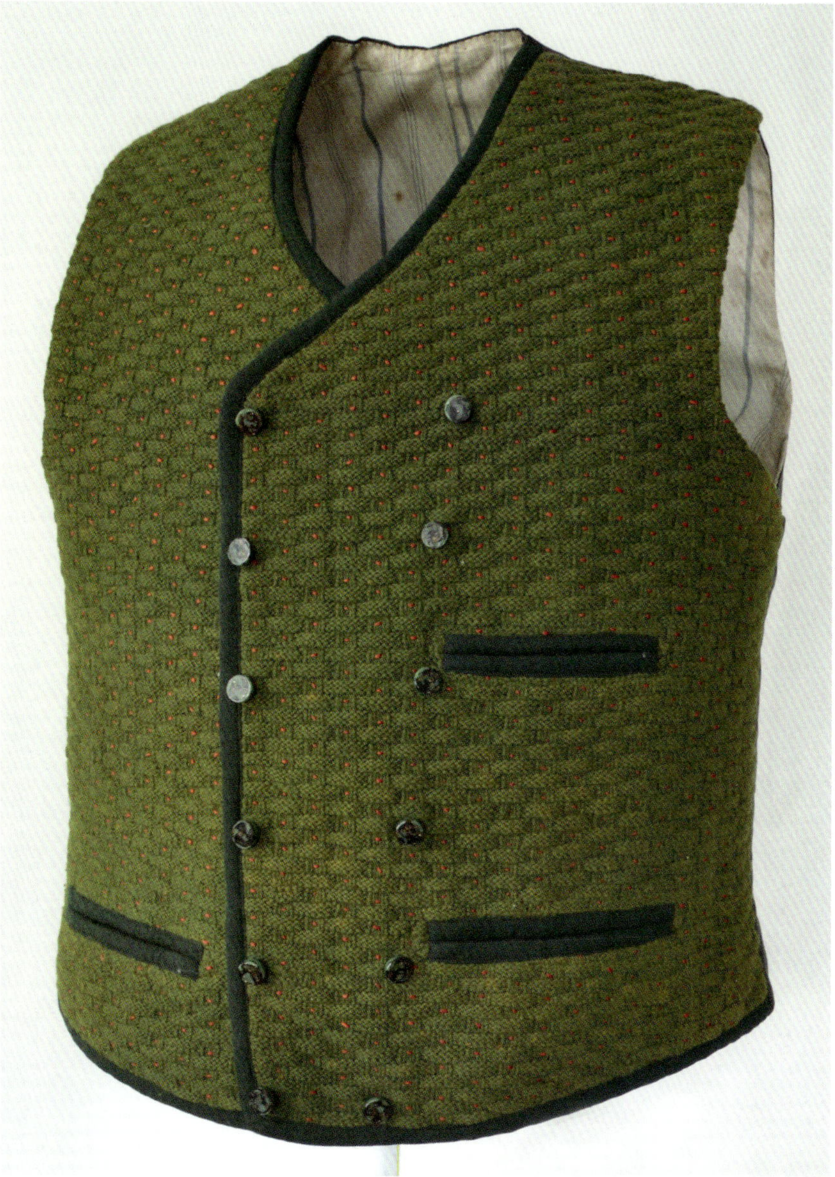

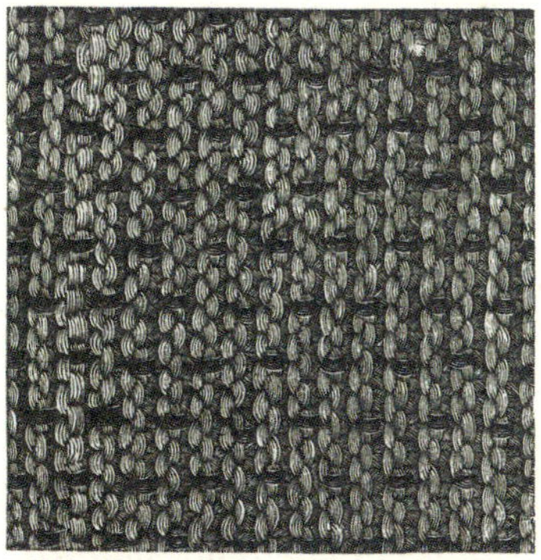

Full Size Working Design of Stitch for Gentleman's Waistcoat.

Above and left: Illustrations to a pattern for a knitted waistcoat in *Weldon's Practical Knitter*, 1898.

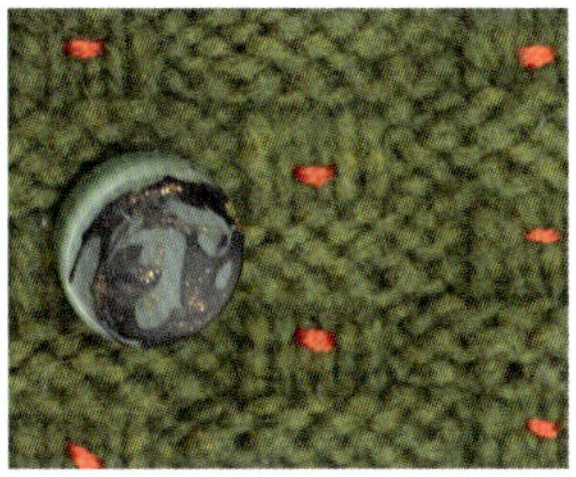

A waistcoat in olive green wool, 1895-1910.
HC.W-3.97

The foreparts are knitted in blocks of plain and purl stitches to give a basket weave pattern, with dots embroidered in red silk. The waistcoat is double-breasted with a fly front, and all the edges are covered in dark green wool. The lining is ivory cotton satin with pale blue stripes, and the back is in black cotton sateen with a backstrap to adjust the waist. The outside buttons are green glass with a black and gold marbled pattern; the ones for fastening are plain.

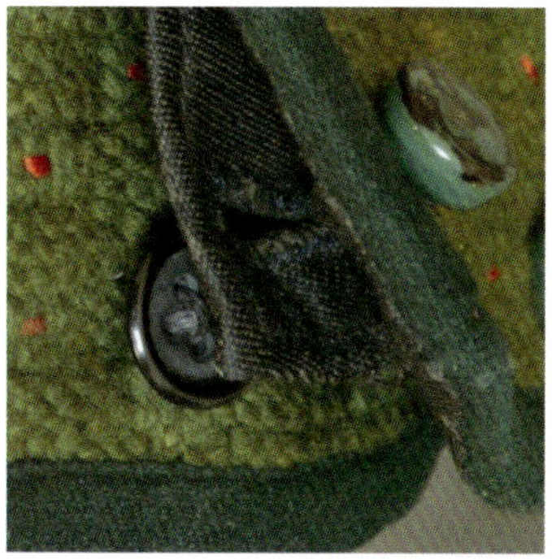

The fly front at the lowest button.

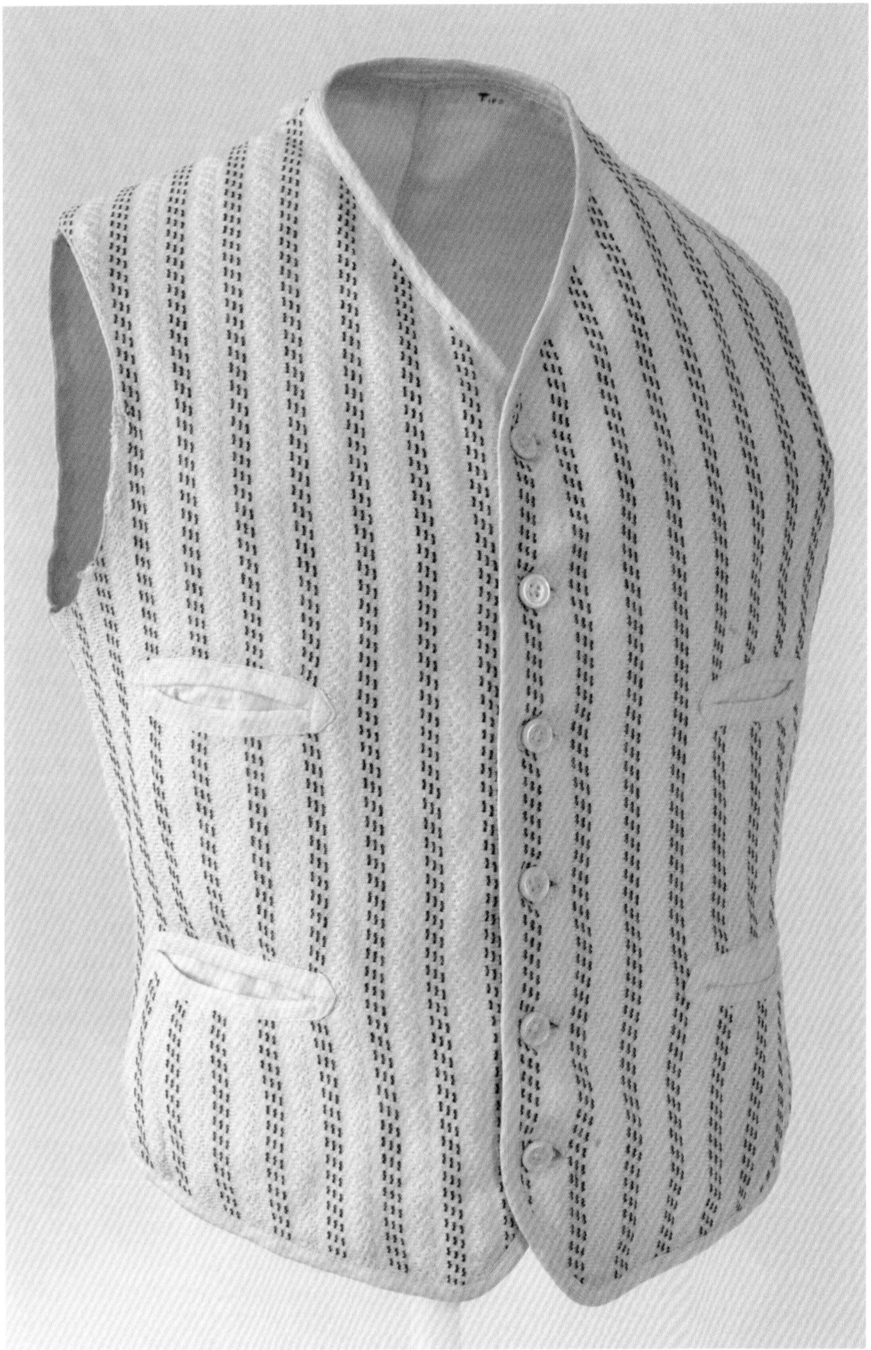

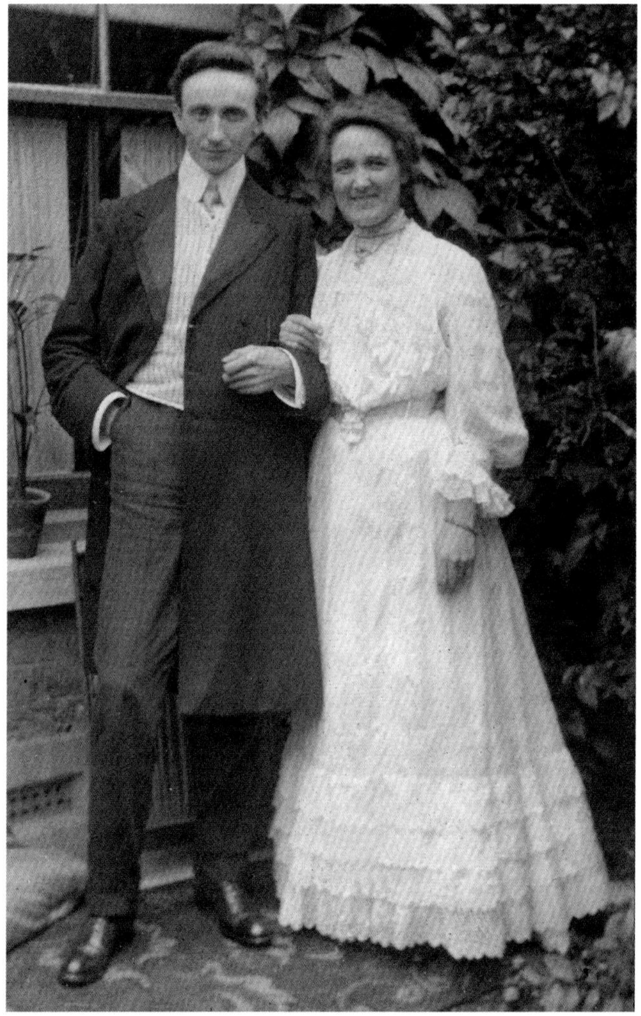

Andrew Gray, a journalist, with Margaret Menzies on their wedding day, 1907.

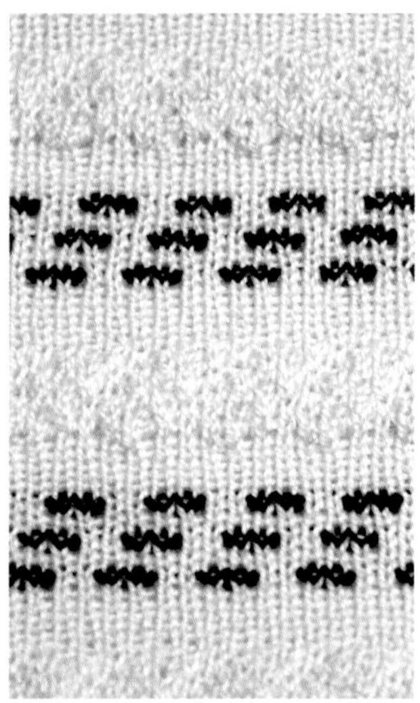

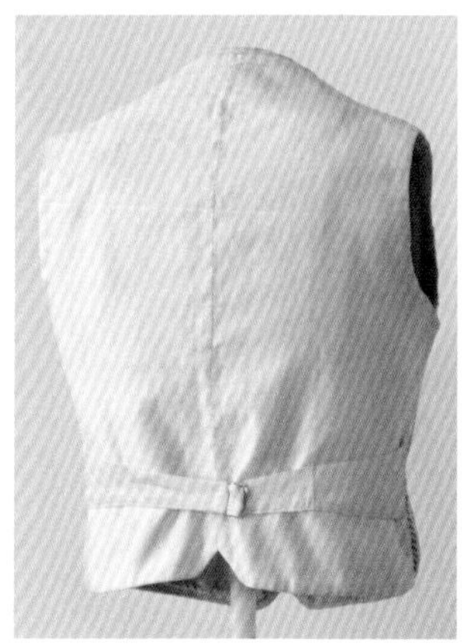

A waistcoat in ivory cotton jersey, 1900-1910. HC.W-0.92

The jersey has raised self stripes with a diagonal texture and broken stripes in black. The waistcoat has been cut sideways across the width of the fabric so that the stripes run from shoulder to hem. The edges of the foreparts, back neck and the edges of the four pockets are bound in ivory silk plaited braid, and a narrow strip of the jersey goes round the back neck. It is lined in plain white cotton, and the back is in white cotton sateen with a backstrap and a white metal buckle (page 210) to adjust the waist. There are six pearl buttons.

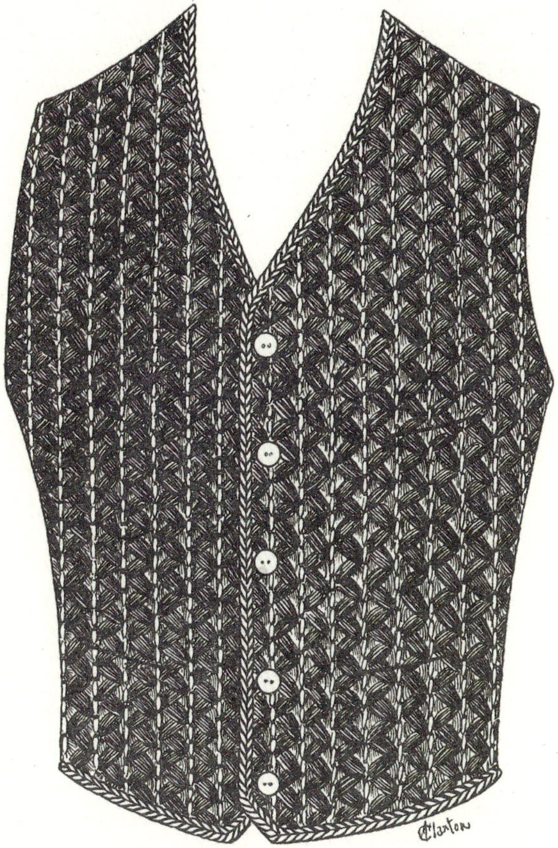

GENTLEMAN'S WAISTCOAT IN SILK, ON CANVAS (ANOTHER PATTERN).

Illustration to a pattern for an embroidered waistcoat in *Pearsall's Illustrated Handbook for Knitting in Silks*, 1902.

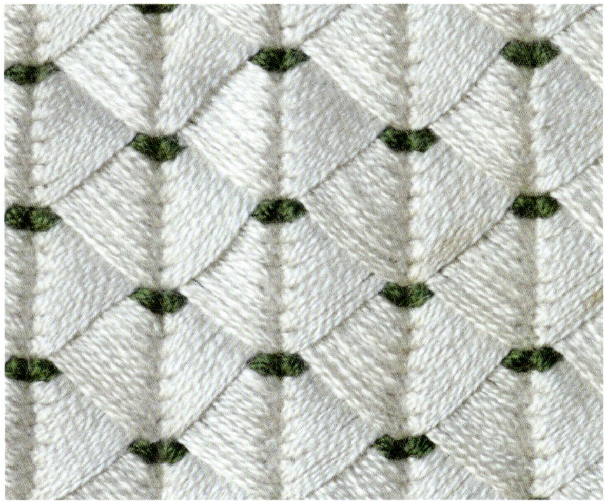

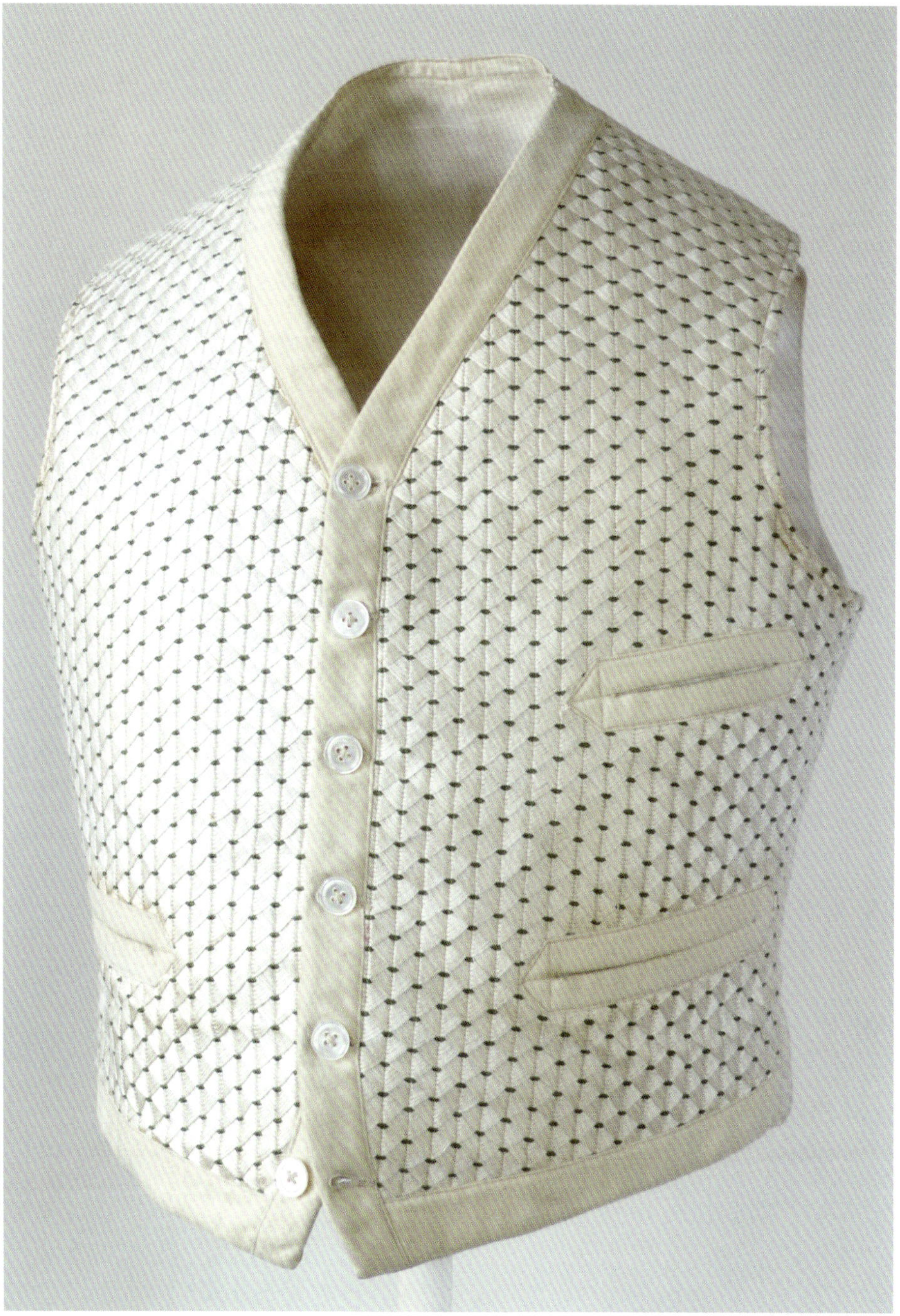

A waistcoat in ivory embroidery, 1900-1910. HC.W-3.01

The ivory silk is embroidered on canvas in a scaly pattern with spots of olive green. The waistcoat foreparts and pockets are edged with ivory wool facecloth, and there are six pearl buttons. It is lined in ivory cotton sateen, and the back is also in the sateen with a backstrap and a white metal buckle to adjust the waist.

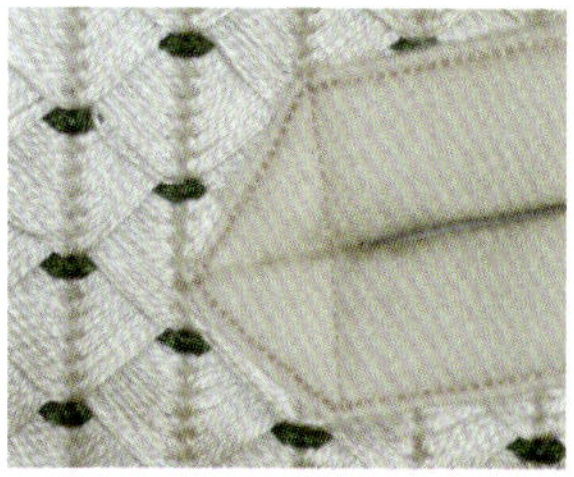

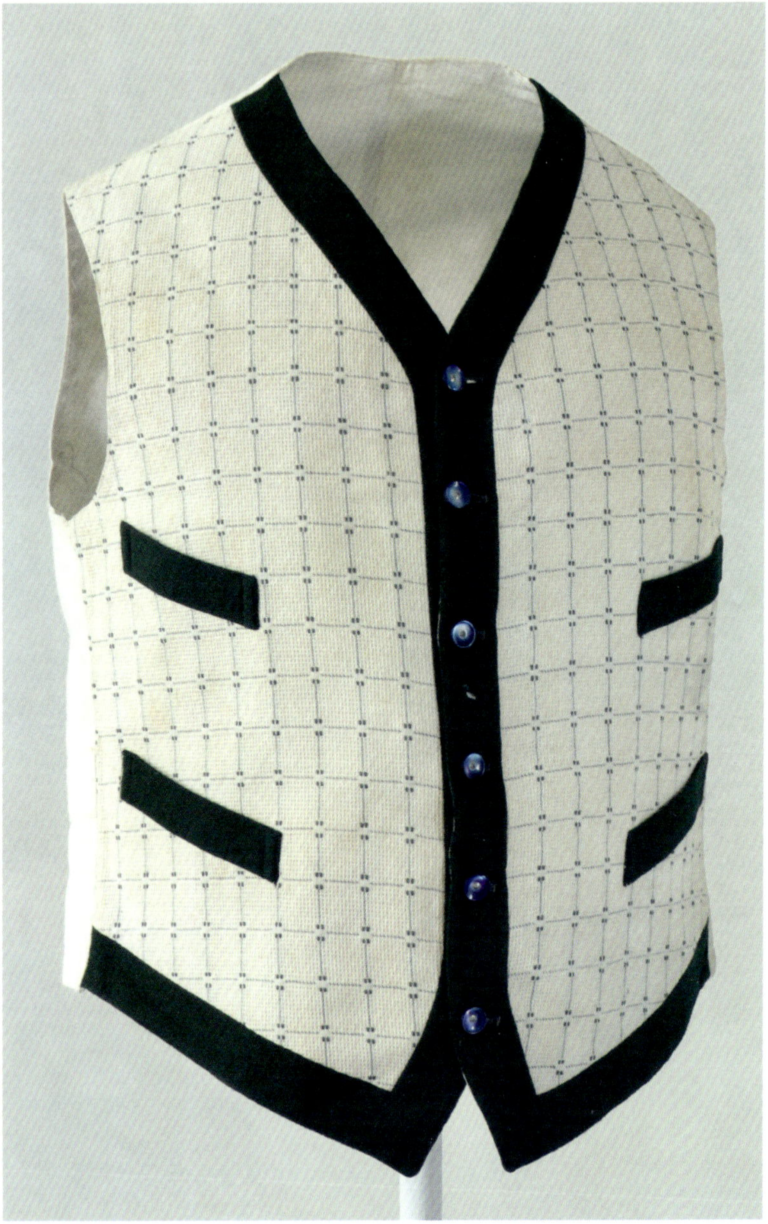

A waistcoat in ivory cotton waffle piqué, 1900-1910. HC.W-0.91

The cotton has window-pane checks in dark green cotton, and the waistcoat foreparts and pockets are edged with dark green wool facecloth. The six removable buttons are saucer-shaped blue pearl, and may not be original; the pins behind them, holding them in place, are covered by a flap of the facing (page 211). The lining is plain white cotton and the hem of the foreparts and front edge facings are in white cotton sateen. The back is in plain white cotton with straps and a removable buckle to adjust the waist; one of the straps has a buttonhole in the end and a button further along, so that the strap can be threaded through the buckle and folded back and fastened on to the button, holding the buckle in place (page 211).

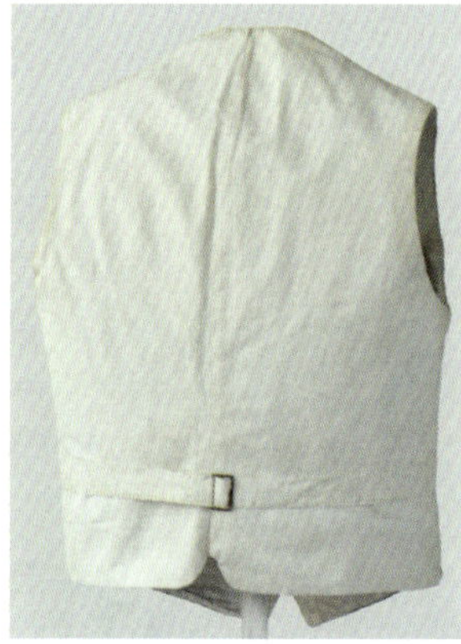

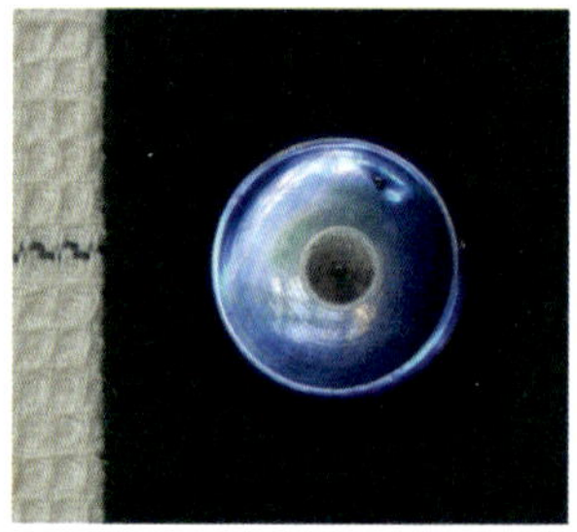

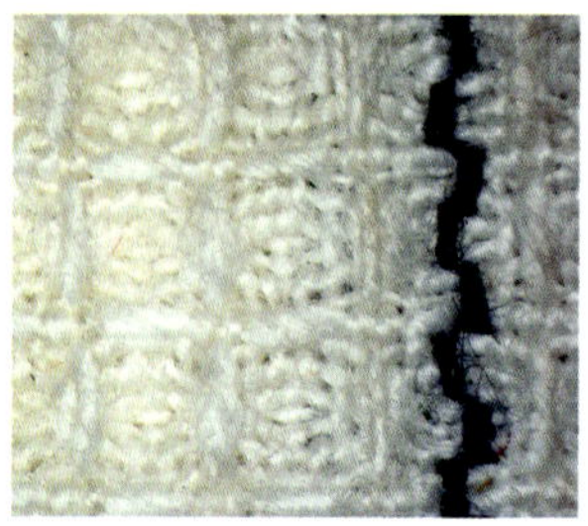

Detail outlined below.

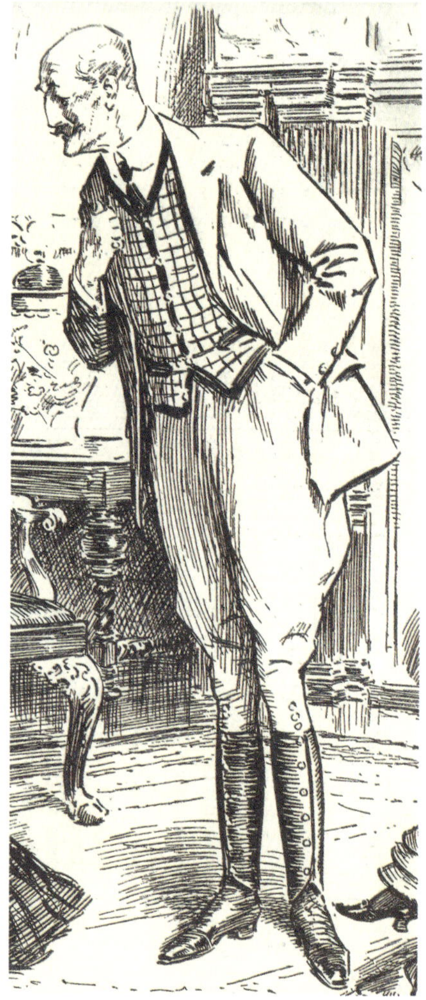

Detail from a cartoon in *Punch*, 1904.

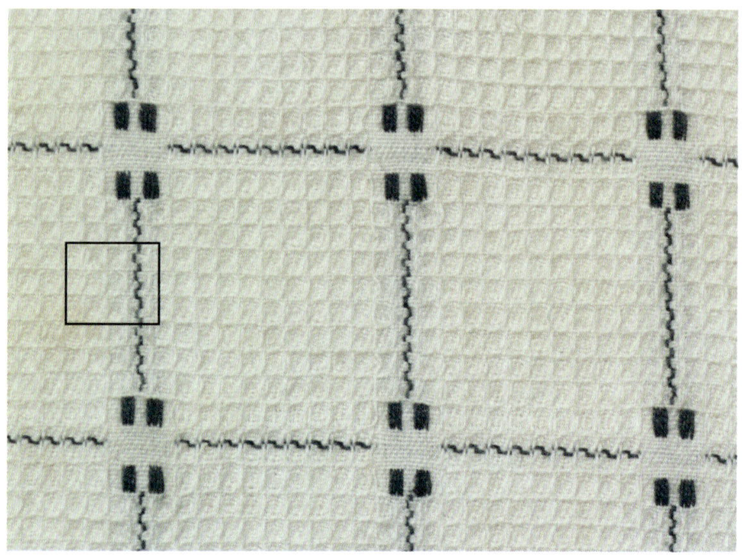

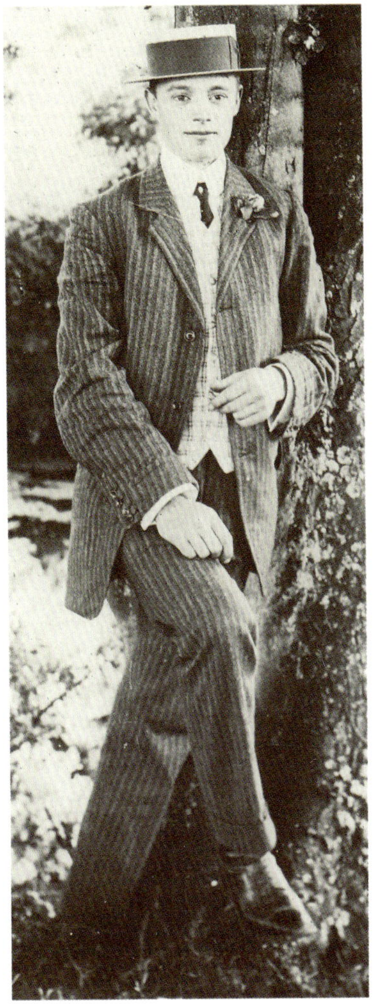

Unknown man, *c.*1900.

A waistcoat in white linen, 1895-1905. HC.W-9.11-2

The linen has a self pattern of window-pane checks and similar black speckled checks. The six pearl buttons are removable and the lining and back are plain white cotton; the back waist adjustment is by straps and a buckle which was removable and the original is missing. The edges of the foreparts and the tops of the pocket welts are bound with ivory silk plaited braid.

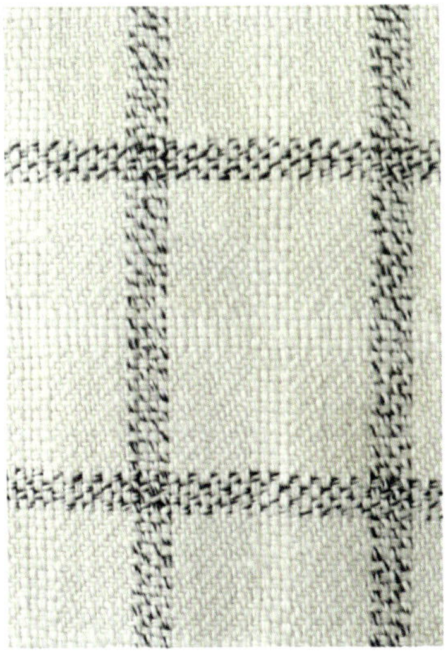

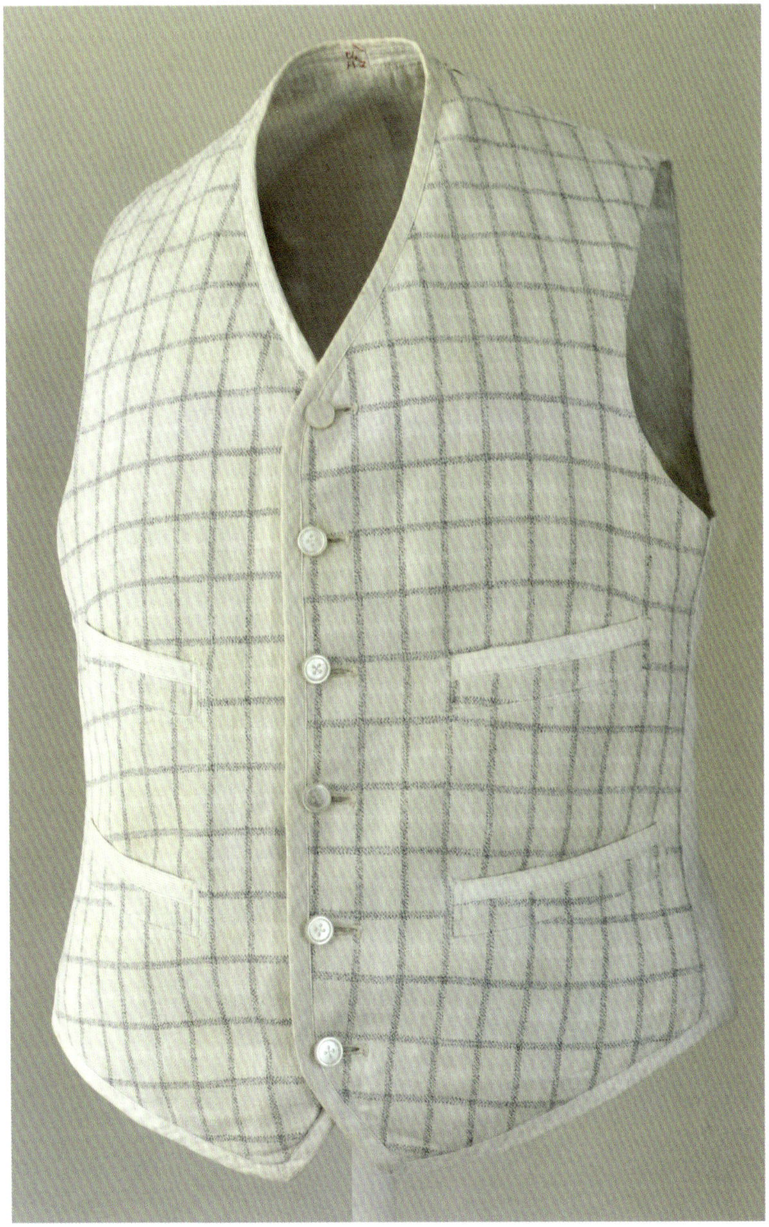

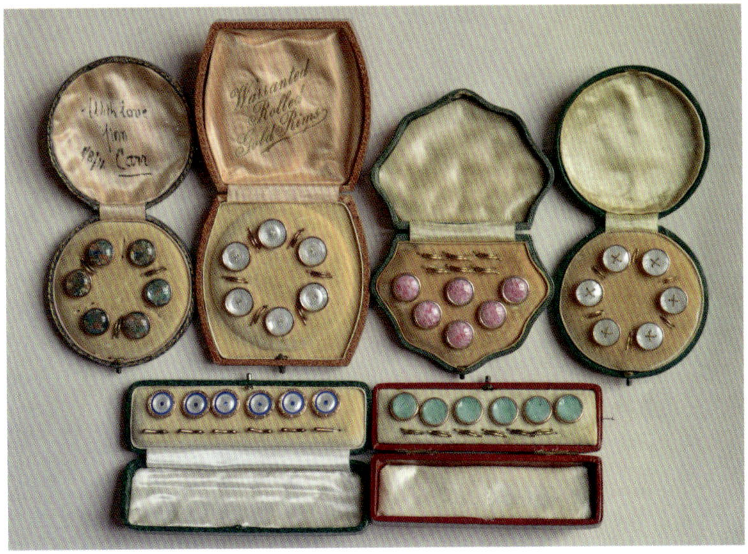

Left: Sets of removable waistcoat buttons in their original boxes, 1900-1930.

Right: A set of removable buttons with pictures of actresses on them, 1900-1910.

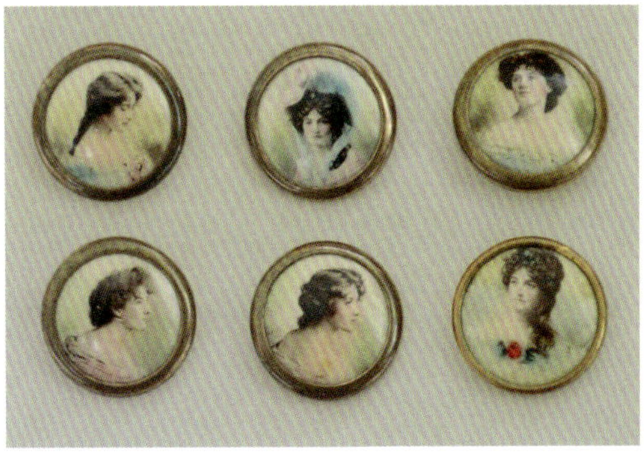

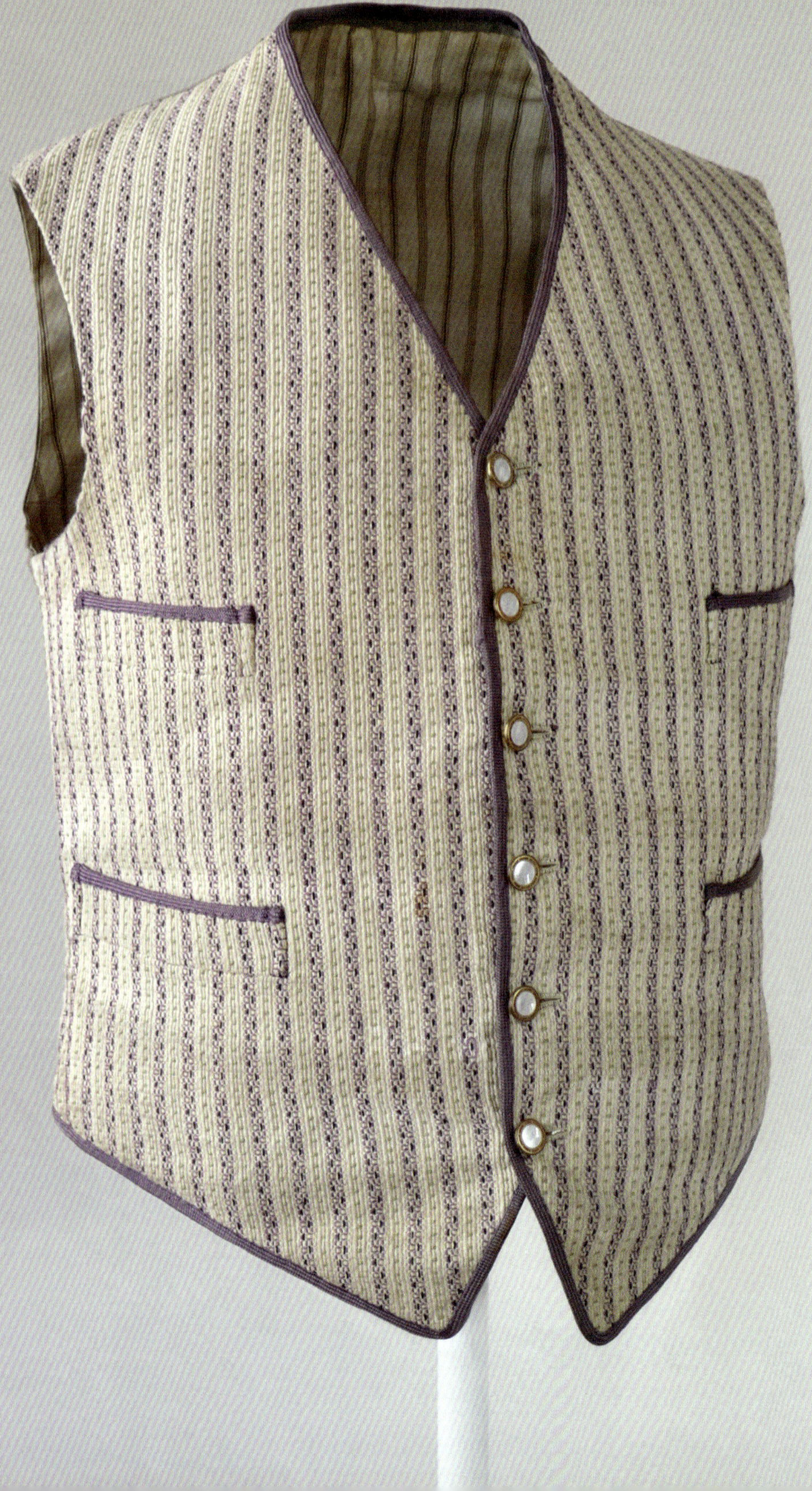

A waistcoat in cream silk, 1910-1920.
HC.W-4.97

The silk is in a corded weave with weft stripes in mauve and black silk threads, which appear to have been darned in, but may be woven, and green silk spots stitched over the ribs. The foreparts have been cut sideways across the width of the fabric, and their edges, the back neck and the tops of the four pocket welts are bound with mauve plaited silk braid. There are six hand-worked eyelets for removable buttons, but the originals are missing; the buttons here are replacements. The waistcoat is lined in cream cotton twill with dark brown printed stripes. The back is in pale grey wool sateen with a backstrap to adjust the waist, and there is a narrow strip of the forepart fabric going round the back neck. The hem of the foreparts and the front facings are also in the pale grey wool; the inner edge of the right facing is not stitched to the lining, and covers the backs of the removable buttons.

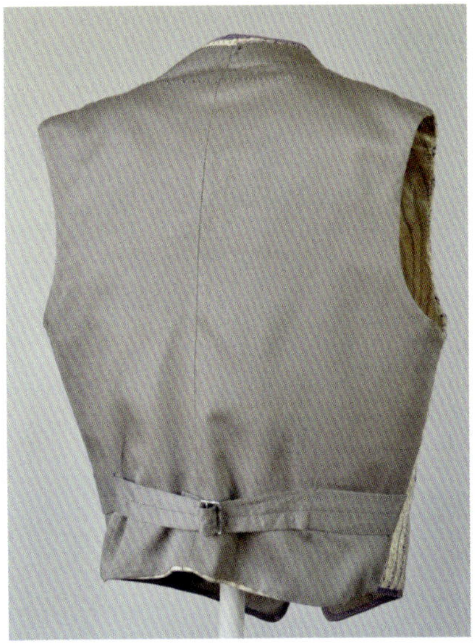

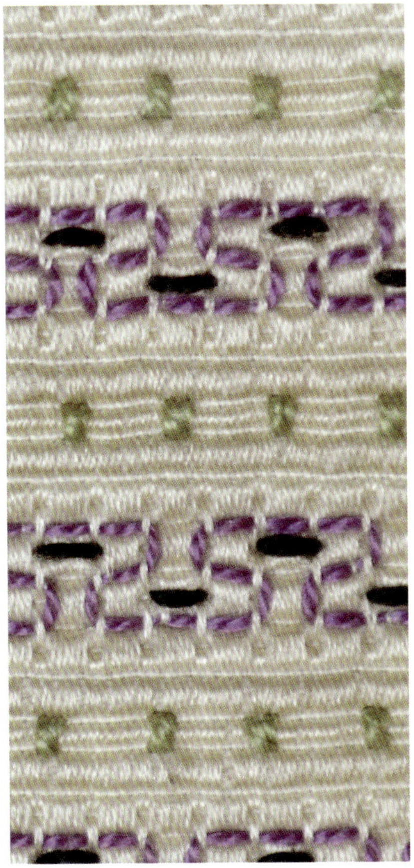

Detail of the fabric, shown warp-wise. The apparent darning of the weft stripes can be seen threading through the warp silk, as well as the green spots over the ribs.

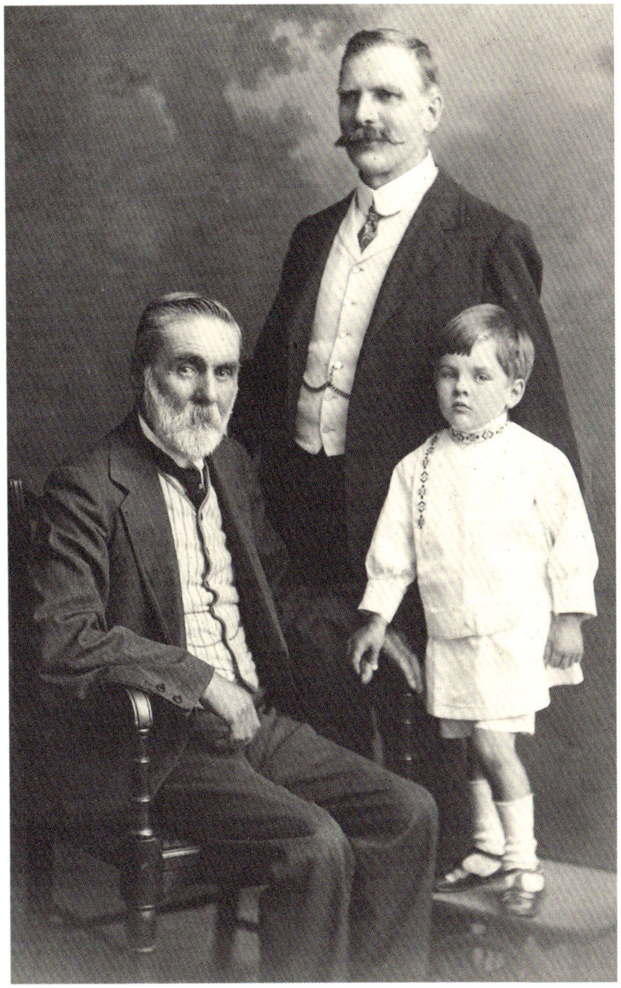

James Joseph Clarke, a retired corn merchant, with his son Edward, an engineer, and grandson Charles, *c.*1915.

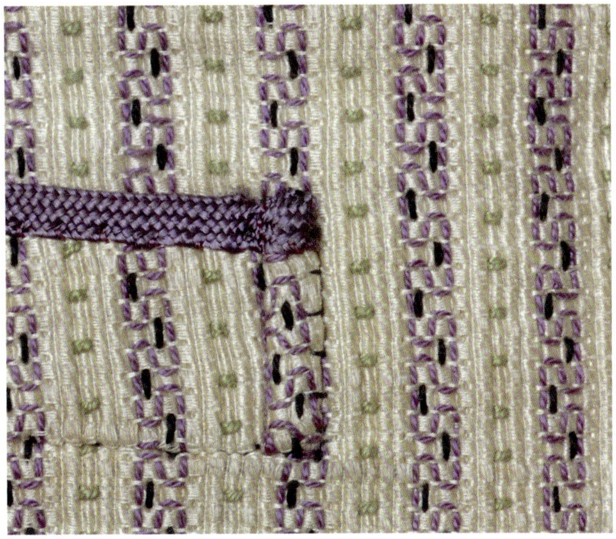

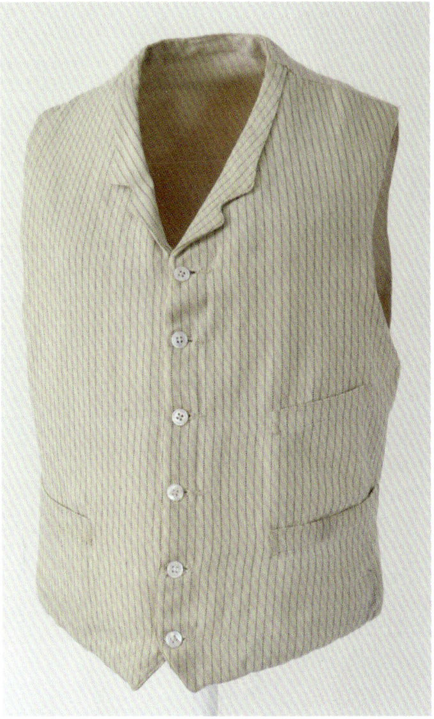

A waistcoat in cream wool twill, 1910-1920. HC.W-11.95

The wool has narrow dark brown stripes. The waistcoat has a narrow step-roll collar and six pearl buttons; the right forepart is cut with a step out at the bottom of the collar for the buttons, so that when the waistcoat is buttoned up the two sides of the collar meet in a V at the bottom of the opening, instead of overlapping. There are three welted pockets. The lining and back are in beige cotton sateen and there is no back waist adjustment.

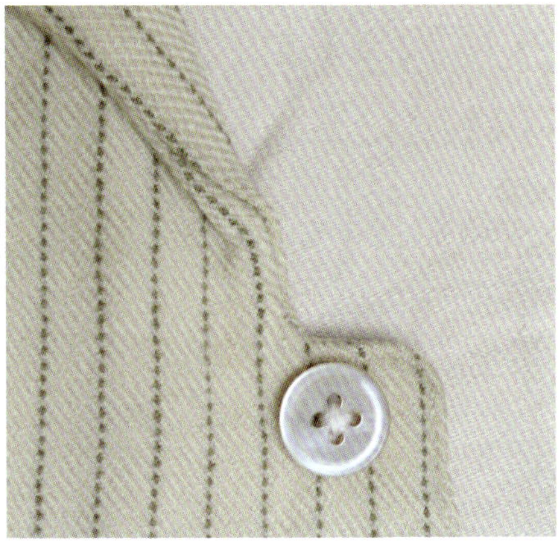

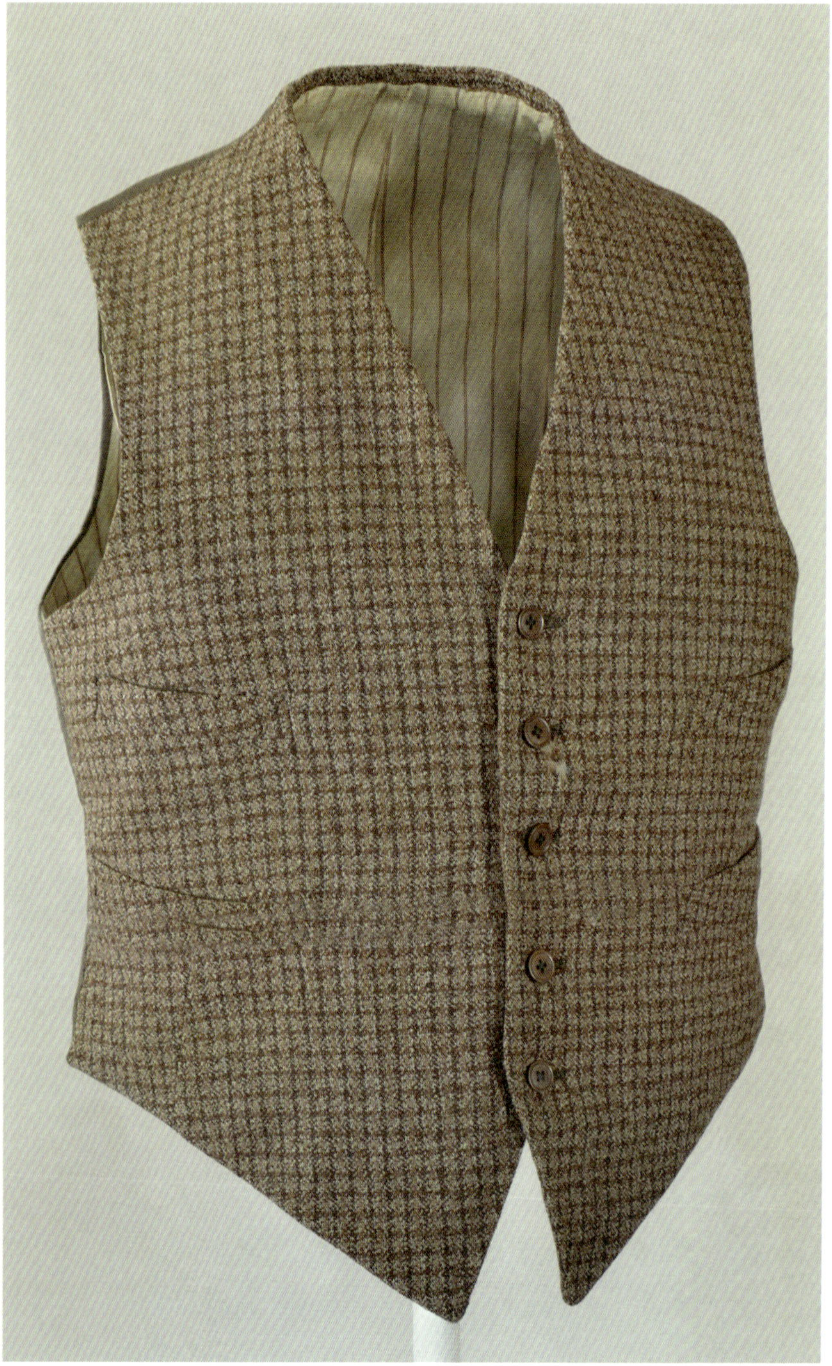

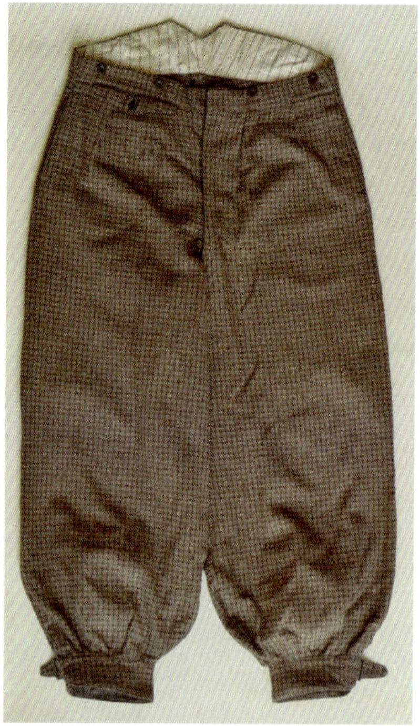

The plus-fours (HC.W-12.82-2) which came with the waistcoat. They are cut 8″ longer than breeches, and when the hem is sewn into a knee-band they hang down 4″ below the knee.

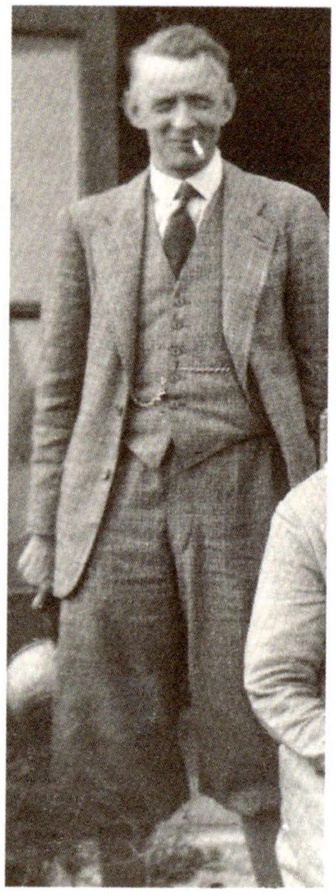

Unknown man, *c.*1932.

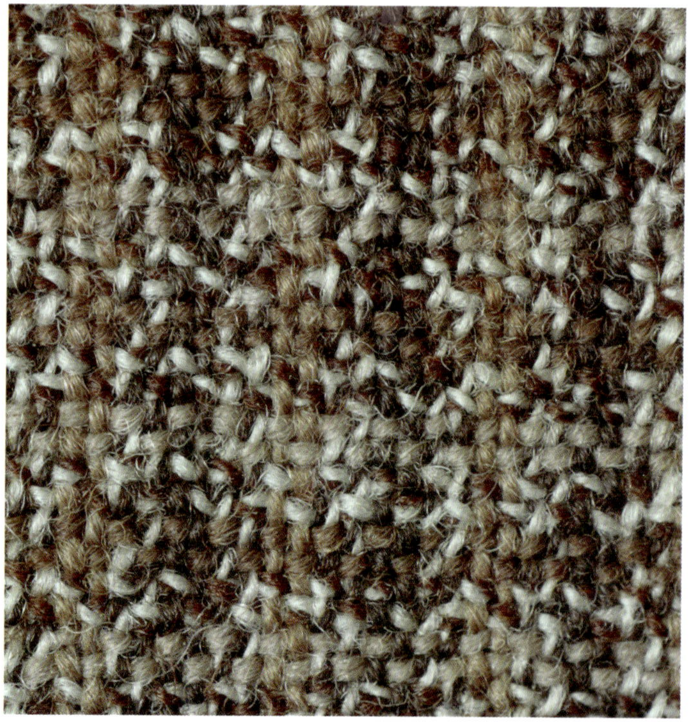

A waistcoat in brown wool, 1920-1935. HC.W-12.82-1

This is a thornproof tweed with checks in shades of brown and white. The waistcoat is lined in cream cotton sateen with a dark brown double narrow stripe, and there is a pocket inside the left front which has a button-down flap to keep it closed. The back is in brown cotton sateen with a backstrap and a buckle to adjust the waist. There are five brown buttons.

It came with a pair of plus-fours, and may have been part of a three-piece suit.

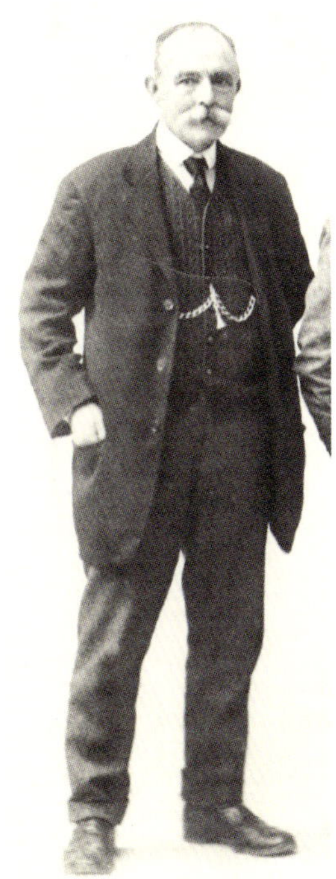

Samuel Cole, a master baker in Plymouth, *c.*1920.

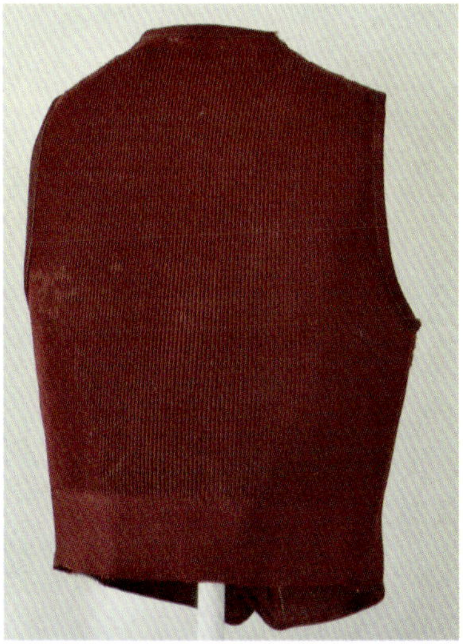

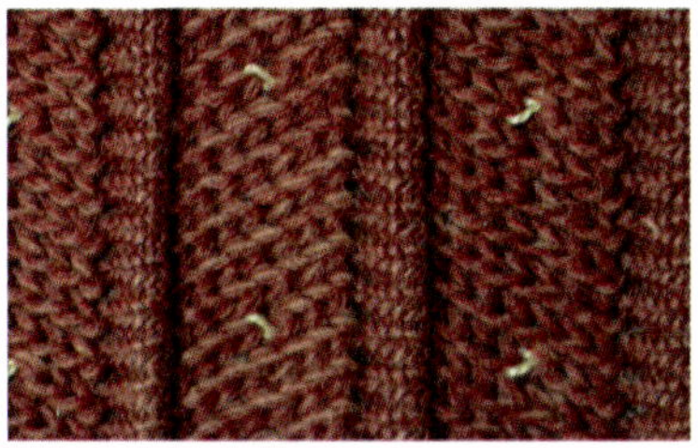

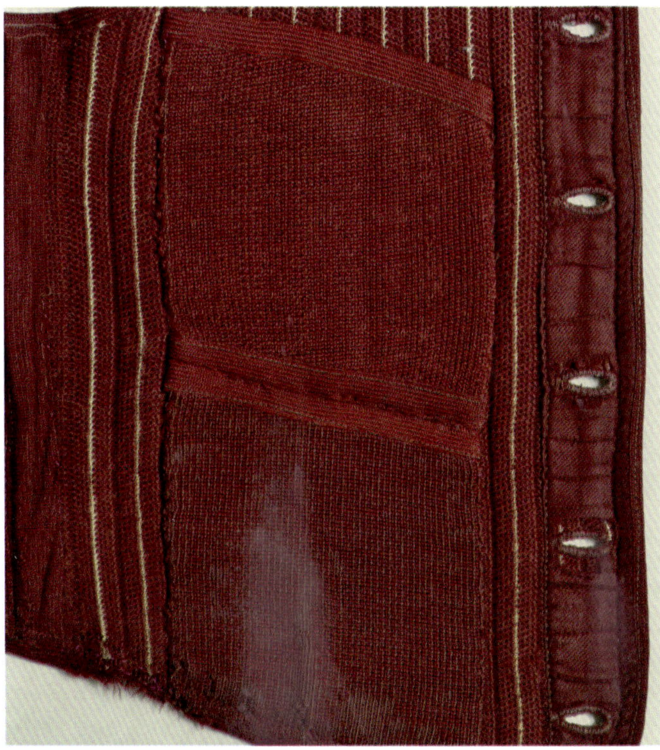

Inside the left front, showing the pocket bags and the rows of ivory silk which appear as dots on the front of the jersey.

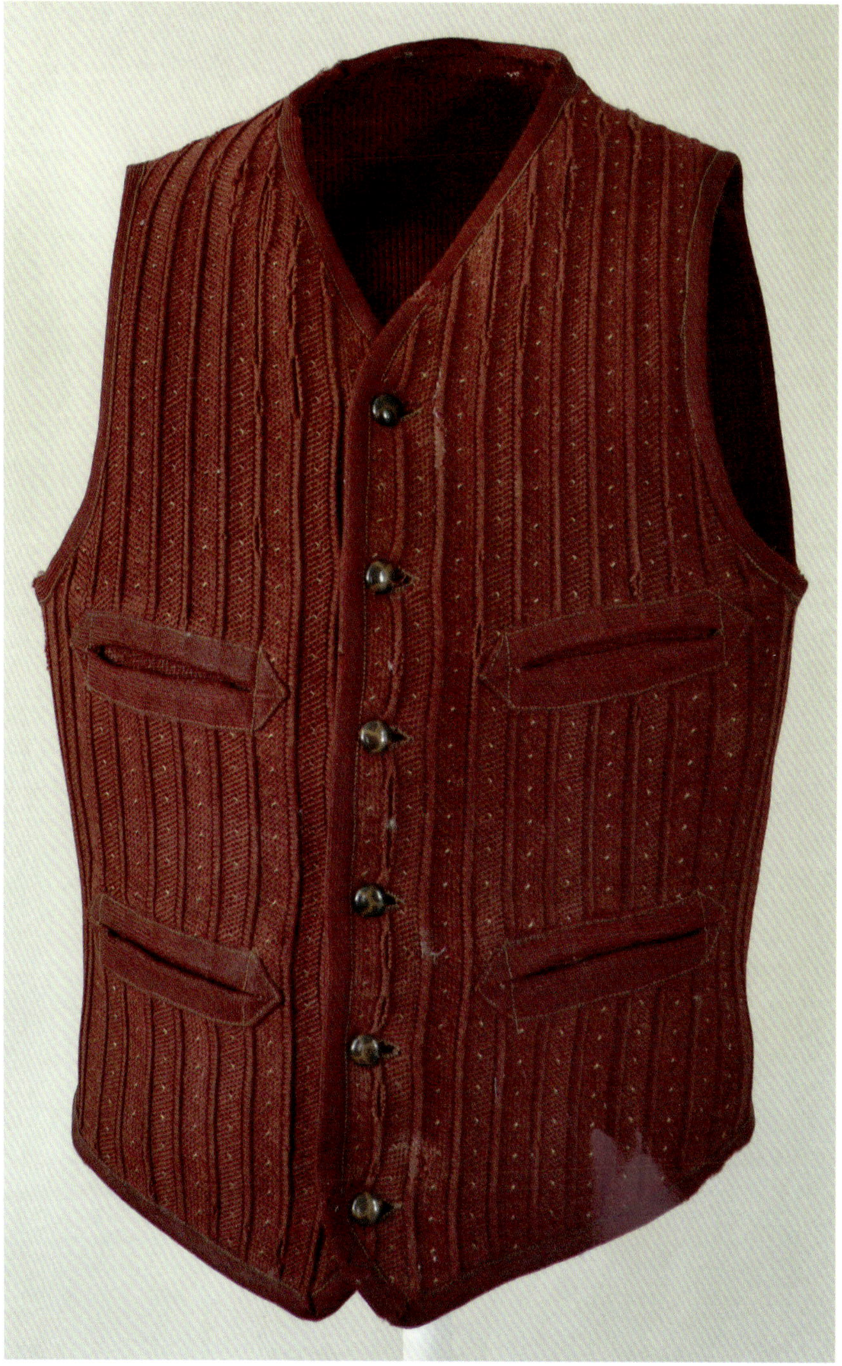

A waistcoat in crimson wool jersey, 1920-1935. HC.W-4.86

It is cut sideways from a length of machine-knitted jersey fabric with the rows of knitting running from shoulder to hem. The knitting zig-zags between ridges, with rows of ivory silk dots. The back is plain ribbed jersey, cut lengthwise. The edges of the foreparts, the back neck and the four pockets are bound with matching wool plaited braid, and there are six mottled brown shallow domed buttons (page 216). It is unlined and the seams are covered in the plaited braid.

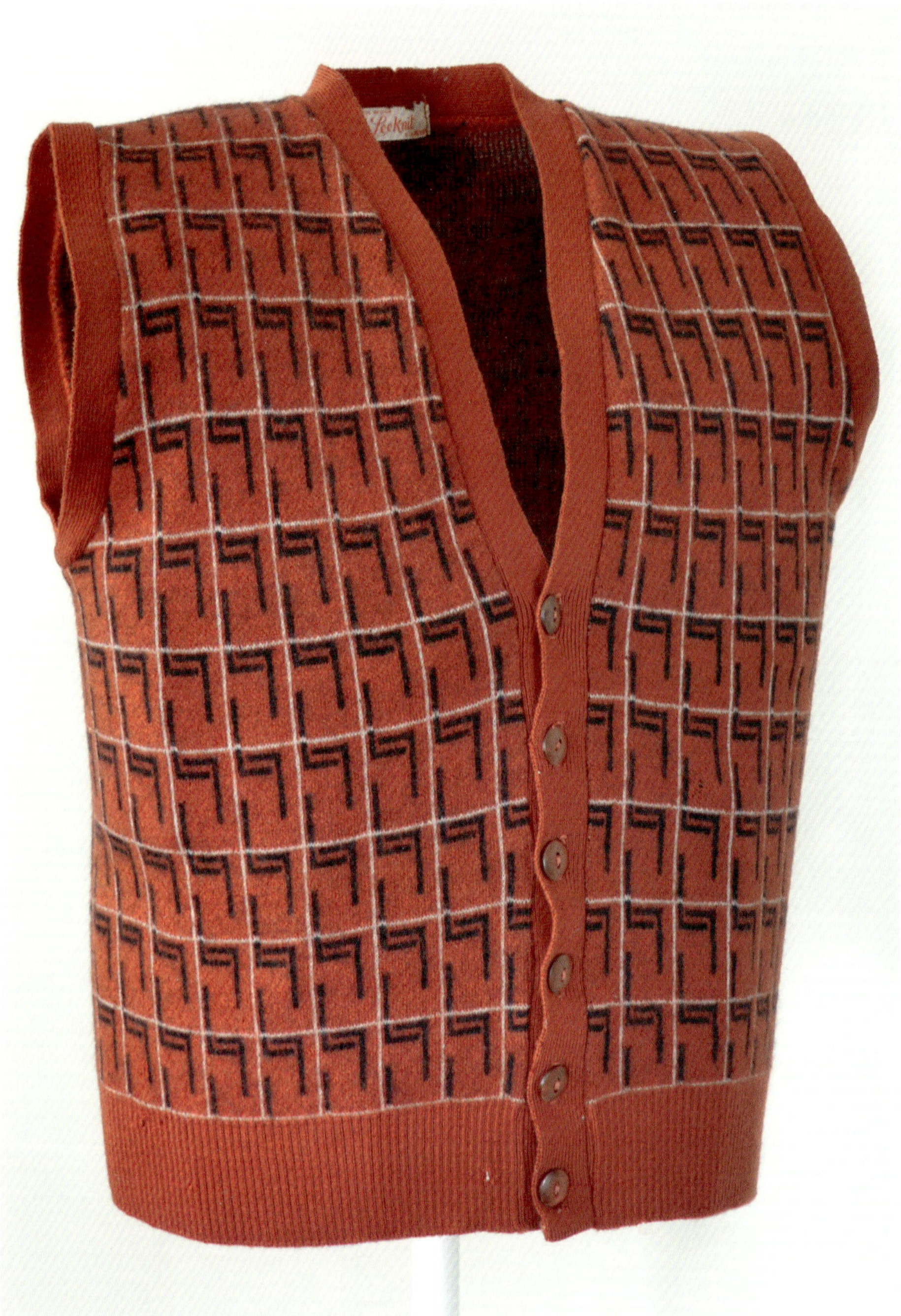

A waistcoat in knitted red wool, 1930-1950. HC.W-0.96

It has a geometric pattern in black and white and is cut from one piece of machine-knitted wool, with no side seams. The ribbing at the bottom has been knitted with the patterned piece and the edges have been seamed on. There are six mottled red buttons, and no lining. The waistcoat has been well washed and has become slightly felted and mis-shapen. It was manufactured with the trade name LeeKnit, for the C.W.S., the Co-operative Wholesale Society, which was the wholesaler for all the individual Co-operative Societies around the country.

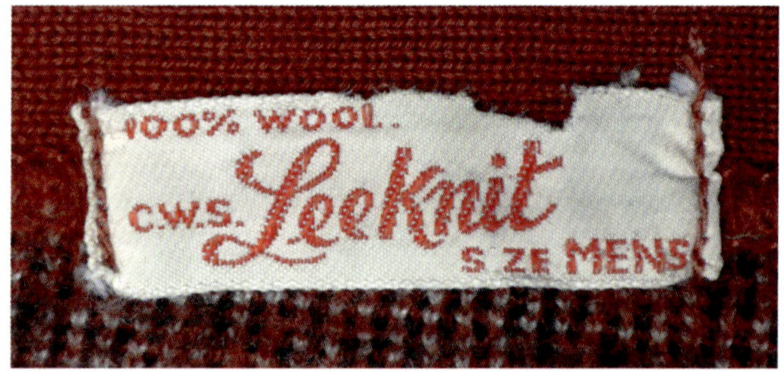

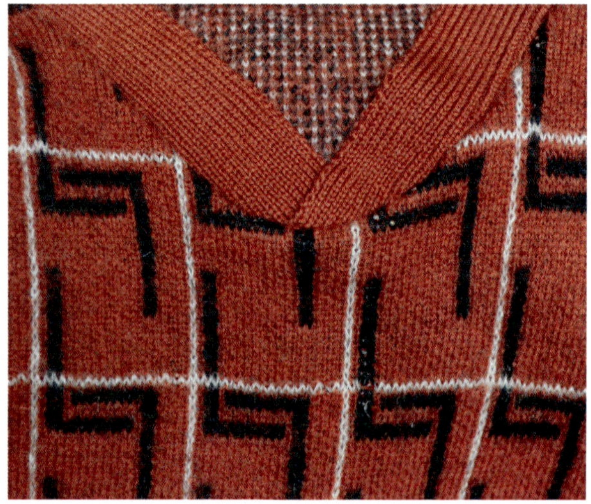

The bottom of one of the armholes, where the knitted edging is sewn in, overlapping; there is no side seam.

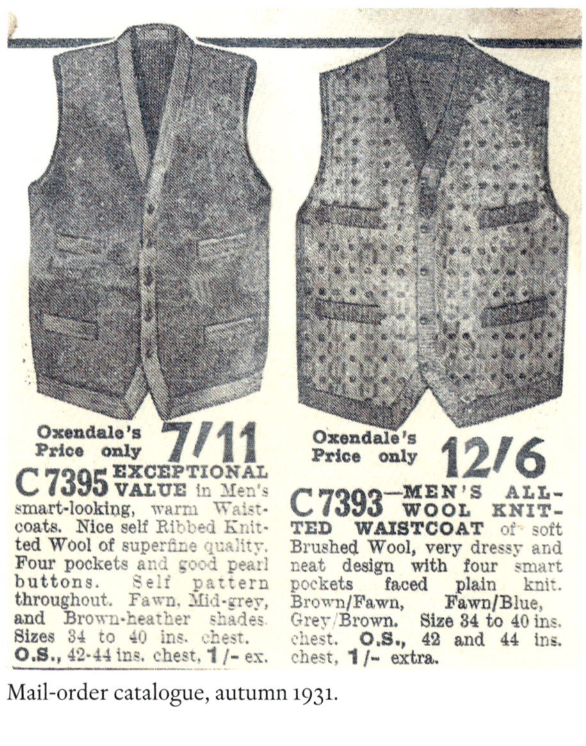

Mail-order catalogue, autumn 1931.

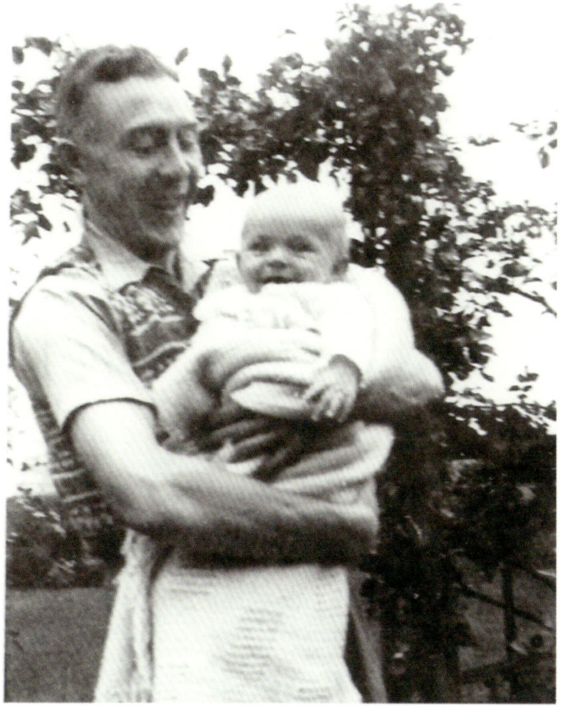

John Hopkins and Moira, 1934.

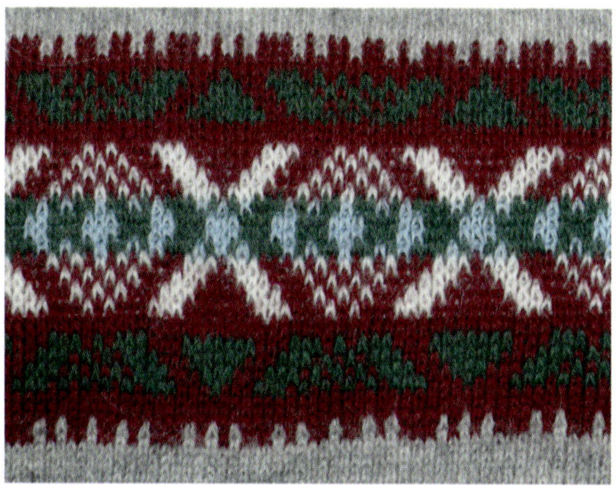

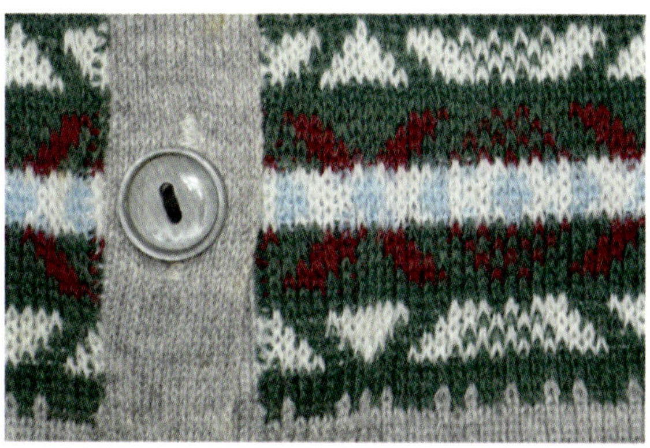

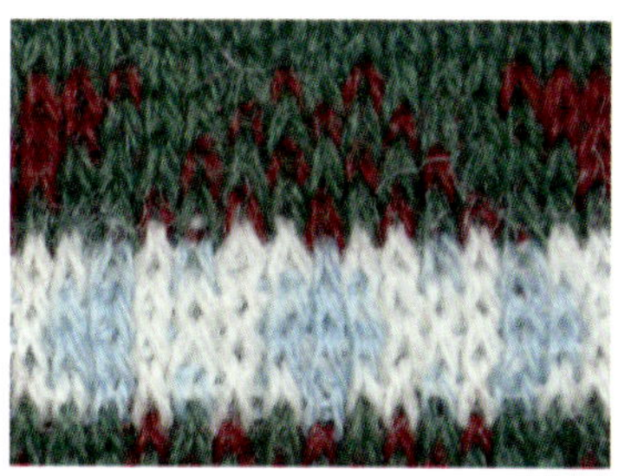

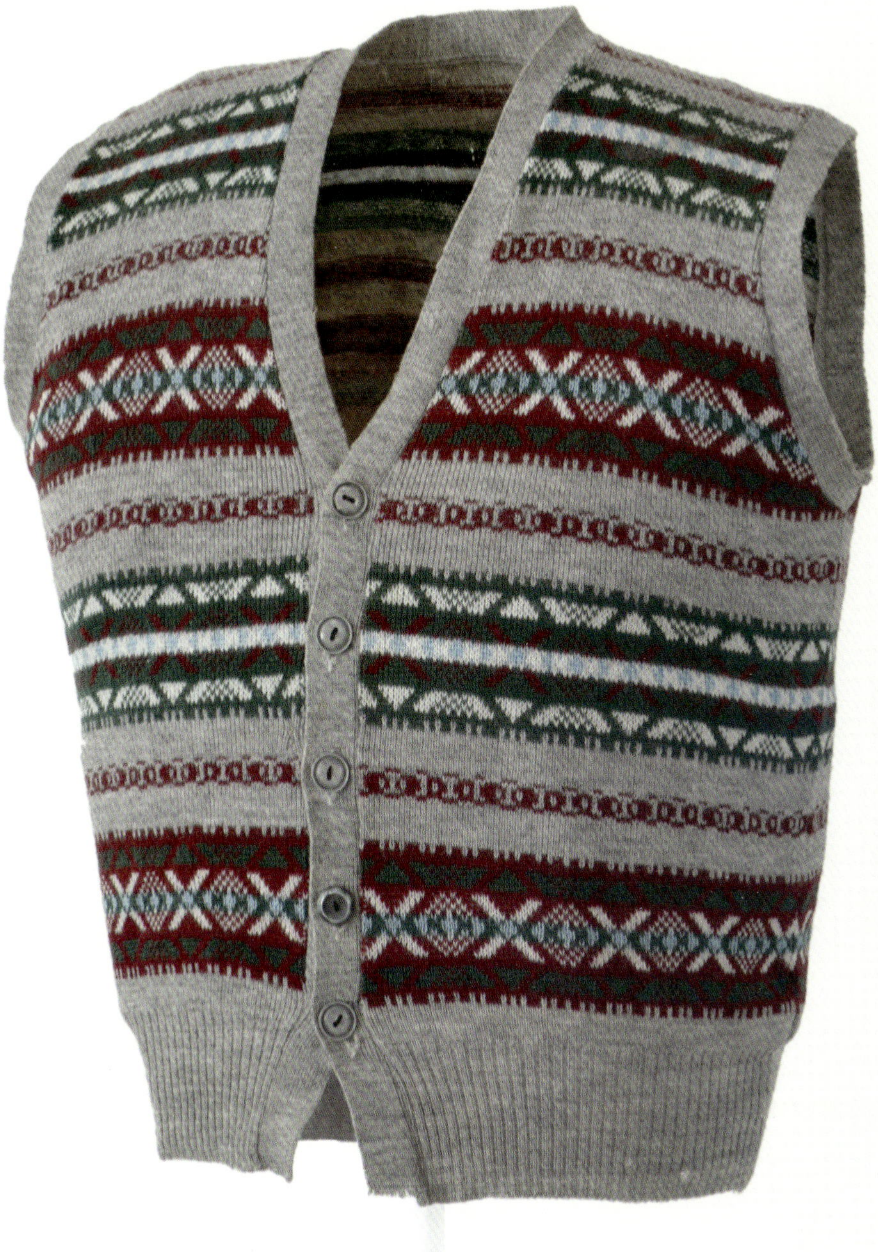

A waistcoat in machine-knitted wool, 1930-1950.
HC.W-8.71

It has a dark green, pale blue, wine and white Fair Isle pattern in stripes on a pale grey ground. The waistcoat is not knitted to shape but cut from knitted panels; the ribbing at the bottom is knitted on to the patterned sections, and the front and armhole edges have been seamed on. There are five grey buttons.

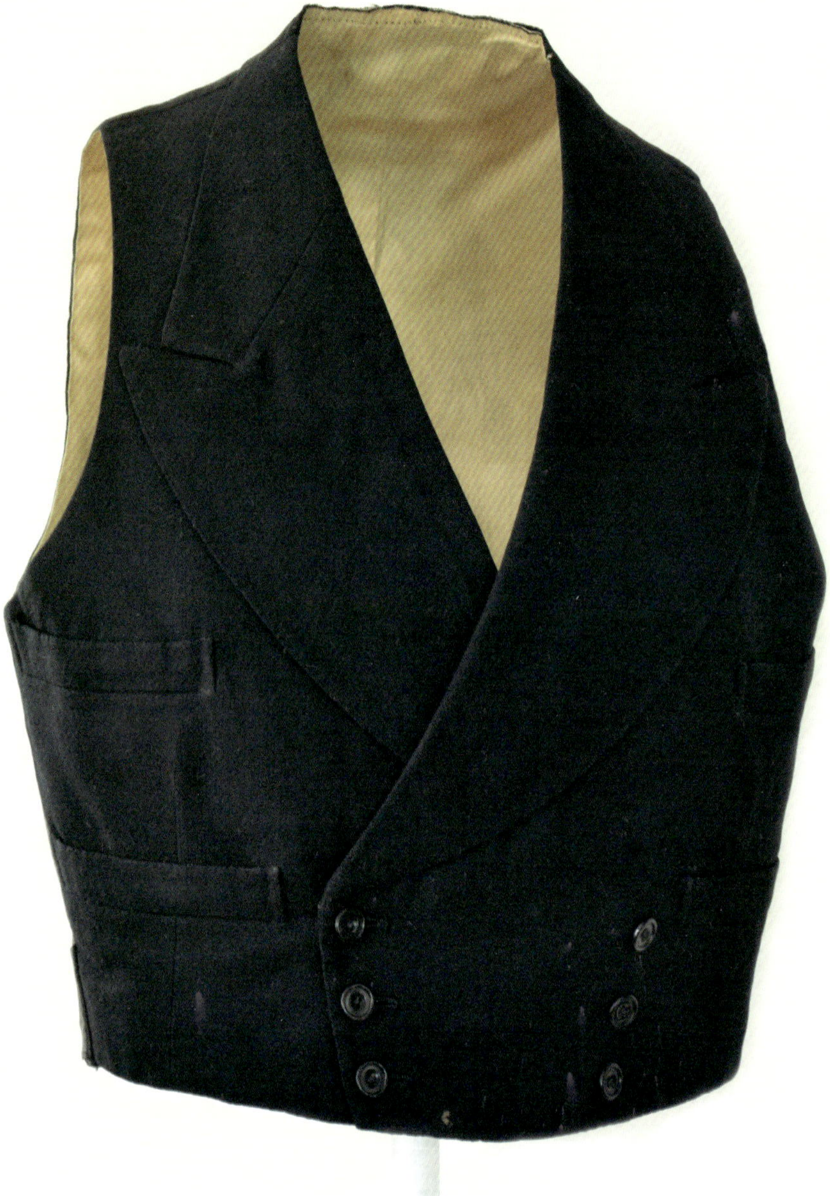

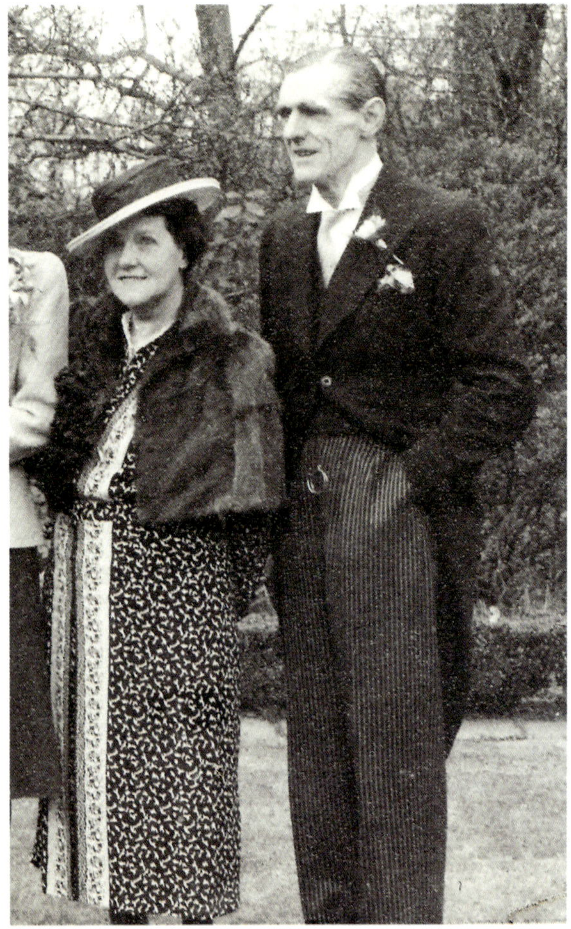

Tom and Dora Clarke at a wedding, 1940. Tom Clarke was an advertising agent in London.

A waistcoat in black wool, 1935. HC.W-5.74-1

The wool is in a narrow herringbone weave. The waistcoat is double-breasted with three pairs of buttons and buttonholes; there are two buttons on the inside of the left forepart to fasten on to the right forepart and keep it in place. The collar does not extend round the back of the neck and the points of the wide curved lapels are stitched down to the foreparts. It is lined with fawn cotton sateen and the back is in black rayon twill with a backstrap to adjust the waist. It was made for Tom Clarke by F. Burrow, whose label is sewn on the inside of one of the straps at the back.

The label of F. Burrow, 5a, New Burlington Street, Regent Street, London W1.

In the City of London, the convention is to wear a black waistcoat with morning dress, instead of the more usual grey.

Right: Illustration in a catalogue for 1933 from High Life Tailor, a tailoring company in Paris.

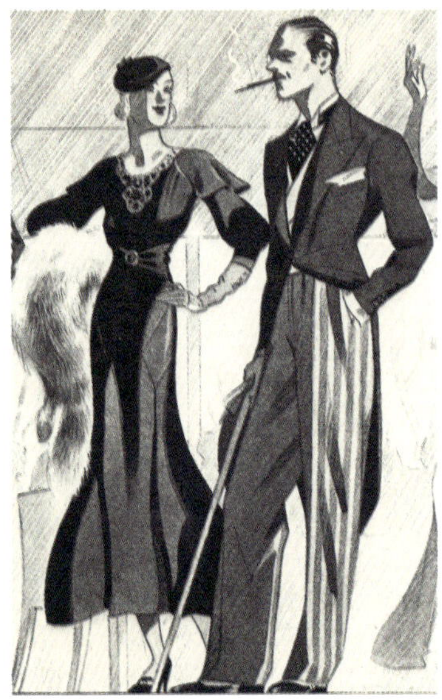

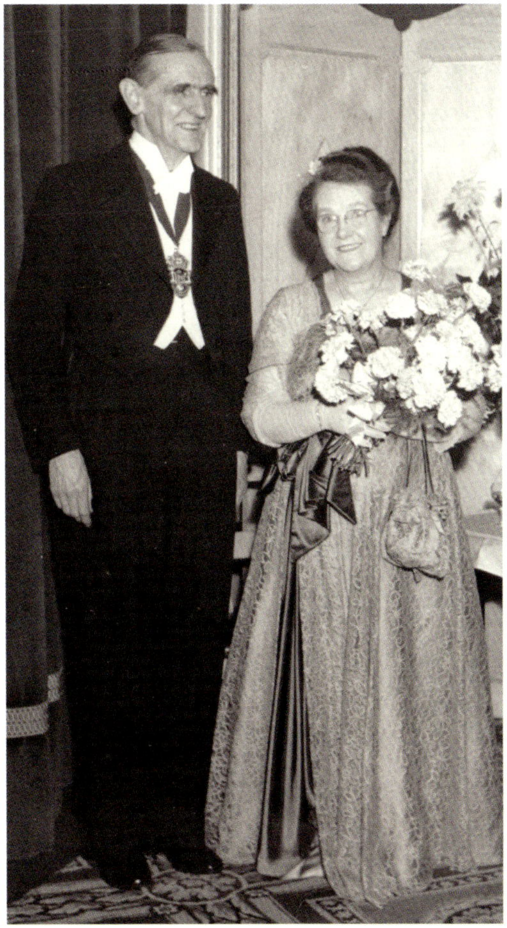

Tom and Dora Clarke at the City Livery Club, London, New Year's Eve 1952. Tom Clarke was President that year.

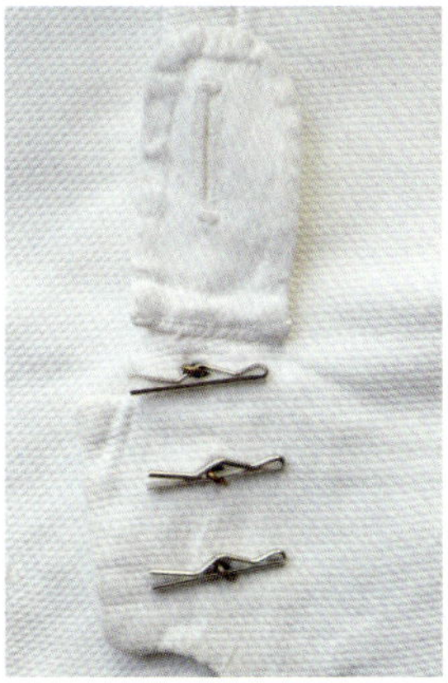

Inside the front, showing the pins holding the buttons; the tab with a buttonhole would be folded down, covering the button pins, and fastening on to the top trouser button to keep the waistcoat in place.

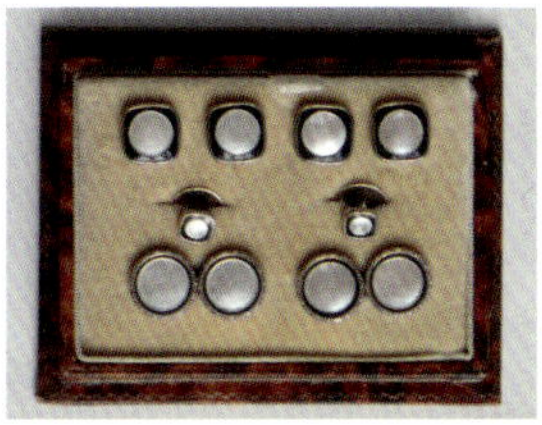

A set of waistcoat buttons, shirt-front studs and cuff links, 1935-1950.

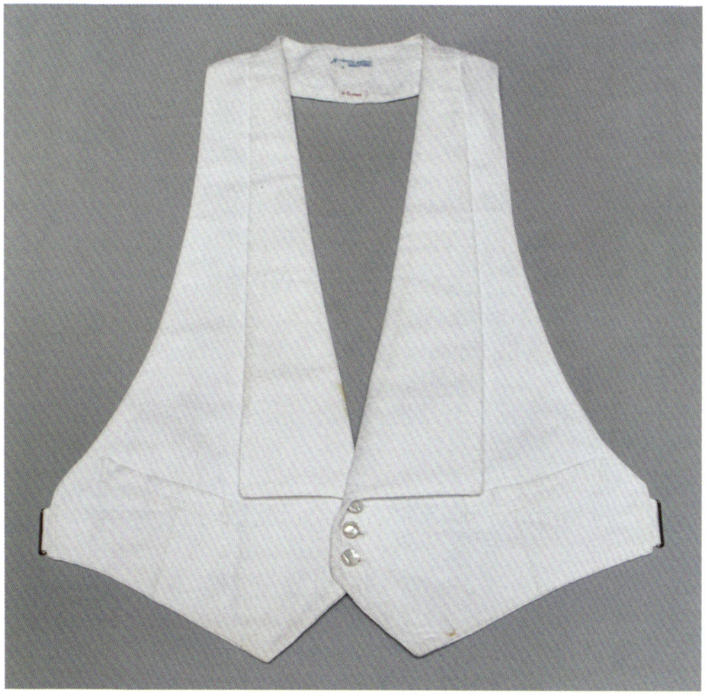

An evening waistcoat in white cotton marcella, 1940-1950. HC.W-5.74-3

This belonged to Tom Clarke, and was made by Austin Reed, a large menswear manufacturer. It is backless, and the foreparts are joined by a band round the back neck; the lining is white cotton with a self diamond pattern. The three pearl buttons are removable, and the back waist straps, which may have been elastic, are missing.

Right: A waistcoat in pale grey self-striped wool, 1930-1950. HC.W-5.74-2

This belonged to Tom Clarke, and it is formal daywear, to be worn with morning dress. It is backless, and double-breasted with two pairs of grey pearl buttons. There are buttonholes on the edge of each forepart and those on the right are to fasten on to fawn bone buttons inside the left forepart, to keep the right forepart in place. The band round the back neck is mushroom-coloured alpaca, as are the straps which fasten round the back waist with a brass buckle. It is lined with cream cotton sateen, and the points of the lapels are stitched to the foreparts.

Backless waistcoats for formal dress appeared around 1930. The foreparts are joined by a band round the back neck, and held in place by a strap and buckle round the back waist, and later, an elastic strap.

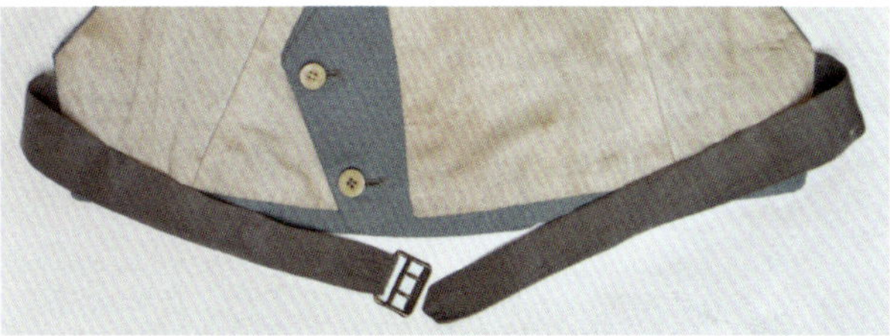

Inside the foreparts, showing the inside buttons and the straps to fasten round the back.

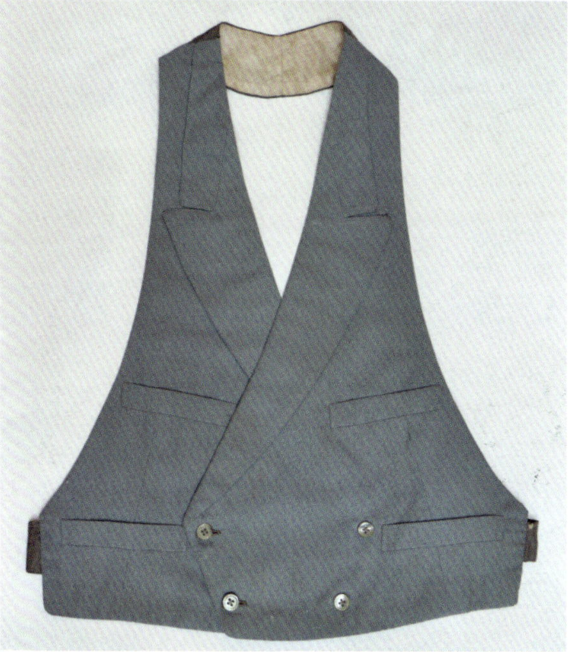

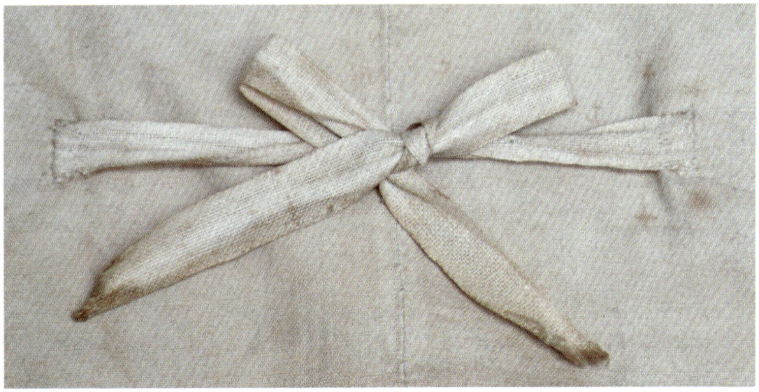

Tape ties, 1810-1820, page 82

Tape ties, to adjust the waist size, appeared during the second half of the eighteenth century. One or two pairs were usual, in cotton or linen. They were still used well into the nineteenth century.

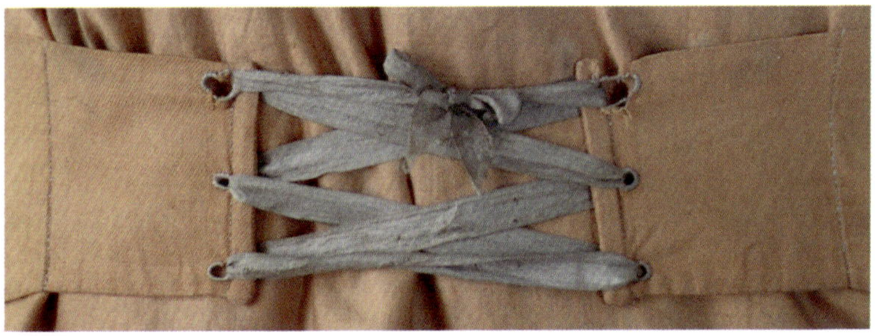

Tabs with hand-worked eyelets for lacing, 1825-1835, page 88

Tabs sewn on to the back waist for lacing appeared in the early nineteenth century; the ends were stiffened with bones or bents, and the eyelets, usually three, were hand-sewn. Cotton or linen tapes, or even narrow silk ribbon were used for the lacing.

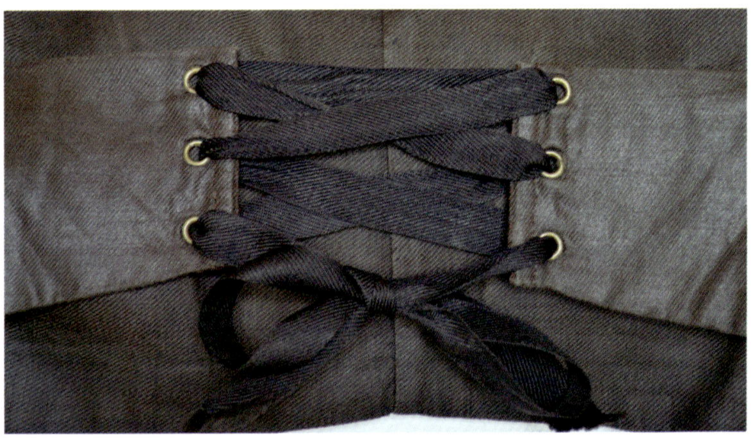

Tabs with metal eyelets for lacing, 1835-1845, page 103

A patent for metallic eyelets was taken out by Thomas Rogers in 1823, and in Paris, Pierre Bonduceau took out a similar patent for their use "for stays and other purposes" in 1829. They were more durable than the hand-sewn eyelets already being used on the lacing tabs.

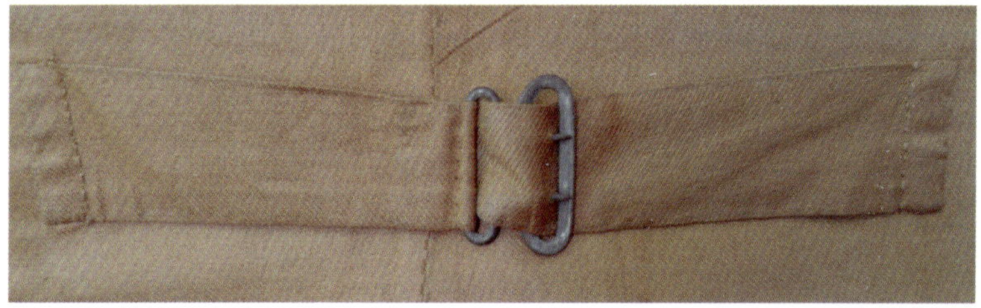

1850-1860, Straps with a buckle, page 138

The backstrap appeared in the 1840s, as a new means of adjusting the waist. The straps were sewn on to the back of the waistcoat at waist level, and later were sewn into the side seams. There were various shapes of buckle to fasten them, made of white metal, brass or black japanned metal, and this form of waist adjustment continues up to the present day. The earliest style was the handle without a crossbar, followed by the handle with a crossbar, and then the rectangular shape, which gradually became standard. The earlier shapes continued to be used through the nineteenth century, although they might have been lying in a tailor's stock for some time. Increasingly, buckles had labels stamped on them. The word "Solide" is often found, which means that the buckle is a solid metal and not plated; sometimes there is a date indicating when the buckle design was registered, and sometimes the name or initials of the buckle-maker. By the end of the nineteenth century well-established tailors had buckles made with their own name on them.

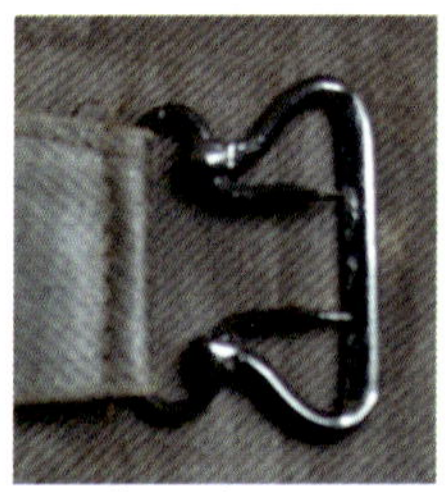

Handle without a crossbar in black japanned metal, 1840-1860, page 131.

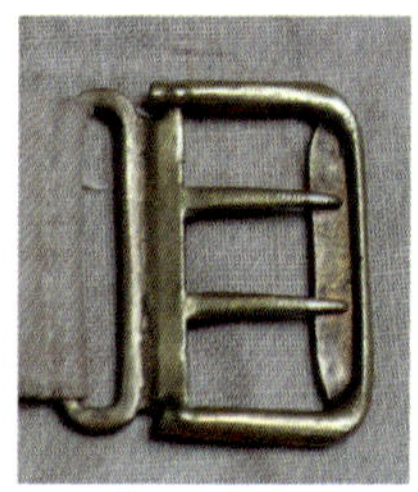

Handle with a crossbar in brass, 1840-1850, page 121, right.

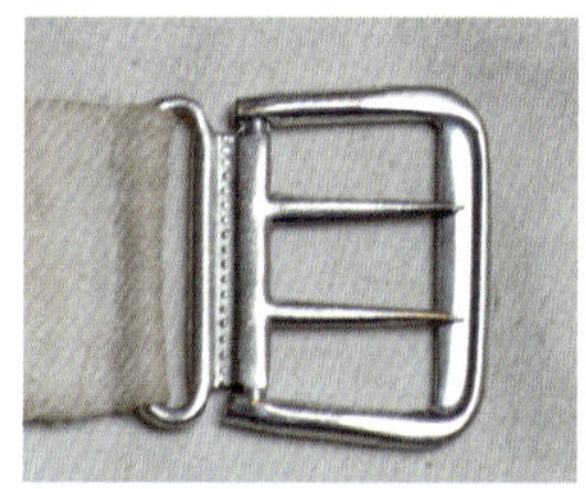

Handle with a crossbar in white metal, 1850-1860, marked J. & D. Holloway, who were buckle-makers in Birmingham, page 151.

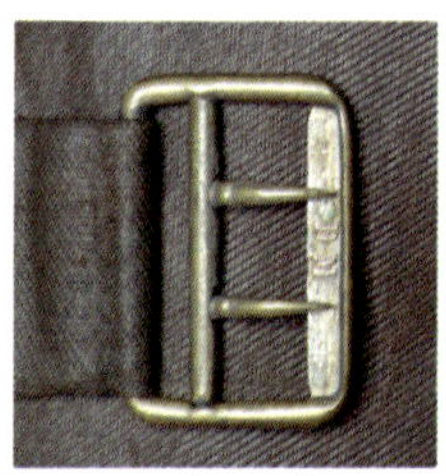

Rectangular in brass, marked with the initials D M, 1865-1875, page 173.

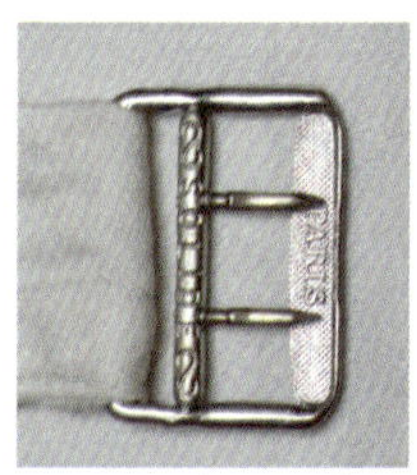

Rectangular in white metal, marked Paris and Solide, 1900-1910, page 198.

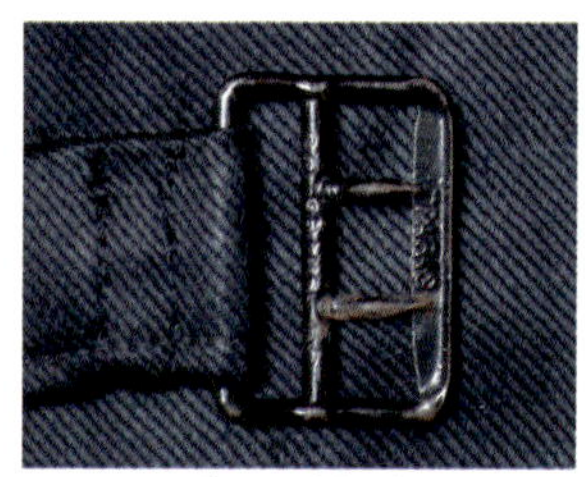

Rectangular in black japanned metal, marked Paris and France, 1890-1900, page 188.

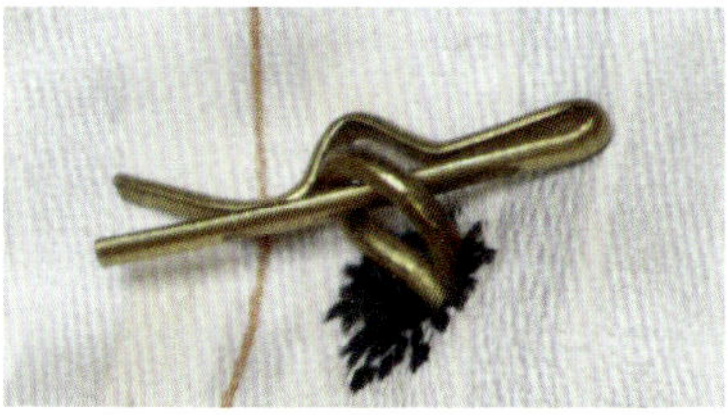

The shank of a removable button held by a split pin, inside the waistcoat on page 190, 1895-1910.

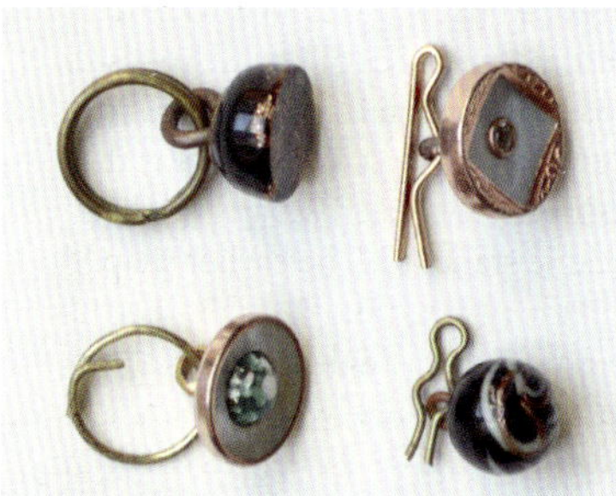

Ring fastenings and split pin fastenings on removable buttons.

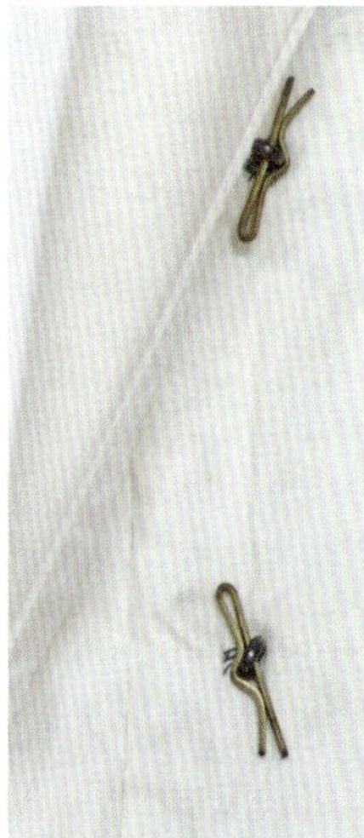

Split pins holding removable buttons under the facing on the waistcoat on page 200, 1900-1910.

"Eyelet holes are worked for the buttons to be fastened on by button fasteners or split rings at the back, the facings being arranged to form a kind of fly and so cover the fastenings." *The Tailor and Cutter*, 1898.

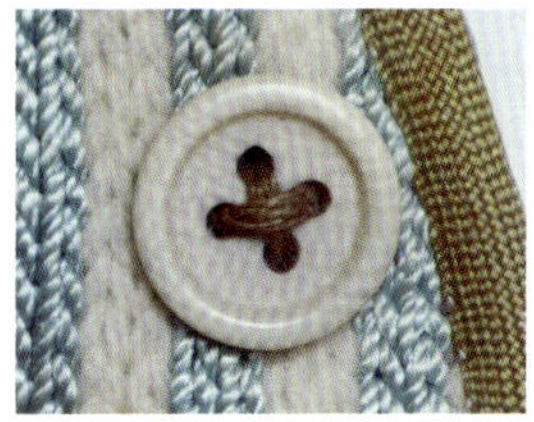

One of the vegetable ivory buttons on the waistcoat on page 186, 1895. The natural grain can be seen.

"Buttons are important factors in the successful production of fancy vests, flat and ball shapes in white and smoke pearl, buffalo, and flaked composite makes being popular, together with the raised fancy twists for black, and navy grounds." *The Tailor and Cutter*, 1898.

Vegetable ivory, also called corozo, comes from the inside of the tagua nut from a South American palm tree, and was widely used for buttons from the late nineteenth century until plastic became common in the twentieth century; it is still used today. It takes dye well and has a natural grain.

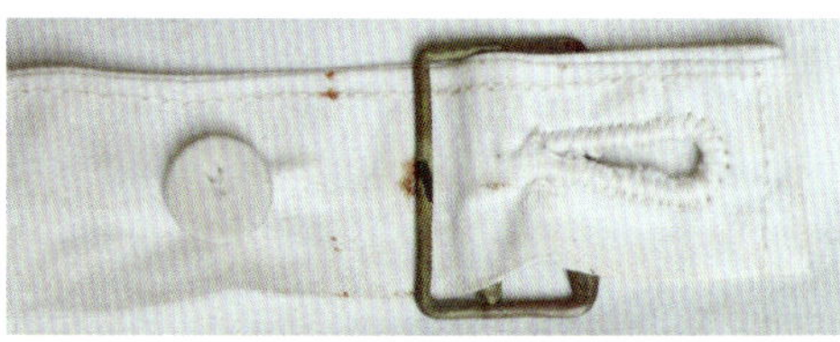

Inside the backstrap for a removable buckle, showing the buttonhole and the linen button, on the back of the waistcoat on page 200, 1900-1910.

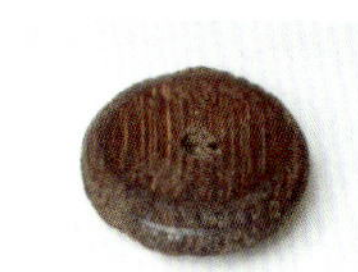

The wooden mould for a button on the waistcoat on page 31, 1760s.

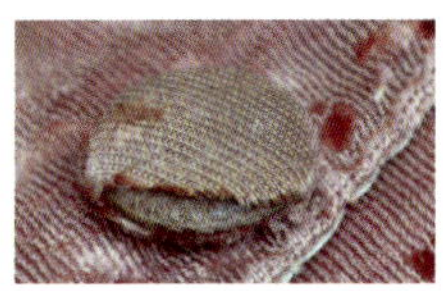

The worn edge of another of the buttons on page 31, revealing the mould.

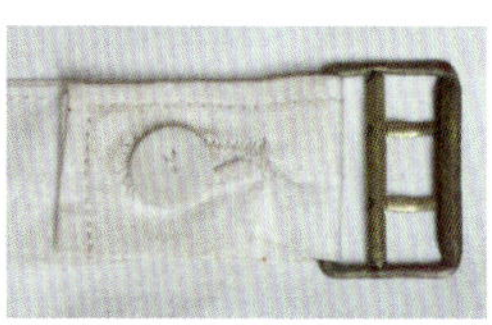

Inside the backstrap, showing the buckle fastened by the strap buttoned up.

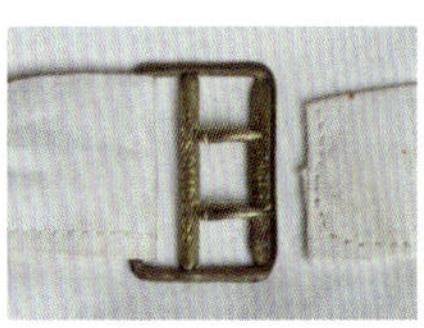

The outside of the backstrap; the end of the other strap is ready to be fastened on to the bucklc.

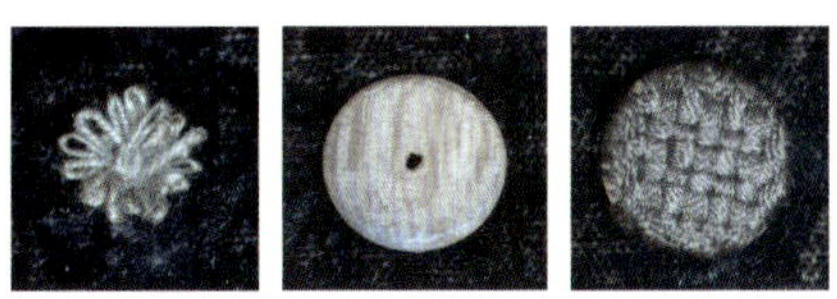

Left to right: The looped base for a thread button on the waistcoat on page 173, 1865–1875; the wooden mould which sits on the base; a button on the waistcoat.

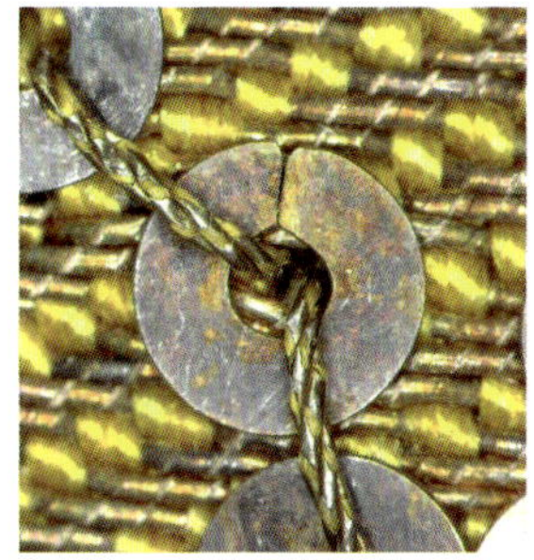

A split ring spangle in silver-gilt; it is made from a cut section of coiled wire, which is flattened. This one is on the braid on the waistcoat on page 36, 1760-1775.

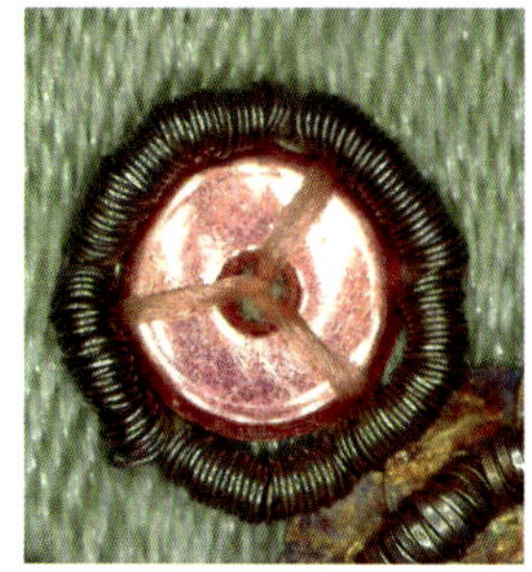

A spangle stamped out from pink enamelled silver foil. It is surrounded by silver-gilt purl and is on the waistcoat foreparts on page 46, 1770-1785.

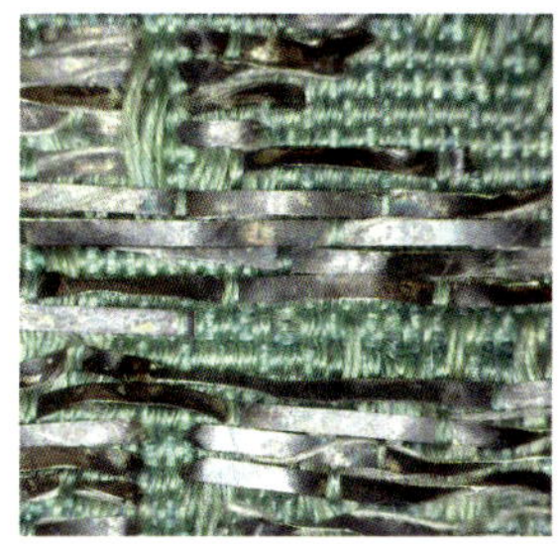

Silver flat strip, here used in weaving the design in the silk fabric of the waistcoat on page 23, 1740-1760.

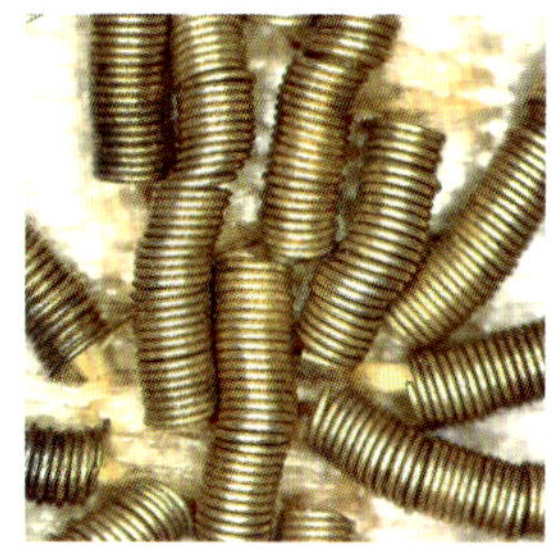

Silver-gilt purl, which is coiled wire, here used on the waistcoat on page 100, 1825-1840.

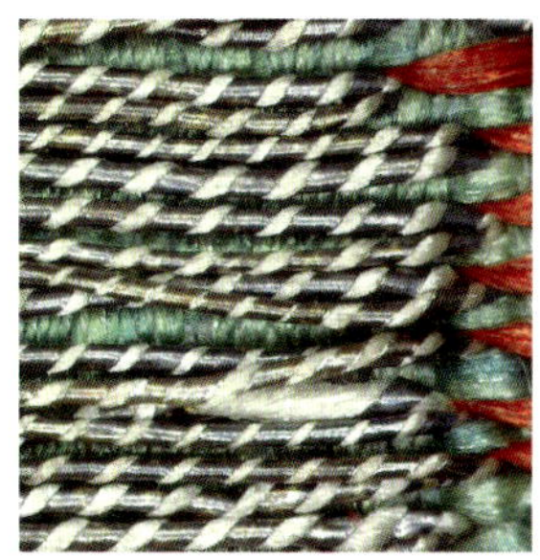

Silver filé, a narrow strip of silver wound round a core of silk thread, here woven in the design in the silk fabric of the waistcoat on pages 23, 1740-1760.

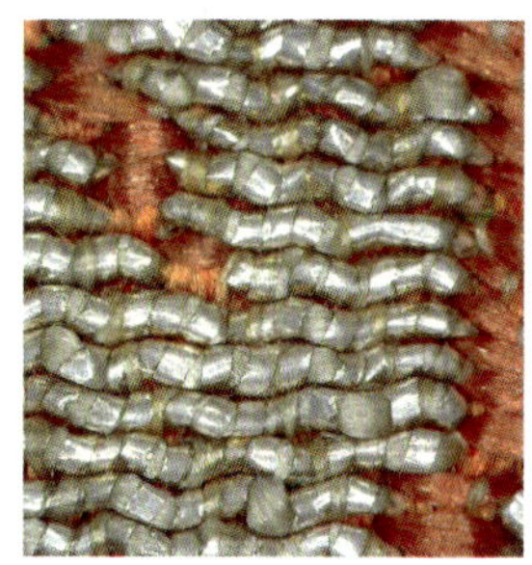

Silver frisé, a curly version of filé, here woven in the brocade of the waistcoat on page 8, 1720-1740.

Glossary

Alpaca: A fabric using the wool of the Alpaca goat in the weft; the warp was silk, and later cotton. It has quite a springy texture and was invented by Sir Titus Salt in 1838.

Ambrotype: This was a collodion positive, an early form of photograph. The image was developed on the glass plate which was mounted on a black background, covered with another piece of glass and sealed into a frame. It was technically a negative, so the clear parts looked black against the black ground; this also meant that the image was laterally reversed like a reflection in a mirror. It was first developed in 1852 but was then superseded in the 1860s by prints on paper.

Appliqué: Small pieces of contrasting fabric sewn on to form part of a design.

Backstrap: A waist adjustment consisting of a pair of straps sewn on to the back of a waistcoat at waist level and meeting at the centre back, with a buckle on the end of one strap through which the end of the other is fastened. From the later nineteenth century they were usually sewn into each side seam.

Baleen: see Bone/Boned/Boning.

Bents: Pieces of dried reed used for stiffening corsets, and the tabs at the back of waistcoats.

Bias: The direction of a fabric which is at an angle between the warp and weft.

Bone/Boned/Boning: Strips of whalebone, or baleen, cut from plates of a horny substance which grows in the upper jaw of certain whales; they are encased in fabric channels on garments, to stiffen them.

Brocade: A fabric, often silk, with a plain coloured ground and a pattern of contrasting coloured extra wefts producing a slightly raised effect. Brocade is now often used to describe any woven-patterned fabric.

Buckram: A strong linen fabric of plain open weave, stiffened with flour paste, china clay and glue.

Calimanco: A heavily glazed worsted fabric, in various weaves.

Cannelé: A silk with the pattern formed by the warp.

Check: **1.** Similar to purl, but made from flat metal strip and faceted.
2. A pattern made by the crossing of vertical and horizontal stripes.

Chenille: A thread with a velvety pile (French for caterpillar).

Collar: A piece of fabric sewn on to finish off the neck of a garment. Sometimes this extends down the front opening.

Cotton piqué: Another name for marcella.

Couched/couching: An embroidery technique where a decorative thread lies on the surface and is secured by a thinner thread stitched over it at intervals.

Cut Velvet: see Velvet.

Damask: A fabric, typically a single colour, using two different weave structures, usually satin and sateen. On the front the ground is in satin and the figure in sateen; this is reversed on the back, with the ground appearing as sateen and the figure as satin. The weaves catch the light differently so the pattern shows as a contrast of textures, and the fabric can be used on either side. It is often all silk, but can be in other fibres, and is sometimes a combination of two different ones.

Dart: A tuck tapering to a point usually taken from an edge or a seam to give three-dimensional shaping to a flat piece of fabric.

Double-breasted: A waistcoat where the foreparts overlap to the extent that, when the buttons are fastened, they are to one side of the centre and there is a corresponding row of decorative buttons on the opposite side of the centre front.

Eyelet: A round hole for laces to pass through, neatened by stitching, and later by metal rings. Thomas Rogers patented a metal eyelet machine in 1823.

Facecloth: A woollen fabric which has been finished in such a way that the surface is completely smooth.

Facing: A piece, usually fabric, sewn on to the inside front edge, or hem, of a garment to neaten and strengthen it.

Faille: A soft silk fabric with a slight transverse rib.

Figured silk: Silk with a small woven pattern, usually geometric and often in a self colour.

Filé: A thread made of a narrow strip of metal wound round a core of silk.

Fly front: An arrangement of the buttonholes on an inside flap of fabric under the front edge, so that they are concealed by the front edge of the garment, and the buttons are not visible when done up.

Foreparts: The front sections of a waistcoat.

Frisé: A curly version of filé.

Fustian: A term used for many types of heavy cotton or cotton and linen fabrics. It often has a raised surface.

Gimp: A thin cord or wire covered with silk, cotton or worsted threads, wound round it.

Grosgrain: A fabric with the weft thicker than the warp, which creates transverse ribs.

Gusset: A small piece of fabric, triangular or diamond-shaped, inserted into a seam, to allow more movement, or to make the garment larger.

Hopsack: Originally this was a heavy rough wool, but now the term has come to be used for a fabric which has two warp threads and two weft threads worked together in a plain weave.

Interlining: A piece of fabric between the outer fabric and the lining of a garment, which adds body or stiffens that section of the garment.

Jersey: A machine-knitted fabric, originally wool, but later cotton, silk or synthetic fibres.

Lapel: The lower part of a step collar, formed by the folded-back facing at the top of the forepart and joined to the front edges of the collar. The collar and the lapel can be cut as one piece as a step-roll collar.

Marcella: see Marseilles cloth.

Marseilles cloth: A technique developed in the eighteenth century to weave fabric resembling quilting. Marseilles was famous for its hand-quilting, so, not wanting to detract from this industry, the French called the new invention *matelassé*. In England it was called Marseilles cloth, later anglicised to marcella.

Matelassé: see Marseilles cloth.

Mercer: A dealer in fabrics, especially silks.

Moiré: A fabric with a weft rib, folded double and passed through heated rollers, causing the ribs to slip about and be flattened unevenly, creating a watered effect which reflects light in different ways.

Mounting: A piece of fabric laid on the inside of the main fabric, the two layers being worked as one; this makes the main fabric firmer.

Ottoman: A transverse corded fabric where the warp passes over a much thicker weft, with one or two rows of flat plain weave between each rib.

Paste: A hard vitreous composition used for making artificial gems.

Pieced/Piecing: A piece of fabric added to a panel of a garment to fill a space where that panel is not quite the size required. When the pattern pieces are laid on the fabric and overlap, one panel would be missing a bit, and so a small piece is sewn in to make the panel the right size. This was often done to minimise the amount of expensive fabric needed for the garment.

Pile: The ends of fibres which project upwards from a woven fabric, forming a smooth surface.

Piped/piping: A narrow strip of fabric folded lengthwise and inserted into a seam or put on an edge. It has a narrow cord lying inside the fold, which sits on top of the seam, or on the edge, as a finish. Sometimes a fine cord is used for the same effect.

Plain weave: The simplest form of weaving where single warp and weft threads pass over and under each other. It can be made with any fibre.

Plush: A fabric with a pile deeper than velvet, made of cotton, silk or wool, sometimes with goat hair.

Polychrome: Having several different colours together making a pattern.

Purl: Metal wire, usually silver or silver-gilt, wound into a coil and used in small sections as decoration.

Quilting: A technique whereby a layer of wadding, cotton or wool, is placed between two pieces of fabric, with stitching to hold it all together. The simplest stitching forms a diamond pattern, but more elaborate designs are often used.

Rayon: A fibre made from cellulose and used to make artificial silk.

Revers: The top section of the front edge of the foreparts turned back to show the facing on the inside surface.

Roll collar: A collar formed of a section of the facing at the top of the front edge of the forepart folded open and extending round the back of the neck with a centre back seam. Sometimes called a shawl collar.

Sateen: A weave producing a fabric whose face is made of closely packed weft threads, looking similar to satin; it is usually cotton. It has a less shiny surface than satin.

Satin: A weave producing a fabric whose face is made of closely packed warp threads; the weft is hardly visible and holds the fabric together from the back. It is often silk, or silk warp and cotton weft, the silk face making a glossy fabric, but it can be cotton, wool or a man-made fibre.

Selvedge: The edge of a woven fabric where the weft threads turn round to go back through the warp. It is often formed of different-coloured and stronger warp threads, and usually in a different weave from the main fabric.

Shag: A fabric with a long pile.

Shagreen: A spot-textured silk fabric with a pebbled surface resembling sharkskin.

Shawl collar: see Roll collar.

Silesia: A glazed linen, later also cotton, usually dark brown, and originally from Silesia, a state in central Europe.

Silver-gilt: Silver which has been plated with gold.

Single-breasted: A waistcoat where the foreparts overlap in the centre just enough for buttonholes on the edge of one side to fasten on to buttons on the edge of the other side.

Spangle: A small piece of metal, usually round, with a hole in the middle, which is sewn on to fabric as decoration. From the late nineteenth century it was increasingly called a sequin.

Stand collar: A collar formed of a straight, or slightly shaped piece of fabric standing up from the neck.

Step collar: A collar formed of the folded-back edge of the forepart showing the facing, which becomes a lapel, joined on to a separate piece of fabric forming the collar which goes round the back of the neck; this produces a notch or step where the pieces join.

Step-roll collar: A collar which is an extension of the front facing, with a notch in the edge, at the point where the seam would be which joined a separate collar to a lapel.

Taffeta: A plain weave silk fabric, where single warp and weft threads pass over and under each other; this is now also made from synthetic fibres.

Tambour embroidery: *Tambour* is French for drum, and fabric stretched on an embroidery frame is reminiscent of this. Tambour work is specifically used to describe embroidery done with a hooked needle pushed through the stretched fabric and pulling up thread from underneath, in loops, forming a chain stitch on the top of the fabric.

Tweed: A heavy twill weave wool, often rough in texture.

Twill: A fabric where the weft threads pass over one and under two warp threads, in a staggered succession; the proportions can vary. This produces a diagonal rib effect on the fabric, and can be made with any fibre.

Uncut velvet: see Velvet.

Vegetable ivory: The inside of the tagua nut from certain South American palm trees, used for buttons from the late nineteenth century until plastic became common.

Velvet: A pile fabric with a second warp which passes over thin rods during weaving, forming loops. The loops are then either cut leaving the threads sticking up as tufts (cut velvet), or left as loops (uncut velvet).

Velveteen: Lightweight cotton velvet with a short pile.

Voided velvet: A fabric with the ground in velvet and the pattern in a flat weave. Sometimes this can be reversed with the ground woven as a flat fabric in a satin, twill or plain weave and a pattern woven in velvet.

Wadding: A thin layer of unspun cotton or wool laid between two fabrics, to give extra warmth or provide shaping.

Waffle piqué: A type of marcella where the pattern forms distinct squares which give more of a texture.

Warp: The threads which run the length of the fabric.

Weft: The threads which run transversely from side to side of the fabric.

Welted pocket: A welt is a narrow strip of fabric put on the top edge of a pocket, or used as a binding.

Worsted: Well-twisted yarn spun from the long fibres of a wool fleece, which have been combed to lay the fibres parallel; it is stronger than other wool threads, and was originally named after the parish of Worstead in Norfolk.

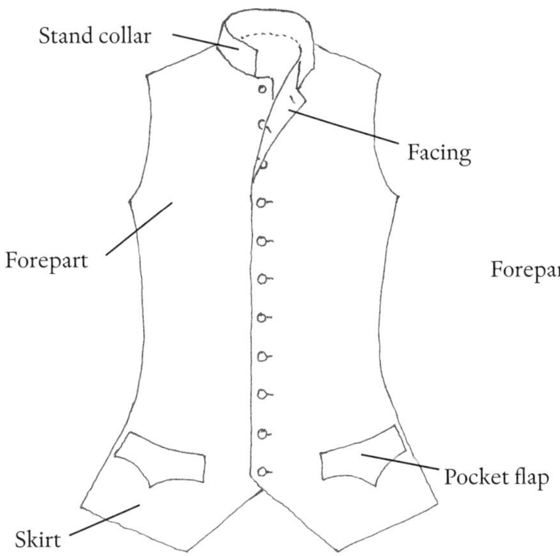

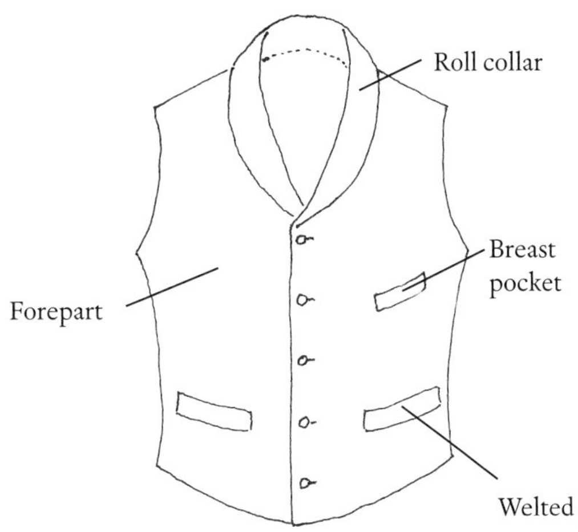

Single Breasted

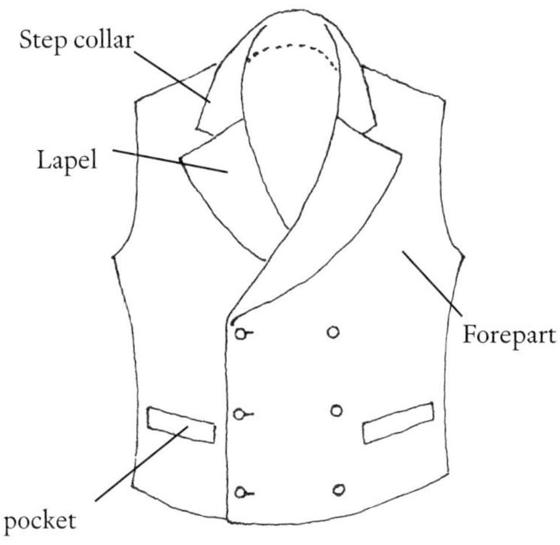

Double breasted

Selected Bibliography

Buck, Anne, *Victorian Costume and Costume Accessories*, London, Herbert Jenkins, 1961.

Buck, Anne, *Dress in Eighteenth-Century England*, London, Batsford, 1979.

Cunnington, C. Willett and Phillis, *Handbook of English Costume in the 19th Century*, London, Faber and Faber 1959.

Cunnington, C. Willett and Phillis, *Handbook of English Costume in the 18th Century*, London, Faber and Faber, 1972.

Evans, Grace, *Fashion in Focus*, Chertsey Museum, 2011.

Mansfield, Alan and Cunnington, Phillis, *Handbook of English Costume in the 20th Century*, London, Faber and Faber, 1973.

Miller, Lesley Ellis, *Selling Silks*, London, V&A Publishing, 2014.

Montgomery, Florence, *Textiles in America, 1650-1870*, New York, W. W. Norton, 1984.

Pietsch, Johannes, *Moden aus dem Rahmen*, Munich, Bayerisches Nationalmuseum, 2014.

Rangström, Lena, *Modelejon Manligt Mode; Lions of Fashion, Male Fashion of the 16th, 17th, 18th Centuries*, Stockholm, Livrustkammaren/The Royal Armoury, 2002.

Rothstein, Natalie, *Silk Designs of the Eighteenth Century*, London, Thames and Hudson, 1990.

Waugh, Norah, *The Cut of Men's Clothes, 1600-1900*, Faber and Faber, 1964.

Source of Illustrations

Janet Arnold Archive: page 83, 95, 97, 108, 111
Bibliothèque Nationale de France: page 174
Bridgeman Images: page 15, 54, 68, 69, 194
Caernarfon Royal Town Council: page 191
Al Cane: page 110
City of London Corporation: page 101
George Clarke: page 77, 152, 165 top centre, 168, 209
Richard Davin: page 197
Dee Atkinson & Harrison: page 98
Jacqueline Durran: page 141
Giana Ferguson: page 187
Peter Headlam-Morley: page 59
Stephen Nye: page 9
John Swannell: page 3
X-radiography by Amwell Veterinary Surgery, London: page 109

All other illustrations are from the Hopkins Collection unless otherwise stated in the caption.

Index

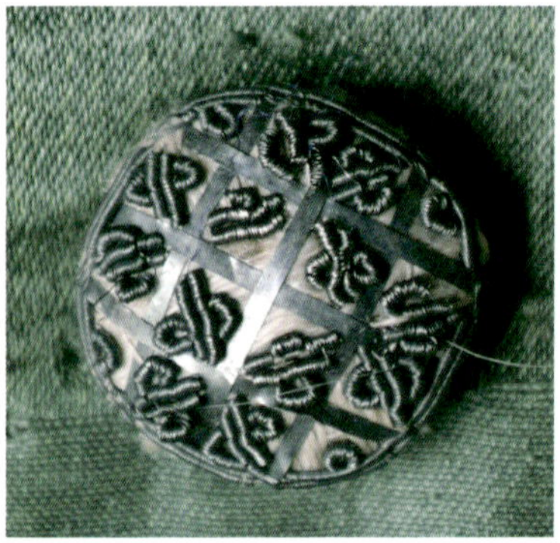

1725-1740, page 12

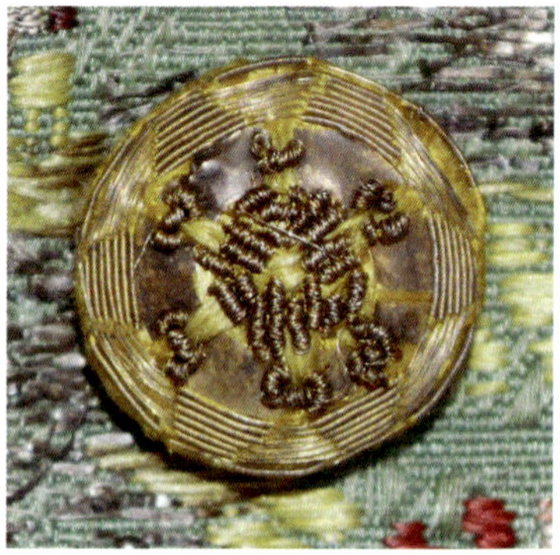

1740-1760, page 23

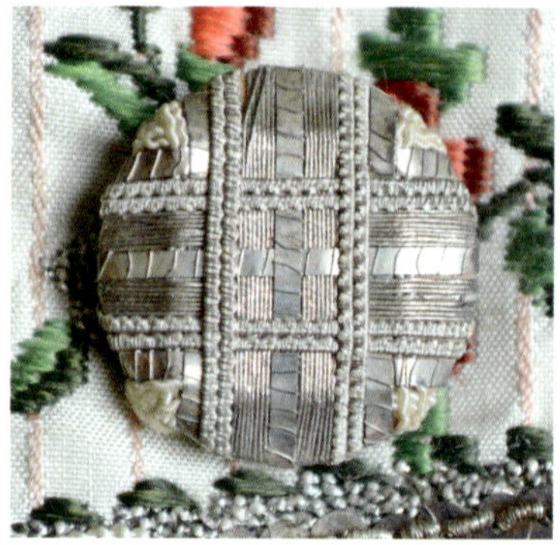

1760-1775, page 33

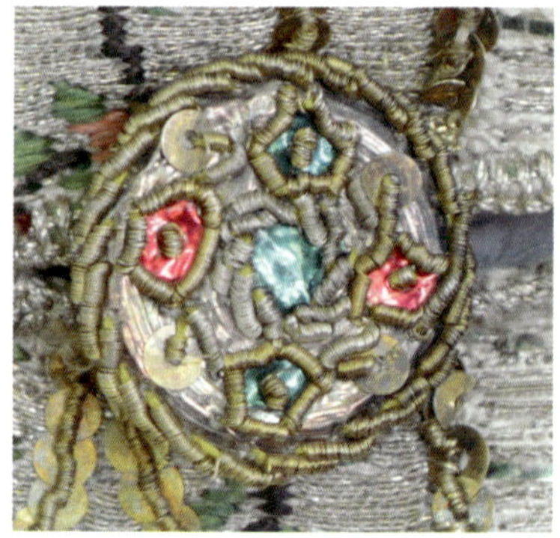

1770-1780, page 44

1770-1785, page 2

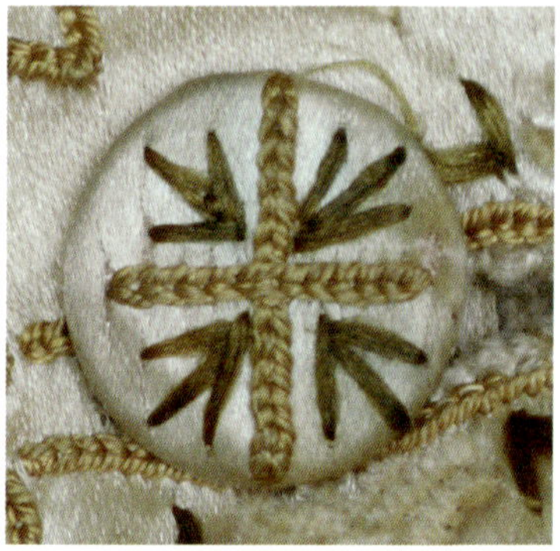

1780-1790, page 62

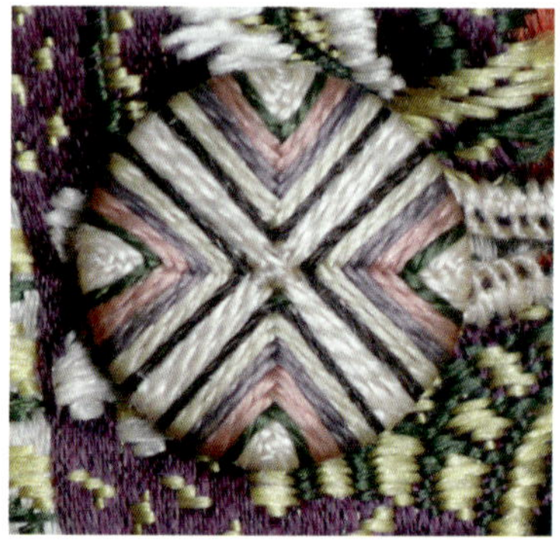

c. 1790-1800, page 72

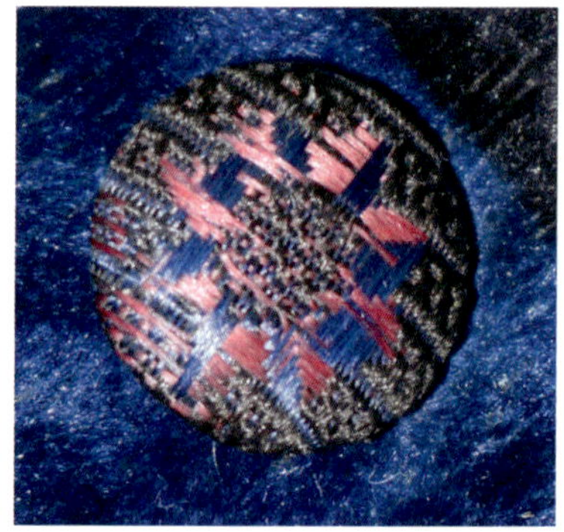

1835-1845, page 111

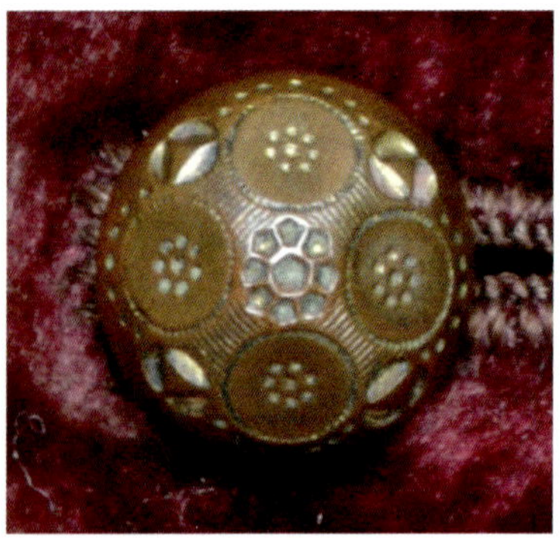

1835-1845, page 116

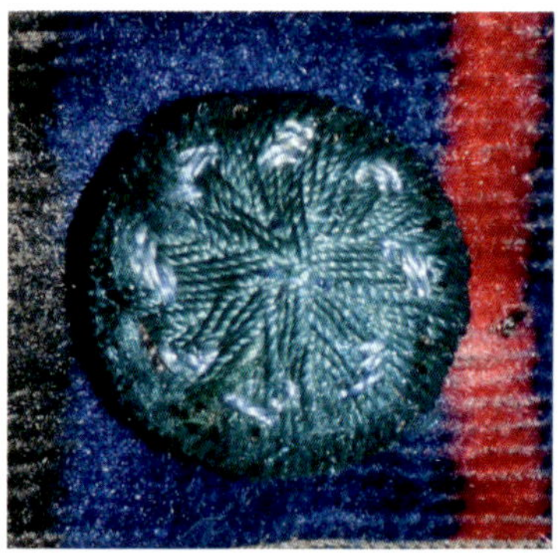

1840-1855, front cover

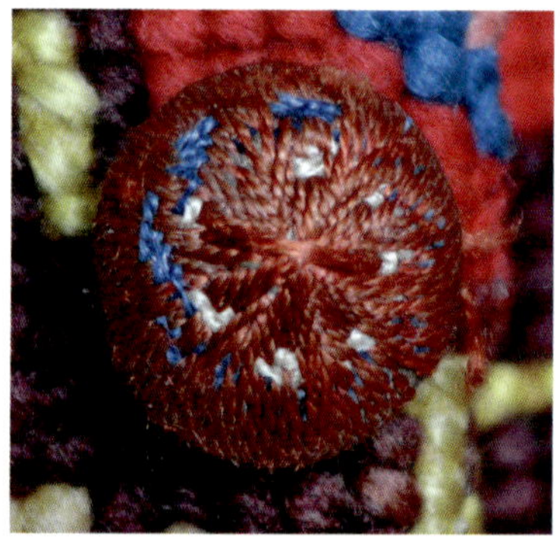

1850-1860, page 146

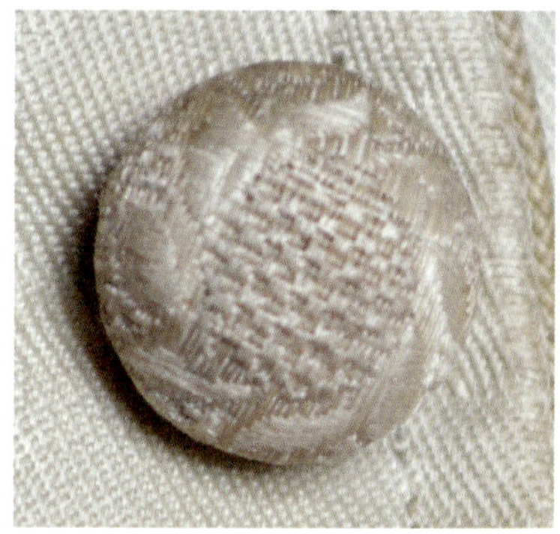

1850-1860, page 151

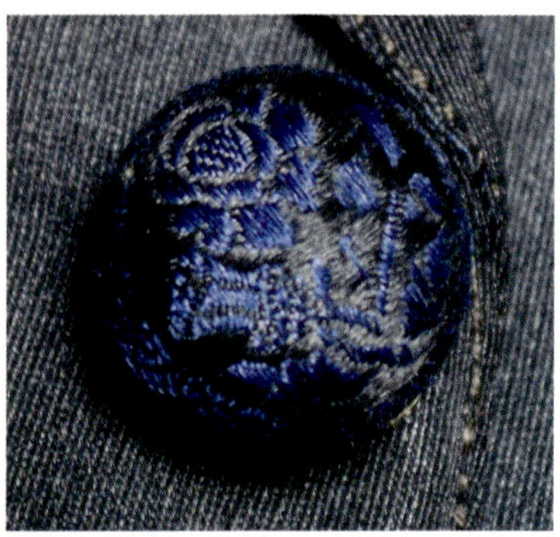

1850-1860, page 152

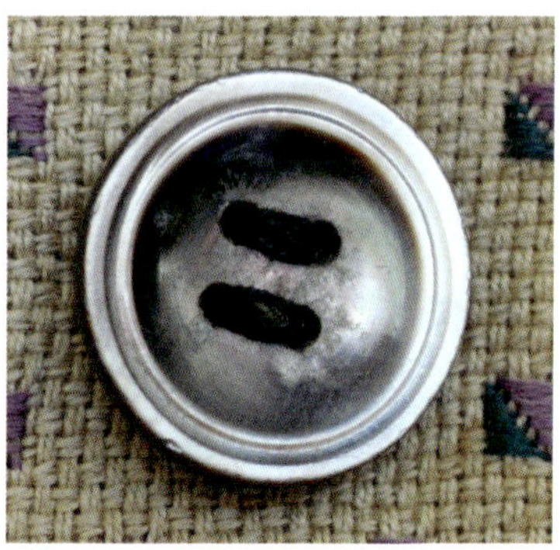

1890-1900, page 189

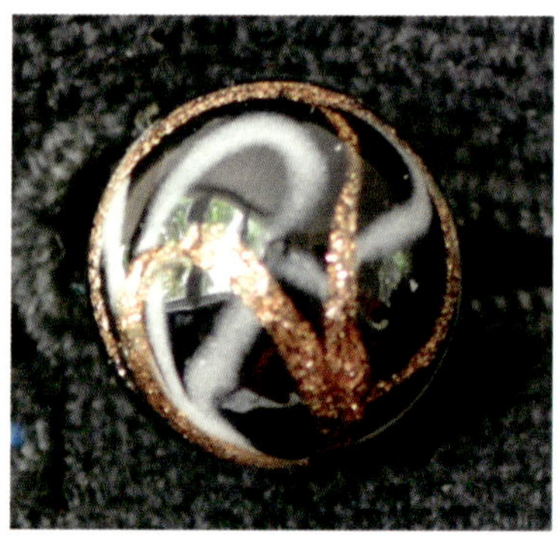

1895-1910, page 192 (left)

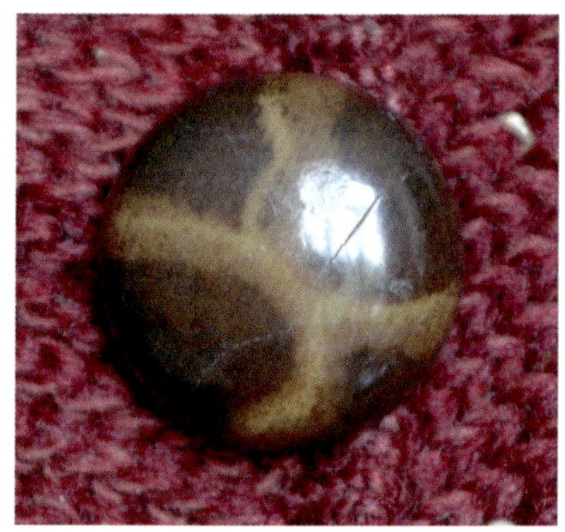

1920-1935, page 205